Staff Credits

EDITORIAL
Project Director: Fannie Safier
Editorial Coordinator: Katie Vignery
Editorial Staff: Lynda Abbott, Sally Ahearn, Judith Austin-Mills, Laura Baci, Amanda Beard, Richard Blake, Susan Britt, Robert Carranza, Kathleen Daniel, Daniela Guggenheim, Scott Hall, Bobbi Hernandez, Constance D. Israel, Susan Lynch, Mary Malone, Jennifer Osborne, Marie Hoffman Price, Sara Schroeder, Amy D.D. Simpson, Atietie O. Tonwe
Editorial Support: Carla M. Beer, Ruth Hooker, Margaret Guerrero
Editorial Permissions: Carrie Jones
Software Development: Armin Gutzmer, Lydia Doty

DESIGN AND PHOTO RESEARCH
Design: Pun Nio, *Senior Art Director;* Richard Metzger, *Design Supervisor;* Diane Motz, *Senior Designer;* Anne Wright, *Designer*
Photo: Debra Saleny, *Photo Research Manager;* V. Sing Griffin Bitzer, Yvonne Gerin, Ann Gillespie, Jeannie Taylor, *Photo Researchers*

PRODUCTION
Beth Prevelige, *Senior Production Manager;* Simira Davis, *Production Assisstant;* Sergio Durante, *Secretary;* George Prevelige, *Production Manager;* Rose Degollado, *Production Coordinator*
Electronic Publishing: Carol Martin, *Electronic Publishing Manager;* Kristy Sprott, *Electronic Publishing Supervisor;* Debra Schorn, *Electronic Publishing Senior Coordinator;* Lana Castle, Denise Haney, David Hernandez, Maria Homic, Barbara Hudgens, Mercedes Newman, Monica Shomos, *Electronic Publishing Staff*

Cover Design: Design 5

ISBN 0-03-098625-7

3 4 5   040   97 96

Adventures

for Readers

AN INTRODUCTION

ATHENA EDITION

HOLT, RINEHART AND WINSTON

Harcourt Brace & Company

Austin • **New York** • Orlando • Atlanta • San Francisco • Boston • Dallas • Toronto • London

Contributors AND Critical Readers

Kay Bevino
Bruner Middle School
Fort Walton Beach, Florida

Scott J. Ewald
Roosevelt Elementary School
Watertown, South Dakota

Barbara Francis
New York, New York

Nancy A. Frese
St. Thomas the Apostle School
Florissant, Missouri

Jan Freeman
Florence, Massachusetts

Patti Grady
St. Thomas More School
Lynnwood, Washington

V. Pauline Hodges
Forgan Public Schools
Forgan, Oklahoma

Linda Ann Lee
Holcomb Bridge Middle School
Alpharetta, Georgia

Carroll Moulton
Formerly of Duke University
Durham, North Carolina

Mary Elizabeth Thomas
Sandy Springs Middle School
Atlanta, Georgia

Acknowledgments

For permission to reprint copyrighted material, grateful acknowledgment is made to the following sources:

American Library Association: From comment by Lloyd Alexander from *Top of the News,* "Editors Notes," January 1968. Copyright © 1968 by the American Library Association.

Arte Público Press: "Petals" by Pat Mora from *Chants* (Houston: Arte Público Press–University of Houston, 1985).

Brent Ashabranner: "The Most Vulnerable People" from *Into a Strange Land* by Brent Ashabranner. Copyright © 1987 by Brent Ashabranner and Melissa Ashabranner.

Atheneum Publishers, an imprint of Macmillan Publishing Company: "Our Washing Machine" from *The Apple Vendor's Fair* by Patricia Hubbell. Copyright © 1963 by Patricia Hubbell. "Beach Stones" from *Something New Begins* by Lilian Moore. Copyright © 1982 by Lilian Moore. "Since Hanna Moved Away" from *If I Were in Charge of the World* by Judith Viorst. Copyright © 1981 by Judith Viorst.

Toni Cade Bambara: From "Rapping About Story Forms" from *Tales and Stories for Black Folks,* edited by Toni Cade Bambara. Copyright © 1971 by Toni Cade Bambara.

The Bancroft Library, University of California, Berkeley: Comment by Yoshiko Uchida.

Susan Bergholz Literary Services: Comment on "Abuelito Who" by Sandra Cisneros. Copyright © 1991 by Sandra Cisneros.

Georges Borchardt, Inc. for the Estate of John Gardner: "Dragon, Dragon" from *Dragon, Dragon and Other Tales* by John Gardner. Copyright © 1993 by Boskydell Artists Ltd.

Bradbury Press, an Affiliate of Macmillan, Inc.: From *Volcano: The Eruption and Healing of Mount St. Helens* by Patricia Lauber. Text copyright © 1988 by Patricia Lauber. From *Hatchet* by Gary Paulsen. Copyright © 1987 by Gary Paulsen.

Betsy Byars: From comment by Betsy Byars from *Something About the Author,* Volume 1. Copyright © 1976 by Betsy Byars. Published by Gale Research Company.

Clarion Books/Houghton Mifflin Co.: From *Lincoln: A Photobiography* by Russell Freedman. Copyright © 1987 by Russell Freedman. All rights reserved.

Ruth Cohen, Inc. on behalf of Lensey Namioka: "The All-American Slurp" by Lensey Namioka. Copyright © 1987 by Lensey Namioka.

Don Congdon Associates, Inc.: "All Summer in a Day" by Ray Bradbury. Copyright © 1954 and renewed © 1982 by Ray Bradbury.

Harold Courlander: "Paul Bunyan's Cornstalk" from *Ride with the Sun* by Harold Courlander. Copyright © 1955 and renewed © 1988 by Harold Courlander.

Creative Arts Book Company: "Momotaro: Boy-of-the-Peach" from *The Dancing Kettle and Other Japanese Folk Tales* by Yoshiko Uchida. Copyright © 1986 by Yoshiko Uchida.

The Crossroad/Continuum Publishing Group: From comment by Maya Angelou from *Black Women Writers at Work,* edited by Claudia Tate. Copyright © 1983 by The Crossroad/Continuum Publishing Group.

Delacorte Press, a division of Bantam Doubleday Dell Publishing Group, Inc.: "The Jacket" from *Small Faces* by Gary Soto. Copyright © 1986 by Gary Soto.

Doubleday, a division of Bantam Doubleday Dell Publishing Group, Inc.: "Good Morning Opponents" and "Who Dressed This Mess?" from *Fatherhood* by Bill Cosby. Copyright © 1986 by William H. Cosby. From *The Diary of Anne Frank: The Critical Edition.* Copyright © 1986 by Anne Frank-Fonds, Basle/Switzerland, for all texts of Anne Frank. "The Waking" from *The Collected Poems of Theodore Roethke.* Copyright 1948 by Theodore Roethke and renewed © 1976 by Beatrice Roethke, Administratrix of the Estate of Theodore Roethke.

The Dramatic Publishing Company: "Act One, Scene Three" (Retitled: "Riddles in the Dark") from *J.R.R. Tolkien's The Hobbit,* dramatized by Patricia Gray. Copyright © 1967 by The Dramatic Publishing Company.

Farrar, Straus & Giroux, Inc.: "The Toaster" from *Laughing Time* by William Jay Smith. Copyright © 1990 by William Jay Smith.

Nikki Giovanni: Comment on "Knoxville, Tennessee" by Nikki Giovanni. Copyright © 1991 by Nikki Giovanni.

Greenwillow Books, a division of William Morrow & Company, Inc.: "The Darkling Elves" from *The Headless Horseman Rides Tonight* by Jack Prelutsky. Copyright © 1980 by Jack Prelutsky.

Gulf Publishing Company: From *The Original Adventures of Hank the Cowdog* by John R. Erikson. Copyright © 1980 by John Erikson.

Harcourt Brace & Company: Adapted definitions from *HBJ School Dictionary,* Second Edition. Copyright © 1985 by Harcourt Brace & Company. "The Rum Tum Tugger" from *Old Possum's Book of Practical Cats* by T. S. Eliot. Copyright 1939 by T. S. Eliot; copyright renewed © 1967 by Esme Valerie Eliot. From "It All Began with a Picture" from *Of Other Worlds: Essays and Stories* by C. S. Lewis, edited by Walter Hooper. Copyright © 1966 by the Executors of the Estate of C. S. Lewis. "Phizzog" from *Good Morning, America* by Carl Sandburg. Copyright 1928 and renewed © 1956 by Carl Sandburg. "The Algonquin Cinderella" from *World Tales, The Extraordinary Coincidence of Stories Told in All Times, in All Places* by Idries Shah. Copyright © 1979 by Technographia, S.A. and Harcourt Brace & Company.

HarperCollins Publishers, Inc.: From *Sounder* by William H. Armstrong. Text copyright © 1969 by William H. Armstrong. "Cynthia in the Snow" and "Narcissa" from *Bronzeville Boys and Girls* by Gwendolyn Brooks. Copyright © 1956 by Gwendolyn Brooks Blakely. From *Julie of the Wolves* by Jean Craighead George. Text copyright © 1972 by Jean Craighead George. "How the Possum Lost the Hair Off His Tail" from *Mules and Men* by Zora Neale Hurston. Copyright 1935 by Zora Neale Hurston; copyright renewed © 1963 by John C. Hurston and Joel Hurston. From *The Land I Lost* by Huynh Quang Nhuong. Text copyright © 1982 by Huynh Quang Nhuong. "January" from *Chicken Soup with Rice: A Book of Months* by Maurice Sendak. Copyright © 1962 by Maurice Sendak. "Sarah Cynthia Sylvia Stout Would Not Take the Garbage Out" and illustrations from *Where the Sidewalk Ends* by Shel Silverstein. Copyright © 1974 by Evil Eye Music, Inc.

HarperCollins Publishers Ltd.: From *The Lion, the Witch and the Wardrobe* (Retitled: "Mr. Tumnus") by C. S. Lewis. Copyright 1950 and renewed © 1978 by the Estate of C. S. Lewis.

Heidelberg Graphics and Leroy V. Quintana: "Legacy II" by Leroy V. Quintana from *The Face of Poetry,* edited by L. H. Clark and Mary MacArthur. Copyright © 1979 by Heidelberg Graphics.

William Heinemann, a division of Reed Book Services: "Why Tortoise's Shell Is Not Smooth" from *Things Fall Apart* by Chinua Achebe. Copyright © 1958 by Chinua Achebe.

Hill and Wang, a division of Farrar, Straus & Giroux, Inc.: From "The Mother of the Gracchi" from *The Big Sea* by Langston Hughes. Copyright © 1940 by Langston Hughes; copyright renewed © 1968 by Arna Bontemps and George Houston Bass.

Holiday House: Cartoon and riddle from *The Dinosaur Princess and Other Prehistoric Riddles* by David A. Adler, illustrated by Loreen Leedy. Text copyright © 1988 by David A. Adler. Illustrations copyright © 1988 by Loreen Leedy.

Henry Holt and Company, Inc.: "The Stone" from *The Foundling and Other Tales of Prydain* by Lloyd Alexander. Copyright © 1973 by Lloyd Alexander. "A Minor Bird" from *The Poetry of Robert Frost,* edited by Edward Connery Lathem. Copyright 1928 and renewed © 1956 by Robert Frost; copyright © 1969 by Holt, Rinehart and Winston. From "When I Was One-and-Twenty" from "A Shropshire Lad" - Authorized Edition - from *The Collected Poems of A. E. Housman.* Copyright 1939,

Contents

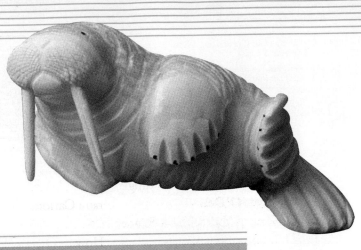

POETRY

NONFICTION

PLAYS

MYTHS AND
FOLK TALES

THE NOVEL

WRITING ABOUT LITERATURE

The Eve of St. John by Peter Hurd (1960). Tempera on board.

A Gallery of Characters

Why do we read? For many readers, the answer to that question is, "To meet new people. To have new experiences. To get information." This unit, like a picture gallery, gives you portraits of several people. One character is a real person who led a dangerous, heroic life. One is a real person whose life is very ordinary. Two are memorable fictional characters. One is even a dog—one of the many unforgettable animal characters in literature.

Writers create lifelike characters for us in six ways:

1. By describing a character's appearance.
2. By letting us hear the character talk.
3. By telling us what the character thinks.
4. By showing us the character's actions.
5. By letting us know how others respond to the character.
6. By telling us directly what the character is like (good, evil, kind, and so on).

Watch for the ways the characters in this unit come alive. Do any of them remind you of people you know—or of yourself?

San Diego Museum of Art.
(Gift of Mr. and Mrs. Norton S. Walbridge)

1

*W*hen you read, you may be sitting quietly, not making a sound. But if you are reading actively, a lot is going on in your head. There are different purposes for reading. When you read a science textbook, for example, you usually read for facts. Your purpose may be to learn how plants convert water and carbon dioxide into sugars and starches. When you read a math book, you may be looking for the information you will need to solve a specific problem.

You may have more than one purpose in reading. You can read a story for pure enjoyment. You can also read to enrich your understanding of other people and yourself.

Guidelines for Close Reading

1. Read actively. Ask questions as you read. Ask about unfamiliar words. Ask about clues that the writer drops. Ask about language or situations that puzzle you.

2. Make predictions as you read. Ask yourself, "What is going to happen next?"

3. Relate what you are reading to your own life and experience. Put yourself in the character's place. Ask yourself how you might act in a similar situation.

4. Put all your responses together. Answer the questions you raised during reading. Find out if your predictions were accurate. Think about the main idea of the selection. Think about your responses to the characters and events.

Here is an excerpt from a novel called *Julie of the Wolves.* The comments in the margin show how one reader has responded to the selection. Note that the reader's very first question has to do with the book's title. If you wish, cover up these comments and take notes of your own as you read. Then compare your responses with the printed comments.

from
Julie of the Wolves

JEAN CRAIGHEAD GEORGE

Miyax pushed back the hood of her sealskin parka and looked at the Arctic sun. It was a yellow disc in a lime-green sky, the colors of six o'clock in the evening and the time when the wolves awoke. Quietly she put down her cooking pot and crept to the top of a dome-shaped frost heave, one of the many earth buckles that rise and fall in the crackling cold of the Arctic winter. Lying on her stomach, she looked across a vast lawn of grass and moss and focused her attention on the wolves she had come upon two sleeps ago. They were wagging their tails as they awoke and saw each other.

Her hands trembled and her heartbeat quickened, for she was frightened, not so much of the wolves, who were shy and many harpoon-shots away, but because of her desperate predicament. Miyax was lost. She had been lost without food for many sleeps on the North Slope of Alaska. The barren slope stretches for three hundred miles from the Brooks Range to the Arctic Ocean, and for more than eight hundred miles from the Chukchi to the Beaufort Sea. No roads cross it; ponds and lakes freckle its immensity. Winds scream across it, and the view in every direction is exactly the same. Somewhere in this cosmos was Miyax; and the very life in her body, its spark and warmth, depended upon these wolves for survival. And she was not so sure they would help.

The Eskimo peoples of Alaska are known for their carving of ivory figures, such as the walrus shown here.
© Chris Arend. Courtesy of Alaska State Council/Alaska Stock Images.

ONE READER'S RESPONSE

How do you say this name? Is she an Eskimo? Who is Julie?

A lime-green sky is weird.

What is a frost heave? (OK. Defined here.) Is she alone? Not a lawn like ours. This is the Arctic.

Two sleeps? Must mean two nights.

She's scared.

Why is she lost? I can't imagine going without food for several days!

A horrible place to be. How did she get here?

Wow—I thought wolves ate people. How could she be dependent on them for food?

How can you tell a wolf you need food?

She is an Eskimo.

But how did he "tell" the wolf?

Well, I see she doesn't know either.

So her father has disappeared. Why is she in this terrible place? Did she get lost hunting? Was she abandoned?

She must know a lot about animals. She is also patient—two days watching wolves!

Miyax stared hard at the regal black wolf, hoping to catch his eye. She must somehow tell him that she was starving and ask him for food. This could be done, she knew, for her father, an Eskimo hunter, had done so. One year he had camped near a wolf den while on a hunt. When a month had passed and her father had seen no game, he told the leader of the wolves that he was hungry and needed food. The next night the wolf called him from far away and her father went to him and found a freshly killed caribou. Unfortunately, Miyax's father never explained to her how he had told the wolf of his needs. And not long afterward he paddled his kayak into the Bering Sea to hunt for seal, and he never returned.

She had been watching the wolves for two days, trying to discern which of their sounds and movements expressed good will and friendship. Most animals had such signals. The little Arctic ground squirrels flicked their tails sideways to notify others of their kind that they were friendly. By imitating this signal with her forefinger, Miyax had lured many a squirrel to her hand. If she could discover such a gesture for the wolves,

Migrating Alaskan caribou.

©Larry B. Jennings/Photo Researchers

Her father's name.

She knows animals very
well. She is kind. I like
her.

What is a "wolverine
ruff"? A ruffle made of
wolf's fur?

She is very patient and
brave. I feel sorry for her.

Her picture is on the book
cover. She's pretty.

I wonder how old she is.
She seems too young to
survive in this awful place
alone.

This is sort of tough. I
think the author is saying
that smaller means
warmer.

What is going to happen
to this girl?

she would be able to make friends with them and share their food, like a bird or a fox.

Propped on her elbows with her chin in her fists, she stared at the black wolf, trying to catch his eye. She had chosen him because he was much larger than the others, and because he walked like her father, Kapugen, with his head high and his chest out. The black wolf also possessed wisdom, she had observed. The pack looked to him when the wind carried strange scents or the birds cried nervously. If he was alarmed, they were alarmed. If he was calm, they were calm.

Long minutes passed, and the black wolf did not look at her. He had ignored her since she first came upon them, two sleeps ago. True, she moved slowly and quietly, so as not to alarm him; yet she did wish he would see the kindness in her eyes. Many animals could tell the difference between hostile hunters and friendly people by merely looking at them. But the big black wolf would not even glance her way.

A bird stretched in the grass. The wolf looked at it. A flower twisted in the wind. He glanced at that. Then the breeze rippled the wolverine ruff on Miyax's parka and it glistened in the light. He did not look at that. She waited. Patience with the ways of nature had been instilled in her by her father. And so she knew better than to move or shout. Yet she must get food or die. Her hands shook slightly and she swallowed hard to keep calm.

Miyax was a classic Eskimo beauty, small of bone and delicately wired with strong muscles. Her face was pearl-round and her nose was flat. Her black eyes, which slanted gracefully, were moist and sparkling. Like the beautifully formed polar bears and foxes of the north, she was slightly short-limbed. The frigid environment of the Arctic has sculptured life into compact shapes. Unlike the long-limbed, long-bodied animals of the south that are cooled by dispensing heat on extended surfaces, all live things in the Arctic tend toward compactness, to conserve heat.

The length of her limbs and the beauty of her face were of no use to Miyax as she lay on the lichen-speckled frost heave in the midst of the bleak tundra.

Looking at Yourself as a Reader

Suppose you were the reader whose thoughts are recorded in the right-hand margins of this story. What would you say about the character of Miyax, as you know it so far?

Remember that a writer can reveal character in six ways:

1. by looks
2. by speech
3. by thoughts
4. by actions
5. by the responses of other people
6. by direct statements

Notice that you commented on Miyax's delicate looks. You thought she was pretty. You worried that she was too fragile to survive. You noted her patient actions. You thought she was brave. You also asked questions about her background: Why is she here? What has happened to put this young girl in this terrible place, where she will soon die if she can't get food?

Are you interested enough in this character to read the whole book? Do you predict that Miyax will survive?

THINKING ABOUT WORDS

USING CONTEXT CLUES

When you are reading and you come across an unfamiliar word, you can often get some clues about the meaning of the word from its context. A word's **context** includes the words and sentences that surround it.

CONTEXT CAN PROVIDE DEFINITIONS

Some contexts even define a word's meaning. For example, in the passage from *Julie of the Wolves* (page 3), the meaning of the term "frost heave" is defined right in context. Below is the passage, with the definition underscored:

> . . . a dome-shaped frost heave, <u>one of the many earth buckles that rise and fall in the crackling cold of the Arctic winter.</u>

CONTEXT CAN PROVIDE "CONTRAST" CLUES

Most contexts, however, do not provide the definition of an unfamiliar word. But many contexts do provide other clues that can give you an idea about the meaning of an unfamiliar word. The next passage from *Julie of the Wolves* does not

define *hostile,* but it does provide a "contrast" clue that gives information about its meaning.

> **... she did wish he would see the kindness in her eyes. Many animals could tell the difference between hostile hunters and friendly people by merely looking at them.**

Thinking It Out. If you don't know what *hostile* means, the context offers a contrast that is helpful. "Hostile hunters" are contrasted with "friendly people." Given this contrast and the situation Miyax is in, it is fairly clear that hostile is the opposite of friendly. In fact, *hostile* means "unfriendly."

CONTEXT CAN PROVIDE OTHER INFORMATION

The next sentence from the same story uses the word *discern.* The context gives you enough information to uncover the meaning of *discern.* Try to figure out what *discern* means by thinking about why Miyax is watching the wolves.

> **She had been watching the wolves for two days, trying to discern which of their sounds and movements expressed good will and friendship.**

Thinking It Out. Miyax is watching the wolves' behavior closely because she wants to know how they communicate friendship to each other. So she is trying to understand what their different sounds and movements mean. By now you've probably figured out that *discern* means "to figure out something." Or, put another way, by now you've probably *discerned* what *discern* means.

When you come across new words as you read, pay attention to their context. Context might help you discern what the words mean. Remember that some contexts give you more information about a word's meaning than others do. But even if a context doesn't give you much information, it can still help you learn something about unfamiliar words. When you learn just a little about a word, you will be ready to learn more about it the next time you see it or hear it.

Mr. Tumnus

C. S. LEWIS

Before You Read

What if another world existed just beyond this one? What if you could enter that world through some kind of magic door? In his famous novel *The Lion, the Witch and the Wardrobe*, C. S. Lewis imagined such a fantasy world in the spooky shadows at the back of a closet.

As the novel begins, Lucy Pevensie and her older sister and brothers have come from London, England, during World War II to stay with an old professor at his very large house in the country. While exploring the professor's house one day, the children enter a spare bedroom and discover a wardrobe—a kind of large cabinet where clothes are kept. But this wardrobe has no back to it, as Lucy discovers when she steps inside it. Suddenly, she finds herself on the other side of the wardrobe in a dark winter wood, walking through falling snow. At a lamppost in the wood, she almost bumps into a faun. Now, a faun, as Lucy knows, is a creature from mythology. It has a man's body, but the shaggy legs, tail, and horns of a goat. *This* faun is wearing a red woolen muffler (scarf) and carrying an umbrella and some packages, as though he had just been Christmas shopping. When the faun sees Lucy, he drops his parcels in surprise.

Read this excerpt from the novel until you get to where the faun tells Lucy his name. Do you predict that Mr. Tumnus will be a friendly character—or an evil one?

A glossary defines words that the reader of a book might find difficult. A glossary usually appears at the back of a book. It looks somewhat like a dictionary. Footnotes are definitions of difficult words or terms and are usually placed at the bottom of the page. This story, set in the fantasy land of Narnia, often refers to creatures from other fantasies and myths: *fauns*, *nymphs*, *dwarfs*, and *dryads*, for example. If you don't understand these references, you can do one of three things: (1) see if the word is defined in a footnote; (2) see if the word is defined in the Glossary, at the back of the book; (3) look for context clues or use your own experience to guess at the term's meaning. Then use these references to help you visualize the fabulous characters who live in Narnia.

"**G**ood evening," said Lucy. But the faun was so busy picking up his parcels that at first he did not reply. When he had finished, he made her a little bow.

"Good evening, good evening," said the faun. "Excuse me—I don't want to be inquisitive—but should I be right in thinking that you are a daughter of Eve?"

"My name's Lucy," said she, not quite understanding him.

"But you are—forgive me—you are what they call a girl?" asked the faun.

"Of course I'm a girl," said Lucy.

"You are in fact human?"

"Of course I'm human," said Lucy, still a little puzzled.

"To be sure, to be sure," said the faun. "How stupid of me! But I've never seen a son of Adam or a daughter of Eve before. I am delighted. That is to say—"

and then he stopped as if he had been going to say something he had not intended but had remembered in time. "Delighted, delighted," he went on. "Allow me to introduce myself. My name is Tumnus."

"I am very pleased to meet you, Mr. Tumnus," said Lucy.

"And may I ask, O Lucy, daughter of Eve," said Mr. Tumnus, "how you have come into Narnia?"

"Narnia? What's that?" said Lucy.

"This is the land of Narnia," said the faun, "where we are now; all that lies between the lamppost and the great castle of Cair Paravel on the eastern sea. And you— you have come from the wild woods of the west?"

"I—I got in through the wardrobe in the spare room," said Lucy.

"Ah!" said Mr. Tumnus in a rather

melancholy voice, "if only I had worked harder at geography when I was a little faun, I should no doubt know all about those strange countries. It is too late now."

"But they aren't countries at all," said Lucy, almost laughing. "It's only just back there—at least—I'm not sure. It is summer there."

"Meanwhile," said Mr. Tumnus, "it is winter in Narnia, and has been for ever so long, and we shall both catch cold if we stand here talking in the snow. Daughter of Eve from the far land of Spare Oom where eternal summer reigns around the bright city of War Drobe, how would it be if you came and had tea with me?"

"Thank you very much, Mr. Tumnus," said Lucy. "But I was wondering whether I ought to be getting back."

"It's only just round the corner," said the faun, "and there'll be a roaring fire—and toast—and sardines[1]—and cake."

"Well, it's very kind of you," said Lucy. "But I shan't be able to stay long."

"If you will take my arm, daughter of Eve," said Mr. Tumnus, "I shall be able to hold the umbrella over both of us. That's the way. Now—off we go."

And so Lucy found herself walking through the wood arm in arm with this strange creature as if they had known one another all their lives.

They had not gone far before they came to a place where the ground became rough and there were rocks all about and little hills up and little hills down. At the bottom of one small valley, Mr. Tumnus turned suddenly aside as if he were going to walk straight into an unusually large rock, but at the last moment Lucy found he was leading her into the entrance of a cave. As soon as they were inside, she found herself blinking in the light of a wood fire. Then Mr. Tumnus stooped and took a flaming piece of wood out of the fire with a neat little pair of tongs, and lit a lamp. "Now we shan't be long," he said, and immediately put a kettle on.

Lucy thought she had never been in a nicer place. It was a little, dry, clean cave of reddish stone with a carpet on the floor and two little chairs ("one for me and one for a friend," said Mr. Tumnus) and a table and a dresser and a mantelpiece over the fire and above that a picture of an old faun with a gray beard. In one corner there was a door which Lucy thought must lead to Mr. Tumnus's bedroom, and on one wall was a shelf full of books. Lucy looked at these while he was setting out the tea things. They had titles like *The Life and Letters of Silenus*[2] or *Nymphs and Their Ways* or *Men, Monks and Gamekeepers: A Study in Popular Legend* or *Is Man a Myth?*

"Now, daughter of Eve!" said the faun.

And really, it was a wonderful tea.

---

1. **sardines:** small fish packed in cans. The British tea is actually a small meal, served around four o'clock in the afternoon.

2. **Silenus** (sī·lē′nəs): the leader of the fauns (also called **satyrs**) in Greek mythology. Silenus is usually shown as a fat, jolly man with pointed ears and a tail.

There was a nice brown egg, lightly boiled, for each of them, and then sardines on toast, and then buttered toast, and then toast with honey, and then a sugar-topped cake. And when Lucy was tired of eating, the faun began to talk. He had wonderful tales to tell of life in the forest. He told about the midnight dances and how the nymphs who lived in the wells and the dryads[3] who lived in the trees came out to dance with the fauns; about long hunting parties after the milk-white stag who could give you wishes if you caught him; about feasting and treasure-seeking with the wild Red Dwarfs in deep mines and caverns far beneath the forest floor; and then about summer, when the woods were green and old Silenus on his fat donkey would come to visit them, and sometimes Bacchus[4] himself, and then the streams would run with wine instead of water and the whole forest would give itself up to jollification for weeks on end. "Not that it isn't always winter now," he added gloomily. Then to

3. **dryads** (drī'əds): nymphs who live in trees.

4. **Bacchus** (bak'əs): the Greek and Roman god of wine and rejoicing. Bacchus had wild parties in the woods with the woodland creatures.

and feeling rather frightened. "What do you mean? I've got to go home at once. The others will be wondering what has happened to me." But a moment later she asked, "Mr. Tumnus! Whatever is the matter?" for the faun's brown eyes had filled with tears, and then the tears began trickling down his cheeks, and soon they were running off the end of his nose; and at last he covered his face with his hands and began to howl.

"Mr. Tumnus! Mr. Tumnus!" said Lucy in great distress. "Don't! Don't! What is the matter? Aren't you well? Dear Mr. Tumnus, do tell me what is wrong." But the faun continued sobbing as if his heart would break. And even when Lucy went over and put her arms round him and lent him her handkerchief, he did not stop. He merely took the handkerchief and kept on using it, wringing it out with both hands whenever it got too wet to be of any more use, so that presently Lucy was standing in a damp patch.

"Mr. Tumnus!" bawled Lucy in his ear, shaking him. "Do stop. Stop it at once! You ought to be ashamed of yourself, a great big faun like you. What on earth are you crying about?"

"Oh—oh—oh!" sobbed Mr. Tumnus. "I'm crying because I'm such a bad faun."

"I don't think you're a bad faun at all," said Lucy. "I think you are a very good faun. You are the nicest faun I've ever met."

"Oh—oh—you wouldn't say that if you knew," replied Mr. Tumnus between his sobs. "No, I'm a bad faun. I don't

cheer himself up he took out from its case on the dresser a strange little flute that looked as if it were made of straw and began to play. And the tune he played made Lucy want to cry and laugh and dance and go to sleep all at the same time. It must have been hours later when she shook herself and said, "Oh, Mr. Tumnus—I'm so sorry to stop you, and I do love that tune—but really, I must go home. I only meant to stay for a few minutes."

"It's no good *now*, you know," said the faun, laying down his flute and shaking his head at her very sorrowfully.

"No good?" said Lucy, jumping up

suppose there ever was a worse faun since the beginning of the world."

"But what have you done?" asked Lucy.

"My old father, now," said Mr. Tumnus, "that's his picture over the mantelpiece. He would never have done a thing like this."

"A thing like what?" said Lucy.

"Like what I've done," said the faun. "Taken service under the White Witch. That's what I am. I'm in the pay of the White Witch."

"The White Witch? Who is she?"

"Why, it is she that has got all Narnia under her thumb. It's she that makes it always winter. Always winter and never Christmas—think of that!"

"How awful!" said Lucy. "But what does she pay *you* for?"

"That's the worst of it," said Mr. Tumnus with a deep groan. "I'm a kidnapper for her, that's what I am. Look at me, daughter of Eve. Would you believe that I'm the sort of faun to meet a poor innocent child in the wood, one that had never done me any harm, and pretend to be friendly with it, and invite it home to my cave, all for the sake of lulling it asleep and then handing it over to the White Witch?"

"No," said Lucy. "I'm sure you wouldn't do anything of the sort."

"But I have," said the faun.

"Well," said Lucy rather slowly (for she wanted to be truthful and yet not to be too hard on him), "well, that was pretty bad. But you're so sorry for it that I'm sure you will never do it again."

"Daughter of Eve, don't you understand?" said the faun. "It isn't something I *have* done. I'm doing it now, this very moment."

"What do you mean?" cried Lucy, turning very white.

"You are the child," said Mr. Tumnus. "I had orders from the White Witch that if ever I saw a son of Adam or a daughter of Eve in the wood, I was to catch them and hand them over to her. And you are the first I ever met. And I've pretended to be your friend and asked you to tea, and all the time I've been meaning to wait till you were asleep and then go and tell *her*."

"Oh, but you won't, Mr. Tumnus," said Lucy. "You won't, will you? Indeed, indeed, you really mustn't."

"And if I don't," said he, beginning to cry again, "she's sure to find out. And she'll have my tail cut off, and my horns sawn off, and my beard plucked out, and she'll wave her wand over my beautiful cloven[5] hoofs and turn them into horrid solid hoofs like a wretched horse's. And if she is extra and especially angry, she'll turn me into stone and I shall be only a statue of a faun in her horrible house until the four thrones at Cair Paravel are filled—and goodness knows when that will happen, or whether it will ever happen at all."

"I'm very sorry, Mr. Tumnus," said Lucy. "But please let me go home."

"Of course I will," said the faun. "Of course I've got to. I see that now. I hadn't

---

5. **cloven:** divided, split in two. A pig has a cloven hoof. A horse has a solid hoof.

known what humans were like before I met you. Of course I can't give you up to the witch, not now that I know you. But we must be off at once. I'll see you back to the lamppost. I suppose you can find your own way from there back to Spare Oom and War Drobe?"

"I'm sure I can," said Lucy.

"We must go as quietly as we can," said Mr. Tumnus. "The whole wood is full

Lucy looked very hard between the trees and could just see in the distance a patch of light that looked like daylight. "Yes," she said, "I can see the wardrobe door."

"Then be off home as quick as you can," said the faun, "and—c–can you ever forgive me for what I meant to do?"

"Why, of course I can," said Lucy, shaking him heartily by the hand. "And I do hope you won't get into dreadful trouble on my account."

"Farewell, daughter of Eve," said he. "Perhaps I may keep the handkerchief?"

"Rather!" said Lucy, and then ran toward the far-off patch of daylight as quickly as her legs would carry her. And presently, instead of rough branches brushing past her, she felt coats, and instead of crunching snow under her feet, she felt wooden boards, and all at once she found herself jumping out of the wardrobe into the same empty room from which the whole adventure had started. She shut the wardrobe her and looked around, It was still raining and voices of the others in

he shouted. "I'm here. all right."

and Discussion

cy discovers Narnia.

always winter in Narnia.

nnus, and why does he invite Lucy to have tea with him?

4. Describe Mr. Tumnus's cave. In what ways does it have "all the comforts of home"?

5. Poor Mr. Tumnus bursts out crying. What is his **conflict**, or problem? How does he solve his problem?

INTERPRETING MEANINGS

6. You never find out here what happens to Mr. Tumnus after Lucy leaves him. Based on what you have learned about Narnia, **predict** what might happen to Mr. Tumnus next.

"This is the land of Narnia, . . . all that lies between the lamppost and the great castle of Cair Paravel on the eastern sea."

Illustration by Pauline Baynes.

7. **Contrast** the trip to the cave with the journey back to the lamppost. Which journey is more relaxed? Which is more exciting? Which is more dangerous?

8. One humorous picture in the story is that of a shaggy faun serving a very proper English tea. Did you find any other details in the story funny?

APPLYING MEANINGS

9. What other stories or movies do you know of in which a character enters another world or dimension? What kind of world does each character discover? (Is it a wish world or a nightmare world?) Think of Alice in Wonderland and Dorothy in Oz for two starters.

Focus on Reading

DISTINGUISHING BETWEEN REALISM AND FANTASY

A **realistic detail** is a true-to-life detail that could be found in the real world. A **fantastic detail** is one that could never be found in real life. *Wearing a red woolen muffler* is a realistic detail. We could see it in real life. But *a faun wearing a red woolen muffler* is a detail that could exist only in fantasy.

A fantasy like *The Lion, the Witch and the Wardrobe* includes both realistic and fantastic details. The realistic details, like snow falling in a wood, make the setting believable. But the fantastic details, like an endless winter controlled by a witch, make the story strange and exciting. Fantastic details spark your imagination.

Write down three fantastic details from this story. Then write down three realistic details that make the setting seem familiar. Add two details of your own telling how you visualize Narnia. Are they fantastic or realistic?

Literary Elements

CHARACTER

At one point in the story, Mr. Tumnus calls himself "a bad faun." Is he really bad? Think of what Mr. Tumnus says, where he lives, and how he behaves. Which of the following words would you use to describe Mr. Tumnus's **character**?

1. Friendly
2. Honest
3. Weak
4. Home-loving
5. Brave
6. Fearful
7. Deceitful
8. Company-loving

Mr. Tumnus is a fantasy character who could not live in the world as we know it. Still, do you think people like him live in our world?

Language and Vocabulary

GLOSSARY AND FOOTNOTES

Here is a list of characters from myths and fairy tales referred to in "Mr. Tumnus." Use the story clues, the Glossary, and the footnotes to match each character with the description on the next page. When you are finished, you might enjoy illustrating each description.

fauns (p. 10) dryads (p. 14)
Bacchus (p. 14) nymphs (p. 13)
dwarfs (p. 14) Silenus (p. 13)

1. The god of wine: _____.
2. Creatures that are part man and part goat: _____.
3. Spiritlike creatures of nature who live in the mountains, water, and woods: _____.
4. Leader of the fauns, who has horse's ears and a tail: _____.
5. Very tiny men who are skilled at mining and crafting precious stones and metals: _____.
6. Beautiful woodland spirits who live in trees: _____.

Focus on Personal Narrative

CHOOSING A TOPIC

How do you think Lucy would have told the story of her meeting with Mr. Tumnus? What do you think Lucy's personal account of her remarkable adventure would have been like?

In a **personal narrative,** you tell about an important experience in your own life. To share this experience, you use details to tell about events in the order in which they happened. In this kind of writing, you normally tell about real events rather than made-up or fantastic ones.

When you choose a topic for a personal narrative, here are guidelines to follow:

1. Write about an experience you remember well.
2. Write about an experience that was important to you.
3. Write about an experience that is not too private to share.

Start to find a topic for a personal narrative by listing ideas and memories on a chart like the one below. You may change one or more of the categories if you wish. Save your notes.

Meetings _____
_____

Scares _____
_____

Travels _____
_____

Animals _____
_____

Holidays _____
_____

Illustration by Pauline Baynes.

About the Author

C. S. Lewis (1898–1963) was born in Belfast, Ireland. As children, Lewis and his brother pretended that each one "owned" a country. Lewis's brother ruled a real country—India. Lewis, who loved to draw "dressed animals," possessed an imaginary place—Animal-Land.

When Lewis was seven, his family moved to a very large house in the country, much like the old professor's house in *The Lion, the Witch and the Wardrobe*. The "New House," as Lewis always called it, was one of the most important places in his life.

"The New House is almost a major character in my story," Lewis once wrote. "I am the product of long corridors, empty sunlit rooms, upstairs indoor silences, attics explored in solitude, distant noises of gurgling cisterns and pipes, and the noise of wind under the tiles. Also, of endless books. . . . In the seemingly endless rainy afternoons, I took volume after volume from the shelves."

This imaginative boy grew up to become a respected medieval scholar and writer. One day, at the age of forty, he found himself writing a story for children. The idea for the story came from a picture he had carried in his head for a long time: "a faun carrying an umbrella and parcels in a snowy wood." The story, of course, became the award-winning novel *The Lion, the Witch and the Wardrobe*. Its success led to six more adventures of Narnia. Lewis said the Narnia books should be read in this order: (1) *The Magician's Nephew*, (2) *The Lion, the Witch and the Wardrobe*, (3) *The Horse and His Boy*, (4) *Prince Caspian*, (5) *The Voyage of the "Dawn Treader,"* (6) *The Silver Chair*, and (7) *The Last Battle*. Of the many books C. S. Lewis wrote, *The Chronicles of Narnia* have proved to be the most memorable and the most popular.

"It all began with a picture . . ."

You must not believe all that authors tell you about how they wrote their books. This is not because they mean to tell lies. It is because a man writing a story is too excited about the story itself to sit back and notice how he is doing it. In fact, that might stop the works; just as, if you start thinking about how you tie your tie, the next thing is that you find you can't tie it. And afterward, when the story is finished, he has forgotten a good deal of what writing it was like.

One thing I am sure of. All my seven Narnian books, and my three science fiction books, began with seeing pictures in my head. At first they were not a story, just pictures. The *Lion* all began with a picture of a faun carrying an umbrella and parcels in a snowy wood. This picture had been in my mind since I was about sixteen. Then one day, when I was about forty, I said to myself: "Let's try to make a story about it."

At first I had very little idea how the story would go. But then suddenly Aslan [a noble lion, the hero of the Narnia stories] came bounding into it. I think I had been having a good many dreams of lions about that time. Apart from that, I don't know where the lion came from or why he came. But once he was there he pulled the whole story together, and soon he pulled the six other Narnian stories in after him.

So you see that, in a sense, I know very little about how this story was born. That is, I don't know where the pictures came from. And I don't believe anyone knows exactly how he "makes things up." Making up is a very mysterious thing. When you "have an idea" could you tell anyone exactly *how* you thought of it?

—C. S. Lewis

Harriet Tubman

ANN PETRY

Harriet Tubman by Robert Savon Pious (1951). Oil on canvas.

Before You Read

This true story takes place during the mid-1800s in the United States, when most Southern states still allowed the practice of slavery. Slavery, or the complete ownership of one person by another person, had been established in the United States in 1619. (Slavery was not abolished until 1865.) The early slaves were brought over to the New World from Africa. They and their descendants had to work hard for their owners and had no rights of their own.

Eventually, many Americans who hated slavery started the Underground Railroad. This was not a railroad and neither was it underground. It was made up of people from the North and South who offered shelter, food, and protection to slaves escaping to freedom in the North. To keep the route secret, the organization used railroad terms, such as "stations" for the houses along the way and "conductors" for the people who offered help.

Harriet Tubman was a slave who became one of the most famous conductors on the Railroad. She helped more than three hundred men, women, and children along the perilous road to freedom.

This is an extract from a *biography*, a story of someone's life. We are introduced to Harriet Tubman when she is a field hand at the Brodas plantation in Maryland. As a young girl, Harriet had received a crushing blow when she refused to help tie up a runaway slave. The injury left a deep scar on her forehead; it also made her fall asleep quite suddenly and uncontrollably. Harriet's husband, John Tubman, was a free man. But, as this excerpt opens, he has made it clear that he will turn his wife in if she tries to escape. Harriet is tormented by fears of being sold off to slave owners farther South.

Before you read, write in your journal how you would feel if you were held in slavery. What would you be unable to do? What dangers and sorrows would you and your family face?

Many English words have multiple meanings. In the third paragraph of this story, for example, the writer says there is fear "in the quarter." The definition of *quarter* in this context is not "a coin worth twenty-five cents." Here, *quarter* means "a district or section of a town or city." This quarter is the place on the plantation where the slaves live. In your reading, when you come across a word that has more than one meaning, the word's context will help you decide which meaning is intended.

One day, in 1849, when Harriet was working in the fields, near the edge of the road, a white woman wearing a faded sunbonnet went past, driving a wagon. She stopped the wagon, and watched Harriet for a few minutes. Then she spoke to her, asked her what her name was, and how she had acquired the deep scar on her forehead.

Harriet told her the story of the blow she had received when she was a girl. After that, whenever the woman saw her in the fields, she stopped to talk to her. She told Harriet that she lived on a farm, near Bucktown. Then one day she said, not looking at Harriet, but looking instead at the overseer,[1] far off at the edge of the fields, "If you ever need any help, Harriet, ever need any help, why you let me know."

That same year the young heir to the Brodas[2] estate died. Harriet mentioned the fact of his death to the white woman in the faded sunbonnet, the next time she saw her. She told her of the panic-stricken talk in the quarter, told her that the slaves were afraid that the master, Dr. Thompson, would start selling them. She said that Doc Thompson no longer permitted any of them to hire their time.[3] The woman nodded her head, clucked to the horse, and drove off, murmuring, "If you ever need any help——"

The slaves were right about Dr. Thompson's intention. He began selling slaves almost immediately. Among the first

---

1. **overseer:** a person who supervises workers; in this case, a slave driver.

2. Edward Brodas, the previous owner of the plantation, died and left his property to his heir, who was not yet old enough to manage it. In the meantime, the plantation was placed in the hands of the boy's guardian, Dr. Thompson.

3. **hire their time:** Some slave owners allowed their slaves to hire themselves out, for pay, to other plantation owners who needed extra help.

ones sold were two of Harriet Tubman's sisters. They went South with the chain gang[4] on a Saturday.

When Harriet heard of the sale of her sisters, she knew that the time had finally come when she must leave the plantation. She was reluctant to attempt the long trip North alone, not because of John Tubman's threat to betray her, but because she was afraid she might fall asleep somewhere along the way and so would be caught immediately.

She persuaded three of her brothers to go with her. Having made certain that John was asleep, she left the cabin quietly, and met her brothers at the edge of the plantation. They agreed that she was to lead the way, for she was more familiar with the woods than the others.

The three men followed her, crashing through the underbrush, frightening themselves, stopping constantly to say, "What was that?" or "Someone's coming."

She thought of Ben[5] and how he had said, "Any old body can go through a woods crashing and mashing things down like a cow." She said sharply, "Can't you boys go quieter? Watch where you're going!"

One of them grumbled, "Can't see in the dark. Ain't got cat's eyes like you."

"You don't need cat's eyes," she retorted. "On a night like this, with all the stars out, it's not black dark. Use your own eyes."

She supposed they were doing the best

they could, but they moved very slowly. She kept getting so far ahead of them that she had to stop and wait for them to catch up with her, lest they lose their way. Their progress was slow, uncertain. Their feet got tangled in every vine. They tripped over fallen logs, and once one of them fell flat on his face. They jumped, startled, at the most ordinary sounds: the murmur of the wind in the branches of the trees, the twittering of a bird. They kept turning around, looking back.

They had not gone more than a mile when she became aware that they had stopped. She turned and went back to them. She could hear them whispering. One of them called out, "Hat!"

"What's the matter? We haven't got time to keep stopping like this."

"We're going back."

"No," she said firmly. "We've got a good start. If we move fast and move quiet——"

Then all three spoke at once. They said the same thing, over and over, in frantic hurried whispers, all talking at once.

They told her that they had changed their minds. Running away was too dangerous. Someone would surely see them and recognize them. By morning, the master would know they had "took off." Then the handbills advertising them would be posted all over Dorchester County. The patterollers[6] would search for them. Even

---

4. **chain gang:** literally, a gang of people (slaves or prisoners) chained together.
5. Ben is Harriet's father. Her mother is called Old Rit.

6. **patterollers:** patrollers.

if they were lucky enough to elude the patrol, they could not possibly hide from the bloodhounds. The hounds would be baying after them, snuffing through the swamps and the underbrush, zigzagging through the deepest woods. The bloodhounds would surely find them. And everyone knew what happened to a runaway who was caught and brought back alive.

She argued with them. Didn't they know that if they went back they would be sold, if not tomorrow, then the next day, or the next? Sold South. They had seen the chain gangs. Was that what they wanted? Were they going to be slaves for the rest of their lives? Didn't freedom mean anything to them?

"You're afraid," she said, trying to shame them into action. "Go on back. I'm going North alone."

Instead of being ashamed, they became angry. They shouted at her, telling her that she was a fool and they would make her go back to the plantation with them. Suddenly they surrounded her, three men, her own brothers, jostling her, pushing her along, pinioning her arms behind her. She fought against them, wasting her strength, exhausting herself in a furious struggle.

She was no match for three strong men. She said, panting, "All right. We'll go back. I'll go with you."

She led the way, moving slowly. Her thoughts were bitter. Not one of them was willing to take a small risk in order to be free. It had all seemed so perfect, so simple, to have her brothers go with her,

sharing the dangers of the trip together, just as a family should. Now if she ever went North, she would have to go alone.

Two days later, a slave working beside Harriet in the fields motioned to her. She bent toward him, listening. He said the water boy had just brought news to the field hands, and it had been passed from one to the other until it reached him. The news was that Harriet and her brothers had been sold to the Georgia trader, and that they were to be sent South with the chain gang that very night.

Harriet went on working but she knew a moment of panic. She would have to go North alone. She would have to start as soon as it was dark. She could not go with the chain gang. She might die on the way, because of those inexplicable sleeping seizures. But then she—how could she run away? She might fall asleep in plain view along the road.

But even if she fell asleep, she thought, the Lord would take care of her. She murmured a prayer, "Lord, I'm going to hold steady onto You and You've got to see me through."

Afterward, she explained her decision to run the risk of going North alone, in these words: "I had reasoned this out in my mind; there was one of two things I had a *right* to, liberty or death; if I could not have one, I would have the other; for no man should take me alive; I should fight for my liberty as long as my strength lasted, and when the time came for me to go, the Lord would let them take me."

Slave Market in Richmond, Virginia, by Eyre Crowe (1852–1853). Oil on canvas.

Mrs. H. J. Heinz III

At dusk, when the work in the fields was over, she started toward the Big House.[7] She had to let someone know that she was going North, someone she could trust. She no longer trusted John Tubman, and it gave her a lost, lonesome feeling. Her sister Mary worked in the Big House, and she planned to tell Mary that she was going to run away, so someone would know.

As she went toward the house, she

saw the master, Doc Thompson, riding up the drive on his horse. She turned aside and went toward the quarter. A field hand had no legitimate reason for entering the kitchen of the Big House—and yet—there must be some way she could leave word so that afterward someone would think about it and know that she had left a message.

As she went toward the quarter, she began to sing. Dr. Thompson reined in his horse, turned around and looked at her. It was not the beauty of her voice that made

---

7. **Big House:** the plantation owner's house.

The Underground Railroad by Charles T. Webber
(1891 or 1893). Oil on canvas.

ons, when she was a child, the same clop-clop of the horses' feet, creak of the wagon, and the feeling of being lost because she did not know where she was going. She did not know her destination this time either, but she was not alarmed. She thought of John Tubman. By this time he must have told the master that she was gone. Then she thought of the plantation and how the land rolled gently down toward the river, thought of Ben and Old Rit, and that Old

Rit would be inconsolable because her favorite daughter was missing. "Lord," she prayed, "I'm going to hold steady onto You. You've got to see me through." Then she went to sleep.

The next morning, when the stars were still visible in the sky, the farmer stopped the wagon. Harriet was instantly awake.

He told her to follow the river, to keep following it to reach the next place where people would take her in and feed her. He said that she must travel only at night, and she must stay off the roads because the patrol would be hunting for her. Harriet climbed out of the wagon. "Thank you," she said simply, thinking how amazing it was that there should be white people who were willing to go to such lengths to help a slave get to the North.

When she finally arrived in Pennsylvania, she had traveled roughly ninety miles from Dorchester County. She had slept on the ground outdoors at night. She had been rowed for miles up the Choptank River by a man she had never seen before. She had been concealed in a haycock,[11] and had, at one point, spent a week hidden in a potato hole in a cabin which belonged to a family of free Negroes. She had been hidden in the attic of the home of a Quaker. She had been befriended by stout German farmers, whose guttural[12] speech surprised her and whose well-kept farms astonished her. She had never before seen barns and fences, farmhouses and outbuildings, so carefully painted. The cattle and horses were so clean they looked as though they had been scrubbed.

When she crossed the line into the free state of Pennsylvania, the sun was coming up. She said, "I looked at my hands to see if I was the same person now I was free. There was such a glory over everything, the sun came like gold through the trees, and over the fields, and I felt like I was in heaven."

---

11. **haycock:** a pile of hay in a field.
12. **guttural** (gut′ər·əl): harsh, rasping.

IDENTIFYING FACTS

1. What did Harriet Tubman discover that made her want to escape?

2. Describe her first attempt to escape. Why did it fail?

3. Why did she decide that she must try to escape again, and this time alone?

4. How did Tubman learn about the Underground Railroad?

5. What did Tubman compare freedom to at the end of her journey?

INTERPRETING MEANINGS

6. Look back at what you wrote in your journal. Would you change anything after reading this biography?

7. The African American slaves used songs as codes to communicate certain forbidden messages. What message was Tubman giving to her sister when she sang about leaving on the chariot? What feelings was she also communicating through the song?

APPLYING MEANINGS

8. The politician Patrick Henry is famous for declaring (in 1775) "Give me liberty, or give me death!" Henry was urging the colonists to arm themselves against the British. Harriet Tubman says (page 26) that "there was one of two things I had a *right* to, liberty or death; if I could not have one, I would have the other; for no man should take me alive." Do you know of other people, in history or living today, who risk death in order to be free?

IDENTIFYING THE SEQUENCE OF EVENTS

Following are six main events from this bi-ography. Number the events in the order in which they happened, starting with (1).

____ Harriet Tubman and three of her brothers attempt to escape.

____ Tubman first meets the white woman in the faded sunbonnet.

____ Tubman sings a song to tell her sister she is going North to freedom.

____ Tubman arrives in Pennsylvania.

____ Tubman hitches a ride with a farmer in a wagon of produce.

____ The woman in the sunbonnet directs Tubman to the first two stops on the Underground Railroad.

Literary Elements

CHARACTER

Think of what you learned about Harriet Tubman in this excerpt. Which of her words, thoughts, or actions reveal these **character traits**?

1. Bravery
2. Closeness to her family
3. Determination
4. Intelligence
5. Faith in God

Think of other heroes you know from stories or from real life. Do they all share these character traits?

Language and Vocabulary

MULTIPLE MEANINGS

Many English words have more than one meaning. Sometimes these multiple mean-ings are related, but sometimes they are not. Use each of the following words from the story of Harriet Tubman in two sentences that show two distinct meanings. (Which words are spelled the same but pronounced differently?)

bitter   bark   produce
post   blow   wind

Harriet Tubman worked as a water girl to cotton pickers; she also worked at plowing, carting, and hauling logs. From *The Harriet Tubman Series* (1939–1940) by Jacob Lawrence. Tempera on hardboard.

Hampton University Museum, Hampton, Virginia.

Focus on Personal Narrative

GATHERING DETAILS

If you want your readers to share and enjoy a personal narrative, you must supply enough **details** so that the experience you tell about becomes clear and vivid. When you write, think about two kinds of details.

Action details tell what happened and how it happened. These details can also include **dialogue,** or the words that people say. For example, notice how Ann Petry uses dialogue and other details to describe Harriet's first attempt to escape with her brothers (page 25).

Sensory details make the experience vivid by appealing to one or more of the five senses: sight, hearing, taste, smell, and touch. Petry uses sensory details in the paragraph beginning "She decided she would take the quilt with her" (page 28).

Choose one of the topics you explored for the writing assignment on page 19, or select a new topic. Gather details by filling in a chart like the one below. Save your notes.

Topic of Narrative: _____

Action Details / Dialogue

_____

_____

_____

Sensory Details

_____

_____

_____

About the Author

Ann Petry (1911–   ) was born in Connecticut. After she graduated from college, she worked as a pharmacist, a reporter, a writer and salesperson for an advertising agency, and an editor. Her first novel, *The Street,* was published in 1946. It was the first novel written by an African American woman to describe the lives of African American women in urban areas. She has written two biographies about slavery for young readers: *Harriet Tubman: Conductor on the Underground Railroad* and *Tituba of Salem Village.* About her biography of Harriet Tubman Petry says, "I came across some references to Harriet Tubman, an escaped slave, who led other slaves to freedom before the Civil War. She seemed to me the epitome [ĭ•pĭtə•mē] of everything that is indomitable in the human spirit. . . ." In addition to biographies and novels, Petry has written short stories and poems.

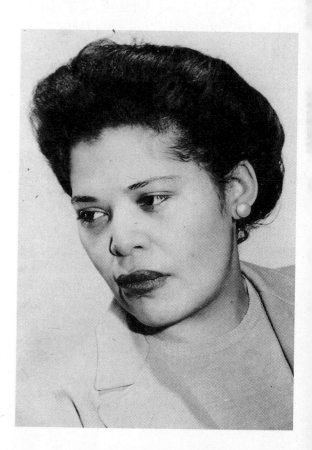

The Underground Railroad

Although organized methods of helping runaway slaves were known as early as 1804, the term *Underground Railroad* was first used in 1831 when a runaway slave mysteriously disappeared just as he was about to be caught. At first the number of routes was limited, but by 1850 numerous lines of the Underground Railroad were in place. An amazing number of people risked imprisonment, financial hardship, and bodily harm in an effort to help slaves find freedom in the North.

Everyone involved in the Underground Railroad understood the great need for secrecy. To evade slave catchers, the routes had to be constantly changed. Many fugitives traveled by foot. Others were disguised and placed on boats and trains. Several accounts tell of slaves being shipped to free states in boxes and crates. Elaborate signals were devised so fugitives could recognize a "safe" house. Slaves were told to look for such things as a quilt hanging on a porch or a smoking chimney. The song "Follow the Drinking Gourd," which was spread from one plantation to the next, contained clues revealing a route to the North. The "Drinking Gourd" represented the constellation of stars known as the "Big Dipper." Upon identifying the Big Dipper, one could find the North Star, which pointed the way to free states in the North.

Many people active in the anti-slavery cause were involved in the Underground Railroad as conductors, like Harriet Tubman and Levi Coffin, an influential Quaker.

Others contributed to the abolitionist cause by speaking and writing against the inhumanities of slavery. Frederick Douglass, an escaped slave, was among those whose personal accounts swayed public opinion against slavery. Harriet Beecher Stowe's bestselling novel, *Uncle Tom's Cabin* (1851–1852), angered numerous slaveowners who argued that Stowe's description of slavery was exaggerated.

Making Connections: Activities

1. Many authors have dramatized the story of fugitive slaves and the Underground Railroad. *When the Rattlesnake Sounds,* a play by Alice Childress, is based on Harriet Tubman's efforts to raise money to help runaway slaves. Read about the Underground Railroad. Two sources are *The Underground Railroad,* by Shaaron Cosner, and *Get on Board: The Story of the Underground Railroad,* by Jim Haskins. Write a short play or a poem based on a historical incident that interests you. If you write a play, create characters and a setting based on events in the life of a historical person, such as Harriet Tubman, Frederick Douglass, or Levi Coffin. Have classmates act in your play.

2. Find a copy of the song "Follow the Drinking Gourd." With a group of other students, identify the clues hidden in the song. Create a series of pictures that show fugitives following the North Star and other specific landmarks detailed in the song. Try to imagine what the journey was like and how slaves felt as they made their way north. Display your art work in the classroom.

The Jacket

GARY SOTO

Before You Read

Have you ever had to wear something that you hated? The narrator of this true story tells about a jacket that he wore long ago—and which he has never forgotten. Notice how the boy's feelings about his clothes reveal a lot about the kind of person he is—or once was.

After you read the first four paragraphs, look back and write down three adjectives that you would use to describe this boy as you know him so far. Do you think you would like him?

A simile is a comparison between two unlike things that uses the words *like* or *as*. When we say "John's voice is like a trumpet," or "Diane is as tall as a giraffe," we are using similes. In the first paragraph of this story, the writer uses a simile when he says the nondancers felt "bitter as a penny toward the happy couples." Have you ever caught the taste of a penny? It has a very ugly and bitter taste. The writer here is comparing the bitter taste of a penny to the boys' unhappiness and bitter envy. Watch for the many similes in this story. Try to visualize their comparisons as you read.

My clothes have failed me. I remember the green coat that I wore in fifth and sixth grades, when you either danced like a champ or pressed yourself against a greasy wall, bitter as a penny toward the happy couples.

When I needed a new jacket and my mother asked what kind I wanted, I described something like bikers wear: black leather and silver studs with enough belts to hold down a small town. We were in the kitchen, steam on the windows from her cooking. She listened so long while stirring dinner that I thought she understood for sure the kind I wanted. The next day when I got home from school, I discovered draped on my bedpost a jacket the color of day-old guacamole.[1] I threw my books on the bed and approached the jacket slowly, as if it were a stranger whose hand I had

to shake. I touched the vinyl sleeve, the collar, and peeked at the mustard-colored lining.

From the kitchen Mother yelled that my jacket was in the closet. I closed the door to her voice and pulled at the rack of clothes in the closet, hoping the jacket on the bedpost wasn't for me but my mean brother. No luck. I gave up. From my bed, I stared at the jacket, I wanted to cry because it was so ugly and so big that I knew I'd have to wear it a long time. I was a small kid, thin as a young tree, and it would be years before I'd have a new one. I stared at the jacket, like an enemy, thinking bad things before I took off my old jacket whose sleeves climbed halfway to my elbow.

I put the big jacket on. I zipped it up and down several times, and rolled the cuffs up so they didn't cover my hands. I put my hands in the pockets and flapped the jacket like a bird's wings. I stood in

---

1. **guacamole** (gwä'kə·mō'lē): a thick sauce made of puréed avocado. The sauce has an olive-green color.

front of the mirror, full face, then profile, and then looked over my shoulder as if someone had called me. I sat on the bed, stood against the bed, and combed my hair to see what I would look like doing something natural. I looked ugly. I threw it on my brother's bed and looked at it for a long time before I slipped it on and went out to the backyard, smiling a "thank you" to my mom as I passed her in the kitchen. With my hands in my pockets I kicked a ball against the fence, and then climbed it to sit looking into the alley. I hurled orange peels at the mouth of an open garbage can, and when the peels were gone, I watched the white puffs of my breath thin to nothing.

I jumped down, hands in my pockets, and in the backyard on my knees I teased my dog, Brownie, by swooping my arms while making bird calls. He jumped at me and missed. He jumped again and again, until a tooth sunk deep, ripping an L-shaped tear on my left sleeve. I pushed Brownie away to study the tear as I would a cut on my arm. There was no blood, only a few loose pieces of fuzz. Darn dog, I thought, and pushed him away hard when he tried to bite again. I got up from my knees and went to my bedroom to sit with my jacket on my lap, with the lights out.

That was the first afternoon with my new jacket. The next day I wore it to fifth grade and got a *D* on a math quiz. During the morning recess, Frankie T., the playground terrorist, pushed me to the ground and told me to stay there until recess was over. My best friend, Steve Negrete, ate an apple while looking at me, and the girls turned away to whisper on the monkey bars. The teachers were no help: they looked my way and talked about how foolish I looked in my new jacket. I saw their heads bob with laughter, their hands half covering their mouths.

Even though it was cold, I took off the jacket during lunch and played kickball in a thin shirt, my arms feeling like Braille[2] from goose bumps. But when I returned to class, I slipped the jacket on and shivered until I was warm. I sat on my hands, heating them up, while my teeth chattered like a cup of crooked dice. Finally warm, I slid out of the jacket but a few minutes later put it back on when the fire bell rang. We paraded out into the yard where we, the fifth-graders, walked past all the other grades to stand against the back fence. Everybody saw me. Although they didn't say out loud, "Man, that's ugly," I heard the buzz-buzz of gossip and even laughter that I knew was meant for me.

And so I went, in my guacamole jacket. So embarrassed, so hurt, I couldn't even do my homework. I received *C*'s on quizzes, and forgot the state capitals and the rivers of South America, our friendly neighbor. Even the girls who had been friendly blew away like loose flowers to follow the boys in neat jackets.

I wore that thing for three years until the sleeves grew short and my forearms stuck out like the necks of turtles. All during that time no love came to me—no little

---

2. **Braille** (brāl): a system of printing and writing for the blind, in which letters are indicated by raised dots which are felt by the fingers.

dark girl in a Sunday dress she wore on Monday. At lunchtime I stayed with the ugly boys who leaned against the chain-link fence and looked around with propellers of grass spinning in our mouths. We saw girls walk by alone, saw couples, hand in hand,

their heads like bookends pressing air together. We saw them and spun our propellers so fast our faces were blurs.

I blame that jacket for those bad years. I blame my mother for her bad taste and her cheap ways. It was a sad time for the heart. With a friend I spent my sixth-grade year in a tree in the alley, waiting for something good to happen to me in that jacket, which had become the ugly brother who tagged along wherever I went. And it was about that time that I began to grow. My chest puffed up with muscle and, strangely, a few more ribs. Even my hands, those fleshy hammers, showed bravely through the cuffs, the fingers already hardening for the coming fights. But that L-shaped rip on the left sleeve got bigger; bits of stuffing coughed out from its wound after a hard day of play. I finally Scotch-taped it closed, but in rain or cold weather the tape peeled off like a scab and more stuffing fell out until that sleeve shriveled into a palsied arm.[3] That winter the elbows began to crack and whole chunks of green began to fall off. I showed the cracks to my mother, who always seemed to be at the stove with steamed-up glasses, and she said that there were children in Mexico who would love that jacket. I told her that this was America and yelled that Debbie, my sister, didn't have a jacket like mine. I ran outside, ready to cry, and climbed the tree by the alley to think bad thoughts and watch my breath puff white and disappear.

But whole pieces still casually flew off my jacket when I played hard, read quietly, or took vicious spelling tests at school. When it became so spotted that my brother began to call me "camouflage," I flung it over the fence into the alley. Later, however, I swiped the jacket off the ground and went inside to drape it across my lap and mope.

I was called to dinner: Steam silvered my mother's glasses as she said grace; my brother and sister, with their heads bowed, made ugly faces at their glasses of powdered milk. I gagged too, but eagerly ate big rips of buttered tortilla that held scooped up beans. Finished, I went outside with my jacket across my arm. It was a cold sky. The faces of clouds were piled up, hurting. I climbed the fence, jumping down with a grunt. I started up the alley and soon slipped into my jacket, that green ugly brother who breathed over my shoulder that day and ever since.

For Study and Discussion

IDENTIFYING FACTS
1. Describe the jacket the narrator asks his mother to buy for him. What kind of jacket does she actually buy?

2. What is the narrator's reaction when he first sees the jacket?

3. List the things that happen to the boy the first day he wears the new jacket to school.

INTERPRETING MEANINGS
4. Why do you think the narrator's mother bought him the jacket she did instead of the one he described to her?

5. Why didn't the boy just get another jacket?

---

3. **palsied arm:** *Palsy* is a form of paralysis resulting in weak muscles. A palsied arm would look limp and thinner than a healthy arm.

6. Do you think people *really* were talking about the boy and laughing at him in his jacket? Do people often get these feelings that they are being laughed at because of what they are wearing?

7. What do you think the narrator means when he describes the jacket as "that green ugly brother who breathed over my shoulder that day and ever since"? How could the jacket still bother him?

APPLYING MEANINGS

8. Have you ever been embarrassed to wear a piece of clothing? (If this has never happened to you, how do you think you would handle the situation if it did?)

Focus on Reading

MAKING INFERENCES

An **inference** is a conclusion based on some kind of evidence. If you see footprints crossing a snowy field, you can **infer** that someone has been walking on the snow. If you see puddles on the sidewalk when you get up in the morning, you can **infer** that it rained overnight. When you read, you naturally make inferences about things the writer *suggests* but does not state directly.

You probably made a lot of inferences as you read "The Jacket." Which of the following inferences about this story are true? (Can you point to evidence in the story that supports each inference?)

1. The ugly green jacket was not the only reason for the boy's troubles in fifth and sixth grades.

2. The playground terrorist Frankie T., the boy's friend Steve, the rest of the fifth

grade, and all the teachers laughed at the boy and made his life miserable because they thought he looked hideous in his green jacket.

3. The boy knows that he must wear the jacket until he grows out of it and that he shouldn't complain.

4. His mother bought him the jacket because she thought he needed to be taught a lesson.

Literary Elements

CHARACTER

This true story is told by an adult who is looking back on his childhood. How would you describe this boy's **character?** Is he likeable? Shy? Outgoing? Angry? Unsure of himself? Selfish? Locate at least one detail in the story to support your answer. Look for examples in the boy's words and actions. Look also at the ways other people respond to the boy.

Is this boy's response to his hated jacket believable? Would you, or would most people you know, have felt this way?

Language and Vocabulary

SIMILES

Similes (sim′ə·lēs) are comparisons of unlike things that use words such as *like* or *as*. Writers use similes to create pictures in our minds. Similes can make us see a familiar object in a new and different way. Below are some similes from "The Jacket." Read them and answer the questions that follow.

1. "I was a small kid, thin as a young tree."

a. What is the narrator comparing himself to?

b. Describe what you think he looked
like.

2. "Even the girls who had been friendly
blew away like loose flowers . . ."

a. What are the girls compared to?

b. What does this comparison suggest
about the way the writer feels about
the girls? (Suppose the writer had said
they'd blown away like clumps of
dust?)

3. ". . . my forearms stuck out like the
necks of turtles."

a. What does the narrator compare his
arms to?

b. What do you think his arms look like?

USING CHRONOLOGICAL ORDER

The narrator in Gary Soto's "The Jacket"
uses chronological order to tell his story. In
chronological or **time order,** you tell events in
the order in which they happened.

To help your readers follow your story,
use **transitional words and phrases.** Transitions show the connections of events and
ideas in your writing. Here is a list of useful
transitions for time order:

after	often
before	soon
finally	then
first, second, third	when
next	

Write a paragraph or two telling about
something funny or interesting that happened at school. Use time order and
transitions to make the sequence of events
clear. Save your writing.

Gary Soto (1952–   ) was born in Fresno,
California. When he was a boy, he worked as
a migrant worker. His book *Small Faces,*
from which "The Jacket" is taken, describes
many of his experiences and feelings growing up as a Mexican American. Other
collections of stories are *Baseball in April*
and *Local News.* Soto has written poetry as
well as essays and short fiction. Soto says
he did not have "any literary aspirations as
a kid. In fact, we were a pretty illiterate
family. We didn't have books, and no one
encouraged us to read. So my wanting to
write poetry was sort of a fluke." He became
interested in writing when he found a book
in the library called *The New American Poetry.* "I discovered this poetry and thought,
This is terrific; I'd like to do something like
this."

Photo of Gary Soto taken by his wife, Carolyn.

from The Adventures of Tom Sawyer

MARK TWAIN

Before You Read

Some of the most popular programs on TV are comedies about characters growing up in America. But the most famous of all American stories about growing up was written by Mark Twain in 1876.

The title of Twain's novel is *The Adventures of Tom Sawyer.* The story takes place in a very small Mississippi River town called St. Petersburg. Tom and his friends go through many of the ordeals that the young characters on TV go through today: They have problems in school, they have conflicts at home, they fall in love, they face prejudice and even violence.

Tom lives with his Aunt Polly, his half-brother Sid, and his cousin Mary. Sid is always good; Tom is always in trouble. Aunt Polly is an unmarried lady who loves Tom dearly, but she often has difficulty understanding him.

After you read the first paragraph of this episode from the novel, stop and be sure you know the answer to this question: What is Tom's problem?

Painting by Norman Rockwell.

Courtesy The Heritage Club, Norwalk, Connecticut.
Richard Cerretti for Mark Twain Museum, Hannibal, Missouri.

from *The Adventures of Tom Sawyer* **43**

Metaphors are a special kind of imaginative language in which one thing is compared to something very different. Metaphors are not literally true. If you say "That movie was a bomb," you are using a metaphor. If you say "New York is the Big Apple," you are using a metaphor. Like most talented writers, Twain uses many metaphors. In the first paragraph, for example, he suggests that Tom's school is a prison. Notice that Twain talks of school in terms of "captivity" and "fetters" (chains). When you read a writer like Mark Twain, you have to let your imagination go. Once you learn to trust your own instincts, most of Twain's language will become clear to you. If you are like millions of other readers, you will also find it very funny.

Dentistry

Monday morning found Tom Sawyer miserable. Monday morning always found him so—because it began another week's slow suffering in school. He generally began that day with wishing he had had no intervening holiday, it made the going into captivity and fetters again so much more odious.[1]

Tom lay thinking. Presently it occurred to him that he wished he was sick; then he could stay home from school. Here was a vague possibility. He canvassed his system. No ailment was found, and he investigated again. This time he thought he could detect colicky symptoms,[2] and he began to encourage them with considerable hope. But they soon grew feeble, and presently died wholly away. He reflected further. Suddenly he discovered something. One of his upper front teeth was loose. This was lucky; he was about to begin to groan, as a "starter," as he called it, when it occurred to him that if he came into court[3] with that argument, his aunt would pull it out, and that would hurt. So he thought he would hold the tooth in reserve for the present, and seek further. Nothing offered for some little time, and then he remembered hearing the doctor tell about a certain thing that laid up a patient for two or three weeks and threatened to make him lose a finger. So the boy eagerly

---

1. **odious** (ō′de·əs): hateful, disgusting.
2. **colicky** (ko′li·kē) **symptoms:** pains in the stomach.

3. In other words, "if he came before his aunt."
   (Twain is comparing Tom's aunt to a judge in court.)

drew his sore toe from under the sheet and held it up for inspection. But now he did not know the necessary symptoms. However, it seemed well worth while to chance it, so he fell to groaning with considerable spirit.

But Sid slept on unconscious.

Tom groaned louder and fancied that he began to feel pain in the toe.

No result from Sid.

Tom was panting with his exertions by this time. He took a rest and then swelled himself up and fetched a succession of admirable groans.

Sid snored on.

Tom was aggravated. He said, "Sid, Sid!" and shook him. This course worked well, and Tom began to groan again. Sid yawned, stretched, then brought himself up on his elbow with a snort, and began to stare at Tom. Tom went on groaning.

Sid said:

"Tom! Say, Tom!" (No response.) "Here, Tom! *Tom!* What is the matter, Tom?" And he shook him and looked in his face anxiously.

Tom moaned out:

"Oh, don't, Sid. Don't joggle me."

"Why, what's the matter, Tom? I must call Auntie."

"No—never mind. It'll be over by and by, maybe. Don't call anybody."

"But I must! *Don't* groan so, Tom, it's awful. How long you been this way?"

"Hours. Ouch! Oh, don't stir so, Sid, you'll kill me."

"Tom, why didn't you wake me sooner? Oh, Tom, *don't!* It makes my flesh

crawl to hear you. Tom, what *is* the matter?"

"I forgive you everything, Sid. (Groan.) Everything you've ever done to me. When I'm gone——"

"Oh, Tom, you ain't dying, are you? Don't, Tom—oh, don't. Maybe——"

"I forgive everybody, Sid. (Groan.) Tell 'em so, Sid. And Sid, you give my window sash and my cat with one eye to that new girl that's come to town, and tell her——"

But Sid had snatched his clothes and gone. Tom was suffering in reality, now, so handsomely was his imagination working, and so his groans had gathered quite a genuine tone.

Sid flew downstairs and said:

"Oh, Aunt Polly, come! Tom's dying!"

"Dying!"

"Yes'm. Don't wait—come quick!"

"Rubbage! I don't believe it!"

But she fled upstairs, nevertheless, with Sid and Mary at her heels. And her face grew white, too, and her lip trembled. When she reached the bedside she gasped out, "You, Tom! Tom, what's the matter with you?"

"Oh, Auntie, I'm——"

"What's the matter with you—what *is* the matter with you, child?"

"Oh, Auntie, my sore toe's mortified!"

The old lady sank down into a chair and laughed a little, then cried a little, then did both together. This restored her and she said:

"Tom, what a turn you did give me.

Now you shut up that nonsense and climb out of this."

The groans ceased and the pain vanished from the toe. The boy felt a little foolish, and he said:

"Aunt Polly, it *seemed* mortified, and it hurt so I never minded my tooth at all."

"Your tooth, indeed! What's the matter with your tooth?"

"One of them's loose, and it aches perfectly awful."

"There, there, now, don't begin that groaning again. Open your mouth. Well— your tooth *is* loose, but you're not going to die about that. Mary, get me a silk thread and a chunk of fire out of the kitchen."

Tom said:

"Oh, please, Auntie, don't pull it out.

"Tom, Tom, I love you so, and you seem to try every way you can to break my old heart with your outrageousness."

From the movie *The Adventures of Tom Sawyer* (1938).

It don't hurt anymore. I wish I may never stir if it does. Please don't, Auntie. *I* don't want to stay home from school."

"Oh, you don't, don't you? So all this row[4] was because you thought you'd get to stay home from school and go a-fishing? Tom, Tom, I love you so, and you seem to try every way you can to break my old heart with your outrageousness." By this time the dental instruments were ready. The old lady made one end of the silk thread fast to Tom's tooth with a loop and tied the other to the bedpost. Then she seized the chunk of fire and suddenly thrust it almost into the boy's face. The tooth hung dangling by the bedpost now.

But all trials bring their compensations. As Tom wended[5] to school after breakfast, he was the envy of every boy he met because the gap in his upper row of teeth enabled him to expectorate[6] in a new and admirable way. He gathered quite a following of lads interested in the exhibition; and one that had cut his finger, and had been a center of fascination and homage up to this time, now found himself suddenly without an adherent,[7] and shorn of his glory. His heart was heavy, and he said with a disdain which he did not feel that it wasn't anything to spit like Tom Sawyer. But another boy said, "Sour grapes!" and he wandered away a dismantled hero.

Huck Finn

Shortly, Tom came upon the juve pariah[8] of the village, Huckleberry Fin son of the town drunkard. Huckleberry was cordially hated and dreaded by all the mothers of the town, because he was idle and lawless and vulgar and bad—and because all their children admired him so, and delighted in his forbidden society, and wished they dared to be like him. Tom was like the rest of the respectable boys in that he envied Huckleberry his gaudy[9] outcast condition, and was under strict orders not to play with him. So he played with him every time he got a chance. Huckleberry was always dressed in the castoff clothes of full-grown men, and they were in perennial bloom and fluttering with rags. His hat was a vast ruin with a wide crescent lopped out of its brim; his coat, when he wore one, hung nearly to his heels and had the rearward buttons far down the back; but one suspender supported his trousers; the seat of the trousers bagged low and contained nothing; the fringed legs dragged in the dirt when not rolled up.

Huckleberry came and went at his own free will. He slept on doorsteps in fine weather and in empty hogsheads[10] in wet; he did not have to go to school or to church, or call any being master or obey anybody; he could go fishing or swimming

---

4. **row** (rou): noise and quarreling.
5. **wended:** traveled.
6. **expectorate** (ik·spek′tə·rāt′): spit.
7. **adherent** (əd·hir′ənt): follower.

8. **pariah** (pə·rī′ə): outcast.
9. **gaudy** (gô′dē): bright and showy, but not considered in "good taste."
10. **hogsheads:** very large barrels.

when and where he chose, and stay as long as it suited him; nobody forbade him to fight; he could sit up as late as he pleased; he was always the first boy that went barefoot in the spring and the last to resume leather in the fall; he never had to wash, nor put on clean clothes; he could swear wonderfully. In a word, everything that goes to make life precious, that boy had. So thought every harassed, hampered, respectable boy in St. Petersburg.

Tom hailed the romantic outcast: "Hello, Huckleberry! . . . Say—what's that?"

"Nothing but a tick."

"Where'd you get him?"

"Out in the woods."

"What'll you take for him?"

"I don't know. I don't want to sell him."

"All right. It's a mighty small tick, anyway."

"Oh, anybody can run a tick down that don't belong to them. I'm satisfied with it. It's a good enough tick for me."

"Sho, there's ticks a-plenty. I could have a thousand of 'em if I wanted to."

"Well, why don't you? Becuz you know mighty well you can't. This is a pretty early tick, I reckon. It's the first one I've seen this year."

"Say, Huck—I'll give you my tooth for him."

"Less see it."

Tom got out a bit of paper and carefully unrolled it. Huckleberry viewed it wistfully. The temptation was very strong. At last he said, "Is it genuwyne?"

Tom lifted his lip and showed the vacancy.

"Well, all right," said Huckleberry, "it's a trade."

Tom enclosed the tick in the percussion-cap box that had lately been the pinch bug's prison,[11] and the boys separated, each feeling wealthier than before.

Becky

When Tom reached the little isolated frame schoolhouse, he strode in briskly, with the manner of one who had come with all honest speed. He hung his hat on a peg and flung himself into his seat with businesslike alacrity.[12] The master, throned on high in his great splint-bottom armchair, was dozing, lulled by the drowsy hum of study. The interruption roused him.

"Thomas Sawyer!"

Tom knew that when his name was pronounced in full, it meant trouble.

"Sir!"

"Come up here. Now, sir, why are you late again, as usual?"

Tom was about to take refuge in a lie, when he saw two long tails of yellow hair hanging down a back that he recognized by the electric sympathy of love. And by that form was *the only vacant place* on the girls' side of the schoolhouse. He instantly said:

"I STOPPED TO TALK WITH HUCKLEBERRY FINN!"

---

11. Tom collects all sorts of things, including bugs and dead cats and teeth.

12. **alacrity** (ə·lak'rə·tē): eagerness and readiness.

The master's pulse stood still, and he stared helplessly. The buzz of study ceased. The pupils wondered if this foolhardy boy had lost his mind. The master said:

"You—you did what?"

"Stopped to talk with Huckleberry Finn."

There was no mistaking the words.

"Thomas Sawyer, this is the most astounding confession I have ever listened to. No mere ferule[13] will answer for this offense. Take off your jacket."

The master's arm performed until it was tired and the stock of switches notably diminished. Then the order followed:

"Now, sir, go and sit with the *girls!* And let this be a warning to you."

The titter that rippled around the room appeared to abash[14] the boy; but in reality, that result was caused rather more by his worshipful awe of his unknown idol and the dread pleasure that lay in his high good fortune. He sat down upon the end of the pine bench, and the girl hitched herself away from him with a toss of her head. Nudges and winks and whispers traversed the room, but Tom sat still, with his arms upon the long, low desk before him, and seemed to study his book.

By and by, attention ceased from him, and the accustomed school murmur rose upon the dull air once more. Presently, the boy began to steal furtive glances at the girl. She observed it, made a mouth at him and gave him the back of her head for the space of a minute. When she cautiously faced around again, a peach lay before her. She thrust it away. Tom gently put it back. She thrust it away again, but with less animosity.[15] Tom patiently returned it to its place. Then she let it remain. Tom scrawled on his slate,[16] "Please take it—I got more." The girl glanced at the words but made no sign. Now the boy began to draw something on the slate, hiding his work with his left hand. For a time, the girl refused to notice. But her human curiosity presently began to manifest itself by hardly perceptible[17] signs. The boy worked on, apparently unconscious. The girl made a sort of noncommittal attempt to see, but the boy did not betray that he was aware of it. At last she gave in and hesitatingly whispered, "Let me see it."

Tom partly uncovered a dismal caricature[18] of a house with two gable ends to it and a corkscrew of smoke issuing from the chimney. Then the girl's interest began to fasten itself upon the work, and she forgot everything else. When it was finished, she gazed a moment, then whispered, "It's nice—make a man."

The artist erected a man in the front

---

13. **ferule** (fer′ool): ruler or flat stick, used to hit children. (In those days, students could be whipped in school by the teacher. For serious offenses, the teacher used a light switch taken from a tree.)
14. **abash**: embarrass.
15. **animosity** (an′ə·mos′ə·tē): dislike.
16. **slate:** In those days, schoolchildren wrote on small chalkboards (or slates) that they carried with them. They did not use paper, as we do today.
17. **perceptible** (pər·sep′tə·bəl): noticeable.
18. **caricature** (kar′i·kə·choor): an exaggerated picture, like a cartoon.

yard, which resembled a derrick.[19] He could have stepped over the house.

But the girl was not hypercritical. She was satisfied with the monster, and whispered, "It's a beautiful man—now make me coming along."

Tom drew an hourglass with a full moon and straw limbs to it and armed the spreading fingers with a portentous[20] fan.

The girl said, "It's ever so nice—I wish I could draw."

"It's easy," whispered Tom, "I'll learn you."

"Oh, will you? When?"

"At noon. Do you go home to dinner?"

"I'll stay if you will."

"Good—that's a whack. What's your name?"

"Becky Thatcher. What's yours? Oh, I know. It's Thomas Sawyer."

"That's the name they lick me by. I'm Tom when I'm good. You call me Tom, will you?"

"Yes."

Now Tom began to scrawl something on the slate, hiding the words from the girl. But she was not backward this time. She begged to see.

Tom said, "Oh, it ain't anything."

"Yes it is."

"No it ain't. You don't want to see."

"Yes I do, indeed I do. Please let me."

"You'll tell."

"No I won't—deed and deed and double deed I won't."

"You won't tell anybody at all? Ever, as long as you live?"

"No, I won't ever tell *any*body. Now let me."

"Oh, *you* don't want to see!"

"Now that you treat me so, I *will* see." And she put her small hand upon his and a little scuffle ensued, Tom pretending to resist in earnest but letting his hand slip by degrees till these words were revealed: *"I love you."*

"Oh, you bad thing!" And she hit his hand a smart rap, but reddened and looked pleased nevertheless.

Just at this juncture[21] the boy felt a slow, fateful grip closing on his ear and a steady lifting impulse. In that vise[22] he was borne across the house and deposited in his own seat, under a peppering fire of giggles from the whole school. Then the master stood over him during a few awful moments, and finally moved away to his throne without saying a word. But although Tom's ear tingled, his heart was jubilant.

As the school quieted down, Tom made an honest effort to study, but the turmoil within him was too great. In turn, he took his place in the reading class and

---

19. **derrick:** a tall tapering framework used to support machinery (like an oil derrick).
20. **portentous** (pôr·ten′təs): large; marvelous.

21. **juncture** (jungk′chər): point in time.
22. **vise** (vīs): a carpenter's tool. Usually, a vise is attached to a workbench and used to grip firmly some object the carpenter is working on. Here, the grip of the schoolmaster is compared to the grip of a vise.

"Let me see it."

Illustration by Worth Brehm.

made a botch of it. Then in the geography class, he turned lakes into mountains, mountains into rivers, and rivers into continents, till chaos was come again. Then in the spelling class, he got "turned down" by a succession of mere baby words, till he brought up the foot[23] and yielded up the pewter medal which he had worn with ostentation for months.

---

23. Tom ended up last in class. Notice that this meant he had to give up a medal he had shown off earlier. (*Ostentation* means "showing off.")

from *The Adventures of Tom Sawyer* **51**

IDENTIFYING FACTS

1. Tom is a character who always seems to have a **problem**. What is his problem as "Dentistry" opens? How does he try to solve his difficulties?

2. Explain how Tom finally loses his tooth.

3. Explain why all the mothers in town hate and dread Huck Finn. Why do all the "respectable" boys want to play with him?

4. Why does the schoolmaster send Tom to sit on the girls' side of the schoolroom?

The romantic outcast, Huck Finn.

Illustration by E. W. Kemble (1884).

INTERPRETING MEANINGS

5. Describe how Tom feels about being sent to sit next to the girls.

6. At the end of the story, the schoolmaster has just dragged Tom by the ear over to his own seat. Why, then, is Tom so jubilant, or happy?

7. Did you find Becky's **character** believable in this excerpt? Why or why not?

8. Tom botches his geography lesson. What does it mean that he turns "lakes into mountains, mountains into rivers, and rivers into continents"? Why does Tom make all these errors?

APPLYING MEANINGS

9. Today, would a teacher punish a boy by sending him to sit with the *girls*? What other things that happened in this schoolroom would *not* happen today?

Focus on Reading

MAKING INFERENCES

An **inference** is an "educated guess." That means that an inference is a conclusion that is based on certain evidence.

Here are some passages from the story about Tom Sawyer. First find each passage and read it in context (that is, read the passages immediately before and after it). Then answer the questions that follow.

1. "Then she seized the chunk of fire and suddenly thrust it almost into the boy's face. The tooth hung dangling by the bedpost now." (Page 47)

   a. What happened when Aunt Polly thrust the fire in Tom's face?

b. Write a sentence supplying the details that are missing between sentences 1 and 2 here.

2. "[Huckleberry] was always the first boy that went barefoot in the spring and the last to resume leather in the fall." (Page 48)

    a. What does Twain mean by "leather" here?

    b. What did the boys wear on their feet in the summer?

3. "The master's arm performed until it was tired and the stock of switches notably diminished." (Page 49)

    a. What is the master doing here?

    b. Explain the action in your own words.

Literary Elements

CHARACTER

Mark Twain's greatest character is Huck Finn. Later, in another novel, Twain lets Huck tell his own story. Look back now at the passage on page 47 where Twain introduces Huck. Make a list of the details that help Huck come alive. Organize your details under these headings:

1. Huck's **appearance.**

2. Huck's **speech.**

3. Huck's **actions.**

4. What **other people** think about Huck.

5. What the writer tells you **directly** about Huck.

Twain says that Huck has "everything that goes to make life precious." In what ways is this definitely not true? Are there children like Huck Finn in our society today?

Language and Vocabulary

METAPHORS

Metaphors are imaginative comparisons which are not literally true. Metaphors compare two things that are basically unlike. For example, in paragraph 2, approaching Aunt Polly with a complaint about a loose tooth is compared with going into court to complain to a judge. (Tom knows he won't win in Polly's court!) Here are some other metaphors in this story.

1. "The master, throned on high in his great splint-bottom armchair, was dozing. . . ."

    a. Which word in this passage suggests a comparison between the schoolmaster and a king?

    b. What does this suggest about the way the master ran his schoolroom?

2. "The buzz of study ceased."

    a. What does Twain compare the sound of studying to?

    b. How might students in a classroom "buzz"?

Dramatizing a Story

(A Group Activity)

Tom Sawyer is great fun to dramatize. Select one of the scenes presented here and write a dramatization for a classroom theater. Here is what you'll have to consider:

1. How many **characters** do you need? List them and write a description of each one.

2. Describe where the **scene** will be set. What scenery will you need?

3. What **costumes** will you need?

from *The Adventures of Tom Sawyer* **53**

4. You will have to assign an individual or a group to write **dialogue**. You should try to use as much of Twain's own dialogue as possible. For a model of how dramatic dialogue is written, see Unit Six.

5. Will you use **music** or any other **sound effects**?

6. What **props** do you need? (*Props* are "properties," or small movable objects used by the actors. Huck's tick is a prop.) Make a list.

Focus on Personal Narrative

USING VIVID LANGUAGE

Mark Twain uses vivid language to bring Tom Sawyer's adventures to life. Here are two kinds of vivid language that will make your own narrative more lively:

Metaphors: imaginative comparisons which are not literally true—for example, "the electric sympathy of love" (page 48) or "a peppering fire of giggles" (page 50).

Vivid action verbs: for example, *rippled, abash, hitched, traversed* in the paragraph on page 49 beginning with "The titter that rippled around the room."

Write a paragraph in which you describe an adventure with a classmate or another friend. Use as many vivid action verbs as you can. Try to include at least two or three metaphors. Save your writing.

About The Author

Mark Twain (1835–1910) is America's greatest comic writer and the author of two famous novels about growing up: *The Adventures of Tom Sawyer* and *The Adventures of Huckleberry Finn.*

"Mark Twain" was born Samuel Langhorne Clemens on the Missouri frontier, and

Mark Twain, 15 years old.

From the Mark Twain Papers. The Bancroft Library, University of California, Berkeley.

he grew up in a town on the Mississippi River. As a boy, he thrived on the teeming river traffic. As an adult, he took his famous pen name from the cry the boatmen made when the water reached the safe depth of two fathoms: "Mark twain!" He later wrote *Life on the Mississippi,* a book about his experiences as a cub pilot on a Mississippi River steamboat.

Twain wrote over a dozen other books and stories. His tales brought him wealth and fame. But he also knew failure and tragedy. Several of his businesses went bankrupt, and he was crushed by the deaths of his wife and two of his three young daughters. As he grew older, the great humorist found it more and more difficult to write.

But today Twain is remembered for the gift of wit and laughter he gave to the American people. He once said that laughter is the best weapon we have against the troubles of life.

Is the Story True?

Behind the Scenes

In his autobiography, Mark Twain talks about some of the experiences from his own life that he used in his novels. Here is how he remembers the boy who inspired the character of Huckleberry Finn. His name was Tom Blankenship.

. . . I have drawn Tom Blankenship exactly as he was. He was ignorant, unwashed, insufficiently fed; but he had as good a heart as ever any boy had. His liberties were totally unrestricted. He was the only really independent person— boy or man—in the community, and by consequence he was tranquilly and continuously happy and was envied by all the rest of us. We liked him; we enjoyed his society. And as his society was forbidden us by our parents, . . . we sought and got more of his society than of any other boy's. I heard, four years ago, that he was justice of the peace in a remote village in Montana and was a good citizen and greatly respected.

—Mark Twain

from Hank the Cowdog

JOHN R. ERICKSON

Before You Read

The next character you'll meet, Hank the Cowdog, will tell you what it's like to have the all-important job of "Head of Ranch Security." As Hank will explain, a cowdog is used on farms and ranches to protect the livestock from coyotes. It's a tough job, and Hank doesn't fool around. You might recognize Hank and his friends from the cartoon made from this book.

After reading the excerpt through once so you're familiar with Hank's lively personality, take turns "being Hank" and read his story aloud. (You'll need one person to play the timid Drover.) Have fun disguising your voices to make the characters of this tough cowdog and his bumbling assistant come to life in your classroom.

Bloody Murder

It's me again, Hank the Cowdog. I just got some terrible news. There's been a murder on the ranch.

I know I shouldn't blame myself. I mean, a dog is only a dog. He can't be everywhere at once. When I took this job as Head of Ranch Security, I knew that I was only flesh and blood, four legs, a tail, a couple of ears, a pretty nice kind of nose that the women really go for, two bushels of hair and another half-bushel of Mexican sandburs.

You add that all up and you don't get Superman, just me, good old easy-going Hank who works hard, tries to do his job, and gets very little cooperation from anyone else around here.

I'm not complaining. I knew this wouldn't be an easy job. It took a special kind of dog—strong, fearless, dedicated, and above all, smart. Obviously Drover didn't fit. The job fell on my shoulders. It was my destiny. I couldn't escape the broom of history that swept through . . . anyway, I took the job.

Head of Ranch Security. Gee, I was proud of that title. Just the sound of it made my tail wag. But now this, a murder, right under my nose. I know I shouldn't blame myself, but I do.

I got the report this morning around dawn. I had been up most of the night patrolling the northern perimeter of ranch headquarters. I had heard some coyotes yapping up there and I went up to check it out. I told Drover where I was going and

he came up lame all of a sudden, said he needed to rest his right front leg.

I went alone, didn't find anything. The coyotes stayed out in the pasture. I figured there were two, maybe three of them. They yapped for a couple of hours, making fun of me, calling me ugly names, and daring me to come out and fight.

Well, you know me. I'm no dummy. There's a thin line between heroism and stupidity, and I try to stay on the south side of it. I didn't go out and fight, but I answered them bark for bark, yap for yap, name for name.

The coyote hasn't been built who can outyap Hank the Cowdog.

A little before dawn, Loper, one of the

The coyote hasn't been built who can outyap Hank the Cowdog.

Courtesy Maverick Books.

cowboys on this outfit, stuck his head out the door and bellered, "Shut up that yapping, you idiot!" I guess he thought there was only one coyote out there.

They kept it up and I gave it back to them. Next time Loper came to the door, he was armed. He fired a gun into the air and squalled, something about how a man couldn't sleep around here with all the dad-danged noise. I agreed.

Would you believe it? Them coyotes yipped louder than ever, and I had no choice but to give it back to them.

Loper came back out on the porch and fired another shot. This one came so close to me that I heard the hum. Loper must have lost his bearings or something, so I barked louder than ever to give him my position, and, you know, to let him know that I was out there protecting the ranch.

The next bullet just derned near got me. I mean, I felt the wind of it as it went past. That was enough for me. I shut her down for the night. If Loper couldn't aim any better than that, he was liable to hurt somebody.

I laid low for a while, hiding in the shelter belt, until I was sure the artillery had gone back to bed. Then I went down for a roll in the sewer, cleaned up, washed myself real good, came out feeling refreshed and ready to catch up on my sleep. Trotted down to the gas tanks and found Drover curled up in my favorite spot.

I growled him off my gunny sack. "Beat it, son. Make way for the night patrol."

He didn't want to move so I went to

sterner measures, put some fangs on him. That moved him out, and he didn't show no signs of lameness either. I have an idea that where Drover is lamest is between his ears.

I did my usual bedtime ritual of walking in a tight circle around my bed until I found just exactly the spot I wanted, and then I flopped down. Oh, that felt good! I wiggled around and finally came to rest with all four paws sticking up in the air. I closed my eyes and had some wonderful twitching dreams about . . . don't recall exactly the subject matter, but most likely they were about Beulah, the neighbor's collie. I dream about her a lot.

What a woman! Makes my old heart pound just to think about her. Beautiful brown and white hair, big eyes, nose that tapers down to a point (not quite as good as mine, but so what?), and nice ears that flap when she runs.

Only trouble is that she's crazy about a spotted bird dog, without a doubt the ugliest, dumbest, worthlessest cur I ever met. What could be uglier than a spotted short-haired dog with a long skinny tail? And what could be dumber or more worthless than a dog that goes around chasing *birds*?

They call him Plato. I don't know why, except maybe because his eyes look like plates half the time, empty plates. He don't know a cow from a sow, but do you think that makes him humble? No sir. He thinks that birdchasing is hot stuff. What really hurts, though, is that Beulah seems to agree.

Don't understand that woman, but I dream about her a lot.

Anyway, where was I? Under the gas tanks, catching up on my sleep. All at once Drover was right there beside me, jumping up and down and giving off that high-pitched squeal of his that kind of bores into your eardrums. You can't ignore him when he does that.

Well, I threw open one eye, kept the other one shut so that I could get some halfway sleep. "Will you please shut up?"

"Hank, oh Hankie, it's just terrible, you wouldn't believe, hurry and wake up, I seen his tracks down on the creek, get up before he escapes!"

I threw open the other eye, pushed myself up, and went nose-to-nose with the noisemaker. "Quit hopping around. Quit making all that racket. Hold still and state your business."

"Okay, Hank, all right, I'll try." He tried and was none too successful, but he did get the message across. "Oh Hank, there's been a killing, right here on the ranch, and we slept through it!"

"Huh?" I was coming awake by then, and the word *killing* sent a jolt clean out to the end of my tail. "Who's been killed?"

"They hit the chickenhouse, Hank. I don't know how they got in but they did, busted in there and killed one of those big leghorn hens, killed her dead, Hank, and oh, the blood!"

Well, that settled it. I had no choice but to go back on duty. A lot of dogs would have just turned over and gone back to sleep, but I take this stuff pretty serious.

We trotted up to the chickenhouse, and Drover kept jumping up and down and talking. "I found some tracks down by the creek. I'm sure they belong to the killer, Hank, I'm just sure they do."

"What kind of tracks?"

"Coyote."

"Hmm." We reached the chickenhouse and, sure enough, there was the hen lying on the ground, and she was still dead. I walked around the body, sniffing it good and checking the signs.

I noticed the position of the body and memorized every detail. The hen was lying on her left side, pointing toward the northeast, with one foot out and the other one curled up under her wing. Her mouth was open and it appeared to me that she had lost some tail feathers.

"Uh huh, I'm beginning to see the pattern."

"What, tell me, Hank, who done it?"

"Not yet. Where'd you see them tracks?" There weren't any tracks around the corpse, ground was too hard. Drover took off in a run and I followed him down into the brush along the creek.

He stopped and pointed to some fresh tracks in the mud. "There they are, Hank, just where I found them. Are you proud of me?"

I pushed him aside and studied the sign, looked it over real careful, sniffed it, gave it the full treatment. Then I raised up.

"Okay, I've got it now. It's all clear. Them's coon tracks, son, not coyote. I can tell from the scent. Coons must have attacked while I was out on patrol. They're sneaky, you've got to watch 'em every minute."

Drover squinted at the tracks. "Are you sure those are coon tracks? They sure look like coyote to me."

"You don't go by the *look,* son, you go by the *smell.* This nose of mine don't lie. If it says coon, you better believe there's a coon at the end of them tracks. And I'm fixing to clean house on him. Stay behind me and don't get hurt."

I threaded my way through the creek willows, over the sand, through the water. I never lost the scent. In the heat of a chase, all my senses come alive and point like a blazing arrow toward the enemy.

In a way I felt sorry for the coon, even though he'd committed a crime and become my mortal enemy. With me on his trail, the little guy just didn't have a chance. One of the disadvantages of being as big and deadly as I am is that you sometimes find yourself in sympathy with the other guy.

But part of being Head of Ranch Security is learning to ignore that kind of emotion. I mean, to hold down this job, you have to be cold and hard.

The scent was getting stronger all the time, and it didn't smell exactly like any coon I'd come across before. All at once I saw him. I stopped dead still and Drover, the little dummy, ran right into me and almost had a heart attack. I guess he thought I was a giant coon or something. It's hard to say what he thinks.

The coon was hiding in some bushes about five feet in front of me. I could hear him chewing on something, and that smell was real strong now.

"What's that?" Drover whispered, sniffing the air.

"Coon, what do you think?" I glanced back at him. He was shaking with fear. "You ready for some combat experience?"

"Yes," he squeaked.

"All right, here's the plan. I'll jump him and try to get him behind the neck. You come in the second wave and take what you can. If you run away like you did last time, I'll sweep the corral with you and give you a whupping you won't forget. All right, let's move out."

I crouched down and crept forward, every muscle in my highly conditioned body taut and ready for action. Five feet, four feet, three feet, two. I sprang through the air and hit right in the middle of the biggest porcupine I ever saw.

It was kind of a short fight.
Courtesy Maverick Books.

Quills: Just Part of the Job

It was kind of a short fight. Coming down, I seen them quills aimed up at me and tried to change course. Too late. I don't move so good in mid-air.

I lit right in the middle of him and *bam,* he slapped me across the nose with his tail, sure did hurt too, brought tears to my eyes. I hollered for Drover to launch the second wave but he had disappeared.

Porcupine took another shot at me but I dodged, tore up half an acre of brush, and got the heck out of there. As I limped back up to the house on pin-cushion feet, my thoughts went back to the murder scene and the evidence I had committed to memory.

It was clear now. The porcupine had had nothing at all to do with the murder because porcupines don't eat anything but trees. Drover had found the first set of tracks he had come to and had started hollering about coyotes. I had been duped into believing the runt.

Yes, it was all clear. I had no leads, no clues, no idea who had killed the hen. What I *did* have was a face-full of porcupine quills, as well as several in my paws. . . .

About the Author

John R. Erickson (1943–) was born in Midland, Texas. *Hank the Cowdog* is the first in the series of Hank the Cowdog books. Erickson has written more than twenty books about the adventures of Hank. Describing his books, Erickson says: "I write my stories to be like an amusement park water slide— once you're on, you can't get off and before you know it, it's over." In addition to writing, Erickson likes ranching and playing a five-string banjo. Two recent books by Erickson are *The Case of the Car-Barkaholic Dog* and *Hank the Cowdog: The Case of the Hooking Bull.*

MAKING GENERALIZATIONS

*T*he **theme** of a story is its main idea or basic meaning. The theme is not the same as the subject. You can usually state the subject of a story in a word or phrase: for example, "childhood" or "escape to freedom." The theme is something the writer wants to reveal about the subject. Use a complete sentence to state a theme.

A **generalization** about the theme of a work is a broad statement that sums up the work's central meaning. The ability to make a generalization can help you enjoy literature more. It can also help you to sum up the meaning of an experience you tell about in a **personal narrative.**

To make a generalization, you need to use sufficient evidence and sound reasoning. Here are some questions to ask when you are trying to find the theme of a story:

- *What is the writer's central purpose?* What is the writer trying to show about life or human nature?
- *How do the characters change through the story?* For example, does a character learn a new lesson or undergo a change in attitude?
- *What major conflicts occur, and how are they resolved?* Do the conflicts end with the characters understanding more about themselves? Do the characters overcome challenges?
- *Does the title give a clue to the theme?*

After you identify the theme of a story, state it in a complete sentence as a generalization about life or human nature. This means that the statement will apply to many people, not just to the characters in the story. For example, the theme of Gary Soto's "The Jacket" (page 35) might be stated as the following generalization: *When we feel insecure, even the smallest problems can seem major.*

Write a complete sentence stating the theme of *one* of the following selections: C. S. Lewis' "Mr. Tumnus" (page 10) or Ann Petry's "Harriet Tubman" (page 22). You can use the questions above as guidelines to help state the theme as a generalization.

WRITING A PERSONAL NARRATIVE

*I*n a **personal narrative** you write about an experience from your own life. In this kind of writing, you tell about events in a clear order. You also express the thoughts and feelings you had about the experience.

Prewriting

1. You will find these hints helpful when you choose a subject for a personal narrative:

   - Choose an experience that is still sharp and clear in your memory.
   - Choose an experience that was important to you.
   - Choose an experience that you are willing to share.

   You can use a chart like the one below to get ideas about topics. What memories does the word at the top of each column prompt in you? (Feel free to use different memory prompts if you wish.)

Movies	Clothes	Family
_____	_____	_____
_____	_____	_____
_____	_____	_____
Teams	Songs	Challenges
_____	_____	_____
_____	_____	_____
_____	_____	_____

   [See **Focus** assignment on page 19.]

2. Think about your purpose and audience. Your **purpose** in a personal narrative is to share one of your experiences with your readers. Make notes while you prewrite about your memories, thoughts, and feelings.

   Your **audience** will probably be your classmates and your teacher. Remember that they may need some background information in order to understand your experience. Make notes about the details that your audience may need.

3. Gather **action details** and **sensory details** that will make your narrative clear and lively. Action details tell what happened and how it happened. These details also include **dialogue,** or the words that people said. Try to use dialogue as often as you can to tell about a situation. You can turn a situation into dialogue by following these simple steps:

   - Visualize the situation as vividly as you can
   - Think about what the people involved in the situation said
   - Consider *how* the people spoke: cheerfully, sadly, quickly, slowly, hesitantly, and so on

   Sensory details appeal to the five senses of sight, hearing, taste, smell, and touch. You can list these details on a chart like the one on the next page.

Details Chart

Action Details	Sensory Details
_____	_____
_____	_____
_____	_____
_____	_____

[See **Focus** assignment on page 32.]

4. Reflect on why the experience was important to you. What were you like before the experience? How did it change you? What did you learn from it? Make a few notes on the overall meaning of the experience.

Writing

1. Follow an outline like the one below to write your narrative.

   I. Beginning: Grab reader's attention and introduce topic.
   II. Body: Tell events in order, giving details, thoughts, and feelings.
   III. Ending: Show the meaning the experience had for you.

   Use **chronological** or **time order** in the body of your narrative. Also plan to use **transitional words and phrases** to show the connections of events and ideas. Some helpful transitions include the following: *after, before, finally, first, next, often, second, soon, then, third,* and *when.* [See **Focus** assignment on page 41.]

2. Make your language as vivid as you can. For example, you can use **metaphors,** or imaginative comparisons that are not literally true. You can also use

vivid action verbs to help your readers see the action. [See **Focus** assignment on page 54.]

Evaluating and Revising

1. When you have finished your first draft, trade papers with a classmate. Read each other's narratives. Then give each other comments and suggestions. Is the order of events clear? Does the narrative help the reader "see" the characters and situations? Does the narrative help the reader understand the meaning of the experience?

   Here is how one writer revised a paragraph from a personal narrative.

Writer's Model

   That Saturday morning I dressed *like an express train and tore* ~~quickly.~~ I went into the kitchen. I was so excited that I ~~couldn't~~ hardly eat breakfast. Uncle Harry was coming at seven o'clock to drive us all to the opening of the state fair in Raleigh. The fair is the most popular entertainment event in our area. *and* I had carefully made a list of the main events and rides. [I overslept. The clock face said 6:45. At first I had no idea what day it was, but soon I realized it was the big weekend I'd been waiting for ever since spring *began*.

2. You may find the following checklist helpful as you revise your narrative.

Checklist for Evaluation and Revision

✔ Does the beginning get the reader's attention and tell the topic?

✔ Do I tell the events in their chronological order?

✔ Do I use vivid action verbs and lively language?

✔ Does the narrative include dialogue to show what people actually said?

✔ Do I include details that show my own thoughts and feelings?

✔ Do I tell or show the overall meaning of the experience?

Proofreading and Publishing

1. Proofread your personal narrative and correct any errors you find in grammar, usage, and mechanics. (Here you may find it helpful to refer to the **Handbook for Revision** on pages 750–785.) Then prepare a final version of your narrative by making a clean copy.

2. Consider some of the following publication methods for your narrative:

   ■ read your narrative orally in a story theater for younger students

   ■ share a copy of your narrative with a relative or friend

   ■ illustrate your narrative with drawings or other art work and then join with a small group to make a collection of narratives

Portfolio If your teacher approves, you may wish to keep a copy of your work in your writing folder or portfolio.

UNIT TWO

Quests

A **quest** is a journey taken in search of something of value. We all know quests from the stories we read as children. Remember all those knights in fairy tales who went on quests to save the kingdom, or to kill the dragon, or to rescue the daughter of the evil king? As you will see from some of the stories that follow, quests are part of everyday life, too. The Pilgrims who voyaged to America were embarked on a quest. The pioneers who made the difficult journey west were embarked on a quest. In Unit Five, you will read about the very recent quest of a Vietnamese boy who crossed a perilous sea for freedom. In fact, some people think that everyone's life can be seen as a "quest story."

Can you think of movies and TV shows that are stories of people on quests?

St. George and the Dragon by Paolo Uccello. Oil on canvas.

National Gallery, London.

*A*ctive readers are always thinking as they read. You are reading actively if you ask questions as you go along: "What will happen next?" or "How could she get herself into this mess?" or "What does that word mean?" Active readers make a lot of guesses, too, and as you know, it's a great feeling when you discover that you've guessed correctly. Active readers draw conclusions from many different clues.

Guidelines for Close Reading

1. Figure out the meaning of an unfamiliar word by using context clues, the words and phrases surrounding the word.

2. Visualize the scene. Use your imagination to picture the time and place of action.

3. Draw conclusions as you read. Look for direct and indirect clues to meaning.

The following excerpt is from the novel *Carlota* by Scott O'Dell. The main character in this novel, Carlota, lives with her father, Don Saturnino (sä•tŏŏr•nē′nō), a wealthy Spanish landowner in California. Her brother Carlos was killed by rivals of their Spanish colony before Carlota was born. Her father named Carlota after his dead son and has brought her up almost as her brother's replacement. As this episode begins, Carlota and her father are making one of their many trips to Blue Beach, where they have found a sunken ship full of gold. The story takes place in the 1800s. Carlota is telling the story.

The comments in the margin show one reader's response to the selection. Ask questions of your own as you read.

from
Carlota

SCOTT O'DELL

ONE READER'S RESPONSE

There were many things to do before the chests could be reached. Usually it took me half a day to bring up a pouch of coins from the sunken ship.

The place where I dove, which was surrounded by jagged rocks and driftwood, was too narrow for my father. He had tried to squeeze through when we first discovered the galleon, but partway down he got stuck and I had to pull him back. It was my task, therefore, to go into the cavelike hole. My father stood beside it and helped me to go down and to come up.

I buckled a strong belt around my waist and to it tied a riata that was ten *varas* long and stout enough to hold a stallion. I fastened my knife to my wrist—a two-edged blade made especially for me by our blacksmith—to protect myself against spiny rays and the big eels that could sting you to death. In the many dives I had made, I never had seen a shark.

Taking three deep breaths, I prepared to let myself down into the hole. In one hand I held a sink-stone, heavy enough to weigh me down. I let out all the air in my chest, took a deep breath, and held it. Then I began the descent.

The sink-stone would have taken me down fast, but the edges of the rocky hole were sharp. I let myself down carefully, one handhold at a time. It took me about a minute to reach the rotted deck where the chests lay. I now had two minutes to pry the coins loose and carry them to the surface. We had tried putting the coins in a leather sack and hoisting them to the surface. But we had trouble with this because of the currents that swept around the wreck.

The coins lay in a mass, stuck together, lapping over each other and solid as rock. They looked, when I first saw them, like something left on the stove too long. I always expected

Sunken treasure! This is my kind of adventure. The girl is doing the diving?

What's a galleon? Another word for ship?

"Jagged rocks," "driftwood," "cavelike"— she must be brave. The diving is dangerous. Is riata rope in Spanish? Varas—must be some kind of measurement.

Maybe this is a hint that she'll meet a shark during this dive. Another danger.

I'm trying to picture these jagged rocks under the water. It's a little confusing. She can hold her breath for three minutes?! I can only hold mine for forty seconds.

Why are the coins stuck together? The ship must have been sunk for a long time.

I can see her walking on the ship's deck with that rocky tunnel above. (It must be hard to walk under water.)

He's smart—I would have agreed with Carlota.

That's nice—they must have a close relationship.

What are barnacles?

I didn't know that. It must be a hard trip up to the surface with all that extra weight.

She does see a shark . . . Oh, but it's not dangerous. So far, so good.

to find them gone, but now as I walked toward the chests, with the stone holding me down, I saw that they were still there. No one had come upon them during the seven months since our last visit.

The first time I had dived and brought up a handful of coins, I said to my father that we should empty both the chests and take the coins home.

"Then everyone would talk," Don Saturnino said. "As soon as they saw the gold coins, the news would spread the length of California."

"We don't need to tell anyone. I can hide them in my chest at home."

"The news would fly out before the sun set. At the ranch there are many eyes."

I still thought it was a better idea to empty the chests before someone else did, but I could see that my father enjoyed these days when the two of us went to the Blue Beach, so I said no more.

The sun was overhead and its rays slanted down through the narrow crevice. There were many pieces of debris on the deck and I had to step carefully. With my knife I pried loose a handful of coins. They were of a dark green color and speckled here and there with small barnacles. I set the coins aside.

My lungs were beginning to hurt, but I had not felt the tug of the riata yet, the signal from my father that I had been down three minutes. I pried loose a second handful and put my knife away. Before the tug came, I dropped my sink-stone and took up the coins. Gold is very heavy, much heavier than stones of the same size.

Fish were swimming around me as I went up through the hole of rocks and tree trunks, but I saw no sting rays or eels. I did see a shark lying back on a ledge, but he was small and gray, a sandshark, which is not dangerous.

On my third trip down, I hauled up about the same number of coins as the other times. The pouch we had brought was now full. I asked my father if we had enough.

"Are you tired?" he said

"Yes, a little."

"Can you go down again?"

"Yes."

"Then go."

I dived twice more. It was on the last dive that I had the trouble. The tug on the riata had not come, but I was tired, so I started away from the chest with one handful of coins. Close to the chests, between them and the hole, I had noticed what seemed to be two pieces of timber covered with barnacles. They looked as if they might be part of a third and larger chest.

I still held my knife and I thrust it at a place where the two

I wonder if he's greedy, or maybe he is just enjoying the adventure of it all.

Now the trouble is coming. What will it be—another shark?

What is it? She's caught.

This means she's been down for three minutes.

I was right—a riata is a rope. Two tugs must be a distress signal.

Horrible! What could be licking her?

Half the height of a man—that means about three feet. A three-foot clam?!

She has to get air soon. She must be about to pass out.

Almost sounds like a science fiction movie. I would be terrified. A maw? Maybe a mouth (a huge mouth).

She's free—I can breathe again.

gray timbers seemed to join. It was possible that I had found another chest filled with coins.

As the knife touched them, the two timbers moved a little. Instantly, I felt pressure upon my wrist. I drew back the hand that held the knife. Rather, I tried to draw it back, but it would not move. The tide had shifted the timbers somehow and I was caught. So I thought.

I felt the tug upon the riata fastened to my waist. It was the signal from my father to come to the surface. I answered him with two quick tugs of the leather rope.

Now I felt a hot pain run up my arm. I tried to open my fingers to drop the knife, but my hand was numb. Then as I stared down into the murky water, I saw a slight movement where my hand was caught. At the same moment I saw a flash of pink, a long fleshy tongue sliding along my wrist.

I had never seen a burro clam, but I had heard the tales about them, for there were many on our coast. Attached to rocks or timbers, they grew to half the height of a man, these gray, silent monsters. Many unwary fishermen had lost their lives in the burros' jaws.

The pain in my arm was not so great now as the hot pains in my chest. I gave a long, hard tug on the riata to let my father know that I was in trouble. Again I saw a flash of pink as the burro opened its lips a little, and the fat tongue slid back and forth.

I dropped the coins I held in my other hand. The burro had closed once more on my wrist. But shortly it began to open again, and I felt a sucking pressure, as if the jaws were trying to draw me inside the giant maw.

Putting my knees against the rough bulge of the shell, as the jaws opened and then began to close, I jerked with all my strength. I fell slowly backward upon the ship's deck. My hand was free. With what breath I had I moved toward the hole. I saw the sun shining above and climbed toward it. The next thing I saw was my father's face and I was lying on the river's sandy bank. He took my knife in his hand.

After I told him what had happened, my father said, ''The

knife saved your life. The burro clamped down upon it. See the mark here. The steel blade kept its jaws open. Enough to let you wrench yourself free.''

He pulled me to my feet and I put on my leather pants and coat.

"Here," he said, passing the reins of his bay gelding to me, "ride Santana. He goes gentler than Tiburón."

"I'll ride my own horse," I said.

"Good, if you wish it."

"I wish it," I said, knowing that he didn't want me to say that my hand was numb.

"Does the hand hurt?"

"No."

"Some?"

"No."

"You were very brave," he said.

My father wanted me to be braver than I was. I wanted to say I was scared, both when the burro had hold of me and now, at this moment, but I didn't because he expected me to be as brave as Carlos. It was at times like this that I was angry at my father and at my dead brother, too.

"It was good fortune," I said.

"Fortune and bravery often go together," Don Saturnino said. "If you do not hurt, let us go."

Looking at Yourself as a Reader

As you look back over this reader's comments, you'll notice:

1. **The reader asks questions about vocabulary.** This reader correctly guesses that *riata* (rē·ä'tä) is the Spanish word for a type of rope. And *varas* is a measurement—equal to about 33 inches. Most of the time, this reader is able to make a good guess at unfamiliar words by using the **context clues,** or the words and phrases surrounding the word. For instance, a *galleon* is a kind of ship—in fact, a large Spanish ship made in the fifteenth and sixteenth centuries. The word *maw* means "oral cavity," or mouth. It is used to refer to the mouth of a large animal.

2. **The reader visualizes the scene.** As she pictures the rocks, she understands the danger of Carlota's quest.

3. **This reader also draws conclusions.** For example, she figures that the ship must have been sunk quite a while for the coins to be stuck together. She calculates the half-height of a man. She concludes that numbness could mean serious trouble after an attack by a burro clam.

Read the excerpt again, this time writing down your own thoughts. After you finish, answer these questions.

1. What kind of person is Carlota? Do you think that she likes being brave and strong and her father's favorite?

2. This reader didn't know why Carlota was angry with her father. What do you think?

3. What might happen next?

THINKING ABOUT WORDS

HOW TO OWN A WORD

What does it mean to know the meaning of a word? You can know nothing or just a little about a word, or you can know a lot about it. When you know a lot about a word, you may feel that you "own" it. To own a word means that you find it easy to understand—not only when you read it, but also when you speak it or write it.

Part of owning a word is figuring out what you already know about it. For instance, *condescend* (kon'di·send') is a word you may know something about. Maybe you've heard someone described as *condescending.* You may realize that people who are *condescending* talk or behave in ways that show they think they are superior to other people.

ORGANIZING WHAT YOU KNOW ABOUT A WORD

Below is a cluster diagram that organizes some ideas about *condescend.* Think of other ideas you might add.

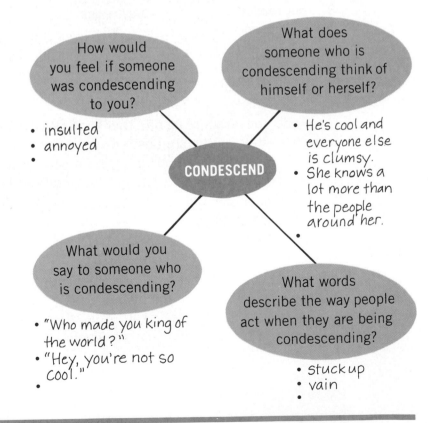

How would you feel if someone was condescending to you?
- insulted
- annoyed
-

What does someone who is condescending think of himself or herself?
- He's cool and everyone else is clumsy.
- She knows a lot more than the people around her.
-

CONDESCEND

What would you say to someone who is condescending?
- "Who made you king of the world?"
- "Hey, you're not so cool."
-

What words describe the way people act when they are being condescending?
- stuck up
- vain
-

In the short story called "The Smallest Dragonboy" in this unit (page 78), you will meet some characters who are *condescending*.

Genuine is an interesting word that you probably know something about. You may know that if something is *genuine* it is real. In the selection you read in the first unit from *The Adventures of Tom Sawyer* (page 42), *genuine* is used twice. When Tom is trying to convince Aunt Polly he is in great pain so he won't have to go to school, the author writes that Tom's "groans had gathered quite a *genuine* tone." Although what Tom does seems *genuine,* he is *not* being *genuine.* Later in the story, when Tom wants to trade his tooth for Huck's tick, Huck wants to make sure the tooth is real and asks, "Is it *genuwyne?*"

MAKING YOUR OWN DIAGRAM

Now you can make your own diagram. On a sheet of paper, copy the ideas listed below. Then list words or phrases that answer the questions about *genuine*. As you think of answers, you'll see how much you really know about the word.

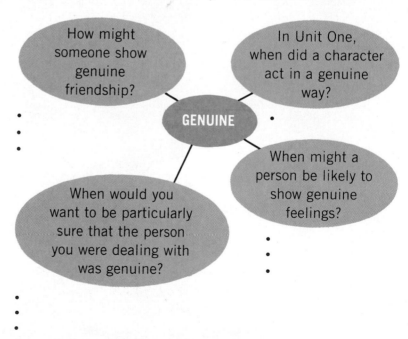

How might someone show genuine friendship?

In Unit One, when did a character act in a genuine way?

GENUINE

When might a person be likely to show genuine feelings?

When would you want to be particularly sure that the person you were dealing with was genuine?

The Smallest Dragonboy

ANNE McCAFFREY

Before You Read

Somewhere in outer space lies the planet Pern, an imaginary world created by Anne McCaffrey. The planet is continually threatened by a deadly force and is protected by the great dragons and their riders who rule its skies. Many of McCaffrey's novels and short stories take place on Pern.

The deadly threat to Pern comes from a dangerous Red Star that rains threadlike plant spores on Pern every two hundred years or so. If the hungry Thread falls on Pern soil and grows there, it will devour every living thing.

To protect their planet, colonists on Pern have developed a race of great winged dragons. These dragons have the telepathic power to travel instantly from one place to another to fight Thread. When fed a special rock called *firestone*, the dragons of Pern breathe flaming tongues of fire that char Thread to ashes in midair. During Threadfall, the dragons and their dragonriders charge into airborne battle, while the other colonists hide safely in their Holds, or cave towns. During the Intervals between Threadfalls, Pern's protectors live inside the cones of old volcanoes, in cave colonies called *weyrs*. The following short story takes place in Benden Weyr, a dragonrider colony in the Benden Mountains.

As the story opens, young Keevan and his fellow candidates for dragonrider are awaiting important news from the Hatching Ground. A clutch of dragon eggs is about to hatch. It is the custom for each newborn dragon to choose its own rider—and lifelong partner—through a kind of telepathic communication called *Impression*.

Impressing a dragon at his first Hatching is vital to Keevan, the youngest dragonboy. How else can he silence the other boys' jeers that he is only "a babe"?

As you read this short story, keep a notepad handy. Write down all the questions you have about Keevan and his quest to become a dragonrider.

Pern has its own people, plants, animals, geography, and weather. To make this imaginary world believable, the writer has created new names, like Keevan, and new words, like *weyr*. She has also combined some familiar English words to make new words, like *dragonrider*. These invented words help you to enter the strange and dangerous world of Pern.

As you read the story, figure out the meanings of the invented words from their **context,** or the words around them. You might make a list of these words to put in a "Pernian" dictionary.

Although Keevan lengthened his walking stride as far as his legs would stretch, he couldn't quite keep up with the other candidates. He knew he would be teased again.

Just as he knew many other things that his foster mother told him he ought not to know, Keevan knew that Beterli, the most senior of the boys, set that spanking pace just to embarrass him, the smallest dragonboy. Keevan would arrive, tail fork-end of the group, breathless, chest heaving, and maybe get a stern look from the instructing wingsecond.

Dragonriders, even if they were still only hopeful candidates for the glowing eggs which were hardening on the hot sands of the Hatching Ground cavern, were expected to be punctual and prepared.

Sloth[1] was not tolerated by the weyrleader of Benden Weyr. A good record was especially important now. It was very near hatching time, when the baby dragons would crack their mottled[2] shells and stagger forth to choose their lifetime companions. The very thought of that glorious moment made Keevan's breath catch in his throat. To be chosen—to be a dragonrider! To sit astride the neck of the winged beast with the jeweled eyes; to be his friend in telepathic communion[3] with him for life; to be his companion in good times and fighting extremes; to fly effortlessly over the lands of Pern! Or, thrillingly, *between* to any point anywhere on the world! Flying *between* was done on dragonback or not at all, and it was dangerous.

---

1. **sloth:** laziness.
2. **mottled:** marked with blotches and spots.
3. **telepathic** (tel′ə·path′ik) **communion:** communication between minds without speaking.

Keevan glanced upward, past the black mouths of the weyr caves in which grown dragons and their chosen riders lived, toward the Star Stones that crowned the ridge of the old volcano that was Benden Weyr. On the height, the blue watch dragon, his rider mounted on his neck, stretched the great transparent pinions[4] that carried him on the winds of Pern to fight the evil Thread that fell at certain times from the sky. The many-faceted rainbow jewels of his eyes glistened momentarily in the greeny sun. He folded his great wings to his back, and the watch-pair resumed their statuesque pose of alertness.

Then the enticing view was obscured as Keevan passed into the Hatching Ground cavern. The sands underfoot were hot, even through heavy wher-hide boots. How the bootmaker had protested having to sew so small! Keevan was forced to wonder again why being small was reprehensible.[5] People were always calling him "babe" and shooing him away as being "too small" or "too young" for this or that. Keevan was constantly working, twice as hard as any other boy his age, to prove himself capable. What if his muscles weren't as big as Beterli's? They were just as hard. And if he couldn't overpower anyone in a wrestling match, he could outdistance everyone in a footrace.

"Maybe if you run fast enough," Beterli had jeered on the occasion when

Keevan had been goaded to boast of his swiftness, "you could catch a dragon. That's the only way you'll make a dragon-rider!"

"You just wait and see, Beterli, you just wait," Keevan had replied. He would have liked to wipe the contemptuous smile from Beterli's face, but the guy didn't fight fair even when the wingsecond was watching. "No one knows what Impresses a dragon!"

"They've got to be able to *find* you first, babe!"

Yes, being the smallest candidate was not an enviable position. It was therefore imperative that Keevan Impress a dragon in his first hatching. That would wipe the smile off every face in the cavern, and accord him the respect due any dragonrider, even the smallest one.

Besides, no one knew exactly what Impressed the baby dragons as they struggled from their shells in search of their lifetime partners.

"I like to believe that dragons see into a man's heart," Keevan's foster mother, Mende, told him. "If they find goodness, honesty, a flexible mind, patience, courage—and you've that in quantity, dear Keevan—that's what dragons look for. I've seen many a well-grown lad left standing on the sands, Hatching Day, in favor of someone not so strong or tall or handsome. And if my memory serves me" (which it usually did—Mende knew every word of every Harper's tale worth telling, although Keevan did not interrupt her to say so), "I don't believe that F'lar, our weyrleader,

4. **pinions** (pin′yənz): wings.
5. **reprehensible** (rep′ri·hen′sə·bəl): deserving of blame.

was all that tall when bronze Mnementh chose him. And Mnementh was the only bronze dragon of that hatching."

Dreams of Impressing a bronze were beyond Keevan's boldest reflections; although that goal dominated the thoughts of every other hopeful candidate. Green dragons were small and fast and more numerous. There was more prestige to Impressing a blue or a brown than a green. Being practical, Keevan seldom dreamed as high as a big fighting brown, like Canth, F'nor's fine fellow, the biggest brown on all Pern. But to fly a bronze? Bronzes were almost as big as the queen, and only they took the air when a queen flew at mating time. A bronze rider could aspire to become weyrleader! Well, Keevan would console himself, brown riders could aspire to become wingseconds, and that wasn't bad. He'd even settle for a green dragon; they were small, but so was he. No matter! He simply had to Impress a dragon his first time in the Hatching Ground. Then no one in the weyr would taunt him anymore for being so small.

"Shells," thought Keevan now, "but the sands are hot!"

"Impression time is imminent,[6] candidates," the wingsecond was saying as everyone crowded respectfully close to him. "See the extent of the striations on this promising egg." The stretch marks *were* larger than yesterday.

Everyone leaned forward and nodded thoughtfully. That particular egg was the one Beterli had marked as his own, and no other candidate dared, on pain of being beaten by Beterli on the first opportunity, to approach it. The egg was marked by a large yellowish splotch in the shape of a dragon backwinging to land, talons outstretched to grasp rock. Everyone knew that bronze eggs bore distinctive markings. And naturally, Beterli, who'd been presented at eight Impressions already and

---

6. **imminent** (im′ə·nənt): about to happen.

was the biggest of the candidates, had chosen it.

"I'd say that the great opening day is almost upon us," the wingsecond went on, and then his face assumed a grave expression. "As we well know, there are only forty eggs and seventy-two candidates. Some of you may be disappointed on the great day. That doesn't necessarily mean you aren't dragonrider material, just that *the* dragon for you hasn't been shelled. You'll have other hatchings, and it's no disgrace to be left behind an Impression or two. Or more."

Keevan was positive that the wingsecond's eyes rested on Beterli, who'd been stood off at so many Impressions already. Keevan tried to squinch down so the wingsecond wouldn't notice him. Keevan had been reminded too often that he was eligible to be a candidate by one day only. He, of all the hopefuls, was most likely to be left standing on the great day. One more reason why he simply had to Impress at his first hatching.

"Now move about among the eggs," the wingsecond said. "Touch them. We don't know that it does any good, but it certainly doesn't do any harm."

Some of the boys laughed nervously, but everyone immediately began to circulate among the eggs. Beterli stepped up officiously to "his" egg, daring anyone to come near it. Keevan smiled, because he had already touched it . . . every inspection day . . . as the others were leaving the Hatching Ground, when no one could see him crouch and stroke it.

Keevan had an egg he concentrated on, too, one drawn slightly to the far side of the others. The shell bore a soft greenish-blue tinge with a faint creamy swirl design. The consensus was that this egg contained a mere green, so Keevan was rarely bothered by rivals. He was somewhat perturbed then to see Beterli wandering over to him.

"I don't know why you're allowed in this Impression, Keevan. There are enough of us without a babe," Beterli said, shaking his head.

"I'm of age." Keevan kept his voice level, telling himself not to be bothered by mere words.

"Yah!" Beterli made a show of standing on his toe tips. "You can't even see over an egg. Hatching Day, you better get in front or the dragons won't see you at all. 'Course, you could get run down that way in the mad scramble. Oh, I forget, you can run fast, can't you?"

"You'd better make sure a dragon sees *you* this time, Beterli," Keevan replied. "You're almost overage, aren't you?"

Beterli flushed and took a step forward, hand half raised. Keevan stood his ground, but if Beterli advanced one more step, he would call the wingsecond. No one fought on the Hatching Ground. Surely Beterli knew that much.

Fortunately, at that moment the wingsecond called the boys together and led them from the Hatching Ground to start on evening chores.

There were "glows" to be replenished in the main kitchen caverns and sleeping cubicles, the major hallways, and the queen's apartment. Firestone sacks had to be filled against Thread attack, and black rock brought to the kitchen hearths. The boys fell to their chores, tantalized by the odors of roasting meat. The population of the weyr began to assemble for the evening meal, and the dragonriders came in from the Feeding Ground or their sweep checks.

It was the time of day Keevan liked best. Once the chores were done, before dinner was served, a fellow could often get close to the dragonriders and listen to their talk. Tonight Keevan's father, K'last, was at the main dragonrider table. It puzzled Keevan how his father, a brown rider and a tall man, could *be* his father—because he, Keevan, was so small. It obviously never puzzled K'last when he deigned[7] to notice his small son: "In a few more turns, you'll be as tall as I am—or taller!"

K'last was pouring Benden drink all around the table. The dragonriders were relaxing. There'd be no Thread attack for three more days, and they'd be in the mood to tell tall tales, better than Harper yarns, about impossible maneuvers they'd done a-dragonback. When Thread attack was closer, their talk would change to a discussion of tactics of evasion, of going *between*, how long to suspend there until the burning but fragile Thread would freeze and crack and fall harmlessly off dragon and man. They would dispute the exact moment to feed firestone to the dragon so he'd have the best flame ready to sear Thread midair

---

7. **deigned** (dānd): here, lowered himself.

and render it harmless to ground—and man—below. There was such a lot to know and understand about being a dragonrider that sometimes Keevan was overwhelmed. How would he ever be able to remember everything he ought to know at the right moment? He couldn't dare ask such a question; this would only have given additional weight to the notion that he was too young yet to be a dragonrider.

"Having older candidates makes good sense," L'vel was saying, as Keevan settled down near the table. "Why waste four to five years of a dragon's fighting prime until his rider grows up enough to stand the rigors?" L'vel had Impressed a blue of Ramoth's first clutch. Most of the candidates thought L'vel was marvelous because he spoke up in front of the older riders, who awed them. "That was well enough in the Interval when you didn't need to mount the full weyr complement to fight Thread. But not now. Not with more eligible candidates than ever. Let the babes wait."

"Any boy who is over twelve turns has the right to stand in the Hatching Ground," K'last replied, a slight smile on his face. He never argued or got angry. Keevan wished he were more like his father. And oh, how he wished he were a brown rider! "Only a dragon . . . each particular dragon . . . knows what he wants in a rider. We certainly can't tell. Time and again the theorists"—and K'last's smile deepened as his eyes swept those at the table—"are surprised by dragon choice. *They* never seem to make mistakes, however."

"Now, K'last, just look at the roster[8] of this Impression. Seventy-two boys and only forty eggs. Drop off the twelve youngest, and there's still a good field for the hatchlings to choose from. Shells! There are a couple of weyrlings unable to see over a wher egg, much less a dragon! And years before they can ride Thread."

"True enough, but the weyr is scarcely under fighting strength, and if the youngest Impress, they'll be old enough to fight when the oldest of our current dragons go *between* from senility."

"Half the weyrbred lads have already been through several Impressions," one of the bronze riders said then. "I'd say drop some of *them* off this time. Give the untried a chance."

"There's nothing wrong in presenting a clutch with as wide a choice as possible," said the weyrleader, who had joined the table with Lessa, the weyrwoman.

"Has there ever been a case," she said, smiling in her odd way at the riders, "where a hatchling didn't choose?"

Her suggestion was almost heretical[9] and drew astonished gasps from everyone, including the boys.

F'lar laughed. "You say the most outrageous things, Lessa."

"Well, *has* there ever been a case where a dragon didn't choose?"

"Can't say as I recall one," K'last replied.

"Then we continue in this tradition,"

---

8. **roster:** list.
9. **heretical** (hə·ret′i·kəl): against the established views.

Lessa said firmly, as if that ended the matter.

But it didn't. The argument ranged from one table to the other all through dinner, with some favoring a weeding out of the candidates to the most likely, lopping off those who were very young or who had had multiple opportunities to Impress. All the candidates were in a swivet,[10] though such a departure from tradition would be to the advantage of many. As the evening progressed, more riders were favoring eliminating the youngest and those who'd passed four or more Impressions unchosen. Keevan felt he could bear such a dictum[11] only if Beterli was also eliminated. But this seemed less likely than that Keevan would be tuffed out, since the weyr's need was for fighting dragons and riders.

By the time the evening meal was over, no decision had been reached, although the weyrleader had promised to give the matter due consideration.

He might have slept on the problem, but few of the candidates did. Tempers were uncertain in the sleeping caverns next morning as the boys were routed out of their beds to carry water and black rock and cover the "glows." Mende had to call Keevan to order twice for clumsiness.

"Whatever is the matter with you, boy?" she demanded in exasperation when he tipped black rock short of the bin and sooted up the hearth.

"They're going to keep me from this Impression."

"What?" Mende stared at him. "Who?"

"You heard them talking at dinner last night. They're going to tuff the babes from the hatching."

Mende regarded him a moment longer before touching his arm gently. "There's lots of talk around a supper table, Keevan. And it cools as soon as the supper. I've heard the same nonsense before every hatching, but nothing is ever changed."

"There's always a first time," Keevan answered, copying one of her own phrases.

"That'll be enough of that, Keevan. Finish your job. If the clutch does hatch today, we'll need full rock bins for the feast, and you won't be around to do the filling. All my fosterlings make dragonriders."

"The first time?" Keevan was bold enough to ask as he scooted off with the rockbarrow.

Perhaps, Keevan thought later, if he hadn't been on that chore just when Beterli was also fetching black rock, things might have turned out differently. But he had dutifully trundled the barrow to the outdoor bunker for another load just as Beterli arrived on a similar errand.

"Heard the news, babe?" asked Beterli. He was grinning from ear to ear, and he put an unnecessary emphasis on the final insulting word.

"The eggs are cracking?" Keevan all but dropped the loaded shovel. Several anxieties flicked through his mind then: He

---

10. **swivet** (swiv′ət): condition of irritation, annoyance.
11. **dictum**: authoritative pronouncement.

his; and dragons hummed when a clutch was being laid or being hatched. Impression! And he was flat abed.

Bitter, bitter disappointment turned the warm broth sour in his belly. Even the small voice telling him that he'd have other opportunities failed to alleviate his crushing depression. *This* was the Impression that mattered! This was his chance to show *everyone* from Mende to K'last to L'vel and even the weyrleaders that he, Keevan, was worthy of being a dragonrider.

He twisted in bed, fighting against the tears that threatened to choke him. Dragonmen don't cry! Dragonmen learn to live with pain. . . .

Pain? The leg didn't actually pain him as he rolled about on his bedding. His head felt sort of stiff from the tightness of the bandage. He sat up, an effort in itself since the numb weed made exertion difficult. He touched the splinted leg, but the knee was unhampered. He had no feeling in his bone, really. He swung himself carefully to the side of his bed and slowly stood. The room wanted to swim about him. He closed his eyes, which made the dizziness worse, and he had to clutch the bedpost.

Gingerly he took a step. The broken leg dragged. It hurt in spite of the numb weed, but what was pain to a dragonman?

No one had said he couldn't go to the Impression. "You are and you aren't," were Mende's exact words.

Clinging to the bedpost, he jerked off his bedshirt. Stretching his arm to the utmost, he jerked his white candidate's tunic from the peg. Jamming first one arm and

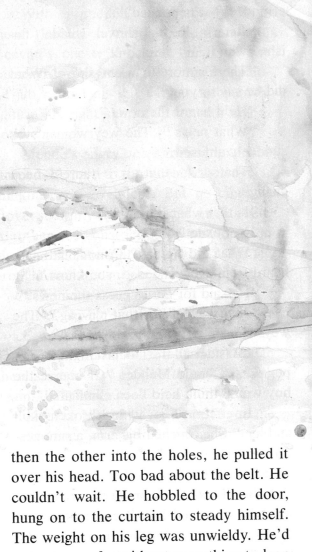

then the other into the holes, he pulled it over his head. Too bad about the belt. He couldn't wait. He hobbled to the door, hung on to the curtain to steady himself. The weight on his leg was unwieldy. He'd not get very far without something to lean on. Down by the bathing pool was one of the long crook-necked poles used to retrieve clothes from the hot washing troughs. But it was down there, and he was on the level above. And there was no one nearby to come to his aid. Everyone would be in the Hatching Ground right now, eagerly waiting for the first egg to crack.

The humming increased in volume and tempo, an urgency to which Keevan responded, knowing that his time was all too limited if he was to join the ranks of the hopeful boys standing about the cracking eggs. But if he hurried down the ramp, he'd fall flat on his face.

He could, of course, go flat on his rear end, the way crawling children did. He sat down, the jar sending a stab of pain through his leg and up to the wound on the back of his head. Gritting his teeth and blinking away the tears, Keevan scrabbled down the ramp. He had to wait a moment at the bottom to catch his breath. He got to one knee, the injured leg straight out in front of him. Somehow he managed to push himself erect, though the room wanted to tip over his ears. It wasn't far to the crooked stick, but it seemed an age before he had it in his hand.

Then the humming stopped!

Keevan cried out and began to hobble frantically across the cavern, out to the bowl of the weyr. Never had the distance between the living caverns and the Hatching Ground seemed so great. Never had the weyr been so silent, breathless. As if the multitude of people and dragons watching the hatching held every breath in suspense. Not even the wind muttered down the steep sides of the bowl. The only sounds to break the stillness were Keevan's ragged breathing and the thump-thud of his stick on the hard-packed ground. Sometimes he had to hop twice on his good leg to maintain his balance. Twice he fell into the sand and had to pull himself up on the stick, his white tunic no longer spotless. Once he jarred himself so badly he couldn't get up immediately.

Then he heard the first exhalation of the crowd, the ooohs, the muted cheer, the susurrus[14] of excited whispers. An egg had cracked, and the dragon had chosen his rider. Desperation increased Keevan's hobble. Would he never reach the arching mouth of the Hatching Ground?

Another cheer and an excited spate of applause spurred Keevan to greater effort. If he didn't get there in moments, there'd be no unpaired hatchling left. Then he was actually staggering into the Hatching Ground, the sands hot on his bare feet.

No one noticed his entrance or his halting progress. And Keevan could see nothing but the backs of the white-robed candidates, seventy of them ringing the area around the eggs. Then one side would surge forward or back and there'd be a cheer. Another dragon had been Impressed. Suddenly a large gap appeared in the white human wall, and Keevan had his first sight of the eggs. There didn't seem to be *any* left uncracked, and he could see the lucky boys standing beside wobble-legged dragons. He could hear the unmistakable plaintive crooning of hatchlings and their squawks of protest as they'd fall awkwardly in the sand.

Suddenly he wished that he hadn't left his bed, that he'd stayed away from the Hatching Ground. Now everyone would see his ignominious[15] failure. He scrambled now as desperately to reach the shadowy walls of the Hatching Ground as he had struggled to cross the bowl. He mustn't be seen.

He didn't notice, therefore, that the shifting group of boys remaining had begun to drift in his direction. The hard pace he had set himself and his cruel disappointment took their double toll on Keevan. He tripped and collapsed sobbing to the warm sands. He didn't see the consternation[16] in the watching weyrfolk above the Hatching Ground, nor did he hear the excited whispers of speculation. He didn't know that the weyrleader and weyrwoman had dropped to the arena and were making their way toward the knot of boys slowly moving in the direction of the archway.

---

14. **susurrus** (sə·sur′əs): rustling sound.

15. **ignominious** (ig′nə·min′ē·əs): shameful; disgraceful.
16. **consternation** (kon′stər·nā′shən): great shock or fear that makes one confused or helpless.

"Never seen anything like it," the weyrleader was saying. "Only thirty-nine riders chosen. And the bronze trying to leave the Hatching Ground without making Impression!"

"A case in point of what I said last night," the weyrwoman replied, "where a hatchling makes no choice because the right boy isn't there."

"There's only Beterli and K'last's young one missing. And there's a full wing of likely boys to choose from. . . ."

"None acceptable, apparently. Where is the creature going? He's not heading for the entrance after all. Oh, what have we there, in the shadows?"

Keevan heard with dismay the sound of voices nearing him. He tried to burrow into the sand. The mere thought of how he would be teased and taunted now was unbearable.

Don't worry! Please don't worry! The thought was urgent, but not his own.

Someone kicked sand over Keevan and butted roughly against him.

"Go away. Leave me alone!" he cried.

Why? was the injured-sounding question inserted into his mind. There was no voice, no tone, but the question was there, perfectly clear, in his head.

Incredulous, Keevan lifted his head and stared into the glowing jeweled eyes of a small bronze dragon. His wings were wet; the tips hung drooping to the sand. And he sagged in the middle on his unsteady legs, although he was making a great effort to keep erect.

Keevan dragged himself to his knees, oblivious to the pain of his leg. He wasn't even aware that he was ringed by the boys passed over, while thirty-one pairs of resentful eyes watched him Impress the dragon. The weyrleaders looked on, amused and surprised at the draconic[17] choice, which could not be forced. Could not be questioned. Could not be changed.

Why? asked the dragon again. *Don't you like me?* His eyes whirled with anxiety, and his tone was so piteous that Keevan staggered forward and threw his arms around the dragon's neck, stroking his eye ridges, patting the damp, soft hide, opening the fragile-looking wings to dry them, and assuring the hatchling wordlessly over and over again that he was the most perfect, most beautiful, most beloved dragon in the entire weyr, in all the weyrs of Pern.

"What's his name, K'van?" asked Lessa, smiling warmly at the new dragonrider. K'van stared up at her for a long moment. Lessa would know as soon as he did. Lessa was the only person who could "receive" from all dragons, not only her own Ramoth. Then he gave her a radiant smile, recognizing the traditional shortening of his name that raised him forever to the rank of dragonrider.

My name is Heath, thought the dragon mildly and hiccuped in sudden urgency. *I'm hungry.*

"Dragons are born hungry," said Lessa, laughing. "F'lar, give the boy a hand. He can barely manage his own legs, much less a dragon's."

---

17. **draconic** (drə·kä′nik): dragon-like.

K'van remembered his stick and drew himself up. "We'll be just fine, thank you."

"You may be the smallest dragonrider ever, young K'van, but you're the bravest," said F'lar.

And Heath agreed! Pride and joy so leaped in both chests that K'van wondered if his heart would burst right out of his body. He looped an arm around Heath's neck and the pair—the smallest dragonboy, and the hatchling who wouldn't choose anybody else—walked out of the Hatching Ground together forever.

IDENTIFYING FACTS

1. What does Keevan want, as the story opens? Why does he fear he won't get it?

2. Describe how the dragonriders are chosen. Why does Keevan fear he'll be kept from this Impression?

3. How does the bully Beterli try to ruin Keevan's chances on Hatching Day?

4. What happens at the Impression that never happened before? What happens to Keevan at the Impression, just when he is most unhappy and discouraged?

INTERPRETING MEANINGS

5. What does shortening Keevan's name to K'van signify?

6. Describe Keevan's **quest** at this stage of his life. What larger quest will he embark on when he is a dragonrider?

7. How do you **predict** Keevan will perform with Heath as a dragonrider? How did you feel about Keevan and Heath?

8. Why do you think no dragon has ever chosen Beterli? Why do you think F'lar called Keevan the bravest dragonboy?

APPLYING MEANINGS

9. List all the women in this story. Do they have powerful positions in Pern society? Or do only men hold power?

10. Pretend you live on Pern and are a candidate for Impression. Which color dragon would you like to Impress? What would be its name? Make up a Pern name for yourself.

DRAWING CONCLUSIONS

One of the challenges of this fantasy is trying to figure out the meanings of the words referring to life on Pern. The writer doesn't tell us directly, for example, what a dragonrider is. But you probably figured out that a dragonrider is someone who has been chosen by a dragon to be its rider for life. Dragonriders fight an enemy called Thread.

1. Based on what you have learned from clues in the story, tell all that you know about Thread. What conclusions would you draw about Thread and its threat to Pern? What do you imagine Thread looks like? (Could you illustrate Thread?)

2. Based on clues in the story, what conclusions can you come to about the dragons of Pern? Compare them with the dragons in old stories, like the one on page 66.

Literary Elements

CONFLICT

Conflict exists in all stories, and especially in stories of quests. **Conflict** is a struggle between two opposing forces. Some conflicts take place between two people. Some take place between a person and a force of nature. Sometimes a person is in conflict with a whole society. At times, a conflict takes place within a person's mind and heart. This might happen when a person has to struggle with fear or sadness or insecurity.

1. What person is Keevan in conflict with?

2. What feelings about himself are causing conflict for Keevan?

from Hatchet

GARY PAULSEN

Before You Read

The character's quest in the next story will keep you on the edge of your seat. As the novel *Hatchet* begins, Brian's parents have just been divorced. Thirteen-year-old Brian is the only passenger aboard a small plane, on his way to visit his father in Canada. Suddenly, with no warning, the pilot of the plane has a heart attack and dies. Brian—who has never flown a plane—is left alone. After a terrifying struggle to keep the plane in the air, he finally manages to crash-land in a lake and swim away from the sinking wreckage.

As this episode opens, Brian has spent two days in the Canadian wilderness with only the clothes on his back and the hatchet on his belt, a parting gift from his mother before he boarded the plane. He has succeeded in turning a rocky ledge into a makeshift shelter. The only food he has found so far are some strange-tasting berries he calls "gut cherries," but they make him violently ill.

Before you read this part of Brian's story, try to imagine what you would do if you suddenly found yourself alone in a wilderness. In your journal write down three problems you think you'd face.

Terry is Brian's good friend back in New York City.

Language and Vocabulary

Description is a kind of writing that helps you see, hear, smell, or taste something, or feel its textures. Even if you have never seen birch trees, you can "see" how they look from Gary Paulsen's vivid description: "They were a beautiful white with bark like clean, slightly speckled paper." As you read, use Paulsen's descriptions to help you visualize Brian's experiences. Does the writer help you feel that "you are there" in the wilderness?

Raspberries.

These he knew because there were some raspberry bushes in the park and he and Terry were always picking and eating them when they biked past.

The berries were full and ripe, and he tasted one to find it sweet, and with none of the problems of the gut cherries. Although they did not grow in clusters, there were many of them and they were easy to pick, and Brian smiled and started eating.

Sweet juice, he thought. Oh, they were sweet, with just a tiny tang, and he picked and ate and picked and ate and thought that he had never tasted anything this good. Soon, as before, his stomach was full, but now he had some sense and he did not gorge or cram more down. Instead he picked more and put them in his wind-breaker, feeling the morning sun on his back and thinking he was rich, rich with food now, just rich, and he heard a noise to his rear, a slight noise, and he turned and saw the bear.

He could do nothing, think nothing. His tongue, stained with berry juice, stuck to the roof of his mouth and he stared at the bear. It was black, with a cinnamon-colored nose, not twenty feet from him and big. No, huge. It was all black fur and huge. He had seen one in the zoo in the city once, a black bear, but it had been from India or somewhere. This one was wild, and much bigger than the one in the zoo and it was right there.

Right there.

The sun caught the ends of the hairs along his back. Shining black and silky, the bear stood on its hind legs, half up, and studied Brian, just studied him, then lowered itself and moved slowly to the left, eating berries as it rolled along, wuffling and delicately using its mouth to lift each berry from the stem, and in seconds it was gone. Gone, and Brian still had not moved. His tongue was stuck to the top of his mouth, the tip half out; his eyes were wide and his hands were reaching for a berry.

Then he made a sound, a low ''Nnnnnnggg.'' It made no sense, was just a sound of fear, of disbelief that something that large could have come so close to him without his knowing. It just walked up to him and could have eaten him, and he could have done nothing. Nothing. And

when the sound was half done, a thing happened with his legs, a thing he had nothing to do with, and they were running in the opposite direction from the bear, back toward the shelter.

He would have run all the way, in panic, but after he had gone perhaps fifty yards, his brain took over and slowed and, finally, stopped him.

If the bear had wanted you, his brain said, he would have taken you. It is something to understand, he thought, not something to run away from. The bear was eating berries.

Not people.

The bear made no move to hurt you, to threaten you. It stood to see you better, study you, then went on its way eating berries. It was a big bear, but it did not want you, did not want to cause you harm, and that is the thing to understand here.

He turned and looked back at the stand of raspberries. The bear was gone, the birds were singing, he saw nothing that could hurt him. There was no danger here that he could sense, could feel. In the city, at night, there was sometimes danger. You could not be in the park at night, after dark, because of the danger. But here, the bear had looked at him and had moved on and—this filled his thoughts—the berries were so good.

So good. So sweet and rich and his body was so empty.

And the bear had almost indicated that it didn't mind sharing—had just walked from him.

And the berries were so good.

And, he thought finally, if he did not go back and get the berries, he would have to eat the gut cherries again tonight.

That convinced him, and he walked slowly back to the raspberry patch and continued picking for the entire morning, although with great caution, and once when a squirrel rustled some pine needles at the base of a tree, he nearly jumped out of his skin.

About noon—the sun was almost straight overhead—the clouds began to thicken and look dark. In moments, it started to rain and he took what he had picked and trotted back to the shelter. He had eaten probably two pounds of raspberries and had maybe another three pounds in his jacket, rolled in a pouch.

He made it to the shelter just as the clouds completely opened and the rain roared down in sheets. Soon the sand outside was drenched and there were rivulets running down to the lake. But inside he was dry and snug. He started to put the picked berries back in the sorted pile with the gut cherries, but noticed that the raspberries were seeping through the jacket. They were much softer than the gut cherries and apparently were being crushed a bit with their own weight.

When he held the jacket up and looked beneath it, he saw a stream of red liquid. He put a finger in it and found it to be sweet and tangy, like pop without the fizz, and he grinned and lay back on the sand, holding the bag up over his face and letting the seepage drip into his mouth.

Outside the rain poured down, but

Brian lay back, drinking the syrup from the berries, dry and with the pain almost all gone, the stiffness also gone, his belly full and a good taste in his mouth.

For the first time since the crash he was not thinking of himself, of his own life. Brian was wondering if the bear was as surprised as he to find another being in the berries.

Later in the afternoon, as evening came down, he went to the lake and washed the sticky berry juice from his face and hands, then went back to prepare for the night.

While he had accepted and understood that the bear did not want to hurt him, it was still much in his thoughts, and as darkness came into the shelter, he took the hatchet out of his belt and put it by his head, his hand on the handle, as the day caught up with him and he slept.

At first he thought it was a growl. In the still darkness of the shelter in the middle of the night, his eyes came open and he was awake and he thought there was a growl. But it was the wind; a medium wind in the pines had made some sound that brought him up, brought him awake. He sat up and was hit with the smell.

It terrified him. The smell was one of rot, some musty rot that made him think only of graves with cobwebs and dust and old death. His nostrils widened and he opened his eyes wider, but he could see nothing. It was too dark, too hard dark, with clouds covering even the small light from the stars, and he could not see. But the smell was alive, alive and full and in the shelter. He thought of the bear, thought of Bigfoot and every monster he had ever seen in every fright movie he had ever watched, and his heart hammered in his throat.

Then he heard the slithering. A brushing sound, a slithering brushing sound near his feet—and he kicked out as hard as he could, kicked out and threw the hatchet at the sound, a noise coming from his throat. But the hatchet missed, sailed into the wall, where it hit the rocks with a shower of sparks, and his leg was instantly torn with pain, as if a hundred needles had been driven into it. "Unnnngh!"

Now he screamed, with the pain and fear, and skittered on his backside up into the corner of the shelter, breathing through his mouth, straining to see, to hear.

The slithering moved again, he thought toward him at first, and terror took him, stopping his breath. He felt he could see a low dark form, a bulk in the darkness, a shadow that lived, but now it moved away; slithering and scraping, it moved away and he saw or thought he saw it go out of the door opening.

He lay on his side for a moment, then pulled a rasping breath in and held it, listening for the attacker to return. When it was apparent that the shadow wasn't coming back, he felt the calf of his leg, where the pain was centered and spreading to fill the whole leg.

His fingers gingerly touched a group of needles that had been driven through his pants and into the fleshy part of his calf.

They were stiff and very sharp on the ends that stuck out, and he knew then what the attacker had been. A porcupine had stumbled into his shelter, and when he had kicked it the thing had slapped him with its tail of quills.

He touched each quill carefully. The pain made it seem as if dozens of them had been slammed into his leg, but there were only eight, pinning the cloth against his skin. He leaned back against the wall for a minute. He couldn't leave them in, they had to come out, but just touching them made the pain more intense.

So fast, he thought. So fast things change. When he'd gone to sleep he had satisfaction and in just a moment it was all different. He grasped one of the quills, held his breath, and jerked. It sent pain signals to his brain in tight waves, but he grabbed another, pulled it, then another quill. When he had pulled four of them, he stopped for a moment. The pain had gone from being a pointed injury pain to spreading in a hot smear up his leg, and it made him catch his breath.

Some of the quills were driven in deeper than others and they tore when they came out. He breathed deeply twice, let half of the breath out, and went back to work. Jerk, pause, jerk—and three more times before he lay back in the darkness, done. The pain filled his leg now, and with it came new waves of self-pity. Sitting alone in the dark, his leg aching, some mosquitoes finding him again, he started crying. It was all too much, just too much, and he couldn't take it. Not the way it was.

I can't take it this way, alone with no fire and in the dark, and next time it might be something worse, maybe a bear, and it wouldn't be just quills in the leg, it would be worse. I can't do this, he thought, again and again. I can't. Brian pulled himself up until he was sitting upright back in the corner of the cave. He put his head down on his arms across his knees, with stiffness taking his left leg, and cried until he was cried out.

He did not know how long it took, but later he looked back on this time of crying in the corner of the dark cave and thought of it as when he learned the most important rule of survival, which was that feeling sorry for yourself didn't work. It wasn't just that it was wrong to do, or that it was considered incorrect. It was more than that—it didn't work. When he sat alone in the darkness and cried and was done, was all done with it, nothing had changed. His leg still hurt, it was still dark, he was still alone, and the self-pity had accomplished nothing.

At last he slept again, but already his patterns were changing and the sleep was light, a resting doze more than a deep sleep, with small sounds awakening him twice in the rest of the night. In the last doze period before daylight, before he awakened finally with the morning light and the clouds of new mosquitoes, he dreamed. This time it was not of his mother, not of the Secret,[1] but of his father at first and then of his friend Terry.

In the initial segment of the dream, his father was standing at the side of a living room, looking at him, and it was clear from his expression that he was trying to tell Brian something. His lips moved but there was no sound, not a whisper. He waved his hands at Brian, made gestures in front of his face as if he were scratching something, and he worked to make a word with his mouth, but at first Brian could not see it. Then the lips made an *mmmmm* shape but no sound came. *Mmmmm—maaaa.* Brian could not hear it, could not understand it, and he wanted to so badly; it was so important to understand his father, to know what he was saying. He was trying to help, trying so hard, and when Brian couldn't understand, he looked cross, the way he did when Brian asked questions more than once, and he faded. Brian's father faded into a fog place Brian could not see and the dream was almost over, or seemed to be, when Terry came.

He was not gesturing to Brian but was sitting in the park at a bench looking at a barbecue pit, and for a time nothing happened. Then he got up and poured some charcoal from a bag into the cooker, then some starter fluid, and he took a flick type of lighter and lit the fluid. When it was burning and the charcoal was at last getting hot, he turned, noticing Brian for the first time in the dream. He turned and smiled and

1. Brian doesn't want to tell his father that his mother is seeing another man.

pointed to the fire as if to say, see, a fire.

But it meant nothing to Brian, except that he wished he had a fire. He saw a grocery sack on the table next to Terry. Brian thought it must contain hot dogs and chips and mustard, and he could think only of the food. But Terry shook his head and pointed again to the fire, and twice more he pointed to the fire, made Brian see the flames, and Brian felt his frustration and anger rise, and he thought, all right, all right, I see the fire, but so what? I don't have a fire. I know about fire; I know I need a fire.

I know that.

His eyes opened and there was light in the cave, a gray dim light of morning. He wiped his mouth and tried to move his leg, which had stiffened like wood. There was thirst, and hunger, and he ate some raspberries from the jacket. They had spoiled a bit, seemed softer and mushier, but still had a rich sweetness. He crushed the berries against the roof of his mouth with his tongue and drank the sweet juice as it ran down his throat. A flash of metal caught his eye and he saw his hatchet in the sand where he had thrown it at the porcupine in the dark.

He scootched up, wincing a bit when he bent his stiff leg, and crawled to where the hatchet lay. He picked it up and examined it and saw a chip in the top of the head.

The nick wasn't large, but the hatchet was important to him, was his only tool, and he should not have thrown it. He should keep it in his hand, and make a tool of some kind to help push an animal away. Make a staff, he thought, or a lance,[2] and save the hatchet. Something came then, a thought as he held the hatchet, something about the dream and his father and Terry, but he couldn't pin it down.

"Ahhh . . ." He scrambled out and stood in the morning sun and stretched his back muscles and his sore leg. The hatchet was still in his hand, and as he stretched and raised it over his head, it caught the first rays of the morning sun. The first faint light hit the silver of the hatchet and it flashed a brilliant gold in the light. Like fire. That is it, he thought. What they were trying to tell me.

Fire. The hatchet was the key to it all. When he threw the hatchet at the porcupine in the cave and missed and hit the stone wall, it had showered sparks, a golden shower of sparks in the dark, as golden with fire as the sun was now.

The hatchet was the answer. That's what his father and Terry had been trying to tell him. Somehow he could get fire from the hatchet. The sparks would make fire.

Brian went back into the shelter and studied the wall. It was some form of chalky granite, or a sandstone, but embedded in it were large pieces of a darker stone, a harder and darker stone. It only took him a moment to find where the hatchet had struck. The steel had nicked into the edge of one of the darker stone pieces. Brian turned the head backward so he would strike with the flat rear of the

---

2. **lance:** long wooden shaft with a sharp metal spear.

hatchet and hit the black rock gently. Too gently, and nothing happened. He struck harder, a glancing blow, and two or three weak sparks skipped off the rock and died immediately.

He swung harder, held the hatchet so it would hit a longer, sliding blow, and the black rock exploded in fire. Sparks flew so heavily that several of them skittered and jumped on the sand beneath the rock, and he smiled and struck again and again.

There could be fire here, he thought. I will have a fire here, he thought, and struck again—I will have fire from the hatchet.

Brian found it was a long way from sparks to fire.

Clearly there had to be something for the sparks to ignite, some kind of tinder or kindling—but what? He brought some dried grass in, tapped sparks into it, and watched them die. He tried small twigs, breaking them into little pieces, but that was worse than the grass. Then he tried a combination of the two, grass and twigs.

Nothing. He had no trouble getting sparks, but the tiny bits of hot stone or metal—he couldn't tell which they were— just sputtered and died.

He settled back on his haunches in exasperation, looking at the pitiful clump of grass and twigs.

He needed something finer, something soft and fine and fluffy to catch the bits of fire.

Shredded paper would be nice, but he had no paper.

"So close," he said aloud, "so close . . ."

He put the hatchet back in his belt and went out of the shelter, limping on his sore leg. There had to be something, had to be. Man had made fire. There had been fire for thousands, millions of years. There had to be a way. He dug in his pockets and found the twenty-dollar bill in his wallet. Paper. Worthless paper out here. But if he could get a fire going . . .

He ripped the twenty into tiny pieces, made a pile of pieces, and hit sparks into them. Nothing happened. They just wouldn't take the sparks. But there had to be a way—some way to do it.

Not twenty feet to his right, leaning out over the water, were birches, and he stood looking at them for a full half-minute before they registered on his mind. They were a beautiful white with bark like clean, slightly speckled paper.

Paper.

He moved to the trees. Where the bark was peeling from the trunks, it lifted in tiny tendrils, almost fluffs. Brian plucked some of them loose, rolled them in his fingers. They seemed flammable, dry and nearly powdery. He pulled and twisted bits off the trees, packing them in one hand while he picked with the other, picking and gathering until he had a wad close to the size of a baseball.

Then he went back into the shelter and arranged the ball of birch-bark peelings at the base of the black rock. As an afterthought he threw in the remains of the twenty-dollar bill. He struck and a stream of sparks fell into the bark and quickly died. But this time one spark fell on one small hair of dry bark—almost a thread of bark—and seemed to glow a bit brighter before it died.

The material had to be finer. There had to be a soft and incredibly fine nest for the sparks.

I must make a home for the sparks, he thought. A perfect home or they won't stay, they won't make fire.

He started ripping the bark, using his fingernails at first, and when that didn't work, he used the sharp edge of the hatchet, cutting the bark in thin slivers, hairs so fine they were almost not there. It was painstaking work, slow work, and he stayed with it for over two hours. Twice he stopped for a handful of berries and once to go to the lake for a drink. Then back to work, the sun on his back, until at last he had a ball of fluff as big as a grapefruit—dry birchbark fluff.

He positioned his spark nest—as he thought of it—at the base of the rock, used his thumb to make a small depression in the middle, and slammed the back of the hatchet down across the black rock. A cloud of sparks rained down, most of them missing the nest, but some, perhaps thirty or so, hit in the depression, and of those six or seven found fuel and grew, smoldered and caused the bark to take on the red glow.

Then they went out.

Close—he was close. He repositioned the nest, made a new and smaller dent with his thumb, and struck again.

More sparks, a slight glow, then nothing.

It's me, he thought. I'm doing something wrong. I do not know this—a cave dweller would have had a fire by now, a Cro-Magnon man would have a fire by now—but I don't know this. I don't know how to make a fire.

Maybe not enough sparks. He settled the nest in place once more and hit the rock with a series of blows, as fast as he could. The sparks poured like a golden waterfall. At first they seemed to take; there were several, many sparks that found life and took briefly, but they all died.

Starved.

He leaned back. They are like me. They are starving. It wasn't quantity—there were plenty of sparks—but they needed more.

I would kill, he thought suddenly, for a book of matches. Just one book. Just one match. I would kill.

What makes fire? He thought back to school. To all those science classes. Had he ever learned what made a fire? Did a teacher ever stand up there and say, "This is what makes a fire . . ."

He shook his head, tried to focus his thoughts. What did it take? You have to have fuel, he thought—and he had that. The bark was fuel. Oxygen—there had to be air.

He needed to add air. He had to fan on it, blow on it.

He made the nest ready again, held the hatchet backward, tensed, and struck four quick blows. Sparks came down and he

leaned forward as fast as he could and blew.

Too hard. There was a bright, almost intense glow, then it was gone. He had blown it out.

Another set of strikes, more sparks. He leaned and blew, but gently this time, holding back and aiming the stream of air from his mouth to hit the brightest spot. Five or six sparks had fallen in a tight mass of bark hair and Brian centered his efforts there.

The sparks grew with his gentle breath. The red glow moved from the sparks themselves into the bark, moved and grew and became worms, glowing red worms that crawled up the bark hairs and caught other threads of bark and grew until there was a pocket of red as big as a quarter, a glowing red coal of heat.

And when he ran out of breath and paused to inhale, the red ball suddenly burst into flame.

"Fire!" he yelled. "I've got fire! I've got it, I've got it, I've got it . . ."

But the flames were thick and oily and burning fast, consuming the ball of bark as fast as if it were gasoline. He had to feed the flames, keep them going. Working as fast as he could, he carefully placed the dried grass and wood pieces he had tried at first on top of the bark and was gratified to see them take.

But they would go fast. He needed more, and more. He could not let the flames go out.

He ran from the shelter to the pines and started breaking off the low, dead small limbs. These he threw in the shelter, went back for more, threw those in, and squatted to break and feed the hungry flames. When the small wood was going well, he went out and found larger wood and did not relax until that was going. Then he leaned back against the wood brace of his door opening and smiled.

I have a friend, he thought—I have a friend now. A hungry friend, but a good one. I have a friend named fire.

"Hello, fire . . ."

The curve of the rock back made an almost perfect drawing flue[3] that carried the smoke up through the cracks of the roof but held the heat. If he kept the fire small, it would be perfect and would keep anything like the porcupine from coming through the door again.

A friend and a guard, he thought.

So much from a little spark. A friend and a guard from a tiny spark.

He looked around and wished he had somebody to tell this thing, to show this thing he had done. But there was nobody.

Nothing but the trees and the sun and the breeze and the lake.

Nobody.

And he thought, rolling thoughts, with the smoke curling up over his head and the smile still half on his face, he thought: I wonder what they're doing now.

I wonder what my father is doing now.

I wonder what my mother is doing now.

I wonder if she is with him.

---

3. **flue:** passage for smoke, such as a chimney.

For Study and Discussion

IDENTIFYING FACTS

1. What big **problem** does Brian encounter when he is picking and eating raspberries? How does he deal with this problem?

2. On the night after Brian finds the raspberries, who is his midnight visitor? Describe Brian's reaction to the intruder.

3. Tell about Brian's efforts to make a fire.

4. In this episode from the novel, how does the hatchet help Brian to survive?

INTERPRETING MEANINGS

5. How would you describe Brian's **quest**? (What is he searching for?)

6. According to Brian, what is the most important rule of survival? How did he reach this conclusion?

7. Describe Brian's dream. In each segment of the dream, what do you think Terry and his father are trying to tell him? (What might his father's "Mmmmm-maaaa" mean?)

8. The ancient Greeks believed that a god named Prometheus (prə·mē′thē·əs) gave the gift of fire to humankind. What qualities of fire make it a precious gift? Why does Brian feel that his fire is his friend?

APPLYING MEANINGS

9. Brian's English teacher once told his class, "You are your most valuable asset. . . . *You* are the best thing you have." Do you agree with that advice or not? Do you think it might have helped Brian?

Focus on Reading

IDENTIFYING THE SEQUENCE OF EVENTS

The account of Brian's attempts to start a fire is important in this part of his story. Following are the key events in that account. Fill in the missing events in the sequence.

1. Tries to set a fire with grass.

2.

3. Tries to set a fire with grass and twigs.

4.

5. Tries birch bark.

6.

7. Blows on fire to give it oxygen.

8.

9. Feeds flames with branches.

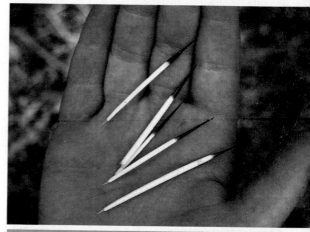

Literary Elements

CONFLICT

Make a list of all of Brian's basic **conflicts**, or struggles, as he faces the wilderness. Be sure to mention the animals or forces of nature that he has to struggle with, which threaten his life and well being.

Then make a list of all the conflicts you can imagine that might exist in his heart and mind. Remember the worries he has about his parents.

Which conflicts of Brian's do you think are most frightening?

Robinson Crusoe with his own hatchet.

Language and Vocabulary

DESCRIPTION AND MOOD

When writers use **description,** they paint word pictures that appeal to our senses of *sight, hearing, touch, taste,* and *smell.* Descriptions often create a certain feeling, or **mood.** For example, when the author describes the bear's fur as "shining black and silky," the bear doesn't seem very threatening. If the writer had described the bear as having "tiny wicked yellow eyes and pointed dirty teeth," we'd feel scared and disgusted.

Try writing a description of your own that creates a mood. Write three sentences. You might describe a locker room, the street in morning, or a fast-food restaurant.

Exchange descriptions with a classmate. On your classmate's paper, write down the feeling that his or her description gives you. (Pleasant? tasty? scary? disgusting? secure? hopeful?)

Focus on Descriptive Writing

USING EXACT WORDS

Exact words help to create bright, clear pictures in a description. Here are some examples of exact words in the paragraph from *Hatchet* beginning with "He made it to the shelter" on page 102:

> made it to the *shelter* (versus *place*)
> the rain *roared* down (versus *came*)
> the sand outside was *drenched* (versus *wet*)
> he was dry and *snug* (versus *comfortable*)
> the raspberries were *seeping* (versus *going*)

Rewrite the message on a postcard that you or someone you know received recently. Use exact nouns, verbs, adjectives, and adverbs. Save your writing.

About the Author

Gary Paulsen (1939–   ) was born in Minneapolis, but his father, who was in the military, moved the family around constantly. Paulsen has written over two hundred short stories and articles, as well as more than forty novels—many of them for adult readers. He is best known to young people for such novels as *The Voyage of the Frog, Tracker,* and *Dogsong.* He wrote *Dogsong* in camp at night while he was training his dogsled team to run a 1,200-mile race in Alaska. Like *Hatchet,* these are survival stories that also tell of adolescents struggling to find themselves. Both *Dogsong* and *Hatchet* have been acclaimed as Honor Books in the annual competition for the Newbery Award—the award given by the American Library Association to the author of the best children's book published in the United States each year. For Paulsen, such awards have a very personal meaning. "It's like things have come full circle," he explains. "I felt like nothing the first time I walked into a library, and now library associations are giving me awards. It means a lot to me." (See "Behind the Scenes" below.)

A First Library Card

Behind the Scenes

I went in to get warm and to my absolute astonishment the librarian walked up to me and asked if I wanted a library card. She didn't care if I looked right, wore the right clothes, dated the right girls, was popular at sports—none of those prejudices existed in the public library. When she handed me the card, she handed me the world. I can't even describe how liberating it was. She recommended westerns and science fiction but every now and then would slip in a classic. I roared through everything she gave me and in the summer read a book a day. It was as though I had been dying of thirst and the librarian had handed me a five-gallon bucket of water. I drank and drank.

—Gary Paulsen

from Sounder

WILLIAM ARMSTRONG

Before You Read

Sounder is a novel about the great power of love to carry people through tragedy. Except for the dog named Sounder, the characters in this fictional family are nameless—perhaps to make them stand for *all* families, everywhere. This family lives in the early 1900s in a nameless place in the rural South.

Sounder begins when the father is forced to steal meat to feed his hungry family. As the father is taken away to jail, the sheriff cruelly shoots the family's beloved dog, Sounder, who has tried to save his master. The mother is now left to support four young children. The oldest son takes his father's place in the fields and grieves and watches for Sounder, who disappeared after he was hurt. Finally, Sounder returns. The dog has healed himself in the woods, but he is changed. He is missing an eye, he is crippled, and he has lost the wonderful mellow voice that gave him his name.

But the father does not return. As the years pass, the boy from time to time searches for his father. All he knows is that his father has been sent far away with a prison work gang. Just before this part of the story opens, the boy had been standing outside the fence of a prison camp. He was searching the faces inside for his father, when a prison guard cruelly smashed his hand.

Read the first two paragraphs of the story, down to the words "He would carry it with him anyway." Pause to write down your own thoughts about why some people are cruel to others.

The stills are from the film Sounder, *made in 1972.*

Language and Vocabulary

Dialect is a special way of speaking used by people who live in a particular part of the country or who belong to a particular group. Dialects differ from standard English in their vocabulary, pronunciation, and grammar. Everybody speaks some kind of dialect. In *Sounder,* the boy and his mother speak a black dialect common to the rural South. For example, the mother says, "Scorchin' to be walkin' and totin' far today." How would your picture of the mother change if she said, "It's awfully hot to have to walk and carry something"?

Later that day, passing along a street in a strange and lonely town, the boy saw a man dump a box of trash into a barrel. He noticed that a large brown-backed book went in with the trash. He waited until the man went back into the building and then took the book from the barrel. It was a book of stories about what people think. There were titles such as Cruelty, Excellent Men, Education, Cripples, Justice, and many others. The boy sat down, leaned back against the barrel, and began to read from the story called Cruelty.

I have often heard it said that cowardice is the mother of cruelty, and I have found by experience that malicious and inhuman animosity and fierceness are usually accompanied by weakness. Wolves and filthy bears, and all the baser beasts, fall upon the dying.[1]

The boy was trying to read aloud, for he could understand better if he heard the words. But now he stopped. He did not understand what it said; the words were too new and strange. He was sad. He thought books would have words like the ones he had learned to read in the store signs, words like his mother used when she told him stories of the Lord and Joseph and David.[2] All his life he had wanted a book. Now he held one in his hands, and it was only making his bruised fingers hurt more. He would carry it with him anyway.

He passed a large brick schoolhouse with big windows and children climbing on little ladders and swinging on swings. No one jeered at him or noticed him because he had crossed the street and was walking close up against the hedge on the other side. Soon the painted houses ran out, and he was walking past unpainted cabins. He

1. The writer is saying that cowardly and weak people can be the cruelest. A *malicious* person is mean. *Animosity* means "hatred."

2. The story of Joseph, who was sold into slavery in Egypt by his brothers, begins in Genesis 37. The boy David kills the giant Goliath with only a slingshot (1 Samuel 17).

always felt better on his travels when he came to the part of town where the unpainted cabins were. Sometimes people came out on the porch when he passed and talked to him. Sometimes they gave him a piece to eat on the way. Now he thought they might laugh and say, "What you carryin', child? A book?" So he held it close up against him.

"That's a school too," the boy said to himself as he stood facing a small unpainted building with its door at the end instead of the side, the way cabin doors were. Besides, he could always tell a school because it had more windows than a cabin.

At the side of the building two children were sloshing water out of a tin pail near a hand pump. One threw a dipper of water on a dog that came from underneath to bark at the boy. The school was built on posts, and a stovepipe came through the wall and stuck up above the rafters. A rusty tin pipe ran from the corner of the roof down to the cistern[3] where the children were playing.

The dog had gone back under the building, so the boy entered the yard and moved toward the children. If one of them would work the pump handle, he could wash the dried blood off his hand. Just when he reached the cistern, a wild commotion of barking burst from under the floor of the school. Half a dozen dogs, which followed children to school and waited patiently for lunchtime scraps and for school to be over, burst from under the

building in pursuit of a pig that had wandered onto the lot. In the wild chase around the building, the biggest dog struck the tin drainpipe, and it clattered down the wall and bounced on the cement top of the cistern. With a pig under the building and the dogs barking and racing in and out, the school day ended.

Two dozen or more children raced out the door, few of them touching the three steps that led from the stoop to the ground. Some were calling the names of dogs and looking under the building. The boy found himself surrounded by strange inquiring eyes. Questions came too fast to answer. "You new here?" "Where you moved to?" "That your book?" "You comin' here to school?" "Kin you read that big a book?" The boy had put his bruised hand into his pocket so no one could see it. Some of the children carried books too, but none were as big as the one he held close against his side.

Just when the commotion was quieting down, a man appeared at the schoolhouse door. The children scattered across the lot in four directions. "Tell your pa that he must keep his pig in the pen," he called to one child.

Then it was quiet. The boy looked at the man in the doorway. They were alone now. The dogs had followed the children. And the pig, hearing a familiar call from the corner of the lot, had come grunting from his sanctuary[4] and gone in the direction of the call.

---

3. **cistern** (sis′tərn): water tank.

4. **sanctuary** (sangk′choo·er′ē): safe, protected place.

The boy's mother was played by Cicely Tyson in the 1972 film.

In his many journeyings among strangers the boy had learned to sniff out danger and spot orneriness[5] quickly. Now, for the first time in his life away from home, he wasn't feared. The lean elderly man with snow-white hair, wearing Sunday clothes, came down the steps. "This pipe is always falling," he said as he picked it up and put it back in place. "I need to wire it up."

"I just wanted to wash my hand. It's got dried blood on it where I hurt my fingers."

"You should have run home."

"I don't live in these parts."

"Here, I'll hold your book, and I'll pump for you." And the mellow eyes of the man began to search the boy for answers, answers that could be found without asking questions.

"We need warm, soapy water," the teacher said. "I live right close. Wait 'til I get my papers and lock the door, and I'll take you home and fix it."

The boy wanted to follow the man into the schoolhouse and see what it was like inside, but by the time he got to the steps, the man was back again, locking the door. "I usually put the school in order after the children leave," he said, "but I'll do it in the morning before they get here."

At the edge of the school lot the man took the road that led away from the town. They walked without much talk, and the boy began to wish the man would ask him a lot of questions. When they had passed several cabins, each farther from the other as they went, the man turned off the road and said, "We're home. I live here alone. Have lived alone for a long time." Fingering the small wire hook on the neatly whitewashed gate which led into a yard that was green, the teacher stopped talking.

A cabin with a gate and green grass in the yard is almost a big house, the boy thought as he followed the man.

Inside the gate the man went along the fence, studying some plants tied up to stakes. He began to talk again, not to the boy, but to a plant that was smaller than the others. "You'll make it, little one, but it'll take time to get your roots set again."

The boy looked at the white-haired old man leaning over like he was listening for the plant to answer him. "He's conjured,"[6] the boy whispered to himself. "Lots of old folks is conjured or addled."[7] He moved backward to the gate, thinking he'd better run away. "Conjured folks can conjure you," the boy's mother always said, "if you get yourself plain carried off by their soft spell-talk."

But before the boy could trouble his mind anymore, the man straightened up and began talking to him. "Some animal dug under the roots and tore them loose from the earth. It was wilted badly and might have died. But I reset it, and I water it every day. It's hard to reset a plant if it's

---

5. **orneriness** (ôr'nər·ē·nes): meanness.

6. **conjured** (kan'jərd): here, someone who practices magic.
7. **addled:** crazy.

wilted too much; the life has gone out of it. But this one will be all right. I see new leaves startin'."

"What grows on it?" the boy asked, thinking it must be something good [obscured] if somebody cared that much about a [obscured]

"It's only a flower," the man [obscured] "I'll water it when the earth has coo[led] little. If you water a plant when the e[arth] is too warm, it shocks the roots."

Inside the cabin the man started a [fire] in the cookstove and heated water. As [he] washed the boy's hand with a soft wh[ite] rag, he said, "You musta slammed the[se] fingers in a awful heavy door or gate." Before the boy could answer, the teacher began to talk about the plant he must remember to water.

He don't wanta know nothin' about me, the boy thought.

"When I saw your book, I thought you were coming to enroll for school. But you don't live in these parts, you say."

"I found the book in a trash barrel. It has words like I ain't used to readin'. I can read store-sign words and some newspaper words."

"This is a wonderful book," said the teacher. "It was written by a man named Montaigne,[8] who was a soldier. But he grew tired of being a soldier and spent his time studying and writing. He also liked to walk on country roads."

The teacher lit two lamps. The boy had never seen two lamps burning in the same room. They made the room as bright as daylight.

"[...]ings," the [...] is all but [...] hear. He [...] o lamps, [...] stoves, [...] y. [...] en two [...] were [...] were [...]s, but [...] man [...] they [...] hich [...] and himself.

Turn to Page

I will read you a little story from your book." The boy watched as the fingers of the man turned the pages one way and then the other until he found what he wanted to read.

"This is a very short story about a king named Cyrus,[9] who wanted to buy the prize horse that belonged to one of his soldiers. Cyrus asked him how much he would sell the horse for, or whether he would exchange him for a kingdom. The soldier said he would not sell his prize horse and he would not exchange him for a kingdom, but that he would willingly give up his horse to gain a friend. . . . But now I have told you the whole story so there's no use for me to read it."

---

8. **Montaigne** (män·tān'): Michel de Montaigne (1533–1592), a great French writer. Montaigne wrote personal essays on hundreds of topics. He is regarded as the "inventor" of the personal essay.

9. **Cyrus** (sī'rəs).

"You've been a powerful good friend to take me in like this," the boy said at last. "My fingers don't hurt no more."

"I am your friend," said the man. "So while I heat some water to soak your hand and make your cot for the night, you tell me all about yourself."

"I had a father and a dog named Sounder," the boy began. . . .

"Who's been kindly to your hurts?" the boy's mother asked as she looked down at the clean white rags that bandaged the boy's fingers. Rocking on the porch, she had seen the white dot swinging back and forth in the sun when the boy wasn't much more than a moving spot far down the road. "For a while I wasn't sure it was you," she said. "Why you walkin' fast? You done found him? Is your hand hurt bad? Is that a Bible somebody's done mistreated?" The woman's eyes had come to rest on the book the boy held in his good hand.

"No. It's a book. I found it in a trash can."

"Be careful what you carry off, child," his mother said. "It can cause a heap o' trouble."

"I got somethin' to tell," the boy said as he sat down on the edge of the porch and ran his bandaged fingers over the head of the great coon dog[10] who had stopped his jumping and whining and lay at the boy's feet with his head cocked to the side,

looking up with his one eye. The younger children sat in a line beside the boy, waiting to hear.

"Is he poorly?" the woman asked slowly. "Is he far?"

"It's about somethin' else," the boy said after a long spell of quiet. "I ain't found him yet."

The boy told his mother and the children about his night in the teacher's cabin. The teacher wanted him to come back and go to school. He had been asked to live in the teacher's cabin and do his chores. The children's eyes widened when they heard the cabin had two lamps, two stoves, and grass growing in a yard with a fence and a gate. He told how the teacher could read and that there were lots of books on shelves in the cabin.

"Maybe he will write letters to the road camps for you," the mother said, "'cause you'll be so busy with schoolin' and cleanin' the schoolhouse for him that you can't go searchin' no more."

"Maybe I'd have time," the boy said. "But he says like you, 'Better not to go. Just be patient and time will pass.'"

"It's all powerful puzzlin' and aggravatin', but it's the Lord's will." The boy noticed that his mother had stopped rocking; the loose boards did not rattle as the chair moved on them.

"The teacher said he'd walk all the way and reason about it if you didn't want me to come to him. You don't want me to go, but I'll come home often as I can. And sometime I might bring word."

"It's a sign; I believes in signs." The

---

10. **coon dog:** "Coon" is a clipped form of raccoon, an animal that is a nuisance to farmers because it breaks into chicken coops and ruins corn crops. A coon dog tracks raccoons.

rocker began to move back and forth, rattling the loose boards in the porch floor. "Go, child. The Lord has come to you."

When he returned to the cabin with books on the shelves and the kind man with the white hair and the gentle voice, all the boy carried was his book with one cover missing—the book that he couldn't understand. In the summers he came home to take his father's place in the fields, for cabin rent had to be paid with field work. In the winter he seldom came because it took "more'n a day's walkin' and sleepin' on the ground."

"Ain't worth it," his mother would say.

Each year, after he had been gone for a whole winter and returned, the faithful Sounder would come hobbling on three legs far down the road to meet him. The great dog would wag his tail and whine. He never barked. The boy sang at his work in the fields; and his mother rocked in her chair and sang on the porch of the cabin. Sometimes when Sounder scratched fleas under the porch, she would look at the hunting lantern and the empty possum[11] sack hanging against the wall. Six crops of persimmons[12] and wild grapes had ripened. The possums and raccoons had gathered them unmolested. The lantern and possum sack hung untouched. "No use to nobody no more," the woman said.

The boy read to his brother and sisters when he had finished his day in the fields.

---

11. **possum:** short for opossum, a small furry animal that lives in trees and is hunted for food.
12. **persimmon** (pər·sim′ən): a kind of sweet fruit.

He read the story of Joseph over and over and never wearied of it. "In all the books in the teacher's cabin, there's no story as good as Joseph's story," he would say to them.

The woman, listening and rocking, would say, "The Lord has come to you, child. The Lord has certainly come to you."

Late one August afternoon the boy and his mother sat on the shaded corner of the porch. The heat and drought of dog days[13] had parched the earth, and the crops had been laid by. The boy had come home early because there was nothing to do in the fields.

"Dog days is a terrible time," the woman said. "It's when the heat is so bad the dogs go mad." The boy would not tell her that the teacher had told him that dog days got their name from the Dog Star[14] because it rose and set with the sun during that period. She had her own feeling for the earth, he thought, and he would not confuse it.

"It sure is hot," he said instead. "Lucky to come from the fields early." He watched the heat waves as they made the earth look like it was moving in little ripples.

Sounder came around the corner of the cabin from somewhere, hobbled back and forth as far as the road several times, and then went to his cool spot under the porch.

"That's what I say about dog days," the woman said. "Poor creature's been addled with the heat for three days. Can't find no place to quiet down. Been down the road nearly out o' sight a second time today, and now he musta come from the fencerows. Whines all the time. A mad dog is a fearful sight. Slobberin' at the mouth and runnin' every which way 'cause they're blind. Have to shoot 'em 'fore they bite some child. It's awful hard."

"Sounder won't go mad," the boy said. "He's lookin' for a cooler spot, I reckon."

A lone figure came on the landscape as a speck and slowly grew into a ripply form through the heat waves. "Scorchin' to be walkin' and totin' far today," she said as she pointed to the figure on the road.

A catbird fussed in the wilted lilac at the corner of the cabin. "Why's that bird fussin' when no cat's prowlin? Old folks has a sayin' that if a catbird fusses 'bout nothin', somethin' bad is comin'. It's a bad sign."

"Sounder, I reckon," the boy said. "He just passed her bush when he came around the cabin."

In the tall locust at the edge of the fence, its top leaves yellowed from lack of water, a mockingbird mimicked the catbird with half a dozen notes, decided it was too hot to sing, and disappeared. The great coon dog, whose rhythmic panting came through the porch floor, came from under the house and began to whine.

As the figure on the road drew near, it took shape and grew indistinct again in the

---

13. **dog days:** the hot, rainless days of August. People used to think the heat drove dogs mad.
14. **Dog Star:** the brightest star in the heavens; also called *Sirius*.

wavering heat. Sometimes it seemed to be a person dragging something, for little puffs of red dust rose in sulfurous[15] clouds at every other step. Once or twice they thought it might be a brown cow or mule, dragging its hooves in the sand and raising and lowering its weary head.

Sounder panted faster, wagged his tail, whined, moved from the dooryard to the porch and back to the dooryard.

The figure came closer. Now it appeared to be a child carrying something on its back and limping.

"The children still at the creek?" she asked.

"Yes, but it's about dry."

Suddenly the voice of the great coon hound broke the sultry[16] August deadness. The dog dashed along the road, leaving three-pointed clouds of red dust to settle back to earth behind him. The mighty voice rolled out upon the valley, each flutelike bark echoing from slope to slope.

"Lord's mercy! Dog days done made him mad." And the rocker was still.

Sounder was a young dog again. His voice was the same mellow sound that had ridden the November breeze from the lowlands to the hills. The boy and his mother looked at each other. The catbird stopped her fussing in the wilted lilac bush. On three legs, the dog moved with the same lightning speed that had carried him to the throat of a grounded raccoon.

Sounder's master had come home.

---

15. **sulfurous** (sul′fər·əs): here, fiery.
16. **sultry:** hot, still, and humid.

For Study and Discussion

IDENTIFYING FACTS

1. What wonderful thing does the boy discover in the trash?

2. What "powerful good friend" does the boy find on his travels? How does the friend help him?

3. What advice finally convinces the boy to stop his search?

4. Describe the father's homecoming. What wonderful change comes over Sounder?

INTERPRETING MEANINGS

5. Before he began his long **quest,** the boy makes this observation: ". . . in Bible-story journeys, ain't no journey hopeless. Everybody finds what they suppose to find." Although he didn't find his father, was the boy's quest hopeless? What did he find instead?

6. After he picks the book out of the trash, the boy reads a passage called Cruelty. Think about this passage (page 116). How would these words make the boy feel about the men who jailed and beat his father for stealing food to feed his hungry children? Do you agree with this analysis of cruelty?

7. On page 119 the teacher talks to a small plant. Which of his words to the little plant could apply to the boy himself?

APPLYING MEANINGS

8. Do you agree that no "journey" is hopeless—that if you make a great effort to do something, you will discover something of value? (Even if it's not what you set out to find.)

SUPPORTING GENERAL STATEMENTS

Below are some general statements about this excerpt from *Sounder*. Find and read aloud the sentences from the story that support each statement.

1. The boy had never owned a book before.

2. The boy could read words, but not very well.

3. On his journeys, the boy feels better when he is traveling through the poorer parts of towns, because people there are kinder to him.

4. The teacher's house is more comfortable than the boy's own home.

5. The boy's mother has great religious faith.

Language and Vocabulary

DIALECT

A **dialect** is the form of a language spoken by people from a certain group or region. Dialects differ from standard English in grammar ("we was" instead of "we were"); in pronunciation ("lickin' " instead of "licking"); and in vocabulary ("I reckon" instead of "I guess"). The following sentences from *Sounder* are spoken by the boy or his mother. Read the sentences aloud and enjoy the sounds of the dialect. Then write the italicized dialect word or expression in standard English. (Some sentences may need rewriting.)

1. "It has words like *I ain't* used to *readin'*. I can read *store-sign* words . . ."

2. "You've been a *powerful good* friend to

take me in like this. . . . My fingers don't hurt *no more*."

3. "Who's been *kindly* to your hurts?"

4. "*Why you walkin'* fast? *You done found* him? Is your hand hurt *bad*? Is that a Bible somebody's *done mistreated*?"

Focus on Descriptive Writing

USING SENSORY DETAILS

Sensory details are words and phrases that appeal to the five senses:

sight   hearing   touch   taste   smell

For example, in the paragraph on page 123 beginning "Each year, after he had been gone for a whole winter," William Armstrong uses details that appeal to sight, hearing, and touch to describe the family's life during the summer.

Working with a small group of your classmates, choose one of the four subjects below for a description. Fill out the **observation chart** with as many sensory details as you can. Save your notes.

a playground   a kitchen
a party   a circus

Observation Chart

Subject: _____

Sight	Hearing	Touch	Smell	Taste
___	___	___	___	___
___	___	___	___	___
___	___	___	___	___
___	___	___	___	___

About the Author

William H. Armstrong (1914–   ) spent many years teaching history to high-school students and writing books and articles on education. But he is best known for his award-winning novel *Sounder*—a story that has been read by countless children, translated into eight languages, and made into a popular Hollywood film.

William Armstrong was born on a farm in the historic Shenandoah Valley near Lexington, Virginia. There he acquired a love for history that has lasted all his life. He grew up riding his horse over the same hills once crossed by General Lee on his horse Traveler, after the Civil War.

When he began to write *Sounder*, Armstrong saw his novel as a kind of history— the personal history of an unforgettable African American teacher he once knew as a child. (See the section "Behind the Scenes" on page 128.)

In 1970, Armstrong's novel was awarded the Newbery Award as the outstanding book for children of that year. In accepting the award, Armstrong read aloud some letters he had received from children. One reader wrote of *Sounder:* "It made me feel very hollow inside. Because we are living comfortable while the boy's family lived uncomfortable. You made me feel like I was watching all this happening right in front of my eyes." Another wrote: "It was sad and a few of us cried silently. At first, I closed my ears to the book, but then I realized that I should listen."

Behind the Scenes

Fifty years ago I learned to read at a round table in the center of a large, sweet-smelling, steam-softened kitchen. My teacher was a gray-haired black man who taught the one-room school several miles away from where we lived in the Green Hill district of the county. He worked for my father after school and in the summer. There were no radios or television sets, so when our lessons were finished, he told us stories. His stories came from Aesop, the Old Testament, Homer, and history.

There was a lasting, magnificent intoxication about the man that has remained after half a century. There was seldom a preacher at the white-washed, clapboard Baptist church in the Green Hill district, so he came often to our white man's church and sat alone in the balcony. Sometimes the minister would call on this eloquent, humble man to lead the congregation in prayer. He would move quietly to the foot of the balcony steps, pray with the simplicity of the Carpenter of Nazareth, and then return to where he sat alone, for no other black people ever came to join him.

He had come to our community from farther south, already old when he came. He talked little, or not at all, about his past. But one night at the great center table after he had told the story of Argus, the faithful dog of Odysseus, he told the story of Sounder, a coon dog.

It is the black man's story, not mine. It was not from Aesop, the Old Testament, or Homer. It was history—*his* history.

That world of long ago has almost totally changed. The church balcony is gone. The table is gone from the kitchen. But the story remains.

—W. H. Armstrong
(1970)

Jody's Discovery

MARJORIE KINNAN RAWLINGS

The stills are from the film The Yearling, *made in 1946.*

Before You Read

The following story is from Marjorie Kinnan Rawlings's novel *The Yearling*, which has been loved by generations of readers. Jody Baxter lives with his family on a small farm in the Florida backwoods, where they grow vegetables and raise hogs and chickens. Their nearest neighbors are the Forresters, who live almost four miles away. Jody is friendly with the youngest Forrester, Fodder-wing, who is handicapped. But aside from that contact, the Baxters and the Forresters are not friendly neighbors. In fact, as this episode opens, Jody and his father are on their way to get back some hogs that the Forresters have stolen from them. Here is a list of characters you will meet in this story:

Jody Baxter
Penny Baxter (Pa) . . . . Jody's father
Ora Baxter (Ma) . . . . Jody's mother
Old Julia and Rip . . . . the Baxters' dogs,
                                          used for hunting
Doc Wilson. . . . . the local doctor, a
                                          good man who drinks
                                          too much

Fodder-wing ⎫
Lem   ⎪
Buck   ⎬ . . . . the Forrester brothers
Mill-wheel   ⎪
Gabby   ⎪
Arch   ⎭

    In this episode, Jody discovers "the yearling," a young deer with whom he develops a strong, mystical bond. As you read, think about Jody and his family. How would you have responded to the disaster that strikes Jody's father?

Dialect **is the form of a language spoken by people in a particular region or social group.** The characters in *Sounder* (page 114) use a Southern black dialect of English. The characters in "Becky and the Wheels-and-Brake Boys" (page 220) speak in a Jamaican dialect. The characters in *The Yearling* use a different dialect, one spoken in the Florida backwoods. Penny Baxter uses dialect when he says, "I seed a man die—" and "Git a move on, young un." Penny uses *seed* for *saw, git* for *get,* and *un* for *one.* Sounds may be dropped from dialect words, as in *he'p* for *help* and *goin'* for *going.* Or sounds may be added, as when Jody says, "Hit's me!" Reading the characters' conversations aloud will help you understand their special dialect and hear how they sound. It will also help you to step into the backwoods with Jody and Penny and share their experiences.

A chill air moved across the scrub[1] and was gone, as though a vast being had blown a cold breath and then passed by. Jody shivered and was grateful for the hot air that fell in behind it. A wild grapevine trailed across the thin-rutted road. Penny leaned to pull it aside.

He said, "When there's trouble waitin' for you, you jest as good go to meet it."

The rattler struck him from under the grapevine without warning. Jody saw the flash, blurred as a shadow, swifter than a martin,[2] surer than the slashing claws of a bear. He saw his father stagger backward under the force of the blow. He heard him give a cry. He wanted to step back, too.

He wanted to cry out with all his voice. He stood rooted to the sand and could not make a sound. It was lightning that had struck, and not a rattler. It was a branch that broke, it was a bird that flew, it was a rabbit running——

Penny shouted, "Git back! Hold the dogs!"

The voice released him. He dropped back and clutched the dogs by the scruff of their necks. He saw the mottled shadow lift its flat head, knee-high. The head swung from side to side, following his father's slow motions. He heard the rattles hum. The dogs heard. They winded. The fur stood stiff on their bodies. Old Julia whined and twisted out of his hand. She turned and slunk down the trail. Her long tail clung to her hindquarters. Rip reared on his hind feet, barking.

---

1. **scrub:** land covered with short, stunted trees or bushes.
2. **martin:** swallow.

He lifted his shotgun and leveled it at the head.
(Gregory Peck is Penny in the film.)

As slowly as a man in a dream, Penny backed away. The rattles sung. They were not rattles—— Surely it was a locust humming. Surely it was a tree frog singing—— Penny lifted his gun to his shoulder and fired. Jody quivered. The rattler coiled and writhed in its spasms. The head was buried in the sand. The contortions moved down the length of the thick body, the rattles whirred feebly and were still. The coiling flattened into slow convolutions,[3] like a low tide ebbing. Penny turned and stared at his son.

He said, "He got me."

He lifted his right arm and gaped at it. His lips lifted dry over his teeth. His throat worked. He looked dully at two punctures in the flesh. A drop of blood oozed from each.

He said, "He was a big un."

Jody let go his hold on Rip. The dog ran to the dead snake and barked fiercely. He made sorties[4] and at last poked the coils with one paw. He quieted and snuffed about in the sand. Penny lifted his head from his staring. His face was like hickory ashes.

He said, "Ol' Death goin' to git me yit."

He licked his lips. He turned abruptly and began to push through the scrub in the direction of the clearing. The road would be shorter going, for it was open, but he headed blindly for home in a direct line. He plowed through the low scrub oaks, the gallberries,[5] the scrub palmettos.[6] Jody panted behind him. His heart pounded so hard that he could not see where he was going. He followed the sound of his father's crashing across the undergrowth. Suddenly the denseness ended. A patch of higher oaks made a shaded clearing. It was strange to walk in silence.

Penny stopped short. There was a stirring ahead. A doe deer leaped to her feet. Penny drew a deep breath, as though breathing were for some reason easier. He lifted his shotgun and leveled it at the head. It flashed over Jody's mind that his father had gone mad. This was no moment to stop for game. Penny fired. The doe turned a somersault and dropped to the sand and kicked a little and lay still. Penny ran to the body and drew his knife from its scabbard. Now Jody knew his father was insane. Penny did not cut the throat, but slashed into the belly. He laid the carcass wide open. The pulse still throbbed in the heart. Penny slashed out the liver. Kneeling, he changed his knife to his left hand. He turned his right arm and stared again at the twin punctures. They were now closed. The forearm was thick-swollen and blackening. The sweat stood out on his forehead. He cut quickly across the wound. A dark blood gushed and he pressed the warm liver against the incision.

He said in a hushed voice, "I kin feel it draw——"

He pressed harder. He took the meat

---

3. **convolutions** (kon′və·lōō′shəns): twistings, coilings.
4. **sortie** (sôr′tē): sudden pounce. Rip thinks the snake is still alive.
5. **gallberries** (gôl′ber·rēz): berries on which a growth ("gall") has appeared.
6. **palmetto** (pal·met′ō): low-growing palm tree.

away and looked at it. It was a venomous green. He turned it and applied the fresh side.

He said, "Cut me out a piece o' the heart."

Jody jumped from his paralysis. He fumbled with the knife. He hacked away a portion.

Penny said, "Another."

He changed the application again and again.

He said, "Hand me the knife."

He cut a higher gash in his arm where the dark swelling rose the thickest. Jody cried out.

"Pa! You'll bleed to death!"

"I'd ruther bleed to death than swell. I seed a man die——"

The sweat poured down his cheeks.

"Do it hurt bad, Pa?"

"Like a hot knife was buried to the shoulder."

The meat no longer showed green when he withdrew it. The warm vitality of the doe's flesh was solidifying in death. He stood up.

He said quietly, "I cain't do it no more good. I'm goin' on home. You go to the Forresters and git 'em to ride to the Branch for Doc Wilson."

"Reckon they'll go?"

"We got to chance it. Call out to 'em quick, sayin', afore they chunk somethin' at you or mebbe shoot."

He turned back to pick up the beaten trail. Jody followed. Over his shoulder he heard a light rustling. He looked back. A spotted fawn stood peering from the edge of the clearing, wavering on uncertain legs. Its dark eyes were wide and wondering.

He called out, "Pa! The doe's got a fawn."

"Sorry, boy. I cain't he'p it. Come on."

An agony for the fawn came over him. He hesitated. It tossed its small head, bewildered. It wobbled to the carcass of the doe and leaned to smell it. It bleated.

Penny called, "Git a move on, young un."

Jody ran to catch up with him. Penny stopped an instant at the dim road.

"Tell somebody to take this road in to our place and pick me up in case I cain't make it in. Hurry."

The horror of his father's body, swollen in the road, washed over him. He began to run. His father was plodding with a slow desperation in the direction of Baxters' Island.[7]

Jody ran down the wagon trail to the myrtle thicket where it branched off into the main road to Forresters' Island. The road, much used, had no growth of weeds or grass to make a footing. The dry shifting sand caught at the soles of his feet and seemed to wrap clinging tentacles around the muscles of his legs. He dropped into a short dogtrot that seemed to pull more steadily against the sand. His legs moved,

---

7. **Baxters' Island:** This island is not surrounded by water, but by scrub. In the Florida backwoods, a patch of rich soil in the midst of dense scrub is called an "island." Each family in the Florida scrub lives on its own "island."

but his mind and body seemed suspended above them, like an empty box on a pair of cartwheels. The road under him was a treadmill.[8] His legs pumped up and down, but he seemed to be passing the same trees and bushes again and again. His pace seemed so slow, so futile, that he came to a bend with a dull surprise. The curve was familiar. He was not far from the road that led directly into the Forrester clearing.

He came to the tall trees of the island. They startled him, because they meant that he was now so close. He came alive and he was afraid. He was afraid of the Forresters. And if they refused him help, and he got safely away again, where should he go? He halted a moment under the shadowy live oaks, planning. It was twilight. He was sure it was not time for darkness. The rain clouds were not clouds, but an infusion of the sky,[9] and had now filled it entirely. The only light was a strand of green across the west, the color of the doe's flesh with the venom on it. It came to him that he would call to his friend Fodder-wing. His friend would hear him and come, and he might be allowed to approach close enough to tell his errand. It eased his heart to think of it, to think of his friend's eyes gentle with sorrow for him. He drew a long breath and ran wildly down the path under the oak trees.

---

8. **treadmill:** an endless belt that moves backward as a person walks forward. (Jody feels as if he's getting nowhere.)
9. **infusion of the sky:** In other words, the clouds filled the sky completely.

He shouted, "Fodder-wing! Fodder-wing! Hit's Jody!"

In an instant now his friend would come to him from the house, crawling down the rickety steps on all fours, as he must do when in a hurry. Or he would appear from the bushes with his raccoon at his heels.

"Fodder-wing! Hit's me!"

There was no answer. He broke into the swept sandy yard.

"Fodder-wing!"

There was an early light lit in the house. A twist of smoke curled from the chimney. The doors and shutters were closed against the mosquitoes and against the nighttime. The door swung open. In the light beyond, he saw the Forrester men rise to their feet, one after the other, as though the great trees in the forest lifted themselves by their roots and stirred toward him. He stopped short. Lem Forrester advanced to the stoop. He lowered his head and turned it a little sideways until he recognized the intruder.

"You leetle varmint. What you after here?"

Jody faltered, "Fodder-wing——"

"He's ailin'. You cain't see him noways."

It was too much. He burst out crying. He sobbed, "Pa—— He's snake-bit."

The Forresters came down the steps and surrounded him. He sobbed loudly, with pity for himself and for his father, and because he was here at last and something was finished that he had set out to do. There was a stirring among the men, as though the leavening[10] quickened in a bowl of bread dough.

"Where's he at? What kind o' snake?"

"A rattlesnake. A big un. He's makin' it for home, but he don't know kin he make it."

"Is he swellin'? Where'd it git him?"

"In the arm. Hit's bad swelled a'ready. Please ride for Doc Wilson. Please ride for him quick, and I won't he'p Oliver[11] agin you no more. Please."

Lem Forrester laughed.

"A skeeter[12] promises he won't bite," he said.

Buck said, "Hit's like not to do no good. A man dies right now, bit in the arm. He'll likely be dead afore Doc kin git to him."

"He shot a doe deer and used the liver to draw out the pizen. Please ride for Doc."

Mill-wheel said, "I'll ride for him."

Relief flooded him like the sun.

"I shore thank you."

"I'd he'p a dog, was snake-bit. Spare your thanks."

Buck said, "I'll ride on and pick up Penny. Walkin's bad for a man is snake-bit. . . . Fellers, we ain't got a drop o' whiskey for him!"

Gabby said, "Ol' Doc'll have some. If he's purty tol'able sober, he'll have some left. If he's drunk all he's got, he kin blow his breath, and that'll make a powerful portion."

Buck and Mill-wheel turned away with torturing deliberation to the lot to saddle their horses. Their leisureliness frightened Jody as speed would not have done. If there was hope for his father, they would be hurrying. They were as slow and unconcerned as though they were burying Penny, not riding for assistance. He stood, desolate. He would like to see Fodder-wing just a moment before he went away. The remaining Forresters turned back up the steps, ignoring him.

Lem called from the door, "Git goin', Skeeter."

Arch said, "Leave the young un be. Don't torment him, and his daddy likely dyin'." . . .

Frightened as he has never been before, Jody runs the four miles home in a driving rainstorm. He is terrified that his father has died of the snake bite. He finds the Forresters in his cabin, sitting by the empty hearth. . . .

Jody was faint. He dared not ask them the question. He walked past them and into his father's bedroom. His mother sat on one side of the bed and Doc Wilson sat on the other. Old Doc did not turn his head. His mother looked at him and rose without speaking. She went to a dresser and took out a fresh shirt and breeches and held them out to him. He dropped his wet bundle and stood the gun against the wall. He walked slowly to the bed.

---

10. **leavening:** a substance, such as yeast, that helps bread dough rise and become light and fluffy.
11. Oliver, a friend of the Baxters, got into a fight with the Forresters, and both Penny and Jody jumped in to help Oliver.
12. **skeeter:** slang for mosquito.

"If he's not dead now, he'll not die."

He thought, "If he's not dead now, he'll not die."

In the bed, Penny stirred. Jody's heart leaped like a rabbit jumping. Penny groaned and retched. Doc leaned quickly and held a basin for him and propped his head. Penny's face was dark and swollen. He vomited with the agony of one who has nothing to emit, but must vomit still. He fell back panting. Doc reached inside the covers and drew out a brick wrapped in flannel. He handed it to Ma Baxter. She laid Jody's garments at the foot of the bed and went to the kitchen to heat the brick again.

Jody whispered, "Is he bad?"

"He's bad, a'right. Looks as if he'd make it. Then again, looks as if he won't."

Penny opened his puffed eyes. The pupils were dilated[13] until his eyes seemed black. He moved his arm. It was swollen as thick as a bullock's[14] thigh.

He murmured thickly, "You'll ketch cold."

Jody fumbled for his clothes and pulled them on. Doc nodded.

"That's a good sign, knowin' you. That's the first he's spoken."

A tenderness filled Jody that was half pain, half sweetness. In his agony, his father was concerned for him. Penny could not die. Not Penny.

He said, "He's obliged to make it, Doc, sir." He added, as he had heard his father say, "Us Baxters is all runty and tough."

Doc nodded.

He called to the kitchen, "Let's try some warm milk now."

With hope, Ma Baxter began to sniffle. Jody joined her at the hearth.

She whimpered, "I don't see as we'd deserve it, do it happen."

He said, "Hit'll not happen, Ma." But his marrow[15] was cold again.

He went outside for wood to hurry the fire. The storm was moving on to the west. The clouds were rolling like battalions[16] of marching Spaniards. In the east, bright spaces showed, filled with stars. The wind blew fresh and cool. He came in with an armful of fatwood.

He said, "Hit'll be a purty day tomorrow, Ma."

"Hit'll be a purty day iffen he's yit alive when day comes." She burst into tears. They dropped on the hearth and hissed. She lifted her apron and wiped her eyes. "You take the milk in," she said. "I'll make Doc and me a cup o' tea. I hadn't et nothin', waitin' for you-all, when Buck carried him in."

He remembered that he had eaten lightly. He could think of nothing that would taste good. The thought of food on his tongue was a dry thought, without nourishment or relish. He carried the cup of hot milk carefully, balancing it in his hands. Doc took it from him and sat close to Penny on the bed.

"Now, boy, you hold his head up while I spoon-feed him."

Penny's head was heavy on the pillow. Jody's arms ached with the strain of lifting it. His father's breathing was heavy, like the Forresters' when they were drunk. His face had changed color. It was green and pallid, like a frog's belly. At first his teeth resisted the intruding spoon.

Doc said, "Open your mouth before I call the Forresters to open it."

The swollen lips parted. Penny swallowed. A portion of the cupful went down. He turned his head away.

Doc said, "All right. But if you lose it, I'm comin' back with more."

Penny broke into a sweat.

Doc said, "That's fine. Sweatin's fine,

---

13. **dilated:** expanded.
14. **bullock** (bŏol′ək): male cow or ox.
15. **marrow:** tissue that fills bone. Jody is chilled to the bone.
16. **battalions** (bə·tal′yəns): large companies of soldiers.

for poison. Lord of the jaybirds, if we weren't all out of whiskey, I'd make you sweat."

Ma Baxter came to the bedroom with two plates with cups of tea and biscuits on them. Doc took his plate and balanced it on his knee. He drank with a mixture of gusto and distaste.

He said, "It's all right, but 'tain't whiskey."

He was the soberest Jody had ever heard of his being.

"A good man snake-bit," he said mournfully, "and the whole county out of whiskey."

Ma Baxter said dully, "Jody, you want somethin'?"

"I ain't hongry."

His stomach was as queasy as his father's. It seemed to him that he could feel the poison working in his own veins, attacking his heart, churning in his gizzard.[17]

Doc said, "Blest if he ain't goin' to keep that milk down."

Penny was in a deep sleep.

Ma Baxter rocked and sipped and nibbled.

She said, "The Lord watches the sparrer's fall. Mought be He'll take a hand for the Baxters."[18] . . .

Night comes and everyone tries to sleep. Jody goes to his father's bedroom.

It seemed to Jody that he was alone with his father. The vigil was in his hands. If he kept awake, and labored for breath with the tortured sleeper, breathing with him and for him, he could keep him alive. He drew a breath as deep as the ones his father was drawing. It made him dizzy. He was light-headed and his stomach was empty. He knew he would feel better if he should eat, but he could not swallow. He sat down on the floor and leaned his head against the side of the bed. He began to think back over the day, as though he walked a road backward. He could not help but feel a greater security here beside his father than in the stormy night. Many things, he realized, would be terrible alone that were not terrible when he was with Penny. Only the rattlesnake had kept all its horror.

He recalled the triangular head, the lightning flash of its striking, the subsidence[19] into alert coils. His flesh crawled. It seemed to him he should never be easy in the woods again. He recalled the coolness of his father's shot, and the fear of the dogs. He recalled the doe and the horror of her warm meat against his father's wound. He remembered the fawn. He sat upright. The fawn was alone in the night, as he had been alone. The catastrophe that might take his father had made it motherless. It had lain hungry and bewil-

---

17. **gizzard:** here, his stomach.
18. Ma is referring to a passage from the Bible about God's love. Jesus reminds the people that not even a sparrow falls to the ground without God's notice (Matthew 10:29).

19. **subsidence** (səb·sīd′əns): sinking or falling back.

"Ol' Death gone thievin' elsewhere."

Illustration by N. C. Wyeth.

dered through the thunder and rain and lightning, close to the devastated body of its dam,[20] waiting for the stiff form to arise and give it warmth and food and comfort. He pressed his face into the hanging covers of the bed and cried bitterly. He was torn with hate for all death and pity for all aloneness. . . .

The next morning Penny is better, and the Forresters are ready to return home. Jody slips in to his father's bedside.

Jody said, "How you comin', Pa?"

"Jest fine, son. Ol' Death gone thievin' elsewhere. But wa'n't it a close squeak!"

"I mean."

Penny said, "I'm proud of you, boy, the way you kept your head and done what was needed."

"Pa——"

"Yes, son."

"Pa, you recollect the doe and the fawn?"

"I cain't never forget 'em. The pore doe saved me, and that's certain."

"Pa, the fawn may be out there yit. Hit's hongry, and likely mighty skeert."

"I reckon so."

"Pa, I'm about growed and don't need no milk. How about me goin' out and seein' kin I find the fawn?"

"And tote it here?"

"And raise it."

Penny lay quiet, staring at the ceiling.

---

20. **dam:** mother of a four-legged animal.

"Boy, you got me hemmed in."

"Hit won't take much to raise it, Pa. Hit'll soon git to where it kin make out on leaves and acorns."

"Dogged if you don't figger the farrest of ary young un I've ever knowed."

"We takened its mammy, and it wa'n't no-ways to blame."

"Shore don't seem grateful to leave it starve, do it? Son, I ain't got it in my heart to say 'No' to you. I never figgered I'd see daylight, come dawn today."

"Kin I ride back with Mill-wheel and see kin I find it?"

"Tell your Ma I said you're to go."

He sidled back to the table and sat down. His mother was pouring coffee for everyone.

He said, "Ma, Pa says I kin go bring back the fawn."

She held the coffeepot in midair.

"What fawn?"

"The fawn belonged to the doe we kilt, to use the liver to draw out the pizen and save Pa."

She gasped.

"Well, for pity sake——"

"Pa says hit'd not be grateful to leave it starve."

Doc Wilson said, "That's right, Ma'am. Nothing in the world don't ever come quite free. The boy's right and his daddy's right."

Mill-wheel said, "He kin ride back with me. I'll he'p him find it."

She set down the pot helplessly.

"Well, if you'll give it your milk—— We got nothin' else to feed it."

"That's what I aim to do. Hit'll be no time, and it not needin' nothin'." . . .

Mill-wheel and Jody set off on a horse. Mill-wheel asks Jody where he wants to get off.

Suddenly Jody was unwilling to have Mill-wheel with him. If the fawn was dead, or could not be found, he could not have his disappointment seen. And if the fawn was there, the meeting would be so lovely and so secret that he could not endure to share it.

He said, "Hits not fur now, but hit's powerful thick for a horse. I kin make it a-foot."

"But I'm daresome to leave you, boy. Suppose you was to git lost, or snake-bit, too?"

"I'll take keer. Hit'll take me likely a long time to find the fawn, if he's wandered. Leave me off right here."

"All right, but you go mighty easy now, pokin' in them palmeeters. This is rattlesnake heaven in these parts. You know north here, and east?"

"There, and there. That fur tall pine makes a bearin'."

"That's right. Now do things go wrong again, you or Buck, one, ride back for me. So long."

"So long, Mill-wheel. I'm shore obliged."

He waved after him. He waited for the sound of the hooves to end, then cut to the right. The scrub was still. Only his own crackling of twigs sounded across the silence. He was eager almost past caution, but he broke a bough and pushed it ahead of him where the growth was thick and the ground invisible. Rattlers got out of the way when they had a chance. Penny had gone farther into the oak thicket than he remembered. He wondered for an instant if he had mistaken his direction. Then a buzzard rose in front of him and flapped into the air. He came into the clearing under the oaks. Buzzards sat in a circle around the carcass of the doe. They turned their heads on their long scrawny necks and hissed at him. He threw his bough at them and they flew into an adjacent tree. Their wings creaked and whistled like rusty pump handles. The sand showed large cat prints, he could not tell whether of wildcat or of panther. But the big cats killed fresh, and they had left the doe to the carrion birds.[21] He asked himself whether the sweeter meat of the fawn had scented the air for the curled nostrils.

He skirted the carcass and parted the grass at the place where he had seen the fawn. It did not seem possible that it was only yesterday. The fawn was not there. He circled the clearing. There was no sound, no sign. The buzzards clacked their wings, impatient to return to their business. He returned to the spot where the fawn had emerged and dropped to all fours, studying the sand for the small hoofprints. The night's rain had washed away all tracks except those of cat and buzzards. But the

---

21. **carrion birds:** birds that feed on *carrion,* the flesh of a dead body.

"It's me."

Illustration by N. C. Wyeth.

cat sign had not been made in this direction. Under a scrub palmetto he was able to make out a track, pointed and dainty as the mark of a ground dove. He crawled past the palmetto.

Movement directly in front of him startled him so that he tumbled backward. The fawn lifted its face to his. It turned its head with a wide, wondering motion and shook him through with the stare of its liquid eyes. It was quivering. It made no effort to rise or run. Jody could not trust himself to move.

He whispered, "It's me."

IDENTIFYING FACTS

1. List the steps Penny takes to fight the poison from the snakebite. Why does he have to kill the doe?

2. Describe the scene in the Baxter cabin when Penny is ill. What is the first hopeful sign that he may recover?

3. After his father gets well, what does Jody want to do? What arguments does he use to convince his father to let him do it?

4. Why does Jody make Mill-wheel leave him when they reach the area where the fawn should be?

INTERPRETING MEANINGS

5. As Jody is sitting by his father's bed, the writer says, "He was torn with hate for all death and pity for all aloneness" (page 141). What is troubling Jody?

6. Jody sets off on a **quest** for the abandoned fawn. Characters on quests often have to face dangers. What dangers does Jody face? How did you feel when he found the fawn?

7. Why do you think Jody feels such a strong bond with an animal he has barely seen? Do you think you would have felt the same way?

APPLYING MEANINGS

8. How did you feel when you read the part of the story about the snakebite and the doe's death? Did you feel it was too violent? Or did you feel that the writer described the events in a sensitive and caring way?

9. Name some other stories or movies or TV shows that focus on a young person who nearly loses (or does lose) a person who is greatly loved. Do you know of other stories about a young person who rescues an animal? Talk about how all these stories make you feel.

Focus on Reading

DRAWING CONCLUSIONS

As you read a story, you understand certain things even though they are not stated directly. You draw these **conclusions** from evidence in the story. For each passage below, choose the conclusion that best fits the evidence.

1. On page 131, when Penny is first bitten, Jody thinks "It was lightning that had struck, and not a rattler. It was a branch that broke, it was a bird that flew, it was a rabbit running—"
   a. Jody is seeing things.
   b. Jody believes that lightning struck his father.
   c. Jody wishes something else had happened, instead of the strike of a deadly snake.

2. On page 136, when Jody gets home after appealing to the Forresters to aid his father, he finds everyone in the cabin. We read: "Jody was faint. He dared not ask them the question."
   a. The question is "Is my father alive?"
   b. The question is "Is there any supper?"
   c. The question is "Did the Forresters fetch Doc Wilson?"

Literary Elements

CHARACTER

There are many strong and memorable characters in *The Yearling.* As you know from Unit One, we can get to know characters by watching their actions, by listening to what they say, and by hearing their thoughts. Think of the details in this story that reveal to you what the people are really like:

1. How does Jody's mother show her faith in God?

2. How do the Forresters show generosity of spirit when their enemy is in trouble?

3. How does Penny show great love for his young son?

4. How does Jody show courage and responsibility?

Did the writer make you care for these characters? Did you dislike any of them?

Language and Vocabulary

DIALECT (An Oral Activity)

With a partner or a small group, choose a **dialogue,** or conversation, from the story that appeals to you. Then prepare this dialogue for oral reading, using as many readers as you need. As you practice your dialogue, be aware of *what* the words are saying. Listen for the rhythm of the speech. Try to make your reading reflect the characters' personalities and feelings. Before you present your "scene" to the class, be sure you have read the conversation aloud at least once. (Don't forget that, depending on your passage, you may have to choose a narrator.)

Focus on Descriptive Writing

ORGANIZING A DESCRIPTION

If you organize the details of your description clearly, you will make it easy to follow. Here are two ways to arrange your details:

Spatial Order: Organize details according to their location: for example, from top to bottom (or bottom to top), or from near to far (or far to near). You will often find this method helpful for describing places and objects.

Order of Importance: Arrange details according to the importance or emphasis you want to give them. You can give the most important detail first or last in order to create the strongest impression on your readers. This method is often useful for describing people or animals. Rawlings uses order of importance in her description of the fawn, where she saves the most important detail for last (see page 143).

Write a paragraph in which you describe a favorite object or animal. Arrange the details of your description in a logical order. Try to create a strong overall impression through specific, vivid details. Save your writing.

About the Author

Marjorie Kinnan Rawlings (1896–1953) introduced millions of readers to the special character of the Florida backwoods in her novel *The Yearling,* which won the Pulitzer Prize in 1939. Rawlings was raised in a big city, where she first worked as a journalist. When she grew unhappy with city living, she bought a huge orange grove near Hawthorn, Florida. Her new home was called Cross Creek. There she began to write short stories and novels inspired by the Florida "piney woods," their people, and their particular way of life. In her book called *Cross Creek,* she wrote: "For myself, the Creek satisfies a thing that had gone hungry and unfed since childhood days. I am often lonely. Who is not? But I should be lonelier in the heart of a city." Both *Cross Creek* and *The Yearling* have been made into successful movies.

The Algonquin Cinderella

Retold by M. R. COX

Buckskin gloves made by the Eastern Woodland Native Americans.

Courtesy Colter Bay Indian Arts Museum, Grand Teton National Park, Wyoming.

Before You Read

People who study literature have discovered that many stories told in different parts of the world are surprisingly similar. No one is certain why this is so. Some people think that certain wishes and fears are so universal that everyone wants to express them in story form.

One of the stories found in many cultures is the Cinderella story. Here is a "Cinderella" story told by the Algonquin (al·gong′kwin) people who lived in the Ottawa River region of Canada.

Before you read this story, take a moment to recall the traditional story. Remember the girl who lived among the ashes and who wanted to attend the prince's ball? What were the other elements of the story? (Remember the cruel stepsisters; the fairy godmother; the girl's ragged clothing; the magical changes?)

This story would be fun to present in a classroom theater. You would need a narrator and these characters:

The sister of the Invisible One
The other girls who try to "see" the Invisible One
Oochigeaskw's sisters
The Invisible One

After you read the story, you might talk in class about the fears or wishes the story expresses.

The Algonquin Cinderella **147**

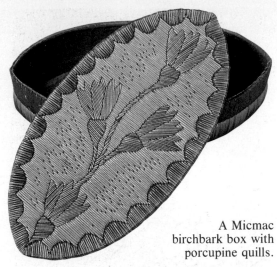

A Micmac
birchbark box with
porcupine quills.

Courtesy The Heard Museum,
Phoenix, Arizona.

There was once a large village belonging
to the Micmac Indians of the Eastern Algonquins, built beside a lake. At the far
end of the settlement stood a lodge, and in
it lived a being who was always invisible.
He had a sister who looked after him, and
everyone knew that the girl who could see
him might marry him. There were very few
girls who did not try to marry him, but it
was very long before anyone succeeded.

This is the way in which the test of
sight was carried out. At evening time,
when the Invisible One was due to return
home, his sister would walk with any girl
who might come down to the lakeshore.
She, of course, could see her brother, since
he was always visible to her. As soon as
she saw him coming, she would say to the
girls:

"Do you see my brother?"

"Yes," they would generally reply—
though some of them did say "No."

To those who said that they could indeed see him, the sister would ask, "What
is his shoulder strap made of?"

Or, some people say that she would
inquire, "What is his moose-runner's
haul?" or "What does he draw his sled
with?"

And they would answer, "A strip of
rawhide" or "A green flexible branch," or
something like that.

Then the sister, knowing that they had
not told the truth, would say, "Very well,
let us return to the wigwam!"

When they went in, she would tell the
girls not to sit in a certain place, because
it belonged to the Invisible One. Then, af-

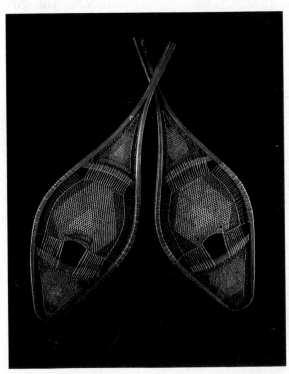

Snowshoes made by Eastern Canadian Native
Americans.

Courtesy Colter Bay Indian Arts Museum,
Grand Teton National Park, Wyoming.

ter they had helped to cook the supper, they would wait with great curiosity to see him eat. They could be sure that he was a real person, for when he took off his moccasins they became visible, and his sister hung them up. But beyond this, they saw nothing of him, not even when they stayed in the place all night, as many of them did.

Now there lived in the village an old man who was a widower, and his three daughters. The youngest girl was very small, weak, and often ill. And yet her sisters, especially the elder, treated her cruelly. The second daughter was kinder and sometimes took her side. But the wicked sister would burn the younger girl's hands and feet with hot cinders. The girl was covered with scars from this treatment. She was so marked that people called her Oochigeaskw, the Rough-Faced-Girl.

When her father came home and asked why the youngest girl had such burns, the bad sister would say at once that it was the girl's own fault, for she had disobeyed orders and gone near the fire and fallen into it.

These two elder sisters decided one day to try their luck at seeing the Invisible One. So they dressed themselves in their finest clothes and tried to look their prettiest. They found the Invisible One's sister and took the usual walk by the water.

When the brother came, and when they were asked if they could see him, they answered, "Of course." And when asked about the shoulder strap or sled cord, they answered, "A piece of rawhide."

Leather pouch with beads and quills made by the Eastern Woodland Native Americans.

Courtesy Colter Bay Indian Arts Museum,
Grand Teton National Park, Wyoming.

But of course they were lying like the others, and they got nothing for their pains.

The next afternoon, when the father returned home, he brought with him many of the pretty little shells from which wampum was made, and the sisters set to work to string them.

That day, poor little Oochigeaskw, who had always gone barefoot, got a pair of her father's moccasins, old ones, and put them into water to soften them so that she could wear them. Then she begged her

Re-created wigwam made of tree bark.

American Indian Archaeological Institute, Washington, Connecticut.

sisters for a few wampum shells. The elder called her a little pest, but the younger one gave her some. Now, since she had no clothes other than her usual rags, the poor little thing went into the woods and got herself some sheets of birch bark. From these, she made a dress and put marks on it for decoration, in the style of long ago. She also made a petticoat and a loose gown, a cap, leggings, and a handkerchief. She put on her father's large old moccasins, which were far too big for her, and went forth to try her luck. She would try, she thought, to see the Invisible One.

She did not begin very well. As she set off, her sisters shouted and hooted, hissed and yelled, and tried to make her stay. And the loafers around the village, seeing the strange little creature, called out "Shame!"

The poor little girl in her strange clothes, with her face all scarred, was an awful sight, but she was kindly received by the sister of the Invisible One. And this was, of course, because this noble lady understood far more about things than simply the mere outside which all the rest of the world knows. As the brown of the evening sky turned to black, the lady took the girl down to the lake.

"Do you see him?" the Invisible One's sister asked.

"I do, indeed—and he is wonderful!" said Oochigeaskw.

The sister asked, "And what is his sled string?"

The little girl said, "It is the Rainbow."

"And, my sister, what is his bow string?"

"It is the Spirit's Road—the Milky Way."

"So you *have* seen him," said his sister. She took the girl home with her and bathed her. As she did so, all the scars disappeared from the girl's body. Her hair grew again, as it was combed, long, like a blackbird's wing. Her eyes were now like stars: In all the world there was no other such beauty. Then, from her treasures, the lady gave her a wedding garment and adorned her.

Then she told Oochigeaskw to take the *wife*'s seat in the wigwam, the one next to where the Invisible One sat, beside the entrance. And when he came in, terrible and beautiful, he smiled and said:

"So we are found out!"

"Yes," said his sister. And so Oochigeaskw became his wife.

Mint, a Pretty Girl by George Catlin (1832). Oil on canvas.

National Museum of American Art, Washington DC/Art Resource, NY

Cradled in the Wind by Luke Simon. Contemporary Micmac sculpture made of buffed clay.

Courtesy Institute of American Indian Art, Santa Fe, New Mexico.

About the Authors

The **Algonquins** lived in the parts of Canada now called Quebec and Ontario. The Algonquins lived in groups of twenty-five or more close relatives, each group living together in one lodge. They believed in a *great spirit,* a very powerful god. They also believed that their lives were influenced by the spirits of plants, animals, and other elements of nature. In 1640, the Algonquins were defeated by their rivals, the Iroquois. Some four thousand Algonquins still live in parts of Canada today.

EXPLORING CONNOTATIONS

*T*he **denotation** of a word is its dictionary definition. A word's **connotations** are the emotions or associations that it has for readers. For example, the three adjectives *thin, slim,* and *skinny* might all be used to describe the same person. Which word would sound most favorable to you? Which word would sound least favorable?

Read the following passage from Gary Paulsen's *Hatchet,* paying special attention to the underlined words. Then use a separate sheet of paper to answer the questions below.

I must make a <u>home</u> for the sparks, he thought. A perfect <u>home</u> or they won't stay, they won't make fire. . . .

He <u>positioned</u> his spark nest—as he thought of it—at the base of the rock, used his thumb to make a small depression in the middle, and <u>slammed</u> the back of the hatchet down across the black rock. A cloud of sparks rained down, most of them missing the nest, but some, perhaps thirty or so, hit in the depression, and of those six or seven found fuel and grew, <u>smoldered</u> and caused the bark to take on the red glow.

Then they went out.

Close—he was close. He repositioned the nest, made a new and smaller dent with his thumb, and struck again.

More sparks, a slight glow, then nothing.

It's me, he thought. I'm doing something wrong. I do not know this—a cave dweller would have had a fire by now, a <u>Cro-Magnon</u> man would have a fire by now—but I don't know this. I don't know how to make a fire.

Exploring Connotations

1. What different associations would you have if Paulsen had used the word *target* rather than *home* in the first paragraph?

2. Explain how the word *placed* (versus *positioned*) would create a different effect at the beginning of the second paragraph.

3. What associations do you have with the verb *slammed*? How would the verb *hit* be different?

4. If the verb *burned* were substituted for *smoldered* toward the end of the second paragraph, what difference would the change make?

5. What if Paulsen had used the word *prehistoric*, rather than *Cro-Magnon*, in the last paragraph?

WRITING A DESCRIPTION

*I*n **descriptive writing,** you use words to create a picture or image of a subject. You can use description in many different forms for a variety of writing purposes. For example, you might want to express yourself in a journal entry, or persuade a friend to see a new movie. You could also use description in a lost-and-found notice or in a piece of creative writing such as a short story. During this unit, you have seen some of the key elements of description. Now you will have the chance to describe a subject of your own choice.

Prewriting

1. Use these guidelines when you start to plan a description:
   - Choose a familiar person, place, or thing.
   - Choose a subject that you can observe directly.
   - Focus and limit your subject so that you have enough space to cover all the important details.

   [See **Focus** assignment on page 96.]

2. Think about your purpose and audience. In a description, your **purpose** is usually to express yourself or to create a mood or feeling. Your **audience** may be your classmates and your teacher. Think about what they may know already about your subject. What might they like to know?

3. Use these techniques to gather details for your description:
   - observing ▪ recalling ▪ imagining

   Pay special attention to **sensory** details—words and phrases that appeal to the five senses: sight, hearing, touch, taste, and smell. Sensory details are especially important in descriptive writing because they help your readers to *see* your subject concretely and vividly. You may wish to use a chart like the one below in order to list sensory details about your subject.

   | Subject of Description: _____ | | | | |
Sight	Hearing	Touch	Smell	Taste
____	____	____	____	____
____	____	____	____	____
____	____	____	____	____
____	____	____	____	____

   [See **Focus** assignment on page 126.]

4. Organize the details for your description in a logical way. Choose one of the two methods listed below:
   - **Spatial Order:** Present details in the order you see them: top to bottom, near to far, left to right.
   - **Order of Importance:** Place the most important details either first or last.

   [See **Focus** assignment on page 145.]

Writing ～

1. As you write the first draft of your description, try to make your words as exact as possible. Using **exact words**—nouns, verbs, adjectives, and adverbs—will help you to present a sharp, vivid picture of the subject. Avoid vague, general words like *move, thing, pretty, rather, very, nice,* and *interesting.* [See **Focus** assignment on page 112.]

2. Use **figures of speech** in your description where they can create special effects. Figures of speech are imaginative comparisons that are not meant to be taken literally.

   ■ A **simile** compares two unlike things, using a word such as *like, as, resembles,* or *than:* "The storm scattered the trees like bowling pins."

   ■ A **metaphor** is a direct comparison between two unlike things in which one thing becomes another thing: "Fame is a trumpet blast."

3. Be sure that all the details you include in your description contribute to a main feeling or overall impression. Leave out any details that do not fit your focus or the mood you are trying to create in your essay.

4. Use **transitional words and phrases** to show the connections between ideas in your paper. Below is a list of useful transitions:

above	first	most important
across	here	over
around	inside	then
before	into	there
behind	last	under
down	mainly	up

Evaluating and Revising ～

1. After you have finished a first draft of your description, put it aside for a while. Then evaluate your draft with fresh eyes. Have you chosen exact words to describe your subject? Do all the details in your paper contribute to a single impression or mood?

2. You may find the following checklist helpful as you revise your writing.

Checklist for Evaluation and Revision

✔ Have I limited my subject so that I can cover it?

✔ Do I clearly identify my subject in the introduction?

✔ Do I help readers "see" my subject by using exact words and sensory details?

✔ Have I used fresh, vivid figures of speech?

✔ Have I organized my details in a logical way that is easy to follow?

✔ Do all the details contribute to a single main impression?

Here is an example of how one writer revised a paragraph in a description.

Russell ~~came slowly~~ *sauntered* out the door and ~~stood~~ *paused* on the porch. He casually glanced at the driveway and then caught his breath in surprise. The brand-new bike's *chrome* handlebars ~~were bright~~ *flashed* in the warm May sunshine. Where had this beautiful bike come from? He had no idea. *it* certainly hadn't been in the Winkler driveway an hour before. As he walked around the bicycle, his nose caught the smell of the leather seat. Then he saw the best part of all: the license plate that was made to order with gold letters on a black background, spelling out "RUSSELL 1." *tr* The rear reflector was red. *a fiery sparkle.*

Proofreading and Publishing

1. Proofread your paper to correct errors in grammar, usage, capitalization, and punctuation. (You may find it helpful to refer to the **Handbook for Revision** on pages 750–785.) Then prepare a final version of your paper by making a clean copy.

2. Consider some of the following ways of publishing and sharing your paper:
   - illustrate your description with drawings or photos and then display your essay on the class bulletin board
   - submit your essay to the school newspaper or magazine
   - together with your classmates, make your essays the basis for a class "radio show" by tape recording your descriptions
   - deliver an oral reading of your paper in class

Portfolio If your teacher approves, you may wish to keep a copy of your work in your writing folder or portfolio.

UNIT THREE

Short Stories

Storytelling is natural to people, just as eating and sleeping are. There is not a group of people on earth who have not told stories. All over the world, stories are built on certain elements. The **plot** is "what happens" in the story. The most important element in the plot is **conflict**, or struggle. This means that a character wants something very much and meets resistance trying to get it. The **characters** in a story are also important. The best stories, in fact, are the ones that create interesting, lifelike characters. Most stories also have a **setting**, a particular time and place in which the action occurs. When you finish a story, you frequently ask: "But what does it MEAN?" What you are looking for is the story's **theme**, or what the story reveals about life. The best stories help us see ourselves and our lives more clearly.

The Wreck of the Ole '97 by Thomas Hart Benton (1943). Egg tempera on gessoed masonite.

Hunter Museum of Art, Chattanooga, Tennessee. Gift of the Benwood Foundation.

Close Reading OF A SHORT STORY

Think of how you read the listing of television programs in a weekly guide or the recipe for a favorite dessert or a letter from a pen pal. You read each of these things in a different way.

Reading literature also requires special skills. Follow these guidelines to become an active reader.

Guidelines for Close Reading

1. Ask questions as you read. Respond to clues and draw inferences from them. Guess at the meaning of unfamiliar words. Draw conclusions from what you have read.

2. Make predictions. Think about what is going to happen next.

3. Relate what you read to your own life and experiences. Put yourself in the main character's place.

4. Try to state the author's overall purpose in your own words.

5. Consider your own responses. What questions remain unanswered? Did your predictions come true? Do you understand your own feelings and actions after reading the selection?

Here is a brief story that has been read carefully by one reader. The comments in the margin show how this reader has responded to the story. If you would like, make notes of your own on a separate sheet of paper, covering up the printed notes as you read. You may wish to compare your responses with these printed comments at a later point.

A Secret for Two

QUENTIN REYNOLDS

Montreal is a very large city, but, like all cities, it has some very small streets. Streets, for instance, like Prince Edward Street, which is only four blocks long, ending in a cul-de-sac.[1] No one knew Prince Edward Street as well as did Pierre Dupin, for Pierre had delivered milk to the families on the street for thirty years now.

During the past fifteen years the horse which drew the milk wagon used by Pierre was a large white horse named Joseph. In Montreal, especially in that part of Montreal which is very French, the animals, like children, are often given the names of saints. When the big white horse first came to the Provincale Milk Company he didn't have a name. They told Pierre that he could use the white horse henceforth. Pierre stroked the softness of the horse's neck; he stroked the sheen of its splendid belly and he looked into the eyes of the horse.

"This is a kind horse, a gentle and a faithful horse," Pierre said, "and I can see a beautiful spirit shining out of the eyes of the horse. I will name him after good St. Joseph, who was also kind and gentle and faithful and a beautiful spirit."

Within a year Joseph knew the milk route as well as Pierre. Pierre used to boast that he didn't need reins—he never touched them. Each morning Pierre arrived at the stables of the Provincale Milk Company at five o'clock. The wagon would be loaded and Joseph hitched to it. Pierre would call *"Bonjour, vieil ami,"*[2] as he climbed into his seat and Joseph would turn his head and the other drivers would smile and say that the horse would smile at Pierre. Then Jacques, the foreman, would say, "All right, Pierre, go on," and Pierre would call softly to Joseph, *"Avance, mon ami,"*[3] and this splendid

---

1. **cul-de-sac** (kul′də·sak′): dead-end street.
2. *Bonjour, vieil ami* (bōn·zhōō′ vē·ā′ ä·mē′): French for "Good morning, old friend."
3. *Avance, mon ami* (ä·väns′ mōn ä·mē): French for "Go forward, my friend."

combination would stalk proudly down the street.

The wagon, without any direction from Pierre, would roll three blocks down St. Catherine Street, then turn right two blocks along Roslyn Avenue; then left, for that was Prince Edward Street. The horse would stop at the first house, allow Pierre perhaps thirty seconds to get down from his seat and put a bottle of milk at the front door and would then go on, skipping two houses and stopping at the third. So down the length of the street. Then Joseph, still without any direction from Pierre, would turn around and come back along the other side. Yes, Joseph was a smart horse.

Pierre would boast at the stable of Joseph's skill. "I never touch the reins. He knows just where to stop. Why, a blind man could handle my route with Joseph pulling the wagon."

So it went on for years—always the same. Pierre and Joseph both grew old together, but gradually, not suddenly. Pierre's huge walrus mustache was pure white now and Joseph didn't lift his knees so high or raise his head quite as much. Jacques, the foreman of the stables, never noticed that they were both getting old until Pierre appeared one morning carrying a heavy walking stick.

"Hey, Pierre," Jacques laughed. "Maybe you got the gout,[4] hey?"

"*Mais oui*,[5] Jacques," Pierre said a bit uncertainly. "One grows old. One's legs get tired."

"You should teach that horse to carry the milk to the front door for you," Jacques told him. "He does everything else."

He knew every one of the forty families he served on Prince Edward Street. The cooks knew that Pierre could neither read nor write, so instead of following the usual custom of leaving a note in an empty bottle if an additional quart of milk was needed they would sing out when they heard the rumble of his wagon wheels over the cobbled street, "Bring an extra quart this morning, Pierre."

---

4. **gout** (gowt): a painful swelling of the feet or hands; like arthritis.
5. *Mais oui* (mā wē′): French for "But yes."

[This is also a clue, but I didn't get it till the end of the story.]

[Another clue: Pierre doesn't have to make out bills. He doesn't have to use his eyes.]

Here is a clue to the title. [At the end of the story you know what this means.]

I don't see any conflict in this story so far. What's going to be its point?

"So you have company for dinner tonight," he would call back gaily.

Pierre had a remarkable memory. When he arrived at the stable he'd always remember to tell Jacques, "The Paquins took an extra quart this morning; the Lemoines bought a pint of cream."

Jacques would note these things in a little book he always carried. Most of the drivers had to make out the weekly bills and collect the money, but Jacques, liking Pierre, had always excused him from this task. All Pierre had to do was to arrive at five in the morning, walk to his wagon, which was always in the same spot at the curb, and deliver his milk. He returned some two hours later, got down stiffly from his seat, called a cheery, *"Au 'voir"*[6] to Jacques and then limped slowly down the street.

One morning the president of the Provincale Milk Company came to inspect the early morning deliveries. Jacques pointed Pierre out to him and said: "Watch how he talks to that horse. See how the horse listens and how he turns his head toward Pierre? See the look in that horse's eyes? You know, I think those two share a secret. I have often noticed it. It is as though they both sometimes chuckle at us as they go off on their route. Pierre is a good man, Monsieur[7] President, but he gets old. Would it be too bold of me to suggest that he be retired and be given perhaps a small pension?" he added anxiously.

"But of course," the president laughed. "I know his record. He has been on this route now for thirty years and never once has there been a complaint. Tell him it is time he rested. His salary will go on just the same."

But Pierre refused to retire. He was panic-stricken at the thought of not driving Joseph every day. "We are two old men," he said to Jacques. "Let us wear out together. When Joseph is ready to retire—then I, too, will quit."

Jacques, who was a kind man, understood. There was

---

6. *Au 'voir* (ō vwär'): French for "good-bye."
7. **Monsieur** (mis·yər'): French word for "sir."

something about Pierre and Joseph which made a man smile tenderly. It was as though each drew some hidden strength from the other. When Pierre was sitting in his seat, and when Joseph was hitched to the wagon, neither seemed old. But when they finished their work, then Pierre would limp down the street slowly, seeming very old indeed, and the horse's head would drop and he would walk very wearily to his stall.

[This is so true! But you don't know till the end.]

Then one morning Jacques had dreadful news for Pierre when he arrived. It was a cold morning and still pitch-dark. The air was like iced wine that morning and the snow which had fallen during the night glistened like a million diamonds piled together.

Something is wrong! I wonder what?

Jacques said, "Pierre, your horse, Joseph, did not wake up this morning. He was very old, Pierre, he was twenty-five and that is like being seventy-five for a man."

"Yes," Pierre said, slowly. "Yes. I am seventy-five. And I cannot see Joseph again."

Joseph has died. How sad! Now what will become of Pierre?

"Of course you can," Jacques soothed. "He is over in his stall, looking very peaceful. Go over and see him."

Pierre took one step forward then turned. "No . . . no

What doesn't Jacques understand? *[You know at the end of the story.]*

Are his eyes this way because he is sad? Or is something wrong with them? *[You know at the end.]*

Is Pierre deaf? No, he heard Jacques talk to him.

What are cataracts?

How did Jacques know the horse knew? *It's a sad story, but I really like it. I wish it didn't have so many French words.*

. . . you don't understand, Jacques.''

Jacques clapped him on the shoulder. ''We'll find another horse just as good as Joseph. Why, in a month you'll teach him to know your route as well as Joseph did. We'll . . .''

The look in Pierre's eyes stopped him. For years Pierre had worn a heavy cap, the peak of which came low over his eyes, keeping the bitter morning wind out of them. Now Jacques looked into Pierre's eyes and he saw something which startled him. He saw a dead, lifeless look in them. The eyes were mirroring the grief that was in Pierre's heart and his soul. It was as though his heart and soul had died.

''Take today off, Pierre,'' Jacques said, but already Pierre was hobbling off down the street, and had one been near one would have seen tears streaming down his cheeks and have heard half-smothered sobs. Pierre walked to the corner and stepped into the street. There was a warning yell from the driver of a huge truck that was coming fast and there was the scream of brakes, but Pierre apparently heard neither.

Five minutes later an ambulance driver said, ''He's dead. Was killed instantly.''

Jacques and several of the milk-wagon drivers had arrived and they looked down at the still figure.

''I couldn't help it,'' the driver of the truck protested, ''he walked right into my truck. He never saw it, I guess. Why, he walked into it as though he were blind.''

The ambulance doctor bent down, ''Blind? Of course the man was blind. See those cataracts? This man has been blind for five years.'' He turned to Jacques, ''You say he worked for you? Didn't you know he was blind?''

''No . . . no . . .'' Jacques said, softly. ''None of us knew. Only one knew—a friend of his named Joseph. . . . It was a secret, I think, just between those two.''

Looking at Yourself as a Reader

Suppose you were this reader, and suppose that now you are reviewing your responses to look for something to write about.

1. You will notice that most of your responses have to do with clues that **foreshadow** or hint at the story's surprise ending. If you want to write about the use of foreshadowing in the story, you might start with this sentence:

    In "A Secret for Two," Quentin Reynolds drops several clues that foreshadow the surprise ending. Here are the clues. (I found most of them only after the story was over.)

2. You might also write about the story's **title.** Notice that you asked right away what the title meant—what *is* the "secret"?

3. Your notes also show that the story had a strong **emotional effect** on you. This could be another topic for a composition. You could also tell if the story reminded you of your own experiences with animals. You might open with this statement:

    After I had finished "A Secret for Two" by Quentin Reynolds, I felt sad about the fates of the two characters who loved each other so much.

Dragon, Dragon

JOHN GARDNER

Before You Read

In most of the old fairy tales we loved to read when we were very young, a big strong hero surprises the evil dragon and kills it with a magic sword. In this story, however, the writer has fun with these old fairy tales. For one thing, cars and their spark plugs appear right alongside the dragon and wizard. For another thing, the wizard, supposedly the brains of the kingdom, has a terrible memory. In what other ways does this story spoof the old fairy tales? You'll find glaring examples in the first paragraph.

Verbs are words that express action or that help make a statement. The action verbs in this story are so vivid they make the action come alive. For example, in the first two paragraphs, the dragon is described as *plaguing* the kingdom and *ravaging* the countryside. *Plaguing* (plāg'ing) means "bringing terrible troubles to." It makes us think of those disgusting diseases (called *plagues*) that used to kill thousands of people (and in some places still do). *Ravaging* (rav'ij·ing) means "violently destroying something." So, a dragon that plagued and ravaged would be pretty bad news.

There was once a king whose kingdom was plagued by a dragon. The king did not know which way to turn. The king's knights were all cowards who hid under their beds whenever the dragon came in sight, so they were of no use to the king at all. And the king's wizard could not help either because, being old, he had forgotten his magic spells. Nor could the wizard look up the spells that had slipped his mind, for he had unfortunately misplaced his wizard's book many years before. The king was at his wit's end.

Every time there was a full moon, the dragon came out of his lair and ravaged the countryside. He frightened maidens and stopped up chimneys and broke store windows and set people's clocks back and made dogs bark until no one could hear himself think.

He tipped over fences and robbed graves and put frogs in people's drinking water and tore the last chapters out of novels and changed house numbers around . . .

He stole spark plugs out of people's cars and put firecrackers in people's cigars and stole the clappers from all the church bells and sprung every bear trap for miles around so the bears could wander wherever they pleased.

And to top it all off, he changed around all the roads in the kingdom so that people could not get anywhere except by starting out in the wrong direction.

"That," said the king in a fury, "is enough!" And he called a meeting of everyone in the kingdom.

Now it happened that there lived in the kingdom a wise old cobbler[1] who had a wife and three sons. The cobbler and his family came to the king's meeting and stood way in back by the door, for the cobbler had a feeling that since he was nobody important there had probably been some mistake, and no doubt the king had

---

1. In most parts of this country, cobblers are called *shoemakers*.

intended the meeting for everyone in the kingdom except his family and him.

"Ladies and gentlemen," said the king when everyone was present, "I've put up with that dragon as long as I can. He has got to be stopped."

All the people whispered amongst themselves, and the king smiled, pleased with the impression he had made.

But the wise cobbler said gloomily, "It's all very well to talk about it—but how are you going to do it?"

And now all the people smiled and winked as if to say, "Well, King, he's got you there!"

The king frowned.

"It's not that His Majesty hasn't tried," the queen spoke up loyally.

"Yes," said the king, "I've told my knights again and again that they ought to slay that dragon. But I can't *force* them to go. I'm not a tyrant."

"Why doesn't the wizard say a magic spell?" asked the cobbler.

"He's done the best he can," said the king.

The wizard blushed and everyone looked embarrassed. "I used to do all sorts of spells and chants when I was younger," the wizard explained. "But I've lost my spell book, and I begin to fear I'm losing my memory too. For instance, I've been trying for days to recall one spell I used to do. I forget, just now, what the deuce[2] it was for. It went something like–

Bimble,
Wimble,
Cha, Cha
CHOOMPF!

Suddenly, to everyone's surprise, the queen turned into a rosebush.

"Oh dear," said the wizard.

"Now you've done it," groaned the king.

"Poor Mother," said the princess.

"I don't know what can have happened," the wizard said nervously, "but don't worry, I'll have her changed back in a jiffy." He shut his eyes and racked his brain for a spell that would change her back.

But the king said quickly, "You'd better leave well enough alone. If you change her into a rattlesnake, we'll have to chop off her head."

Meanwhile the cobbler stood with his hands in his pockets, sighing at the waste of time. "About the dragon . . ." he began.

"Oh yes," said the king. "I'll tell you what I'll do. I'll give the princess's hand in marriage to anyone who can make the dragon stop."

"It's not enough," said the cobbler. "She's a nice enough girl, you understand. But how would an ordinary person support her? Also, what about those of us that are already married?"

"In that case," said the king, "I'll offer the princess's hand or half the kingdom or both—whichever is most convenient."

The cobbler scratched his chin and considered it. "It's not enough," he said at

---

2. **what the deuce:** an expression meaning something like "what in the world."

last. "It's a good enough kingdom, you understand, but it's too much responsibility."

"Take it or leave it," the king said.

"I'll leave it," said the cobbler. And he shrugged and went home.

But the cobbler's eldest son thought the bargain was a good one, for the princess was very beautiful and he liked the idea of having half the kingdom to run as he pleased. So he said to the king, "I'll accept those terms, Your Majesty. By tomorrow morning the dragon will be slain."

"Bless you!" cried the king.

"Hooray, hooray, hooray!" cried all the people, throwing their hats in the air.

The cobbler's eldest son beamed with pride, and the second eldest looked at him enviously. The youngest son said timidly, "Excuse me, Your Majesty, but don't you think the queen looks a little unwell? If I were you, I think I'd water her."

"Good heavens," cried the king, glancing at the queen who had been changed into a rosebush, "I'm glad you mentioned it!"

Now the cobbler's eldest son was very clever and was known far and wide for how quickly he could multiply fractions in his head. He was perfectly sure he could slay the dragon by somehow or other playing a trick on him, and he didn't feel that he needed his wise old father's advice. But he thought it was only polite to ask, so he went to his father, who was working as usual at his cobbler's bench, and said, "Well, Father, I'm off to slay the dragon. Have you any advice to give me?"

The cobbler thought a moment and replied, "When and if you come to the dragon's lair, recite the following poem:

Dragon, dragon, how do you do?
I've come from the king to murder you.

Say it very loudly and firmly, and the dragon will fall, God willing, at your feet."

"How curious!" said the eldest son. And he thought to himself, "The old man is not as wise as I thought. If I say something like that to the dragon, he will eat me up in an instant. The way to kill a dragon is to outfox him." And keeping his opinion to himself, the eldest son set forth on his quest.

When he came at last to the dragon's lair, which was a cave, the eldest son slyly disguised himself as a peddler and knocked on the door and called out, "Hello there!"

"There's nobody home!" roared a voice.

The voice was as loud as an earthquake, and the eldest son's knees knocked together in terror.

"I don't come to trouble you," the eldest son said meekly. "I merely thought you might be interested in looking at some of our brushes. Or if you'd prefer," he added quickly, "I could leave our catalogue with you and I could drop by again, say, early next week."

"I don't want any brushes," the voice roared, "and I especially don't want any brushes next week."

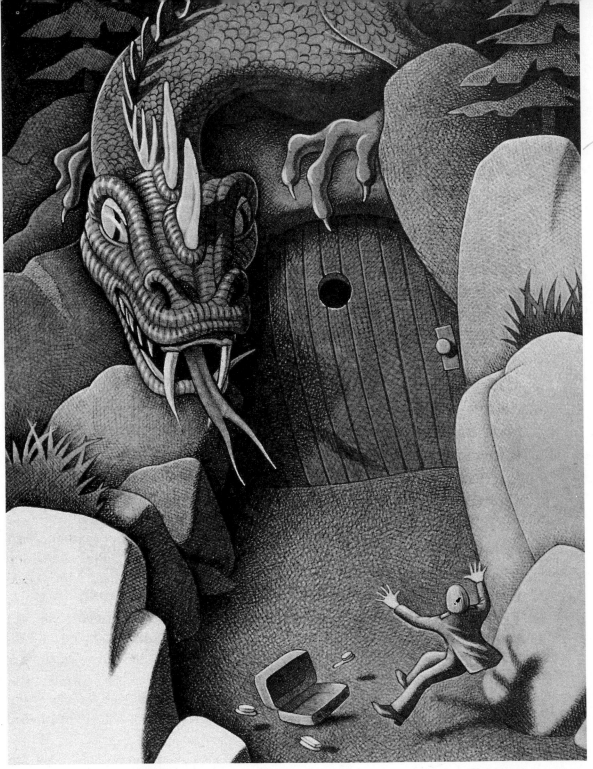

Suddenly a great shadow fell over him . . .

Illustration by Charles Shields.

"Oh," said the eldest son. By now his knees were knocking together so badly that he had to sit down.

Suddenly a great shadow fell over him, and the eldest son looked up. It was the dragon. The eldest son drew his sword, but the dragon lunged and swallowed him in a single gulp, sword and all, and the eldest son found himself in the dark of the dragon's belly. "What a fool I was not to listen to my wise old father!" thought the eldest son. And he began to weep bitterly.

"Well," sighed the king the next morning, "I see the dragon has not been slain yet."

"I'm just as glad, personally," said the princess, sprinkling the queen. "I would have had to marry that eldest son, and he had warts."

Now the cobbler's middle son decided it was his turn to try. The middle son was very strong and was known far and wide for being able to lift up the corner of a church. He felt perfectly sure he could slay the dragon by simply laying into him, but he thought it would be only polite to ask his father's advice. So he went to his father and said to him, "Well, Father, I'm off to slay the dragon. Have you any advice for me?"

The cobbler told the middle son exactly what he'd told the eldest.

"When and if you come to the dragon's lair, recite the following poem:

Dragon, dragon, how do you do?
I've come from the king to murder you.

Say it very loudly and firmly, and the dragon will fall, God willing, at your feet."

"What an odd thing to say," thought the middle son. "The old man is not as wise as I thought. You have to take these dragons by surprise." But he kept his opinion to himself and set forth.

When he came in sight of the dragon's lair, the middle son spurred his horse to a gallop and thundered into the entrance, swinging his sword with all his might.

But the dragon had seen him while he was still a long way off, and being very clever, the dragon had crawled up on top of the door so that when the son came charging in, he went under the dragon and onto the back of the cave and slammed into the wall. Then the dragon chuckled and got down off the door, taking his time, and strolled back to where the man and the horse lay unconscious from the terrific blow. Opening his mouth as if for a yawn, the dragon swallowed the middle son in a single gulp and put the horse in the freezer to eat another day.

"What a fool I was not to listen to my wise old father," thought the middle son when he came to in the dragon's belly. And he, too, began to weep bitterly.

That night there was a full moon, and the dragon ravaged the countryside so terribly that several families moved to another kingdom.

"Well," sighed the king in the morning, "still no luck in this dragon business, I see."

"I'm just as glad, myself," said the princess, moving her mother, pot and all, to the window where the sun could get at her. "The cobbler's middle son was a kind of humpback."

Now the cobbler's youngest son saw that his turn had come. He was very upset and nervous, and he wished he had never been born. He was not clever, like his eldest brother, and he was not strong, like his second-eldest brother. He was a decent, honest boy who always minded his elders.

He borrowed a suit of armor from a friend of his who was a knight, and when the youngest son put the armor on, it was so heavy he could hardly walk. From another knight he borrowed a sword, and that was so heavy that the only way the youngest son could get it to the dragon's lair was to drag it along behind his horse like a plow.

When everything was in readiness, the youngest son went for a last conversation with his father.

"Father, have you any advice to give me?" he asked.

"Only this," said the cobbler. "When and if you come to the dragon's lair, recite the following poem:

Dragon, dragon, how do you do?
I've come from the king to murder you.

Say it very loudly and firmly, and the dragon will fall, God willing, at your feet."

"Are you certain?" asked the youngest son uneasily.

"As certain as one can ever be in these matters," said the wise old cobbler.

And so the youngest son set forth on his quest. He traveled over hill and dale[3] and at last came to the dragon's cave.

The dragon, who had seen the cobbler's youngest son while he was still a long way off, was seated up above the door, inside the cave, waiting and smiling to himself. But minutes passed and no one came thundering in. The dragon frowned, puzzled, and was tempted to peek out. However, reflecting that patience seldom goes unrewarded, the dragon kept his head up out of sight and went on waiting. At last, when he could stand it no longer, the dragon craned his neck and looked. There at the entrance of the cave stood a trembling young man in a suit of armor twice his size, struggling with a sword so heavy he could lift only one end of it at a time.

At sight of the dragon, the cobbler's youngest son began to tremble so violently that his armor rattled like a house caving in. He heaved with all his might at the sword and got the handle up level with his chest, but even now the point was down in the dirt. As loudly and firmly as he could manage, the youngest son cried—

Dragon, dragon, how do you do?
I've come from the king to murder you.

"What?" cried the dragon, flabbergasted.[4] "You? *You?* Murder *Me???*" All at once he began to laugh, pointing at the little cobbler's son. *"He he he ho ha!"* he

---

3. **dale:** valley.
4. **flabbergasted:** greatly surprised.

"Dragon, dragon, how do you do?"

Illustration by Charles Shields.

roared, shaking all over, and tears filled his eyes. *"He he he ho ho ho ha ha!"* laughed the dragon. He was laughing so hard he had to hang onto his sides, and he fell off the door and landed on his back, still laughing, kicking his legs helplessly, rolling from side to side, laughing and laughing and laughing.

The cobbler's son was annoyed. "I *do* come from the king to murder you," he said. "A person doesn't like to be laughed at for a thing like that."

"He he he!" wailed the dragon, almost sobbing, gasping for breath. "Of course not, poor dear boy! But really, *he he,* the *idea* of it, *ha ha ha!* And that simply ridiculous *poem!"* Tears streamed from the dragon's eyes and he lay on his back perfectly helpless with laughter.

"It's a good poem," said the cobbler's youngest son loyally. "My father made it up." And growing angrier, he shouted, "I want you to stop that laughing, or I'll—I'll——" But the dragon could not stop for the life of him. And suddenly, in a terrific rage, the cobbler's son began flopping the sword end over end in the direction of the dragon. Sweat ran off the youngest son's forehead, but he labored on, blistering mad, and at last, with one supreme heave, he had the sword standing on its handle a foot from the dragon's throat. Of its own weight the sword fell, slicing the dragon's head off.

"He he ho huk," went the dragon—and then he lay dead.

The two older brothers crawled out and thanked their younger brother for saving their lives. "We have learned our lesson," they said.

Then the three brothers gathered all the treasures from the dragon's cave and tied them to the back end of the youngest brother's horse, and tied the dragon's head on behind the treasures, and started home. "I'm glad I listened to my father," the youngest son thought. "Now I'll be the richest man in the kingdom."

There were hand-carved picture frames and silver spoons and boxes of jewels and chests of money and silver compasses and maps telling where there were more treasures buried when these ran out. There was also a curious old book with a picture of an owl on the cover, and inside, poems and odd sentences and recipes that seemed to make no sense.

When they reached the king's castle, the people all leaped for joy to see that the dragon was dead, and the princess ran out and kissed the youngest brother on the forehead, for secretly she had hoped it would be him.

"Well," said the king, "which half of the kingdom do you want?"

"My wizard's book!" exclaimed the wizard. "He's found my wizard's book!" He opened the book and ran his finger along under the words and then said in a loud voice, "Glmuzk, shkzmlp, blam!"

Instantly the queen stood before them in her natural shape, except she was soaking wet from being sprinkled too often. She glared at the king.

"Oh dear," said the king, hurrying toward the door.

For Study and Discussion

IDENTIFYING FACTS

1. Name four things that this dragon does to annoy people.

2. Describe what happens when the wizard tries to remember one of his old spells.

3. What advice does the cobbler give his sons before they go off to fight the dragon? How do they feel about the father and his advice?

4. Tell why the youngest son is successful. What is his reward?

5. One of the comical things about this fairy tale is that it combines details from modern life with regular fairy-tale details. Find three details that are out of place in a fairy tale (like the novels and house numbers in paragraph 3).

INTERPRETING MEANINGS

6. What do you think the queen will do next?

7. The **plots** of most fairy tales end happily ever after. Does this one? What happens to the two older brothers? the dragon killer? the queen? the wizard?

8. Characters and their actions often seem funny because the writer uses **exaggeration.** For example, this wizard is clumsy. If he were clumsy in an ordinary way, he might just have stayed in his palace room all day trying to remember his spells. But, instead, he is *so* clumsy that when he bungles a spell, he turns the queen into a rosebush. Tell about another character in the story who is funny because some characteristic is exaggerated.

APPLYING MEANINGS

9. This story teaches a **message** about wisdom. In real life, is it always the experts (like this wizard) who are wise? Or does wisdom often come from humble, unexpected sources? Who is wise in this story? Talk about the wise people you know.

Literary Elements

A STORY MAP

Just as you can draw a map of a section of the world to show its main features, so can you draw a map of a story to show its main elements. Following is a chart containing an outline for a "story map." Write this outline on a separate piece of paper and fill in the details. When you have finished, compare your story map to those of your classmates. Do your maps agree on the details?

Story Map
Title and author:
Setting:
Characters:
Main events in the plot: 1. 2. 3. and so on.
Conflict faced by the characters:
Solution to the conflict:
Story's message to me:

Language and Vocabulary

VIVID VERBS

"Dragon, Dragon" uses striking verbs that make the humorous details in the story come alive. For instance, the writer says that the middle son "*thundered* into the entrance" of the dragon's cave. If he had written that the son "rode into the entrance," the action would have been the same. But the verb *thundered* makes us imagine that the son galloped into the cave with a lot of noise (like thunder).

The verbs in the following sentences are underlined. All of them are weak, tame verbs. Rewrite each sentence using a stronger verb—one that makes the action juicier, noisier, more exciting, more active. Exchange your papers in class. How many vivid verbs has your class thought of for each tame verb?

1. The dragon <u>said</u>, "I am the fiercest, toughest dragon around!"

2. The queen <u>dislikes</u> being a rosebush.

3. The youngest son <u>cuts off</u> the dragon's head.

4. The princess <u>comes out</u> of the palace to greet her hero.

events you have witnessed
people you have met or imagined
stories you have heard
daydreams
pictures in magazines or albums

The characters in good stories usually face a **conflict** or problem. The **plot** of a story reaches a **climax,** or turning point, when the outcome of the conflict is decided one way or another. This is the point of greatest excitement or tension. In Gardner's story, the climax occurs when the cobbler's youngest son kills the dragon.

Working with a partner, brainstorm some story ideas together with a main conflict. Try building a plot around this conflict by filling out a chart like the one below. Save your notes.

Introduction	
Conflict	Climax
	Resolution

Focus on Writing a Short Story

BUILDING A PLOT FROM A STORY IDEA

John Gardner builds his story on old fairy tales. To find your own story ideas, think first about your own experiences. Here are some possible sources for story ideas:

Dramatizing the Story

(A Group Activity)

This dragon-slaying story would be fun to act out in the classroom. Before you present the play, you will have to take the following steps:

1. List the **characters** you will need. Write a brief description of what each one should look like.

2. Block out your **scenes**. For example, you might decide to have these scenes:
   a. An opening scene in which a narrator tells the audience the background for the action.
   b. Scene 1: The Meeting
   c. Scene 2: The Eldest Son
   d. Scene 3: The Middle Son
   e. Scene 4: The Youngest Son
   f. Scene 5: Back at the Castle

3. Write your **dialogue.** Be sure to include some descriptions of how people are to say their lines (such as angrily, meekly, stupidly).

4. List your **props** (short for "properties"). These are all the movable items the actors will need (for example, the rosebush that was once the queen).

5. Plan your **costumes.** One of your challenges will be dressing the dragon.

Examples of plays can be found in Unit Six.

About the Author

John Gardner (1933–1982) is best known as a scholar and novelist. The story you have just read is from *Dragon, Dragon, and Other Tales*, his first collection for young readers. Each of the four stories in the collection gives a traditional fairy tale a humorous twist. For instance, in "The Tailor and the Giant," the beautiful princess is won not by the handsome prince but by the "timid little tailor." Gardner also wrote the popular *Child's Bestiary*, a collection of humorous verses about animals. His famous book for adults, *Grendel*, is based on the well-known old English epic tale *Beowulf*. The tale is about the hero Beowulf, who battles and finally defeats the monster Grendel. Like his fairy tale spoofs, Gardner twists this tale by telling *his* story from the monster's point of view. Gardner said that his favorite authors when he was young were Charles Dickens and Walt Disney. He said "both created wonderful cartoon images, told stories as direct as fairy tales, knew the value of broad comedy, spiced up with a little weeping." He kept a statue of Dickens's head in his study "to keep me honest." Gardner was only forty-nine years old when he died in a motorcycle accident.

President Cleveland, Where Are You?

ROBERT CORMIER

Before You Read

This is a story about *want*. It takes place during the Depression of the 1930s, a period when many businesses failed and many people were out of work. It was a period when the whole nation was "in want." This story concerns eleven-year-old Jerry, who wants a particular thing.

Jerry's "want" creates the simple conflict that draws us into the story. We all know that feeling of wanting something so badly it hurts. Most of us have believed at one time or another that if only we could have that baseball mitt or that skateboard or that red dress, our life would become happy.

You'll see that in many ways, life was different in the 1930s. Boys and girls didn't collect baseball cards; they collected cowboy cards. Cowboys in the movies were big heroes then, just as sports figures are today. It costs Jerry only ten cents to see a movie, and only five cents to buy a candy bar.

Before you read about Jerry, write in your journal at least three sentences telling about something you once wanted so very badly it almost hurt.

Grover Cleveland

Calvin Coolidge

Context refers to all the words or phrases or sentences that surround a particular word. You will probably come across some unfamiliar words in this story. Don't let this discourage you. Grappling with new words is the best way to increase your vocabulary. If a dictionary isn't handy, you can often guess a word's meaning by looking carefully at its context. Here are two kinds of context clues:

1. Sometimes a synonym (sin′ə·nim) of the word appears in the sentence. **Synonyms** are words with the same or nearly the same meanings.

2. Sometimes an antonym (an′tə·nim) appears in the sentence. **Antonyms** are words with opposite meanings. For example, in the third paragraph, Jerry says that Rollie Tremaine "did not live in a tenement but in a big white birthday cake of a house on Laurel Street." If you don't know what a *tenement* is, the context of this whole paragraph will give you a general idea. The sentence says that a tenement is different from a "big white birthday cake of a house." You can figure that a tenement is a place to live, and that it is not as desirable as that big white fancy house.

That was the autumn of the cowboy cards—Buck Jones and Tom Tyler and Hoot Gibson and especially Ken Maynard. The cards were available in those five-cent packages of gum: pink sticks, three together, covered with a sweet white powder. You couldn't blow bubbles with that particular gum, but it couldn't have mattered less. The cowboy cards were important— the pictures of those rock-faced men with eyes of blue steel.

On those wind-swept, leaf-tumbling afternoons, we gathered after school on the sidewalk in front of Lemire's Drugstore, across from St. Jude's Parochial School, and we swapped and bargained and matched for the cards. Because a Ken Maynard serial was playing at the Globe every Saturday afternoon, he was the most popular cowboy of all, and one of his cards was worth at least ten of any other kind. Rollie Tremaine had a treasure of thirty or so, and he guarded them jealously. He'd match you for the other cards, but he risked his Ken Maynards only when the other kids threatened to leave him out of the competition altogether.

You could almost hate Rollie Tremaine. In the first place, he was the only son of Auguste Tremaine, who operated the Uptown Dry Goods Store, and he did not live in a tenement but in a big white birthday cake of a house on Laurel Street. He was too fat to be effective in the football games between the Frenchtown Tigers and the North Side Knights, and he made us constantly aware of the jingle of coins in his pockets. He was able to stroll into Lemire's and casually select a quarter's worth of cowboy cards while the rest of us watched, aching with envy.

Once in a while I earned a nickel or dime by running errands or washing windows for blind old Mrs. Belander, or by finding pieces of copper, brass, and other valuable metals at the dump and selling them to the junkman. The coins clutched in my hand, I would race to Lemire's to buy a cowboy card or two, hoping that Ken Maynard would stare boldly out at me as I opened the pack. At one time, before a disastrous matching session with Roger Lussier (my best friend, except where the cards were involved), I owned five Ken Maynards and considered myself a millionaire, of sorts.

One week I was particularly lucky; I had spent two afternoons washing floors

for Mrs. Belander and received a quarter. Because my father had worked a full week at the shop, where a rush order for fancy combs had been received, he allotted[1] my brothers and sisters and me an extra dime along with the usual ten cents for the Saturday afternoon movie. Setting aside the movie fare, I found myself with a bonus of thirty-five cents, and I then planned to put Rollie Tremaine to shame the following Monday afternoon.

Monday was the best day to buy the cards because the candy man stopped at Lemire's every Monday morning to deliver the new assortments. There was nothing more exciting in the world than a fresh batch of card boxes. I rushed home from

school that day and hurriedly changed my clothes, eager to set off for the store. As I burst through the doorway, letting the screen door slam behind me, my brother Armand blocked my way.

He was fourteen, three years older than I, and a freshman at Monument High School. He had recently become a stranger to me in many ways—indifferent to such matters as cowboy cards and the Frenchtown Tigers—and he carried himself with a mysterious dignity that was fractured now and then when his voice began shooting off in all directions like some kind of vocal fireworks.[2]

"Wait a minute, Jerry," he said. "I want to talk to you." He motioned me out

---

1. **allotted:** gave as a share.

2. **vocal fireworks:** many different levels of sounds— very deep one minute, high the next. (Armand's voice is changing because of his age.)

of earshot of my mother, who was busy supervising the usual after-school skirmish in the kitchen.

I sighed with impatience. In recent months Armand had become a figure of authority, siding with my father and mother occasionally. As the oldest son he sometimes took advantage of his age and experience to issue rules and regulations.

"How much money have you got?" he whispered.

"You in some kind of trouble?" I asked, excitement rising in me as I remembered the blackmail plot of a movie at the Globe a month before.

He shook his head in annoyance. "Look," he said, "it's Pa's birthday tomorrow. I think we ought to chip in and buy him something . . ."

I reached into my pocket and caressed the coins. "Here," I said carefully, pulling out a nickel. "If we all give a nickel, we should have enough to buy him something pretty nice."

He regarded me with contempt.[3] "Rita already gave me fifteen cents, and I'm throwing in a quarter. Albert handed over a dime—all that's left of his birthday money. Is that all you can do—a nickel?"

"Aw, come on," I protested. "I haven't got a single Ken Maynard left, and I was going to buy some cards this afternoon."

"Ken Maynard!" he snorted. "Who's more important—him or your father?"

His question was unfair because he knew that there was no possible choice— "my father" had to be the only answer. My father was a huge man who believed in the things of the spirit. . . . He had worked at the Monument Comb Shop since the age of fourteen; his booming laugh—or grumble—greeted us each night when he returned from the factory. A steady worker when the shop had enough work, he quickened with gaiety on Friday nights . . . and he was fond of making long speeches about the good things in life. In the middle of the Depression, for instance, he paid cash for a piano, of all things, and insisted that my twin sisters, Yolande and Yvette, take lessons once a week.

I took a dime from my pocket and handed it to Armand.

"Thanks, Jerry," he said. "I hate to take your last cent."

"That's all right," I replied, turning away and consoling myself with the thought that twenty cents was better than nothing at all.

When I arrived at Lemire's I sensed disaster in the air. Roger Lussier was kicking disconsolately[4] at a tin can in the gutter, and Rollie Tremaine sat sullenly on the steps in front of the store.

"Save your money," Roger said. He had known about my plans to splurge on the cards.

"What's the matter?" I asked.

"There's no more cowboy cards," Rollie Tremaine said. "The company's not making any more."

---

3. **contempt:** (kən·tempt′): disgust or scorn.

4. **disconsolately** (dis·kon′sə·lit·lē): unhappily.

"They're going to have President cards," Roger said, his face twisting with disgust. He pointed to the store window. "Look!"

A placard in the window announced: "Attention, Boys. Watch for the New Series. Presidents of the United States. Free in Each 5-Cent Package of Caramel Chew."

"President cards?" I asked, dismayed.

I read on: "Collect a Complete Set and Receive an Official Imitation Major League Baseball Glove, Embossed[5] with Lefty Grove's Autograph."

Glove or no glove, who could become excited about Presidents, of all things?

Rollie Tremaine stared at the sign. "Benjamin Harrison,[6] for crying out loud," he said. "Why would I want Benjamin Harrison when I've got twenty-two Ken Maynards?"

I felt the warmth of guilt creep over me. I jingled the coins in my pocket, but the sound was hollow. No more Ken Maynards to buy.

"I'm going to buy a Mr. Goodbar," Rollie Tremaine decided.

I was without appetite, indifferent even to a Baby Ruth, which was my favorite. I thought of how I had betrayed Armand and, worst of all, my father.

"I'll see you after supper," I called over my shoulder to Roger as I hurried away toward home. I took the shortcut behind the church, although it involved leaping over a tall wooden fence, and I zigzagged recklessly through Mr. Thibodeau's garden, trying to outrace my guilt. I pounded up the steps and into the house, only to learn that Armand had already taken Yolande and Yvette uptown to shop for the birthday present.

I pedaled my bike furiously through the streets, ignoring the indignant horns of automobiles as I sliced through the traffic. Finally I saw Armand and my sisters emerge from the Monument Men's Shop. My heart sank when I spied the long, slim package that Armand was holding.

"Did you buy the present yet?" I asked, although I knew it was too late.

"Just now. A blue tie," Armand said. "What's the matter?"

"Nothing," I replied, my chest hurting.

He looked at me for a long moment. At first his eyes were hard, but then they softened. He smiled at me, almost sadly, and touched my arm. I turned away from him because I felt naked and exposed.

"It's all right," he said gently. "Maybe you've learned something." The words were gentle, but they held a curious dignity, the dignity remaining even when his voice suddenly cracked on the last syllable.

I wondered what was happening to me, because I did not know whether to laugh or cry.

Sister Angela was amazed when, a week before Christmas vacation, everybody in the class submitted a history essay worthy

---

5. **embossed** (im·bôst′): printed with letters that are raised above the surface.
6. **Benjamin Harrison:** the twenty-third President of the United States. (He served from 1889 to 1893.)

of a high mark—in some cases as high as *A*-minus. (Sister Angela did not believe that anyone in the world ever deserved an *A*.) She never learned—or at least she never let on that she knew—we all had become experts on the Presidents because of the cards we purchased at Lemire's. Each card contained a picture of a President, and on the reverse side, a summary of his career. We looked at those cards so often that the biographies imprinted themselves on our minds without effort. Even our street-corner conversations were filled with such information as the fact that James Madison was called "The Father of the Constitution," or that John Adams had intended to become a minister.

The President cards were a roaring success and the cowboy cards were quickly forgotten. In the first place we did not receive gum with the cards, but a kind of chewy caramel. The caramel could be tucked into a corner of your mouth, bulging your cheek in much the same manner as wads of tobacco bulged the mouths of baseball stars. In the second place the competition for collecting the cards was fierce and frustrating—fierce because everyone was intent on being the first to send away for a baseball glove, and frustrating because although there were only thirty-two Presidents, including Franklin Delano Roosevelt,[7] the variety at Lemire's was at a minimum. When the deliveryman

Franklin D. Roosevelt

left the boxes of cards at the store each Monday, we often discovered that one entire box was devoted to a single President—two weeks in a row the boxes contained nothing but Abraham Lincolns. One week Roger Lussier and I were the heroes of Frenchtown. We journeyed on our bicycles to the North Side, engaged three boys in a matching bout and returned with five new Presidents, including Chester Alan Arthur, who up to that time had been missing.

Perhaps to sharpen our desire, the card company sent a sample glove to Mr. Lemire, and it dangled, orange and sleek, in the window. I was half sick with longing, thinking of my old glove at home, which I had inherited from Armand. But Rollie Tremaine's desire for the glove outdistanced my own. He even got Mr. Lemire to agree to give the glove in the window to the first person to get a complete set of cards, so

---

7. **Franklin Delano Roosevelt:** Roosevelt was elected to the presidency four different times. (He died in 1944 during his fourth term.)

that precious time wouldn't be wasted waiting for the postman.

We were delighted at Rollie Tremaine's frustration, especially since he was only a substitute player for the Tigers. Once after spending fifty cents on cards—all of which turned out to be Calvin Coolidge—he threw them to the ground, pulled some dollar bills out of his pocket and said, "The heck with it. I'm going to buy a glove!"

"Not that glove," Roger Lussier said. "Not a glove with Lefty Grove's autograph. Look what it says at the bottom of the sign."

We all looked, although we knew the words by heart: "This Glove Is Not For Sale Anywhere."

Rollie Tremaine scrambled to pick up the cards from the sidewalk, pouting more than ever. After that he was quietly obsessed with the Presidents, hugging the cards close to his chest and refusing to tell us how many more he needed to complete his set.

I, too, was obsessed with the cards, because they had become things of comfort

in a world that had suddenly grown dismal. After Christmas a layoff at the shop had thrown my father out of work. He received no paycheck for four weeks, and the only income we had was from Armand's after-school job at the Blue and White Grocery Store—a job he lost finally when business dwindled[8] as the layoff continued.

Although we had enough food and clothing—my father's credit had always been good, a matter of pride with him—the inactivity made my father restless and irritable. . . . The twins fell sick and went to the hospital to have their tonsils removed. My father was confident that he would return to work eventually and pay off his debts, but he seemed to age before our eyes.

When orders again were received at the comb shop and he returned to work, another disaster occurred, although I was the only one aware of it. Armand fell in love.

I discovered his situation by accident, when I happened to pick up a piece of paper that had fallen to the floor in the bedroom he and I shared. I frowned at the paper, puzzled.

"Dear Sally, When I look into your eyes the world stands still . . ."

The letter was snatched from my hand before I finished reading it.

"What's the big idea, snooping around?" Armand asked, his face crimson. "Can't a guy have any privacy?"

He had never mentioned privacy before. "It was on the floor," I said. "I didn't know it was a letter. Who's Sally?"

He flung himself across the bed. "You tell anybody and I'll muckalize you," he threatened. "Sally Knowlton."

"A girl from the North Side?" I asked, incredulous.[9]

He rolled over and faced me, anger in his eyes, and a kind of despair too.

"What's the matter with that? Think she's too good for me?" he asked. "I'm warning you, Jerry, if you tell anybody . . ."

"Don't worry," I said. Love had no particular place in my life; it seemed an unnecessary waste of time. And a girl from the North Side was so remote that for all practical purposes she did not exist. But I was curious. "What are you writing her a letter for? Did she leave town, or something?"

"She hasn't left town," he answered. "I wasn't going to send it. I just felt like writing to her."

I was glad that I had never become involved with love—love that brought desperation to your eyes, that caused you to write letters you did not plan to send. Shrugging with indifference, I began to search in the closet for the old baseball glove. I found it on the shelf, under some old sneakers. The webbing was torn and the padding gone. I thought of the sting I would feel when a sharp grounder slapped into the glove, and I winced.[10]

---

8. **dwindled** (dwin′dəld): steadily shrank.

9. **incredulous** (in-krej′ə·ləs): unbelieving.
10. **winced:** twisted his face with pain.

"You tell anybody about me and Sally and I'll—"

"I know. You'll muckalize me."

I did not divulge his secret and often shared his agony, particularly when he sat at the supper table and left my mother's special butterscotch pie untouched. I had never realized before how terrible love could be. But my compassion was short-lived because I had other things to worry about: report cards due at Eastertime; the loss of income from old Mrs. Belander, who had gone to live with a daughter in Boston; and, of course, the Presidents.

Because a stalemate[11] had been reached, the President cards were the dominant force in our lives—mine, Roger Lussier's, and Rollie Tremaine's. For three weeks, as the baseball season approached, each of us had a complete set—complete except for one President, Grover Cleveland. Each time a box of cards arrived at the store, we hurriedly bought them (as hurriedly as our funds allowed) and tore off the wrappers, only to be confronted by James Monroe or Martin Van Buren or someone else. But never Grover Cleveland, never the man who had been the twenty-second *and* the twenty-fourth President of the United States. We argued about Grover Cleveland. Should he be placed between Chester Alan Arthur and Benjamin Harrison as the twenty-second President, or did he belong between Benjamin Harrison and William McKinley as

the twenty-fourth President? Was the card company playing fair? Roger Lussier brought up a horrifying possibility—did we need *two* Grover Clevelands to complete the set?

Indignant, we stormed Lemire's and protested to the harassed storeowner, who had long since vowed never to stock a new series. Muttering angrily, he searched his bills and receipts for a list of rules.

"All right," he announced. "Says here you only need one Grover Cleveland to finish the set. Now get out, all of you, unless you've got money to spend."

Outside the store, Rollie Tremaine picked up an empty tobacco tin and scaled it across the street. "Boy," he said. "I'd give five dollars for a Grover Cleveland."

When I returned home I found Armand sitting on the piazza[12] steps, his chin in his hands. His mood of dejection mirrored my own, and I sat down beside him. We did not say anything for a while.

"Want to throw the ball around?" I asked.

He sighed, not bothering to answer.

"You sick?" I asked.

He stood up and hitched up his trousers, pulled at his ear, and finally told me what the matter was—there was a big dance next week at the high school, the Spring Promenade, and Sally had asked him to be her escort.

I shook my head at the folly of love. "Well, what's so bad about that?"

---

11. **stalemate:** a draw where neither side can win.

12. **piazza** (pē·az′ə): in the United States, a large, covered porch.

"How can I take Sally to a fancy dance?" he asked desperately. "I'd have to buy her a corsage . . . and my shoes are practically falling apart. Pa's got too many worries now to buy me new shoes or give me money for flowers for a girl."

I nodded in sympathy. "Yeah," I said. "Look at me. Baseball time is almost here, and all I've got is that old glove. And no Grover Cleveland card yet . . ."

"Grover Cleveland?" he asked. "They've got some of those up on the North Side. Some kid was telling me there's a store that's got them. He says they're looking for Warren G. Harding."

"Holy smoke!" I said. "I've got an extra Warren G. Harding!" Pure joy sang in my veins. I ran to my bicycle, swung into the seat—and found that the front tire was flat.

"I'll help you fix it," Armand said.

Within half an hour I was at the North Side Drugstore, where several boys were matching cards on the sidewalk. Silently but blissfully, I shouted, "President Grover Cleveland, here I come!"

After Armand had left for the dance, all dressed up as if it were Sunday, the small green box containing the corsage under his arm, I sat on the railing of the piazza, letting my feet dangle. The neighborhood was quiet because the Frenchtown Tigers were at Daggett's Field, practicing for the first baseball game of the season.

I thought of Armand and the ridiculous expression on his face when he'd stood before the mirror in the bedroom. I'd avoided looking at his new black shoes. "Love," I muttered.

Spring had arrived in a sudden stampede of apple blossoms and fragrant breezes. Windows had been thrown open and dust mops had banged on the sills all day long as the women busied themselves with housecleaning. I was puzzled by my lethargy.[13] Wasn't spring supposed to make everything bright and gay?

I turned at the sound of footsteps on the stairs. Roger Lussier greeted me with a sour face.

"I thought you were practicing with the Tigers," I said.

"Rollie Tremaine," he said. "I just couldn't stand him." He slammed his fist against the railing. "Jeez, why did *he* have to be the one to get a Grover Cleveland? You should see him showing off. He won't let anybody even touch that glove . . ."

I felt like Benedict Arnold[14] and knew that I had to confess what I had done.

"Roger," I said, "I got a Grover Cleveland card up on the North Side. I sold it to Rollie Tremaine for five dollars."

---

13. **lethargy** (leth′ər·jē): a condition of feeling dull, tired, lifeless.
14. **Benedict Arnold**: a famous traitor in the American Revolutionary War.

"Are you crazy?" he asked.

"I needed that five dollars. It was an—an emergency."

"Boy!" he said, looking down at the ground and shaking his head. "What did you have to do a thing like that for?"

I watched him as he turned away and began walking down the stairs.

"Hey, Roger!" I called.

He squinted up at me as if I were a stranger, someone he'd never seen before.

"What?" he asked, his voice flat.

"I had to do it," I said. "Honest."

He didn't answer. He headed toward the fence, searching for the board we had loosened to give us a secret passage.

I thought of my father and Armand and Rollie Tremaine and Grover Cleveland and wished that I could go away someplace far away. But there was no place to go.

Roger found the loose slat in the fence and slipped through. I felt betrayed: Weren't you supposed to feel good when you did something fine and noble?

A moment later two hands gripped the top of the fence and Roger's face appeared. "Was it a real emergency?" he yelled.

"A real one!" I called. "Something important!"

His face dropped from sight and his voice reached me across the yard: "All right."

"See you tomorrow!" I yelled.

I swung my legs over the railing again. The gathering dusk began to soften the sharp edges of the fence, the rooftops, the distant church steeple. I sat there a long time, waiting for the good feeling to come.

IDENTIFYING FACTS

1. Jerry says that "you could almost hate Rollie Tremaine." List the reasons Jerry gives for feeling this way about Rollie.

2. After the cowboy cards were phased out, what was the topic of street-corner talk and essays for Sister Angela?

3. Name the two disasters that occurred while Jerry was busy collecting President cards.

4. What does Jerry finally do with the President card he had so longed for?

INTERPRETING MEANINGS

5. Describe Armand's **conflict** when Sally asks him to the Spring dance. (What does he want? What is keeping him from getting it?)

6. Describe Jerry's **conflicts.** (What does he want? What keeps him from getting it?)

7. When Jerry learns that Lemire's store will sell President cards rather than cowboy cards, he says, "I felt the warmth of guilt creep over me." (Page 183) Why does Jerry feel guilty?

8. When Jerry catches up with Armand and finds that his brother and sisters have already bought their father's gift, Armand says, "Maybe you've learned something." (Page 183) What might Jerry have learned?

9. An **inference** is a guess you make based on evidence in the story. What inference can you make about why Jerry sold the President Cleveland card to Rollie?

10. At the end, Jerry says, "I sat there a long time, waiting for the good feeling to come." Why doesn't he feel good right away? Do you think eventually he *will* feel good about what he did?

APPLYING MEANINGS

11. In this story, Jerry makes a great sacrifice for his brother. Did you find his action believable? Did Armand deserve this good turn?

DRAWING CONCLUSIONS ABOUT CHARACTERS

A **conclusion** is a general statement about people and events. You make ("or draw") a conclusion based on what you learn in the story. For example, the list below gives information about Jerry's father's actions:

1. He works hard at the comb shop.

2. He buys his twin daughters a piano and pays for their lessons even though there is little money in the family.

3. When he works a full week, he gives his children an extra dime.

What can you conclude about Jerry's father?

Share your ideas with others in the class. You might want to edit your own conclusions after hearing what others have to say.

CHARACTER

As you recall from Unit One, writers can create characters in six ways. Think of how Robert Cormier created Jerry's character. Fill in the chart that follows with details that bring Jerry to life. Can you find at least one detail for every box?

You might want to brainstorm in class and fill out the chart as a group.

How the writer reveals Jerry's character	
1. His appearance.	
2. His speech.	
3. His thoughts.	
4. His actions.	
5. The way he affects other people.	
6. Telling us directly what Jerry is like.	

CONTEXT CLUES

Use context clues to figure out the meanings of these italicized words from the story. Look for (1) synonyms for the unfamiliar word, and (2) definitions contained right in the sentence. Your guesses will be rough; be sure to check them in a dictionary.

1. "He smiled at me, almost sadly, and touched my arm. I turned away from him because I felt naked and *exposed*."

2. "Monday was the best day to buy the cards because the candy man stopped at Lemire's every Monday morning to deliver the new *assortments*. There was nothing more exciting in the world than a fresh batch of card boxes."

3. "After Christmas a *layoff* at the shop had thrown my father out of work."

4. " 'How can I take Sally to a fancy dance?' he asked desperately. 'I'd have to buy her a *corsage* . . . and my shoes are practically falling apart. Pa's got too many worries now to buy me new shoes or give me money for flowers for a girl.' "

Focus on Writing a Short Story

IMAGINING CHARACTERS

In his story Robert Cormier uses many details to help you "see" the main characters: Jerry, Armand, Roger, and Rollie. When you plan your own story, try to form a mental picture of the characters. Feel free to use people you know in real life as models for characters in your story. Describe their looks, speech, and actions as vividly as you can.

Review the notes you made for the assignment on page 176 or choose another story idea. Create at least two characters for your story by filling out a chart like the **Literary Elements** chart for Jerry on the left. Save your notes.

About the Author

Robert Cormier (1925–   ) is well known for his novels and stories for young adults. In his novels, heroes who find themselves isolated from friends and adults must struggle to cope with difficult problems on their own. For example, in *The Chocolate War* (1974), the hero, also called Jerry, attends a private school. Each year, the students sell chocolates to raise money for the school, even though they dislike doing it. One year, however, Jerry takes a stand and refuses to sell the candy. Two of Cormier's novels, *I am the Cheese* and *The Chocolate War,* have been made into movies.

Cormier is often recognized for his outstanding writing by such publications as *The New York Times.* He lives today in Leominster, Massachusetts.

A Marvelous Moment

Behind the Scenes

There's a sentence in "President Cleveland, Where Are You?" which is probably the most significant I have written in terms of my development as a writer. The sentence echoes back to a lost and half-forgotten story I wrote in the days when I was scribbling stories in pencil at the kitchen table. The story was about a boy from the poorer section of a town who falls desperately in love with a girl from the other side of town where the people live, or so he thinks, grandly and affluently. The story was told in the first person, the narrator was a twelve-year-old boy.

The problem concerned description. The narrator (and I, the writer) faced the problem of describing the girl's house, a thing of grandeur and beauty, white and shining, alien to the three-story tenement building in which the boy lived. How to describe such a house? I knew little about architecture, next to nothing at all. The house had an aura of graceful antiquity—was it a relic of some earlier era? It seemed that I had seen such houses in books—but what books? I knew nothing about researching such a subject and, anyway, I didn't want to burden the narrative with a long description of the house. In fact, this would not only be fatal to the forward thrust of the story, but would also not be consistent with what a twelve-year-old boy would know about architecture. Yet, I wanted to describe it as more than just a big white house.

The problem brought the story to a complete halt. I walked my hometown streets, desolated by the thought of all the things I did not know. How could someone so ignorant about so much ever become a writer? Back home, chewing at the pencil, I read and reread the words I had written. The lean clean prose of Ernest Hemingway and the simplicity of William Saroyan had affected me deeply, and I always told myself: Keep it simple, don't get too technical. So, let's apply those principles to the girl's house. Forget architecture—what did the house look like? Not what did it *really* look like, but what did it look like to this twelve-year-old boy?

Yes, that was the key—the viewpoint of the boy and not the writer. And from somewhere the description came. It looked like a big white birthday cake of a house! I knew this was exactly the kind of image I had sought. I felt the way Columbus must have felt when he sighted land.

In that moment, I had discovered simile and metaphor, had learned that words were truly tools, that figures of speech were not just something fancy to dress up a piece of prose but words that could evoke scene and event and emotion. Until that discovery at the kitchen table, I had been intimidated [frightened] by much of what I encountered in books of grammar, including the definitions of similes and metaphors. Suddenly, the definitions didn't matter. What mattered was using them to enrich my stories—not in a "Look, Ma, how clever I am" way, but to sharpen images, pin down emotions, create shocks of recognition in the reader.

At any rate, the story of the boy and the birthday cake of a house has been lost through the years. I doubt if it was ever published. In "President Cleveland, Where Are You?" I resurrected the description. It occurs in the second sentence of the third paragraph, a tribute to a marvelous moment in my hesitant journey toward becoming a writer.

—Robert Cormier

All Summer in a Day

RAY BRADBURY

Before You Read

Have you ever thought about living on a different planet? Have you wondered what the weather might be like on that planet? What the plants would look like? What people would have to do in order to survive there? What they would eat?

Ray Bradbury has always been curious about life on other planets. (You may have heard of his collection of stories about Mars, called *The Martian Chronicles*.) The children in this Bradbury story live on Venus. (That is, Venus as Bradbury imagines it!) Most of the children have never known the planet Earth.

This famous story has an ending that many people find surprising. Read through to this sentence on page 197: "Now she stood, separate, staring at the rain and the loud wet world beyond the huge glass." Then write down three possible ways this story might end. What might happen to the children? What might happen to Margot? Do the illustrations give away anything that might happen later in the story?

Keep your notes and talk about them with your classmates after you finish the story.

This story contains many **similes** (sim′ə·lēs), that is, comparisons between two unlike things using the words *like* or *as*. Margot uses a simile when she says that the sun is "like a penny." This may seem an odd comparison at first. But think of the shape and color of a brand-new penny—it is round, coppery, and glints just like the sun. Watch for other similes as you read. Use them to visualize the story's setting. Do the similes sometimes make the story sound like poetry?

"**R**eady?"

"Ready."

"Now?"

"Soon."

"Do the scientists really know? Will it happen today, will it?"

"Look, look; see for yourself!"

The children pressed to each other like so many roses, so many weeds, intermixed, peering out for a look at the hidden sun.

It rained.

It had been raining for seven years; thousands upon thousands of days compounded and filled from one end to the other with rain, with the drum and gush of water, with the sweet crystal fall of showers and the concussion[1] of storms so heavy they were tidal waves come over the islands. A thousand forests had been crushed under the rain and grown up a thousand times to be crushed again. And this was the way life was forever on the planet Venus, and this was the schoolroom of the children of the rocket men and women who had come to a raining world to set up civilization and live out their lives.

"It's stopping, it's stopping!"

"Yes, Yes!"

Margot stood apart from them, from these children who could never remember a time when there wasn't rain and rain and rain. They were all nine years old, and if there had been a day, seven years ago, when the sun came out for an hour and showed its face to the stunned world, they could not recall. Sometimes, at night, she heard them stir, in remembrance, and she knew they were dreaming and remembering gold or a yellow crayon or a coin large enough to buy the world with. She knew they thought they remembered a warmness, like a blushing in the face, in the body, in the arms and legs and trembling hands. But then they always awoke to the tatting drum, the endless shaking down of clear bead necklaces upon the roof, the walk, the gardens, the forests, and their dreams were gone.

All day yesterday they had read in

---

1. **concussion** (kən·kush′ən): violent shaking.

class about the sun. About how like a lemon it was, and how hot. And they had written small stories or essays or poems about it:

> I think the sun is a flower,
> That blooms for just one hour.

That was Margot's poem, read in a quiet voice in the still classroom while the rain was falling outside.

"Aw, you didn't write that!" protested one of the boys.

"I did," said Margot. "I *did*."

"William!" said the teacher.

But that was yesterday. Now the rain was slackening,[2] and the children were crushed in the great thick windows.

"Where's teacher?"

"She'll be back."

"She'd better hurry, we'll miss it!"

They turned on themselves, like a feverish wheel, all tumbling spokes.

Margot stood alone. She was a very frail girl who looked as if she had been lost in the rain for years and the rain had washed out the blue from her eyes and the red from her mouth and the yellow from her hair. She was an old photograph dusted from an album, whitened away, and if she spoke at all, her voice would be a ghost. Now she stood, separate, staring at the rain and the loud wet world beyond the huge glass.

"What're *you* looking at?" said William.

Margot said nothing.

_____

2. **slackening:** falling off, lessening.

"Speak when you're spoken to." He gave her a shove. But she did not move; rather, she let herself be moved only by him and nothing else.

They edged away from her; they would not look at her. She felt them go away. And this was because she would play no games with them in the echoing tunnels of the underground city. If they tagged her and ran, she stood blinking after them and did not follow. When the class sang songs about happiness and life and games, her lips barely moved. Only when they sang about the sun and the summer did her lips move as she watched the drenched windows.

And then, of course, the biggest crime of all was that she had come here only five years ago from Earth, and she remembered the sun and the way the sun was and the sky was when she was four in Ohio. And they, they had been on Venus all their lives, and they had been only two years old when last the sun came out and had long since forgotten the color and heat of it and the way it really was. But Margot remembered.

"It's like a penny," she said once, eyes closed.

"No it's not!" the children cried.

"It's like a fire," she said, "in the stove."

"You're lying, you don't remember!" cried the children.

But she remembered and stood quietly apart from all of them and watched the patterning windows. And once, a month ago, she had refused to shower in the school shower rooms, had clutched her hands to her ears and over her head, screaming the water mustn't touch her head. So after that, dimly, dimly, she sensed it, she was different and they knew her difference and kept away.

There was talk that her father and mother were taking her back to Earth next year. It seemed vital to her that they do so, though it would mean the loss of thousands of dollars to her family. And so, the children hated her for all these reasons of big and little consequence.[3] They hated her pale snow face, her waiting silence, her thinness, and her possible future.

"Get away!" The boy gave her another push. "What're you waiting for?"

Then, for the first time, she turned and looked at him. And what she was waiting for was in her eyes.

"Well, don't wait around here!" cried the boy savagely. "You won't see nothing!"

Her lips moved.

"Nothing!" he cried. "It was all a joke, wasn't it?" He turned to the other children. "Nothing's happening today. *Is* it?"

They all blinked at him and then, understanding, laughed and shook their heads. "Nothing, nothing!"

"Oh, but," Margot whispered, her eyes helpless. "But this is the day, the scientists predict, they say, they *know*, the sun . . ."

"All a joke!" said the boy, and seized her roughly. "Hey, everyone, let's put her in a closet before teacher comes!"

"No," said Margot, falling back.

They surged about her, caught her up and bore her, protesting, and then pleading, and then crying, back into a tunnel, a room, a closet, where they slammed and locked the door. They stood looking at the door and saw it tremble from her beating and throwing herself against it. They heard her muffled cries. Then, smiling, they turned and went out and back down the tunnel, just as the teacher arrived.

"Ready, children?" She glanced at her watch.

"Yes!" said everyone.

"Are we all here?"

"Yes!"

The rain slackened still more.

They crowded to the huge door.

The rain stopped.

It was as if, in the midst of a film concerning an avalanche, a tornado, a hurricane, a volcanic eruption, something had, first, gone wrong with the sound apparatus,[4] thus muffling and finally cutting off all noise, all of the blasts and repercussions and thunders, and then, second, ripped the film from the projector and inserted in its place a peaceful tropical slide which did not move or tremor. The world ground to a standstill. The silence was so immense and unbelievable that you felt

---

3. **consequence** (kän′sə·kwens′): importance.

4. **apparatus** (ap′ə·rat′əs): device. (The author refers to the part of the film projector that controls sound.)

your ears had been stuffed or you had lost your hearing altogether. The children put their hands to their ears. They stood apart. The door slid back and the smell of the silent, waiting world came in to them.

The sun came out.

It was the color of flaming bronze and it was very large. And the sky around it was a blazing blue tile color. And the jungle burned with sunlight as the children, released from their spell, rushed out, yelling, into the springtime.

"Now, don't go too far," called the teacher after them. "You've only two hours, you know. You wouldn't want to get caught out!"

But they were running and turning their faces up to the sky and feeling the sun on their cheeks like a warm iron; they were taking off their jackets and letting the sun burn their arms.

"Oh, it's better than the sun lamps, isn't it?"

"Much, much better!"

They stopped running and stood in the great jungle that covered Venus, that grew and never stopped growing, tumultuously,[5] even as you watched it. It was a nest of octopi,[6] clustering up great arms of flesh-like weed, wavering, flowering in this brief spring. It was the color of rubber and ash, this jungle, from the many years without sun. It was the color of stones and white cheeses and ink, and it was the color of the moon.

The children lay out, laughing, on the jungle mattress, and heard it sigh and squeak under them, resilient[7] and alive. They ran among the trees, they slipped and fell, they pushed each other, they played hide-and-seek and tag, but most of all they squinted at the sun until tears ran down

---

5. **tumultuously** (too·mul′choo·wəs·lē): wildly.
6. **octopi** (ok′tə·pī): the plural of *octopus*.

7. **resilient** (ri·zil′yənt): springy. (See page 165.)

their faces, they put their hands up to that yellowness and that amazing blueness and they breathed of the fresh, fresh air and listened and listened to the silence which suspended them in a blessed sea of no sound and no motion. They looked at everything and savored[8] everything. Then, wildly, like animals escaped from their caves, they ran and ran in shouting circles. They ran for an hour and did not stop running.

And then——

In the midst of their running, one of the girls wailed.

Everyone stopped.

The girl, standing in the open, held out her hand.

"Oh, look, look," she said, trembling.

They came slowly to look at her opened palm.

In the center of it, cupped and huge, was a single raindrop.

She began to cry, looking at it.

They glanced quietly at the sky.

"Oh. Oh."

A few cold drops fell on their noses and their cheeks and their mouths. The sun faded behind a stir of mist. A wind blew cool around them. They turned and started to walk back toward the underground house, their hands at their sides, their smiles vanishing away.

A boom of thunder startled them, and like leaves before a new hurricane, they tumbled upon each other and ran. Lightning struck ten miles away, five miles away,

a mile, a half-mile. The sky darkened into midnight in a flash.

They stood in the doorway of the underground for a moment until it was raining hard. Then they closed the door and heard the gigantic sound of the rain falling in tons and avalanches, everywhere and forever.

"Will it be seven more years?"

"Yes. Seven."

Then one of them gave a little cry.

"Margot!"

"What?"

"She's still in the closet where we locked her."

"Margot."

They stood as if someone had driven them, like so many stakes, into the floor. They looked at each other and then looked away. They glanced out at the world that was raining now and raining and raining steadily. They could not meet each other's glances. Their faces were solemn and pale. They looked at their hands and feet, their faces down.

"Margot."

One of the girls said, "Well . . . ?"

No one moved.

"Go on," whispered the girl.

They walked slowly down the hall in the sound of cold rain. They turned through the doorway to the room in the sound of the storm and thunder, lightning on their faces, blue and terrible. They walked over to the closet door slowly and stood by it.

Behind the closet door was only silence.

They unlocked the door, even more slowly, and let Margot out.

8. **savored:** delighted in.

IDENTIFYING FACTS

1. At the beginning of the story, why are the children so excited?

2. Most of the children have not seen the sun for seven years. How do they know about the sun?

3. The children in this story live on Venus. What is the most important fact about this **setting**?

4. How is Margot different from the other children? Describe what Margot looks like.

5. What happens on the outside while Margot is in the closet?

INTERPRETING MEANINGS

6. Describe what you think Margot will say or do now. What would you do if you were in her situation?

7. Differences among people often cause **conflicts,** or problems. What causes the conflict between Margot and the other children? Why does Margot keep to herself?

8. **Characters** in a story usually behave in certain ways for certain reasons. Why do you think the children lock Margot in the closet when they know how much the sun means to her?

9. On page 202, the children remember that Margot is still in the closet. The narrator says that the children's faces "were solemn and pale. They looked at their hands and feet, their faces down." What does this tell you about how the children feel?

APPLYING MEANINGS

10. The narrator says that Margot's parents may soon take Margot back to Earth. Leaving Venus, however, will cost them "thousands of dollars." Which would be more important to you: going home to the sunshine, or setting up a civilization on Venus, where the money is?

11. Do you think the hardships faced by pioneers like these people on Venus are worth it? Would you volunteer to be a colonist on a distant planet?

Focus on Reading

PREDICTING OUTCOMES

When you start to read a story, you almost automatically begin to predict its outcome. This means that you begin to make guesses at how the conflict will end. You begin to guess about what will become of various characters. Making predictions is one of the great pleasures of reading.

When you make predictions, you look for clues left by the writer. If the story is illustrated, you also look for clues in the illustrations. (Some people "cheat" and read the last paragraph of a story to find out before they start how the story ends!)

What predictions did you make before you completed this story? What clues did you base them on? Did the illustrations affect your predictions?

Do you like any of your predictions better than Bradbury's conclusion?

Suppose the ending was different. How would that affect your feelings about the story?

Literary Elements

THEME

Theme is the heart of a story. Theme is what the story reveals about our lives. Theme is different from plot. **Plot** is "what happens" in a story. **Theme** is what a story means. When you are asked to summarize a plot, you can start out by saying, "The major events in this story are . . ." When you are asked to summarize a theme, you can start out by saying "This story revealed to me that . . ."

Some stories have stronger themes than others. This story has a particularly strong theme. Write at least one sentence telling what the story reveals about the reasons people sometimes hurt one another.

Always think about how a theme relates to your own life. Think about whether you agree with the theme. (You don't have to agree with what every writer says.) Can you think of times in real life when a group would hurt an outsider like Margot?

Do you think it is easier to be cruel to someone when you are a member of a group than when you are acting alone?

Language and Vocabulary

SIMILES

A **simile** compares two very different things, using words such as *like* or *as*. Below are two sentences from "All Summer in a Day" that use similes. Answer the questions about each simile.

1. "But they were running and turning their faces up to the sky and feeling the sun on their cheeks like a warm iron. . . ."
   a. What is the sun compared to?
   b. Write another simile about an iron that would be unpleasant.

2. "A boom of thunder startled them, and like leaves before a new hurricane, they tumbled upon each other and ran."
   a. What are the running children compared to?
   b. Make up another simile describing how the running children looked.

3. Write some similes of your own. You might start out like this:
   a. I am like a _____ (name a flower or a tree).
   b. I am as _____ as a _____ (name a piece of furniture).
   c. At times I resemble _____ (you might base your simile on cars, foods, or mechanical objects).
   d. I can _____ (name some action) like a _____ (think of an animal or bird).

Focus on Writing a Short Story

EXPLORING A THEME

The **theme** of a story is its central idea about life. Some writers start a story with a theme in mind. Others discover a theme part way through the writing process.

Choose a theme for a short story of your own. Here are some ideas:

Never give up.
Love is stronger than hate.
Look before you leap.

Make some notes about a plot and some characters that you might use to develop the theme you have chosen into a story. Save your notes.

Ray Bradbury (1920–　　) has been called the world's greatest science fiction writer. Encouraged by his teachers, Bradbury was sending science fiction stories to magazines by the time he was fifteen. He even began his own little magazine. Since then, Bradbury has written more than thirty books and hundreds of stories, poems, and radio, television, and movie scripts. He has been a frequent writer for the TV series *Alfred Hitchcock Presents* and Rod Serling's *The Twilight Zone.* He is best known for his books *The Martian Chronicles, The Illustrated Man,* and *Fahrenheit 451.*

Unlike many science fiction writers, Bradbury is not much concerned with the machines and gadgets of the future. Instead, he often writes about the loneliness that might await us in the world of the future. Bradbury encourages young people to explore the universe. "The stars are yours," he says, "if you have the head, the hands, and the heart for them."

Fact Versus Fiction

In "All Summer in a Day," Bradbury creates an imaginary setting for the planet Venus. Because Venus lacks oxygen, an important element in the water molecule, the average temperature on the planet is above 850 degrees Fahrenheit! If water did exist on Venus, it would boil away immediately. Scientists now speculate that Venus may at one time have had oceans and life forms but that the "greenhouse effect"—a process in which heat becomes trapped at the planet's surface—may have changed the face of Venus.

Making Connections: Activities

1. Imagine that people could take trips to Venus or another planet and, while unable to land or stay very long, they could orbit its surface. After collecting information in the library, create a travel brochure or pamphlet that describes the interesting things people would see and experience while orbiting Venus. On the front of your brochure, provide a colored illustration of the planet. Describe Venus' surface and conditions (weather, temperature, sunlight, clouds, gases). See if other members of the class would like to do similar projects for other planets.

2. Astronomers and scientists have speculated that Venus may have had swamps and living things millions of years ago, but the planet underwent drastic changes. Many people fear that Earth is now undergoing a "greenhouse effect." Working with a partner or a group of students, prepare a report that explains the process and efforts to stop its damaging effects on Earth.

The Stone

LLOYD ALEXANDER

Before You Read

Have you ever asked your friends, "If you were granted
one wish, what would it be?" It's a question that could
keep you thinking for hours. The next story starts out normally enough, until the main character has a chance to
change his life with a wish. Before you read the story,
write in your journal your response to this question: How
would you like to remain forever at the age you are now?

One of the ways you can analyze words is by examining their parts. For example, this story opens on a day that is "cloudless." You probably know that -*less* is a **suffix** meaning "not, or without," and that *cloudless* means "without clouds." The suffix -*less* is used quite a lot in this story. You'll find a toothless baby, a calfless cow, and a fruitless tree. In fact, the whole story is about what it means to be "changeless." Do you know what *that* would be like?

There was a cottager named Maibon, and one day he was driving down the road in his horse and cart when he saw an old man hobbling along, so frail and feeble he doubted the poor soul could go many more steps. Though Maibon offered to take him in the cart, the old man refused; and Maibon went his way home, shaking his head over such a pitiful sight, and said to his wife, Modrona:

"Ah, ah, what a sorry thing it is to have your bones creaking and cracking, and dim eyes, and dull wits. When I think this might come to me, too! A fine, strong-armed, sturdy-legged fellow like me? One day to go tottering, and have his teeth rattling in his head, and live on porridge, like a baby? There's no fate worse in all the world."

"There is," answered Modrona, "and that would be to have neither teeth nor porridge. Get on with you, Maibon, and stop borrowing trouble. Hoe your field or you'll have no crop to harvest, and no food for you, nor me, nor the little ones."

Sighing and grumbling, Maibon did as his wife bade him. Although the day was fair and cloudless, he took no pleasure in it. His ax-blade was notched, the wooden handle splintery; his saw had lost its edge; and his hoe, once shining new, had begun to rust. None of his tools, it seemed to him, cut or chopped or delved as well as they once had done.

"They're as worn out as that old codger I saw on the road," Maibon said to himself. He squinted up at the sky. "Even the sun isn't as bright as it used to be, and doesn't warm me half as well. It's gone threadbare as my cloak. And no wonder, for it's been there longer than I can remember. Come to think of it, the moon's been looking a little wilted around the edges, too.

"As for me," went on Maibon, in dismay, "I'm in even a worse state. My appetite's faded, especially after meals. Mornings, when I wake, I can hardly keep myself from yawning. And at night, when I go to bed, my eyes are so heavy I can't hold them open. If that's the way things are now, the older I grow, the worse it will be!''

In the midst of his complaining, Maibon glimpsed something bouncing and tossing back and forth beside a fallen tree in a corner of the field. Wondering if one of his piglets had squeezed out of the sty and gone rooting for acorns, Maibon hurried across the turf. Then he dropped his ax and gaped in astonishment.

There, struggling to free his leg which had been caught under the log, lay a short, thickset figure: a dwarf with red hair bristling in all directions beneath his round, close-fitting leather cap. At the sight of

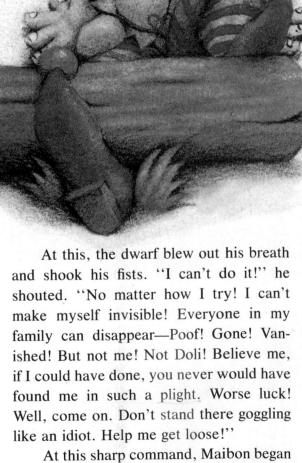

Maibon, the dwarf squeezed shut his bright red eyes and began holding his breath. After a moment, the dwarf's face went redder than his hair; his cheeks puffed out and soon turned purple. Then he opened one eye and blinked rapidly at Maibon, who was staring at him, speechless.

''What,'' snapped the dwarf, ''you can still see me?''

''That I can,'' replied Maibon, more than ever puzzled, ''and I can see very well you've got yourself tight as a wedge under that log, and all your kicking only makes it worse.''

At this, the dwarf blew out his breath and shook his fists. ''I can't do it!'' he shouted. ''No matter how I try! I can't make myself invisible! Everyone in my family can disappear—Poof! Gone! Vanished! But not me! Not Doli! Believe me, if I could have done, you never would have found me in such a plight. Worse luck! Well, come on. Don't stand there goggling like an idiot. Help me get loose!''

At this sharp command, Maibon began tugging and heaving at the log. Then he stopped, wrinkled his brow, and scratched his head, saying:

"Well, now, just a moment, friend. The way you look, and all your talk about turning yourself invisible—I'm thinking you might be one of the Fair Folk."

"Oh, clever!" Doli retorted. "Oh, brilliant! Great clodhopper! Giant beanpole! Of course I am! What else! Enough gabbling. Get a move on. My leg's going to sleep."

"If a man does the Fair Folk a good turn," cried Maibon, his excitement growing, "it's told they must do one for him."

"I knew sooner or later you'd come round to that," grumbled the dwarf. "That's the way of it with you ham-handed, heavy-footed oafs. Time was, you humans got along well with us. But nowadays, you no sooner see a Fair Folk than it's grab, grab, grab! Gobble, gobble, gobble! Grant my wish! Give me this, give me that! As if we had nothing better to do!

"Yes, I'll give you a favor," Doli went on. "That's the rule, I'm obliged to. Now, get on with it."

Hearing this, Maibon pulled and pried and chopped away at the log as fast as he could, and soon freed the dwarf.

Doli heaved a sigh of relief, rubbed his shin, and cocked a red eye at Maibon, saying:

"All right. You've done your work, you'll have your reward. What do you want? Gold, I suppose. That's the usual. Jewels? Fine clothes? Take my advice, go for something practical. A hazelwood twig to help you find water if your well ever goes dry? An ax that never needs sharpening? A cook pot always brimming with food?"

"None of those!" cried Maibon. He bent down to the dwarf and whispered eagerly, "But I've heard tell that you Fair Folk have magic stones that can keep a man young forever. That's what I want. I claim one for my reward."

Doli snorted. "I might have known you'd pick something like that. As to be expected, you humans have it all muddled. There's nothing can make a man young again. That's even beyond the best of our skills. Those stones you're babbling about? Well, yes, there are such things. But greatly overrated. All they'll do is keep you from growing any older."

"Just as good!" Maibon exclaimed. "I want no more than that!"

Doli hesitated and frowned. "Ah—between the two of us, take the cook pot. Better all around. Those stones—we'd sooner not give them away. There's a difficulty——"

"Because you'd rather keep them for yourselves," Maibon broke in. "No, no, you shan't cheat me of my due. Don't put me off with excuses. I told you what I want, and that's what I'll have. Come, hand it over and not another word."

Doli shrugged and opened a leather pouch that hung from his belt. He spilled a number of brightly colored pebbles into his palm, picked out one of the larger stones, and handed it to Maibon. The dwarf then jumped up, took to his heels, raced across the field, and disappeared into a thicket.

Laughing and crowing over his good fortune and his cleverness, Maibon hurried back to the cottage. There, he told his wife what had happened, and showed her the stone he had claimed from the Fair Folk.

"As I am now, so I'll always be!" Maibon declared, flexing his arms and thumping his chest. "A fine figure of a man! Oho, no gray beard and wrinkled brow for me!"

Instead of sharing her husband's jubilation, Modrona flung up her hands and burst out:

"Maibon, you're a greater fool than ever I supposed! And selfish into the bargain! You've turned down treasures! You didn't even ask that dwarf for so much as new jackets for the children! Nor a new apron for me! You could have had the roof mended. Or the walls plastered. No, a stone is what you ask for! A bit of rock no better than you'll dig up in the cow pasture!"

Crestfallen and sheepish, Maibon began thinking his wife was right, and the dwarf had indeed given him no more than a common field stone.

"Eh, well, it's true," he stammered, "I feel no different than I did this morning, no better nor worse, but every way the same. That redheaded little wretch! He'll rue the day if I ever find him again!"

So saying, Maibon threw the stone into the fireplace. That night he grumbled his way to bed, dreaming revenge on the dishonest dwarf.

Next morning, after a restless night, he yawned, rubbed his eyes, and scratched

his chin. Then he sat bolt upright in bed, patting his cheeks in amazement.

"My beard!" he cried, tumbling out and hurrying to tell his wife. "It hasn't grown! Not by a hair! Can it be the dwarf didn't cheat me after all?"

"Don't talk to me about beards," declared his wife as Maibon went to the fireplace, picked out the stone, and clutched it safely in both hands. "There's trouble enough in the chicken roost. Those

eggs should have hatched by now, but the hen is still brooding on her nest.''

"Let the chickens worry about that,'' answered Maibon. "Wife, don't you see what a grand thing's happened to me? I'm not a minute older than I was yesterday. Bless that generous-hearted dwarf!''

"Let me lay hands on him and I'll bless him,'' retorted Modrona. "That's all well and good for you. But what of me? You'll stay as you are, but I'll turn old and gray, and worn and wrinkled, and go doddering into my grave! And what of our little ones? They'll grow up and have children of their own. And grandchildren, and great-grandchildren. And you, younger than any of them. What a foolish sight you'll be!''

But Maibon, gleeful over his good luck, paid his wife no heed, and only tucked the stone deeper into his pocket. Next day, however, the eggs had still not hatched.

"And the cow!" Modrona cried. "She's long past due to calve, and no sign of a young one ready to be born!"

"Don't bother me with cows and chickens," replied Maibon. "They'll all come right, in time. As for time, I've got all the time in the world!"

Having no appetite for breakfast, Maibon went out into his field. Of all the seeds he had sown there, however, he was surprised to see not one had sprouted. The field, which by now should have been covered with green shoots, lay bare and empty.

"Eh, things do seem a little late these days," Maibon said to himself. "Well, no hurry. It's that much less for me to do. The wheat isn't growing, but neither are the weeds."

Some days went by and still the eggs had not hatched, the cow had not calved, the wheat had not sprouted. And now Maibon saw that his apple tree showed no sign of even the smallest, greenest fruit.

"Maibon, it's the fault of that stone!" wailed his wife. "Get rid of the thing!"

"Nonsense," replied Maibon. "The season's slow, that's all."

Nevertheless, his wife kept at him and kept at him so much that Maibon at last, and very reluctantly, threw the stone out the cottage window. Not too far, though, for he had it in the back of his mind to go later and find it again.

Next morning he had no need to go looking for it, for there was the stone sitting on the window ledge.

"You see?" said Maibon to his wife.

"Here it is back again. So, it's a gift meant for me to keep."

"Maibon!" cried his wife. "Will you get rid of it! We've had nothing but trouble since you brought it into the house. Now the baby's fretting and fuming. Teething, poor little thing. But not a tooth to be seen! Maibon, that stone's bad luck and I want no part of it!"

Protesting it was none of his doing that the stone had come back, Maibon carried it into the vegetable patch. He dug a hole, not a very deep one, and put the stone into it.

Next day, there was the stone above ground, winking and glittering.

"Maibon!" cried his wife. "Once and for all, if you care for your family, get rid of that cursed thing!"

Seeing no other way to keep peace in the household, Maibon regretfully and unwillingly took the stone and threw it down the well, where it splashed into the water and sank from sight.

But that night, while he was trying vainly to sleep, there came such a rattling and clattering that Maibon clapped his hands over his ears, jumped out of bed, and went stumbling into the yard. At the well, the bucket was jiggling back and forth and up and down at the end of the rope; and in the bottom of the bucket was the stone.

Now Maibon began to be truly distressed, not only for the toothless baby, the calfless cow, the fruitless tree, and the hen sitting desperately on her eggs, but for himself as well.

"Nothing's moving along as it should," he groaned. "I can't tell one day from another. Nothing changes, there's nothing to look forward to, nothing to show for my work. Why sow if the seeds don't sprout? Why plant if there's never a harvest? Why eat if I don't get hungry? Why go to bed at night, or get up in the morning, or do anything at all? And the way it looks, so it will stay for ever and ever! I'll shrivel from boredom if nothing else!"

"Maibon," pleaded his wife, "for all our sakes, destroy the dreadful thing!"

Maibon tried now to pound the stone to dust with his heaviest mallet; but he could not so much as knock a chip from it. He put it against his grindstone without so much as scratching it. He set it on his anvil and belabored it with hammer and tongs, all to no avail.

At last he decided to bury the stone again, this time deeper than before. Picking up his shovel, he hurried to the field. But he suddenly halted and the shovel dropped from his hands. There, sitting cross-legged on a stump, was the dwarf.

"You!" shouted Maibon, shaking his fist. "Cheat! Villain! Trickster! I did you a good turn, and see how you've repaid it!"

The dwarf blinked at the furious Maibon. "You mortals are an ungrateful crew. I gave you what you wanted."

"You should have warned me!" burst out Maibon.

"I did," Doli snapped back. "You wouldn't listen. No, you yapped and yammered, bound to have your way. I told you we didn't like to give away those stones. When you mortals get hold of one, you stay just as you are—but so does everything around you. Before you know it, you're mired in time like a rock in the mud. You take my advice. Get rid of that stone as fast as you can."

"What do you think I've been trying to do?" blurted Maibon. "I've buried it, thrown it down the well, pounded it with a hammer—it keeps coming back to me!"

"That's because you really didn't want to give it up," Doli said. "In the back of your mind and the bottom of your heart, you didn't want to change along with the

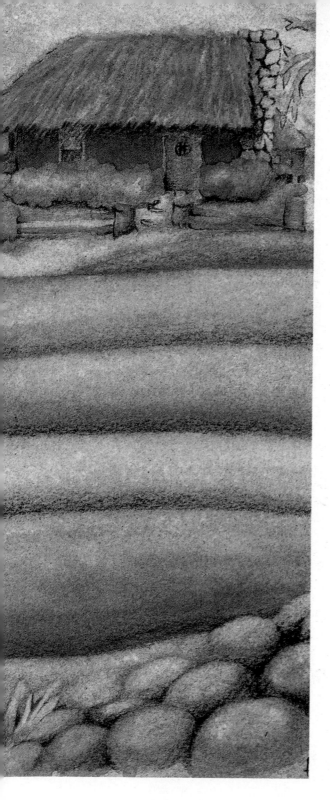

rest of the world. So long as you feel that way, the stone is yours.''

"No, no!" cried Maibon. "I want no more of it. Whatever may happen, let it happen. That's better than nothing happening at all. I've had my share of being young, I'll take my share of being old. And when I come to the end of my days, at least I can say I've lived each one of them."

"If you mean that," answered Doli, "toss the stone onto the ground, right there at the stump. Then get home and be about your business."

Maibon flung down the stone, spun around, and set off as fast as he could. When he dared at last to glance back over his shoulder, fearful the stone might be bouncing along at his heels, he saw no sign of it, nor of the redheaded dwarf.

Maibon gave a joyful cry, for at that same instant the fallow field was covered with green blades of wheat, the branches of the apple tree bent to the ground, so laden were they with fruit. He ran to the cottage, threw his arms around his wife and children, and told them the good news. The hen hatched her chicks, the cow bore her calf. And Maibon laughed with glee when he saw the first tooth in the baby's mouth.

Never again did Maibon meet any of the Fair Folk, and he was just as glad of it. He and his wife and children and grandchildren lived many years, and Maibon was proud of his white hair and long beard as he had been of his sturdy arms and legs.

"Stones are all right, in their way," said Maibon. "But the trouble with them is, they don't grow."

IDENTIFYING FACTS

1. What does Maibon think is the worst thing that can happen to him?

2. Who is Doli, and why does he grant Maibon a wish?

3. What does Doli suggest Maibon wish for? What wish does Maibon insist on?

4. How does the magic stone work? List all the effects it has on Maibon's household.

5. How does Maibon finally resolve his **conflict,** or problem?

INTERPRETING MEANINGS

6. How would you describe Maibon's **character**? (Is he impulsive? stupid? selfish? hard-working?) How is Maibon's wife different?

7. Maibon's troubles start when he sees a wizened old man in the road. Do you agree that Maibon "borrows trouble," as his wife puts it?

8. Doli makes some guesses about what Maibon will wish for. What does Doli think about human values, or at least the values of Maibon's society? How would Doli be surprised if Modrona had rescued him and had been granted the wish?

APPLYING MEANINGS

9. On a sheet of paper, write the heading "Doli, the Wish Granter, will grant one wish to each of those below." Pass the paper around and have your classmates write down their wishes. Are any wishes the same? Would Doli approve or disapprove of these wishes?

PREDICTING OUTCOMES

As you read this story, did you guess that Maibon's wish might not turn out the way he expected? Did you guess how the magic stone was actually keeping him from changing? As we read, we naturally make guesses about what's going to happen next. Look back over the story now and make a list of all the clues you found at the beginning of the story that **foreshadowed,** or hinted at, Maibon's foolishness. Then make a list of the clues that told you that the stone was working its magic. One reader has already filled in two clues, below.

Maibon's wish will be a mistake
1. Doli, who has experience in wish-making, thinks Maibon's choice is dumb.
2.
3.

The stone *is* magic
1. The first thing Maibon notices is that his beard doesn't grow.
2.
3.

THEME

The **theme** of a story is its main idea, or the message the writer is sending you. This story has a very strong theme that should be easy to pick up. In fact, the story concludes with a statement that almost sums up its theme. To put you on the right track as you try to discover the story's theme, answer the questions below.

1. Why does Maibon quickly become disenchanted with his immortality?

2. When is Maibon truly able to throw the stone away without its coming back to him?

3. Explain what Maibon means when he says at the end, "Stones are all right, in their way. But the trouble with them is, they don't grow."

4. State the theme of "The Stone" in your own words. (A theme always has to be stated in a complete sentence.)

5. What do you think of the story's message or theme? If you were Maibon, how would you have felt about living forever?

Language and Vocabulary

PREFIXES AND SUFFIXES
As you know, **prefixes** are added to the front of words to alter their meanings. **Suffixes** are added to the ends of words to alter their meanings. Here are some useful prefixes and suffixes:

Prefixes:
in- "in, into," or "not"
un- "not, to do the opposite of"
pre- "before"
ante- "before"
anti- "against"

Suffixes:
-less "not, without"

-ish "of, belonging to, like"
-let "small, little, ornament"
-ful "full of, able to"

Use these prefixes and suffixes to answer the following questions:

1. How would you use a prefix to describe someone who cannot be seen?

2. How would you use a suffix to describe someone who is not at all scared?

3. What would you call a very small pig?

4. How would you use a suffix to describe someone who is full of gratitude?

5. How would you use a prefix and suffix to describe someone who has no feelings of gratitude at all?

6. If someone is said to be *antiwar,* is that person *against* war, or was that person born *before* a war?

7. If someone has a *prewar* house, was the house built *before* or *after* the war?

Writing About Literature

DESCRIBING A WISH THAT GOES WRONG
Doli advises Maibon to wish for something practical and then gives him several suggestions. Choose one of Doli's suggestions, and write a story about how that wish could go wrong. (For instance, would the hazelwood twig find water not only when Maibon needed it but also when he didn't?) Make up your own "wish that goes wrong" if you don't want to use one of Doli's. You can use Maibon and his wife as the characters in your story if you like, or you can invent new characters.

Lloyd Alexander (1924–   ) decided to become a poet at the early age of fifteen. His parents were unable to send him to college, so he found a job as a messenger in a bank after he graduated from high school. He spent most of his free time writing and trying to get his stories published. In 1943 he joined the army because, as he put it, "Adventure, I decided, was the best way to learn writing." After the war, Alexander wrote for a total of seventeen years before he found success by writing fantasy books for children. His most popular series is called the *Prydain Chronicles*. "The Stone" is taken from *The Foundling and Other Tales of Prydain*.

Alexander says he likes to write fantasy books because ". . . a wish is certainly a good way to start. There's no law in the fantasy world or in the real world that says some wishes can't come true. If fantasy is a kind of hopeful dream, it's nevertheless one that we made up ourselves."

Some of Alexander's recent titles are *The Hedera Adventure, The Philadelphia Adventure,* and *The Remarkable Journey of Prince Jen.*

Connecting Cultures

Wishes in Folklore

The wish is a familiar theme in the folklore of many cultures. A popular figure in the Russian *Baba Yaga* tales is the wise old woman who lives in the woods and has the power to make wishes come true. A similar character named Adivinadora appears in the folk tales of Spain. The genie in the Arabian tale "Aladdin and the Wonderful Lamp" is perhaps one of the most famous wish granters in literature.

Sometime during the nineteenth century, the Grimm brothers in Germany collected many popular European folk tales. Several of these classics center on the fulfillment of a wish, such as the tales about Cinderella, Sleeping Beauty, and Rumpelstiltskin.

Other folk tales you might like to read are China's "Chen Ping and His Magic Axe," Africa's "Pot Full of Luck" (Ashanti), and the Cherokee legend "Ahyoka and the Talking Leaves."

Making Connections: Activities

1. Read one of the stories listed above or one of the following. In a short report describe the character whose wish comes true. How does the granting of the wish change the character's life?

   Tuck Everlasting, a novel by Natalie Babbit

   "The Monkey's Paw," a short story by W. W. Jacobs

   "The Fisherman and His Wife," a fairy tale by Jakob and Wilhelm Grimm

   The Greek myth about King Midas (available in many collections of Greek mythology)

2. Choose a story that you and a few friends know well, such as the tale of Cinderella or Rumpelstiltskin. Using a cassette player, record the story as you remember it. Let each person tell a different part of the story. Compare the group's version with a printed version of the tale. What new and interesting details are introduced in the oral retelling of a familiar story?

Behind the Scenes

I was always a hungry reader—in more ways than one. I gobbled up stories and never had my fill. At the same time, I wanted a real taste of whatever food the people in the stories were eating. Reading about the Mad Tea Party in *Alice in Wonderland,* I pleaded for a cup of tea, bread and butter, and treacle. (Treacle, I guessed, was something like pancake syrup.) My poor mother! How did she ever find patience to put up with her son's reading-and-eating habits!

In *Treasure Island* (you'll be reading it soon), bloodthirsty pirates nearly find young Jim Hawkins hiding in an apple barrel. So, of course, I had to munch an apple. . . .

However, when Robin Hood and his Merry Men dined on venison washed down with flagons of brown October ale, I could only make believe with a hamburger and a glass of root beer. A dish of cornmeal mush took the place of Indian maize when, sitting cross-legged under our living room lamp, I devoured *The Song of Hiawatha.* Our neighborhood grocer never sold—nor had we money to buy—anything like the rich feasts at *King Arthur's Round Table.* Instead of the roast goose of *A Christmas Carol,* I gnawed a chicken leg. The pages of *Winnie-the-Pooh,* along with my fingers, got sticky with honey. My mother's cookbook held no recipe for the nectar and ambrosia of Greek mythology; I settled for corn flakes and grape juice. Zeus must have smiled at that.

In time, to sighs of relief from my parents, I lost the habit of eating what I read about, but never my hunger for reading. I think the stories we love as children stay with us, somewhere in our hearts, to feed our imaginations. We never outgrow our need for them, any more than we outgrow our need for food. But, to me, the books I love are better than a feast.

—Lloyd Alexander

Becky and the Wheels-and-Brake Boys

JAMES BERRY

Before You Read

Like the earlier story by Robert Cormier, this story about
a Jamaican girl is about *want*. Becky has a terrible craving
for a bicycle and for the boys' world it will open for her.
In spite of her family's lack of money, and the sensible
advice of her mother and grandmother, Becky goes right
on wanting—and in the end, working out a clever plan to
try to get what she wants.

Jamaica is an island in the Caribbean Sea. Much of
the island consists of farms where sugarcane, bananas, and
coconut palm trees are grown. Becky's father used to work
on one of these farms, but he has died before this story
opens.

Before you read, write in your journal a response to
this question: In your world, what activities do people feel
girls should *not* do? What activities do they feel boys *should*,
and *should not*, do? Or aren't there any differences?

Even my own cousin Ben was there—riding away, in the ringing of bicycle bells down the road. Every time I came to watch them—see them riding round and round enjoying themselves—they scooted off like crazy on their bikes.

They can't keep doing that. They'll see!

I only want to be with Nat, Aldo, Jimmy, and Ben. It's no fair reason they don't want to be with me. Anybody could go off their head for that. Anybody! A girl can not, not, let boys get away with it all the time.

Bother! I have to walk back home, alone.

I know total-total that if I had my own bike, the Wheels-and-Brake Boys wouldn't treat me like that. I'd just ride away with them, wouldn't I?

Over and over I told my mum I wanted a bike. Over and over she looked at me as if I was crazy. "Becky, d'you think you're a boy? Eh? D'you think you're a boy? In any case, where's the money to come from? Eh?"

Of course I know I'm not a boy. Of course I know I'm not crazy. Of course I know all that's no reason why I can't have a bike. No reason! As soon as I get indoors I'll just have to ask again—ask Mum once more.

At home, indoors, I didn't ask my mum.

It was evening time, but sunshine was still big patches in yards and on housetops. My two younger brothers, Lenny and Vin, played marbles in the road. Mum was taking measurements of a boy I knew, for his new trousers and shirt. Mum made clothes for people. Meggie, my sister two years younger than me, was helping Mum on the veranda.[1] Nobody would be pleased with me not helping. I began to help.

Granny-Liz would always stop fanning herself to drink up a glass of ice water. I gave my granny a glass of ice water, there in her rocking chair. I looked in the kitchen to find shelled coconut pieces to cut into small cubes for the fowls' morning feed. But Granny-Liz had done it. I came and started tidying up bits and pieces of cut-off material around my mum on the floor. My sister got nasty, saying she was already helping Mum. Not a single good thing was happening for me.

With me even being all so thoughtful of Granny's need of a cool drink, she started up some botheration against me.

Listen to Granny-Liz: "Becky, with you moving about me here on the veranda, I hope you dohn have any centipedes or scorpions in a jam jar in your pocket."

"No, mam," I said sighing, trying to be calm. "Granny-Liz," I went on, "you forgot. My centipede and scorpion died." All the same, storm broke against me.

"Becky," my mum said. "You know I don't like you wandering off after dinner. Haven't I told you I don't want you keeping company with those awful riding-about bicycle boys? Eh?"

"Yes, mam."

"Those boys are a menace. Riding bicycles on sidewalks and narrow paths together, ringing bicycle bells and braking at people's feet like wild bulls charging anybody, they're heading for trouble."

"They're the Wheels-and-Brake Boys, mam."

"The what?"

"The Wheels-and-Brake Boys."

"Oh! Given themselves a name as well, have they? Well, Becky, answer this. How d'you always manage to look like you just escaped from a hair-pulling battle? Eh? And don't I tell you not to break the backs down and wear your canvas shoes like slippers? Don't you ever hear what I say?"

"Yes, mam."

"D'you want to end up a field laborer? Like where your father used to be overseer?"[2]

"No, mam."

"Well, Becky, will you please go off and do your homework?"

Everybody did everything to stop me. I was allowed no chance whatsoever. No chance to talk to Mum about the bike I dream of day and night! And I knew exactly the bike I wanted. I wanted a bike like Ben's bike. Oh, I wished I still had even my scorpion on a string to run up and down somebody's back!

I answered my mum. "Yes, mam." I went off into Meg's and my bedroom.

I sat down at the little table, as well as I might. Could homework stay in anybody's head in broad daylight outside? No. Could I keep a bike like Ben's out of my

---

1. **veranda** (və·ran′də): a long, open, outdoor porch.

2. **overseer**: someone who supervises laborers at their work.

head? Not one bit. That bike took me all over the place. My beautiful bike jumped every log, every rock, every fence. My beautiful bike did everything cleverer than a clever cowboy's horse, with me in the saddle. And the bell, the bell was such a glorious gong of a ring!

If Dad was alive, I could talk to him. If Dad was alive, he'd give me money for the bike like a shot.

I sighed. It was amazing what a sigh could do. I sighed and tumbled on a great idea. Tomorrow evening I'd get Shirnette to come with me. Both of us together would be sure to get the boys interested to teach us to ride. Wow! With Shirnette they can't just ride away!

Next day at school, everything went sour. For the first time, Shirnette and me had a real fight, because of what I hated most.

Shirnette brought a cockroach to school in a shoepolish tin. At playtime she opened the tin and let the cockroach fly into my blouse. Pure panic and disgust nearly killed me. I crushed up the cockroach in my clothes and practically ripped my blouse off, there in open sunlight. Oh, the smell of a cockroach is the nastiest ever to block your nose! I started running with my blouse to go and wash it. Twice I had to stop and be sick.

I washed away the crushed cockroach stain from my blouse. Then the stupid Shirnette had to come into the toilet, falling about laughing. All right, I knew the cockroach treatment was for the time when I made my centipede on a string crawl up Shirnette's back. But you put fair-is-fair aside. I just barged into Shirnette.

When it was all over, I had on a wet blouse, but Shirnette had one on, too.

Then, going home with the noisy flock of children from school, I had such a new, new idea. If Mum thought I was scruffy, Nat, Aldo, Jimmy, and Ben might think so, too. I didn't like that.

After dinner I combed my hair in the bedroom. Mum did her machining on the veranda. Meggie helped Mum. Granny sat there, wishing she could take on any job, as usual.

I told Mum I was going to make up a quarrel with Shirnette. I went, but my friend wouldn't speak to me, let alone come out to keep my company. I stood alone and watched the Wheels-and-Brake Boys again.

This time the boys didn't race away past me. I stood leaning against the tall coconut palm tree. People passed up and down. The nearby main road was busy with traffic. But I didn't mind. I watched the boys. Riding round and round the big flame tree, Nat, Aldo, Jimmy, and Ben looked marvelous.

At first each boy rode round the tree alone. Then each boy raced each other round the tree, going round three times. As he won, the winner rang his bell on and on, till he stopped panting and could laugh and talk properly. Next, most reckless and fierce, all the boys raced against each other. And, leaning against their bicycles, talking and joking, the boys popped soft drinks open, drank, and ate chipped bananas.

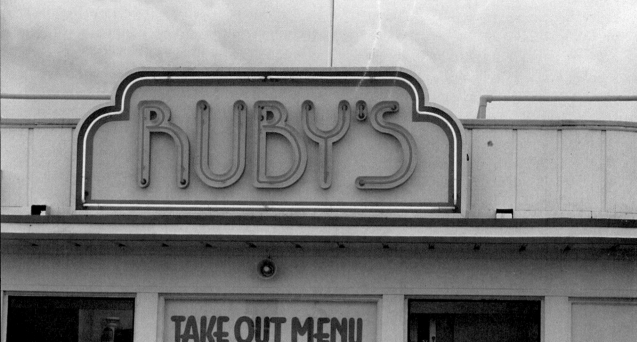

and Ben got on their bikes and rode off. I wasn't at all cross with them. I only wanted to be riding out of the playground with them. I knew they'd be heading into the town to have ice cream and things and talk and laugh.

Mum was sitting alone on the veranda. She sewed buttons onto a white shirt she'd made. I sat down next to Mum. Straightaway, "Mum," I said, "I still want to have a bike badly."

"Oh, Becky, you still have that foolishness in your head? What am I going to do?"

Mum talked with some sympathy. Mum knew I was honest. "I can't get rid of it, mam," I said.

Mum stopped sewing. "Becky," she said, staring in my face, "how many girls around here do you see with bicycles?"

"Janice Gordon has a bike," I reminded her.

"Janice Gordon's dad has acres and acres of coconuts and bananas, with a business in the town as well."

I knew Mum was just about to give in. Then my granny had to come out onto the veranda and interfere. Listen to that Granny-Liz. "Becky, I heard you mother tell you over and over she cahn[3] afford to buy you a bike. Yet you keep on and on. Child, you're a girl."

"But I don't want a bike because I'm a girl."

"D'you want it because you feel like a bwoy?" Granny said.

I walked up to Nat, Aldo, Jimmy, and Ben and said, "Can somebody teach me to ride?"

"Why don't you stay indoors and learn to cook and sew and wash clothes?" Jimmy said.

I grinned. "I know all that already," I said. "And one day perhaps I'll even be mum to a boy child, like all of you. Can you cook and sew and wash clothes, Jimmy? All I want is to learn to ride. I want you to teach me."

I didn't know why I said what I said. But everybody went silent and serious.

One after the other, Nat, Aldo, Jimmy,

---

3. **cahn:** can't.

"No. I only want a bike because I want it and want it and want it."

Granny just carried on. "A tomboy's like a whistling woman and a crowing hen, who can only come to a bad end.[4] D'you understand?"

I didn't want to understand. I knew Granny's speech was an awful speech. I went and sat down with Lenny and Vin, who were making a kite.

By Saturday morning, I felt real sorry for Mum. I could see Mum really had it hard for money. I had to try and help. I knew anything of Dad's—anything—would be worth a great mighty hundred dollars.

I found myself in the center of town, going through the busy Saturday crowd. I hoped Mum wouldn't be too cross. I went into the fire station. With lots of luck I came face to face with a round-faced man in uniform. He talked to me. "Little miss, can I help you?"

I told him I'd like to talk to the head man. He took me into the office and gave me a chair. I sat down. I opened out my brown paper parcel. I showed him my dad's sun helmet. I told him I thought it would make a good fireman's hat. I wanted to sell the helmet for some money toward a bike, I told him.

The fireman laughed a lot. I began to laugh, too. The fireman put me in a car and drove me back home.

Mum's eyes popped to see me bringing home the fireman. The round-faced fireman laughed at my adventure. Mum laughed, too, which was really good. The fireman gave Mum my dad's hat back. Then—mystery, mystery—Mum sent me outside while they talked.

My mum was only a little cross with me. Then—mystery and more mystery—my mum took me with the fireman in his car to his house.

The fireman brought out what? A bicycle! A beautiful, shining bicycle! His nephew's bike. His nephew had been taken away, all the way to America. The bike had been left with the fireman-uncle for him to sell it. And the good, kind fireman-uncle decided we could have the bike—on small payments. My mum looked uncertain. But in a big, big way, the fireman knew it was all right. And Mum smiled a little. My mum had good sense to know it was all right. My mum took the bike from the fireman Mr. Dean.

And guess what? Seeing my bike much, much newer than his, my cousin Ben's eyes popped with envy. But he took on the big job. He taught me to ride. Then he taught Shirnette.

I ride into town with the Wheels-and-Brake Boys now. When she can borrow a bike, Shirnette comes too. We all sit together. We have patties and ice cream and drink drinks together. We talk and joke. We ride about, all over the place.

And, again, guess what? Fireman Mr. Dean became our best friend, and Mum's especially. He started coming around almost every day.

---

4. **tomboy's . . . end:** an old expression meaning that just as a hen does not crow, a woman shouldn't whistle. (Whistling was thought to be unladylike.)

For Study and Discussion

IDENTIFYING FACTS

1. The story has an unusual **title.** Who are the Wheels-and-Brake Boys?

2. What does Becky want so badly? Why does she want it? What keeps her from getting it?

3. What steps does Becky take to solve her problem, or **conflict?** How does life change for her at the story's end?

INTERPRETING MEANINGS

4. Name two good things that result from Becky's meeting with the fireman.

5. Becky knows that her family doesn't have much money. Yet she keeps asking her mother for the bike. Make a list of the events that lead up to Becky's thinking, "I could see Mum really had it hard for money." (Page 227)

6. Granny says to Becky, "A tomboy's like a whistling woman and a crowing hen . . ." (Page 227) What is Granny's message? Why does Becky say it was an "awful speech"? Do you agree?

7. Other characters in this story besides Granny have firm ideas about the roles males and females should play. What are some of these ideas? How does Becky rebel against them?

APPLYING MEANINGS

8. Many people in this story think that Becky should not have a bicycle because she is a girl. Name other things that some people believe girls should *not* have. Then name things that some people think *boys* should not have. What do you think of these ideas?

9. This story is **set** in Jamaica. Could it happen where you live? What details in the story would change if its setting were your own town or city?

10. If you want to play a trick on a friend in Jamaica, you can pick up a bug on the way to school. What jokes do children play on each other in your neighborhood? Can any of them become cruel or harsh?

Focus on Reading

READING ALOUD (A Group Project)

Prepare this story for oral reading. First, you will have to decide how many readers you will need. You might want to assign one narrator to read Becky's voice and have separate readers read each of the other characters' lines.

Next, be sure you practice the dialect before you present your reading. How will one character's voice be different from another's?

Finally, decide who your audience will be. Your presentation to a group of younger children might be quite different from your presentation to parents or a group of boys and girls who are your own age.

Literary Elements

POINT OF VIEW

Point of view refers to the vantage point from which a story is told. Many stories are told from an **omniscient** (om·nish′ənt) point of view, that is, by someone who knows everything about every character and every event, past, present, and future. *Omniscient* means "all-knowing." The omniscient narrator is just that: all-knowing, like a god.

Many stories are told from the **first-person** point of view. This means that an "I" tells the story, someone who is a character in the story. Becky tells this story using the first-person pronoun *I*.

Becky's story would be very different if it were told by an omniscient narrator.

Take the first five paragraphs of the story, down to "I'd just ride away with them, wouldn't I?" Rewrite these paragraphs as if they are being told by an omniscient narrator. You will have to drop the "I." You will have to drop Becky's dialect. Here is how the opening could be rewritten:

Even Becky's own cousin Ben was there.

Which point of view is "President Cleveland, Where Are You?" (page 178) told from? How can you tell?

"Dragon, Dragon" (page 166) is told by an omniscient narrator. Take the first five paragraphs of that story and retell them in the first person. Who will be the first-person narrator, or the "I" of your story? Will it be the dragon, or some other character?

Language and Vocabulary

DIALECT

Dialect is a way of speaking that is particular to a region or group of people. If you know anyone who was born in the Caribbean islands, you'll know that James Berry is very good at imitating the musical way Jamaicans speak English. If this story had been written in standard English, we would have had a very different feel for Becky and her world. For instance, the Jamaican Becky says in the third paragraph, "It's no fair reason they don't want to be with me. Anybody could go off their head for that." A Becky in Missouri might have said instead, "It's not fair that they don't want to be with me. Anybody would be upset about that." See how a

change in dialect makes Becky a different person?

In the following passages from the story, some expressions characteristic of Jamaican dialect are underlined. How would you "translate" these expressions into your own dialect, or way of speaking?

1. "With me even being all so thoughtful of Granny's need of a cool drink, she started up some botheration against me."

2. " 'Haven't I told you I don't want you keeping company with those awful riding-about bicycle boys?' "

3. " 'And one day perhaps I'll even be mum to a boy child, like all of you.' "

4. "I could see Mum really had it hard for money."

5. "I knew anything of Dad's—anything— would be worth a great mighty hundred dollars."

About the Author

James Berry (1925–   ), who was born in Jamaica, writes short stories, children's fiction, and poetry. "Becky and the Wheels-and-Brake Boys" is from a collection of short stories he wrote for children called *A Thief in the Village and Other Stories.* In a review of this collection, one critic wrote that the nine stories in this collection evoke in precise detail Caribbean village life, where young people carry wood and water before they go to school, the arrival of the city bus gives shape to the day, and people wash their donkeys in the sea early on Sunday morning. Another popular book by Berry is a collection of West Indian folk tales called *Anancy—Spiderman.*

Focus on Writing a Short Story

EXPERIMENTING WITH POINT OF VIEW
Choose a story idea. For example, you might want to retell the story of a movie or TV show you saw recently. Then write the first paragraph for your story in two different ways. In one version, use **first-person point of view** by having a character in your tale tell the story. In the second version, use **omniscient point of view**—that is, refer to the characters either by their names or with third-person pronouns like *she, he,* and *they.*

Get together with a classmate to compare paragraphs. Save your writing.

Nancy

ELIZABETH ENRIGHT

Before You Read

This is a story about outsiders. Before you read, write a few ideas in your journal about outsiders. What is an outsider? Why do some individuals feel like outsiders? Can whole families or groups of people feel like outsiders? This is also a story about our need for friends. In your journal, describe the way you'd feel if you were seven years old and lonely for friends.

Though this story takes place many years ago, Fiona is just like children you know today. As you read, notice the differences between Fiona's home life and the Fadgins' home life. Why do you think the writer calls the story "Nancy" instead of "Fiona"?

The use of words to describe sights, sounds, tastes, smells, and textures is called imagery. As Fiona lies down to take a nap, she notices sounds and smells around her. She hears the snoring of the adults and the rattling of Nana's newspaper. Through the window, she hears the sound of insects and she smells the grass. As you read, notice all the images that help you visualize Fiona's grandparents' house. Then look for contrasting images that help you experience life at the Fadgins' house. Try to put yourself into these two settings.

Fiona Farmer was seven years old. Her mother was forty-six, her father was fifty-five, her nurse was sixty-one, and her grandmother and grandfather, with whom they were all spending the summer, had reached such altitudes of age that no one remembered what they were. From these great heights, Fiona was loved and directed.

She wore her hair as her mother had worn it in 1914, braided tight and tied back in pretzel loops with big stiff ribbons. In winter, she was the only girl at school to wear a flannel petticoat and underwear with sleeves. Her mother read her all the books she had loved in her childhood: *Rebecca of Sunnybrook Farm*, and *The Five Little Peppers*, and *Under the Lilacs*. Her grandmother read her the books *she* had loved as a child: *Macé's Fairy Tales*, and *Grimm's Fairy Tales*, and *The Princess and Curdie*. On this mixed diet of decorum[1] and

brutality, Fiona was rapidly turning into a "quaint little creature." She was a pensive[2] child with large attentive eyes and rather elderly manners; all her play was quiet, accompanied at times by nothing noisier than a low continuous murmuring, so it was strange that the ranks of dolls on her nursery shelves were scalped and eyeless.

"What on earth does she do to them?" her mother said to Nana, the nurse. "Why, when I was little, my dollies were really like babies to me. I took such *care* of them, I *loved* them so. . . ."

"I honestly don't know, Mrs. Farmer," Nana said. "She'll be as quiet as a mouse in here for hours at a time, and then I'll come in and find all this—this destruction! It seems so unlike her!"

Fiona's grandmother reproached her quietly. "How would you like it if your dear mother pulled all your hair out of your head and broke your arms and legs? Your

---

1. **decorum** (di·kôr′əm): proper behavior.

2. **pensive** (pen′siv): thoughtful.

dolls are your little responsibilities, your *children* in a way. . . ."

Her admonishments,[3] though frequent, were always mild. When Fiona scratched her head or picked her nose, she would say, "That's not very pretty, dear, is it? We don't do those things, do we?" She was a lofty, dignified, conventional lady, and she smelled like an old dictionary among whose pages many flowers have been dried and pressed. She taught Fiona how to make a sachet and a pomander ball and play Parcheesi.[4]

Fiona liked her grandfather the best. He was a man of wonderful patience and politeness, deaf as a post. Every morning she followed him out to the vegetable garden where, in his old loose button-down-the-front sweater and his white canvas golf hat that sagged in a ruffle around his head, he worked along the rows of beets and cabbages with his hoe and rake. Fiona followed at his heels, speaking ceaselessly. It did not matter to her that he never heard a word she said; she told him everything. Now and then, he would stop, resting on his hoe handle, and look down at her appreciatively. "Well," he would say. "You're a pleasant little companion, aren't you?" Then he would reach out his old parched hand (he was so old that he never sweated anymore) and give her a brittle tap or two on the shoulder or head, and he and Fiona would smile at each other out of a mutual feeling of benevolence.[5]

Sooner or later, though, Nana's voice would begin to caw, "Fee-ona! Fee-ona!" and she would have to go back to the house to pick up her toys, or change her dress, or eat a meal, or do some other dull thing.

Her grandparents' house was big and cool inside. All the rooms were full of greenish light reflected from the maple trees outdoors; the floors were dark and gleaming, the carpets had been taken up for the summer, and the furniture had linen dresses on. There was no dust anywhere, not even in the corners of the empty fireplaces, for Cora and Mary, the maids who had been there for thirty years, spent their lives seeing that there was not.

Cora had arthritis, and on Sundays when Fiona had noon dinner with the whole family, she marveled at the extreme slowness with which the maid moved about the table, like a running-down toy. Her face looked very still and concentrated then, relaxing only when she served Fiona, whispering, "Eat it all up now, dear, every bit, so I can tell Mary."

Oh, food! People were always speaking of food to Fiona; the Sunday dinners were a trial to toil through. "Eat it all up, dear," and "Clean your plate" were phrases that were ugly in her ears.

After Sunday dinner everyone went to

---

3. **admonishments** (ad·mon′ish·mənts): mild scoldings.
4. A **sachet** (sa·shā′) is a bag of perfumed powder; a **pomander** (pō′man·dər) **ball** is a mixture of sweet-smelling substances shaped like a ball; and **Parcheesi** (pär·chē′zē) is a board game played with dice.
5. **benevolence** (bə·nev′ə·ləns): goodwill.

sleep for a while and the house droned with different pitches of snoring. Wearing nothing but a pink wrapper, Fiona would lie on the big white bed while Nana sat in an armchair by the window rattling the Sunday paper. Out of doors the cicadas[6] sounded hot as drills. The lazy air coming in the window brought a smell of grass, and Fiona wished that Nana would fall asleep so that she could get up and find something to play with, but Nana would not fall asleep.

But once she did.

Once on Sunday after the usual slow, massive[7] dinner, as Fiona lay in the extremity of boredom counting mosquito bites and listening to herself yawn, she heard another sound: a new one that might promise much. Quietly she raised herself to her elbows, hardly daring to believe, and saw that the impossible had happened at last. Nana lay in the armchair, abandoned, with her head thrown back and her hair coming down and her mouth wide open like that of a fish. A faint guttural sound came out of it each time she breathed.

A great light seemed to flood the room, and a voice from on high addressed Fiona: "Get up and dress, but do not put on your shoes. Carry them in your hand till you get outside, and close the front door quietly behind you."

Fiona got up at once, dressed with the silence and speed of light, and departed.

The upstairs hall hummed and trumpeted with the noises of sleeping; no one heard her running down the stairs.

Out of doors it was bright and hot; she sat on the front step and put on her sandals with her heart galloping in her chest. Though old, the members of her family were tall, their legs were long as ladders, and if they came after her, they would surely catch her. Leaving the sandal straps unbuckled, Fiona ran out of the gate and down the street, terrified and exhilarated. She ran till she was giddy[8] and breathless, but when at last she stopped and looked behind her, the street on which she found herself was still and empty; steeped[9] in Sunday.

She walked for a long time. Her heart stopped racing and her breathing became comfortable again. Her fear, too, gave way to pleasure and pride. It was a beautiful afternoon. The street was very high with elms. The light that came through their roof of leaves was green and trembling like light through water. Fiona became a little crab crawling among the roots of seaweed. The parked cars were fishes which would eat her up, danger was everywhere. . . . She walked sideways, made claws out of her thumbs, hid behind trees, and felt that her eyes grew out on stems. But not for long. Suddenly, as sometimes happened, the fancy[10] collapsed, betrayed her completely. There was no danger; the cars were cars

---

6. **cicadas** (si·kā′dəs): large insects with transparent wings. The males make shrill sounds, like crickets.
7. **massive**: large, heavy.

8. **giddy** (gid′ē): here, dizzy.
9. **steeped**: here, absorbed.
10. **fancy**: imaginative idea. (Fiona was creating a make-believe world.)

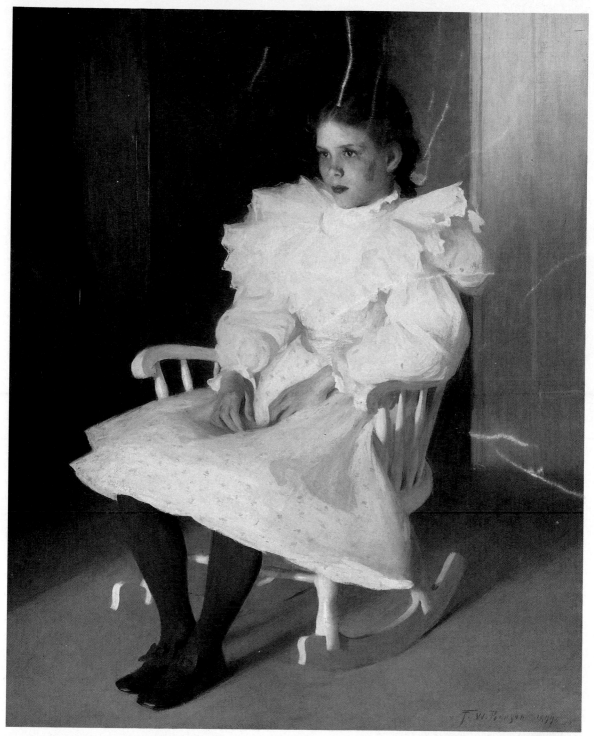

Gertrude by Frank Weston Benson (1899).

Museum of Fine Arts, Boston, Massachusetts.
Gift of Mrs. William Rodman Fay.

only. Nothing was any better than real. In the end, somebody would catch her and take her home, or she would return of her own accord, driven by hunger or conscience, and everything would be as it had always been.

The houses sat back from their green laps of lawn, silent and substantial, regarding her like people wearing glasses. There was a smell of privet[11] and hot asphalt in the still air; a boring smell. Intolerable[12] boredom amounting to anguish drove Fiona to turn abruptly and kick the iron palings[13] of a fence that she was passing— a kick that hurt right through her shoe.

The big street came to an end finally at a small Civil War monument and branched out beyond it in three roads. She chose the right-hand one because there was a dog asleep on the sidewalk there; but when she got to him, she saw the flies strolling up and down his face and he looked up at her balefully[14] with a low ripple of sound in his throat, and she hurried on.

This street had few trees; it was broader, and the houses, while farther apart, were shabbier. The afternoon sun was in her eyes, drawing her along the gilded[15] road. The wind had sprung up, too, warm and lively, blowing from the west.

On the outskirts of the town she came upon her destination, though at first she did not realize it. For some time the wind had been bringing her great blasts of radio music; and she saw now that these had their source in a gray frame house that fairly trembled with melody. Though not small, this was the seediest of all the houses. It stood in the middle of a yard as full of tall grass as a field. There were paths through the field and bald patches where people had stamped and trampled, and many souvenirs abandoned and half grown over: a rusted little wagon with no wheels, somebody's shoe, an old tire.

The house had a queer shape, fancy, but with everything coming off or breaking. Some of the shutters hung by one hinge only; the cupola[16] on top was crooked, and so was the porch from which half the palings were gone. The fence, too, had lost many of its pickets and stood propped against the tangle like a large comb with teeth missing. But it had kept its gate, and hanging onto this and swinging slowly back and forth were three little girls. Fiona walked more slowly.

One of the girls had a bandanna tied tightly around her head, but the other two regarded her from under untrimmed dusty bangs, like animals peering out from under ferns. The gate gave a long snarl of sound as they pushed it forward.

---

11. **privet** (priv′it): a kind of hedge that has a strong odor.
12. **intolerable** (in·tol′ər·ə·bəl): unbearable.
13. **palings** (pā′lingz): pickets of a fence.
14. **balefully** (bāl′fəl·lē): threateningly.
15. **gilded** (gild′id): as if inlaid with gilt, or gold.

16. **cupola** (kyo͞o′pə·lə): a circular dome-shaped roof.

"Where are you going?" said the tallest one.

Fiona could not be sure of the tone of this question: Was it a friendly or a hostile challenge? She moved still more slowly, touching each picket with her forefinger.

"No place," she said guardedly.

"What's your name?" demanded the girl with the bandanna. She smelled of kerosene.[17]

"Fiona Farmer," said Fiona.

"That's a funny name. My name's Darlene, and hers is Pearl, and *hers* is Merle. Nancy is a nice name."

Fiona saw that all of them were wearing red nail polish and asked a question of her own.

"Are you all three sisters?"

"Yes, and there's more of us. *Them,*" said Pearl, the tallest girl, jerking her head. "In the swing."

Beyond the house Fiona now saw for the first time an old double-rocker swing full of boys.

"There's Norman and Stanley and Earl," Darlene said. "And in the house we got a baby sister named Marilyn, and down to the picture theater we got a big sister named Deanna. Come on in."

"Will they let me swing in the swing?" said Fiona.

"Sure they will. *What* did you say your name was?"

"Fiona," she admitted. "Fiona Farmer."

"Gee," said Pearl.

"We'll call her Nancy," said Darlene, who, though younger, seemed to be a leader in her way. "Come on, Nancy, you wanna swing on the gate? Get off, Merle."

Merle got off obediently, sucking her thumb.

"I would like to swing in the *swing,*" Fiona said.

She came into the yard, gazing up at the tipsy cupola. "Can you get up there into that kind of little tower?"

"Sure," said Darlene. "Come on up and we'll show you."

Fiona followed them through the interesting grass in which she now saw a broken doll, somebody's garter, somebody's hat, and many weathered corncobs and beer cans.

On the porch which swayed when they walked on it there was a tough-looking baby buggy, two sleds, a bent tricycle, a lot of chairs and boxes and bushel baskets and peck baskets and a baby pen and a wagon wheel and some kindling wood. The screen door was full of holes, and instead of a doorknob, there was a wooden thread spool to turn.

The noise of music was stunning as they went indoors; it kept the Mason jars[18] ringing on the shelves. They walked right into it, into the thrilling heart of noise which was the kitchen, where a woman was sitting nursing a baby and shouting random conversation at an old, old woman with a beak nose.

---

17. **kerosene:** fuel oil that is sometimes used as a home treatment for head lice.

18. **Mason jars:** jars used for preserving fruits and vegetables.

The music ceased with a flourish and the radio announcer's tremendous tones replaced it, but this did not stop the shouted discourse of the woman with the baby. As the girls crossed the kitchen, she turned for a moment to look at them, saw Fiona, and said, "Who's she?"

"She's Nancy," called Darlene, against the radio.

"Who?"

"Nancy! She dropped in."

"That's Mom," Pearl said.

Fiona went over to the lady to shake her hand. She made her usual curtsy and said, "How do you do?"

Mom's hand felt limp and rather damp and startled. She was a big woman with a wide face and tired blue eyes.

"The old one's Gramma," Darlene said, so Fiona curtsied to the old lady too, and shook her hand, which felt like a few twigs in a glove.

"And that's my father," Darlene added a few seconds later when they had gone up the loud bare stairs to the next floor. Fiona peeked in the doorway of the dim, strong-smelling room, but all she saw of *him* was the soles of his socks, and she heard him snoring.

"Just like at home," she said. "Sunday afternoon they all sleep."

"He sleeps all *day* on Sundays," Darlene said, and Fiona felt a little humiliated for her own father.

"This is Gramma's room." Pearl threw open the door. "She likes flowers."

The room was a jungle steeped in musky twilight. A vine of some kind had

crawled all over the window and parts of the wall, and on the sill, the sash, and the floor below were pots and jars and coffee tins in which stout lusty plants were growing and flowering.

"How does she open the window at night?" Fiona wondered.

"*She* don't open no windows day or night," Darlene said. "She's *old*, she's gotta stay *warm*."

They went up another flight of stairs,

narrow steep ones, crowded with magazines and articles of clothing and decayed toys. "Up here's where we sleep," Darlene said. "Us girls, all of us except Marilyn. Pearl and me and Merle sleep in the big bed and Deanna she sleeps in the cot. This is the attic like."

The big bed was made of iron with the post knobs missing. It dipped in the middle like a hammock, and there, Fiona knew, the little girls would lie at night, dumped together in a tangle, quarreling or giggling in whispers.

"Look at all the comic books!" she cried, and indeed they lay everywhere in tattered profusion, a drift of stained, disordered leaves.

"We got about a hundred or a thousand of 'em, I guess," Pearl said. "You want some?"

"Could I really, Pearl? Could you spare them?"

"*Atom Annie*'s a good one," Pearl said. "We got a lot about her, and here's one called *Hellray* that's real good, real scary. Take these."

Fiona looked at them longingly. "I don't know if my mother—she doesn't like for me to have comics."

"Heck, why not?"

"Well, maybe this time she won't mind," Fiona said, taking the books, determined that everything would be all right for once. "Thank you very, very much, Darlene and Pearl."

"Here's the stairs to the lookout," Darlene said. "Get out of the way, Merle, you wait till last."

They climbed the ladder steps in the middle of the room, Pearl pushed open the trap door, and one by one they ascended into the tiny chamber.

It was a tipped little cubicle like a ship's cabin in stiff[19] weather, and stiflingly hot. It seemed remote, high, cozy, and its four soiled windows showed four different views of the town, faded and reduced as pictures in an old book. Flies buzzed and butted at the hot glass. Fiona felt disappointed when she saw the steeple of the church that stood across the street from her grandfather's house. She had not thought it was so near.

"Jump!" cried Darlene. They all began to jump, and the cupola jarred and trembled under the pounding.

"Won't it break?" cried Fiona, pounding with the rest. "Won't it fall off?"

"Naw, it won't break," Darlene called back. "It never did yet."

"But it might someday, though," shouted Pearl encouragingly.

It was fun to jump riotously and yell, as the tiny tower rocked and resounded.

There was an interruption from below.

"Get out of there!" bawled Mom up the stairs. "How many times I told you kids to stay down out of there! You want to get your backs broke? You want to get killed? You scram down!"

"Get out of the way, Merle, let Nancy go first," Pearl said.

Mom stood at the foot of the steps wearing the baby around her neck. Anxiety had made her furious. "That place ain't safe, you know that!" she cried. "How many times have I told you?" She gave Pearl a slap on the cheek and would have given one to Darlene, too, if Darlene had not bent her neck adroitly.[20]

"You let me catch you up there one more time and I'll get your father to lick you good!"

"Aw, climb a tree," said Darlene.

Fiona was aghast. What would happen now?

But nothing happened. Merle still quietly sucked her thumb, Darlene and Pearl seemed cool and jaunty, and as they descended through the house, Mom's anger dried up like dew.

"You kids want a snack?" she said. "You didn't eat since breakfast."

"Can Nancy stay?"

---

19. **stiff:** rough.

20. **adroitly** (ə·droit′lē): skillfully.

"Why, sure, I guess. Why not?"

"Oh, thank you very, very much. . . ."

The kitchen, like the rest of the house, had a rich, bold, musty smell. It smelled of constant usage and memories of usage. It was crowded and crusted with objects: pots, pans, kettles, boxes, jars, cans, buckets, dippers. There were two alarm clocks, one lying on its side, and both asserting a different hour, and four big Coca-Cola calendars on the wall, none for the current year. The radio was still thundering music, and close beside it warming herself at the noise sat Gramma, dark as a crow, chewing and chewing on her empty gums.

The stove was named Ebony Gem, and behind it in a cardboard box there was something alive; something moved. . . .

"It's kittens," said Merle, removing her thumb from her mouth and speaking for the first time. "Our cat had kittens."

"Oh, let me see!" Fiona knelt by the box. There inside it lay a bland[21] and happy group: mother cat with her yellow eyes half closed and her paws splayed out in pleasure; kittens lined up all along her, sucking.

Merle put out her little forefinger with its chipped red nail polish, stroking first one infant, then the next. "The black one's name is Blackie and the white one's name is Whitey and we call *this* one Butch because he's so——"

"My father usually drowns them, all but one," Darlene interrupted. She bent her kerchiefed head close to Fiona's, so

that there was a blinding smell of kerosene. "Tomorrow probly," she whispered. "We don't tell Merle, it makes her feel so bad." Then she raised her voice. "She knows it's going to happen but she don't know when, huh, Merle?"

"You could take one, Nancy," Merle said, still gazing at the kittens. "You could keep it and be good to it."

"Do you mean honestly and truly?" Fiona's joy was suffocating.

"Any one? Any one at all?"

"Except Butch," Darlene said. "We're going to keep him to help with the rats."

"Could I have Blackie? Really for keeps?"

Merle plucked the dark little thing from the mother as if she were plucking off a burr and gave it to Fiona.

"I can feel its little tiny heart," Fiona said. "I'll give it milk all the time and brush its fur and it can sleep in the doll cradle. Oh look at its ears, oh Merle, oh thank you!"

Shamed by gratitude, Merle put her thumb back in her mouth and looked away.

"You kids get out from under my feet," Mom said. "Sit up to the table now, it's all ready. Come on, Mama, come on, *boys!*" She opened the screen door and put her head out, shouting so hard that great cords stood out on her neck.

They sat around the big table with its oilcloth cover, everything in easy reach: cereal in paper boxes, sugar, catsup. . . . They had cornflakes and milk, Swiss cheese sandwiches with catsup, cream

---

21. **bland**: mild.

Irish Girl (Mary O'Donnell) by Robert Henri (1913).

soda in bottles, and little cakes out of a box with pink and green beads on them. Fiona ate everything.

"Nancy eats good, don't she, Mom?" Darlene said.

"I never had catsup before," said Fiona. "My, it certainly is delicious, isn't it?"

The table was a family battlefield. Fiona had never seen anything like it in her life. Stanley and Norman threw pieces of sandwich at each other; Earl took one of Merle's cakes and Merle cried and Mom slapped Earl; Darlene stole big swigs from Pearl's soda bottle, was loudly accused, and loudly defended herself.

"You kids shut up," Mom said, eating over Marilyn's head and giving her occasional bits of cake dipped in tea. Gramma was the only quiet one; she sat bent over, all wrapped and absorbed in her old age, gazing into her cup as she drank from it with a long purring sound. Blackie was quiet too, asleep in Fiona's lap. She kept one hand on his little velvet back.

Mom pointed at Fiona with her spoon. "Looks like Margaret O'Brien[22] used to, don't she? The ribbons and all."

"Margaret who?" said Fiona.

"O'Brien. _You_ know, the kid in the movies," Darlene said.

"Oh, I never go to movies," said Fiona. "I'm not allowed."

"Not allowed!" cried Darlene incred-
ulously. "We go all the time, don't we, Mom? Even Deanna goes. We could take Nancy with us sometimes, couldn't we, Mom?"

"Maybe, if her folks say yes."

"Oh, if I went with _you_, it would be all right, I'm sure," cried Fiona joyously. Drunk with noise, strange flavors, gifts, and new friendship, she really believed this.

Afterward, still with catsup on their upper lips, they went outdoors to play hide-and-seek.

"You be her partner, Stanley," ordered Darlene, who was "it." "You kind of look after her, she don't know our places to hide."

Then she hid her eyes with her arm, cast herself against a tree like a girl in grief, and began to count out loud.

"The cellar," hissed Stanley, grabbing Fiona's hand. He was a big eight-year-old boy, and still clutching the kitten, Fiona ran with him willingly, hesitating only for a second at sight of the dark abyss.[23] On the steps were many cans and crates, but Stanley led her safely down among these and into the black deep tunnel beyond. Fiona could feel that there were solid things all around them—probably more boxes, more crates—but she could see nothing. Stanley's hand was warm and firm, it just fitted hers, and she liked having him lead her.

---

22. **Margaret O'Brien**: a child movie star in the 1940s and 1950s. (She often wore her hair in looped braids tied with ribbons.)

23. **abyss** (ə·bis'): bottomless space.

"We can stop now," he said, "but keep quiet."

Darlene could still be heard, faintly. Her counting voice sounded deserted and defiant: "*Ninety*-five, *ninety*-six, *ninety*-seven" . . . The blackness throbbed and shimmered and the air had a dense aged smell.

"Coming, ready or not!" called the faraway defiant voice.

"We're safe here anyways," Stanley said. "She won't come down *here*, she's scared to." He laughed silently and gave Fiona's hand a squeeze. "There's rats down here."

"Oh no, oh no! Oh, Stanley, let's go up again," cried Fiona, tears of panic in her voice.

But Stanley held onto her hand. "You going to be a sissy, too?" he demanded. "We got the *cat,* ain't we?"

Fiona strained the tiny kitten to her chest. Her heart was banging terribly and she wanted to cry, but she would not. All around the rats were closing in, large as dogs and smiling strangely; smiling like people. She almost sobbed when Stanley said, "Now we can go, hurry up, and keep still!"

They were the first ones back.

For a long time they played and Stanley always was her partner. He knew the best places to hide: up in the boughs of a pear tree, under the porch steps, in the fearful little dark privy with its different-sized "family accommodations," and flat on their stomachs under the folded-back cellar door. Darlene was "it" till she caught Merle, and Merle was "it" for hours. Fiona got spiderwebs in her mouth and gnats up her nose, tore her dress, scraped her knee, lost one hair ribbon, and gave the other to Merle, who had admired it.

When they were through with hide-and-seek, they all got into the rocker swing and played gangsters. The swing leapt to and fro, to and fro, screaming wildly at the joints; surely it would break, and soon! That was the thrilling thing about this place: So many features of it—the tower, the swing, the porch—trembled at the edge of ruin, hung by a thread above the fatal plunge.

Earl and Stanley and Norman leaned over the back of one of the seats firing at the enemy. "Step on it, you guys," yelled Stanley, "they got a gat!"

"They got a rod!" yelled Norman. "They got a lotta rods!"

"What's a rod?" cried Fiona. "What's a gat?"

"Guns he means," Darlene told her. "Rods and gats is guns."

"Shoot 'em, Stanley," yelled Fiona. "With your gat, shoot the eyes out of 'em!"

Clutching the clawing kitten to her collarbone, her hair in her open mouth, she bawled encouragement to them. The swing accelerated ever more wildly. Soon it would take off entirely, depart from its hinges, fly through the air, burn a hole through the sky! . . .

"Fee-ona Farmer!"

The cry was loud enough to be heard

above all sounds of war and wind and radio music.

Beside the swing stood Nana, so tall, so highly charged with hurry and emotion, that the children stopped their play at once.

"Who's she?" Stanley asked.

"She's my nurse," Fiona murmured.

"Your nurse! What's the matter, are you sick?"

"No . . . she just—takes care of me."

"Takes *care* of you!"

"You get out of that swing and come this in-stant!"

Having struck the bottom of disgrace, Fiona stepped down and slowly went to Nana. From the swing the others watched as still as children posing for a photograph.

"Put down that cat and come at once."

"Oh no!" Fiona said. "It's mine, they gave it to me."

"Put. Down. That. Cat."

Darlene came to stand beside Fiona. "But we did give it to her. We want for her to have it."

Nana struck the kitten from Fiona's arms. "You will not take that creature home! It's filthy, it has fleas!"

"Oh my kitty!" shrieked Fiona, diving after Blackie, but Nana caught her wrist.

"You come!"

Fiona pulled, struggled, cast a glare of anguish at all the rapt[24] photograph-faces in the swing.

"You should be punished. You should be whipped. Whipped!" Nana whistled the

cruel words; Nana, who was never cruel! Her fingers on Fiona's wrist were hard.

"Let me say good-bye to them, Nana, let me say good-bye to their *mother!* You said I should *always* say good-bye to the mother!"

"Not this time, this time it doesn't matter," Nana said. "You're going straight home and into the tub. Heavens knows what you will have caught!" Upon Fiona's friends she turned a single brilliant glance like one cold flash from a lighthouse.

There was nothing to commend Fiona's departure; dragged by the hand, whimpering, she looked back at her friends in desperation. "Oh, Darlene!"

But it was easy to see that Darlene had detached herself. "Good-bye, Nancy," she said, not without a certain pride. She did not smile or say anything else, but her attitude showed Fiona and Nana that she had no need for either of them, could not be hurt by them, and would not think of them again. As they went out the gate, she turned her back and skipped away, and Fiona heard the rocker swing resume its screaming tempo.

Halfway home, Nana's recriminations[25] began to modify, gradually becoming reproaches: "How could you have, Fiona, run away like that. Why it's only by the grace of God I ever found you at all! And all the time I was half sick with worry I never said a word to your father and mother! I didn't want *them* to worry!"

Somewhere deep inside her Fiona

---

24. **rapt**: absorbed.

25. **recriminations** (ri·krim′ə·nā′shəns): accusations.

understood exactly why Nana had said nothing to her parents, but she just kept on saying, "I want my kitty, I want my kitty."

Finally Nana said, "If you're a good girl, maybe we'll get you another kitten."

"I don't want another, I want that one."

"Oh for pity's sakes, it had fleas; or worse. Anything belonging to the Fadgins would be bound to have—"

"Do *you* know them?"

"I know *about* them, everybody does. They're the dirtiest, the shiftlessest, the most down-at-the-heel tribe in this whole town!"

"They are not, they're nice, I love them!"

Nana relented a little. "Maybe it's hard not to be shiftless when you're that poor."

"*They* aren't poor. You should see all the things they've got! More than Grandmother's got in her whole house!"

"All right now, dearie, all right. We'll forget about it, shall we? It will be our secret and we'll never tell anyone because we don't want them to worry, do we? But you must promise me never, never to do such a thing again, hear?"

"I want my kitty," droned Fiona.

Her grandparents' house smelled cool and sweetish. There was a bowl of white and pink stock[26] on the hall table, and her grandmother's green linen parasol leaned in a corner among the pearly company of her grandfather's canes.

---

26. **stock**: a kind of flower.

In the shaded living room, Fiona saw her mother knitting and her grandmother at the piano playing the same kind of music she always played, with the loose rings clicking on her fingers.

"Is that my baby?" called her mother—but Nana answered hastily, "I'm getting her right into her bath, Mrs. Farmer. She's sim-ply fil-thy."

Upstairs Nana went in to run the water in the tub. Fiona kicked off one sandal, then the other. A terrible pain took hold of her; it began in her mind and spread down to her stomach. She had never been homesick before and did not know what ailed her. She knew only that she wanted to sleep at night in a big twanging bed full of children and to eat meals at a crowded table where people threw bread at each other and drank pop. She wanted Stanley's hand to guide her and Darlene's voice to teach her and Blackie's purr to throb against her chest. . . .

Beyond the window she saw her grandfather's wilted golf hat bobbing among the cornstalks, and escaped again, running on bare feet down the back stairs and out of doors across the billowing lawn which seemed to be colliding with the trees and sky and shadows, all flooded and dazzled with tears. Blindly she flung open the garden gate and pushed her way through the green-paper corn forest to her grandfather, who dropped his hoe and held out his arms when he saw her face.

"Come here now," he said in his gentle deaf voice. "Well, well, this won't do, no it won't, not at all. Come sit here with

Grandpa, sit here in the arbor. Did you hurt yourself?''

He led her to the seat under the green grape trellis where he sometimes rested from the hot sun. He put his arm around her shoulders, offering himself as a support for grief, and Fiona howled against his waistcoat till the wet tweed chapped her cheek and there was not a tear left in her. He did not interrupt or ask questions but kept patting her shoulder in a sort of sympathetic accompaniment to her sobs, which he could not hear but which he felt. What's the cause of it all, he wondered. A broken toy? A scolding? Children's tragedies, he thought, children's little tragedies. There are bigger ones in store for you, Fiona, a world of them. The thought did not move him deeply, everyone must suffer, but for an instant he was not sorry to be old.

Fiona leaned against him and after a while, between the hiccups left from sobbing, she could hear the ancient heart inside his chest tick-tocking steadily, as tranquil and unhurried as he was himself. All the wild performance of her sorrow had not quickened its tempo by a single beat, and this for some reason was a comfort.

The sound of her grandmother's music, sugary and elegant, came sparkling from the house, and upstairs in the bedroom or the hall Nana began to call. ''Fee-ona?'' she cried. ''Oh, Fee-*ona*?'' There was a hint of panic in her voice now, but no response came from under the green trellis: Fiona's grandfather could not hear the calling, and Fiona, for the time being, did not choose to answer.

IDENTIFYING FACTS

1. One **setting** in the story is the grandparents' house. Explain why Fiona finds life there boring.

2. We see a very different **setting** when we get to the Fadgins' house. Describe their house and yard.

3. Fiona has many new experiences with the Fadgin children. Name three or four of her adventures. How does she respond to her newfound friends?

4. Fiona's nurse says that she ''knows about'' the Fadgins. What does she know about them?

INTERPRETING MEANINGS

5. This is a story about several outsiders. How are the Fadgins outsiders? How is Fiona also an outsider?

6. Fiona's grandparents and the Fadgins have very different lifestyles. Describe the meal at the grandparents' house. Then describe ''snacktime'' at the Fadgins' house. Why do you think Fiona so loves being with the disorderly Fadgins?

7. A **character trait** is a quality that describes how a person thinks, feels, or behaves. (For example, a character can be outgoing, shy, or clever.) List at least three character traits that could describe Fiona. What traits does she show when she becomes ''Nancy''?

8. Why do you think Fiona from time to time destroys her dolls? (What could this show about her feelings?)

9. Why do you think the author chose "Nancy" for the **title** of this story?

APPLYING MEANINGS

10. Do you think it's true that people like Fiona's Nana often disapprove of people like the Fadgins? What are the various reasons we sometimes reject or fear other people?

Focus on Reading

DISTINGUISHING BETWEEN FACT AND OPINION

A **fact** is a statement that can be proved right or wrong. The proof may be taken from details in the story, from your own experience, or from some outside source, like an encyclopedia or newspaper. It is a fact, for example, that Nancy's mother is forty-six years old. This is stated in the first paragraph of the story.

An **opinion,** on the other hand, is a personal belief. It cannot be proved right or wrong. One reader's opinion might be: "It's not fair that Fiona's parents keep her cooped up in the house all day." Sometimes two people look at the very same facts and have different opinions. That's when things get interesting.

Identify each statement below as fact (F) or opinion (O). Do all your classmates agree?

1. The Fadgins' house is falling apart because they are lazy.

2. The Fadgins' yard is littered with a hat, a broken doll, and some corncobs.

3. The Fadgins lead exciting and adventurous lives.

4. The Fadgins are poor.

5. Three of the Fadgin girls sleep in the same bed.

6. It's wrong that Darlene Fadgin talks back to her mother.

7. Darlene has head lice.

Language and Vocabulary

IMAGERY AND FEELINGS

Images are words that describe sights, sounds, smells, and tastes. They also describe textures, or things that you touch. The author of this story uses images to help you create mental pictures of two settings. Images often reveal a writer's feelings. Images can reveal pleasure or disgust, happiness or sadness.

The images are underlined in the passages below. For each underlined word or group of words, substitute different words to change the feeling of the image. For instance, in the first sentence in the first passage, you might say "Her grandparents' house was tiny and hot inside."

1. "Her grandparents' house was big and cool inside. All the rooms were full of greenish light reflected from the maple trees outdoors; the floors were dark and gleaming, the carpets had been taken up for the summer, and the furniture had linen dresses on. There was no dust anywhere. . . ."

2. "The kitchen, like the rest of the house, had a <u>rich, bold, musty smell</u>. It smelled of <u>constant usage</u> and <u>memories of usage</u>. It was <u>crowded</u> and <u>crusted</u> with objects: <u>pots, pans, kettles, boxes, jars, cans, buckets, dippers</u>. . . . The <u>radio was still thundering music</u>, and close beside it warming herself at the noise sat Gramma, <u>dark as a crow, chewing and chewing on her empty gums</u>."

Focus on Writing a Short Story

LISTING DETAILS OF SETTING

Setting is the time and place of a story. The setting can help to create atmosphere or mood. For example, compare the mood in the description of Fiona's grandparents' house (page 235) with the mood created by the details about the Fadgins' kitchen (page 243).

Create a setting for a short story of your own by filling out a chart like the one below. List as many descriptive details as you can. Save your notes.

Setting Chart
Place: _____
Time: _____
Weather: _____
Time of Year/Time of Day: _____
Objects: _____
Sights/Sounds/Smells: _____
_____
_____
Overall Atmosphere/Mood: _____

About the Author

Elizabeth Enright (1909–1968) wrote books about children who have unusual adventures. Four of those books, *The Saturdays, The Four-Story Mistake, Spiderweb for Two,* and *Then There Were Five* are about the Melendy children. Four of the Melendy children grow up in a home without a mother near New York City. In describing the children's adventures, Enright writes, "They discovered a secret room, built a tree house, found a diamond, escaped from dangers, effected rescues . . . got lost, and did many other striking things. . . ."

Where the Buffaloes Begin

OLAF BAKER

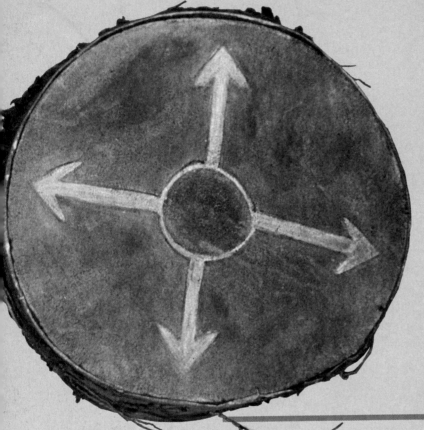

Toy tepee of buckskin and painted sticks. Made by the Sioux between 1900 and 1910.

Werner Forman Archive/Robinson Museum, Pierre, South Dakota.

Dance drum made out of painted hide from South Dakota.

Robinson Museum, Pierre, South Dakota/Museum of the American Indian, Heye Foundation.

Before You Read

This story tells how a boy becomes a hero to his people. Little Wolf lives long ago on the great western prairie of North America. He has heard a tale about where the buffaloes came from, and one day he sets off on a quest to find out if the old tale is true. The strange things that happen to Little Wolf become an addition to the old legend.

Before you read, describe in your journal your favorite setting. What is the weather like there? What do you see and hear there? How does this place make you feel?

Description is the use of language that appeals to our senses of sight, smell, taste, hearing, and touch. Description often creates a mood or feeling. This writer uses specific details to appeal to your five senses and to create a powerful mood or feeling. As you read, let the descriptive details work their magic. Let them help you experience what it was like to live with Little Wolf and his people on this vast windy prairie, in a world of nature that has almost disappeared with the shaggy buffaloes themselves.

Over the blazing campfires, when the wind moaned eerily through the thickets of juniper and fir, they spoke of it in the Indian tongue—of the strange lake to the south whose waters never rest. And Nawa, the wise man, who had lived such countless moons that not even the oldest member of the tribe could remember a time when Nawa was not old, declared that if you arrived at the right time, on the right night, you would see the buffaloes rise out of the middle of the lake and come crowding to the shore; for there, he said, was the sacred spot where the buffaloes began. It was not only Nawa who declared that the buffaloes had their beginnings beneath the water and were born in the depths of the lake. The Indian legend, far older even than Nawa, said the same thing. Nawa was only the voice that kept the legend alive.

Often in the winter, when the wind drove with a roar over the prairies and came thundering up the creek, making the tepees shudder and strain, Little Wolf would listen to the wind and think it was the stampede of the buffaloes. Then he would snuggle warmly under the buffalo robe that was his blanket and would be thankful for the shelter of his home. And sometimes he would go very far down the shadow ways of sleep and would meet the buffaloes as they came up from the lake, with the water shining on their shaggy coats and their black horns gleaming in the moon. And the buffaloes would begin by being very terrible, shaking their great heads at him as if they intended to kill him there and then. But later they would come up close, and smell him, and change their minds, and be friendly after all.

Little Wolf was only ten years old, but he could run faster than any of his friends. And the wildest pony was not too wild for him to catch and ride. But the great thing about him was that he had no fear. He knew that if an angry bull bison or a pack of prairie wolves ran him down, there would be nothing left of him but his bones. And he was well aware that if he fell into the hands of his people's enemies, the Assiniboins,[1] he would be killed and scalped as neatly as could be. Yet none of these things terrified him. Only, being wise for his age, he had a clear understanding that, for the present, it was better to keep out of their way.

But of all the thoughts that ran this way and that in his quick brain, the one that galloped the hardest was the thought of the great lake to the south where the buffaloes began. And as the days lengthened and he could smell springtime on the warm blowing air, the thought grew bigger and bigger in Little Wolf's mind. At last it was so very big that Little Wolf could not bear it any longer. And so, one morning, very early, before the village was awake, he crept out of the tepee and stole along below the junipers and tall firs till he came to the spot where the ponies were hobbled.[2]

The dawn was just beginning to break, and in the gray light the ponies looked like dark blotches along the creek. But Little Wolf's eyes were very sharp, and soon he

had singled out his own pony, because it had a white forefoot and a white patch on its left side. When Little Wolf spoke, calling softly, the animal whinnied in answer and allowed itself to be caught. Little Wolf unhobbled the pony, slipped on the bridle he had brought with him, and leaped lightly upon its back. A few minutes afterward, horse and rider had left the camp behind them and were out on the prairie, going due south.

When the sun rose, they had already traveled far. Little Wolf's eyes constantly swept the immense horizon, searching for danger, moving or in half-concealed ambush. Far off, just on the edge of his sight, there was a dim spot on the yellowish gray of the prairie. Little Wolf reined in his pony and watched to see if it moved. If it did, it crept so slowly as to seem absolutely still. He decided that it was a herd of antelope feeding and that there was nothing to fear.

On he went, hour after hour, never ceasing to watch. The prairie grouse[3] got up almost under the pony's feet. Larks and sparrows filled the air with their singing, and everywhere wild roses were in bloom. It seemed as if nothing but peace would ever find its way among these singing birds and flowers. Yet Little Wolf knew well that his enemies, the Assiniboins, could come creeping along the hollows of the prairie

---

1. **Assiniboins** (ə·sin'ə·boins): members of the Sioux group of people, who lived in northeast Montana and parts of Canada.
2. **hobbled:** Two of a pony's legs would be tied loosely together, which prevented the pony from running away.

3. **grouse** (grous): plump birds.

It was late in the afternoon when, at last, he sighted the lake. It lay, a gray sheet with a glint of silver, glimmering under the sun. Little Wolf looked eagerly on all sides for any sign of buffaloes, but far and wide the prairies lay utterly deserted, very warm and still in the white shimmer of the air. As he drew nearer, however, he saw trails, many trails, all going in one direction and leading toward the lake. Antelope and coyote, wolf and buffalo—all had left traces behind them as they went to the water and returned. But it was the buffalo trails that were most numerous and most marked, and Little Wolf noted them above all the others.

When he was quite close to the lake, he dismounted; hobbling the pony, he turned it loose to graze. Then Little Wolf lay down behind some tussocks[4] of prairie grass, above the low bank at the edge of the lake, and waited. From this position he could overlook the lake without being seen. He gazed far over its glittering expanse, very still now under the strong beams of the sun. It was disappointingly still. Scarcely a ripple broke on the shore. Little Wolf could not possibly imagine that the buffaloes were struggling underneath. Where was the movement and the mysterious murmur of which Nawa had spoken? But Little Wolf was not impatient. He could afford to wait and listen for hours, if need be.

The time went on. Slowly the sun dipped westward, and the shadows of the

like wolves, and that there is no moment more dangerous than when there is no hint of danger.

All this time he had not seen a single buffalo, but he told himself that this was because the herds had taken some other way and that he would probably not see them until he was near the lake. He lost sight of the shadowy spot that had been so far away. If he had known that it was a party of Assiniboins on the way to his village, he would have thought twice about continuing to the lake and would probably have returned along the trail to give warning to his people. But his head was too full of the singing of birds and the breath of roses, and, above all, of the great thought of the buffaloes, fighting below the lake.

---

4. **tussocks:** clumps.

grass grew longer. The lake kept its outward stillness, and nothing happened. At last the sun reached the horizon; it lay there a few moments, a great ball of flame, then sank out of sight. Twilight fell, and all over the vast wilderness crept a peculiar silence, like a wild creature stealing from its lair. Far in the west there lingered the strange orange light that belongs to the prairie skies alone when the sun is down and the night winds sigh along the grass. Little Wolf could not tell whether it was the sighing of the wind or not, but there came to him along the margin of the lake a strange, low murmur that died away and rose again. As the night deepened, the sound grew clearer; Little Wolf was certain now that it was not the wind but a murmur that came from the center of the lake. For hours he lay and listened, but the mysterious murmur never ceased. Sometimes it was a little louder, sometimes a little softer; but always it was plain to hear—a wonderful and terrible thing in the silence of the night. And as Little Wolf lay watching under the stars, the words of Nawa kept singing in his head:

> Do you hear the noise that never
>   ceases?
> It is the Buffaloes fighting far
>   below.
> They are fighting to get out upon
>   the prairie.
> They are born below the Water but
>   are fighting for the Air,
> In the great lake in the Southland
>   where the Buffaloes begin!

Suddenly, Little Wolf lifted himself up. He could not tell whether he had been asleep or not, but there in the lake he saw a wonderful sight: *the buffaloes!*

There they were, hundreds and hundreds of them, rising out of the water. He could not see the surface anymore. Instead, he saw a lake of swaying bodies and heads that shook; and on their horns and tossing heads the water gleamed in the moonlight, as it had done in his dreams.

Little Wolf felt the blood run along his body. He clutched at the prairie grass, crushing it in his hot hands. With staring eyes he drank in the great vision. And not only with his eyes but also with his ears and his nose: for his ears were filled with the trampling and snorting of the herd and the flash of the water as it moved under their hooves. And his nose inhaled the sharp moist smell of the great beasts as they crowded in on one another—the smell the wolves know well when it comes dropping down the wind.

Little Wolf never knew what came to him, what spirit of the wild whispered in his ear; but suddenly he leaped to his feet and cried out. And when he cried, he flung his arms above his head. And then he cried out again.

At the first cry, a shiver passed through the herd. As if they were one beast, the buffaloes threw up their heads and listened, absolutely still. Above the margin of the lake they saw, in the white light of the moon, a little wild boy making swift motions with his arms. He seemed to speak with his arms—to talk to them with

Buffalo Hunt by George Catlin (1835).
Oil on canvas.

the ripple of his muscles and the thrust of his fingers in the air. They had never seen such a thing before. Their eyes fastened on the boy excitedly, and shot out sparks of light. And when he cried out again, there swept through the stillness of the herd a stir, a movement, a ripple that Little Wolf could see. And the ripple became a wave, and the wave a swell. It was a swell of buffaloes that began on the outskirts of the herd and broke along the margin of the lake in a terrifying roar.

It was a wonderful sound, that roar of the buffaloes on the edge of a stampede. It rolled far out on the prairie in the hollow silence of the night. Wandering wolves caught it, threw their long noses to the moon, and howled an answering cry.

It was the hour when, on the lonely prairie, sound carries an immense distance. But the ears it might have warned—the quick ears of Assiniboin warriors—did not catch it, for they were too far away on the northern trail.

On moccasins noiseless as the padded feet of the wolves, as intent, and almost more cruel, these painted warriors were stealthily approaching the camp of Little Wolf's people, determined to wipe them out before the Dog Star faded in the dawn.

But now the buffaloes had received the strange message that the Indian boy waved to them from the margin of the lake. Little Wolf did not understand this message. He had cried out to the buffaloes because he could not help himself, because he loved them as the creatures of his dreams. But when he saw and heard their answer, when they came surging out of the lake like a mighty flood, bellowing and stamping and tossing their heads, a wild excitement possessed him. For the first time in his life, he knew the meaning of fear.

Swift as the wolf for whom he was named, he darted toward his pony. To unhobble it and leap upon its back took but a moment. Then he was off, riding for his life!

Behind him came the terrible sound of the buffaloes as they swept out of the lake. Little Wolf threw a quick glance behind to see which way they took and saw the dark surging mass heave itself onto the prairie and gallop due north.

Chee-ah-ka-tchee, Wife of Not-to-way by George Catlin (1835–1836). Oil on canvas.

National Museum of American Art, Washington DC / Art Resource, NY

Little Wolf tried to escape the middle rush of the herd by turning the pony's head slightly westward. Once the buffaloes surrounded him, he did not know what might happen. If the pony had been fresh, Little Wolf could easily have outstripped them, but after a long day the animal was tired, and was going at half its usual speed. Little Wolf again glanced over his shoulder. The buffaloes were gaining! He cried out to the pony—little, short cries that made a wild note in the night.

As they swept along, the leaders of the left flank of the herd drew so close that Little Wolf could hear the snorting sound of their breath. Then they were beside him, and the pony and the buffaloes were galloping together. Yet they did nothing to harm him. They did not seem to have any other desire but to gallop on into the night.

Soon Little Wolf was completely surrounded by the buffaloes. In front, behind, and on both sides of him, a heaving mass of buffaloes billowed like the sea. Again, as when he had cried out beside the lake, a wild feeling of excitement seized him, and he felt the blood stir along his scalp. And once again he shouted a cry—a long, ringing cry—flinging his arms above his head. And the buffaloes replied, bellowing a wild answer that rolled like thunder along the plains.

Northward the great gallop swept— down the hollows, over the swells of the prairie, below the lonely ridges with their piles of stones that mark where Indians leave their dead. Crashing through the alder thickets beside the creeks and

Carved statue of a buffalo. Made by the Plains Native Americans. Green quartzite.

through the shallow creeks themselves, churning the water into a muddy foam, the mighty herd rolled on its way; and the thunder of its coming spread terror far and wide. The antelopes were off like the wind; the badgers and coyotes slunk into their holes. Even the wolves heeded the warning, vanishing shadowlike along the hollows to the east and west.

Little Wolf was beside himself with excitement and joy. It seemed as if he, too, were a member of the herd, as if the buffaloes had adopted him and made him their own.

Suddenly he saw something ahead. He could not see clearly because of the buffaloes in front of him, but it looked like a band of men. They were not mounted but were running swiftly on foot, as if to regain their ponies. At first, Little Wolf thought they were his own people; he knew by the outline of the country that the camp could not be far off. But then he saw that the men were not running toward the camp but away from it. Very swiftly, the thought flashed on him: They were Assiniboins, the deadly enemies of his tribe. They must have left their ponies some distance away in order to approach the camp unseen through the long grass and attack Little Wolf's people as they slept!

Little Wolf knew well that unless his enemies reached their ponies in time, the buffaloes would cut off their retreat. Once that great herd hurled itself upon them, nothing could save them from being trampled. He saw the Assiniboins making desperate efforts to escape. He cried shrilly, hoping that it would excite the buffaloes even more. The buffaloes seemed to answer his cries. They bore down upon the fleeing men at a terrible gallop, never slackening speed. One by one the Assiniboins were overtaken, knocked down, and trampled underfoot.

Suddenly, Little Wolf's pony went down too. The boy leaped clear as the animal fell. By this time they were on the outskirts of the herd, and before Little Wolf could get to his fallen pony, the last buffalo had passed. The pony struggled to its feet, trembling but unharmed, and with his arm around its neck, Little Wolf watched the herd disappear into the night . . .

Over the blazing campfires, when the wind moans eerily through the thickets of juniper and fir, they still speak of the great lake to the south where the buffaloes begin. But now they always add the name of Little Wolf to the legend, for he is the boy who led the buffaloes and saved his people.

IDENTIFYING FACTS

1. According to the legend, where did the buffaloes begin?

2. Explain why Little Wolf rides to the lake one morning.

3. What causes the buffaloes to stampede out of the water?

4. Tell how Little Wolf saves his people from their enemies.

INTERPRETING MEANINGS

5. Which events in this story of Little Wolf could really have happened? Which events could not happen in the world as we know it?

6. Suppose you wanted to tell this as a realistic story. How would you explain the fantastic details of Little Wolf's experience?

APPLYING MEANINGS

7. How do you think heroes are created today? Name three people you think are heroes or heroines.

8. Suppose that Little Wolf were living today. Suppose, in fact, that he has always lived in your town and that he attends your school. What kind of a "modern" boy do you think he might be?

9. Look through a newspaper; ask some of your relatives. Can you find a modern story of a heroic deed that might someday make a good legend? Do you know of any heroic legends that people keep passing on today?

FOLLOWING A SEQUENCE OF EVENTS

In a story, or **narrative,** clue words and phrases like *first, later, the next day,* and *at last* help you know when each event takes place. List the clue words and phrases that signal when the following events take place.

1. "At last it was so very big that Little Wolf could not bear it any longer. And so, one morning, very early, before the village was awake, he crept out of the tepee . . ."

2. "It was late in the afternoon when, at last, he sighted the lake."

3. "Suddenly, Little Wolf lifted himself up."

SETTING

A few stories could take place in any setting at all, but most stories take place in very particular settings. In fact, most stories would not be the same if they were set someplace else. Review the following stories. Tell where each one is set. Could any of these stories be set someplace else and still be the same? (Use the **Index of Authors and Titles** at the back of this book to locate the page on which each story begins.)

1. "Mr. Tumnus": could this story take place in Miami, Florida, in the year 2000?

2. "The Adventures of Tom Sawyer": could this story take place anywhere in the United States in the year 2000?

3. "Sounder": could this story take place in any modern city?

4. "All Summer in a Day": could this story take place in a modern suburb in the United States?

Language and Vocabulary

SENSORY DETAILS

Writers use description to create a feeling or mood. Vivid description is made up of **sensory details,** that is, words and phrases that appeal to your senses of sight, hearing, touch, taste, and smell.

Beaded moccasins.
Made by the Dakota,
Blackfoot, or Assiniboin
people.

National Museum of
the American Indian,
Smithsonian Institution.

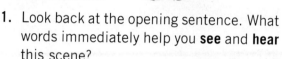

1. Look back at the opening sentence. What words immediately help you **see** and **hear** this scene?

2. Look back at the seventh paragraph beginning "On he went." What do you **see** and **hear** on the prairie? How does this description make you **feel** about the prairie setting?

3. Look back at the ninth paragraph, beginning "It was late in the afternoon." What words make you **see, hear,** and **feel** what it would be like to stand with Little Wolf on this late afternoon and look at the lake?

4. Look at the paragraph on page 257 that opens "Little Wolf felt the blood . . ." In this paragraph and the following ones, find the words that help you **see** and **hear** and **smell** the buffaloes and the great stampede. How does the writer make you **feel** about these great beasts?

Writing About Literature

WRITING FROM A DIFFERENT POINT OF VIEW
Imagine that you are a twelve-year-old Assiniboin who went along on the raiding party. You are the only one who managed to escape the buffalo stampede. You struggle back to your own camp. Write a paragraph telling what you would say to your people there.

Use the first-person pronoun *I.* Tell your people what happened. Try to use descriptive details telling what you **saw, heard, smelled,** and **felt** during the stampede.

About the Author

Olaf Baker was born in England in the 1870s. After leaving school, he traveled to the United States and spent many years traveling throughout the West. One of his favorite places was the vast Northern Plains area of the Midwest, which had been the territory of the Blackfoot, Crow, Sioux, Assiniboin, and Pawnee peoples. Baker wrote several stories and novels about Native Americans. "Where the Buffaloes Begin" was first published in 1915 by *St. Nicholas Magazine,* a very popular children's magazine of the time. When the story was republished in book form in 1981, it won the Caldecott Medal for its illustrations.

The All-American Slurp

LENSEY NAMIOKA

This comical short story is told by a young Chinese American girl. Her story is divided into six parts. You might use several readers and present parts of the story to the class. Before you present the story, decide how you will say the word *slurp*. How will you imitate the sounds of people eating celery *(crunch),* or the sounds of threads coming off the celery stalk *(z-z-zip)*? How will you say *shloop*, which is the sound of a slurp in any language?

The first time our family was invited out to dinner in America, we disgraced ourselves while eating celery. We had emigrated to this country from China, and during our early days here we had a hard time with American table manners.

In China we never ate celery raw, or any other kind of vegetable raw. We always had to disinfect the vegetables in boiling water first. When we were presented with our first relish tray, the raw celery caught us unprepared.

We had been invited to dinner by our neighbors, the Gleasons. After arriving at the house, we shook hands with our hosts and packed ourselves into a sofa. As our family of four sat stiffly in a row, my younger brother and I stole glances at our parents for a clue as to what to do next.

Mrs. Gleason offered the relish tray to Mother. The tray looked pretty, with its tiny red radishes, curly sticks of carrots, and long, slender stalks of pale green celery. "Do try some of the celery, Mrs. Lin," she said. "It's from a local farmer, and it's sweet."

Mother picked up one of the green stalks, and Father followed suit. Then I picked up a stalk, and my brother did too. So there we sat, each with a stalk of celery in our right hand.

Mrs. Gleason kept smiling. "Would you like to try some of the dip, Mrs. Lin? It's my own recipe: sour cream and onion flakes, with a dash of Tabasco sauce."

Most Chinese don't care for dairy products, and in those days I wasn't even ready to drink fresh milk. Sour cream sounded perfectly revolting. Our family shook our heads in unison.

Mrs. Gleason went off with the relish tray to the other guests, and we carefully watched to see what they did. Everyone seemed to eat the raw vegetables quite happily.

Mother took a bite of her celery. *Crunch.* "It's not bad!" she whispered.

Father took a bite of his celery. *Crunch.* "Yes, it *is* good," he said, looking surprised.

I took a bite, and then my brother. *Crunch, crunch.* It was more than good; it was delicious. Raw celery has a slight sparkle, a zingy taste that you don't get in cooked celery. When Mrs. Gleason came around with the relish tray, we each took another stalk of celery, except my brother. He took two.

There was only one problem: Long strings ran through the length of the stalk, and they got caught in my teeth. When I help my mother in the kitchen, I always pull the strings out before slicing celery.

I pulled the strings out of my stalk. *Z-z-zip, z-z-zip.* My brother followed suit. *Z-z-zip, z-z-zip, z-z-zip.* To my left, my parents were taking care of their own stalks. *Z-z-zip, z-z-zip, z-z-zip.*

Suddenly I realized that there was dead silence except for our zipping. Looking up, I saw that the eyes of everyone in the room were on our family. Mr. and Mrs. Gleason, their daughter Meg, who was my friend, and their neighbors the Badels—they were all staring at us as we busily pulled the strings off our celery.

That wasn't the end of it. Mrs. Gleason announced that dinner was served and invited us to the dining table. It was lavishly covered with platters of food, but we couldn't see any chairs around the table. So we helpfully carried over some dining chairs and sat down. All the other guests just stood there.

Mrs. Gleason bent down and whispered to us, "This is a buffet[1] dinner. You help yourselves to some food and eat it in the living room."

Our family beat a retreat back to the sofa as if chased by enemy soldiers. For the rest of the evening, too mortified to go back to the dining table, I nursed a bit of potato salad on my plate.

Next day Meg and I got on the school bus together. I wasn't sure how she would feel about me after the spectacle our family made at the party. But she was just the same as usual, and the only reference she made to the party was, "Hope you and your folks got enough to eat last night. You certainly didn't take very much. Mom never tries to figure out how much food to prepare. She just puts everything on the table and hopes for the best."

I began to relax. The Gleasons' dinner party wasn't so different from a Chinese meal after all. My mother also puts everything on the table and hopes for the best.

Meg was the first friend I had made after we came to America. I eventually got acquainted with a few other kids in school, but Meg was still the only real friend I had.

My brother didn't have any problems making friends. He spent all his time with some boys who were teaching him baseball, and in no time he could speak English much faster than I could—not better, but faster.

I worried more about making mistakes, and I spoke carefully, making sure I could say everything right before opening my mouth. At least I had a better accent than my parents, who never really got rid of their Chinese accent, even years later. My parents had both studied English in

---

1. **buffet** (boŏ·fā′).

school before coming to America, but what they had studied was mostly written English, not spoken.

Father's approach to English was a scientific one. Since Chinese verbs have no tense, he was fascinated by the way English verbs changed form according to whether they were in the present, past imperfect, perfect, pluperfect, future, or future perfect tense. He was always making diagrams of verbs and their inflections,[2] and he looked for opportunities to show off his mastery of the pluperfect and future perfect tenses, his two favorites. "I shall have finished my project by Monday," he would say smugly.

Mother's approach was to memorize lists of polite phrases that would cover all possible social situations. She was constantly muttering things like "I'm fine, thank you. And you?" Once she accidentally stepped on someone's foot, and hurriedly blurted, "Oh, that's quite all right!" Embarrassed by her slip, she resolved to do better next time. So when someone stepped on *her* foot, she cried, "You're welcome!"

In our own different ways, we made progress in learning English. But I had another worry, and that was my appearance. My brother didn't have to worry, since Mother bought him blue jeans for school, and he dressed like all the other boys. But she insisted that girls had to wear skirts.

By the time she saw that Meg and the other girls were wearing jeans, it was too late. My school clothes were bought already, and we didn't have money left to buy new outfits for me. We had too many other things to buy first, like furniture, pots, and pans.

The first time I visited Meg's house, she took me upstairs to her room, and I wound up trying on her clothes. We were pretty much the same size, since Meg was shorter and thinner than average. Maybe that's how we became friends in the first place. Wearing Meg's jeans and T-shirt, I looked at myself in the mirror. I could almost pass for an American—from the back, anyway. At least the kids in school wouldn't stop and stare at me in the hallways, which was what they did when they saw me in my white blouse and navy blue skirt that went a couple of inches below the knees.

When Meg came to my house, I invited her to try on my Chinese dresses, the ones with a high collar and slits up the sides. Meg's eyes were bright as she looked at herself in the mirror. She struck several sultry poses, and we nearly fell over laughing.

The dinner party at the Gleasons' didn't stop my growing friendship with Meg. Things were getting better for me in other ways too. Mother finally bought me some jeans at the end of the month, when Father got his paycheck. She wasn't in any hurry about buying them at first, until I worked on her. This is what I did. Since we didn't

---

2. **inflections** (in·flek′shəns): changes in the form of a verb to indicate things like tense or speaker (*am, are, was, were*, for examples, are just a few of the inflections of the verb *to be*).

have a car in those days, I often ran down to the neighborhood store to pick up things for her. The groceries cost less at a big supermarket, but the closest one was many blocks away. One day, when she ran out of flour, I offered to borrow a bike from our neighbor's son and buy a ten-pound bag of flour at the big supermarket. I mounted the boy's bike and waved to Mother. "I'll be back in five minutes!"

Before I started pedaling, I heard her voice behind me. "You can't go out in public like that! People can see all the way up to your thighs!"

"I'm sorry," I said innocently. "I thought you were in a hurry to get the flour." For dinner we were going to have pot-stickers (fried Chinese dumplings), and we needed a lot of flour.

"Couldn't you borrow a girl's bicycle?" complained Mother. "That way your skirt won't be pushed up."

"There aren't too many of those around," I said. "Almost all the girls wear jeans while riding a bike, so they don't see any point buying a girl's bike."

We didn't eat pot-stickers that evening, and Mother was thoughtful. Next day we took the bus downtown and she bought me a pair of jeans. In the same week, my brother made the baseball team of his junior high school, Father started taking driving lessons, and Mother discovered rummage sales. We soon got all the furniture we needed, plus a dart board and a 1,000-piece jigsaw puzzle (fourteen hours later, we discovered that it was a 999-piece jigsaw puzzle). There was hope that the Lins might become a normal American family after all.

Then came our dinner at the Lakeview restaurant.

The Lakeview was an expensive restaurant, one of those places where a headwaiter dressed in tails[3] conducted you to your seat, and the only light came from candles and flaming desserts. In one corner of the room a lady harpist played tinkling melodies.

Father wanted to celebrate, because he had just been promoted. He worked for an electronics company, and after his English started improving, his superiors decided to appoint him to a position more suited to his training. The promotion not only brought a higher salary but was also a tremendous boost to his pride.

Up to then we had eaten only in Chinese restaurants. Although my brother and I were becoming fond of hamburgers, my parents didn't care much for western food, other than chow mein.

But this was a special occasion, and Father asked his coworkers to recommend a really elegant restaurant. So there we were at the Lakeview, stumbling after the headwaiter in the murky dining room.

At our table we were handed our menus, and they were so big that to read mine I almost had to stand up again. But why bother? It was mostly in French, anyway.

Father, being an engineer, was always

---

3. **tails:** short for coattails. The expression refers to the long coattails on formal suit jackets.

systematic. He took out a pocket French dictionary. "They told me that most of the items would be in French, so I came prepared." He even had a pocket flashlight, the size of a marking pen. While Mother held the flashlight over the menu, he looked up the items that were in French.

"*Pâté en croûte,*"[4] he muttered. "Let's see . . . *pâté* is paste . . . *croûte* is crust . . . hmm . . . a paste in crust."

The waiter stood looking patient. I squirmed and died at least fifty times.

At long last Father gave up. "Why don't we just order four complete dinners at random?" he suggested.

"Isn't that risky?" asked Mother.

"The French eat some rather peculiar things, I've heard."

"A Chinese can eat anything a Frenchman can eat," Father declared.

The soup arrived in a plate. How do you get soup up from a plate? I glanced at the other diners, but the ones at the nearby tables were not on their soup course, while the more distant ones were invisible in the darkness.

Fortunately, my parents had studied books on western etiquette before they came to America. "Tilt your plate," whispered my mother. "It's easier to spoon the soup up that way."

She was right. Tilting the plate did the trick. But the etiquette book didn't say anything about what you did after the soup

---

4. *pâté en croûte* (pä·tā′ onh kro͞ot).

reached your lips. As any respectable Chinese knows, the correct way to eat your soup is to slurp. This helps to cool the liquid and prevent you from burning your lips. It also shows your appreciation.

We showed our appreciation. *Shloop,* went my father. *Shloop,* went my mother. *Shloop, shloop,* went my brother, who was the hungriest.

The lady harpist stopped playing to take a rest. And in the silence, our family's consumption of soup suddenly seemed unnaturally loud. You know how it sounds on a rocky beach when the tide goes out and the water drains from all those little pools? They go *shloop, shloop, shloop.* That was the Lin family, eating soup.

At the next table a waiter was pouring wine. When a large *shloop* reached him, he froze. The bottle continued to pour, and red wine flooded the tabletop and into the lap of a customer. Even the customer didn't notice anything at first, being also hypnotized by the *shloop, shloop, shloop.*

It was too much. "I need to go to the toilet," I mumbled, jumping to my feet. A waiter, sensing my urgency, quickly directed me to the ladies' room.

I splashed cold water on my burning face, and as I dried myself with a paper towel, I stared into the mirror. In this perfumed ladies' room, with its pink-and-silver wallpaper and marbled sinks, I looked completely out of place. What was I doing here? What was our family doing in the Lakeview restaurant? In America?

The door to the ladies' room opened. A woman came in and glanced curiously at me. I retreated into one of the toilet cubicles and latched the door.

Time passed—maybe half an hour, maybe an hour. Then I heard the door open again, and my mother's voice. "Are you in there? You're not sick, are you?"

There was real concern in her voice. A girl can't leave her family just because they slurp their soup. Besides, the toilet cubicle had a few drawbacks as a permanent residence. "I'm all right," I said, undoing the latch.

Mother didn't tell me how the rest of the dinner went, and I didn't want to know. In the weeks following, I managed to push the whole thing into the back of my mind, where it jumped out at me only a few times a day. Even now, I turn hot all over when I think of the Lakeview restaurant.

But by the time we had been in this country for three months, our family was definitely making progress toward becoming Americanized. I remember my parents' first PTA meeting. Father wore a neat suit and tie, and Mother put on her first pair of high heels. She stumbled only once. They met my homeroom teacher and beamed as she told them that I would make honor roll soon at the rate I was going. Of course, Chinese etiquette forced Father to say that I was a very stupid girl and Mother to protest that the teacher was showing favoritism toward me. But I could tell they were both very proud.

The day came when my parents announced that they wanted to give a dinner party. We had invited Chinese friends to eat with us before, but this dinner was going to be different. In addition to a Chinese-American family, we were going to invite the Gleasons.

"Gee, I can hardly wait to have dinner at your house," Meg said to me. "I just *love* Chinese food."

That was a relief. Mother was a good cook, but I wasn't sure if people who ate sour cream would also eat chicken gizzards stewed in soy sauce.

Mother decided not to take a chance with chicken gizzards. Since we had western guests, she set the table with large dinner plates, which we never used in Chinese meals. In fact we didn't use individual plates at all, but picked up food from the platters in the middle of the table and brought it directly to our rice bowls. Following the practice of Chinese-American restaurants, Mother also placed large serving spoons on the platters.

The dinner started well. Mrs. Gleason exclaimed at the beautifully arranged dishes of food: the colorful candied fruit in the sweet-and-sour pork dish, the noodle-thin shreds of chicken meat stir-fried with tiny peas, and the glistening pink prawns[5] in a ginger sauce.

At first I was too busy enjoying my food to notice how the guests were doing. But soon I remembered my duties. Sometimes guests were too polite to help themselves and you had to serve them with more food.

---

5. **prawns:** shellfish, something like large shrimp.

I glanced at Meg, to see if she needed more food, and my eyes nearly popped out at the sight of her plate. It was piled with food: The sweet-and-sour meat pushed right against the chicken shreds, and the chicken sauce ran into the prawns. She had been taking food from a second dish before she finished eating her helping from the first!

Horrified, I turned to look at Mrs. Gleason. She was dumping rice out of her bowl and putting it on her dinner plate. Then she ladled prawns and gravy on top of the rice and mixed everything together, the way you mix sand, gravel, and cement to make concrete.

I couldn't bear to look any longer, and I turned to Mr. Gleason. He was chasing a pea around his plate. Several times he got it to the edge, but when he tried to pick it up with his chopsticks, it rolled back toward the center of the plate again. Finally, he put down his chopsticks and picked up the pea with his fingers. He really did! A grown man!

All of us, our family and the Chinese guests, stopped eating to watch the activities of the Gleasons. I wanted to giggle. Then I caught my mother's eyes on me. She frowned and shook her head slightly, and I understood the message: The Gleasons were not used to Chinese ways, and they were just coping the best they could. For some reason I thought of celery strings.

When the main courses were finished, Mother brought out a platter of fruit. "I hope you weren't expecting a sweet des-

sert," she said. "Since the Chinese don't eat dessert, I didn't think to prepare any."

"Oh, I couldn't possibly eat dessert!" cried Mrs. Gleason. "I'm simply stuffed!"

Meg had different ideas. When the table was cleared, she announced that she and I were going for a walk. "I don't know about you, but I feel like dessert," she told me, when we were outside. "Come on, there's a Dairy Queen down the street. I could use a big chocolate milkshake!"

Although I didn't really want anything more to eat, I insisted on paying for the milkshakes. After all, I was still hostess.

Meg got her large chocolate milkshake and I had a small one. Even so, she was finishing hers while I was only half done. Toward the end she pulled hard on her straws and went *shloop, shloop*.

"Do you always slurp when you eat a milkshake?" I asked, before I could stop myself.

Meg grinned. "Sure. All Americans slurp."

Lensey Namioka (1929–   ) was born in Beijing, China, and came to the United States with her parents when she was nine. As a child, she liked to make up stories about princes, dragons, and magical powers. Namioka studied and taught mathematics before she began writing stories for young people. She has written a series of novels about two young samurai warriors, Matsuko and Zenta, in feudal Japan. She is also the author of *Who's Hu?,* a humorous story about a Chinese American teenager, and *The Phantom of Tiger Mountain,* a mystery set in China. A recent book, *The Loyal Cat,* is based on a story told by her husband's uncle, a priest at a "cat temple" in Japan.

EVALUATING SHORT STORIES

You have studied some key elements of short stories in this unit. Below are some standards that you can use to **evaluate,** or judge, the quality of any short story you read. Use a separate sheet of paper to answer the questions marked with this symbol: ∎.

Plot

1. *Is the conflict in the story clear and believable? Does the plot hold the reader's interest?* Even stories with elements of fantasy, such as John Gardner's "Dragon, Dragon," should include a well-developed conflict.

   ∎ What structure does Gardner use in "Dragon, Dragon" (page 166) to draw out the conflict and to create suspense?

Character

2. *Do the characters' actions match their words and thoughts? Are their actions clearly motivated by events in the story? Are the characters lifelike and believable?*

   ∎ Think about Jerry in "President Cleveland, Where Are You?" (page 178). How does Robert Cormier reveal Jerry as a complex individual, different from any other character in the story?

Setting

3. *What role does the setting play? Is the setting realistic or fantastic? Does the*
setting have an important connection to the plot, or could the story have been set in any time and place?

   ∎ In Elizabeth Enright's "Nancy" (page 233), how is the setting related to the central conflict of the story? How does the setting help to create atmosphere or mood in this story?

Point of View

4. *What point of view is used and what is its purpose?* For example, James Berry uses first-person point of view in "Becky and the Wheels-and-Brake Boys" (page 220) to help us understand why Becky wants a bicycle.

   ∎ How do you think Lloyd Alexander's "The Stone" (page 206) might have been different if Maibon had told the story from his own point of view?

Theme

5. *Does the story offer an important idea or message about people or about life?* Some stories are written purely for entertainment. From others, however, the reader can draw an important or valuable lesson. More often than not, readers draw a conclusion about the theme from what happens in the story.

   ∎ Choose *one* of the following stories: Ray Bradbury's "All Summer in a Day" (page 194) or Olaf Baker's "Where the Buffaloes Begin" (page 252). How would you state the message or theme of the story you have chosen? Test your statement by seeing if it includes all the important aspects of the story.

- Do you think Lensey Namioka's story "The All-American Slurp" (page 264) is purely humorous entertainment? Or does a more serious theme lie behind the comedy? How would you state Namioka's central message?

Use the questions on page 274 to evaluate the following story.

Rolls for the Czar

Robin Kinkead

This is a tale of the days of the Czars, of ermine and gold and pure white bread.

In Saint Petersburg[1] the Czar held his court with pomp and ceremony that dazzled peasants and ambassadors alike. His Winter Palace covered acres by the side of the frozen Neva.[2] It had pillars of lapis lazuli[3] and of rare stone from the Urals. Its halls held treasures from all the world.

Once a year the Czar paid a visit of state to Moscow, where the rich merchants lived, trade center of the Imperial Domain. Here he would sit in the throne room of the Kremlin,[4] where his ancestors once ruled warring Muscovy.[5]

There was another great man in Moscow—a baker, Markov by name. The master bakers of the city were famous, and Markov was prince among them. His cakes and pastry were renowned throughout all the Russias, but his rolls were the best of all: pure white, like the driven snow of the steppes, a crust just hard enough to crunch, the bread not too soft, but soft enough to hold the melted butter.

Merchant princes from the gold rivers of Siberia, chieftains from the Caucasus in high fur hats, nobles from their feudal estates in the country, all came to Moscow to eat Markov's rolls.

The Czar himself was a mighty eater and especially fond of Markov's delicacies. So one day in February, when it came time for a visit to Moscow, he was thinking of Markov and his art, anticipating the rolls. His private car bore the imperial coat of arms. The rest of the train was filled with grand dukes, princes of the blood, and noble ladies. The railroad track ran straight as an arrow five hundred miles through the snow, the white birch forests, and the pines.

The train chuffed into the Moscow station, into a morning of sun and frost. The sun sparkled on the gold domes of churches, it glittered on the cuirasses[6] of a regiment of guards, all men of noble birth.

---

1. **Saint Petersburg:** city in northwest Russia.
2. **Neva** (Nē′və, nyĕ·vă′): a river.
3. **lapis lazuli** (lăp′ĭs lăz′yo͞o·lē): an azure-blue gemstone.
4. **Kremlin** (krĕm′lən): the fortress of Moscow.
5. **Muscovy** (mŭs′kə·vē): the Russian Empire.

---

6. **cuirasses** (kwĭ·răs′əs): armor for the breast and back.

Smoke rose straight up from chimneys. Twin jets of steam snorted from the nostrils of the three horses of the Czar's troika.[7] The Czar has a fine appetite.

The horses' hoofs kicked up gouts of snow as they galloped over the moat and through the gate in the Kremlin wall. The Czar walked up the royal staircase, carpeted in red and lined with bowing servants. He was thinking of the rolls.

He went through the formal greetings with a distracted look, then sat down eagerly at the breakfast table. Not a glance did he give the caviar, the smoked sterlets,[8] the pheasant in aspic. He watched the door. When a royal footman came through carrying a silver platter loaded with rolls, the Czar smiled. All was well.

The Czar rubbed his hands and took a steaming roll. He broke it open and the smile vanished from his face. A dead fly lay embedded in the bread. Courtiers crowded around to look.

"Bring Markov here!" said the Czar, with one of his terrible glances.

The banquet room was silent in tense horror. Markov came in puffing slightly but bearing himself with the pride of a master artist.

"Look at this, Markov," said the Czar, pointing at the fly, "and tell me what it is."

Markov looked and stood frozen for a moment. Princes, nobles, and servants all leaned forward waiting for doom to strike him. The Czar could bend horseshoes in his bare hands. A word from him and the bleak wastes of Siberia lay waiting.

No man could tell what Markov thought, but they knew that a fly had endangered his life. He reached to the platter and picked up the fly. He put it in his mouth and ate it. Every eye watched him swallow.

"It is a raisin, Sire," he said.

Wrath faded from the Czar's face. He broke out laughing and the nobles relaxed.

"Markov," he said, "we grant you a coat of arms with a fly as the motif.[9] A fly imperiled your life and a fly saved your life."

And the Czar went on with his rolls.

---

7. **troika** (troi′kə): a small carriage drawn by a team of three horses.
8. **sterlets** (stûr′lĭts): sturgeon, a source of caviar.

9. **motif** (mō·tēf′): main figure in the design.

WRITING A SHORT STORY

*I*n a **short story** you entertain your readers by creating lifelike characters, together with a well-developed plot and a specific setting. In this unit you have studied some of the important elements of short stories. Now you will have the chance to write a story of your own.

Prewriting ᴧᴧ

1. Start to find a story idea by thinking of familiar people, places, and situations. Notice a person or problem—and give your imagination free rein. You might want to ask yourself some "What if?" questions such as the following:

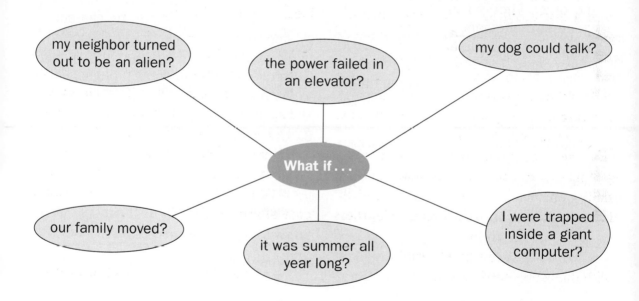

my neighbor turned out to be an alien?

the power failed in an elevator?

my dog could talk?

What if . . .

our family moved?

it was summer all year long?

I were trapped inside a giant computer?

You can also use these methods to find a story idea:

- brainstorming with classmates
- reviewing notes for this unit
- looking at family albums
- skimming news stories
- observing people in a park or mall

2. Work on turning your story idea into a

plot by making some notes on the following key plot elements:

- introduction
- conflict
- climax
- resolution

Pay special attention to the main **conflict** or problem. Plan to introduce this conflict early in your story in order to grab the reader's attention. Here are three types of conflict to consider:

- a person versus another person (external conflict)
- a person versus a force of nature (external conflict)
- a struggle or problem within a character's mind (internal conflict)

When you have identified the key conflict of your story, decide what the **climax** or **high point** will be—the point where the conflict is settled one way or the other. This is usually the point of greatest excitement or tension: for example, the moment in Lloyd Alexander's "The Stone" when Maibon is finally able to throw away the magic stone (page 215). [See **Focus** assignment on page 176.]

3. Make some notes about the **characters** for your story. Fill out a character chart like the one below for each person you create:

Character Chart
Name: _____ Age: _____
Physical Appearance: _____
Way of Moving and Speaking: _____
Personality Traits: _____
Likes and Dislikes: _____
Habits: _____

[See **Focus** assignment on page 191.]

4. Make a list of details for the **setting** of your story—the time and place of the events. Pay special attention to **sensory details** when you imagine the setting: details that appeal to sight, hearing, taste, smell, and touch. Think about the possible relationship between setting and mood in your story. [See **Focus** assignment on page 251.]

5. Decide on the **point of view,** or vantage point, from which you will tell your story. In **first-person point of view,** your narrator will be a character in the story and will use the first-person pronouns *I, me,* and *my.* In **third-person point of view,** the narrator will be outside the story. The narrator will be an omniscient or "all-knowing" storyteller who knows everything about the characters and their problems. If you choose this point of view, you will refer to your characters with third-person pronouns such as *he, she,* and *they.* [See **Focus** assignment on page 231.]

6. Use all the notes you have made so far to create a **story map,** a plan that lists all the main elements of your story. [For a sample story map, see **Literary Elements** on page 175.]

Writing

1. When you write your story, use **chronological** or **time order** to tell events. Remember that **transitions** can help your readers to follow your story better. Here are some helpful **transitional words and phrases:**

after	finally	soon
at once	first	suddenly
before	meanwhile	then
eventually	next	when

2. You can make your story more lifelike if you use **dialogue,** or the words that characters actually say. Say the words

aloud, and decide if they sound like real conversation. When you write dialogue, feel free to use brief phrases, contractions, and slang.

3. Remember that **vivid action verbs** and **sensory details** are two powerful tools a writer has to make a story lively.

Evaluating and Revising

1. When you have finished your first draft, put it aside for a while. Then reread your writing; remember that your audience wants to be entertained. Pay attention to using exact, vivid words. Here is how one writer revised a passage from a short story.

Writer's Model

Raven knew that he might have only ~~a short time~~ minutes to save the President's life. He ~~looked at~~ frantically scanned the computer printout, ~~He~~ Searching ~~looked~~ for initials that matched the code letters for the world's top terrorists. ~~He~~ When He came up blank. ~~He~~ took a deep breath.

"Something's ~~strange,~~ wrong," he murmured. "I'm just not ~~understanding~~ getting one piece of ~~this situation.~~ puzzle."

2. You may find the following checklist helpful as you revise your short story.

Checklist for Evaluation and Revision

✔ Do I grab the reader's attention at the beginning?
✔ Do I present a strong conflict for one of the main characters?
✔ Are the characters lifelike and believable?
✔ Do I tell the events in chronological order?
✔ Is there a clear climax or turning point?
✔ Is the setting clear?
✔ Does the resolution of the story make sense?

Proofreading and Publishing

1. Proofread your short story and correct any errors you find in grammar, usage, and mechanics. (Here you may find it helpful to refer to the **Handbook for Revision** on pages 750–785.) Then prepare a final version of your story by making a clean copy.

2. Consider some of the following publication methods for your story:

   - join with classmates to produce a "story hour" for younger children
   - illustrate your story with drawings or other art work and post it on the class bulletin board
   - submit your story to the school or community newspaper

Portfolio If your teacher approves, you may wish to keep a copy of your work in your writing folder or portfolio.

Poetry

Inside a Poem
EVE MERRIAM

It doesn't always have to rhyme,
but there's the repeat of a beat,
    somewhere
an inner chime that makes you want to
tap your feet or swerve in a curve;
a lilt, a leap, a lightning-split:—
thunderstruck the consonants jut,
while the vowels open wide as waves in
    the noon-blue sea.

You hear with your heels, your eyes feel
what they never touched before:
fins on a bird, feathers on a deer;
taste all colors, inhale
memory and tomorrow and always the
    tang is today.

Mt. Fuji from Kajikazawa in the Province of Kai,
from *The Thirty-six Views of Fuji* by Hokusai.

The Metropolitan Museum of Art, New York, Rogers Fund,
1922. (JP1327)

*P*oetry is the shortest kind of writing, but it can be the most demanding to read. This is because poets pack a lot of meaning into a very few words. Here is how one reader responded to this very short poem. Do you think it has more than one layer of meaning?

The Darkling Elves

JACK PRELUTSKY

ONE READER'S RESPONSE

What does "darkling" mean? Dark? Are elves good or bad?

I like the sounds of the poem.

I like the beat. It's fun.

Good pictures in the poem. (What is "garish"?)

Gross! They eat you?

Hungry for what? This is repeated.

The rhymes are good.

Again. Same line. They eat people? Or bite them?

They must be tiny. Whom is the poet talking to?

Again! I just had an idea. Maybe these elves are mosquitoes? Or bats? Maybe the poem is meant to be funny? Or is it really scary? What do others think?

In wildest woods, on treetop shelves,
sit evil beings with evil selves—
they are the dreaded darkling elves
and they are always hungry.

In garish garb of capes and hoods,   5
they wait and watch within their woods
to peel your flesh and steal your goods
for they are always hungry.

Through brightest days and darkest nights
these terrifying tiny sprites   10
await to strike and take their bites
for they are always hungry.

Watch every leaf of every tree,
for once they pounce you cannot flee—
their teeth are sharp as sharp can be . . .   15
and they are always hungry.

Looking at Yourself as a Reader

Suppose you were this reader. How would you sum up this little poem?

1. You might say that it has **sounds** you like. You noticed that the poem **rhymes** and that it has a good **beat.**

2. You might say that you noticed that one line is **repeated** four times. The line gave you a scary feeling.

3. You might say that at the end of the poem you had an idea: You thought that maybe the poet was talking about mosquitoes or bats that attack people in the woods.

Read the poem over again, this time aloud. Do you have any other ideas about it?

Compare your response with the responses of your classmates. What do you agree on? What do you disagree about? Would you recommend the poem to anyone else?

The Lawrence Tree
by Georgia O'Keeffe
(1929). Oil on canvas.
Wadsworth Atheneum,
Hartford, Connecticut.
The Ella Gallup Sumner
and Mary Catlin Sumner
Collection.

STORY POEMS

Centuries ago, all stories were told in poetry. In ancient Greece, stories about the post-war wanderings of the soldier Odysseus were told in poetry. At one time in the United States, people used to read long stories in poetry the way we read best-selling novels today. Story poems often have a strong beat and strong rhymes. They often use a lot of repetition. All of these elements help the storyteller remember the lines. They also help keep the listener interested. Here are two lively story poems, which are also wonderful nonsense. Be sure to read them aloud.

Fantastic creatures are the characters in this poem, which moves at a gallop from start to finish, with lots of hilarious action along the way. You've probably guessed, if you haven't already peeked, that the poet is Dr. Seuss. "The Sneetches," like some of his other poems, is meant for both children and adults. Perhaps you read this poem when you were a little child. But did you realize that under the clever wordplay there is a very important idea? "The Sneetches" must be read aloud. Perhaps you can share it with a younger student.

The Sneetches   DR. SEUSS (THEODOR GEISEL)

Now, the Star-Belly Sneetches
Had bellies with stars.
The Plain-Belly Sneetches
Had none upon thars.

Those stars weren't so big. They were really so small   5
You might think such a thing wouldn't matter at all.

But, because they had stars, all the Star-Belly Sneetches
Would brag, "We're the best kind of Sneetch on the beaches."
With their snoots in the air, they would sniff and they'd snort
"We'll have nothing to do with the Plain-Belly sort!"   10
And whenever they met some, when they were out walking,
They'd hike right on past them without even talking.

When the Star-Belly children went out to play ball,
Could a Plain Belly get in the game . . . ? Not at all.
You only could play if your bellies had stars   15
And the Plain-Belly children had none upon thars.

When the Star-Belly Sneetches had frankfurter roasts
Or picnics or parties or marshmallow toasts,
They never invited the Plain-Belly Sneetches.
They left them out cold, in the dark of the beaches.   20
They kept them away. Never let them come near.
And that's how they treated them year after year.

Then ONE day, it seems . . . while the Plain-Belly Sneetches
Were moping and doping alone on the beaches,
Just sitting there wishing their bellies had stars . . .   25
A stranger zipped up in the strangest of cars!

"My friends," he announced in a voice clear and keen,
"My name is Sylvester McMonkey McBean.
And I've heard of your troubles. I've heard you're unhappy.
But I can fix that. I'm the Fix-it-Up Chappie.   30
I've come here to help you. I have what you need.
And my prices are low. And I work at great speed.
And my work is one hundred per cent guaranteed!"

Then, quickly, Sylvester McMonkey McBean
Put together a very peculiar machine.   35
And he said, "You want stars like a Star-Belly Sneetch . . . ?
My friends, you can have them for three dollars each!"

"Just pay me your money and hop right aboard!"
So they clambered inside. Then the big machine roared
And it klonked. And it bonked. And it jerked. And it berked
And it bopped them about. But the thing really worked!
When the Plain-Belly Sneetches popped out, they had stars!
They actually did. They had stars upon thars!

Then they yelled at the ones who had stars at the start,
"We're exactly like you! You can't tell us apart.   45
We're all just the same, now, you snooty old smarties!
And now we can go to your frankfurter parties."

"Good grief!" groaned the ones who had stars at the first.
"We're *still* the best Sneetches and they are the worst.
But, now, how in the world will we know," they all frowned,   50
"If which kind is what, or the other way round?"

Then up came McBean with a very sly wink
And he said, "Things are not quite as bad as you think.
So you don't know who's who. That is perfectly true.
But come with me, friends. Do you know what I'll do?   55
I'll make you, again, the best Sneetches on beaches
And all it will cost you is ten dollars eaches."

"Belly stars are no longer in style," said McBean.
"What you need is a trip through my Star-*Off* Machine.
This wondrous contraption will take *off* your stars   60
So you won't look like Sneetches who have them on thars."
And that handy machine
Working very precisely
Removed all the stars from their tummies quite nicely.

Then, with snoots in the air, they paraded about   65
And they opened their beaks and they let out a shout,
"We know who is who! Now there isn't a doubt.
The best kind of Sneetches are Sneetches without!"

Then, of course, those with stars all got frightfully mad.
To be wearing a star now was frightfully bad.   70
Then, of course, old Sylvester McMonkey McBean
Invited *them* into his Star-Off Machine.

Then, of course from THEN on, as you probably guess,
Things really got into a horrible mess.

All the rest of that day, on those wild screaming beaches,   75
The Fix-it-Up Chappie kept fixing up Sneetches.
Off again! On again!
In again! Out again!
Through the machines they raced round and about again,
Changing their stars every minute or two.   80
They kept paying money. They kept running through
Until neither the Plain nor the Star-Bellies knew
Whether this one was that one . . . or that one was this one
Or which one was what one . . . or what one was who.

Then, when every last cent
Of their money was spent,
The Fix-it-Up Chappie packed up
And he went.

And he laughed as he drove
In his car up the beach,
"They never will learn.
No. You can't teach a Sneetch!"

But McBean was quite wrong. I'm quite happy to say
That the Sneetches got really quite smart on that day,
The day they decided that Sneetches are Sneetches
And no kind of Sneetch is the best on the beaches.
That day, all the Sneetches forgot about stars
And whether they had one, or not, upon thars.

For Study and Discussion

IDENTIFYING DETAILS

1. A **conflict** is introduced right at the beginning of this story poem. Why do the Star-Bellies feel that they are better than the Plain-Bellies? How do the Star-Bellies treat the Plain-Bellies?

2. Who is McBean? What does he say he can do for the Plain-Bellies? What does he think of the Sneetches?

3. At the end of the poem, how have the Sneetches changed? What caused them to change?

INTERPRETING MEANINGS

4. In your own words, explain this story poem's **lesson** or **moral.** Do you think it is an important lesson?

APPLYING MEANINGS

5. What real-life people behave like the Sneetches or like Sylvester McMonkey McBean?

Literary Elements

RHYTHM

The **rhythm** of a poem is the repetition of stressed and unstressed syllables in each line. In the following lines, the syllables that get heavy stresses are marked with a (´).

Read the lines aloud and exaggerate the stressed sounds:

> Now, the Star-Belly Sneetches
> Had bellies with stars.

"The Sneetches" is told in very regular sing-song rhythms. Read the poem aloud to feel its beat. Does the poem move quickly or slowly? Does its rhythm make the story more fun to read? Practice reading the poem aloud, as if you were going to read it to a young child. Can you vary the way you read some verses, making them either fast or slow, loud or soft?

Language and Vocabulary

WORDPLAY

To make his lines rhyme, and to add to the fun, Dr. Seuss sometimes changed a spelling, added a new ending sound, or even invented a word. Find the funny words that Dr. Seuss made up in lines 4, 40, and 57. What word does each made-up word rhyme with?

Make up another line of poetry to rhyme with the following line. (You will have to invent a rhyming word because no word in English rhymes with *orange.*)

> Eva was eating an orange

Writing About Literature

DESCRIBING AND ILLUSTRATING A FANTASTIC CREATURE

Write three sentences describing a creature who lives on an imaginary world and who thinks he or she is superior to other creatures. Make up a name for your creature. If you like, draw its picture in the style of Dr. Seuss.

Dr. Seuss, whose real name was Theodor Seuss Geisel (1904–1991), was born in Springfield, Massachusetts. He began drawing fantastic animals while he was still a child. (His father ran the local zoo.) An art teacher told him that he would never learn to draw, and twenty-nine publishers rejected his first children's book, *And to Think That I Saw It on Mulberry Street.* But Dr. Seuss went on to write and illustrate more than forty books for children. Judged by the number of books he has sold—at least eighty million copies—he is perhaps the most popular writer in the world. ("Dr." is a title that he gave himself. He also wrote under the name Theo LeSieg—"Geisel" spelled backward.) When asked the question "What is rhyme?" Dr. Seuss replied, "A rhyme is something without which I would probably be in the dry-cleaning business!"

Behind the Scenes

"Dr. Seuss"

The "Dr. Seuss" name is a combination of my middle name and the fact that I had been studying for my doctorate when I quit to become a cartoonist. My father had always wanted to see a Dr. in front of my name, so I attached it. I figured by doing that, I saved him about ten thousand dollars.

—Theodor Geisel

Most members of the middle and upper classes in nine-teenth-century England were highly serious, proper folk. Then along came Edward Lear. Lear was a professional artist, but he also loved words and nonsense.

You probably have a sieve (siv) in your kitchen at home. It's also called a sifter or strainer. The main thing to know about a sieve is that it is full of holes.

The Jumblies

EDWARD LEAR

1

They went to sea in a Sieve, they did,
  In a Sieve they went to sea:
In spite of all their friends could say,
On a winter's morn, on a stormy day,
  In a Sieve they went to sea!   5
And when the Sieve turned round and round,
And everyone cried, "You'll all be drowned!"
They called aloud, "Our Sieve ain't big,
But we don't care a button! we don't care a fig!
  In a Sieve we'll go to sea!"   10
    Far and few, far and few,
      Are the lands where the Jumblies live;
    Their heads are green, and their hands are blue,
    And they went to sea in a Sieve.

2

They sailed away in a Sieve, they did,   15
  In a Sieve they sailed so fast,
With only a beautiful pea-green veil
Tied with a ribbon by way of a sail;
  To a small tobacco-pipe mast;
And everyone said, who saw them go,   20

"O won't they be soon upset, you know!
For the sky is dark, and the voyage is long,
And happen what may, it's extremely wrong
   In a Sieve to sail so fast!"
      Far and few, far and few,   25
        Are the lands where the Jumblies live;
      Their heads are green, and their hands are blue,
        And they went to sea in a Sieve.

3

The water it soon came in, it did,
   The water it soon came in;   30
So to keep them dry, they wrapped their feet
In a pinky paper all folded neat,
   And they fastened it down with a pin.
And they passed the night in a crockery jar,
And each of them said, "How wise we are!   35
Though the sky be dark, and the voyage be long,
Yet we never can think we were rash or wrong,
   While round in our Sieve we spin!"
      Far and few, far and few,
        Are the lands where the Jumblies live;   40
      Their heads are green, and their hands are blue,
        And they went to sea in a Sieve.

4

And all night long they sailed away;
   And when the sun went down,
They whistled and warbled a moony song   45
To the echoing sound of a coppery gong,
   In the shade of the mountains brown.
"O Timballoo! How happy we are,
When we live in a Sieve and a crockery jar,
And all night long in the moonlight pale,   50
We sail away with a pea-green sail,
   In the shade of the mountains brown!"
      Far and few, far and few,

Are the lands where the Jumblies live;
  Their heads are green, and their hands are blue,   55
    And they went to sea in a Sieve.

5

They sailed to the Western Sea, they did,
  To a land all covered with trees,
And they bought an Owl, and a useful Cart,
And a pound of Rice, and a Cranberry Tart,   60
  And a hive of silvery Bees.
And they bought a Pig, and some green Jackdaws,
And a lovely Monkey with lollipop paws,
And forty bottles of Ring-Bo-Ree,
  And no end of Stilton Cheese.   65
    Far and few, far and few,
      Are the lands where the Jumblies live;
    Their heads are green, and their hands are blue,
      And they went to sea in a Sieve.

6

And in twenty years they all came back,   70
  In twenty years or more,
And everyone said, "How tall they've grown!
For they've been to the Lakes, and the Torrible Zone,
  And the hills of the Chankly Bore'';
And they drank their health, and gave them a feast   75
Of dumplings made of beautiful yeast;
And everyone said, "If we only live,
We too will go to sea in a Sieve,—
  To the hills of the Chankly Bore!''
    Far and few, far and few,   80
      Are the lands where the Jumblies live;
    Their heads are green, and their hands are blue,
      And they went to sea in a Sieve.

For Study and Discussion

IDENTIFYING DETAILS

1. What do the Jumblies look like?

2. Describe the Jumblies' "boat."

3. Which lines tell how the sailing Jumblies feel about themselves?

4. Where did the Jumblies land and what did they buy there?

INTERPRETING MEANINGS

5. **Nonsense** is Lear's trademark. What is nonsensical about the Jumblies' boat and the way they keep their feet dry? Find two examples of nonsensical place names. How would you sing a "moony song" (line 45)? How would you illustrate "lollipop paws" (line 63)?

APPLYING MEANINGS

6. Many English people in Lear's day traveled to very exotic parts of the world. They brought back to England the most amazing souvenirs. How are the Jumblies like those travelers? Are the Jumblies like tourists today?

Literary Elements

ALLITERATION

Alliteration gives this story poem a lively, happy feeling. It also makes us laugh. **Alliteration** is the repetition of consonant sounds, especially at the beginning of words placed close together. An example of alliteration is the repeated *s* sound in:

> In a Sieve they went to sea

Find at least two other examples of alliteration in the **refrain,** the four lines that end each stanza. Can you find the alliteration in lines 32—33? In lines 44—45? In line 63?

Write three sentences of your own using silly alliteration.

Focus on Writing a Poem

FINDING A SUBJECT

You can find a subject for a poem of your own by thinking about people and things you know best. For example, "The Jumblies" is a poem about a journey. Would one of your own journeys be a good subject for a poem?

Here are some more examples of subjects you might consider:

riding a bike	an apple
a mouse	a snowflake
a crowded mall	playing baseball
a good friend	a relative

Make your own list of three possible subjects for a poem. Get together with a partner and exchange lists. Brainstorm with each other about how you might develop each subject. What words could you use to describe your subject? Save your notes.

About the Author

Many people believe that **Edward Lear** (1812—1888) is the world's greatest writer and illustrator of nonsense verse. Lear began writing funny verses as a hobby, but his nonsense became a safety valve for a life plagued by sickness and lack of money. Lear was the youngest of twenty-one children. He began earning his living as a commercial artist when he was only fifteen. Like the Jumblies, Lear loved to travel. He is said to have written letters regularly to 444 people. Lear's first *Book of Nonsense,* a collection of five-line humorous poems called **limericks,** was written to amuse a friend's children. "The Jumblies" is from his second book, *Nonsense Songs, Stories, Botany, and Alphabets.*

Sound effects are important to poets. In fact, poets often recite their poetry as they write so that they can hear the sounds of the words. A poet can use many kinds of sound effects in a poem.

1. **Rhymes:** chiming sounds, especially at the ends of words (*shelves/selves/elves*).

2. **Rhythm:** the repetition of stressed and unstressed syllables in a line ("In garish garb of capes and hoods").

3. **Refrain:** the repetition of a word or phrase or line throughout a poem.

4. **Alliteration:** the repetition of consonant sounds in several words ("in wildest woods").

5. **Onomatopoeia:** the use of words with sounds that echo their meaning (*sizzle, smack, drip, plunk, ticktock).*

How do you think snow sounds? Here is a poem that uses sound effects to help you "hear snow." Be sure to read it aloud.

Cynthia in the Snow

GWENDOLYN BROOKS

It SUSHES.
It hushes
The loudness in the road.
It flitter-twitters,
And laughs away from me.
It laughs a lovely whiteness,

And whitely whirs away,
To be
Some otherwhere,
Still white as milk or shirts.
So beautiful it hurts.

Here is a bold little girl's voice telling everyone how brave she is. But *is* she as brave as she sounds? Before you read the poem, make a list of three things that you think frighten most small children—even those who really have nothing to be afraid of at all.

Kept In by Edward Lamson Henry (1888). Oil on canvas.

New York State Historical Association, Cooperstown.

Life Doesn't Frighten Me

MAYA ANGELOU

Shadows on the wall
Noises down the hall
Life doesn't frighten me at all
Bad dogs barking loud
Big ghosts in a cloud   5
Life doesn't frighten me at all.

Mean old Mother Goose
Lions on the loose
They don't frighten me at all
Dragons breathing flame   10
On my counterpane°
That doesn't frighten me at all.

I go boo
Make them shoo
I make fun   15
Way they run
I won't cry
So they fly
I just smile
They go wild   20
Life doesn't frighten me at all.

Tough guys in a fight
All alone at night
Life doesn't frighten me at all.
Panthers in the park   25
Strangers in the dark
No, they don't frighten me at all.

That new classroom where
Boys all pull my hair
(Kissy little girls   30
With their hair in curls)
They don't frighten me at all.

Don't show me frogs and snakes
And listen for my scream,
If I'm afraid at all   35
It's only in my dreams.

I've got a magic charm
That I keep up my sleeve,
I can walk the ocean floor
And never have to breathe.   40

Life doesn't frighten me at all
Not at all
Not at all.
Life doesn't frighten me at all.

---

11. **counterpane:** quilt.

1. What is the refrain in this poem?

2. Do you think it carries the speaker's main message?

3. Would you recite the refrain exactly the same way each time it occurs?

For Study and Discussion

IDENTIFYING DETAILS

1. List all the things this brave girl is *not* afraid of.

2. When *is* she afraid?

3. What does her magic charm do?

INTERPRETING MEANINGS

4. Do you think that, with all her boldness and brave remarks, this speaker is not so brave after all? Talk about your responses.

5. Why do you think the speaker calls Mother Goose "mean"?

6. What do you think she means by "kissy little girls"?

7. Which of the little girl's fears might come from her imagination? Which are real?

APPLYING MEANINGS

8. Where do you think children's imaginary fears come from? What do you think of the old Mother Goose stories and fairy tales? Do you think that most small children are seriously frightened by them?

Literary Elements

REFRAIN

A **refrain** is a word or a phrase or a line that is repeated over and over again in a poem or song. Think of songs that are popular today, and you'll probably be able to find a refrain in every one. Can you make a list of at least three popular refrains?

Often refrains carry the main message of a song or poem.

Focus on Writing a Poem

EXPERIMENTING WITH REFRAIN

Have you ever found yourself humming a tune or repeating a phrase that you just couldn't get out of your head?

Working with a small group of partners, try building a short poem around a repeated phrase, or **refrain.** First, choose a phrase that the group likes. Then brainstorm to find images, examples, or incidents that fit the phrase. Save your notes.

If you wish, choose one phrase from the list below to get your group started:

They're so cool	Put on a smile
Life's a peach	Tell it out!
Baseball fever	Grrrr!

EXPLORING RHYMES IN COUPLETS

Not all poems have to rhyme, but exploring rhymes can be fun and can give you ideas for poems. You can explore rhymes by writing **couplets,** or pairs of rhyming lines like this one:

Dan, Dan, the ice cream man,
Drives a blue and silver van.

Write two or three couplets of your own and then share them with a partner. Save your writing.

As everyone knows who has read the first volume of her autobiography, called *I Know Why the Caged Bird Sings,* **Maya Angelou** (1928–   ) grew up with her grandmother in the small town of Stamps, Arkansas. She went on to become a dancer, an actress, a writer, and a TV producer. The second and third volumes of her autobiography are called *Gather Together in My Name* and *Singin' and Swingin' and Gettin'*

Merry Like Christmas. Four books of her poetry are called *Just Give Me a Cool Drink of Water 'Fore I Diiie, Oh Pray My Wings Are Gonna Fit Me Well, And Still I Rise,* and *Shaker, Why Don't You Sing?* Her lively titles show that Angelou loves words and the colorful rhythms and slang of everyday speech. Her titles also show that she was nourished on African American music, especially gospel songs, spirituals, and blues. In 1993 she recited her poem "On the Pulse of Morning" at President Clinton's inauguration.

"All things are possible . . ."

Behind the Scenes

I believe all things are possible for a human being, and I don't think there's anything in the world I can't do. Of course, I can't be five foot four because I'm six feet tall. I can't be a man because I'm a woman. The physical gifts are given to me, just like having two arms is a gift. In my creative source, wherever that is, I don't see why I can't sculpt. Why shouldn't I? Human beings sculpt. I'm a human being.

All my work, my life, everything is about survival. All my work is meant to say, "You may encounter many defeats, but you must not be defeated." In fact, the encountering may be the very experience which creates the vitality and the power to endure.

—Maya Angelou

Habits of the Hippopotamus

ARTHUR GUITERMAN

The hippopotamus is strong
    And huge of head and broad of bustle;
The limbs on which he rolls along
    Are big with hippopotomuscle.

He does not greatly care for sweets   5
    Like ice cream, apple pie, or custard,
But takes to flavor what he eats
    A little hippopotomustard.

The hippopotamus is true
    To all his principles, and just;   10
He always tries his best to do
    The things one hippopotomust.

He never rides in trucks or trams,
    In taxicabs or omnibuses,
And so keeps out of traffic jams   15
    And other hippopotomusses.

IDENTIFYING DETAILS

1. What *are* the habits of the hippopotamus?

2. Much of the humor in the poem comes from portmanteau (pôrt·man·tō′) words. A portmanteau is a suitcase that opens into two sections. **Portmanteau** words are invented by combining words. For example, *smog* is a portmanteau word; it is a combination of *smoke* and *fog*. Find four silly portmanteau words in the poem.

INTERPRETING MEANINGS

3. A bustle (bus′l) is a framework or padding worn many years ago by women to puff out their long skirts at the rear. Some bustles were huge. What does the poet mean when he says the hippo is "broad of bustle"?

4. Think of what a hippo looks like (see the handsome fellow on page 306). Is this the way you would expect a hippo to behave if it were a person? How would you have described the habits of the hippo?

Literary Elements

RHYME SCHEME

Words that rhyme end in the same sound or sounds, like *strong* and *along*. A **rhyme scheme** is the pattern of rhyming words at the ends of lines in a poem. Suppose you give each new rhyme in stanza 1 a letter. You will get this pattern of rhyme: **abab.** What is the rhyme scheme in the other three stanzas?

The Granger Collection, New York.

Colored engraving by Gustave Doré.

Focus on Writing a Poem

PLAYING WITH WORDS

Some poets, as you see from Guiterman's verses, like to make up comical words. But we all have these impulses to play with language. The following story plays with words by exchanging the first letter of one word for the first letter of another. After you read this story aloud (if you can stand it), write your own fairy tale in Prinderella style.

Prinderella and the Cinch

Twonce upon a wime there was a gritty little pearl named Prinderella who lived with her two sugly isters and her sticked weptmother, who made her pine the shots and shans and do all the other wirty dirk around the house.

Well, one day the Ping issued a Kroclamation saying that all geligible irls were invited to the Palace for a drancy fess ball. Well the two sugly isters and the sticked weptmother were going but Prinderella couldn't go because she didn't have a drancy fess. But along came her Gary Fodmother and she changed a cumpkin into a poach and hice into morses and her rirty dags into a drancy fess. And she sent her off to the palace saying "Now, Prinderella, you come home at the moke of stridnight or—your drancy fess will be turned into rirty dags again." So Prinderella went to the stalace and she pranced all night with the Cinch.

But at the moke of stridnight she ran down the stalace peps and on the bottom pep she slopped her dripper—now wasn't that a shirty dame?

The next day the Ping issued another Kroclamation saying that all geligible irls should sly on the tripper. Well, the two sugly isters and the sticked weptmother, they slied on the tripper but it fiddent dit. Prinderella slied on the tripper and it fid dit.

So Prinderella and the Cinch mot garried and hived lappily ever after.

About the Author

Arthur Guiterman (gē'tər·man) (1871–1943) was born in Vienna, Austria, but his parents were American citizens. The family returned to New York before Guiterman started school. Even as a child, Guiterman loved animals. Many of his clever animal poems first appeared in *Life* magazine and *The New Yorker.* Guiterman also wrote the words for many songs and operas.

The Rum Tum Tugger   *T. S. ELIOT*

Narrator **Girls' chorus**	The Rum Tum Tugger is a Curious Cat: If you offer him pheasant he would rather have grouse.° If you put him in a house he would much prefer a flat, If you put him in a flat then he'd rather have a house. If you set him on a mouse then he only wants a rat, 5 If you set him on a rat then he'd rather chase a mouse.

Narrator	Yes the Rum Tum Tugger is a Curious Cat—
	   And there isn't any call for me to shout it:
	     For he will do
	     As he do do 10
	       And there's no doing anything about it!

Narrator **Boys' chorus**	The Rum Tum Tugger is a terrible bore: When you let him in, then he wants to be out; He's always on the wrong side of every door, And as soon as he's at home, then he'd like to get about. 15 He likes to lie in the bureau drawer, But he makes such a fuss if he can't get out.

Narrator	Yes the Rum Tum Tugger is a Curious Cat—
	   And it isn't any use for you to doubt it:
	     For he will do 20
	     As he do do
	       And there's no doing anything about it!

2. **pheasant . . . grouse:** birds used for food, considered delicacies.

The Cat by an unknown American painter (c. 1840).

National Gallery of Art, Washington, D.C. Gift of Edgar William and Bernice Chrysler Garbisch.

Narrator	The Rum Tum Tugger is a curious beast:
Girls' chorus	His disobliging ways are a matter of habit.
	If you offer him fish then he always wants a feast;
	When there isn't any fish then he won't eat rabbit.
Boys' chorus	If you offer him cream then he sniffs and sneers,
	For he only likes what he finds for himself;
	So you'll catch him in it right up to the ears,
	If you put it away on the larder shelf.
Girls' chorus	The Rum Tum Tugger is artful and knowing,
	The Rum Tum Tugger doesn't care for a cuddle;
	But he'll leap on your lap in the middle of your sewing,
	For there's nothing he enjoys like a horrible muddle.
	Yes the Rum Tum Tugger is a Curious Cat—
Narrator	And there isn't any need for me to spout it:
	For he will do
	As he do do
	And there's no doing anything about it!

25

30

35

For Study and Discussion

IDENTIFYING DETAILS

1. The Tugger is a curious cat (meaning an "odd" cat). Find at least three examples of the Tugger's peculiar behavior in stanza 1.

2. Why is the Tugger also a bore, according to stanza 2?

3. How does the Tugger show that he is not interested in obliging or pleasing his owner, according to stanza 3?

APPLYING MEANINGS

4. It is said that all of T. S. Eliot's cat poems are really about people. Do you know any people who are like the Tugger? Tell about them.

5. The long-running Broadway musical *CATS* is based on Eliot's cat poems. In the show, the Rum Tum Tugger is portrayed as a rock singer. What do you think of that? What other human occupation would the Tugger like?

Language and Vocabulary

SOUNDS AND SPELLINGS

You may think it is simple to find rhyming words, but it is not always easy to work good rhymes or funny rhymes into a poem. For example, in lines 24 and 26, Eliot rhymes *habit* and *rabbit*. Can you think of any other word in the whole English language that also rhymes with *habit/rabbit*?

Some words look as if they should *not* rhyme, but they do. Complete each entry in

Terry Mann as the Rum Tum Tugger in the Broadway Musical *CATS*.

the list below with words that rhyme with *know* and *sew* or *door* and *bore*, but look as if they shouldn't.

1. know/sew/s_/n_/t_____/t__/g_/h__/J__

2. bore/door/f___/f__/o__/l___/n__/p___/r___

Focus on Writing a Poem

EXPERIMENTING WITH SOUND EFFECTS

If you participated in a group reading of "The Rum Tum Tugger," you know how important **sound effects** can be in a poem. Here are some sound effects that you can use in your own poems:

rhyme	repetition
rhythm	alliteration

Experiment with sound effects by choosing *two* of the four devices listed above. Write a few lines of prose or poetry in which you use each device.

For example, you might create a sentence with alliteration like the following: "Cheerfully Charles charged into the Chinese restaurant." If you choose rhythm, you might write two lines of verse like these:

Colder nights are lasting longer,
Winter's bite is in the air.

After you have finished, share your experiments with classmates. Save your writing.

About the Author

T. S. Eliot (1888–1965) was born in St. Louis, Missouri, and studied literature at Harvard, but he lived in England for most of his life. Eliot wrote the most famous poem of the twentieth century, called *The Wasteland*. Eliot collected his cat poems in a book called *Old Possum's Book of Practical Cats*. ("Old Possum" is the nickname given to him by his friend and fellow poet Ezra Pound.) These poems imitate the "thumping rhythms" of poetry he heard as a child. Eliot clearly loved and understood cats. His own pets had names like Pettipaws, Wiscus, and George Pushdragon.

Suppose that you are a very young child looking at the bright, full moon for the first time. You have no idea what the moon is. What might you imagine it to be? Jot down one or two ideas. Then see what this poet imagines the moon is.

You'll notice the unusual way this poem is printed on the page. It's as if the poem is saying "Pay attention to me! Look at each and every one of my words!"

who knows if the moon's
E. E. Cummings

who knows if the moon's
a balloon,coming out of a keen city
in the sky—filled with pretty people?
(and if you and i should

get into it,if they   5
should take me and take you into their balloon,
why then
we'd go up higher with all the pretty people

than houses and steeples and clouds:
go sailing   10
away and away sailing into a keen
city which nobody's ever visited,where

always
        it's
                Spring)and everyone's   15
in love and flowers pick themselves

A Carnival Evening by Henri Rousseau.
Oil on canvas.

Philadelphia Museum of Art. Stern Collection.

IDENTIFYING DETAILS

1. What does the speaker suggest the moon is? Where does it come from?

2. Inside the parentheses, the speaker imagines a journey. Who would go on the journey? Where would they go?

INTERPRETING MEANINGS

3. What details make the "keen city" sound like a wonderful place?

4. Whom do you think the speaker is talking to in this poem?

5. Cummings capitalizes a word only if he wants to emphasize it. In line 4, which word, usually capitalized, does he *not* capitalize? Which word in the poem gets the most emphasis?

APPLYING MEANINGS

6. Why do you suppose poets usually associate love and joy with spring? If you were describing a perfect place, what season would you assign to it? Why?

Literary Elements

RHYTHM

E. E. Cummings wrote his poems so that they looked very unusual on the page. You are supposed to read some of Cummings's lines very fast, some very slowly.

Look at lines 2, 5, and 12. Why do you think the word following the comma bumps right up to it? Look at line 15. Why do you think the parenthesis is all jammed up between two words? Would you read these lines quickly, or slowly?

Which lines in the poem would you definitely read slowly?

Write two lines in imitation of Cummings. Write one line in such a way that the reader knows it should be read very fast. Write the other line so that the reader would know that it should be read very slowly.

Language and Vocabulary

SLANG

Slang is informal language that is often popular with certain groups. Many slang words are "in" (fashionable) for just a year or two. For example, *groovy* was a popular slang word in the 1960s, but it's not used today at all. Some other once-popular slang words are *cool, uptight, mellow, dig it, bug off, far-*

out. (Do you use any of these words today?) In "who knows if the moon's," Cummings uses the word *keen* as slang to mean "good" or "fine." Do you know anyone today who uses *keen* in this way? What do you mean when you say a knife is "keen"? Or when you say someone has a "keen intelligence"?

Think of three slang words popular today. (Perhaps use your favorite ones.) Write a definition of each slang word and use it in a sentence.

Focus on Writing a Poem

EXPERIMENTING WITH VISUAL EFFECTS

E. E. Cummings was a pioneer in his experiments with punctuation and capital letters. You have seen how the way a poem looks on the page can be related to what it means and how it should be read aloud.

Write a poem of your own describing either a pet or a wild animal with whose habits you are familiar. You can identify and organize details for your description by filling out a chart like the one below.

Details Chart
Animal's Name: _____
Setting/Habitat: _____
Physical Appearance: _____ _____
Action/Movements: _____ _____

In your poem, experiment with visual effects by running letters or words together, capitalizing important words, omitting punctuation, or arranging words to form a picture on the page. Save your writing.

About the Author

E. E. Cummings (1892–1962) was born in Cambridge, Massachusetts, and completed his education at Harvard. Cummings is famous for the unusual way his poems look on the page. By experimenting with punctuation and capital letters, he surprises readers into paying attention to every word. In his anthology *Sleeping on the Wing,* the poet Kenneth Koch writes this about Cummings: ". . . almost every poem seems like some kind of experiment, like another investigation into the use of words. His poetry constantly breaks all the rules. . . . His way of writing seems to call attention to the sense of each word, so that each word counts and is important in the poem."

In Greek mythology, Narcissus was a young man who was very proud of his own good looks and would not marry. Angry at his selfishness, the goddess of love made him fall in love with his reflection in a lake. Narcissus looked at himself for so long that he wasted away. The first narcissus flowers grew in the spot where he died.

Is this little Narcissa anything like that Greek boy?

Narcissa

GWENDOLYN BROOKS

Some of the girls are playing jacks.
Some are playing ball.
But small Narcissa is not playing
Anything at all.

Small Narcissa sits upon   5
A brick in her back yard
And looks at tiger lilies,
And shakes her pigtails hard.

First she is an ancient queen
In pomp and purple veil.   10
Soon she is a singing wind.
And, next, a nightingale.

How fine to be Narcissa,
A-changing like all that!
While sitting still, as still, as still   15
As anyone ever sat!

For Study and Discussion

IDENTIFYING DETAILS

1. Narcissa is not playing, but she is very busy all the same. What does small Narcissa "change" into?

INTERPRETING MEANINGS

2. To someone just looking at her, Narcissa seems to be "not playing / Anything at all." However, someone—like the speaker of the poem—who really knows Narcissa can tell what she is doing in her imagination. What game is Narcissa playing?

3. Do you see any connection between Narcissa and the boy in the Greek myth? Or do you think the poet chose this name just by accident? What do you think of the name?

Marble Players by Allan Rohan Crite (1938). Oil on canvas.

The Boston Athenaeum. Gift of the artist.

APPLYING MEANINGS

4. What qualities in Narcissa might some-day help her to be a good writer, if that's what she wants to be?

Literary Elements

RHYMES AND ALLITERATION

The music of a poem is created by its rhymes and by other sound effects. Write out the words at the ends of the lines of this poem that rhyme. What **internal rhymes,** or rhymes within the lines, can you hear in lines 2–3 and 11–12?

Music in this poem is also created by **alliteration,** the repetition of consonant sounds. Find where the poet uses alliteration in lines 3, 5, 6, 7, 10, 11, 12, 15, and 16.

Read the lines aloud to hear the musical effects of all these repeated sounds.

Focus on
Writing a Poem

PLANNING A POEM

"Narcissa" is from a collection of poems for children called *Bronzeville Boys and Girls.* Each poem in this book tells about the thoughts and feelings of a different city child. The title of each poem is a child's name. For example, "Skipper" is about the way a child feels when his pet dies. Here is how you might plan a similar poem:

1. Think of an interesting name for a little boy or girl. (Do not use the name of anyone you know.)

2. Next, think about a feeling that your young child might have.

3. Then think about where (at what place or event) the child would have that feeling. For example, a child might feel happy about going to a birthday party, or angry about being left with a babysitter.

On a sheet of paper, copy this planning chart and fill it in. Using this information, you can now write your poem whenever you want.

Child's name (two or three ideas) _____
_____
Feeling _____
_____
Place or event _____
_____

About the Author

Gwendolyn Brooks (1917–   ) is a major American poet. The "Bronzeville" that she writes about is a black neighborhood in Chicago, a city she has lived in for most of her life. In her autobiography, *Report from Part One,* Brooks writes that she "dreamed a lot" when she was a child, perhaps just like Narcissa. "As a little girl I dreamed freely, often on the top step of the back porch—morning, noon, sunset, deep twilight. I loved clouds . . . I loved the gold worlds I saw in the sky . . . I was writing all the time." Brooks's many prizes include the Pulitzer Prize for poetry, which she received for *Annie Allen,* her collection of adult poems. In addition to writing, Brooks seeks out and encourages young poets. Her advice to young writers is to get as much education as possible, read widely, and "live richly with eyes open, and heart, too."

Poets try to create very precise pictures of what they experience. This means that they search for words to create pictures in our minds. Words that create pictures are called **images.** Images can also appeal to other senses. They can help us hear how something sounds, tastes, or smells, or even how something feels to the touch (hot, cold, rough, smooth, slimy). As you read a poem, you want to enter the poet's world. Images will help you share the poet's imagination.

Before You Read

Have you ever found something beautiful outside? This poet writes about an experience that has happened to many of us. Notice how she shows you a sequence of carefully drawn pictures. As you read, be aware of the feelings that each word-picture gives you.

Beach Stones

LILIAN MOORE

When these small
stones
were
in clear pools and
nets of weed   5

tide-tumbled
teased by spray

they glowed
moonsilver,
glinted sunsparks on   10
their speckled
skins.

Spilled on the
shelf
they were   15
wet-sand jewels
wave-green
still flecked with
foam.

Now   20
gray stones
lie
dry and dim.

Why did we bring them home?

For Study and Discussion

IDENTIFYING DETAILS

1. What happened to the stones when they were brought home?

2. This poem doesn't have rhymes, but it does contain the kind of sound echoes called alliteration. **Alliteration** is the repetition of consonant sounds in words that are close together. Alliteration makes lines more musical and memorable. (Advertisers often use alliteration in their slogans.) Read aloud your favorite example of alliteration in this poem.

INTERPRETING MEANINGS

3. How does the speaker feel about the stones now? Which line of the poem tells you?

APPLYING MEANINGS

4. What other things can you think of that look beautiful when you see them in nature, but which change after you "bring them home"?

Literary Elements

IMAGERY

Images are details that help you **see** something, **smell** it, **hear** it, **taste** it, or **feel** its textures or temperatures. List three details that help you see what these stones looked like when they were wet.

Focus on Writing a Poem

GATHERING IMAGES

Choose a subject for a poem and make a chart like the one below. Save your notes.

Subject _____	
Sense	**Image**
sight	_____
hearing	_____
smell	_____
taste	_____
touch	_____

About the Author

Lilian Moore (1909–   ) was born in New York City, where she went to Hunter College and Columbia University. For many years, she was a teacher and a reading specialist in the New York City schools. She also wrote many stories and poems for young people. *See My Lovely Poison Ivy* is her collection of poems about ghosts and witches. Moore is a founding member of the Council on Interracial Books for Children.

a2

A Poem's Roots

Sometimes poems come with long roots. The poem "Beach Stones" comes out of feelings that go back to my childhood. I loved many things I found at the beach, but beach stones had a special fascination. As they lay washed up on the beach or in small tide pools, they seemed to be magically colored, and even then they looked to me like jewels of the sea. I gathered them eagerly and it was always hard to choose. One seemed more beautiful than another.

Several times I brought them home to have forever. What a disappointment to see them fade into plain gray stones! After a while I learned that some things can't be moved. They have to be enjoyed where they are.

—Lilian Moore

If you have ever traveled in Mexico or in parts of the Southwest, you might have seen older women selling souvenirs to tourists. See what the speaker in the poem thinks about an old woman selling paper flowers in an open-air market, probably in Mexico.

Calluses are those rough, hard places on our skin that are caused by things like hard labor or shoes that don't fit. You have to read the title as the first line.

Petals   *PAT MORA*

have calloused her hands,
brightly colored crepe paper: turquoise,
yellow, magenta, which she shapes
into large blooms for bargain-hunting tourists
who see her flowers, her puppets, her baskets,
but not her—small, gray-haired woman
wearing a white apron, who hides behind
blossoms in her stall at the market,
who sits and remembers collecting wildflowers
as a girl, climbing rocky Mexican hills
to fill a straw hat with soft blooms
which she'd stroke gently, over and over again
with her smooth fingertips.

Flower Day by Diego Rivera (1925).
Encaustic on canvas.

Los Angeles County Museum of Art.
Los Angeles County Funds.

For Study and Discussion

IDENTIFYING DETAILS

1. What does the woman in the marketplace sell? Whom does she sell to?

2. What have calloused her hands?

3. What **images** do the tourists see? What *don't* they see?

4. What does this woman remember? How were her hands different then?

INTERPRETING MEANINGS

5. How do you feel about the woman in this poem?

6. List the five **images** of color in the poem. What colors are similar to turquoise and magenta?

APPLYING MEANINGS

7. Can you think of other people like this flower seller, whose humanity is ignored by those who pass by?

Illustrating the Poem

This poem is full of color. You might collaborate with a group of classmates to produce a collage (kə·läzh´) illustrating the objects, people, and events you see in this little scene. Be sure to include the five colors in the poem. (A **collage** is made up of pictures and objects from all sources: photographs from magazines, words from newspapers, stones, flowers, sand, seeds, leaves, cloth, and so on. What makes a collage interesting is the way all these images are put together.)

About the Author

Pat Mora (1942–   ) is a Mexican American. Much of her poetry is about the blending of Hispanic culture into American society. Mora has a particular interest in writing for children. She says, "Writing is a way of thinking about what I see and feel. In words I save images of people and of scenes. Writing is not exactly like a picture album, though, because when I write I have to think about why I want to save those images, how I feel about them."

Concrete Cat   *DORTHI CHARLES*

A   A
  e   r   e   r

eYe   eYe   stripestripestripestripe
whisker   whisker   stripestripestripe   t a i l / t a i l
whisker m   h whisker   stripestripestripestripes
         o   t whisker   stripestripestripe
         U   stripestripestripestripe

   paw paw   paw paw   ǝsnoɯ

   dishdish   litterbox
                               litterbox

INTERPRETING MEANINGS

1. List all the words the poet has used. Can you think of any that might be added? Where would you put them?

2. Why do you think the word *mouse* is upside down? Explain why *dishdish* and

   litterbox
   litterbox

   are printed the way they are.

3. What do you think the capital letters *A, Y,* and *U* represent?

APPLYING MEANINGS

4. What other subjects do you think might be good for a concrete poem? List three subjects that, in your opinion, would be *poor* choices for a concrete poem. (Do your classmates all agree?)

Language and Vocabulary

CONCRETE WORDS

You have learned that *concrete* is a word used to describe a poem that has the shape of an actual thing. *Concrete* is also used to describe words that refer to actual things that can be seen, touched, tasted, smelled, or heard. Concrete words are words like *cat, paw, mouse,* and *litterbox.* Each of these words names something that can be seen. The opposite of *concrete* is *abstract.* Abstract words name ideas or qualities. Some examples of abstract words are *beauty, power, democracy,* and *peace.* Poets are usually more interested in concrete words than in abstract ones.

Write down two concrete words or phrases that appeal to each of these senses.

1. sight		4. hearing	
2. smell		5. touch	
3. taste			

Focus on Writing a Poem

WRITING A CONCRETE POEM

First, think of a subject. For your first concrete poem, you may want to use just one word, such as *dog, rain, slide, wave,* or *pizza.* Next, decide what kind of shape your subject suggests to you. Finally, think of words associated with your subject. Remember that how you arrange the words should have something to do with what they mean.

About the Author

Dorthi Charles is a penname that X. J. Kennedy (1929–   ) used when he began writing poems for young people. X. J. Kennedy's true first name is Joseph. He says he uses the initial *X* to distinguish himself from the Kennedys of political fame. X. J. Kennedy was born in New Jersey and began writing and publishing homemade comic books when he was in the seventh grade. He has taught in college and has written several best-selling textbooks. He and his wife, Dorothy M. Kennedy, began making up verses and stories to amuse their own five children. Their *Knock at a Star* introduces children to different types of poetry and encourages them to write their own poems. Two of X. J. Kennedy's books of poetry are *Brats* and *The Phantom Ice Cream Man.* His first novel for young people is called *The Owlstone Crown.*

The most famous form of Japanese poetry is called *haiku* (hī'kōō). Haiku are always three lines long. Often they are about a particular season. Haiku try to capture a moment with a few quick, sharp pictures. As you read these haiku, try to put yourself in the scene along with the poet. What do you see? What do you hear? How do you feel about the moment expressed?

Haiku

A heavy cart rumbles,
And from the grass
Flutters a butterfly.
    —Kuroyanagi Shōha

A chilling moon
As I walk alone:
Clatter of the bridge.
    —Tan Taigi

Winter rain:
A farmhouse piled with firewood,
A light in the window.
    —Nozawa Bonchō

Bad-tempered, I got back:
Then, in the garden,
The willow tree.
    —Ōshima Ryōta

View of Kondrai by Hokusai. Woodcut.

Museum Chiossone, Geneva, Switzerland.

In the Japanese language, a haiku has just seventeen syllables: five syllables in lines 1 and 3 and seven syllables in line 2. The translators of these haiku have not tried to imitate the rule of seventeen syllables.

Here are some other "rules" for writing a haiku. (Not all haiku follow all these rules.)

1. A haiku is about daily life.

2. A haiku describes particular things, often two contrasting things.

3. A haiku records a moment of enlightenment—a sudden discovery about life.

4. A haiku is usually about a season of the year. Often a haiku contains a *kigo,* a "season" word.

That is quite a lot to get into only seventeen syllables! But to Japanese poets, the challenge of the haiku is part of its pleasure.

INTERPRETING MEANINGS

1. What season might each haiku describe?

2. List three **images** in these haiku that help you **see** something. List two **images** that help you **hear** sounds.

3. Which haiku present **contrasting images?**

4. Did any of the images make you feel lonely? Cozy? Happy? Fearful? Which haiku reveals how nature can change a person's bad mood?

5. In Japan, there are poetry contests in which judges award prizes to the best haiku. Suppose you are one of the judges. Which of these haiku would you give the prize to? Why?

Focus on Writing a Poem

WRITING A HAIKU

Haiku are fun to write. You may not be able to create a poem as forceful as one of these Japanese haiku, but you can still produce images that you will be pleased with. Before you write, review the "rules" for writing haiku. (You can skip the rule about the seventeen syllables.) Then keep filling out charts like the one below until you have images and a feeling that you think will work. You might try to open with a word stating your season. Be sure to list some contrasting images in your chart. One important rule: You must limit your poem to three lines.

Haiku ideas	
Season	
Sight images	
Sound images	
Touch images	
Smell images	
Taste images	
Feeling or discovery I want to express	

MAKING COMPARISONS

We all use comparisons every day. We might say that some-body is "white as a ghost" or that someone "wormed out of an invitation" or that someone is "as light as a feather." In these everyday expressions, we are comparing someone's pale face to the whiteness of a ghost; we are comparing someone who gets out of a tight spot to a worm slithering out of a hole; we are comparing someone's weight with the lightness of a feather.

Here are the two major kinds of comparisons used by poets:

1. **Simile:** a comparison made between two very unlike things that uses a specific word of comparison such as *like* or *as* or *resembles* ("cheeks like roses," "skin like marble," "feet as big as boats").

2. **Metaphor:** a comparison made between two very unlike things that omits the specific word of comparison ("cheeks are roses," "skin is marble," "boats for feet").

Why do poets use so many comparisons? Some people believe it is because they want to show that everything in the world is "one."

The Shore of the Turquoise Sea (detail)
by Albert Bierstadt (1878). Oil on canvas.

The Manoogian Collection, Detroit, Michigan.

Before You Read

After you read the title of the next poem, stop for a moment. In your journal, describe the picture that comes to your mind. What sounds do you hear in your imagination? As you read the poem, compare the sights and sounds you saw and heard with the ones James Reeves gives you.

The Sea

JAMES REEVES

The sea is a hungry dog,
Giant and gray.
He rolls on the beach all day.
With his clashing teeth and shaggy jaws
Hour upon hour he gnaws   5
The rumbling, tumbling stones,
And "Bones, bones, bones!"
The giant sea dog moans,
Licking his greasy paws.

And when the night wind roars   10
And the moon rocks in the stormy cloud,
He bounds to his feet and snuffs and sniffs,
Shaking his wet sides over the cliffs,
And howls and hollos long and loud.

But on quiet days in May or June,   15
When even the grasses on the dune
Play no more their reedy tune,
With his head between his paws
He lies on the sandy shores,
So quiet, so quiet, he scarcely snores.   20

For Study and Discussion

IDENTIFYING DETAILS

1. A **metaphor** compares two things that are basically very different. The poet wants you to see how these two different things are similar in some way. In "The Sea," the poet identifies the sea as a dog. Describe what you see the sea dog doing in each stanza.

INTERPRETING MEANINGS

2. This poem is an **extended metaphor**—that is, it states a very unusual comparison and then extends it throughout several lines. See if you can find all the ways the sea is like a dog.
   a. How is the sea like a "hungry" dog?
   b. How would the sea "roll" on the beach?
   c. What would its "clashing teeth and shaggy jaws" be?

   d. What are the "bones" the sea dog gnaws?
   e. When the sea dog is "licking its greasy paws," what is the sea doing?
   f. In stanza 2, what does the poet imagine the sea spray is?
   g. When the sea dog "howls and hollos," what would the sea really be doing?
   h. What sound of the sea is compared to the dog's quiet snore?

3. If the sea is a "hungry" dog in the first two stanzas, what kind of dog is it in stanza 3? Find two details in the third stanza that are a striking contrast to details in stanzas 1 and 2.

APPLYING MEANINGS

4. Can you think of any other animals the sea might remind someone of? What animal would a volcano remind you of? How about a tornado?

Language and Vocabulary

ONOMATOPOEIA

Onomatopoeia (on·ə·mat′ə·pē′ə) is a word that came into English from the Greek language. The Greek words that it comes from mean "name-making." In English, onomatopoeia refers to the use of a word whose sound suggests its meaning. For example, the words *bark, woof, ticktock,* and *crash* imitate the sounds they name. Poets use onomatopoeia to create sound effects that echo the meaning of a poem. Three of the words in "The Sea" that sound like what they mean are *clashing, roars,* and *rumbling.* Can you find one more example of onomatopoeia in each stanza?

Fill in the blank in each sentence below with a word that sounds like what it means. Then compare your choices with those of your classmates.

1. The bacon _____.
2. The crowd _____.
3. The bee _____.
4. The wind _____.

Writing About Literature

CREATING METAPHORS

Write a list of at least three metaphors, in which you say one thing *is* another very different thing (it has to be a noun).

A smile is . . .   Happiness is . . .
My brain is . . .   A walnut is . . .
My handwriting is . . . Jealousy is . . .
I am . . .   Love is . . .
My life is . . .   Home is . . .

About the Author

James Reeves (1909–   ) was born in a small town near London. As a child, he loved to read; he wrote his first poem when he was only eleven. For many years, Reeves was a teacher in England. He has had a lifelong interest in traditional stories of all kinds. His love of folk tales and myths led to his best-known prose works, *The Shadow of the Hawk* and *The Cold Flame.*

Poets use imaginative comparisons to help you see the ordinary world in brand-new ways. The speaker in "The Sea" made you see the sea as a dog. The speaker in this poem gives you a different way of looking at something very ordinary—something you may use every day.

The Toaster
WILLIAM JAY SMITH

A silver-scaled Dragon with jaws flaming red
Sits at my elbow and toasts my bread.
I hand him fat slices, and then, one by one,
He hands them back when he sees they are done.

For Study and Discussion

IDENTIFYING DETAILS

1. What is the speaker's action in this poem?

INTERPRETING MEANINGS

2. The speaker in "The Toaster" identifies the toaster as a dragon. What part of the toaster is the dragon's silver scales? What part of the toaster is the dragon's jaws?

3. Suppose this poem had no title. What clues would have helped you decide what this dragon really was?

4. According to legend, what can a dragon do that makes it easy—if somewhat surprising—to imagine one disguised as a toaster?

Language and Vocabulary

HOMOPHONES

Homophones are words that sound alike but have different meanings. Homophones are also spelled differently. For example, *to, too,* and *two* are homophones. You can usually figure out which spelling to use from the word's context (the words surrounding it in the sentence). "The Toaster" contains several words that have homophones. Think of homophones for the words *red, bread, one, by, sees.* Now make up three sentences using at least two homophones in each sentence. Here is an example:

> The dragon ate eight knights in two nights.

Writing About Literature

LETTING AN OBJECT SPEAK

Think of something like a garden hose, a refrigerator, a computer, or a TV. Write a brief paragraph in which you let the object speak as "I," revealing its true personality. Here are some details you might want the object to talk about:

> My true name (known only to me)
> Where I live
> What my family is like
> My work
> My appearance
> What I like about my job
> What I don't like about it
> What I wish I were
> What I like to do on weekends

About the Author

William Jay Smith (1918–   ) has Choctaw ancestors on his mother's side. His father was a corporal in the Sixth Infantry Band. In a few years, you might want to read *Army Brat*, the poet's fascinating account of growing up in an Army family. Smith attended Washington University in St. Louis. He also studied at Columbia University, Oxford University (where he was a Rhodes scholar), and the University of Florence. He has been a college teacher, a translator of Russian and French poetry, and a member of the Vermont legislature. *Laughing Time* is a collection of his poems. Smith is also co-editor (with Louise Bogan) of *The Golden Journey: Poems for Young People.*

A subway is a train that runs under the ground of a city and takes people from station to station. When this poet worked in New York City, she rode the subway at least twice a day. As you read, compare this poem to "The Toaster."

Things To Do
If You Are a Subway

BOBBI KATZ

Pretend you are a dragon.
Live in underground caves.
Roar about underneath the city.
Swallow piles of people.
Spit them out at the next station.
Zoom through the darkness.
Be an express.
Go fast.
Make as much noise as you please.

rhythm that match the feeling in the poem you chose. Write three or four sentences telling which poem you have decided on, which musical piece you have chosen to go with it, and why you made that choice. Share your ideas in class. Have any of you set the same poem to very different music?

About the Author

Langston Hughes (1902–1967) was born in Joplin, Missouri. He was brought up by his mother, who was a schoolteacher, and his grandmother, who had attended Oberlin College before the Civil War. An avid reader since second grade, Hughes wrote his first poem when he was fourteen. When he was sixteen, he visited his father in Mexico and learned to speak and read Spanish. Later, Hughes moved to Harlem in New York City and attended Columbia University. Although his travels took him all over the world, Hughes always considered Harlem his home. His best writing was inspired by the people, music, and art he found there. Until he could support himself from his writing, Hughes worked as a seaman, dishwasher, busboy, cook, and café bouncer. Throughout his life, he encouraged and helped many young black poets, including Gwendolyn Brooks (see pages 301 and 318). Arna Bontemps, a poet and biographer, wrote about Hughes: "His sources are street music. . . . He is an American original."

The Class Poet

Behind the Scenes

I was the Class Poet. . . . The day I was elected, I went home and wondered what I should write. Since we had eight teachers in our school, I thought there should be one verse for each teacher, with an especially good one for my favorite teacher, Miss Ethel Welsh. And since the teachers were to have eight verses, I felt the class should have eight, too. So my first poem was about the longest poem I ever wrote—sixteen verses, which were later cut down. In the first half of the poem, I said that our school had the finest teachers there ever were. And in the latter half, I said our class was the greatest class ever graduated. So at graduation, when I read the poem, naturally everybody applauded loudly. That was the way I began to write poetry.

—Langston Hughes

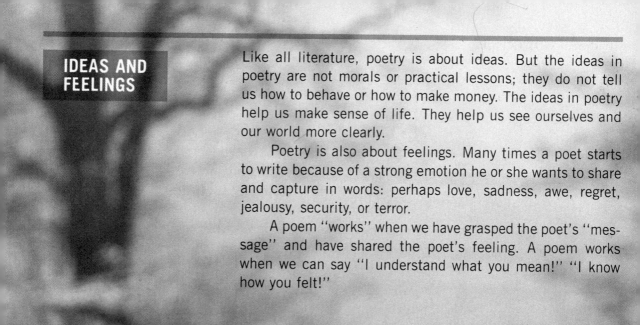

IDEAS AND FEELINGS

Like all literature, poetry is about ideas. But the ideas in poetry are not morals or practical lessons; they do not tell us how to behave or how to make money. The ideas in poetry help us make sense of life. They help us see ourselves and our world more clearly.

Poetry is also about feelings. Many times a poet starts to write because of a strong emotion he or she wants to share and capture in words: perhaps love, sadness, awe, regret, jealousy, security, or terror.

A poem "works" when we have grasped the poet's "message" and have shared the poet's feeling. A poem works when we can say "I understand what you mean!" "I know how you felt!"

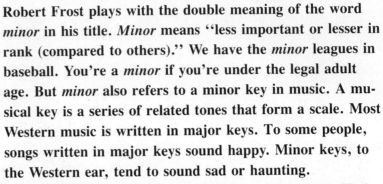

Before You Read

Robert Frost plays with the double meaning of the word *minor* in his title. *Minor* means "less important or lesser in rank (compared to others)." We have the *minor* leagues in baseball. You're a *minor* if you're under the legal adult age. But *minor* also refers to a minor key in music. A musical key is a series of related tones that form a scale. Most Western music is written in major keys. To some people, songs written in major keys sound happy. Minor keys, to the Western ear, tend to sound sad or haunting.

But Frost isn't really writing about music here. He is expressing an idea about something else. Look for what he learns in the second half of this poem.

A Minor Bird

ROBERT FROST

I have wished a bird would fly away,
And not sing by my house all day;

Have clapped my hands at him from the door
When it seemed as if I could bear no more.

The fault must partly have been in me.
The bird was not to blame for his key.

And of course there must be something wrong
In wanting to silence any song.

For Study and Discussion

IDENTIFYING DETAILS
1. What has the speaker wished?

2. What is it about the bird that the speaker dislikes?

3. Who does the speaker say is partly at fault? What two reasons does he give?

INTERPRETING MEANINGS
4. What do you think is the poet's **message** in "A Minor Bird"?

5. Describe the **feelings** the poet expresses in this poem. (Regret? Irritation? Self-blame? Delight?)

APPLYING MEANINGS
6. Do you agree with the last two lines of this poem? Tell why or why not.

Literary Elements

COUPLETS
Notice that each pair of lines in this poem is a couplet. A **couplet** is made up of two rhyming lines that follow one another and that form a complete unit. Sum up the idea in each of Frost's couplets.

Writing About Literature

WRITING A JOURNAL ENTRY
Suppose you are Frost and you have not yet written this poem. You are trying to work, and you hear a bird. Write a journal entry about your experience. Tell the season of the year, your mood, where you are, what the bird sounded like, and why it irritated you.

About the Author

Robert Frost (1874–1963) was born in San Francisco, but his ancestors had been New Englanders for nine generations. After the death of his father, eleven-year-old Robert moved to Massachusetts with his sister and mother. There in high school, he combined writing poetry with playing varsity football. Later, his grandfather gave him a small farm, and Frost tried to support his family by raising chickens for eleven long years. In 1912, after the deaths of two of his children, he and his family moved to England. There, Frost had success: His first two poetry collections were published. Frost eventually returned to New Hampshire and spent the rest of his long life writing poetry, lecturing, giving public readings, and farming. The plain speech and simple, everyday subjects of his poems disguise their complex thoughts. Frost won four Pulitzer Prizes. He is one of the few modern poets who appeal to a great variety of readers.

Suppose that you are grown up. What day from your
childhood do you think you will remember most? As you
read this poem, see if the day you remember is anything
like the day that "stands out forever" in this poet's memory. (The poet's parents were Armenian.)

That Day

DAVID KHERDIAN

Just once
my father stopped on the way
into the house from work
and joined in the softball game
we were having in the street,   5
and attempted to play in *our*
game that *his* country had never
known.

Just once
and the day stands out forever   10
in my memory
as a father's living gesture
to his son,
that in playing even the fool
or clown, he would reveal   15
that the lines of their lives
were sewn from a tougher fabric
than the son had previously known.

Boy with Baseball by George
Luks. Oil on canvas.

The Metropolitan Museum of Art.
The Edward Joseph Gallagher III
Memorial Collection. Gift of
Edward J. Gallagher, Jr., 1954.
(54.10.2)

For Study and Discussion

IDENTIFYING DETAILS

1. Whose game does the speaker mean when he says *"our* game"? How do you know that the speaker's father was born in a different country?

2. Why does the day stand out forever in the speaker's memory?

INTERPRETING MEANINGS

3. A "gesture" is an action that shows a feeling or an idea. For example, in many countries, a bow is a gesture of respect. What was the father's "living gesture"?

4. What **feeling** did the father show for his son? How does the son feel about his father?

5. A **metaphor** at the end compares the life of this family with tough fabric. Does this suggest family strength? Or weakness?

APPLYING MEANINGS

6. Suppose your father or mother or guardian joined in a game with you and your friends and played badly enough to look silly. How would you feel? Can you think of other things parents or guardians might do as gestures of love and solidarity?

Literary Elements

FREE VERSE

This poem is a good example of free verse. **Free verse** is "free" of all regular patterns of rhythm. Often free verse is also free of a regular rhyme scheme. But poets writing in free verse still have to find ways of making their poems sound rhythmical. You will notice in this poem that Kherdian uses repetition to create rhythm. Read the poem aloud. What words does he repeat? Variety in line length also can create rhythm. Where does Kherdian vary his lines?

Do you prefer free-verse poems? Or do you prefer poems with a strong pattern of rhythm, like that in "A Minor Bird" (page 354)?

Focus on Writing a Poem

IMITATING THE POEM

Imitate the structure of this poem and write a poem about something that happened with a member of your family that was especially memorable. Open with the poet's words:

> Just once
> and the day stands out forever
> in my memory:

Try to use one **metaphor** in your poem, that is, use some very unusual comparison that describes a person or feeling, or the way something looked or sounded on that memorable day.

Before you write, read what Kherdian says about poetry (opposite). Try to find an incident that *touched* you, in the way that this incident touched him.

David Kherdian (1931–   ) was born in Racine, Wisconsin, and brought up in the Armenian culture of his parents. He learned English after he started school. Kherdian served in the Army and graduated from the University of Wisconsin. Between the ages of nineteen and thirty-eight, he remembers being always on the move: "the army and college and Europe and an endless series of odd jobs: unloading boxcars, shoe clerking, magazine selling, rug merchanting, office help . . . and always secretly scribbling: waiting for the stuff to become good enough to spring on the world."

The Story Behind the Poem

Behind the Scenes

In many ways my father and I were strangers to each other. At home I was his Armenian son, but in the streets I was an American stranger. I'm putting this a little bluntly. I'm exaggerating. So far as I knew, children did not play games in the Old Country. Therefore I did not believe that he understood any of the games I was involved in. And then, one day, while walking home from work, along the street where we were playing a pick-up game of softball, he stopped and either pitched the ball, or picked up the bat and tried to give the ball a hit. He was *intentionally* participating, he was joining in, and by doing so he was sharing with me something that was of value in my life that I did not believe had any importance in his life. I was deeply touched by this, though why I was touched, or where I was touched, or even how I was touched, was beyond my understanding at the time. Which brings me to poetry and why I write: but that's another story, and has to do with why I wrote *all* of my poems, not just the one you are looking at today.

—David Kherdian

Usually we think of a legacy as money or property handed down from a relative who has died. Before you read this poem, talk about all the kinds of "legacies" people might pass on. Can people pass on nonmaterial things—values like wisdom, faith, or honesty?

Quintana is a Mexican American; you will find four Spanish words in the poem.

Legacy II

LEROY V. QUINTANA

Grandfather never went to school
spoke only a few words of English,
a quiet man; when he talked
talked about simple things

planting corn or about the weather   5
sometimes about herding sheep as a
    child.
One day pointed to the four directions
taught me their names

      El Norte

Poniente   Oriente   10

     El Sur

He spoke their names as if they were
one of only a handful of things
a man needed to know

Now I look back   15
only two generations removed
realize I am nothing but a poor fool
who went to college

trying to find my way back
to the center of the world   20
where Grandfather stood
that day

The Dry River by Peter Hurd. Egg tempera on board.   Roswell Museum and Art Center. Roswell, New Mexico.
Gift of Mr. and Mrs. Daniel Longwell. Photo by Richard Faller.

IDENTIFYING DETAILS

1. Who is **speaking** to you in the poem? What do you find out about this person?

2. What do you learn about Grandfather?

3. What is the speaker trying to do now?

INTERPRETING MEANINGS

4. How does the speaker **feel** about his Grandfather?

5. What do you think Grandfather's legacy is?

6. Find the lines in the poem that look different from the other lines. How does the shape of these lines help you to understand the Spanish words? What do the words mean?

APPLYING MEANINGS

7. What is the **message** the poet is sharing with you? Does his message apply to your own life?

Literary Elements

FREE VERSE

This poem is written in **free verse.** This means that the lines don't have a regular rhythmic beat. Read the poem aloud. Does it sound natural—the way someone would speak? When you read the poem aloud, pause briefly at the ends of lines that do not have marks of punctuation. Make a nearly full pause when you come to a comma and a full pause when you reach a period. How would you read the four directions aloud?

Language and Vocabulary

SPANISH WORDS

Some Spanish words look and sound a little like English words. That's because Spanish and English belong to the same family of languages. Have you ever heard someone speaking Japanese, Finnish, or Arabic? It's more difficult for an English speaker to learn those languages because each of them belongs to a family of languages that is different from the English language family.

You probably had no trouble figuring out that *el norte* (nôr'tā) means "the north," and *el sur* (pronounced like "sore") means "the south." Grandfather chose two words that are beautiful ways of saying east and west in Spanish. *Oriente* (ôr·ē·en'tā) means not just "the east," but also "the beginning." *Poniente* (pōn·ē·en'tā) means not just "the west," but also "the setting or the ending."

At first glance, you may think that *oriente* and *poniente* aren't much like English. But here are some English words that are related to them:

Oriente: the Orient (the Far East—China, Japan, Indonesia)
to orient (to adjust to a situation)
orientation (a period of introduction and adjustment)

Poniente: position (from the Latin verb *ponere* meaning "to place")
ponderous (very weighty)

Many Spanish words have been adopted into the English language. We eat foods such as enchiladas and burritos. We watch broncos and rodeos. We yell "Adios!" to our friends. Because English and Spanish are related, we can often figure out the meaning of an unfamiliar Spanish word by thinking about English words that resemble it. Become a language detective. Find an English dictionary that tells what language words come from. Then look up the following Spanish words and (1) give the original Spanish word for each and (2) list one or two English words that resemble that word. To do this, you can either look in the dictionary or use your own experience with words.

Spanish Word	Origin	Related English Words
sombrero	sombra (shade)	somber umbrella
cafeteria		
stampede		
bonanza		

Writing About Literature

INTERVIEWING AN OLDER PERSON

Find out as much as you can about the way someone you know well lived at least fifty years ago. Perhaps you can interview one of your grandparents to discover what was important to him or her a half-century ago. Find out what this person liked to talk about. Think about what this person taught you. Then write a paragraph summarizing what you learned about this person's life. Before you conduct your interview, be sure to write down at least three questions you want to ask.

About the Author

Leroy V. Quintana (1944—   ) was born in Albuquerque, New Mexico. He has worked as a journalist, a counselor, and a teacher. In 1982 his book *Sangre* (Blood) received the American Book Award for poetry from the Before Columbus Foundation. Quintana says, "I was raised by my grandparents and my major form of entertainment was the old *cuentos* (stories) I was told. I have always enjoyed stories—I read comic books by the hundreds, went to the movies, and recited the stanzas in the back of the catechism religiously." Quintana uses Mexican folklore and traditional storytelling techniques in his poetry. "In many ways," he says, "I'm still basically a small-town New Mexico boy carrying on the oral tradition."

Maudelle Sleet's Magic Garden by Romare
Bearden (c. 1978). Collage on board.

Collection of Mr. and Mrs. Gerhard Stebich.
Courtesy The Estate of Romare Bearden.

Before You Read

What's your favorite season? Imagine it is that season now. Close your eyes for a few seconds. What sounds do you hear? What tastes and smells do you connect with that time of year? What activities and people do you think of? When you read Nikki Giovanni's poem, see if she mentions any of your memories and associations.

This poet was born in Knoxville, Tennessee, but later moved to Cincinnati, Ohio. After the move, she loved to return to Knoxville in the summer. Her beloved grandmother lived there, and visiting her was always like coming home.

Knoxville, Tennessee

NIKKI GIOVANNI

I always like summer
best
you can eat fresh corn
from daddy's garden
and okra
and greens
and cabbage
and lots of
barbecue
and buttermilk
and homemade ice cream
at the church picnic
and listen to
gospel music
outside
at the church
homecoming
and go to the mountains with
your grandmother
and go barefooted
and be warm
all the time
not only when you go to bed
and sleep

For Study and Discussion

IDENTIFYING DETAILS

1. Find an **image** or word-picture in this poem that appeals to each of these senses: sight, sound, taste, and touch.

INTERPRETING MEANINGS

2. How does the speaker feel about Knoxville and her grandmother?

3. Could the word *warm* in line 21 refer to the warmth of love and security, as well as to actual heat? Talk about your answers.

APPLYING MEANINGS

4. In a poem called "Nikki-Rosa," Giovanni writes that "Black love is Black wealth." How does that idea apply to "Knoxville, Tennessee"? How does it apply to all people?

Literary Elements

FREE VERSE

Like "That Day" (page 356), this poem is also written in **free verse,** that is, in poetry that is free from a regular pattern of rhythm. But how does this poet make her poem sound like a poem, and not like prose? Read the poem aloud.

1. Is there any punctuation in the poem at all? Would you pause at the end of each line? Or sometimes would you run your voice right on to the next line?

2. What words are repeated to create rhythm?

3. What are the most important lines?

Focus on Writing a Poem

MAKING A LIST-POEM

Imitate the way Nikki Giovanni starts her poem. First, copy her opening sentence and fill in your own favorite season.

> I always like _____
> best

Then list the tastes, smells, sights, sounds, and activities that make this time of year special to you.

WRITING A FUNNY POEM

If you prefer to write a funny poem, here is one way to do it. First, think of the season you dislike most. Then list all of the reasons why you dislike it. Follow the same form that Giovanni used. Here is an example:

> I always like summer
> least
> there are so many mosquitoes
> my ice cream melts
> you can smell garbage
> rotting

Nikki Giovanni (1943–   ) was born in Knoxville and grew up in Cincinnati, Ohio. She graduated with honors from Fisk University in Nashville, Tennessee. She has taught at Queens College in New York, at Rutgers University in New Jersey, and at Ohio State University. In addition to her own writing, she has edited and collected the writings of other African American authors. Three of her collections for children are *Spin a Soft Black Song, Ego Tripping & Other Poems for Young Readers,* and *Vacation Time.* Giovanni has recorded her poems, using gospel music as background.

Behind the Scenes

A Favorite Place

"Knoxville, Tennessee" is one of my favorite poems because it's one of my favorite places. Though I was born in Knoxville, our family moved to Cincinnati, Ohio, shortly after my birth. Knoxville always represented summer and warmth and sitting on porches overhearing the stories and gossip of my grandparents. Even though I liked snow and playing in it, I preferred the summer games, and still do, that take me outdoors.

I simply tried to recall and capture the summertime fun of reading books because I want to, not because they are school reports, making and baking clay figures (a few of which have survived) at camp. . . the summertime freedom that all adults know is all too short.

My language is really quite literal though I do believe literal language conveys figurative thoughts.

The poem is fun to me because the experience was fun. And sometimes happiness is a good enough reason to write a poem.

—Nikki Giovanni

Before You Read

"Phizzog" (fiz·og′) or "phiz" (fiz) was a slang word in the 1920s and 1930s. It was short for *physiognomy* (fiz′ē·og′nə·mē), which means "face." The word usually refers to facial features and expressions that are supposed to reveal character. Have you ever wished you could trade in your face for another one? Carl Sandburg thought about that question. As you read this poem, decide how he would answer it.

Phizzog

CARL SANDBURG

This face you got,
This here phizzog you carry around,
You never picked it out for yourself,
   at all, at all—did you?
This here phizzog—somebody handed it
   to you—am I right?
Somebody said, "Here's yours, now go see
   what you can do with it."
Somebody slipped it to you and it was like
   a package marked:
"No goods exchanged after being taken away"——
This face you got.

For Study and Discussion

IDENTIFYING DETAILS

1. According to the poet, how do people get their faces?

INTERPRETING MEANINGS

2. Who do you think Sandburg implies that "Somebody" is?

3. How do you think Sandburg feels about his own face?

4. What do you think is the **idea** behind this poem? Do you think the poem's message is important?

APPLYING MEANINGS

5. Suppose that someday plastic surgery costs very little. Do you think that most

Carl Sandburg by Edward Steichen (1936).
Photographic montage.

National Portrait Gallery, Washington, D.C./Art Resource,
NY/with permission of Joanna T. Steichen.

people would want to change their faces?
Imagine that thousands of people choose
the same face. What might happen then?
(Rod Serling once wrote an episode on
this idea for his long-running, eerie suspense series *The Twilight Zone.*)

Writing About Literature

DESCRIBING YOUR PHIZZOG
Bring to school a picture of yourself when
you were a baby. Write about how you have
changed in the past ten or eleven years. Be
sure to include a description of how your
face has changed. (If you can't find a baby
picture of yourself, ask some of your relatives or family friends to describe how you
looked when you were a baby.)

About the Author

Carl Sandburg (1878–1967) is one of the
best-loved American poets. He was born in
Galesburg, Illinois, the son of immigrants
from Sweden. Forced to leave school at age
thirteen, he rode trains all around the country looking for jobs. While working as a
newspaper editor and writer in Chicago, he
had several poems published. *Chicago
Poems*, his collection of free-verse poetry
about Chicago and its people, made him
famous. The best-known poem in that book
is the one about the fog in Chicago coming
in on little cat feet. Sandburg traveled
throughout the United States, reciting his
poems, playing his guitar, and gathering
folksongs that he later published in the book
American Songbag. He was awarded the Pulitzer Prize in history for the last four
volumes of his six-volume biography of Abraham Lincoln. Sandburg also received the
Pulitzer Prize in poetry. His two books of
poems for young people are called *Early
Moon* and *Wind Song*. His autobiography is
titled *Always the Young Strangers*. Sandburg
once described what he wanted out of life:
"to eat regular, . . . to get what I write
printed, . . . a little love at home and a little
nice affection hither and yon over the American landscape, . . . [and] to sing every
day."

Do you remember Cinderella? According to the old fairy
tale, Cinderella was treated very badly by her stepmother
and two unattractive stepsisters. But since she was the her-
oine of a fairy tale, life turned out well for Cinderella. She
married a handsome prince and lived happily ever after.
This poem presents another point of view on Cinderella.
The first thing you must do as you read is decide who the
speaker is.

Interview

SARA HENDERSON HAY

Yes, this is where she lived before she won
The title Miss Glass Slipper of the Year,
And went to the ball and married the king's son.
You're from the local press, and want to hear
About her early life? Young man, sit down.   5
These are my *own* two daughters; you'll not find
Nicer, more biddable° girls in all the town,   7. **biddable:** eager to obey, docile.
And lucky, I tell them, not to be the kind

That Cinderella was, spreading those lies,
Telling those shameless tales about the way   10
We treated her. Oh, nobody denies
That she was pretty, if you like those curls.
But looks aren't everything, I always say.
Be sweet and natural, I tell my girls,
And Mr. Right will come along, someday.   15

IDENTIFYING DETAILS

1. Who is the speaker? Whom is this person speaking to? Who else is at the interview?

2. What advice does the speaker give her girls?

3. How does the speaker **feel** about Cinderella? Why would she feel this way?

INTERPRETING MEANINGS

4. Perhaps the **message** in this poem is that there are two sides to every story. Whose side of this story do you tend to believe? Explain why.

5. Do you think that the speaker really believes what she is saying about Cinderella and her own girls? What do you suppose her own girls look like?

APPLYING MEANINGS

6. One **idea** in this poem might be that stepmothers and stepsisters are portrayed unfairly in fairy tales. Talk about your responses to this idea.

7. Another Cinderella story appears on page 147. This one was told by the Algonquin people of North America. How do the two stories compare? Why do you think the Cinderella story is so popular?

Literary Elements

TONE

Tone is the speaker's or writer's attitude. When you listen to people, you can often tell from their voices and faces how they feel. You usually know whether they are bored, serious, sarcastic, worried, or self-satisfied. But when you read a poem or story, you have to depend on words alone to discover the speaker's attitude. After you've read this poem to yourself a couple of times, think about the character who is speaking.

1. Which word would you use to describe her tone in lines 1–3: sarcastic or admiring?

2. How would you describe her tone in lines 6–9: joking or serious?

3. How would you describe her tone in lines 11–13: sad or jealous?

4. In lines 14–15, is the speaker's tone optimistic or wishful?

Read the poem aloud to reveal the speaker's feelings. Decide how you will change your voice to show where the speaker's tone changes.

About the Author

Sara Henderson Hay (1906–1987) was born in Pittsburgh and lived there and in the South for most of her life. Hay published six collections of poetry. "Interview" is from the collection called *Story Hour,* which offers surprising and often humorous twists on several old stories. Another poem in that collection, "The Builders," tells the story of the Three Little Pigs from the point of view of the sensible pig who used bricks to build his home.

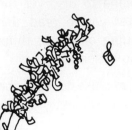

Before You Read

Do you think poetry has to be about beautiful things? If you've ever read any of Shel Silverstein's poems, you won't be surprised to find that he once wrote a poem about garbage. Read this poem aloud or you'll miss a lot of the fun.

Sarah Cynthia Sylvia Stout Would Not Take the Garbage Out

SHEL SILVERSTEIN

Sarah Cynthia Sylvia Stout
Would not take the garbage out!
She'd scour the pots and scrape the pans,
Candy the yams and spice the hams,
And though her daddy would scream and shout,   5
She simply would not take the garbage out.
And so it piled up to the ceilings:
Coffee grounds, potato peelings,
Brown bananas, rotten peas,
Chunks of sour cottage cheese.   10
It filled the can, it covered the floor,
It cracked the window and blocked the door
With bacon rinds and chicken bones,
Drippy ends of ice cream cones,
Prune pits, peach pits, orange peel,   15
Gloppy glumps of cold oatmeal,
Pizza crusts and withered greens,
Soggy beans and tangerines,
Crusts of black burned buttered toast,
Gristly bits of beefy roasts . . .   20

The garbage rolled on down the hall,
It raised the roof, it broke the wall . . .
Greasy napkins, cookie crumbs,
Globs of gooey bubble gum,
Cellophane from green baloney,   25
Rubbery blubbery macaroni,
Peanut butter, caked and dry,
Curdled milk and crusts of pie,
Moldy melons, dried-up mustard,
Eggshells mixed with lemon custard,   30
Cold french fries and rancid meat,
Yellow lumps of Cream of Wheat.
At last the garbage reached so high
That finally it touched the sky.
And all the neighbors moved away,   35
And none of her friends would come to play.
And finally Sarah Cynthia Stout said,
"OK, I'll take the garbage out!"
But then, of course, it was too late . . .
The garbage reached across the state,   40
From New York to the Golden Gate.
And there, in the garbage she did hate,
Poor Sarah met an awful fate,
That I cannot right now relate
Because the hour is much too late.   45
But children, remember Sarah Stout
And always take the garbage out!

Original illustrations by Shel Silverstein from *Where the Sidewalk Ends*, Harper & Row, Publishers © 1974.

About the Author

Shel Silverstein (1932–1999) was born in Chicago, where he still lives sometimes. He also lives in Key West, Florida, in New York City, and on a houseboat off the coast of California. Besides writing and illustrating poetry and prose for children and adults, Silverstein is a folksinger and songwriter. (His best-known song is "A Boy Named Sue.") His first poetry collection, *Where the Sidewalk Ends*, which includes "Sarah Cynthia Sylvia Stout . . .," converted many people of all ages who thought they didn't like poetry. His second collection of humorous verse, *A Light in the Attic*, was on *The New York Times* adult best-seller list for three years. His prose works include *The Giving Tree* and *A Giraffe and a Half*.

PORTRAITS OF IMAGINATION

WRITING YOUR OWN POEMS

A poem is like a portrait. You visualize something in your mind, and to share that vision with someone else, you may draw a picture or write about it. A poem or a picture shows your imagination at work.

Poets follow certain rules and use certain patterns to send their messages. Since poets work under these limitations, every word is important. As a poet, you want to paint that picture as carefully as possible so that your reader understands what you are trying to say.

Two elements are very important in poetry: one is the **image,** or a picture created by words. The other is the **metaphor,** or an unusual comparison made between two very different things. As you write your poems, images and metaphors will help you express your own unique imagination.

The following exercises are suggested to get you started, to help you share your imagination with your friends and classmates.

1. Metaphor Poems

Metaphors compare one thing with another very different thing. We go through life making all kinds of comparisons. Usually we use the words *like* or *as* to make a comparison; this produces a simile. A metaphor is a comparison that does not use *like* or *as.*

Similes: The child was as quiet as a mouse.
The road looked like a ribbon of black.

Metaphors: The child was a quiet mouse.
The road was a ribbon of black.
They drove along the black ribbon of highway.

Write a metaphor poem using the following structure, or something like it:

Line 1 says that you are something else.
Line 2 says that a friend is something else.
Line 3 says that your life is something else.

My days are a crowded mall
My life is an untied knot holding
a brick
My brain is an overflowing
pool.

—Elan Dobbs
6th grade

My handwriting is a junkyard
My friend's handwriting is a
blooming flower
My hand is a grasping crane.

—Jim Philippou
6th grade

My eyes are the sky
My friend's eyes are dirt
My heart is a stomping foot.

—Megan Morelli
6th grade

2. Acrostic Poems

An **acrostic poem** is a series of lines in which the first, last, or special letters spell out a word or a phrase. The name poem is a kind of acrostic that describes *you,* the writer. First, write the letters of your name vertically, in very bold print. Skip a space between your first and your last name. Then write a characteristic of yourself beside each letter. The trick is to find something to say about yourself that begins with the right letter. You can choose physical characteristics, attitudes, or relationships.

Erica: That's me, I
Reject blondes
I also hate airheads
Can't stand the Cougars and boys
named John
And I like:

Boys: Only the cute ones
Ongoing notes
Talking on the phone
Terrorizing Gus Splittorf especially
Sand, sun, surfing, and the stars.

—Erica Botts
6th grade

3. Japanese-Lantern Poems

A lantern gives off light. A Japanese-lantern poem is said to be light and airy, and a lantern can easily be drawn around it if you center each line. A lantern poem should create pictures with words. It should also create a feeling. The pattern of the poem is this:

Line 1 has one syllable.
Line 2 has two syllables.
Line 3 has three syllables.
Line 4 has four syllables.
Line 5 has one syllable, just like line 1.

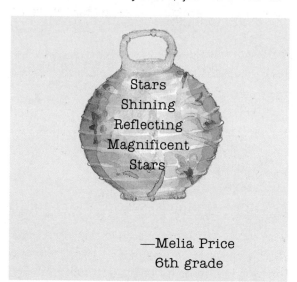

Stars
Shining
Reflecting
Magnificent
Stars

—Melia Price
6th grade

4. Cinquains

A **cinquain** (sin'kān) has five lines. (The name comes from the French word for "five.") The inventor of the cinquain was influenced by the Japanese haiku. Each line of our cinquain will have a special function:

Line 1 is a title; it has one word with two syllables.

Line 2 has four syllables that describe the title.

Line 3 has six syllables and shows action.

Line 4 has eight syllables and expresses a feeling.

Line 5 has two syllables and gives another name for the title.

Thunder
loud claps scaring
comes, goes, shrieks, scares, frightens
dark, loud, lonely, sacred, lovely
Beauty

—Erica Botts
6th grade

Reading
Bathing the mind
Interesting, still fun
Expressing messages or thoughts
Knowledge

—Elan Dobbs
6th grade

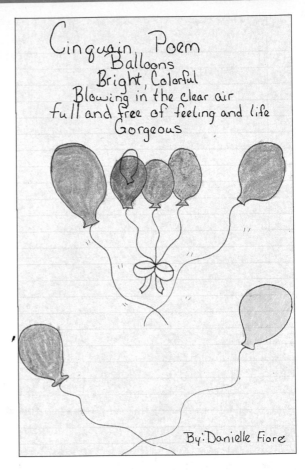

Cinquain Poem
Balloons
Bright, Colorful
Blowing in the clear air
full and free of feeling and life
Gorgeous

By: Danielle Fiore

5. Sense Poems

A **sense poem** is good to write when you feel a strong emotion: when you are happy, sad, angry, mellow, excited—whatever. First, you name your emotion and give it a color. Second, you tell how it smells. Third, you tell how it tastes. Next, you tell how it sounds. Finally, you tell how it feels. In this poem, you can use **similes** (comparisons between two different things using *like* or *as*) or **metaphors** (comparisons between two different things without using *like* or *as*). Here are some student "sense" poems:

Embarrassment is pink.
It smells like vinegar.
It tastes like pickle juice out of a
jar.
It sounds like a horn blowing in
your ear.
And it feels like a mosquito bite
that doesn't stop itching.

—Kelly Burke
6th grade

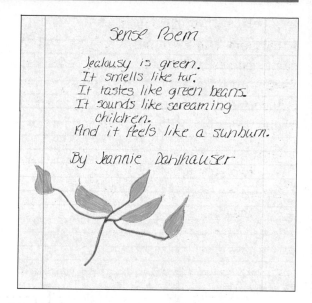

Sense Poem

Jealousy is green.
It smells like tar.
It tastes like green beans.
It sounds like screaming
children.
And it feels like a sunburn.

By Jeannie Dahlhauser

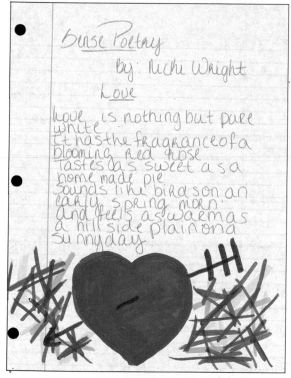

Sense Poetry
By: Nichi Wright
Love

Love is nothing but pure
white
It has the fragrance of a
blooming Red rose
Tastes as sweet as a
home made pie
Sounds like birds on an
early spring morn'
And feels as warm as
a hill side plain on a
sunny day

The students' poems on these pages were written
for Jane Meyer Lee's classes at Safety Harbor
Middle School, Pinellas County, Florida.

Friendship is violet.
It smells like blooming roses.
It tastes like candy.
It sounds like laughter.
It feels like a mother's kiss.

—Cindy Duncan
6th grade

Think of an emotion as a gift that you have.
In your poem, you use this gift to let other
people know how you feel about them or the
world around you. In your poem, you are
expressing real things that you like and do
not like. Be truthful when you write this
poem. Open the gift package that surrounds
you.

6. Parts-of-Speech Poems

Parts-of-speech poems help reinforce your
understanding of the eight parts of speech.
You should follow this structure:

Line 1 consists of an article and a noun.

Line 2 consists of two adjectives joined by a conjunction.

Line 3 has two verbs joined by a conjunction.

Line 4 has an adverb.

Line 5 has a noun that relates to the first line.

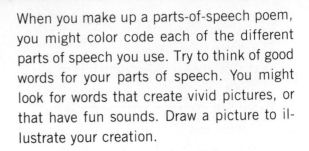

A tree
   green and tall
grows and dies
   daily.
Oak
—Megan Morelli
  6th grade

An elephant
   smelly and big
tramples and stomps
   constantly.
Pacaderm
   —Elan Dobbs
    6th grade

When you make up a parts-of-speech poem, you might color code each of the different parts of speech you use. Try to think of good words for your parts of speech. You might look for words that create vivid pictures, or that have fun sounds. Draw a picture to illustrate your creation.

7. Couplets

Couplets are the simplest rhymed poems. A couplet has two rhyming lines. Couplets are often funny. Here is one couplet by a famous humorous poet:

> The cow is of the bovine ilk;
> One end is moo, the other, milk.
>   —Ogden Nash

Couplets can be put together to make a longer poem. Here is Nash again:

> Behold the duck.
> It does not cluck.
> A cluck it lacks.
> It quacks.
> It is specially fond
> Of a puddle or pond.
> When it dines or sups,
> It bottoms ups.
>   —Ogden Nash

Here is a sixth grader's couplet poem:

Dan Dan the ice cream man
He drives a purple polka dot van
He plays his music round the clock
But all it really is is rock
You can hear his bells all over
    town
His lights flash round and then
    down
Even though it's very scary
He only sells strawberry.

—Michelle Kraft
6th grade

8. Limericks

A **limerick** is a humorous verse form that takes its name from the City of Limerick, Ireland. No one knows how the limerick originated, but it is a five-line poem with a special rhythm and a definite rhyme pattern. Lines 1, 2, and 5 rhyme, and lines 3 and 4 rhyme. Lines 1, 2, and 5 have three strong beats, and lines 3 and 4 have only two.

There once was a girl, oh so cool,
She never thought much about school.
    She stayed home a lot.
    What she learned she forgot.
Now all she can do is play pool.

Some nursery rhymes follow the pattern of a limerick. "Hickory Dickory Dock" is an example.

Many limericks put a place name at the end of their first line and open with the words "There once was." Here are two famous limericks:

There once was a man from Nantucket
Who kept all his cash in a bucket.
    But his daughter named Nan
    Ran away with a man,
And as for the bucket, Nantucket.

There was an old man of Tarentum,
Who gnashed his false teeth till he bent
    'em:
    And when asked for the cost
    Of what he had lost,
Said, "I really can't tell, for I rent 'em."

RELATING SOUND TO MEANING

*T*he sounds of the words in a poem are often closely related to the poem's meaning and mood. Sound devices in poetry include rhyme, repetition, alliteration, refrain, rhythm, and onomatopoeia.

Read the following poem aloud. Then join with a small group of classmates for the activity that follows.

The Waking

I strolled across
An open field;
The sun was out;
Heat was happy.

This way! This way!   5
The wren's throat shimmered,
Either to other,
The blossoms sang.

The stones sang,
The little ones did,   10
And flowers jumped
Like small goats.

A ragged fringe
Of daisies waved;
I wasn't alone   15
In a grove of apples.

Far in the wood
A nestling sighed;
The dew loosened
Its morning smells.   20

I came where the river
Ran over stones:
My ears knew
An early joy.

And all the waters   25
Of all the streams
Sang in my veins
That summer day.

                                   —Theodore Roethke

Relating Sound to Meaning

1. Working in small groups, use a sheet of paper to list all the sound devices that contribute to the description in this poem. List one or more specific examples from the poem for each sound device. Identify each example you list by line number.

2. Discuss with your group how you would describe the speaker's mood in this poem.

3. Now discuss with the group what you think the poet's overall message or theme is in "The Waking."

4. Do you think this poem would have been more effective if the poet had used rhyming lines? Why or why not?

WRITING A POEM

*P*oets use only a few words to offer their readers many layers of meaning. Poetry is fun to read and write because poems often present new ways of looking at the world. In this unit you have studied some of the basic elements of poetry. Now you will have the chance to express *your* way of looking at the world by writing a short poem.

Prewriting

1. Here are some techniques to use when you look for a subject:

    - brainstorm with a group of class-mates
    - draw a sketch of a person or object
    - focus on visualizing a favorite mem-ory

    Remember that almost anything can be a good subject for a poem. In fact, you may find it easier to write something fresh and original about an unexpected subject: a tomato, for instance!

    To jump-start your imagination, try listing the associations you have with the following:

    - a slice of pizza
    - ice-cold water
    - wearing a scarf
    - washing clothes
    - helping a friend
    - skateboarding
    - the color green
    - lightning
    - birds
    - shoveling snow
    - lions
    - a red hat

    [See **Focus** assignment on page 299.]

2. You can also get ideas for poems by

exploring patterns for a poem's struc-ture. Here are three kinds of patterns you can explore:

Metaphor poems use a metaphor in all three lines.
(See Poem 1b on page 383.)
Sense poems name a strong emotion and give it a color in the first line. The next four lines use similes or metaphors to tell how that emotion smells, tastes, sounds, and feels.
(See the poems on page 377.)
Cinquains have five lines. (The name comes from the French word for "five.") Each line has a special func-tion:
Line 1 is a title; it has one word with two syllables.
Line 2 has four syllables that de-scribe the title.
Line 3 has six syllables and shows action.
Line 4 has eight syllables and ex-presses a feeling.
Line 5 has two syllables and gives another name for the title.
(See the poems on page 376.)
Parts-of-speech poems have five lines and follow this pattern:
Line 1 consists of an article and a noun.
Line 2 consists of two adjectives joined by a conjunction.
Line 3 consists of two verbs joined by a conjunction.

Line 4 has an adverb.
Line 5 has a noun that relates to the first line.

Here is an example of a parts-of-speech poem:

> A tree
>   green and tall
> grows and dies
> daily.
> Oak

3. After you have chosen a subject, explore it further by listing some **sensory details.** Fill out an **image chart** like the one below:

Sense	Image
Sight	_____
Hearing	_____
Smell	_____
Taste	_____
Touch	_____

4. **Figures of speech** are words or phrases that describe one thing in terms of another. Think about how you could use one or more of the figures of speech below to make the language in your poem more interesting.

- **Simile** uses *like* or *as* to compare two different things.
  Example: The road looked like a ribbon of black.
- **Metaphor** compares two different things directly.
  Example: The road was a black ribbon.

- **Personification** gives human qualities to something nonhuman.
  Example: The road guided us steadily onward.

[See **Focus** assignment on page 347.]

5. Experiment with **sound effects.** Here are some of the devices you can use:

- repetition
- refrain
- rhyme
- alliteration
- rhythm
- onomatopoeia

[See **Focus** assignments on pages 304, 308, and 313.]

6. Use one of the following methods to organize the details for your poem. If you wish, make an **outline** of your poem in note form.

- chronological order
- spatial order
- order of importance

Writing

1. Write a first draft of your poem. You do not need to use rhyme or regular rhythm, although you can use either or both for special effects. As you write, concentrate on making every word count. Choose precise, specific words. Make your writing as vivid as you can.

2. Feel free to be as inventive as you want in your poem. Here are three ideas you can use:

- Make up some new words, like "hippopotomuscle" (page 307) or "phizzog" (page 368)
- Use foreign words for special effects, the way Leroy Quintana does in "Legacy II" (see page 360)

- Experiment with punctuation, capitalization, and the layout of words on the page (see pages 314 and 328)
3. Make sure that all the details you include in your poem contribute to the same overall impression or main idea.
4. Give your poem a title that describes the subject or conveys your overall meaning.

Evaluating and Revising

1. Put your first draft aside for a while. Then reread it and evaluate it as objectively as you can. Add, cut, reorder, or replace words. Trade papers with a partner, and offer each other suggestions.

Compare these two versions of the poem that appears on page 374. Why is the second version better?

Writer's Model

1a. My days are a mall

My life is a knot holding a brick

My brain is overflowing.

1b. My days are a crowded mall

My life is an untied knot holding a

brick

My brain is an overflowing pool.

2. You may find the following checklist helpful as you revise your poem:

Checklist for Evaluation and Revision

- ✓ Have I created a single main impression in the poem?
- ✓ Do I use precise, concrete words?
- ✓ Do I use fresh, clear images that appeal to the senses?
- ✓ Have I used figures of speech?
- ✓ Do I use sound effects that contribute to the meaning?

Proofreading and Publishing

1. Proofread your poem and correct any errors you find in grammar, usage, and mechanics. (Here you may find it helpful to refer to the **Handbook for Revision** on pages 750–785.) Then prepare a final version of your poem by making a clean copy.
2. Consider some of the following publication methods for your poem:
   - read your poem aloud to the class
   - post your poem on the class bulletin board
   - send your poem to the school newspaper or magazine
   - join with a group of classmates and create a poetry anthology

Portfolio If your teacher approves, you may wish to keep a copy of your work in your writing folder or portfolio.

UNIT FIVE

Nonfiction

Nonfiction is writing that is based on fact, but like other forms of literature, it appeals to the imagination. Nonfiction includes biography (the story of someone's life), autobiography (the story of the writer's own life), articles, diaries, journals, speeches, interviews, true adventures, and travel literature.

Imagine yourself at the scene shown in this painting of whalers trapped in ice somewhere in the Arctic. If you were one of the whalers keeping a record of your journey, how would you describe the scene shown here? Write a brief journal entry about what you see.

Compare your responses with those of other students. Evaluate your work. What details have others seen that you missed? Are you more aware of any elements in the painting after writing down your ideas and listening to others' responses?

Whalers Trapped in Arctic Ice by William Bradford (c. 1870–1880). Oil on canvas.

The Manoogian Collection, Detroit, Michigan.

Close Reading OF NONFICTION

The subjects of nonfiction are as broad as the world itself: people, animals, environment, exploration, adventure, science, arts, politics, current events, history, personal opinions. Nonfiction can take many forms. An autobiographical narrative, for example, may combine true adventure, scientific observations, historical accounts, and interpretations. When you read nonfiction, you must determine whether the facts and conclusions presented by the author are reliable and complete.

Guidelines for Close Reading

1. Read actively, asking questions as you read. Think about any details or passages that puzzle you. Ask yourself what might happen next.

2. Guess the meaning of unfamiliar words by using context clues. Look up any words or references you don't understand.

3. Think about how the selection relates to your own experience or to things you have already learned. What reactions do you have during and after reading?

4. What impression do you have of the writer? Do you agree or disagree with the writer's ideas?

5. Note the writer's use of language. Are there any images that appeal to you? Is the writer using formal language or a conversational style?

6. Ask yourself what the writer's overall purpose might be. Is it to give information, to entertain the reader, to present a particular interpretation, or some combination of these objectives?

The following excerpt is from *Gorillas in the Mist* by Dian Fossey, a naturalist who spent a number of years observing mountain gorillas in a part of Africa. In addition to recording her scientific observations and discoveries about gorillas, Fossey gives an account of her adventures. At one point she took care of two orphan gorillas, whom she named Pucker and Coco. Her object was to train these baby gorillas so that they could be returned to their natural home in the wild.

The notes in the margin represent one reader's responses. If you wish, cover these notes and write your own comments on a separate sheet of paper as you read. Then at a later point compare your own responses with the printed comments.

from
Gorillas in the Mist
DIAN FOSSEY

One day while walking in a new area, Pucker suddenly ran toward a large cluster of *Hagenia* trees on the edge of the forest leading to the mountain. Coco leapt from my arms in rapid pursuit—which was unusual. I thought they were making a dash for the mountain and was hastily taking out the bananas when both infants halted below one of the largest trees. They peered up at the tree like children looking up a chimney on Christmas eve. I had never seen them so fascinated by a tree, nor could I determine what it was that so strongly attracted them. Suddenly the two began frenziedly climbing the huge trunk, leaving me even more puzzled. About thirty feet above the ground they stopped, pig-grunted at one another, and avidly started biting into a large bracket fungus. Previously I had noted these shelf-like growths, which protrude from *Hagenia* tree trunks and rather resemble overgrown solidified mushrooms. They are rare throughout the forest, and before acquiring Coco and Pucker I had never observed wild gorillas being interested in them. Try as they might, neither Coco nor Pucker could pry the fungus from its anchorage on the trunk,

I guess the bananas would bring them back.

I didn't know that gorillas eat fungus.

What's an "elixir"?

This must have been an important discovery.

I like watching animals in a zoo, but I'm not sure I'd like to live next to them!

so they had to content themselves with gnawing chunks out of it. A half-hour later only a remnant remained. Reluctantly they descended, but as we walked on they gazed longingly back at the tree with the fungus elixir. Needless to say, the next day everyone in camp was asked to search the forest for bracket fungus!

Another rare food item that evoked squabbles between Coco and Pucker was the parasitic flowering shrub *Loranthus luteo-aurantiacus* belonging in the mistletoe family. Fortunately for the gorillas, the staff knew exactly where to find abundant supplies of the delicacy.

My studies with the gorillas showed that larvae and grub matter were often obtained from the inner hollow dead stalk material, but I was amazed to see the two captives ignore such treats as blackberries to search for worms and grubs. They often appeared to know exactly where to peel the slabs from live and dead tree trunks to find abundant deposits of larvae. Even while licking one slab clean, purring with pleasure over their feast, they were ripping off another slab for more burrowed protein sources. Worms, when discovered, were immediately torn in half—a rather revolting sight to watch—and each half was chewed with gusto, though not always ingested. After realizing that Coco and Pucker craved such food I included boiled hamburger in their diet, which they ate before any of their cherished foliage or fruit.

Coco and Pucker's outdoor freedom carried over into the security of their room, where eventually nearly every conceivable item of natural gorilla food was introduced three times a day, along with medicine given on a routine schedule.

Usually the pair awoke voluntarily around 7:00 A.M. They weren't the least bit reticent about informing me they were awake by boisterously banging on the wire door between our rooms. After the three of us exchanged good morning hugs, I gave them their milk formulas in two separate pans bolted down to the top of the playpen. Then, food such as bananas and wild blackberries was tossed into the outside run to get rid of the babies during the time it took us to scrub the floor and shelves of the room and discard every bit of vegetation and other debris left over from the previous day. During that time other members of the staff were collecting fresh vegetation for feeding and nesting purposes, so that when the runway door into the room was finally opened the gorillas could return to a "fresh forest," albeit one that smelled slightly of disinfectant.

If the weather was overcast or cold, they spent about an hour feeding contentedly before making their nests in the new vegetation. If it was sunny, they demanded to be taken outdoors, where they could unleash their pent-up energy in roughhouse wrestling, chasing, and tree-climbing.

Between 12:30 P.M. and 1:00 P.M. I would bring them back to the cabin to repeat the early morning routine of medication, favorite food, and fresh foliage. Afternoon activities were again dictated by weather, though the two ruffians were more content to rest during this time of day. At 4:00 P.M. old foliage was discarded for new along with piles of leafy *Vernonia* saplings for me, and later for them, to use as their night-nesting materials. The 5:00 P.M. schedule was much the same except that the youngsters were left alone for an hour to feed. During this time their croons of pleasure and belch vocalizations nearly drowned out the noise of my typewriter in the adjoining room, lending an air of serenity and contentment to the near end of each day.

Once Coco and Pucker had eaten their fill, the four of us, including Cindy, set the cabin frame shaking as we chased, tumbled, and wrestled within the miniforest of their room. I recall those hours as some of the most joyful I have ever known at camp, because Pucker, somewhat inhibited during the day when other people were around the cabin, became ebullient and outgoing when just the four of us were alone together.

During these relaxed sessions I learned a great deal about

Dian Fossey shown with Pucker and Coco.

What are "belch vocalizations"? Have to look that up.

It sounds like they made a mess of the place but didn't get in trouble for it.

I think the word ebullient must mean something like "enthusiastic." Will check.

gorilla behavior that I had not gained previously from the free-ranging animals who had yet to become totally habituated to my presence. Tickling between Coco and Pucker provoked many loud play chuckles and also lengthened their play sessions. Tentatively, I first tried out tickling Coco, and after receiving a very receptive response tried it later with Pucker. After a few weeks I changed approaches from mild "tickle-tickles" to drawn-out "oouchy-gouchy-goo-zoooom" tickles,

She found out that gorillas like to tickle each other. I'll have to watch for that when I visit the zoo.

She has mixed emotions—she doesn't want to lose them but knows how unfair it would be to keep them. I admire her.

much like those given by parents or grandparents when zeroing in with a teasing finger for a child's belly button. The term "oouchy-gouchy-goo-zoooom" is not in any dictionary, yet it seems to be an international and interspecific term that can evoke laughter and smiles from both human and nonhuman primates. Later I had occasion to tickle free-living gorilla youngsters in the same manner and was able to elicit the same delighted responses that Coco and Pucker had given. This was done very rarely for it was always necessary to keep in mind that the observer should not interfere with the behavior of the wild subjects.

When I felt that they were tiring from our strenuous sessions, I broke off the leafy tops of the *Vernonia* branches to place on fresh beds of moss on the highest storage shelf. The final positioning of the foliage signaled night-nest time to the infants. After about seven weeks, Coco and Pucker were able to construct their own night nests and showed selectivity in their choice of the fullest branches for their nests. That was exactly the type of independent behavior I had been hoping for, a necessity if the two were going to be reintroduced to the wild. During the night stillness I often was saddened by the thought of the inevitable separation between myself and the two captives, yet thrilled to imagine them as members of Group 8, free to spend the remainder of their lives in the forests of their birth.

Looking at Yourself as a Reader

Think about your responses to this selection from Fossey's book. Did you enjoy reading it? Did you learn something from it? Would you be interested in reading more of this book?

If you wrote your own responses while you were reading the selection, compare your notes with the printed notes. Did you have similar reactions or not? Did the printed responses clarify any of your own reactions?

Which of the following statements best expresses the central idea of the selection? If you don't agree with any of the choices, state your own idea in a sentence or two.

1. Gorillas can be trained as house pets, just like cats and dogs.
2. Gorillas need to learn routines the way small children do.
3. A naturalist must guard against changing the natural behavior of creatures in the wild.
4. Gorillas eat a variety of foods besides fruit and vegetation.

from The Diary of a Young Girl

ANNE FRANK

Before You Read

A diary is very private. In a diary, a writer can be as personal and honest as he or she wants to be. After all, a diary is not usually read by anyone except the writer. To keep their diaries private, some writers have even written them in a code that only they can read.

One of the most famous diaries in the world was kept by a teenaged girl, who hid in an attic during World War II. Anne Frank was a German Jewish girl whose family had fled to the Netherlands in 1933 to escape the Nazi persecutions against the Jews in Germany. Then trouble started in the Netherlands too. The freedom of Jews was brutally limited there by the occupying Nazis. Some Jewish families fled the country. Some went into hiding. Anne's diary, kept from June 14, 1942, till August 1, 1944, provides a touching human record of what it was like to hide, terrified, in a small crowded attic for two years.

Before you read, write in your own journal how you think you would feel if you had to hide for two years in a few small rooms on the top of an office building. You can never go outside. You are totally dependent on a few people who bring you food and news. How would you pass the time? What would you miss most?

Prefixes are word parts added to the front of a word. If you add the prefix *anti-* (meaning "against") to the word *war*, you get the word *antiwar*, "against war." Anne and her family were victims of *anti-Semitism*, which means "being against people because they are Jewish." The Franks often used to hear *antiaircraft* guns—guns directed "against" aircraft. Knowing prefixes will help you as you figure out the meanings of new words.

Saturday, June 20, 1942

I haven't written for a few days, because I wanted first of all to think about my diary. It's an odd idea for someone like me to keep a diary; not only because I have never done so before, but because it seems to me that neither I—nor for that matter anyone else—will be interested in the unbosomings[1] of a thirteen-year-old schoolgirl. Still, what does that matter? I want to write, but more than that, I want to bring out all kinds of things that lie buried deep in my heart.

There is a saying that "paper is more patient than man"; it came back to me on one of my slightly melancholy days, while I sat chin in hand, feeling too bored and limp even to make up my mind whether to go out or stay at home. Yes, there is no doubt that paper is patient and as I don't intend to show this cardboard-covered notebook, bearing the proud name of "diary," to anyone, unless I find a real friend, boy or girl, probably nobody cares. And now I come to the root of the matter, the reason for my starting a diary: it is that I have no such real friend.

Let me put it more clearly, since no one will believe that a girl of thirteen feels herself quite alone in the world, nor is it so. I have darling parents and a sister of sixteen. I know about thirty people who one might call friends—I have strings of boy friends, anxious to catch a glimpse of me and who, failing that, peep at me through mirrors in class. I have relations, aunts and uncles, who are darlings too, a good home, no—I don't seem to lack anything. But it's the same with all my friends, just fun and joking, nothing more. I can never bring myself to talk of anything outside the common round. We don't seem to be able to get any closer, that is the root of the trouble. Perhaps I lack confidence, but anyway, there it is, a stubborn fact and I don't seem to be able to do anything about it.

Hence, this diary. In order to enhance in my mind's eye the picture of the friend for whom I have waited so long, I don't

---

1. **unbosomings** (un·bŏŏz′əm·ingz): confidences.

want to set down a series of bald facts in a diary like most people do, but I want this diary itself to be my friend, and I shall call my friend Kitty.

Wednesday, July 8, 1942

Dear Kitty,

Years seem to have passed between Sunday and now. So much has happened, it is just as if the whole world had turned upside down. But I am still alive, Kitty, and that is the main thing, Daddy says.

Yes, I'm still alive, indeed, but don't ask where or how. You wouldn't understand a word, so I will begin by telling you what happened on Sunday afternoon.

At three o'clock (Harry[2] had just gone, but was coming back later) someone rang the front doorbell. I was lying lazily reading a book on the veranda in the sunshine, so I didn't hear it. A bit later, Margot appeared at the kitchen door looking very excited. "The S.S.[3] have sent a call-up notice for Daddy," she whispered. "Mummy has gone to see Mr. Van Daan already." (Van Daan is a friend who works with Daddy in the business.) It was a great shock to me, a call-up; everyone knows what that means. I picture concentration camps and lonely cells—should we allow him to be doomed to this? "Of course he won't go," declared Margot, while we waited together. "Mummy has gone to the Van Daans to discuss whether we should move into our hiding place tomorrow. The Van Daans are going with us, so we shall be seven in all." Silence. We couldn't talk anymore, thinking about Daddy, who, little knowing what was going on, was visiting some old people in the Joodse Invalide;[4] waiting for Mummy, the heat and suspense, all made us very overawed and silent.

Suddenly the bell rang again. "That is Harry," I said. "Don't open the door." Margot held me back, but it was not necessary as we heard Mummy and Mr. Van Daan downstairs, talking to Harry, then they came in and closed the door behind them. Each time the bell went, Margot or I had to creep softly down to see if it was Daddy, not opening the door to anyone else.

Margot and I were sent out of the room. Van Daan wanted to talk to Mummy alone. When we were alone together in our bedroom, Margot told me that the call-up was not for Daddy, but for her. I was more frightened than ever and began to cry. Margot is sixteen; would they really take girls of that age away alone? But thank goodness she won't go, Mummy said so herself; that must be what Daddy meant when he talked about us going into hiding.

Into hiding—where would we go, in a town or the country, in a house or a cottage, when, how, where . . . ?

These were questions I was not allowed to ask, but I couldn't get them out of my mind. Margot and I began to pack

---

2. **Harry:** a friend of Anne's.
3. **S.S.:** the dreaded Secret Police of the Nazis.

4. **Joodse Invalide** (yood'sə in·val·ēd'): the Jewish hospital.

some of our most vital belongings into a school satchel. The first thing I put in was this diary, then hair curlers, handkerchiefs, schoolbooks, a comb, old letters; I put in the craziest things with the idea that we were going into hiding. But I'm not sorry, memories mean more to me than dresses.

At five o'clock Daddy finally arrived, and we phoned Mr. Koophuis[5] to ask if he could come around in the evening. Van Daan went and fetched Miep.[6] Miep has been in the business with Daddy since 1933 and has become a close friend, likewise her brand-new husband, Henk. Miep came and took some shoes, dresses, coats, underwear, and stockings away in her bag, promising to return in the evening. Then silence fell on the house; not one of us felt like eating anything, it was still hot and everything was very strange. We let our large upstairs room to a certain Mr. Goudsmit, a divorced man in his thirties, who appeared to have nothing to do on this particular evening; we simply could not get rid of him without being rude; he hung about until ten o'clock. At eleven o'clock Miep and Henk Van Santen arrived. Once again, shoes, stockings, books, and underclothes disappeared into Miep's bag and Henk's deep pockets, and at eleven-thirty they too disappeared. I was dog tired and although I knew that it would be my last night in my own bed, I fell asleep immediately and didn't wake up until Mummy called me at five-thirty the next morning. Luckily it was not so hot as Sunday; warm rain fell steadily all day. We put on heaps of clothes as if we were going to the North Pole, the sole reason being to take clothes with us. No Jew in our situation would have dreamed of going out with a suitcase full of clothing. I had on two vests, three pairs of pants, a dress, on top of that a skirt, jacket, summer coat, two pairs of stockings, lace-up shoes, woolly cap, scarf, and still more; I was nearly stifled before we started, but no one inquired about that.

Margot filled her satchel with schoolbooks, fetched her bicycle, and rode off behind Miep into the unknown, as far as I was concerned. You see I still didn't know where our secret hiding place was to be. At seven-thirty the door closed behind us. Moortje,[7] my little cat, was the only creature to whom I said farewell. She would have a good home with the neighbors. This was all written in a letter addressed to Mr. Goudsmit.

There was one pound of meat in the kitchen for the cat, breakfast things lying on the table, stripped beds, all giving the impression that we had left helter-skelter. But we didn't care about impressions, we only wanted to get away, only escape and arrive safely, nothing else. Continued tomorrow. . . .

Yours, Anne

5. **Mr. Koophuis** (kōp′hūs): a business associate of Mr. Frank's.

6. **Miep** (mēp).

7. **Moortje** (mōort′jə).

Dit is een foto, zoals
ik me zou wensen,
altijd zo te zijn.
Dan had ik nog wel
een kans om naar
Holywood te komen.
AnneFrank.
10 Oct. 1942

"This is a photo as I would wish myself to look all the time.
Then I would maybe have a chance to come to Hollywood."

Anne Frank, October 10, 1942

Monday, July 19, 1943

Dear Kitty,
North Amsterdam was very heavily bombed on Sunday. The destruction seems to be terrible. Whole streets lie in ruins, and it will take a long time before all the people are dug out. Up till now there are two hundred dead and countless wounded; the hospitals are crammed. You hear of children lost in the smoldering ruins, looking for their parents. I shudder when I recall the dull droning rumble in the distance, which for us marked the approaching destruction.

Yours, Anne

Friday, July 23, 1943

Dear Kitty,
Just for fun I'm going to tell you each person's first wish, when we are allowed to go outside again. Margot and Mr. Van Daan long more than anything for a hot bath filled to overflowing and want to stay in it for half an hour. Mrs. Van Daan wants most to go and eat cream cakes immediately. Dussel thinks of nothing but seeing Lotje, his wife; Mummy of her cup of coffee; Daddy is going to visit Mr. Vossen first; Peter the town and a cinema, while I should find it so blissful, I shouldn't know where to start! But most of all, I long for a home

of our own, to be able to move freely and to have some help with my work again at last, in other words—school. . . .

Yours, Anne

Monday evening, November 8, 1943

Dear Kitty,

If you were to read my pile of letters one after another, you would certainly be struck by the many different moods in which they are written. It annoys me that I am so dependent on the atmosphere here, but I'm certainly not the only one—we all find it the same. If I read a book that impresses me, I have to take myself firmly in hand, before I mix with other people;

The building where the Franks and their friends hid is now called the Anne Frank House.

otherwise they would think my mind rather queer. At the moment, as you've probably noticed, I'm going through a spell of being depressed. I really couldn't tell you why it is, but I believe it's just because I'm a coward, and that's what I keep bumping up against.

This evening, while Elli was still here, there was a long, loud, penetrating ring at the door. I turned white at once, got a tummy ache and heart palpitations,[8] all from fear. At night, when I'm in bed, I see myself alone in a dungeon, without Mummy and Daddy. Sometimes I wander by the roadside or our "Secret Annexe" is on fire, or they come and take us away at night. I see everything as if it is actually taking place, and this gives me the feeling that it may all happen to me very soon! Miep often says she envies us for possessing such tranquillity here. That may be true, but she is not thinking about all our fears. I simply can't imagine that the world will ever be normal for us again. I do talk about "after the war," but then it is only a castle in the air, something that will never really happen. If I think back to our old house, my girl friends, the fun at school, it is just as if another person lived it all, not me.

I see the eight of us with our "Secret Annexe" as if we were a little piece of blue heaven, surrounded by heavy black rain clouds. The round, clearly defined spot where we stand is still safe, but the clouds gather more closely about us and the circle

---

8. **palpitations** (pal′pə·tā′shənz): rapid heartbeats.

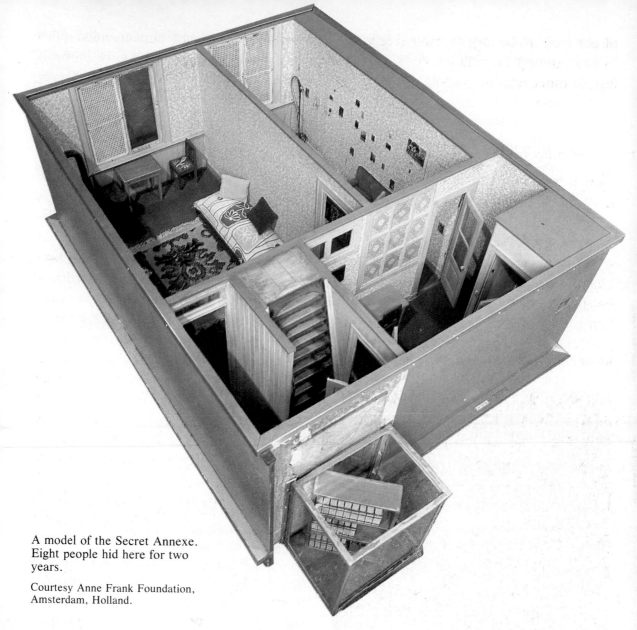

A model of the Secret Annexe. Eight people hid here for two years.

Courtesy Anne Frank Foundation, Amsterdam, Holland.

which separates us from the approaching danger closes more and more tightly. Now we are so surrounded by danger and darkness that we bump against each other, as we search desperately for a means of escape. We all look down below, where people are fighting each other, we look above, where it is quiet and beautiful, and meanwhile we are cut off by the great dark mass, which will not let us go upward, but which stands before us as an impenetrable wall; it tries to crush us, but cannot do so yet. I can only cry and implore: "Oh, if only the black circle could recede and open the way for us!"

Yours, Anne

from The Diary of a Young Girl **399**

For Study and Discussion

IDENTIFYING FACTS

1. On June 20, 1942, what reason does Anne give for starting a diary?

2. Summarize the events reported by Anne on July 8, 1942.

3. What happened on July 19, 1943, that made Anne shudder?

4. What did Anne wish on July 23, 1943?

5. What fears does Anne confide to her diary on November 8, 1943? Describe how she visualizes the eight people in the Secret Annexe.

INTERPRETING MEANINGS

6. Do you think "Kitty" did become the friend Anne longed for? Do you think Anne succeeded in bringing out things that lay buried in her heart?

APPLYING MEANINGS

7. How did this diary make you feel about Anne and about what eventually happened to her and her family? (See About the Author, page 401.)

8. Read your responses to the questions at the bottom of page 393. Are they the same as or different from Anne's responses?

9. How would Anne's story be different if it were told by a historian or biographer?

Focus on Reading

DISTINGUISHING BETWEEN FACTS AND OPINIONS

In her entry for June 20, 1942, Anne says "I don't want to set down a series of bald facts in a diary like most people do." Anne wants instead to "bring out all kinds of things that lie buried deep in my heart."

Below are several quotations from Anne's diary on July 8, 1942. Which are factual statements: that is, statements that could be proved true? Which are opinion statements: that is, statements that express Anne's feelings?

1. ". . . it is just as if the whole world had turned upside down."

2. "Miep has been in the business with Daddy since 1933 and has become a close friend . . ."

3. "At seven-thirty the door closed behind us."

Find three other expressions of Anne's feelings in these diary entries.

Literary Elements

TONE

Tone means a speaker's or writer's attitude. Here are some words that can describe tone: sarcastic, serious, critical.

When we speak, we can indicate tone by using our voices and facial expressions. In writing we can reveal tone only through words. We can't rely on our voices or facial expressions.

1. How would you describe Anne's tone when she says toward the end of the entry for July 8, 1942:
   "I was nearly stifled before we started, but no one inquired about that."
   Is she being sarcastic? Comic? Or just straightforward?

2. How would you describe Anne's tone on July 19, 1943? (Frightened? Confident? Sarcastic?)

3. How would you describe Anne's tone on November 8, 1943? (Fearful? Hopeless? Angry?)

Focus on Informative Writing

PLANNING A BIOGRAPHICAL REPORT

In a **biographical report,** you present information about a person's life and achievements.

When you choose a subject for a report, ask yourself these questions:

What is interesting or special about the person?

What has the person accomplished?

Can I get the information I need?

To gather details for a report, you need to use **sources** about your subject. If she or he is a celebrity, you can use books or articles in newspapers and magazines. If you are writing about a family member or a friend, you may be able to **interview** the person.

Choose a subject for a biographical report: for example, a famous person from history such as Anne Frank, a current celebrity, or a family member or friend you admire. Fill out a chart like the one below. Save your notes.

Biographical Report Chart

Subject: _____

Date and Place of Birth: _____

Childhood/Education: _____

Job/Profession: _____

Achievements/Special Awards: _____

Opinions/Outlook on Life: _____

Statements/Quotations: _____

Overall Importance: _____

About the Author

The life of **Anne Frank** (1929–1945) was tragically short. She was born in Frankfurt-am-Main in Germany on June 12, 1929, and she died in a concentration camp in March 1945. Anne lived only 16 years. Tragically, only two months after Anne died, the Allies liberated her camp. The last entry in Anne's diary is August 1, 1944. It was three days after this date that the Nazis raided the Secret Annexe. All the occupants of the attic were sent off to concentration camps. Of all the occupants of the Secret Annexe, only Mr. Frank survived. Anne's red-checked diary was later found by Miep, lying among a pile of old books, magazines, and newspapers in the Secret Annexe. If you are interested in knowing more about Anne, you should read her diary. A play and a movie have also been made about Anne. Miep Gies tells the story in her own words in *Anne Frank Remembered.*

A Backwoods Boy

RUSSELL FREEDMAN

Before You Read

This is the second chapter of a Newbery-Award-winning "photobiography" of Abraham Lincoln. The book is called a "photobiography" because many historical photographs illustrate the text. Lincoln, as every American schoolchild knows, was born in the backwoods and became President of the United States in 1861. Before you begin reading, talk about the Presidents that you know something about. What were their backgrounds? Do you think a person born very, very poor could get to be President today?

A replica of Lincoln's Kentucky birthplace.
Illinois State Historical Library, Springfield

A suffix is a word part that is added to the end of a word. Suffixes can create whole new words. (For example, a suffix makes the verb *toddle* into the noun *toddler* in the third paragraph of this selection.) Suffixes are often useful when you have to figure out the meaning of a new word. They are also useful in writing, since they can help you say something in fewer words. For example, it is much simpler to say "Abe Lincoln was still a toddler," than to say "Abe Lincoln was still a baby who would toddle around."

It is a great piece of folly to attempt to make anything out of my early life. It can all be condensed into a simple sentence, and that sentence you will find in Gray's "Elegy"—"the short and simple annals[1] of the poor." That's my life, and that's all you or anyone else can make out of it.
—*Abraham Lincoln*

Abraham Lincoln never liked to talk much about his early life. A poor backwoods farm boy, he grew up swinging an ax on frontier homesteads in Kentucky, Indiana, and Illinois.

He was born near Hodgenville, Kentucky, on February 12, 1809, in a log cabin with one window, one door, a chimney, and a hardpacked dirt floor. His parents named him after his pioneer grandfather. The first Abraham Lincoln had been shot dead by hostile Indians in 1786, while planting a field of corn in the Kentucky wilderness.

Young Abraham was still a toddler when his family packed their belongings and moved to another log-cabin farm a few miles north, on Knob Creek. That was the first home he could remember, the place where he ran and played as a barefoot boy.

He remembered the bright waters of Knob Creek as it tumbled past the Lincoln cabin and disappeared into the Kentucky hills. Once he fell into the rushing creek and almost drowned before he was pulled out by a neighbor boy. Another time he caught a fish and gave it to a passing soldier.

Lincoln never forgot the names of his first teachers—Zachariah Riney followed by Caleb Hazel—who ran a windowless log schoolhouse two miles away. It was called a "blab school." Pupils of all ages sat on rough wooden benches and bawled out

---

1. **annals** (an′əlz): yearly records.

their lessons aloud. Abraham went there with his sister Sarah, who was two years older, when they could be spared from their chores at home. Holding hands, they would walk through scrub trees and across creek bottoms to the schoolhouse door. They learned their numbers from one to ten, and a smattering of reading, writing, and spelling.

Their parents couldn't read or write at all. Abraham's mother, Nancy, signed her name by making a shakily drawn mark. He would remember her as a thin, sad-eyed woman who labored beside her husband in the fields. She liked to gather the children around her in the evening to recite prayers and Bible stories she had memorized.

His father, Thomas, was a burly, barrel-chested farmer and carpenter who had worked hard at homesteading since marrying Nancy Hanks in 1806. A sociable fellow, his greatest pleasure was to crack jokes and swap stories with his chums. With painful effort, Thomas Lincoln could scrawl his name. Like his wife, he had grown up without education, but that wasn't unusual in those days. He supported his family by living off his own land, and he watched for a chance to better himself.

In 1816, Thomas decided to pull up stakes again and move north to Indiana, which was about to join the Union as the nation's nineteenth state. Abraham was seven. He remembered the one-hundred-mile journey as the hardest experience of his life. The family set out on a cold morning in December, loading all their possessions on two horses. They crossed the Ohio River on a makeshift ferry, traveled through towering forests, then hacked a path through tangled underbrush until they reached their new homesite near the backwoods community of Little Pigeon Creek.

Thomas put up a temporary winter shelter—a crude, three-sided lean-to of logs and branches. At the open end, he kept a fire burning to take the edge off the cold and scare off the wild animals. At night, wrapped in bearskins and huddled by the fire, Abraham and Sarah listened to wolves howl and panthers scream.

Abraham passed his eighth birthday in the lean-to. He was big for his age, "a tall spider of a boy," and old enough to handle an ax. He helped his father clear the land. They planted corn and pumpkin seeds between the tree stumps. And they built a new log cabin, the biggest one yet, where Abraham climbed a ladder and slept in a loft beneath the roof.

Soon after the cabin was finished, some of Nancy's kinfolk arrived. Her aunt and uncle with their adopted son Dennis had decided to follow the Lincolns to Indiana. Dennis Hanks became an extra hand for Thomas and a big brother for Abraham, someone to run and wrestle with.

A year later, Nancy's aunt and uncle lay dead, victims of the dreaded "milk sickness" (now known to be caused by a poisonous plant called white snake root). An epidemic of the disease swept through the Indiana woods in the summer of 1818. Nancy had nursed her relatives until the

Abraham Lincoln in June 1860, when he was a presidential candidate. Photograph by Alexander Hessler. Gelatin silver print.

National Portrait Gallery. Smithsonian Institution, Washington, D.C.

Sarah Bush Lincoln.

Illinois State Historical Library,
Springfield, Illinois.

Thomas Lincoln.

The Abraham Lincoln Museum,
Harrogate, Tennessee.

end, and then she too came down with the disease. Abraham watched his mother toss in bed with chills, fever, and pain for seven days before she died at the age of thirty-four. "She knew she was going to die," Dennis Hanks recalled. "She called up the children to her dying side and told them to be good and kind to their father, to one another, and to the world."

Thomas built a coffin from black cherry wood, and nine-year-old Abraham whittled the pegs that held the wooden planks together. They buried Nancy on a windswept hill, next to her aunt and uncle. Sarah, now eleven, took her mother's place, cooking, cleaning, and mending clothes for her father, brother, and cousin Dennis in the forlorn and lonely cabin.

Thomas Lincoln waited for a year. Then he went back to Kentucky to find himself a new wife. He returned in a four-horse wagon with a widow named Sarah Bush Johnston, her three children, and all her household goods. Abraham and his sister were fortunate, for their stepmother was a warm and loving person. She took the motherless children to her heart and raised them as her own. She also spruced up the neglected Lincoln cabin, now shared by eight people who lived, ate, and slept in a single smoky room with a loft.

Abraham was growing fast, shooting

up like a sunflower, a spindly youngster with big bony hands, unruly black hair, a dark complexion, and luminous gray eyes. He became an expert with the ax, working alongside his father, who also hired him out to work for others. For twenty-five cents a day, the boy dug wells, built pigpens, split fence rails, felled trees. "My how he could chop!" exclaimed a friend. "His ax would flash and bite into a sugar tree or a sycamore, and down it would come. If you heard him felling trees in a clearing, you would say there were three men at work, the way the trees fell."

Meanwhile, he went to school "by littles," a few weeks one winter, maybe a month the next. Lincoln said later that all his schooling together "did not amount to one year." Some fragments of his schoolwork still survive, including a verse that he wrote in his homemade arithmetic book: "Abraham Lincoln/his hand and pen/he will be good but/god knows When."

As I would not be a _slave_, so I would not be a _master_. This expresses my idea of democracy — Whatever differs from this, to the extent of the difference, is no democracy —

A. Lincoln —

A copy of a fragment of a manuscript containing Lincoln's idea of democracy. The fragment is undated but might have been written around 1858. No one knows where the original fragment is today.

For Study and Discussion

IDENTIFYING FACTS

1. This biography of Lincoln is crammed with facts. Skim the selection again. Then close your book and write down three facts you learned about Lincoln's childhood.

INTERPRETING MEANINGS

2. Write down one **general statement** you would make about Lincoln's early life.

3. What do you think was the hardest part of Lincoln's early life?

4. Can you find any hints in Lincoln's childhood of the great man he was to become?

APPLYING MEANINGS

5. The quotation that opens this excerpt was written by Lincoln himself. He quotes in turn from a long poem by Thomas Gray called "Elegy in a Country Churchyard." How does Lincoln sum up his early life? What other people in the history of America could also sum up their lives this way?

6. What **message** do you think the story of Lincoln's childhood has for young people? Do similar hardships exist for boys or girls today?

Literary Elements

IRONY

We feel a sense of **irony** when *we* know something that a character does *not* know. For instance, suppose we read that Reggie Jackson as a young boy once said sadly, "I'll just never be able to hit that ball." *We* know that this boy went on to become a famous ball-player. This knowledge gives us a sense of irony. We know something that the character did *not* know at the time. Lincoln wrote in his arithmetic book that he "will be good" sometime, "but god knows When." What do *we* know now, that Lincoln *didn't* know then?

We also feel irony when something happens that is totally different from what most people expect. For instance, Lincoln had about one year of school. What do most people expect would become of someone with so little formal education?

Language and Vocabulary

SUFFIXES

Suffixes are word parts added to the ends of words. Here are some useful suffixes and their meanings:

-*dom* "state, rank, or condition"
-*ism* "manner, doctrine"
-*less* "lacking, without"
-*ful* "full of"

1. Which suffix would you use to make another noun from the noun *king?*

2. Which suffix would you add to a word to describe a place that had no windows?

3. Which suffix would you add to a word to describe a situation that is full of pain?

4. What political systems are described using the suffix -*ism?*

Focus on
Informative Writing

ORGANIZING A BIOGRAPHICAL REPORT

When you write a biographical report, you should follow **chronological** or **time order.** With this method, you tell events in the order in which they happen.

You can help your reader follow your report more easily if you use **transitional words and phrases.** For example, notice how Russell Freedman uses these transitions to show time order in the paragraph describing Nancy's death: *a year later, until, then, before* (see pages 404–406).

Write an outline like the one below for a biographical report of three paragraphs. Save your notes.

I. Introduction
   A. Attention grabber: _____
   _____
   _____
   B. Statement of subject and main idea:
   _____
   _____
   _____

II. Body
   Facts/Anecdotes about subject:
   _____
   _____
   _____

III. Conclusion
   A. Restatement of main idea: _____
   _____
   _____
   B. Summary of person's importance:
   _____
   _____
   _____

About the Author

Russell Freedman (1929–   ) lives in New York City. He has written over thirty books for children and young adults, including *Children of the Wild West, Immigrant Kids,* and *Two Thousand Years of Space Travel.* His book on Lincoln won the Newbery Award for the most distinguished contribution to children's literature in 1988. Before writing that book, Freedman read widely, including all of Lincoln's letters and his notes. At the end of the book, Freedman has a section called "In Lincoln's Footsteps." There he lists all the historical sites he visited, places that played a part in Lincoln's life. You yourself can follow this Lincoln Heritage Trail through Kentucky, Indiana, Illinois, Pennsylvania, and Washington, D.C.

The Land I Lost

HUYNH QUANG NHUONG

Before You Read

In 1961, the United States began sending military advisors
to South Vietnam, a country in Southeast Asia. Within a
few years, the United States was fully involved in South
Vietnam's war against the Communists in North Vietnam.
The war tore Vietnam apart. People in the United States
were deeply divided over this country's involvement in the
Vietnam war, and traces of this conflict still persist today.
Here is one former South Vietnamese soldier's recollection
of a more peaceful time in his beautiful country. These essays are from his book called *The Land I Lost*.

Before you read, write in your journal three things
that you think of when you hear the word *Vietnam*.

(The writer's name is pronounced whyng quong
nuong.)

Context clues are clues contained in a sentence or passage which help you figure out the meaning of an unfamiliar word. If the context does not actually define an unfamiliar word, it will often give you enough information about the word so that you can make a pretty good guess about its meaning.

In the very first sentence of this story, for example, the writer says he lived in a small *hamlet*. If you do not know what a hamlet is, you will find clues in the first three paragraphs. There are houses in a hamlet. Some hamlets have shops and marketplaces. People travel to distant hamlets for certain supplies. By this time, you would be pretty sure that a hamlet is a town or village. As you read, use information in the context to help you figure out the meanings of any unfamiliar words.

I was born on the central highlands of Vietnam in a small hamlet on a riverbank that had a deep jungle on one side and a chain of high mountains on the other. Across the river, rice fields stretched to the slopes of another chain of mountains.

There were fifty houses in our hamlet, scattered along the river or propped against the mountainsides. The houses were made of bamboo and covered with coconut leaves, and each was surrounded by a deep trench to protect it from wild animals or thieves. The only way to enter a house was to walk across a "monkey bridge"—a single bamboo stick that spanned the trench. At night we pulled the bridges into our houses and were safe.

There were no shops or marketplaces in our hamlet. If we needed supplies—medicine, cloth, soaps, or candles—we had to cross over the mountains and travel to a town nearby. We used the river mainly for traveling to distant hamlets, but it also provided us with plenty of fish.

During the six-month rainy season, nearly all of us helped plant and cultivate fields of rice, sweet potatoes, Indian mustard, eggplant, tomatoes, hot peppers, and corn. But during the dry season, we became hunters and turned to the jungle.

Wild animals played a very large part in our lives. There were four animals we feared the most: the tiger, the lone wild hog, the crocodile, and the horse snake. Tigers were always trying to steal cattle. Sometimes, however, when a tiger became old and slow it became a maneater. But a lone wild hog was even more dangerous than a tiger. It attacked every creature in sight, even when it had no need for food. Or it did crazy things, such as charging into the hamlet in broad daylight, ready to kill or to be killed.

The river had different dangers: crocodiles. But of all the animals, the most hated and feared was the huge horse snake. It was sneaky and attacked people and cattle just for the joy of killing. It would either crush its victim to death or poison it with a bite.

Like all farmers' children in the hamlet, I started working at the age of six. My seven sisters helped by working in the kitchen, weeding the garden, gathering eggs, or taking water to the cattle. I looked after the family herd of water buffaloes. Someone always had to be with the herd because no matter how carefully a water buffalo was trained, it always was ready to nibble young rice plants when no one was looking. Sometimes, too, I fished for the family while I guarded the herd, for there were plenty of fish in the flooded rice fields during the rainy season.

I was twelve years old when I made my first trip to the jungle with my father. I learned how to track game, how to recognize useful roots, how to distinguish edible mushrooms from poisonous ones. I learned that if birds, raccoons, squirrels, or monkeys had eaten the fruits of certain trees, then those fruits were not poisonous. Often they were not delicious, but they could calm a man's hunger and thirst.

My father, like most of the villagers, was a farmer and a hunter, depending upon the season. But he also had a college education, so in the evenings he helped to teach other children in our hamlet, for it was too small to afford a professional schoolteacher.

My mother managed the house, but during the harvest season she could be found in the fields, helping my father get the crops home; and as the wife of a hunter, she knew how to dress and nurse a wound and took good care of her husband and his hunting dogs.

I went to the lowlands to study for a while because I wanted to follow my father as a teacher when I grew up. I always planned to return to my hamlet to live the rest of my life there. But war disrupted my dreams. The land I love was lost to me forever.

These stories are my memories. . . .

So Close

My grandmother was very fond of cookies made of banana, egg, and coconut, so my mother and I always stopped at Mrs. Hong's house to buy these cookies for her on our way back from the marketplace. My mother also liked to see Mrs. Hong because they had been very good friends since grade-school days. While my mother talked with her friend, I talked with Mrs. Hong's daughter, Lan. Most of the time Lan asked me about my older sister, who was married to a teacher and lived in a nearby town. Lan, too, was going to get married—to a young man living next door, Trung.

Trung and Lan had been inseparable playmates until the day tradition did not allow them to be alone together anymore. Besides, I think they felt a little shy with each other after realizing that they were man and woman.

Lan was a lively, pretty girl who attracted the attention of all the young men of our hamlet. Trung was a skillful fisherman who successfully plied[1] his trade on the river in front of their houses. Whenever Lan's mother found a big fish on the kitchen windowsill, she would smile to herself. Finally she decided that Trung was a fine young man and would make a good husband for her daughter.

Trung's mother did not like the idea of her son giving good fish away, but she liked the cookies Lan brought her from time to time. Besides, the girl was very helpful; whenever she was not busy at her house, Lan would come over in the evening and help Trung's mother repair her son's fishing net.

Trung was happiest when Lan was helping his mother. They did not talk to each other, but they could look at each other when his mother was busy with her work. Each time Lan went home, Trung looked at the chair Lan had just left and secretly wished that nobody would move it.

One day when Trung's mother heard her son call Lan's name in his sleep, she decided it was time to speak to the girl's mother about marriage. Lan's mother

---

1. **plied** (plīd): worked at.

agreed they should be married and even waived[2] the custom whereby the bridegroom had to give the bride's family a fat hog, six chickens, six ducks, three bottles of wine, and thirty kilos[3] of fine rice, for the two families had known each other for a long time and were good neighbors.

The two widowed mothers quickly set the dates for the engagement announcement and for the wedding ceremony. Since their decision was immediately made known to relatives and friends, Trung and Lan could now see each other often. . . .

At last it was the day of their wedding. Friends and relatives arrived early in the morning to help them celebrate. They brought gifts of ducks, chickens, baskets filled with fruits, rice wine, and colorful fabrics. Even though the two houses were next to each other, the two mothers observed all the proper wedding day traditions.

First Trung and his friends and relatives came to Lan's house. Lan and he prayed at her ancestors' altars and asked for their blessing. Then they joined everyone for a luncheon.

After lunch there was a farewell ceremony for the bride. Lan stepped out of her house and joined the greeting party that was to accompany her to Trung's home. Tradition called for her to cry and to express her sorrow at leaving her parents behind and forever becoming the daughter of her husband's family. In some villages the bride was even supposed to cling so tightly to her mother that it would take several friends to pull her away from her home. But instead of crying, Lan smiled. She asked herself, why should she cry? The two houses were separated by only a garden; she could run home and see her mother anytime she wanted to. So Lan willingly followed Trung and prayed at his ancestors' altars before joining everyone in the big welcome dinner at Trung's house that ended the day's celebrations.

Later in the evening of the wedding night Lan went to the river to take a bath. Because crocodiles infested the river, people of our hamlet who lived along the riverbank chopped down trees and put them in the river to form barriers and protect places where they washed their clothes, did their dishes, or took a bath. This evening, a wily crocodile had avoided the barrier by crawling up the riverbank and sneaked up behind Lan. The crocodile grabbed her and went back to the river by the same route that it had come.

Trung became worried when Lan did not return. He went to the place where she was supposed to bathe, only to find that her clothes were there but she had disappeared. Panic-stricken, he yelled for his relatives. They all rushed to the riverbank with lighted torches. In the flickering light they found traces of water and crocodile claw prints on the wet soil. Now they knew that a crocodile had grabbed the young bride and dragged her into the river.

Since no one could do anything for the girl, all of Trung's relatives returned to the

---

2. **waived** (wāvd): gave up voluntarily.
3. **kilos** (kēl′ōz): A kilogram is about 2.2 pounds.

house, urging the bridegroom to do the same. But the young man refused to leave the place; he just stood there, crying and staring at the clothes of his bride.

Suddenly the wind brought him the sound of Lan calling his name. He was very frightened, for according to an old belief, a crocodile's victim must lure a new victim to his master; if not, the first victim's soul must stay with the beast forever.

Trung rushed back to the house and woke all his relatives. Nobody doubted he thought he had heard her call, but they all believed that he was the victim of a hallucination. Everyone pleaded with him and tried to convince him that nobody could survive when snapped up by a crocodile and dragged into the river to be drowned and eaten by the animal.

The young man brushed aside all their arguments and rushed back to the river. Once again, he heard the voice of his bride in the wind, calling his name. Again he rushed back and woke his relatives. Again they tried to persuade him that it was a hallucination, although some of the old folks suggested that maybe the ghost of the young girl was having to dance and sing to placate[4] the angry crocodile because she failed to bring it a new victim.

No one could persuade Trung to stay inside. His friends wanted to go back to the river with him, but he said no. He resented them for not believing him that there were desperate cries in the wind.

Trung stood in front of the deep river alone in the darkness. He listened to the sound of the wind and clutched the clothes Lan had left behind. The wind became stronger and stronger and often changed direction as the night progressed, but he did not hear any more calls. Still he had no doubt that the voice he had heard earlier was absolutely real. Then at dawn, when the wind died down, he again heard, very clearly, Lan call him for help.

Her voice came from an island about six hundred meters away. Trung wept and prayed: "You were a good girl when you were still alive, now be a good soul. Please protect me so that I can find a way to kill the beast in order to free you from its spell and avenge your tragic death." Suddenly, while wiping away his tears, he saw a little tree moving on the island. The tree was jumping up and down. He squinted to see better. The tree had two hands that were waving at him. And it was calling his name.

Trung became hysterical and yelled for help. He woke all his relatives and they all rushed to his side again. At first they thought that Trung had become stark mad. They tried to lead him back to his house, but he fiercely resisted their attempt. He talked to them incoherently[5] and pointed his finger at the strange tree on the island. Finally his relatives saw the waving tree. They quickly put a small boat into the river and Trung got into the boat along with two other men. They paddled to the island and

---

4. **placate** (plā′kāt): calm the anger of.

5. **incoherently** (in′kō·hir′ənt·lē): not clearly; in a confused way.

discovered that the moving tree was, in fact, Lan. She had covered herself with leaves because she had no clothes on.

At first nobody knew what had really happened because Lan clung to Trung and cried and cried. Finally, when Lan could talk they pieced together her story.

Lan had fainted when the crocodile snapped her up. Had she not fainted, the crocodile surely would have drowned her

the crocodile's jaw, she regained consciousness. The crocodile smashed her against the ground a few more times, but Lan played dead. Luckily the crocodile became thirsty and returned to the river to drink. At that moment Lan got up and ran to a nearby tree and climbed up it. The tree was very small. Lan stayed very still for fear that the snorting, angry crocodile, roaming around trying to catch her again, would find her and shake her out of the tree. Lan stayed in this frozen position for a long time until the crocodile gave up searching for her and went back to the river. Then she started calling Trung to come rescue her.

Lan's body was covered with bruises, for crocodiles soften up big prey before swallowing it. They will smash it against the ground or against a tree, or keep tossing it into the air. But fortunately Lan had no broken bones or serious cuts. It was possible that this crocodile was very old and had lost most of its teeth. Nevertheless, the older the crocodile, the more intelligent it usually was. That was how it knew to avoid the log barrier in the river and to snap up the girl from behind.

Trung carried his exhausted bride into the boat and paddled home. Lan slept for hours and hours. At times she would sit up with a start and cry out for help, but within three days she was almost completely recovered.

Lan's mother and Trung's mother decided to celebrate their children's wedding a second time, because Lan had come back from the dead.

before carrying her off to the island. Lan did not know how many times the crocodile had tossed her in the air and smashed her against the ground, but at one point, while being tossed in the air and falling back onto

The Most Vulnerable People

BRENT ASHABRANNER

Before You Read

The next selection is also a true story from Vietnam. The Vietnam war (1957–1979) ravaged the country. It left many people stripped of their possessions and desperate to leave the country. Like so many other refugees, many Vietnamese made the difficult voyage to America. Since 1975, thousands of refugees have come from Vietnam and other war-torn countries of Southeast Asia.

Most of the Vietnamese refugees escape their homeland in small fishing boats. They usually travel through the South China Sea to Thailand, where they stay temporarily in refugee camps. Though the boats are small and the trip is very dangerous, the passage is expensive. Often a Vietnamese family can only afford to send one person—usually, this is the oldest son. In this essay from his nonfiction book *Into a Strange Land*, Brent Ashabranner writes the true story of one Vietnamese boy, Tran, and what he endured to be free.

Before you read Tran's story, write two or three sentences in your journal telling what you think it would be like to be torn from your family suddenly, without warning. Do you know of any people who have had this experience?

The waves were not big now. Tran sat in the middle of the boat, crowded next to an old woman. She had put her arm around him during the night when the spray from the high waves was cold. He did not know her name. The boat was packed with people standing, sitting, a few lying down, but Tran could see no familiar face. Even now, on their third day at sea, he could not think clearly. He could not really believe what had happened. He knew he was not having a bad dream, but still he hoped he would wake up and be at his home in Vietnam.

The beginning had been good. Late in the afternoon, four days ago, Tran's father had told him they were going fishing, just the two of them. Tran was very happy because he had never been fishing with his father before. Tran's brother, who was ten, and four years younger than Tran, cried

and the man poled them away from the shore. After a while, Tran saw a big boat anchored in the bay. They headed toward it, and Tran saw other small boats going in the same direction.

"When are we going to fish?" Tran asked.

"Soon," his father said, "from the big boat."

Tran did not understand, but he said nothing more. Their boat came alongside the big boat; his father and the boatman grabbed a rope ladder from the big boat and pulled their own boat close. Tran's father handed Tran a small plastic bag.

"Climb up the ladder and do not lose the bag," he said.

Tran's eyes widened with fear. "No," he said. "I don't want to."

His father picked him up and swung him to the rope ladder. "I will follow," he said.

Then Tran climbed the ladder, gripping the bag tightly in one hand. When he reached the big boat's rail, two men waiting there swung him onto the deck. Tran saw that the deck was crowded with people. Most were men, but there were also women and children.

Tran looked down and saw that his father was still in the small boat. His father looked up at Tran and raised his hand. "Do not lose the bag," he said.

Then the boatman pushed the small boat away, and soon it was lost in the darkness. Tran cried out to his father, but one of the men standing beside him gripped him roughly by the shoulder. "Do not make noise," he said.

because his father would not let him come. Tran remembered that his mother stood in the doorway of their house and watched them leave.

An hour later, when it was almost dark, Tran's father led them to a place on the beach where a man was waiting in a small boat. "Hurry," the man said. "You are late."

Tran and his father got into the boat,

Tran clutched the boat's rail and stared into the night. His heart pounded. Perhaps his father had forgotten something and would return. But in only a few minutes, the big boat's engine started up, and the boat moved quickly out to sea. Tran spun away from the rail and tried to run, but people were all around him, and he could hardly move. He held the plastic bag close, and he began to tremble.

After that, time ran together. During the dark night, the boat began to roll, and Tran became seasick. He vomited until there was nothing in his stomach and then continued to retch until all the muscles of his body hurt. He lay on the deck and called for his mother. All around him people were sick; he could hear their moans over the noise of the boat's engine.

When at last the sun came up, the sea was calmer, and the boat did not roll so much. Tran was no longer sick, but he was terribly thirsty. He whispered for water, but no one heard him or paid any attention. Finally, a man came around with a bucket of water and gave everyone a single cupful. Tran drank his in a few gulps and then he was sick again. Sometime after that another man came around with a bucket of rice. He gave Tran a cupful, but Tran could not eat even one bite.

Now the sun overhead was hot and burned into Tran's skin. He cradled his head in his arms and slept all day on the deck. That night, when the waves came high again, he crawled to the middle of the boat and found a place beside the old woman.

It was not until the third day that Tran opened the plastic bag, although it had not been out of his hand, even for a moment. Some of his clothes were in the bag, and there was an envelope. He opened it and found a picture of his family that had been taken last year. He was in the picture with his mother and father, his two sisters, and his brother, Sinh.

A letter from his mother was also in the bag. The letter said she was sorry they could not tell him he was going away. She said the boat would take him to a refugee camp[1] in a place called Thailand.[2] She told him to tell the people who ran the camp that he wanted to go to America. She said she hoped someday the whole family could come, or at least his brother when he was older.

Tran held the letter in his hand and stared at it. He knew about refugees. You could not live in Vietnam and not know about them. He had even thought that someday he might be a refugee, but had never imagined that he would leave Vietnam without his family.

"Are you alone?" the old woman asked.

For a moment Tran could not speak. At last he said, "I want to go home."

"Pray that we reach the refugee camp," the woman told him. "Do not even think about anything else.". . .

---

1. **refugee camp:** *Refugees* are people who flee their country because of persecution or danger. Many countries have *camps,* or places where refugees from a particular country are grouped together.
2. **Thailand** (tī′land): a country in southeast Asia, close to Vietnam.

For Study and Discussion

IDENTIFYING FACTS
1. Where does this story take place?

2. Why is Tran on the boat?

INTERPRETING MEANINGS
3. Why do you think Tran's father was so anxious that Tran not lose the plastic bag?

4. Brent Ashabranner calls refugee children like Tran "the most vulnerable people." What does that title suggest to you? Why are refugee children like Tran so vulnerable to harm?

5. Tran's family suddenly uprooted him and sent him alone to a far-distant country. Do you think they were cruel to do this? Or do you think they were making a sacrifice to help their son? Explain.

Volcano

PATRICIA LAUBER

Before You Read

How should you read scientific articles and books? Here are some suggestions:

1. Look for imaginative ways the writer explains or describes things that might be strange to you. Scientific writers, just like fiction writers, often use imaginative comparisons, or figures of speech, to clarify difficult ideas.
2. Look for cause-and-effect relationships. How is one event connected to another?
3. When you come across new scientific words, check the context for their definitions. Or, try to figure out their meanings from other clues in the passage.
4. Look for graphic aids—those tables, charts, graphs, photographs, diagrams, maps and their captions that will help you visualize what the author is saying.

Here is a section of an exciting, prize-winning book on volcanoes. Before you read, write down in your journal three facts you already know (or think you know) about that monster of nature, the volcano.

Many words in science have interesting histories. For example, some scientific words come from the names of gods, goddesses, and other characters from ancient Greek and Roman mythology. The word *volcano,* for example, comes from Vulcanus, the Roman god of fire. The Romans imagined that Vulcanus, or Vulcan, was the gods' blacksmith and that he lived and worked in a mountain in Italy. Blacksmiths work with hot iron, mostly to make shoes for horses. The ancient myth makers imagined that when Vulcan stirred the underground fires which he needed for his blacksmith's forge, terrible clanking, roaring noises, and steam, smoke, and fire came from the mountain. They imagined that when Vulcan pounded the iron on his anvil to shape it, the mountain exploded. As you read the following article, think about why the ancients imagined that a volcanic eruption was caused by the activity of Vulcan.

The Volcano Wakes

For many years the volcano slept. It was silent and still, big and beautiful. Then the volcano, which was named Mount St. Helens, began to stir. On March 20, 1980, it was shaken by a strong earthquake. The quake was a sign of movement inside St. Helens. It was a sign of a waking volcano that might soon erupt again.

Mount St. Helens was built by many eruptions over thousands of years. In each eruption hot rock from inside the earth forced its way to the surface. The rock was so hot that it was molten, or melted, and it had gases trapped in it. The name for such rock is magma. Once the molten rock reaches the surface it is called lava. In some eruptions the magma was fairly liquid. Its gases escaped gently. Lava flowed out of the volcano, cooled, and hardened. In other eruptions the magma was thick and sticky. Its gases burst out violently, carrying along sprays of molten rock. As it blasted into the sky, the rock cooled and hardened. Some of it rained down as ash—tiny bits of rock. Some rained down as pumice—frothy rock puffed up by gases.

Together the lava flows, ash, and pumice built a mountain with a bowl-shaped crater at its top. St. Helens grew to a height of 9,677 feet, so high that its peak was often hidden by clouds. Its big neighbors were built in the same way. Mount St. Helens is part of the Cascade Range, a chain of volcanoes that runs from northern California into British Columbia.

In the middle 1800s a number of small eruptions took place. Between 1832 and 1857 St. Helens puffed out clouds of steam and ash from time to time. It also gave off small flows of lava. Then the mountain fell still.

For well over a hundred years the volcano slept. Each spring, as winter snows

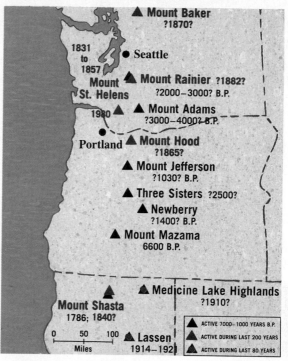

(*Opposite*) Map shows the Cascade Range in the United States and the periods in which each volcano last erupted. Question marks mean that dates are not certain. *B.P.* means "before present."

(*Below*) A volcano is a place where hot, molten rock from inside the earth comes to the surface. Mount St. Helens was built by many eruptions over thousands of years.

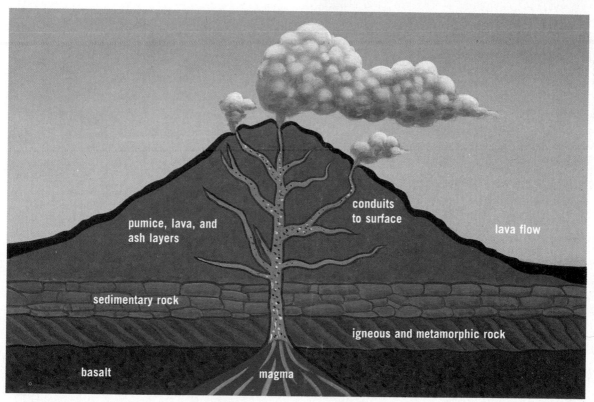

Before: Visitors enjoyed the sight of wild animals, forested slopes, and clear cold waters.

melted, its slopes seemed to come alive. Wildflowers bloomed in meadows. Bees gathered pollen and nectar. Birds fed, found mates, and built nests. Bears lumbered out of their dens. Herds of elk and deer feasted on fresh green shoots. Thousands of people came to hike, picnic, camp, fish, paint, bird watch, or just enjoy the scenery. Logging crews felled tall trees and planted seedlings.

These people knew that Mount St. Helens was a volcano, but they did not fear it. To them it was simply a green and pleasant mountain, where forests and firs stretched up the slopes and streams ran clear and cold.

The mountain did not seem so trustworthy to geologists, scientists who study the earth. They knew that Mount St. Helens was dangerous. It was a young volcano and one of the most active in the Cascade Range. In 1975 two geologists finished a study of the volcano's past eruptions. They predicted that Mount St. Helens would erupt again within 100 years, perhaps before the year 2000.

The geologists were right. With the earthquake of March 20, 1980, Mount St. Helens woke from a sleep of 123 years. Magma had forced its way into the mountain, tearing apart solid rock. The snapping of that rock set off the shock waves that shook St. Helens. That quake was followed by many others. Most of them were smaller, but they came so fast and so often that it was hard to tell when one quake ended and another began.

On March 27, people near Mount St. Helens heard a tremendous explosion. The volcano began to blow out steam and ash that stained its snow-white peak. Small explosions went on into late April, stopped, started again on May 7, and stopped on May 14.

The explosions of late March opened up two new craters at the top of the mountain. One formed inside the old crater. The other formed nearby. The two new craters grew bigger. Soon they joined, forming one large crater that continued to grow during the next few weeks. Meanwhile, the north face of the mountaintop was swelling and cracking. The swelling formed a bulge that grew outward at a rate of five to six feet a day.

Geologists were hard at work on the waking volcano. They took samples of ash and gases, hoping to find clues to what was happening inside. They placed instruments on the mountain to record earthquakes and the tilting of ground. They kept measuring the bulge. A sudden change in its rate of growth might be a sign that the volcano was about to erupt. But the bulge grew steadily, and the ash and gases yielded no clues.

By mid-May the bulge was huge. Half a mile wide and more than a mile long, it had swelled out 300 feet.

On Sunday morning, May 18, the sun inched up behind the Cascades, turning the sky pink. By 8 A.M. the sun was above the mountains, the sky blue, the air cool. There was not one hint of what was to come.

At 8:32 Mount St. Helens erupted. Billowing clouds of smoke, steam, and ash hid the mountain from view and darkened the sky for miles.

The eruption went on until evening. By its end a fan-shaped area of destruction stretched out to the north, covering some 230 square miles. Within that area 57 people and countless plants and animals had died.

Geologists now faced two big jobs. One was to keep watch on the mountain, to find out if more eruptions were building up. If so, they hoped to learn how to predict the eruptions.

The other job was to find out exactly what had happened on May 18. Most volcanic eruptions start slowly. Why had Mount St. Helens erupted suddenly? What events had caused the big fan-shaped area of destruction? What had become of the mountaintop, which was now 1,200 feet lower?

The answers to these questions came slowly, as geologists studied instrument records and photographs, interviewed witnesses, and studied the clues left by the eruption itself. But in time they pieced together a story that surprised them. This eruption turned out to be very different from the ones that built Mount St. Helens.

The Big Blast

The May 18 eruption began with an earthquake that triggered an avalanche. At 8:32 A.M. instruments that were miles away registered a strong earthquake. The pilot and passengers of a small plane saw the north side of the mountain rippling and churning.

After: The mountain disappeared in billowing clouds of hot gas, ash, and rock.

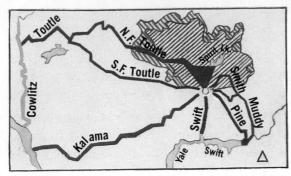

Red stripes mark the area of destruction caused by the blast. Yellow stripes mark the area where trees were left standing but were killed by heat. Solid red shows the avalanche path.

Shaken by the quake, the bulge was tearing loose. It began to slide, in a huge avalanche that carried along rock ripped from deep inside Mount St. Helens.

The avalanche tore open the mountain. A scalding blast shot sideways out of the opening. It was a blast of steam, from water heated by rising magma.

Normally, water cannot be heated beyond its boiling point, which is 212 degrees Fahrenheit at sea level. At boiling point, water turns to a gas, which we call steam. But if water is kept under pressure, it can be heated far beyond its boiling point and still stay liquid. (That is how a pressure cooker works.) If the pressure is removed, this superheated water suddenly turns, or flashes, to steam. As steam it takes up much more room—it expands. The sudden change to steam can cause an explosion.

Before the eruption, Mount St. Helens was like a giant pressure cooker. The rock inside it held superheated water. The water stayed liquid because it was under great pressure, sealed in the mountain. When the mountain was torn open, the pressure was suddenly relieved. The superheated water flashed to steam. Expanding violently, it shattered rock inside the mountain and exploded out the opening, traveling at speeds of up to 200 miles an hour.

The blast flattened whole forests of 180-foot-high firs. It snapped off or uprooted the trees, scattering the trunks as if they were straws. At first, this damage was puzzling. A wind of 200 miles an hour is not strong enough to level forests of giant trees. The explanation, geologists later discovered, was that the wind carried rocks ranging in size from grains of sand to blocks as big as cars. As the blast roared out of the volcano, it swept up and carried along the rock it had shattered.

The result was what one geologist described as "a stone wind." It was a wind of steam and rocks, traveling at high speed. The rocks gave the blast its great force. Before it, trees snapped and fell. Their stumps looked as if they had been sandblasted. The wind of stone rushed on. It stripped bark and branches from trees and uprooted them, leveling 150 square miles of countryside. At the edge of this area other trees were left standing, but the heat of the blast scorched and killed them.

The stone wind was traveling so fast that it overtook and passed the avalanche. On its path was Spirit Lake, one of the most beautiful lakes in the Cascades. The blast stripped the trees from the slopes surrounding the lake and moved on.

Meanwhile, the avalanche had hit a ridge and split. One part of it poured into Spirit Lake, adding a 180-foot layer of rock and dirt to the bottom of the lake. The slide of avalanche into the lake forced the water out. The water sloshed up the slopes, then fell back into the lake. With it came thousands of trees felled by the blast.

The main part of the avalanche swept down the valley of the North Fork of the Toutle River. There, in the valley, most of the avalanche slowed and stopped. It covered 24 square miles and averaged 150 feet thick.

The blast itself continued for ten to fifteen minutes, then stopped. Minutes later, Mount St. Helens began to erupt up-ward. A dark column of ash and ground-up rock rose miles into the sky. Winds blew the ash eastward. Lightning flashed in the ash cloud and started forest fires. In Yakima, Washington, some 80 miles away, the sky turned so dark that street lights went on at noon. Ash fell like snow that would not melt. This eruption continued for nine hours.

Shortly after noon, the color of the ash column changed. It became lighter, a sign that the volcano was now throwing out mostly new magma. Until then, much of the ash had been made of old rock.

The blast leveled forests of huge firs. The tiny figures of two scientists (lower right) give an idea of scale.

An eruption on March 19, 1982, melted snow and caused this mudflow. The smaller part of the flow went into Spirit Lake (lower left), while the larger part traveled down the Toutle River.

At the same time the volcano began giving off huge flows of pumice and ash. The material was very hot, with temperatures of about 1,000 degrees Fahrenheit, and it traveled down the mountain at speeds of 100 miles an hour. The flows went on until 5:30 in the afternoon. They formed a wedge-shaped plain of pumice on the side of the mountain. Two weeks later, temperatures in the pumice were still 780 degrees.

Finally, there were the mudflows, which started when heat from the blast melted ice and snow on the mountaintop. The water mixed with ash, pumice, ground-up rock, and dirt and rocks of the avalanche. The result was a thick mixture that was like wet concrete, a mudflow. The mudflows traveled fast, scouring the landscape and sweeping down the slopes into river valleys. Together, their speed and thickness did great damage.

The largest mudflow was made of avalanche material from the valley of the North Fork of the Toutle River. It churned down the river valley, tearing out steel bridges, ripping houses apart, picking up boulders and trucks and carrying them along. Miles away it choked the Cowlitz River and blocked shipping channels in the Columbia River.

When the sun rose on May 19, it showed a greatly changed St. Helens. The mountain was 1,200 feet shorter than it had been the morning before. Most of the old top had slid down the mountain in the avalanche. The rest had erupted out as shattered rock. Geologists later figured that

Crack in dome shows red-hot molten rock just below the surface.

the volcano had lost three quarters of a cubic mile[1] of old rock.

The north side of the mountain had changed from a green and lovely slope to a fan-shaped wasteland.

At the top of Mount St. Helens was a big, new crater with the shape of a horseshoe. Inside the crater was the vent, the opening through which rock and gases erupted from time to time over the next few years.

In 1980 St. Helens erupted six more times. Most of these eruptions were explosive—ash soared into the air, pumice swept down the north side of the mountain. In the eruptions of June and August, thick pasty lava oozed out of the vent and built a dome. But both domes were destroyed by the next eruptions. In October the pattern changed. The explosions stopped, and thick lava built a dome that was not destroyed. Later eruptions added to the dome, making it bigger and bigger.

During this time, geologists were learning to read the clues found before eruptions. They learned to predict what St. Helens was going to do. The predictions helped to protect people who were on and near the mountain.

Among these people were many natural scientists. They had come to look for survivors, for plants and animals that had lived through the eruption. They had come to look for colonizers, for plants and animals that would move in. Mount St. Helens had erupted many times before. Each time life had returned. Now scientists would have a chance to see how it did. They would see how nature healed itself.

1. **cubic mile:** the amount of space in a cube one mile long, one mile wide, and one mile high.

For Study and Discussion

IDENTIFYING FACTS

1. What was the first sign that something was going on inside Mount St. Helens?

2. Describe the process which built Mount St. Helens and neighboring volcanoes.

3. After the eruption that took place on May 18, what two big jobs did the geologists face?

4. What three questions did the geologists want answered after the May 18 eruption? How did they get the answers? What did they learn?

5. This writer very carefully defines several scientific terms in **context.** Skim the opening of the selection to find where the following ''volcano terms'' are defined. Write out their definitions:
   a. magma
   b. lava
   c. pumice

INTERPRETING MEANINGS

6. The writer contrasts St. Helens before the eruption with St. Helens after the eruption. Describe some of these before-and-after **images.** How did the writer make you feel about what happened to people, animals, and land as a result of the explosion?

7. Just as fiction writers do, scientific writers build up **suspense.** They want to make us eager to read on to find out ''what happens next.'' Where in this selection did the writer build up your suspense? At these moments, what questions did she plant in your mind?

8. Scientific writers, like all nonfiction writers, have to know their **audience.** This book about volcanoes was written for young adults. Do you think the writer succeeded in making difficult scientific concepts clear? Was anything unclear?

APPLYING MEANINGS

9. If you lived in the area around Mount St. Helens and were warned that it was going to erupt some time within the next five years, would you continue to live there? Explain.

Focus on Reading

USING GRAPHIC AIDS: MAPS AND CAPTIONS

To help you understand a science article, an author will usually include **graphic aids,** such as charts, graphs, diagrams, maps, and photographs. These graphic aids often are accompanied by **captions,** which explain what the aids are about.

Use the map and caption on page 433 to answer the following questions.

1. What does the map show?

2. Which is farther away from Mount Jefferson, Mount Shasta or Mount Rainier?

3. What do the letters *B.P.* stand for?

4. Which is closer to Mount Mazama, Lassen or Three Sisters?

5. Which volcano is between Mount Hood and Three Sisters?

Literary Elements

FIGURES OF SPEECH

When science writers need to explain ideas that are unfamiliar to their readers, they may compare those ideas to things their readers already know. Comparisons between two unlike things are called **figures of speech.**

The very first sentence of this selection uses a figure of speech when the writer says "For many years the volcano slept." Obviously, a volcano cannot close its eyes and snooze. This figure of speech makes us visualize the volcano as a sleeping giant— something that will be dangerous when it "wakes up."

1. Find other passages in which this writer describes the volcano in terms of a sleeping person.

2. "Before the eruption, Mount St. Helens was like a giant pressure cooker."
   a. What is the mountain compared with here?
   b. Is this a good comparison? Why?

3. "It snapped off or uprooted the trees, scattering the trunks as if they were straws."
   a. What are the tree trunks compared with?
   b. In your opinion, is this a good comparison? Why?

4. What do you think nature is compared with in the very last sentence?

Focus on Informative Writing

EXPLAINING A PROCESS
In a **process explanation,** you tell your readers how something works or how to do something. For example, in "Volcano" Patricia Lauber explains the process that leads to an eruption. She also explains how geologists work.

To find a topic for a process explanation, ask yourself questions like these:
What do I like to do?
What can I do best?
What might interest my audience?

Get together with a small group. Brainstorm with your classmates to find *two* topics for informative papers. One topic should focus on how to do something. The other should focus on how something works. Here are some possible topics for your group to consider:

How to do X	*How X Works*
how to make a kite	how blood circulates
how to make salsa	how VCRs work

For each topic your group chooses, make a chart like the one below. List each step or stage of the process in the correct order. Save your notes.

Topic: _____
Steps/Stages
1. _____
2. _____
3. _____
4. _____

About the Author

Patricia Lauber (1924–   ) is best known for her informational books on a variety of topics, including animals, rivers, planets, robots, and cattle ranching. She has been praised for her skill in presenting clearly and with colorful detail subjects that young people often think are boring. She says that the greatest reward in writing scientific books for young readers comes from children who write her letters asking for "more."

Myths and Scientific Words

Many words in science have their beginnings in the mythologies of ancient Greece and Rome. You have already seen that the word *volcano* comes from the name of the Roman god Vulcan. Nearly all the planets in our solar system are named after Roman gods, and a number of constellations are named after Greek figures. The names of several chemical elements come from figures in Greek mythology.

Making Connections: Activities

Use a dictionary, an encyclopedia, or other reference book to discover how the meaning of each of the following words is associated with a figure in classical mythology. Can you add to this list other scientific words named after mythological persons?

arachnid	plutonium
heliosphere	chronometer
Mercury	selenium
ocean	typhoon
medusa	echidna

Behind the Scenes

A "Spinachlike" Reputation

To many people an "appealing" science book is a contradiction in terms, for science tends to have a spinachlike reputation. . . . Readers of science books are unlikely to feel the hair rise on the backs of their necks or to laugh or cry, except perhaps for highly personal reasons. They may well have to work hard to understand the content. And so science is often viewed as being somewhat unpalatable [not tasty]—but good for you . . .

Yet, that is an adult view. Children are not born turned off by science, and if they grow up that way, it is because they have "caught" that attitude, along with the common cold and other scourges. Children are born curious, wanting and needing to understand the world around them, wanting to know why, how, and what: the very questions that scientists ask.

—Patricia Lauber

Snapshot of a Dog

JAMES THURBER

Before You Read

A famous animal character can be as vivid and memorable as a human character. Just think of the many well-known animals created in the movies (like Lassie), on television (like Alf), or in cartoons (like Garfield). What famous animals do you know from books you have read?

James Thurber characterized and even drew a "breed" of dog called the Thurber dog, or Thurberhound. In this essay he remembers a real dog his family once owned. Do you think these events are all absolutely true, or has Thurber exaggerated a little to make you smile?

After reading the first paragraph, sketch Rex. Compare your "snapshots" with those of your classmates.

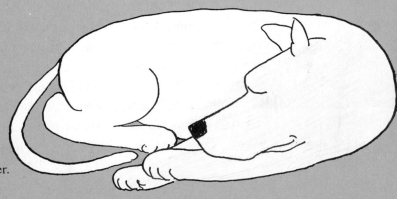

A sketch of Rex by James Thurber.

Courtesy Rosemary Thurber.

Descriptive details help us see something, taste it, smell it, hear its sounds, and feel its textures. A snapshot is an informal picture taken with a camera. Here, Thurber is *writing* a snapshot, using descriptive details to help us form a clear, and comical, picture of his pet Rex. (Just looking at your drawings of Rex will show you how many details you picked up from Thurber's description.) As you read, be aware of the descriptions of Rex that make him come bounding off the page.

I ran across a dim photograph of him the other day, going through some old things. He's been dead twenty-five years. His name was Rex (my two brothers and I named him when we were in our early teens) and he was a bull terrier. "An American bull terrier," we used to say, proudly; none of your English bulls. He had one brindle[1] eye that sometimes made him look like a clown and sometimes reminded you of a politician with derby hat and cigar. The rest of him was white except for a brindle saddle that always seemed to be slipping off and a brindle stocking on a hind leg. Nevertheless, there was a nobility about him. He was big and muscular and beautifully made. He never lost his dignity even when trying to accomplish the extravagant tasks my brothers and myself used to set for him. One of these was bringing a ten-foot wooden rail into the yard through the back gate. We would throw it out into the alley and tell him to go get it. Rex was as powerful as a wrestler, and there were not many things that he couldn't manage somehow to get hold of with his great jaws and lift or drag to wherever he wanted to put them, or wherever we wanted them put. He could catch the rail at the balance[2] and lift it clear of the ground and trot with great confidence toward the gate. Of course, since the gate was only four feet wide or so, he couldn't bring the rail in broadside.[3] He found that out when he got a few terrific jolts, but he wouldn't give up. He finally figured out how to do it, by dragging the rail, holding onto one end, growling. He got a great, wagging satisfaction out of his work. We used to bet kids who had never seen Rex in action that he could catch a baseball thrown as high as they could throw it. He almost never let us down. Rex

---

1. **brindle:** streaks or spots of a darker color.

2. **at the balance:** in the middle.
3. **broadside:** here, with the length of the pole facing front.

could hold a baseball with ease in his mouth, in one cheek, as if it were a chew of tobacco.

He was a tremendous fighter, but he never started fights. I don't believe he liked to get into them, despite the fact that he came from a line of fighters. He never went for another dog's throat but for one of its ears (that teaches a dog a lesson), and he would get his grip, close his eyes, and hold on. He could hold on for hours. His longest fight lasted from dusk until almost pitch-dark, one Sunday. It was fought in East Main Street in Columbus with a large, snarly nondescript[4] that belonged to a big neighborhood handyman. When Rex finally got his ear grip, the brief whirlwind of snarling turned to screeching. It was frightening to listen to and to watch. The man boldly picked the dogs up somehow and began swinging them around his head, and finally let them fly like a hammer in a hammer throw, but although they landed ten feet away with a great plump, Rex still held on.

The two dogs eventually worked their way to the middle of the car tracks, and after a while two or three streetcars were held up by the fight. A motorman tried to pry Rex's jaws open with a switch rod; somebody lighted a fire and made a torch of a stick and held that to Rex's tail, but he paid no attention. In the end, all the residents and storekeepers in the neighborhood were on hand, shouting this, suggesting that. Rex's joy of battle, when battle was joined, was almost tranquil. He had a kind of pleasant expression during fights, not a vicious one, his eyes closed in what would have seemed to be sleep had it not been for the turmoil of the struggle. The Oak Street Fire Department finally had to be sent for—I don't know why nobody thought of it sooner. Five or six pieces of apparatus arrived, followed by a battalion[5] chief. A hose was attached and a powerful stream of water was turned on the dogs. Rex held on for several moments more while the torrent buffeted him about like a log in a freshet.[6] He was a hundred yards away from where the fight started when he finally let go.

The story of that Homeric[7] fight got all around town, and some of our relatives looked upon the incident as a blot on the family name. They insisted that we get rid of Rex, but we were very happy with him, and nobody could have made us give him up. We would have left town with him first, along any road there was to go. It would have been different, perhaps, if he'd ever started fights, or looked for trouble. But he had a gentle disposition. He never bit a person in the ten strenuous years that he lived, nor ever growled at anyone except prowlers. He killed cats, that is true, but

---

4. **nondescript:** here, no particular breed of dog.

5. **battalion:** here, a group of firefighters.
6. **freshet:** a sudden stream of water.
7. **Homer** was a Greek poet of the eighth century B.C. who was famous for a long story-poem called the *Iliad,* about a ten-year-long battle.

quickly and neatly and without especial malice, the way men kill certain animals. It was the only thing he did that we could never cure him of doing. He never killed, or even chased, a squirrel. I don't know why. He had his own philosophy about such things. He never ran barking after wagons or automobiles. He didn't seem to see the idea in pursuing something you couldn't catch, or something you couldn't do anything with, even if you did catch it. A wagon was one of the things he couldn't tug along with his mighty jaws, and he knew it. Wagons, therefore, were not a part of his world.

Swimming was his favorite recreation. The first time he ever saw a body of water (Alum Creek), he trotted nervously along the steep bank for a while, fell to barking wildly, and finally plunged in from a height of eight feet or more. I shall always remember that shining, virgin dive. Then he swam upstream and back just for the pleasure of it, like a man. It was fun to see him battle upstream against a stiff current, struggling and growling every foot of the way. He had as much fun in the water as any person I have known. You didn't have to throw a stick in the water to get him to go in. Of course, he would bring back a stick to you if you did throw one in. He would even have brought back a piano if you had thrown one in.

That reminds me of the night, way after midnight, when he went a-roving in the light of the moon and brought back a small chest of drawers that he found somewhere—how far from the house nobody ever knew; since it was Rex, it could easily have been half a mile. There were no drawers in the chest when he got it home, and it wasn't a good one—he hadn't taken it out of anybody's house; it was just an old cheap piece that somebody had abandoned on a trash heap. Still, it was something he wanted, probably because it presented a nice problem in transportation. It tested his mettle.[8] We first knew about his achievement when, deep in the night, we heard him trying to get the chest up onto the porch. It sounded as if two or three people were trying to tear the house down. We came downstairs and turned on the porch light. Rex was on the top step trying to pull the thing up, but it had caught somehow and he was just holding his own. I suppose he would have held his own till dawn if we hadn't helped him. The next day we carted the chest miles away and threw it out. If we had thrown it out in a nearby alley, he would have brought it home again, as a small token of his integrity in such matters. After all, he had been taught to carry heavy wooden objects about, and he was proud of his prowess.

I am glad Rex never saw a trained police dog jump. He was just an amateur jumper himself, but the most daring and tenacious I have ever seen. He would take on any fence we pointed out to him. Six feet was easy for him, and he could do eight by making a tremendous leap and hauling himself over finally by his paws, grunting and straining; but he lived and died without

---

8. **mettle:** spirit or courage.

knowing that twelve- and sixteen-foot walls were too much for him. Frequently, after letting him try to go over one for a while, we would have to carry him home. He would never have given up trying.

There was in his world no such thing as the impossible. Even death couldn't beat him down. He died, it is true, but only, as one of his admirers said, after "straight-arming[9] the death angel" for more than an hour. Late one afternoon he wandered home, too slowly and too uncertainly to be the Rex that had trotted briskly homeward up our avenue for ten years. I think we all knew when he came through the gate that he was dying. He had apparently taken a terrible beating, probably from the owner of some dog that he had got into a fight with. His head and body were scarred. His heavy collar with the teeth marks of many a battle on it was awry;[10] some of the big brass studs in it were sprung loose from the leather. He licked at our hands and, staggering, fell, but got up again. We could see that he was looking for someone. One of his three masters was not home. He did not get home for an hour. During that hour the bull terrier fought against death as he had fought against the cold, strong current of Alum Creek, as he had fought to climb twelve-foot walls. When the person he was waiting for did come through the gate, whistling, ceasing to whistle, Rex walked a few wobbly paces toward him, touched his hand with his muzzle, and fell down again. This time he didn't get up.

---

9. **straight-arming:** pushing away with the arm outstretched (like a tackler in football).

10. **awry** (ə·rī′): leaning or turned to one side.

A Thurberhound.

Courtesy Rosemary Thurber.

For Study and Discussion

IDENTIFYING FACTS
1. Describe Rex's extraordinary talents. What feats do Thurber and his brothers get Rex to accomplish?

2. Describe Rex's Homeric fight with the nondescript dog. What does it take to finally break them up?

3. Why does Thurber think Rex decided to bring home the chest of drawers?

4. Describe Rex's last hours. What was his final brave struggle?

INTERPRETING MEANINGS
5. How did Thurber feel about his pet? How did he make you feel about Rex?

6. What descriptions or events do you think Thurber has **exaggerated** in this snapshot of Rex?

APPLYING MEANINGS

7. One of Thurber's famous dogs went around biting everyone and everything. His name was Muggs. When Muggs died, Thurber wrote this for his tombstone: "*Cave canem*," which means "Beware of the dog" in Latin. What would you write on Rex's tombstone? (It doesn't have to be in a foreign language.)

Literary Elements

CHARACTER

Think for a minute about Rex's unusual character. Then go back through the story and list at least three things Thurber says Rex *did*.

Next, list at least three things Thurber says Rex did *not* do.

Finally, list at least three direct statements that Thurber makes about Rex's character. (For example, at the beginning of the essay, Thurber says "there was a nobility about him.")

All of these details taken together should give you a good summary of Rex's character. Did Rex remind you of any pets you have known and loved?

Language and Vocabulary

DESCRIPTION

When you want to help a reader see something, or smell it, taste it, hear its sounds or feel its textures, you use **description**.

Thurber uses many descriptive details to make Rex jump off the page, as if he were alive. Reread paragraphs 1, 2, and 3 from the essay. Then make a list of the descriptive details from one of these paragraphs that help you **see** Rex and **hear** the sounds that result from his adventures.

Writing About Literature

WRITING YOUR OWN SNAPSHOT

Pick a favorite animal (or far-out creature, if you like) and write your own "Snapshot of a _____." You can choose your animal or creature from real life, or from a movie, book, or TV show. Use Thurber's snapshot as a model. Start out by describing your animal's physical appearance. Then go on to describe some actions that will give your reader a good idea of your animal's character. Before you write, you might want to brainstorm some ideas in a chart such as the one below. One writer filled in a few details.

Name of animal or creature: ___Sneegle___

Appearance	Actions
Has rolls of furry fat.	Is always getting stuck in small places. Once I had to pull him out of the neighbor's flowerpot.
Is orange-and-brown-striped.	
Has smart, beady eyes.	

James Thurber (1894—1961) was once asked to write an autobiographical sketch. He started out this way: "James Thurber was born on a night of wild portent and high wind in the year 1894, at 147 Parsons Avenue, Columbus, Ohio." Thurber grew up to be the greatest humorist of his time. In addition to humorous stories and essays, he was famous for his hilarious cartoons of people and animals. In 1925 he began his long-term association with *The New Yorker* magazine. Among his many famous works are "The Secret Life of Walter Mitty"; a children's fantasy called *Many Moons*; and a collection of essays called *The Middle-Aged Man on the Flying Trapeze*, from which this story about Rex is taken. Thurber loved dogs. "If I have any beliefs at all about immortality," he once said (exaggerating as usual), "it is that certain dogs I have known will go to heaven, and very, very few persons will be there. I am pretty sure that heaven will be densely populated with bloodhounds, for one thing."

A dog and a turtle by James Thurber.

Courtesy Rosemary Thurber.

Fatherhood

BILL COSBY

Before You Read

Who hasn't heard of Bill Cosby, the star of the TV show that was a top-running hit for many years? If you've seen the re-runs, do you remember how Bill Cosby is always running into family problems? (Usually they're funny ones—though not always.) In his best-selling book of essays called *Fatherhood,* he talks about similar situations that have happened in real life with his own five children. As you read aloud, you will surely hear Bill Cosby's own unique voice coming through. You will probably also find yourself imagining how these situations could take place right on *The Cosby Show.*

Good Morning, Opponents

If a family wants to get through the day with a minimum of noise and open wounds, the parents have to impose order on the domestic scene. And such order should start with breakfast, which we all know is the most important meal of the day. My wife certainly thinks so. A few weeks ago, she woke me at six o'clock in the morning and said, "I want you to go downstairs and cook breakfast for the children."

"But, dear," I said with an incredulous[1] look at the clock, "it's six in the morning."

"You tell time very nicely. Now go down and cook breakfast for the children. They have to go to school."

"But to eat at six . . . isn't that bad for the stomach? I mean, they just ate twelve hours ago."

"Bill, get out of this bed and go downstairs and cook breakfast for your children!"

I would like to repeat a point I made before: I am not the boss of my house. I don't know how I lost it and I don't know where I lost it. I probably never had it to begin with. My wife is the boss, and I do not understand how she is going to outlive me.

"But here's the thing, dear," I said, now a desperate man, "I don't know what they want to eat."

"It's *down* there."

I went back to sleep. I dreamed I was with Scott in the Antarctic, perhaps because my wife was pouring ice water over my head.

"Have you given any more thought to cooking breakfast?" she said as I awoke again.

And so, downstairs I went, wondering about the divorce laws in my state, and I started slamming things around. I had bacon, sausages, and eggs all lined up when my four-year-old arrived, looking so adorable with her cute face and little braids.

"Morning, Daddy," she said.

"Okay," I said, "what do *you* want for breakfast?"

"Chocolate cake," she replied.

"Chocolate *cake*? For *breakfast*? That's ridiculous."

Then, however, I thought about the ingredients in chocolate cake: milk and eggs and wheat, all part of good nutrition.

"You want chocolate cake, honey?" I said, cutting a piece for her. "Well, here it is. But you also need something to drink."

And I gave her a glass of grapefruit juice.

When the other four children came downstairs and saw the four-year-old eating chocolate cake, they wanted the same, of course; and since I wanted good nutrition for them too, I gave each of them a piece.

So there my five children sat, merrily eating chocolate cake for breakfast, occasionally stopping to sing:

Dad is the greatest dad you can make!
For breakfast he gives us chocolate cake!

---

1. **incredulous** (in·krej′ə·ləs): disbelieving.

The party lasted until my wife appeared, staggered slightly, and said, "Chocolate cake for *breakfast?* Where did you all get *that?*"

"*He* gave it to us! *He* made us eat it!" said my five adorable ingrates[2] in one voice; and then my eight-year-old added, "*We* wanted eggs and cereal."

Who Dressed This Mess?

The father of a daughter, especially one in her teens, will find that she doesn't like to be seen walking with him on the street. In fact, she will often ask him to walk a few paces behind. The father should not take this outdoor demotion personally; it is simply a matter of clothes. His are rotten. Every American daughter is an authority on fashion, and one of the things she knows is that her father dresses like somebody in the Mummers Parade.

In schools, you can always identify the children who were dressed by their fathers. Such children should have signs pinned on their strange attire that say:

Please do not scorn or mock me. I was dressed by my father, who sees colors the way Beethoven heard notes.[3]

Whenever I travel with my kids, the moment I open my suitcase in a hotel, I see the instructions from my wife:

The red blouse goes with the gray skirt.

Do not *let her wear the green striped shirt with the purple plaid pants.*

The pink paisley pants and pink paisley sweater go together.

They may jog or sleep in their sweat suits, but no *one is to wear a sweat suit into the hotel dining room.*

The problem is that men are less studied than women about the way they dress. They never see what a woman sees—for example, that those khaki pants do not cover their ankles. Therefore, the child who goes out to be seen by the public represents the mother; and if this child is out of fashion, an observer will say, "Who dressed that little girl? Some woman at Ringling Brothers?"

"No," will come the answer. "That is Mrs. Cosby's child."

"You're kidding! In spite of her choice of husband, I've always thought that woman had taste."

"It must have been Bill who dressed the child today."

"Oh no, he's not allowed to dress them."

Unless he happens to work for Halston,[4] the American father cannot be trusted to put together combinations of clothes. He is a man who was taught that the height of fashion was to wear two shoes that matched; and so, children can easily convince him of the elegance of whatever they do or don't want to wear.

---

2. **ingrates**: people who are ungrateful for something that's been done for them.
3. **Beethoven** (bā′tō·vən) (1770–1827) was a great German composer who became completely deaf.
4. **Halston** was a famous designer.

Bill Cosby and his TV family, the Huxtables.

"Dad, I don't want to wear socks to-day."

"Fine."

"Or a shirt."

"That's fine, too."

Mothers, however, are relentless in dressing children and often draw tears.

"Young lady, you are not going to wear red leotards outside this house unless you're on your way to dance *Romeo and Juliet*."

"But, Mom, everyone at *school* is wearing them."

"Then I'm helping you keep your individuality. You're wearing that nice gray skirt with the blue sweater and the white lace blouse."

"But, Mom, I *hate* that white lace blouse. It makes me look like a *waitress*."

"Which is what you will be if you don't wear it 'cause you won't be leaving the house to go to school, and a restaurant job will be *it*."

And now come the tears, which move a father deeply. His heart breaks for this child crying at seven in the morning, and he fears that this moment will leave a scar on her psyche. He wonders if Blue Cross covers psychiatry. Couldn't his wife back off a bit? After all, *he* would allow red leotards. He would *also* allow green combat boots.

However, a few minutes later at breakfast, where his darling little girl appears with swollen eyes, a runny nose, and the white lace blouse, she and her mother are getting along beautifully.

Of course, it is not hard to get along beautifully with my wife—certainly not for *me*. After twenty-two years of marriage, she is still as feminine as a woman can be; she has fine taste, especially in husbands; and we have many things in common, the greatest of which is that we are both afraid of the children. (The sternness with which she disciplines them is just a front.) I am happiest when she is happy, which means I am happy most of the time. . . .

About the Author

Bill Cosby (1937–   ) was born and grew up in Philadelphia. He is most famous now for his TV comedy show about the Huxtable family. Cosby started his career as a stand-up comic in the coffeehouses in Philadelphia, playing for five dollars a night. Now four records feature his jokes, with such titles as *Bill Cosby Is a Very Funny Fellow . . . Right?* and *I Started Out as a Child*.

When Cosby was twenty-three, he enrolled in Temple University in Philadelphia on an athletic scholarship (despite his high IQ, he had dropped out of high school in the tenth grade). Cosby majored in physical education (he played halfback on Temple's football team), but he chose comedy over sports as his career.

As on his sitcom, Cosby in real life has five children, and all of their names begin with the letter "E." Cosby compares his humor to jazz solos: "To me, a joke is a tune that has a beginning, a middle, and an end. I'm the soloist, and my chord changes are the punch lines that make people laugh."

UNDERSTANDING CAUSE AND EFFECT

A **cause** is a reason that something happens. An **effect** is a result of something that happens. Writers often develop their ideas by explaining or discussing causes and effects.

Read this passage from "Volcano" by Patricia Lauber carefully. Then answer the questions that follow.

> Before the eruption, Mount St. Helens was like a giant pressure cooker. The rock inside it held superheated water. The water stayed liquid because it was under great pressure, sealed in the mountain. When the mountain was torn open, the pressure was suddenly relieved. The superheated water flashed to steam. Expanding violently, it shattered rock inside the mountain and exploded out the opening, traveling at speeds of up to 200 miles an hour.
>
> The blast flattened whole forests of 180-foot-high firs. It snapped off the trunks as if they were straws. At first, this damage was puzzling. A wind of 200 miles an hour is not strong enough to level forests of giant trees. The explanation, geologists later discovered, was that the wind carried rocks ranging in size from grains of sand to blocks as big as cars. As the blast roared out of the volcano, it swept up and carried along the rock it had shattered.

Understanding Cause and Effect

1. What caused the water to stay liquid, even though it was superheated?

2. List *three* effects of the sudden relief of pressure when the mountain was torn open.

3. What explanation does the writer give for the fact that the wind could level forests of giant trees?

WRITING AN INFORMATIVE PAPER

In **informative writing,** your purpose is to share information. In a **how-to paper,** you explain how to do a process or how something works. In a **cause-and-effect paper,** you explore the reasons and/or the results of an event or situation. In a **biographical report,** you share information about a person's life, personality, and achievements.

Prewriting

1. To find a subject for a process or "how-to" paper, ask yourself questions like these:

   - What do I like to do?
   - What do I do well?

   If you want to write a cause-and-effect explanation, start with these questions:

   - Have I ever wondered why . . . ?
   - What would happen if . . . ?

   If your assignment is to write a biographical report, ask:

   - What is special about this person?
   - What has this person done that would interest my readers?

2. Gather **details** for your informative paper. If you are writing a how-to explanation, list the steps or stages of a process carefully. Remember to list them in exact order. Then list any materials that people may need to perform the process. [See **Focus** assignment on page 444.]

To identify details for a cause-and-effect explanation, fill out a chart like the one below.

Cause
_____
_____
_____
Event/Problem/Situation:
Effects
_____
_____
_____

When you fill out your chart, remember that one event or situation may have more than one cause and may result in more than one effect. [See **Focus** assignment on page 428.]

For a biographical report, fill out a chart like the one below.

Details Chart for a Biographical Report
Date and Place of Birth: _____
Education: _____
Job/Career: _____
Achievements/Special Awards: _____
Family Life: _____
Statements/Quotations: _____
Overall Importance: _____

[See **Focus** assignment on page 401.]

3. Develop a **main idea** for your paper. Use the hints below to write your main idea in one sentence.

Main Ideas in Informative Writing

How-to paper ⟶ state reason for learning process

"If you follow these simple steps, you can save money on groceries."

Cause-and-effect paper ⟶ summarize what follows

"There are three important reasons for not closing the playground."

Biographical report ⟶ state reason for person's importance

"Jack Benny was one of the most talented comedians of his time."

Writing 〜〜

1. Follow an **outline** when you write your first draft. Below are three samples.

Process Paper

I. Introduction
   A. Grab reader's attention
   B. State reason for learning process
II. Body
   A. List necessary materials
   B. Explain each step
III. Conclusion
   Summarize value of process

Cause-and-Effect Explanation

I. Introduction
   A. Grab reader's attention
   B. State main idea
II. Body
   Discuss causes/effects in a logical order
III. Conclusion
   Sum up main points and add comment

Biographical Report

I. Introduction
   A. Grab reader's attention
   B. State main idea
II. Body
   Give facts/anecdotes in chronological order
III. Conclusion
   A. Restate main idea
   B. Summarize person's importance

2. Remember to arrange the details in the body of your paper in a logical order. In an informative paper, you will usually find it convenient to use **chronological** or time order. In a process paper, you explain the steps of a process in the exact order in which they occur. In a cause-and-effect explanation, you can help the reader to follow a sequence or chain of causes and effects by using time order. Finally, in a biographical report, you will usually want to give the facts and/or anecdotes about a person's life or achievements in correct time order.

3. Help your readers to understand the connections of facts and ideas in your paper by using **transitions.** Here are some useful words and phrases.

Transitions in Informative Writing

How-to paper: after, before, first, next, then, when

Cause-and-effect paper: as a result, because, for, since, therefore

Biographical report: after, before, finally, next, often, then, until

[See **Focus** assignment on page 409.]

Evaluating and Revising

1. When you have finished a first draft, put it aside for a while. Then look it over for places that need improvement. Pay special attention to evaluating your details and the order in which you present them. Have you included all the necessary details? Have you arranged them in a sensible order that is easy to follow?

   Here is how one writer revised a paragraph in an informative paper on washing clothes.

Writer's Model

Place one load of clothes in the washing machine. ~~First separate the light-colored clothes from the dark-colored ones.~~ **Next,** Select the proper wash cycle. Wait two or three minutes until the load is completely wet. Then add detergent. at the end of the cycle remove the clothes from the washer promptly.

2. Use the following checklist when you revise your paper.

Checklist for Evaluation and Revision

✔ Do I grab the reader's interest at the beginning?

✔ Do I state my main idea in the first paragraph?

✔ Do I list any necessary materials that readers may need in order to perform a process?

✔ Do I present the details for my paper in a sensible order?

✔ Is all my information accurate?

✔ Do I conclude my paper with a clear summary statement?

Proofreading and Publishing

1. Proofread your paper and correct any errors you find in grammar, usage, and mechanics. (Here you may find it helpful to refer to the **Handbook for Revision** on pages 750–785.) Then prepare a final version of your paper by making a clean copy.

2. Consider some of the following publication methods for your paper:
   - send your essay to the school newspaper or magazine
   - illustrate your essay with maps, diagrams, or charts, and then post it on the class bulletin board
   - stage a "How-to Day" or a "I Wonder Why Day" or a "Celebrity Day" in your class and read your essays aloud

Portfolio If your teacher approves, you may wish to keep a copy of your work in your writing folder or portfolio.

The Broadway production of *Peter Pan*, with Sandy Duncan playing the lead (1979).

UNIT SIX

Plays

Drama may be the oldest form of storytelling. We don't know how or when drama began, but we can guess that people as long ago as prehistoric times started acting out an exciting story. Like any story, drama has a plot, conflict, and characters. But reading a story is basically a private act. Drama, on the other hand, is meant to be performed. Bringing a drama to life requires the creative effort of many people—the playwright, actors, directors, set designers, and many others.

Today you can attend a live performance of a play, you can watch television, or you can go to a movie theater. Why do people love drama so much? Probably for the same reasons we enjoy any form of storytelling: Stories allow us to meet people, to witness actions, and to feel emotions that broaden our experience of life. But even more than that, dramas allow us to share the storytelling experience with the people who sit with us in the living room, the movie house, or the theater.

Close Reading OF A PLAY

*J*ust like a story or poem, a play demands active reading and the exercise of your imagination. The most important feature of a play is its dialogue—what the actors and actresses say. But there is more to reading a play than simply reading dialogue. You also have to read stage directions. Stage directions (or in the case of television plays and movie scripts, camera directions) reveal where the scene is set, how the characters read their lines, and how they should act.

Guidelines for Close Reading

1. Read actively and thoughtfully. Look for conflict and clues to characterization. Ask questions. Make predictions. Try to relate the play to your own experiences. When you're finished, see if all your questions have been answered. See if any of your predictions have come true. Think about your overall response to the play. Try to state the main idea of the play in one or two sentences.

2. Read the stage directions or camera directions carefully. These directions are usually in parentheses or brackets.

3. Use your imagination to visualize the play just as if you were watching it on stage or on the movie or television screen.

    Here is the first act of a teleplay called *The Monsters Are Due on Maple Street.* This television play was produced in 1960 for the famous television series *The Twilight Zone.* Alongside the selection you will find one reader's response.

from
The Monsters Are Due on Maple Street

ROD SERLING

Act One

Scene 1:

Fade-in on shot of the night sky. The various heavenly bodies stand out in sharp, sparkling relief. As the camera begins a slow pan across the heavens, we hear the narrator.

NARRATOR: (*offstage*) There is a fifth dimension beyond that which is known to man. It is a dimension as vast as space, and as timeless as infinity. It is the middle ground between light and shadow—between science and superstition. And it lies between the pit of man's fears and the summit of his knowledge. This is the dimension of imagination. It is an area which we call the Twilight Zone.

Scene 2:

The camera begins to pan down until it passes the horizon and stops on a sign which reads "Maple Street." It is daytime. Then we see the street below. It is a quiet, tree-lined, small-town American street. The houses have front porches on which people sit and swing on gliders, talking across from house to house. STEVE BRAND *is polishing his car, which is parked in front of his house. His neighbor,* DON MARTIN, *leans against the fender watching him. A Good Humor man riding a bicycle is just in the process of stopping to sell some ice cream to a couple of kids. Two women gossip on the front lawn. Another man is watering his lawn with a garden hose. At this moment* TOMMY, *one of the two boys buying ice cream from the vendor, looks up to listen to a tremendous screeching roar from over-head. A flash of light plays on the faces of both boys and then moves down the street and disappears. Various people leave their porches or stop what they are doing to stare at the sky.* STEVE BRAND, *the man who has been polishing his car, stands there transfixed, staring upward. He looks at* DON MARTIN, *his neighbor from across the street.*

STEVE: What was that? A meteor?

DON: That's what it looked like. I didn't hear any crash though, did you?

STEVE: Nope. I didn't hear anything except a roar.

MYRA: (*from her porch*) Steve? What was that?

STEVE: (*raising his voice and looking toward the porch*) Guess it was a meteor, honey. Came awful close, didn't it?

MYRA: Too close for my money! Much too close.

[*The camera pans across the various porches to people who stand there watching and talking in low conversing tones.*]

NARRATOR: Maple Street. Six forty-four P.M. on a late September evening. (*A pause*) Maple Street in the last calm and reflective moment . . . before the monsters came!

[*The camera takes us across the porches again. A man is replacing a light bulb on a front porch. He gets down off his stool to flick the switch and finds that nothing happens. Another man is working on an electric power mower. He plugs in the plug, flicks the switch of the mower off and on; but nothing happens. Through a window we see a woman pushing her finger back and forth on the dial hook of a telephone. Her voice sounds far away.*]

WOMAN ONE: Operator, operator, something's wrong on the phone, operator!

[MYRA BRAND *comes out on the porch and calls to* STEVE.]

MYRA: (*calling*) Steve, the power's off. I had the soup on the stove and the stove just stopped working.

WOMAN ONE: Same thing over here. I can't get anybody on the phone either. The phone seems to be dead.

[*We look down again on the street. Small, mildly disturbed voices creep up from below.*]

VOICE ONE: Electricity's off.
VOICE TWO: Phone won't work.
VOICE THREE: Can't get a thing on the radio.
VOICE FOUR: My power mower won't move, won't work at all.
VOICE FIVE: Radio's gone dead!

[PETE VAN HORN, *a tall, thin man, is seen standing in front of his house.*]

PETE: I'll cut through the back yard . . . see if the power's still on, on Floral Street. I'll be right back!

[*He walks past the side of his house and disappears into the back yard. The camera pans down slowly until we are looking at ten or eleven people standing around the street and overflowing to the curb and sidewalk. In the background is* STEVE BRAND'S *car.*]

STEVE: Doesn't make sense. Why should the power go off all of a sudden *and* the phone line?
DON: Maybe some kind of an electrical storm or something.
CHARLIE: That don't seem likely. Sky's just as blue as anything. Not a cloud. No lightning. No thunder. No nothing. How could it be a storm?
WOMAN ONE: I can't get a thing on the radio. Not even the portable.

[*The people again murmur softly in wonderment.*]

CHARLIE: Well, why don't you go downtown and check with the police, though they'll probably think we're crazy or something. A little power failure and right away we get all flustered and everything——
STEVE: It isn't just the power failure, Charlie. If it was, we'd

> These people are completely cut off now. If something happens, they can't get help.

> I wonder if he'll come back?

> What's the portable?

> I notice Charlie isn't going himself!

still be able to get a broadcast on the portable.

[*There is a murmur of reaction to this.* STEVE *looks from face to face and then over to his car.*]

STEVE: I'll run downtown. We'll get this all straightened out.

[*He walks over to the car, gets in, and turns the key. Looking through the open car door, we see the crowd watching* STEVE *from the other side. He starts the engine. It turns over sluggishly and then stops dead. He tries it again, and this time he can't get it to turn over. Then very slowly he turns the key back to "off" and gets out of the car. The people stare at* STEVE. *He stands for a moment by the car and then walks toward them.*]

STEVE: I don't understand it. It was working fine before——
DON: Out of gas?
STEVE: (*shakes his head*) I just had it filled up.
WOMAN ONE: What's it mean?
CHARLIE: It's just as if . . . as if everything had stopped. (*Then he turns toward* Steve.) We'd better walk downtown.

[*Another murmur of assent to this.*]

STEVE: The two of us can go, Charlie. (*He turns to look back at the car.*) It couldn't be the meteor. A meteor couldn't do this.

[*He and* CHARLIE *exchange a look. Then they start to walk away from the group.* TOMMY *comes into view. He is a serious-faced young boy in spectacles. He stands halfway between the group and the two men who start to walk down the sidewalk.*]

TOMMY: Mr. Brand . . . you'd better not!
STEVE: Why not?
TOMMY: They don't want you to.

[STEVE *and* CHARLIE *exchange a grin and* Steve *looks back toward the boy.*]

I guess a portable radio would be battery-operated. It shouldn't be affected by a power loss. What's going on?

Steve seems to be a major character. He seems like a good guy.

It definitely is more than just a power failure. The "monsters" must be doing this. They seem powerful. Something like this happened in that movie Close Encounters of the Third Kind.

I already figured that.

What's the look? Do they suspect something horrible?

Does he know something? How does he know?

STEVE: *Who* doesn't want us to?

TOMMY: (*jerks his head in the general direction of the distant horizon*) Them!

STEVE: Them?

CHARLIE: Who are *them*?

TOMMY: (*intently*) Whoever was in that thing that came by overhead.

[STEVE *knits his brows for a moment, cocking his head questioningly. His voice is intense.*]

STEVE: What?

TOMMY: Whoever was in that thing that came over. I don't think they want us to leave here.

[STEVE *leaves* CHARLIE, *walks over to the boy, and puts his hand on the boy's shoulder. He forces his voice to remain gentle.*]

STEVE: What do you mean? What are you talking about?

TOMMY: They don't want us to leave. That's why they shut everything off.

STEVE: What makes you say that? Whatever gave you *that* idea?

WOMAN ONE: (*from the crowd*) Now isn't that the craziest thing you ever heard?

TOMMY: (*persistent but a little frightened*) It's always that way, in every story I ever read about a ship landing from outer space.

WOMAN ONE: (*to the boy's mother,* Sally, *who stands on the fringe of the crowd*) From outer space yet! Sally, you better get that boy of yours up to bed. He's been reading too many comic books or seeing too many movies or something!

SALLY: Tommy, come over here and stop that kind of talk.

STEVE: Go ahead, Tommy. We'll be right back. And you'll see. That wasn't any ship or anything like it. That was just a . . . a meteor or something. Likely as not——(*He turns to the group, now trying very hard to sound more optimistic than he*

He's seen something. The monsters!

Did he see a spaceship?

Sure looks like it!

Steve is really nervous.

This is getting creepy. Who is "they"?

It figures. No one ever believes kids.

He's really nervous. He knows there's more to it than that.

I've heard this about sunspots. What does "raise Cain" mean?

I notice that this Don isn't volunteering to go! They're all scared.

I wonder if they'll make it back?

I can't wait to read what happens next. I hope the monsters are really horrible. Maybe Tommy is part of their plan to take over.

feels.) No doubt it did have something to do with all this power failure and the rest of it. Meteors can do some crazy things, like sunspots.

DON: (*picking up the cue*) Sure. That's the kind of thing—like sunspots. They raise Cain with radio reception all over the world. And this thing being so close—why, there's no telling the sort of stuff it can do. (*He wets his lips, smiles nervously.*) Go ahead, Charlie. You and Steve go into town and see if that isn't what's causing it all.

[STEVE *and* CHARLIE *walk away from the group down the sidewalk, as the people watch silently.* TOMMY *stares at them, biting his lips, and finally calls out again.*]

TOMMY: Mr. Brand!

[*The two men stop.* TOMMY *takes a step toward them.*]

TOMMY: Mr. Brand . . . please don't leave here.

Looking at Yourself as a Reader

1. After reading the first part of the play, which of these questions are you able to answer:
   a. What is the name of the town where the action takes place?
   b. What do the adults think has caused the bright light passing overhead?
   c. Which character insists that a ship has come from outer space?
   d. Why do Steve and Charlie go into town?

2. *Foreshadowing* is the use of hints or clues to suggest that something is going to happen. List three specific events that foreshadow the trouble that lies ahead on Maple Street.

3. *Suspense* is the feeling of uncertainty about what is going to happen next. Which character creates suspense toward the end of the excerpt?

4. What do you think will happen to the people on Maple Street? Share your predictions with a partner.

THINKING ABOUT WORDS

COMPARING WORDS: SEMANTIC FEATURES

Comparing words is a good way to learn about words. Doing a semantic features chart is an interesting way to compare words. A "semantic features chart" may sound hard, but it's really easy and can be fun to do.

Semantics means "the study of the meanings of words." To do a semantic features chart, you "take apart" the meanings of some words and compare the parts. If you do this carefully, you'll see that words that seem different can be alike in surprising ways. Or, you may see what is different about words that have similar meanings.

In a semantic features chart the words themselves are listed down the left-hand side. Various features, definitions, or meanings of the words are listed along the top. If a word usually has that feature or meaning, mark +. If it usually does *not* have that feature or meaning, mark −. Below is a semantic features chart comparing two very different foods that you probably know well.

	hot	delicious	sweet	spicy	good for breakfast	a good lunch
pizza	+	+	−	+	−	+
cocoa	+	+	+	−	+	−

Now let's try a semantic features analysis with some words you will meet as you read Unit Six. These are all words telling how characters can feel. Let's begin by taking a look at their definitions.

melancholy: "a strong feeling of quiet sadness that lasts a long time"

tranquillity: "a pleasant feeling of calm and peace"

frenzy: "a wildly excited or upset feeling"

Here is a semantic features analysis for these words. The chart helps you see that both *melancholy* and *tranquillity* are quiet feelings, but one feeling is sad while the other is peaceful. It also helps you see that both *melancholy* and *frenzy* are feelings people might have if something bad happens.

	sad	quiet	peaceful	wildly upset	the feeling you have when you hear soft music	the feeling you'd have if your pet ran away
melancholy	+	+	−	−	+	+
tranquillity	−	+	+	−	+	−
frenzy	−	−	−	+	−	+

DO IT YOURSELF

Now try to do a semantic chart of your own. The chart below uses two more words from Unit Six. A hint: The results of your chart will show that someone who is arrogant *can* be caustic. (Both words are defined in the Glossary at the back of the book.)

	proud	mean	feeling superior to others	intending to hurt someone
arrogant				
caustic				

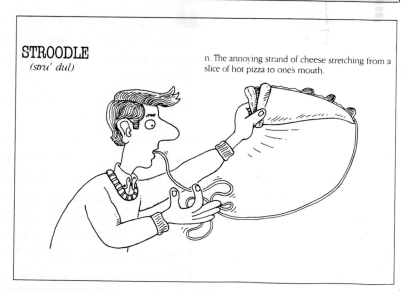

STROODLE
(stru' dul)

n. The annoying strand of cheese stretching from a slice of hot pizza to one's mouth.

Sniglets are those funny made-up words you use to describe something when a dictionary word just won't do. Here is a funny sniglet about pizza. (You might read some other funny ones Rich Hall comes up with in his book *Sniglets*.)

The Secret Garden

Dramatized by BLANCHE HANALIS,
based on the novel by FRANCES HODGSON BURNETT

Before You Read

This television play is based on a very popular young-adult
novel. The play is one huge flashback. A flashback is an
interruption in a story that flashes backward to tell you
what happened at an earlier time. As the play opens, the
main character, Mary, is an adult. She is returning to her
childhood home in Yorkshire, a county in northern England. It is 1918, just at the end of World War I. The bulk
of the play, however, takes place in the early 1900s, when
Mary is a child.

 As Act One begins, Mary is remembering her childhood. Her first memory is of her parents' home in New
Delhi, the capital of India, a country that was then under
British rule. At that time, many British officers, like Mary's
father, were stationed in India. Their families lived in India
with them, where they enjoyed lavish lifestyles and had
many native Indians as their servants.

 Epidemics of various diseases were common during
those years. Without modern medicines, sicknesses spread
easily and killed many people. Cholera (kol′ər·ə) epidemics, like the one at the beginning of this play, really
happened. Cholera is an intestinal disease that is often fatal. It spreads quickly through food and drinking water
and is even carried by flies.

 Before you read, write your responses to this question
in your journal: Suppose you were sent far away from
home to a strange mansion, where there were no other
children to play with and where you heard sounds of weeping at night. How would you feel?

All stills illustrating the play are from the television production of *The Secret Garden* (November 30, 1987).

Rosemont Productions, Ltd., and CBS-TV Reading Program.

Teleplay Terms

Scripts written for television or the movies are different from scripts written for the stage. A **teleplay** (a script written for TV) or a **screenplay** (a script written for the movies) will contain these camera directions.

Fade-in: the picture appears on the screen.

Fade-out: the pictures goes away.

Cut to: a sudden change from one scene or character to another.

Tight shot: a close-up camera shot.

Ext.: exterior (outdoors).

Int.: interior (indoors).

Long shot: a camera shot from far off.

Pan: a swiveling movement of the camera, from one side to the other.

Montage: several images appear on the screen at once.

Beat: pause.

Day: daytime scene.

Night: nighttime scene.

Cast of Characters

(in order of appearance)

BEN WEATHERSTAFF: the gardener at Misselthwaite Manor in England.

MARY LENNOX: an orphaned English girl who is sent from India to live at Misselthwaite Manor.

CAPTAIN LENNOX
MRS. LENNOX } Mary's parents.

MRS. CRAWFORD: a friend of the Lennoxes in India.

COL. MCGRAW AND
LIEUT. BARNEY } British officers serving in India.

MRS. MEDLOCK: housekeeper for Archibald Craven.

JOHN: footman for Archibald Craven.

PITCHER: servant for Archibald Craven.

DICKON SOWERBY: a boy of about twelve.

His family is large and poor and lives in a cottage near Misselthwaite Manor.

MARTHA SOWERBY: a servant for Archibald Craven; Dickon's sister.

BETTY: scullery maid at Misselthwaite Manor.

ARCHIBALD CRAVEN: master of Misselthwaite Manor; a bitter widower who is also an invalid.

COLIN CRAVEN: Archibald's only child, about twelve years old.

DR. CRAVEN: Colin's doctor; Archibald's cousin.

MRS. GORDY: cook at Misselthwaite Manor.

NURSE BOGGS: Colin's nurse.

Act One

Fade-in:

Opening titles appear over a succession of exterior shots.

1. **Ext.—Yorkshire moor—day**

   Wide on a moor with a stone gazebo[1] off in the distance.

2. **Ext. roadway—day**

   An open touring car[2] moves swiftly up the roadway toward the camera.

3. **Ext. signpost—day**

   The signpost reads: "Misselthwaite Manor." The touring car drives past and we see that the car bears a large Red Cross on the door.

4. **Ext. roadway—day**

   The car continues on its way, crossing a stone bridge.

5. **Ext. Misselthwaite Manor—day**

   A large imposing mansion that has seen better days. A tight shot of the centuries-old house reveals boarded windows and a building that is much in need of repair. The camera pans, and comes to a stop on BEN WEATHERSTAFF, *who is holding a black cat in his arms. About eighty,* BEN'S *rheumy[3] eyes and shaggy brows*

give him an almost sinister appearance. Watching the approaching car, he seems angered by the intrusion.

6. **Ext. roadway—day**

   The car continues on its way, passing the brick gazebo, which is also in a state of disrepair. BEN *peeks out around the corner of the house, staring at the approaching car.*

7. **Ext. touring car—day**

   Camera is tight on the driver of the car, MARY LENNOX, *a beautiful young woman in her early twenties. The car comes to a stop outside the manor.*

8. **Ext. Misselthwaite Manor—day**

   As she exits the car, we see that MARY *is wearing the uniform of a British Red Cross transport driver.* BEN *continues to watch* MARY *as she walks. Suddenly, the black cat he has been holding leaps from* BEN'S *arms and streaks away.*

9. **Ext. vegetable garden—day**

   As MARY *passes through shot, the camera cuts to the cat moving along a wall—seemingly stalking* MARY. MARY *continues walking and there is suddenly heard the faint sound, filtered through time, of a little girl giggling. Again, the camera cuts to the cat as it continues to stalk* MARY. MARY *continues walking and there is suddenly the sound from the past of a little girl's voice.*

LITTLE GIRL'S VOICE: I never had any friends. When will it be spring? . . . We'll

---

1. **gazebo** (gə·zē′bō): outdoor roofed structure, like an open porch.
2. **touring car:** open, luxurious car. During World War I, these touring cars were donated to the Red Cross for use in transporting the wounded.
3. **rheumy** (rōōm′ē): watery (a condition that often comes with old age).

be driven out, like from the Garden of Eden.

10. Ext. secret garden path—day

MARY *moves to a brick wall, pushes the ivy aside, and pulls a loose brick out of the wall. Whatever she expected to find inside the niche isn't there. Disappointed, she replaces the brick, moves to a tree, and leans against it. Lost in revery, remembering another time, she touches the heart-shaped locket at her throat. Once again, there is the sound of a young girl speaking.*

LITTLE GIRL'S VOICE: I shall wear it always.

[Camera cuts to the cat, now in the tree just above MARY *poising to leap. As the cat leaps, we hear a scream.]*

Cut to:

11. Int.—bedroom—(New Delhi, India, 1906)—on Mary—night

MARY, *ten years old, bolts upright in her bed, awakened by a scream. She's a thin, dark-haired, rather "plain" little girl whose arrogance and imperious[4] manner do little to enhance her appearance.* MARY *calls her ayah:*[5]

MARY: Saidie?[6]

[There's no response.]

MARY: (*continuing*) Saidie? (*Angry now*) You're supposed to come when I call you!

[Frustrated and angry, MARY *pushes the netting of her bed[7] aside and gets up from the bed. In the distance there is the sound of adult laughter. She slowly crosses the room and we see a collection of children's dolls. Clutching her robe, she starts for the door, then looks back at a photograph on the bureau. The photo is a picture of* MARY'S *parents,* CAPTAIN *and* MRS. LENNOX. MRS. LENNOX *is a luscious, dark-haired beauty.* CAPT. LENNOX, *a dashing young man in British Army dress uniform, is dark-haired with a waxed dark moustache.]*

12. Int. hallway—night

MARY *walks slowly down the hall as the laughter of the adults grows louder. She peeks through the slats of a door leading into a dining room area. Through the slats, the camera reveals a group of eight adults seated at a formal dinner setting. All the women wear lovely gowns and the men are in British Army dress uniforms.*

13. Int. dining room—night

MRS. LENNOX *sits at one end of the table,* CAPT. LENNOX *at the other.* MRS. LENNOX, *as superficial as she is beautiful, ignores her other guests as she flirts with the handsome young officer to her right.* CAPT. LENNOX *is either oblivious or indifferent. His face*

---

4. **imperious** (im·pĭr'ē·əs): proud and haughty.
5. **ayah** (ä'yə): native Indian nursemaid or lady's maid.
6. **Saidie** (sā'dē)

7. People in India and other tropical climates put netting around their beds to protect them from mosquitoes.

is damp with perspiration and he looks ill. He suddenly looks up to see his wife's flirtation. Camera cuts back to show MARY *looking through the slats of the door.* CAPT. LENNOX *reaches for his glass of wine and can barely raise it. He is obviously very sick. Camera on* MARY. *Angry at her mother for humiliating her father,* MARY *leaves the door and returns to her room.*

14. Int. Mary's bedroom—night

As MARY *enters and moves to the bed, she vents her anger at her mother on her absent nurse.*

MARY: I'll fix Saidie in the morning! I'll put a snake in her millet![8]

[MARY *sits in a chair with one of her dolls in her lap. She speaks to the doll.*]

MARY: I'm going to read this lovely story about a rajah[9] and a tiger.

Cut to:

15. Int. dining room—night

MRS. LENNOX *is speaking animatedly.*

MRS. LENNOX: I just had the most marvelous idea! After the Governor's Ball, why don't we go for a breakfast picnic along the river?

[MRS. CRAWFORD, *one of the dinner guests, speaks out.*]

MRS. CRAWFORD: I doubt I'll feel much like a picnic after dancing all night.

MRS. LENNOX: Nonsense.

MRS. CRAWFORD: Besides, I shan't be going to the ball. Steven's booked passage for me to England. He says there's some kind of plague in the provinces.

MRS. LENNOX: (*gaily*) Oh, there's always some kind of plague in the provinces, Mrs. Crawford. I wouldn't let that stop me from going to the ball.

[MRS. LENNOX *lifts the small bell next to her plate. Rings it.* CAPT. LENNOX *wipes perspiration from his brow.* CAPT. LENNOX *rises. He stares blindly at his wife, then pitches face-down on the table. Everyone with the exception of* MRS. LENNOX *races to be of help.*]

Cut to:

16. Ext. blazing sky—sunset

A horn is being blown against the blood-red setting sun.

17. Ext. street outside compound wall[10]—day

Natives are fleeing the city, some on foot, others in carts pulled by bullocks.[11] Dust stirred up by the exodus[12] casts a yellow haze. The sound is that of the bullocks, the creaking carts, and the whips of the drivers. The frightened natives have

---

8. **millet** (mil'it): here, cereal.
9. **rajah** (rä'jə): Indian prince.

10. **compound wall:** wall built around the officers' compound, or community, where Mary and her family live.
11. **bullocks** (bŏŏl'əks): steers or oxen.
12. **exodus** (ek'sə·dəs): departure of a large group of people.

only one thought: to escape the cholera that kills.

18. Int. Mary's bedroom—day
MARY *awakens and calls out for her nurse.*

MARY: Saidie . . . Saidie!

[*There is no response and* MARY *moves to the window. From her point of view we again see the hundreds of natives fleeing the city.*]

Cut to:

19. Int. servants' quarters—day
MARY'S *nurse lies dead on the bed.* MARY *is curious but not frightened. She's seen death before. Beggars often die in the streets of New Delhi.*

20. Int. parents' room—day
MARY'S *father is lying comatose[13] on the bed. Her mother, lying at the foot of the bed, is also feeling the final deadly effects of cholera.* MARY *enters the room.*

MARY: Mama, Saidie is dead and there's no one to dress me or give me breakfast.

[MRS. LENNOX *groans.*]

21. Int. dining room—day
The remains of the interrupted dinner are scattered on the table. Flies buzz around the platters of food. Some of the wineglasses are full, others have spilled and stained the damask cloth.[14]

There's evidence of hasty departure: a woman's wrap, a fan, an overturned chair.

MARY *comes into shot. She helps herself to food off the plates and drinks a glass of wine. Still thirsty, she drinks another.*

22. Int. Mary's bedroom—day
MARY *enters. The wine has gone to her head. She can barely walk and looks as if she is about to be sick. She stumbles toward the bed.*

MARY: I'm sick.

[*She plops herself down on the bed and goes to sleep.*]

23. Ext. bungalow compound—day
Natives are busily burning furniture, which people believed had been contaminated by the cholera. COL. MCGRAW *and* LIEUT. BARNEY *enter the compound.*

LIEUT. BARNEY: The servants may have taken the child with them. (*Suddenly spotting* MARY *standing in the doorway of her home*) She's here, Colonel . . . she's alive!
MARY: (*annoyed*) Of course I'm alive, but Saidie is dead, so I shall need a new ayah.
COL. MCGRAW: (*distressed*) Poor child . . .
MARY: (*haughty*) I am not a poor child. I am Mary Lennox and my father has a very important position at Government House.
LIEUT. BARNEY: (*shaken*) She doesn't know, Colonel.

[COL. MCGRAW *hesitates, trying to find a way to soften the blow.*]

---

13. **comatose** (kō′mə·tōs′): in a coma (an unconscious state).
14. **damask** (dam′əsk) **cloth:** fine table linen.

COL. MCGRAW: (*compassionate*) I'm afraid there's no easy way to tell you this, child. I'm very sorry, my dear, but your parents are dead.

[*In the turmoil surrounding the three of them,* MARY *accidentally drops her favorite doll. She tries to go back for it, but a native scoops it up and the doll is thrown into the fire.*]

MARY: (*screaming*) My doll . . . no, stop . . . give me my doll!
LIEUT. BARNEY: She doesn't understand, Colonel.
COL. MCGRAW: Well, it's hardly surprising. Look, we'll take you to Mrs. Crawford. She can look after you until other arrangements can be made.
MARY: (*screaming*) Give me my doll, my doll!

[MARY *looks back in tears as her doll begins to burn. Riding off on horseback with* COL. MCGRAW, *she continues to stare back at the burning doll.*]

Cut to:
24. *Int. hotel dining room—dusk*
    MARY *and* MRS. CRAWFORD *are seated at a table.* MARY *is ignoring her food as she stares ahead, stone-faced. She wears mourning,*[15] *a black jumper and black shoes and stockings. Her thin black coat is across the back of her chair and her black bonnet hangs from a spindle*[16] *by its ribbons.* MRS. CRAWFORD *is in a smart traveling suit and hat, and has a small fur around her shoulders.*

MRS. CRAWFORD: (*kind*) Mary, you haven't touched your tea. Aren't you hungry?
MARY: (*curt*) No.

[*A woman in her late sixties, tall and spare, enters the room and speaks to the head waiter. She is* MRS. MEDLOCK, *and at first glance she's a formidable-looking*[17] *woman. She approaches the table where* MRS. CRAWFORD *and* MARY *are seated.*]

MRS. MEDLOCK: Mrs. Crawford?
MRS. CRAWFORD: (*warmly*) You must be Mrs. Medlock. Please, do sit down.

[*As* MRS. MEDLOCK *seats herself, she glances at* MARY, *curious about her.*]

MRS. CRAWFORD: (*continuing*) Mary, this is Mrs. Medlock, who is going to take you to Yorkshire tomorrow.

[MARY *ignores the introduction.* MRS. MEDLOCK *manages to hide her annoyance at* MARY'S *rudeness, but only barely.*]

MRS. MEDLOCK: (*to* MRS. CRAWFORD) Mr. Craven said to thank you for bringing the little girl, ma'am.
MRS. CRAWFORD: It would have been unkind not to since I was returning to England anyway.

---

15. **mourning:** black clothes worn as an expression of grief for the dead.

16. **spindle:** knob on the chair.
17. **formidable** (fôr'mi·də·bəl): causing fear or dread.

[MARY *looks at* MRS. CRAWFORD *with contempt.*]

MRS. CRAWFORD: (*continuing*) Will you have some tea?

MRS. MEDLOCK: No, thank you.

MRS. CRAWFORD: What time will you be calling for Mary tomorrow?

MRS. MEDLOCK: The train leaves at seven, so I'll be here at six.

MRS. CRAWFORD: So early?! Mary, will you be good enough to ask the desk clerk to send a porter up for your trunk a little before six?

[*Rising,* MARY *stares directly at* Mrs. Medlock *without saying a word. She then moves from the table.*]

MRS. CRAWFORD: She's a difficult child, Mrs. Medlock. But to be fair, it's not entirely her fault. If her mother had carried her pretty face into the nursery more often, Mary might not be quite so recalcitrant.[18]

MRS. MEDLOCK: Neglected her, did she?

MRS. CRAWFORD: I know one shouldn't speak ill of the dead, but Mrs. Lennox was a very silly and shallow woman. She was embarrassed that Mary was plain, at least in her eyes, and Mary knew it.

MRS. MEDLOCK: Pity.

MRS. CRAWFORD: Yes. (*Warmly*) It's kind of Mr. Craven to take Mary, especially since they're not related.

MRS. MEDLOCK: There's no living relatives, but since Mr. Craven's and Capt. Lennox's father were dear friends till they both passed on, young Mr. Craven felt obliged to give the little girl a home.

Cut to:

25. **Ext. English countryside—long shot—train—day**
Though it's March and the fields are still fallow,[19] *the gently rolling landscape is lovely.*

MRS. MEDLOCK'S VOICE: I've got some nice watercress sandwiches. Would you like one?

MARY'S VOICE: (*curt*) I don't like English food, only Indian.

MRS. MEDLOCK'S VOICE: Well, English food is all you'll be getting at Misselthwaite Manor, so you'd better get used to it.

Cut to:

26. **Ext. roadway—dusk**
Carriage carrying MARY *and* MRS. MEDLOCK *to Misselthwaite Manor.*

MRS. MEDLOCK'S VOICE: Oh, it was different when Mrs. Craven was alive. She had cook make all sorts of foreign dishes. They took the recipes out of a book.

27. **Int. carriage—dusk**

MRS. MEDLOCK: (*continuing*) Mr. Archibald—Mr. Craven, that is—didn't mind. She was such a sweet pretty thing. Nobody thought she'd marry him, not with that hump on his back, but she did.

[MARY'S *intrigued in spite of herself.*]

---

18. **recalcitrant** (ri·kal′sə·trənt): stubbornly disobedient.

19. **fallow:** plowed, but not planted for the summer.

MARY: That's like a French fairy tale I once read, "Riquet de la Houppe."[20] It was about a hunchback and a beautiful princess.

MRS. MEDLOCK: So there is something that interests you.

MARY: (*coldly*) I didn't say I was interested.

28. Ext. roadway—dusk

MRS. MEDLOCK: These are the moors.

MARY: The moors are ugly!

[MRS. MEDLOCK's *patience is wearing thin, though she tries to cover.*]

MRS. MEDLOCK: Did your father ever tell you about Misselthwaite Manor?

MARY: (*bitter*) Why should he? He didn't know he was going to die and I'd have to live there.

MRS. MEDLOCK: Very well . . . I will. Misselthwaite Manor is a grand place. It was built ages ago and has over one hundred rooms.

MARY: (*caustic*) I don't care how many rooms there are.

MRS. MEDLOCK: (*dryly*) Your manners could use improving.

MARY: (*curt*) I don't have to be polite to servants.

MRS. MEDLOCK: (*sharp*) Mind yourself, Missy. I'm Mr. Craven's housekeeper and servant to no one. I'll overlook your bad manners for now, seeing you've gone through so much sadness. Not that you'll find much joy at Misselthwaite Manor. Mr. Archibald still grieves for his wife and won't trouble himself with anyone.

29. Ext. Misselthwaite Manor—night
Various shots of the carriage as it approaches the main entrance of Misselthwaite Manor.

30. Ext. Misselthwaite Manor—night
As the carriage pulls into shot, JOHN, *a young footman, hurries out of the house.*

JOHN: Have a good trip, Mrs. Medlock?

MRS. MEDLOCK: I've had worse. Fetch Miss Mary's trunk. (*Stern*) And use the back stairs.

JOHN: (*grinning*) I'll tiptoe all the way. Wouldn't want to wake the dead.

[MRS. MEDLOCK's *too tired to chastise* JOHN *for his flippant remark. She also knows what lies behind it.*]

31. Int. manor—entry hall—night
The hall, though richly furnished, has a cold, unlived-in look. Dimly lit, the tapestries on the walls recede into darkness. A staircase leads to the upper floors, and PITCHER, *an elderly, too-thin man, descends the stairs. He doesn't waste any time on amenities.*[21]

PITCHER: You're to take her directly to her

---

20. **"Riquet de la Houppe"** (ri·kā′ de la ōōp): Riquet is the hunchback's name. *Houppe* literally means "tuft."

21. **amenities** (ə·men′ə·tēz): niceties of conversation; good manners.

rooms. He doesn't want to see her, and he'll be leaving for London in the morning.

MRS. MEDLOCK: As long as I know what's expected of me, Mr. Pitcher.

PITCHER: (*terse*) What's expected, Mrs. Medlock, is that you make certain Mr. Archibald is not disturbed and that he doesn't see what he doesn't want to see.

MRS. MEDLOCK: (*dryly*) Well . . . there's a revelation. (*To* MARY) Come on.

[MARY *and* MRS. MEDLOCK *start up the stairs.*]

32. Int. bedroom—night
MARY *and* MRS. MEDLOCK *enter from the hall corridor.*

MRS. MEDLOCK: This is where you're going to live, Miss Mary. This is your bedroom, and the sitting room's just through there.

[MARY *makes no response.*]

MRS. MEDLOCK: (*continuing*) The rooms were especially prepared for you.

[*Still no reaction from* MARY.]

MRS. MEDLOCK: (*continuing*) I see a little supper has been laid out for you. You must be tired, so eat it and go to bed.

[MARY *looks at* MRS. MEDLOCK *with barely veiled contempt.* MRS. MEDLOCK *has had her fill of* MARY *for the moment.*]

MRS. MEDLOCK: (*continuing*) Good night.

[MRS. MEDLOCK *moves to the door, opens it, pauses, then turns to* MARY. *She's grim now and her words carry a veiled threat.*]

MRS. MEDLOCK: (*continuing*) You can go anywhere you like in this wing of the house, but you're not to go poking about anywhere else. Mr. Archibald won't have it and neither will I. Is that understood?

[*Over the eerie, disembodied sound of a child crying:*]

Cut to:

33. *Ext. the moors—night*
    The pale moon, high in the sky now, illuminates the Martian-like landscape.

34. *Int. Mary's bedroom—night*
    MARY, *lying awake in bed, suddenly*

hears the sound of a crying child. As the sound, filled with pain and despair, rises to a crescendo,[22] MARY *sits up and listens, obviously somewhat frightened.*

Fade-out.

---

22. **crescendo** (krə·shen′dō): the peak of a gradual increase in loudness.

For Study and Discussion

IDENTIFYING FACTS

1. Act One takes place in three different times and places. What are these three different **settings**?

2. Explain why Mary is taken to England.

3. According to Mrs. Crawford, why has Mary's mother neglected Mary?

4. What do we learn about Archibald Craven in Act One?

INTERPRETING MEANINGS

5. What is our first picture of Mary Lennox? List some of her **character traits,** or qualities. (Is she a likable character?)

6. Why do you think Mary is so unpleasant toward Mrs. Medlock? (How might Mary feel about what has just happened to her?)

7. List all the **questions** you have about the story so far.

APPLYING MEANINGS

8. How would you feel if you were Mary at this point in the play?

Act Two

Fade-in:

35. Ext. the moors—day—(dawn)

DICKON, *a boy of about twelve, sits near the moor path, fingering a panpipe.[1] A crow is perched on* DICKON's *shoulder, a little lamb snuggles against him, a small red fox lies at his feet, and a squirrel is nestled in his pocket. There's a sweetness about* DICKON, *a forever-innocence, yet we sense in him a wisdom that transcends time.*

DICKON: (*beaming*) Mornin', Mr. Weatherstaff.

BEN: Mornin', Dickon. (*Teasing*) Wishin' the day in with a song?

DICKON: Just sayin' hello to the mornin'. (*Eager*) If you got a minute, I'll show you a trick I just learned.

BEN: I've work waitin' on me at the Manor.

DICKON: Please . . .

[DICKON *looks disappointed.* BEN *hesitates. Despite his dour appearance and usually gruff manner,* BEN *is fond of* DICKON *and finds it hard to disappoint him.*]

BEN: (*continuing*) Guess the work will wait till I get there.

[DICKON's *delighted.*]

DICKON: (*to crow*) Take yourself elsewhere, Soot.

---

1. **panpipe:** a musical instrument made of tubes of different sizes. It is played by blowing across the tubes.

[*The crow obligingly hops down from* DICKON's *shoulder and settles on a rock.* DICKON *puts the panpipe in his mouth and plays a one-note "song" as he walks on his hands. He moves a few feet and falls over.*]

BEN: (*laughing*) Good trick, especially the last part.

[DICKON *grins.*]

BEN: (*continuing*) I'm off. See you around, Dickon.

DICKON: See you about, Mr. Weatherstaff.

36. Ext. establishing shot—Misselthwaite Manor—day

37. Int. sitting room—day

MARTHA, *a pretty, fresh-faced girl of about seventeen, wearing a starched white pinafore and a little ruffled cap, is setting out breakfast on the table. As* MARY *enters from the bedroom,* MARTHA *greets her with a warm smile.*

MARTHA: Mornin', miss.

MARY: Who are you?

MARTHA: Martha. Martha Sowerby.

MARY: Are you going to be my servant?

MARTHA: (*amused*) I'm to do the cleanin' up here an' a bit of waitin' on you, though judgin' on your size, you won't need much waitin' on, will ya?

MARY: (*curt*) Of course I'll need to be waited on. Someone has to dress me.

MARTHA: (*confused*) Can you not dress yourself?

MARY: Of course I can, but in India my ayah dressed me!

MARTHA: (*wry*) Well, you're in Yorkshire now, an' here children dress themselves soon's they're out of nappies.[2] You'll find some lovely new garments in the cupboard, warm ones bought by Mrs. Medlock on Mr. Archibald's orders.

MARY: (*sarcastic*) I thought he troubled himself with no one.

MARTHA: He don't. It was Mrs. Medlock who told him you'd not have proper clothing for the cold since you was comin' from India. An' it was she who had these rooms fixed up all pretty for ya. (*Kind*) I know you was wore out from your journey, so I hope you had a good sleep.

MARY: (*caustic*) How could I sleep with all that crying and moaning. This is a haunted house, isn't it?

MARTHA: (*flustered*) It was the wind you heard wutherin'[3] across the moors. It often makes a mournful sound. You best eat your breakfast 'fore it gets cold.

MARY: I don't like English food.

MARTHA: (*cajoling*) I've nine little brothers an' sisters who'd eat the table clean in a minute.

MARY: (*startled*) Nine brothers and sisters?

MARTHA: No doubt there'd be more if my dad hadn't died in his prime.[4] Feedin' that brood's hard on my mother, but Dickon's a help.

MARY: Who's Dickon?

MARTHA: He's one of our gaggle of children. He leaves what food there is for the others an' feeds hisself out on the moors. He says the wild goats give him their milk, an' there's lovely greens an' berries his for the takin'.

MARY: (*dryly*) He sounds peculiar.

MARTHA: (*laughing*) He's a rare boy, Dickon. He talks to animals an' they talk back.

MARY: That's the silliest thing I ever heard.

[MARTHA's *enjoying herself too much to stop now.*]

MARTHA: And when he plays his panpipe, wild animals stop and listen.

MARY: (*contemptuous*) Animals can't talk and they don't listen to music.

MARTHA: (*teasing*) I told ya Dickon was a rare boy.

[MARTHA *starts toward the bedroom.*]

MARY: (*curt*) I didn't dismiss you.

MARTHA: (*innocently*) You'll be makin' your own bed up then.

MARY: (*haughty*) You have my permission to go on with your work.

MARTHA: (*admiring*) The Queen couldn't of said it better herself.

[*As* MARTHA *starts out:*]

MARY: I have nothing to do.

[MARTHA *reappears.*]

MARTHA: There's plenty of gardens you can go and play in, except for the one that's locked.

MARY: (*sarcastic*) How can a garden be locked?

---

2. **nappies:** British term for diapers.
3. **wutherin':** *wuthering* is Yorkshire dialect meaning "blowing with a dull roar."
4. **in his prime:** at the peak of his life, probably in his thirties.

MARTHA: It can if there's a high wall 'round it. Dress warm if you're goin' out. March can be a cruel month in Yorkshire.

Cut to:

38. *Ext. vegetable garden—Ben—day*

BEN *is using a shovel to break the still-frozen ground. A wheelbarrow and other garden tools are nearby.* MARY *comes into shot. She's wearing her new warm coat and matching bonnet.*

MARY: What are you doing?

BEN: (*testy*) You got eyes. I'm turnin' the earth for plantin' vegetables when spring comes.

MARY: (*haughty*) It doesn't surprise me you're rude. All the servants here seem to be rude.

BEN: (*dryly*) I take it you're the little wench just come from India.

MARY: I'm not a little wench. I'm Mary Lennox, and you may call me Miss Mary, if you like. Where are the flower gardens?

BEN: (*curt*) Other side, but naught blooms this time of year.

MARY: Where's the locked-up garden?

BEN: (*glaring*) There's no door into it, so you can save yourself the trouble of lookin'!

MARY: (*contemptuous*) Of course there's a door. If there wasn't, it wouldn't be locked.

BEN: Don't go pokin' your nose where it's no cause to go!

MARY: I think everyone in Yorkshire's mad as a hatter . . .

[*A robin sitting in a tree begins to chirp.* BEN *addresses the bird affectionately.*]

BEN: Ho, ho, you cheeky little beggar. Has you started courtin' this early in the season?

[*The robin chirps in response.* MARY'S *astounded.*]

MARY: He answered you!

BEN: (*gruff, but pleased*) Considers hisself my friend.

MARY: I never had any friends.

BEN: (*dryly*) Then we're a good deal alike, neither of us good-lookin' an' both as sour as we look.

[MARY *ignores the insult. For the first time she lowers her guard.*]

MARY: (*wistfully*) Do you think he'd mind being my friend too? (*To the robin*) If you'll be my friend, I'll be yours.

BEN: (*grudging*) You said that as nice an' human as Dickon talks to his wild creatures.

MARY: You know Dickon?

BEN: The very blackberries an' heather-bells know Dickon. The foxes show him where their cubs lie an' the skylarks don't hide their nests from him (*Embarrassed*) Off with you. I've work to do.

MARY: I think I shall look for the door into the locked garden.

BEN: All you'll find are brambles and thorns.

MARY: We shall see . . . shan't we?

[*A series of shots follows:* MARY *skipping along the moor, tossing a rock into the water;* MARY *walking slowly through various gardens;* MARY *sitting quietly next to the fire in her bedroom.*]

39. Ext. the moors—day

MARY *walks along the shore of the moors. Suddenly* MARY *spots* DICKON *and his animal friends.*

MARY: You're Dickon, aren't you?

DICKON: Aye. (*Smiles*) I was waitin' for you, Miss Mary.

MARY: (*confused*) How do you know my name? And how did you know I was going to be here when I didn't know it myself?

DICKON: (*matter-of-fact*) Sometimes wishin' makes things happen. (*Introducing his "creatures"*) The crow is Soot, the fox is Captain, the lamb is Lady, the squirrel is Nut. (*Grins*) The rabbit just happened to be passin'.

MARY: Those are strange names for animals.

DICKON: It's what they asked to be called.

MARY: (*sarcastic*) Animals and birds can't talk.

DICKON: There's ways of talkin' that don't take words. (*Rising*) I've gathered some wild mustard seeds for Ben Weatherstaff, so if you don't mind company, I'll walk back to the Manor with you . . .

[DICKON *pauses.*]

DICKON: (*gently*) You're sad an' lonely now, but in time, you'll find happiness in Misselthwaite Manor.

MARY: No . . . I shall never be happy there! And I don't want your company nor anyone else's!

[MARY *moves off swiftly. She fights to hold back her tears, too proud to admit even to herself that she is lonely and unhappy.*]

Cut to:

40. Int. sitting room—Mary—night

The wind is howling. MARY, *in her nightgown, stands at the window looking out.* MARTHA *emerges from the bedroom.*

MARTHA: (*cheerful*) Your bed's turned down an' the room's all cozy. Listen to that wind!

MARY: I looked for the door into the locked garden again today, but I couldn't find it.

MARTHA: Why trouble yourself when there's so many other gardens you can go and play in?

MARY: I like to know about things. Why was the garden locked up?

MARTHA: (*sobering*) But for the garden, Mr. Archibald wouldn't be the way he is.

MARY: What do you mean?

[MARTHA *hesitates; then:*]

MARTHA: You'll not repeat what I tell you?

MARY: You know I've no one to talk to except you!

MARTHA: All right, then. But mind you, I'm only tellin' what Mrs. Medlock said 'cause this happened long before I came to work here. Mrs. Craven had that garden made when she first came to Misselthwaite as a bride. She an' Mr. Archibald would shut themselves inside for hours an' hours, like two lovebirds.

MARY: Well, if the garden was such a happy place, why was it locked up?

MARTHA: Because it's where the accident happened. There was an old tree in the garden with a high branch bent like a seat. Mrs. Craven—Lilias was her name—she loved to climb up an' sit on the branch an' read when she was alone. One day the branch broke an' she fell an' she hurt so bad she died the next day.

MARY: (dramatically) And Mr. Craven was so wild with grief that he locked up the garden and threw away the key!

MARTHA: (startled) That's what Mrs. Medlock said, but how did you know?

MARY: (triumphantly) I didn't, you just told me. And if there's a key, there must be a door, and I intend to find it . . .

[Suddenly a great draft blows the door open. As MARTHA hurries to the door, for a fleeting moment we hear the sound of a crying child. MARTHA closes the door.]

MARTHA: Someone must have left the door downstairs open to cause such a terrible draft!

MARY: You heard it, too, didn't you?

MARTHA: I heard what?

MARY: Someone crying.

MARTHA: (flustered) I told you the wind often makes a mournful sound . . .

MARY: (coldly) No, it wasn't the wind. It was human . . . and if it wasn't human, it was a ghost.

MARTHA: (nervous) It was the wind you heard wutherin' across the moors. Good night, Miss Mary.

[As MARTHA hurries to the door and exits, MARY looks after her, unconvinced.]

Cut to:

41. **Int. Mary's bedroom—Mary—night**
MARY, shaken, is sitting up in bed listening to the distant, heart-rending sound of a child crying. MARY gets out of bed, opens the door, and looks down the corridor.

42. **Int. corridor outside Mary's room—night**
Dimly lit by a single gas lamp, the corridor stretches off into darkness. MRS. MEDLOCK emerges out of the darkness. She's in her nightgown, a shawl over her shoulders. She hurries to the stairway and starts down. MARY steps into the corridor and listens, and the sound of a child crying grows louder.

Cut to:

43. **Ext. manor house—Dickon and Ben—day**
BEN sits at the base of a tree as DICKON approaches. DICKON hands a small napkin-covered basket to BEN.

DICKON: Mornin', Mr. Weatherstaff. From my mother. She baked this mornin'.

[BEN takes the napkin off, revealing a small loaf of bread.]

BEN: (pleased) My thanks to her. There's nobody bakes better bread than Susan Sowerby.

DICKON: (grinning) She'll be pleased to hear it.

[DICKON *looks off. Sobers.* BEN *follows his gaze.*]

44. *Ext. manor house—day—point of view—long shot—Mary*

MARY *has just emerged from the manor and is moving away swiftly.*

45. *Ext. manor house—day*

DICKON *and* BEN *looking after* MARY.

BEN: There's not a day she don't go lookin' for the door into the locked garden, but she'll not find it. (*Bitter*) An' 'tis better so.
DICKON: Have you been in the garden, Mr. Weatherstaff?
BEN: (*grim*) We'll not talk about that garden.
DICKON: (*thoughtful*) Well, Miss Mary won't give up. There's a stubbornness in her, but there's also a need. I'm off. See you about, Mr. Weatherstaff.

46. *Int. sitting room—day*

MARY *stands at the window watching the rain come down in sheets.* MARTHA *is dusting the furniture.* MARY *turns to her.*

MARY: I've nothing to do when it rains.
MARTHA: Mrs. Medlock has wool to spare. You could knit.
MARY: I don't know how.
MARTHA: You could read.
MARY: I haven't any books.
MARTHA: There's thousands of books in Mr. Archibald's library.
MARY: (*caustic*) Mrs. Medlock said I wasn't to go anywhere except in this wing.
MARTHA: The library's in this wing, but findin' it is a bit trickish, so I'll tell you how.

47. *Int. portrait gallery—day*

MARY *slowly enters the portrait gallery. The walls of the long gallery are hung with portraits of people long gone; men, women, and children in sixteenth- and seventeenth-century garb.* MARY *slowly looks up at the various portraits. The gallery interests her. She pauses, studies a portrait of a boy about twelve years old. He's a beautiful child with a pale, sensitive face and shock of black hair. He wears a velvet suit with a lace collar, the elegant apparel of seventeenth-century children. Intrigued,* MARY *studies the portrait for a long moment, then continues on.*

48. *Int. Lilias's bedroom—day—Mary's point of view*

MARY *enters the elegant bedroom. Maintained as though it were a shrine,*[5] *the room is exquisitely feminine. The furniture is inlaid and the bed is draped in pastel silk. Gilt chairs are done in needlepoint. A rare Aubusson carpet covers the floor. A silk-draped dressing table is crowded with crystal perfume bottles. Against one wall, a tall, glass-fronted curio cabinet displays its treasures. Everywhere vases and bowls are filled with hothouse flowers.*

Entranced, MARY *moves slowly around the room. She pauses as she reaches the dressing table, picks up one of the perfume bottles, and shakes*

---

5. **shrine:** sacred place.

it. *The bottle is empty.* MARY *takes the stopper out of the bottle and sniffs it. The scent still lingers.* MARY *seems shaken now. As she stares into the mirror remembering another time, another place:*

Flashback: parents' bedroom—(New Delhi)—night

MRS. LENNOX, *wearing a lacy peignoir,*[6] *sits at her dressing table touching perfume to her throat and ears.* MARY, *in her nightgown, appears in the mirror behind her mother.* MARY *smiles, taking pride in her pretty mother. As* MRS. LENNOX *sees her in the mirror, she gestures impatiently that* MARY's *to go away.*

Lilias's bedroom—day

MARY *stares at the mirror, hurt by the remembrance. As she replaces the perfume bottle, it clinks against another bottle and the sound triggers another memory:*

Flashback: dining room—(New Delhi)—night

CAPT. LENNOX, *his face damp with perspiration, his hand trembling, lowers his wineglass and it clinks against another glass.*

Lilias's bedroom—day

MARY, *remembering, hurts for her father.*

Dissolve to:

49. Int. tapestry corridor—day

A ceiling-to-floor tapestry hangs on the wall at the end of the short corridor. MARY *comes into shot. She pauses, aware she's reached a dead end.* MARY *freezes. The sound seems to be coming from behind the tapestry. As* MARY *moves slowly, nervously, toward the tapestry,* MRS. MEDLOCK *emerges from behind it. The shock is mutual. Then:*

MRS. MEDLOCK: (*furious*) What are you doing here?!

MARY: (*coldly*) You don't have to shout. I got lost going to the library. (*Looking at the tapestry*) I heard someone crying . . .

MRS. MEDLOCK: Old houses are full of strange sounds.

MARY: (*softly*) I know what I heard, and it was someone crying.

[MRS. MEDLOCK, *aware* MARY's *not to be put off, manages a smile of sorts.*]

MRS. MEDLOCK: Perhaps you're right. Betty, who works in the scullery,[7] has been carrying on all day because she has a toothache. Come. I'll take you to your rooms.

MARY: Toothache?

Cut to:

50. Int. manor—back stairs—Betty—day

BETTY, *a perky girl of about eighteen, carrying a breakfast tray, is going up the stairs.*

51. Int. Mary's sitting room—day

MARY, *still in her nightgown, stands at the window looking out.* BETTY *enters.*

---

6. **peignoir** (pān·wär'): robe.

7. **scullery** (skul'ər·ē): in big old-fashioned houses, a room off the kitchen where the dirty work is done.

BETTY: Mornin', miss.

MARY: Who are you?

BETTY: Betty. It's Martha's free day an' she's gone to the cottage to give her mum a hand.

[As BETTY *starts to lay out* MARY's *breakfast,* MRS. MEDLOCK *enters.*]

MARY: (*dryly, to* BETTY) Is your toothache gone?

BETTY: (*confused*) Toothache?

MARY: (*too sweetly*) The toothache you didn't have.

MRS. MEDLOCK: Betty, cook wants you at the scullery.

[BETTY *takes the empty tray and hurries out.*

The exchange about BETTY's *nonexistent toothache has made* MRS. MEDLOCK *somewhat uncomfortable. She manages a smile of sorts to cover.*]

MRS. MEDLOCK: (*continuing*) It's terribly muddy out because of the rain. I thought we'd go into the village this morning and buy you a sturdier pair of shoes.

[MARY *studies* MRS. MEDLOCK, *her face expressionless.*]

MRS. MEDLOCK: (*continuing*) It will be a nice little outing for you as well. I know you're lonely. When Mr. Archibald comes back, I shall speak to him. I'll ask him to get a governess[8] for you.

---

8. **governess** (guv′ər·nis): a woman who teaches children in a private home.

MARY: (*curt*) I had governesses in India. None of them stayed very long. They didn't like me.

MRS. MEDLOCK: Well, I'm sure that's not true.

MARY: Well, I don't lie, you do.

MRS. MEDLOCK: What a dreadful thing to say!

MARY: It's true! You lied to me yesterday about Betty having a toothache! There's something behind that tapestry and you don't want me to know about it.

[MARY *and* MRS. MEDLOCK *stare at one another.*]

Fade-out.

For Study and Discussion

IDENTIFYING FACTS

1. Who is Dickon?

2. Tell what you've learned about the secret garden in this act.

3. As Mary walks around Lilias Craven's bedroom, she experiences a **flashback** within the flashback of the main action of the play. What is she reminded of?

4. What mysterious sound does Mary hear at Misselthwaite Manor? How does Mrs. Medlock explain the noise?

INTERPRETING MEANINGS

5. Dickon says about Mary, "There's a stubbornness in her, but there's also a need." What do you think he means? (What might Mary need or want?)

Act Three

Fade-in:

52. Ext. fountain garden—day

MARY *is seen skipping rope in the garden, counting as she skips. She comes upon* BEN WEATHERSTAFF, *who is pruning trees.*

MARY: (*proudly*) I only got the skipping rope from Martha last night and I'm already very good at it.

BEN: (*dryly*) Maybe there's some child's blood in your veins after all.

[MARY's *too pleased with herself to take offense.*]

MARY: I have decided to skip one hundred times now without stopping.

[*As* MARY *skips away*, BEN *calls after her:*]

BEN: Pride goeth before a fall!

53. Ext. path outside the secret garden

MARY *skips into shot, counting aloud:*

MARY: Ninety-five, ninety-six, ninety-seven . . .

[*As* MARY *approaches the stone bench under the tree:*]

MARY: (*counting; teasing*) Have you begun courting yet, you cheeky little beggar?

[*A robin is on the ground pecking at a small mound of dirt.*]

MARY: (*counting; laughing*) Are you looking for food?

[*The robin flies off. The wind suddenly blows away the leaves from the ground and a small rusted ring protrudes from the mound.* MARY *picks up the ring; a rusted key encrusted with dirt emerges.* MARY *brushes the dirt away. Stares at the key.*]

MARY: The key . . . (*Elated*) And if there's a key, there *must* be a door!

[*A sudden gust of wind hurls leaves into* MARY's *face. Looking up, she sees that the wind has separated the ivy surrounding the secret garden. Elated, she spots the door leading to the garden.* MARY *races to the door, pushes aside the ivy, and inserts the key. The door to the secret garden slowly opens and* MARY *sneaks inside.*]

54. Ext. the secret garden—day

Once inside, we see a nightmare. The high walls are covered with dead ivy, and the thorny, leafless stems of dead rose vines are so thick they're matted. Dead brown grass chokes dead bushes. The branches of dead-looking trees are gaunt against the sky. Soggy leaves, the accumulation of years, form a spongy, rotting carpet. Everywhere, what were once climbing roses have spread and fastened themselves to trees and bushes, creating an ugly, thorny web. Stone urns that once held flowers are now filled with rotting debris. MARY *slowly, carefully walks around the garden, when something suddenly catches her eye. A tiny green shoot has poked*

through the layers of dead rotting leaves. Camera pulls back to include MARY staring down at the shoot. It's the first living thing she's seen in the garden. She kneels and scoops the dead leaves away until the dead choking grass around the shoot is revealed.

A dozen or so tender young shoots are now revealed. Camera pulls back to include MARY looking down at the shoots. MARY smiles. In the midst of death, she found life . . . minimal, fragile . . . but life.

55. **Ext. secret garden path—garden door—day**

MARY emerges from the garden. As she closes the door, pulling it firmly, a small piece of mortar falls from one of the bricks in the wall adjacent to the door.

MARY: It's my garden now. My own secret garden.

[MARY tugs the brick and it comes loose. She's found a place to hide the key. She puts the key in the niche and replaces the brick. Then she pulls the ivy over the door and steps back to study the result. The door is now completely hidden again.]

Cut to:

56. **Int. sitting room—Mary and Martha—night**

MARY, in her long white nightdress, sits at the small table eating her supper. MARTHA sits beside her.

MARY: Is Dickon good at making things grow?

MARTHA: (laughing) He can make things grow just by whisperin' to them.

MARY: When will it be spring?

MARTHA: Spring comes on sudden in Yorkshire. You'll wake up one mornin' an' the moors'll be all purple with heather. I'll go and turn down your bed now . . .

[As MARTHA starts toward the bedroom:]

MARY: I wish I had a little spade.

[MARTHA pauses, surprised.]

MARY: (casually) If I had a spade, I could make a garden. (Quickly) A vegetable garden. I'd make it next to the big vegetable garden. It would give me something to do.

MARTHA: There's a little shop in Thwaite Village has garden sets for children, a spade an' rake an' fork all tied together, but it would cost two shillings.

MARY: Oh, I've got more than that. Much more. My mother always gave me money on my birthday so I could buy a present for myself, but I never did.

[MARTHA barely manages to contain her anger at a mother who had so little interest in her child.]

MARTHA: Well, if you give me the two shillings, I'll give it to the butcher boy when he comes an' he'll pass it on to Dickon. Dickon'll go and get your garden set for you.

[As MARTHA goes into the bedroom, MARY looks after her, elated now. With *the garden tools, she can accomplish much more in her secret garden.*]

57. *Ext. secret garden path—day*
DICKON *sits under the tree next to the bench playing his pipe. The garden set, tied with a string, is on the ground beside him. As* MARY, *eager and filled with anticipation, hurries into shot,* DICKON *stops playing, picks up the garden set, and rises.*

DICKON: (*beaming*) I've brought your garden set. If you'll show me where you want to make your garden, I'll be pleased to help you start it.

[MARY *hesitates. She hates lying, and there's a sweetness and openness about* DICKON *that makes it even more difficult.*]

MARY: If I tell you a secret, will you promise not to tell anyone else?
DICKON: Aye, if it's what you want.
MARY: I've stolen a garden.

[DICKON *looks confused.*]

MARY: (*continuing*) I had to. It was locked up and no one's taken care of it for ages and ages and I'm not giving it back!
DICKON: A garden's not for givin' or takin'. A garden belongs to all. (*Studying* MARY) You found the door.

[MARY *nods.*]

DICKON: (*continuing*) It was meant to be.

58. *Ext. the secret garden—day*
MARY *and* DICKON *enter the garden.*

MARY: I was hoping it would look different than before, but it doesn't. Everything still looks dead.

[DICKON's *eyes move over the garden.*]

DICKON: It's how I thought it'd be . . .

[DICKON *moves to a bush and snaps off a cutting. He shows the cutting to* MARY.]

DICKON: (*continuing*) If you look deep, you'll see it still has a green heart. (*Looking around*) Could be others is wick, too.
MARY: (*confused*) Wick?
DICKON: In Yorkshire, *wick* means 'live.
MARY: Even the thorny ones?!
DICKON: Aye. They've run wild an' attached themselves everywhere an' some will've died. But the strong ones will be wick, an' once the dead wood's cut away, there'll be roses.

[MARY's *eyes move over the "dead" garden. She's filled with wonder now, already visualizing the roses.*]

MARY: There'll be roses . . .

59. *Int. sitting room—Mrs. Medlock—day*
MRS. MEDLOCK *paces and* MARY *enters.*

MRS. MEDLOCK: Where have you been? Mr. Archibald is back and he wants to see you!

[MARY *tenses, fearful her guardian's discovered she's been inside the locked garden.*]

MARY: (*almost afraid to ask*) Why? Why does he want to see me?

MRS. MEDLOCK: I imagine it's about the governess. I mentioned it to Mr. Pitcher and he said he'd pass it on to Mr. Archibald.

60. Int. library—evening

Ever so slowly, MARY *opens the door to the library and quietly enters. She walks farther into the room, staring at the beautiful overhead ceiling. She places her small hand on the arm of a chair. Suddenly an adult hand reaches out from the chair and clasps her hand.* MARY *jumps back in fright.* ARCHIBALD CRAVEN *slowly rises from the chair. Tall and gaunt to the point of emaciation,[1] his black coat strains against the hump on his back. Though he's not yet forty, his dark hair is streaked with white. His skin is pale and chalky. Pain from a debilitating*

---

1. **emaciation** (i·mā′sē·ā′shən): abnormal thinness.

illness[2] has etched his face with lines and created dark smudges under his eyes. A closer look would reveal fine, sensitive features.

MARY *stands frozen, unable to take her eyes from* ARCHIBALD. *He beckons her.*

ARCHIBALD: Come here . . .

[MARY *stands rooted, unable to move.*]

ARCHIBALD: (*continuing*) Don't be afraid. (*Bitter*) I know children usually find me frightening, but I'm quite harmless, I assure you.

[MARY *edges forward nervously.* ARCHIBALD *studies her.*]

ARCHIBALD: (*continuing*) You're too thin . . .
MARY: (*frantic*) I'm getting fatter!

[ARCHIBALD *continues to study* MARY. *Finally:*]

ARCHIBALD: You resemble your father. I only met him once, when we were boys, but I remember him. I envied him because he was on his way to Harrow[3] and I was too ill to go away to school.

[ARCHIBALD *moves slowly to the fireplace. He holds his forehead.*]

ARCHIBALD: (*continuing*) Ill. I have always been ill . . .

[MARY *manages to find her voice.*]

---

2. **debilitating** (di·bil′ə·tāt·ing) **illness:** illness that has made him weak and feeble.
3. **Harrow:** a famous preparatory school for boys in England.

MARY: I'm sorry.
ARCHIBALD: Yes. Are they taking good care of you?

[MARY *looks away.* ARCHIBALD *moves to the winged chair next to the fireplace and seats himself.*]

ARCHIBALD: (*continuing*) You find me repulsive, don't you?

[MARY *is shaken, but from somewhere inside herself she finds the courage to speak honestly.*]

MARY: You . . . you look different from other people . . . not repulsive.
ARCHIBALD: (*bitter*) Different. Yes, I look different. If we met in the dark, would you scream and run away?

[*Again,* MARY *finds it impossible to be anything but honest.*]

MARY: I might, but it would only be because it was the first time.

[ARCHIBALD *manages a shadow of a smile.*]

ARCHIBALD: Honesty is rare. I value it. (*Beat*) Are you happy here?
MARY: I like India better.

[ARCHIBALD *stares into the fire. After a long moment:*]

ARCHIBALD: This is a sad house for a child . . . (*Beat*) We accept what we must. (*Beat*) Oh, I meant to get a governess for you, I forgot. I'll see to it now.

[MARY *tries to hide her distress. She doesn't want a governess. A governess*

MARY: (*nervous*) Please, could I go without a governess for a while?

ARCHIBALD: Why?

[MARY *searches for a safe answer.*]

MARY: Well, I'm just getting used to being here. And when I came here, I wasn't very well . . . but now I'm getting better. And it's because I'm out a lot. And, well, if I had lessons, I wouldn't be out as much. And besides, I'm ahead on my studies. I know French, I'm good at history, and I read a lot.

ARCHIBALD: Very well. The governess can wait. Is there anything you need or want?

[ARCHIBALD *has given* MARY *an opportunity to ease her conscience about the secret garden.*]

MARY: Please, could I have a bit of earth to make a garden? I love gardens.

[ARCHIBALD *looks at* MARY *with shocked disbelief. Then he rises, moves to the window, and stands with his back to the room.* MARY'S *shaken. She's upset, perhaps angered, her guardian and she doesn't know why. After a long moment,* ARCHIBALD *turns to* MARY. *Pain and grief are mirrored in his face. He finds it difficult to speak.*]

ARCHIBALD: There was once someone, someone very dear to me, who loved gardens, too. Take your bit of earth wherever you like. (*Turning back to the window*) Go now. Leave me . . .

[MARY *understands.*]

MARY: (*whispers*) Thank you.

[*She hurries out of the room.* ARCHIBALD *watches her go, fighting to hold back his tears.*]

61. Int. corridor outside library—day
As MARY *moves into the corridor, she meets* MRS. MEDLOCK.

MRS. MEDLOCK: Miss Mary . . .

[MARY *simply stares up at her.*]

MRS. MEDLOCK: Well . . .

MARY: I think he's the saddest man I've ever seen, like the Hunchback of Notre Dame who died because he loved Esmerelda.[4]

[MRS. MEDLOCK *looks at* MARY *with surprise. This is the first time she's heard* MARY *express concern or compassion for another.*]

Cut to:

62. Int. Mary's bedroom—night
MARY *stands by her nightstand, listening once again to the sound of the child crying. Though frightened, she is now determined to find the source of the weeping. Taking a candle, she steps out into the corridor.*

---

4. **The Hunchback of Notre Dame** is a famous novel written in 1831 by the French writer Victor Hugo. The hunchback, called Quasimodo, is a handicapped bell-ringer. **Esmerelda** is a beautiful gypsy dancer.

63. Int. portrait gallery—night

The pale light from MARY's candle precedes her as she enters the gallery. In the wavering half-light, the portraits seem alive and menacing. A sudden clap of thunder followed by lightning frightens MARY even more. The crying of the child gets louder. The entire house is now filled with the menacing thunder and lightning.

64. Int. tapestry corridor—night

The sound of weeping is close. MARY appears at the top of the stairs. She looks toward the tapestry. A thin line of light is visible at the bottom of the tapestry. Suddenly the wind blows out the candle. Now, only the lightning is left to light up the corridor. Slowly, MARY inches toward the tapestry. Taking a moment to gather her courage, she pulls the tapestry aside and slowly moves inside.

65. Int. Colin's bedroom—night

The large room is crowded with handsome old furniture. MARY's eyes focus on the bed. The crying comes from someone rolling on the bed, covered by the bedcovers. Suddenly, the crying stops. Whoever is in the bed slowly drops the covers. MARY finds herself staring at a boy of about twelve. It is the boy who has been crying. As the boy sees MARY, he stares at her in shocked disbelief. MARY, equally shocked, stares back.

Fade-out.

For Study and Discussion

IDENTIFYING FACTS

1. Describe the **setting** of the secret garden when Mary first enters it. Why does Mary smile when she finds the green shoot?

2. Whom does Mary finally share her secret with? Why?

3. Describe Mary's meeting with Archibald Craven. Why is he impressed with her?

4. Besides the secret garden, what other **discovery** does Mary make in this act?

INTERPRETING MEANINGS

5. Ben calls after Mary, as she is skipping rope, "Pride goeth before a fall!" Ben is warning Mary that bragging can sometimes be followed by failure. In what other ways does Mary's pride get in her way—with making friends, for instance?

6. Mary's **character** begins to **change** in Act Three. How does it change? What important incident in this act marks the change?

7. In a play, the action moves forward when a character wants something and takes steps to get it. What does Mary want? What steps has she taken in this act to get what she wants?

8. What **questions** do you have at the end of this act?

APPLYING MEANINGS

9. Do you know people like Mary? What has happened in her life to make her the way she is?

Act Four

Fade-in:

66. *Int. Colin's bedroom—Mary and Colin—night*

For a long moment, MARY *and* COLIN *stare at each other. Then:*

COLIN: (*frightened*) Are you a ghost?
MARY: No. I thought you were.

[*As* MARY *starts toward the bed:*]

COLIN: Stay away from me!
MARY: (*continuing to the bed*) I'm Mary Lennox. I came here from India so Mr. Archibald Craven could be my guardian.
COLIN: (*trembling*) Are you sure you're not a ghost?

[MARY *extends her hand as she moves to the side of the bed and sits.*]

MARY: Touch me. If I'm a ghost, your hand will go right through mine.

[COLIN's *hand trembles as it touches* MARY's.]

COLIN: You feel real . . .
MARY: I am. Who are you?
COLIN: Colin Craven. My father's master of Misselthwaite Manor.
MARY: Your father?! Why didn't somebody tell me he had a son?!
COLIN: Because no one's allowed to talk to me!
MARY: Why?
COLIN: Because I won't have it . . . neither will my father.

MARY: Why?
COLIN: Because I'm going to have a hump on my back like he has!
MARY: Is that why you cry all the time?
COLIN: Yes.
MARY: Don't you ever go out of this room?
COLIN: No. If people look at me, I have a fit and get a fever.
MARY: I'm looking at you and you're not having a fit.
COLIN: (*glaring*) I might.
MARY: Well, you can save yourself the trouble. Now that I know you're human, not a spirit or a ghost, I'm going back to bed.
COLIN: (*imperious*) You'll stay. I've no one to talk to except my nurse, and she's away on holiday.
MARY: I don't have to stay if I don't want to.
COLIN: You said you came from India. I want to know about India.
MARY: You can read about India in books.
COLIN: (*petulant*) Reading makes my head ache.
MARY: (*tartly*) Well, if I were your father, I'd make you read so you could learn about things.
COLIN: No one can make me do anything!
MARY: Why not?
COLIN: Because I'm sick and I probably won't live to grow up!
MARY: (*interested now*) Do you want to live?

[COLIN *bursts into tears.*]

COLIN: Not if I'm going to have a lump on my back like my father . . .

MARY: You are the cryingest boy I've ever seen! I'm going back to bed!

[COLIN's *so angry he stops crying and glares at* MARY.]

COLIN: You'll stay till I say you can go!

MARY: (*haughty*) You can't make me stay if I don't want to.

COLIN: Yes, I can! Everyone has to do as I say because I'm going to die!

MARY: People who always talk about dying are boring. I'm going.

[*As* MARY *starts toward the door,* COLIN *realizes he's met his match.*]

COLIN: (*grandly*) You may go now, but you will come again tomorrow.

MARY: (*shrugging*) I might if I don't have anything else to do.

[MARY *exits. Despite the heated exchange,* COLIN *is pleased and excited.* MARY *is his first contact with another child.*]

67. Int. Colin's bedroom—night
Angle on ceiling as a large shadow looms into view. The shadow belongs to ARCHIBALD, COLIN's *father.*

ARCHIBALD *stands next to the bed, looking down at his sleeping son. He grieves for* COLIN . . . *but there's bitterness as well.*

Cut to:
68. Int. Mary's bedroom—Mary and Martha—day (morning)
MARY *sits on the bed tying her shoelaces.* MARTHA *is distraught.*

MARTHA: You shouldn't 've done it, Miss Mary! You shouldn't 've gone looking for Master Colin!

MARY: (*tartly*) Well, if you'd told me Mr. Craven had a boy, I wouldn't have gone looking for who was crying.

MARTHA: But no one's allowed to talk about him or see him!

MARY: (*dryly*) Then how do you know I saw him?

MARTHA: Because Master Colin told me! I'm the one has to look after him when his nurse is away.

[MARTHA's *on the verge of tears now.*]

MARTHA: (*continuing*) I'll be blamed for tellin' you an' I'll lose my place here.

MARY: (*impatient*) You won't lose your place because I won't tell anyone I saw him. No one's going to know except you.

MARTHA: But Master Colin said if you don't come now, he'll scream and scream till he brings the house down!

MARY: (*outraged*) We'll see about that!

69. Int. Colin's room—day

COLIN: (*furious*) You said you'd come!

MARY: (*just as furious*) I said I might! Might is only *maybe*, and I don't care if you scream till you're blue in the face!

[COLIN *turns away. He looks so frail, so miserable,* MARY's *moved in spite of herself.*]

MARY: (*continuing*) I suppose as long as I'm here I might as well stay.

COLIN: (*eager now*) Bring a stool and sit next to me.

[MARY *moves to get the stool.*]

MARY: I never had to do anything for myself in India. English people are the lords and masters there, you know.

COLIN: No, I didn't know.

MARY: (*dryly*) You don't know anything, do you?

[MARY *looks between* COLIN's *back and the pillows.*]

COLIN: (*depressed*) You're trying to see the lump on my back, aren't you?

MARY: Bother your lump. I was just thinking how different you are from Dickon.

COLIN: (*confused*) Dickon?

MARY: He's Martha's brother. If she wasn't so scared of you, she probably would have told you about him. Dickon's not like anyone in the world.

COLIN: Why?

MARY: Because he can charm animals and birds. He talks to them and they talk back.

COLIN: (*overwhelmed*) That's magic.

MARY: (*proudly*) Dickon's my friend, the first friend I've ever had.

COLIN: (*imperious*) Then I shall order him to be my friend, too.

MARY: (*contemptuous*) You don't know anything, do you? You can't order someone to be your friend. They have to want to be . . .

[*Suddenly,* MRS. MEDLOCK *and* DR. CRAVEN *enter.* MRS. MEDLOCK *is stunned, speechless, as she sees* MARY. DR. CRAVEN, *a tall, sensitive-looking man in his early forties, holds his medical bag. A gifted and dedi-*

cated physician, he barely manages to contain his anger now.]

DR. CRAVEN: (*to* MRS. MEDLOCK) How dare you permit a stranger in the sickroom?

[*Before* MRS. MEDLOCK *can defend herself:*]

COLIN: She's not a stranger and I want her here!

DR. CRAVEN: (*stern*) Calm yourself, Master Colin. You know excitement makes you ill.

COLIN: You're the one who's making me so ill, so go away!

[*Though* DR. CRAVEN *is sensitive to* COLIN's *rudeness, his first concern is for his patient. A confrontation will do* COLIN *more harm than good.*]

DR. CRAVEN: You're to rest now. I insist. (*To* MRS. MEDLOCK) The vicar's ailing, so I'll get on to him and return tomorrow.

MRS. MEDLOCK: Yes, Doctor.

[MRS. MEDLOCK *looks back at* MARY *and* COLIN. *She is still shocked as she leaves the bedroom.*]

70. Int. kitchen—day

MRS. MEDLOCK *sits at the table drinking a cup of tea to settle her frazzled nerves.* BETTY *stands nearby.* MRS. GORDY, *the cook, a plump, middle-aged woman, looks dismayed.*

MRS. GORDY: So Miss Mary found our little tyrant . . .

MRS. MEDLOCK: Master Colin actually wanted her there.

BETTY: I always said what Master Colin needs is the company of another child.

MRS. GORDY: (*tartly*) What Master Colin needs is a father who don't treat him like another plague that's been visited on him.

MRS. MEDLOCK: Anyway, it's done, and to tell the truth, I'm relieved in a way. It's been no easy thing trying to keep Miss Mary from finding out about Master Colin. Still, it's fortunate Mr. Archibald left for Cornwall this morning. Dr. Craven saw Miss Mary with Master Colin.

BETTY: He won't tell. He's Mr. Archibald's cousin an' down to inherit the manor someday, so he's not about to get Mr. Archibald angry.

MRS. MEDLOCK: (*sharp*) We'll have none of that. I've known Dr. Craven since he and Mr. Archibald were boys. (*Continues*) It was seeing Mr. Archibald suffer that turned Dr. Craven to medicine. So you just watch yourself, my girl.

71. Ext. church—day

The church bells are pealing as parishioners stream out of the church. MRS. SOWERBY, *a motherly-looking woman in her forties, wearing a neat but shabby dress, walks from the church with two of her children.*

MRS. SOWERBY: Go and see what's keepin' your brothers and sisters.

[*As the older boy starts back toward the church,* MRS. MEDLOCK *approaches* MRS. SOWERBY.]

MRS. SOWERBY: (*continuing warmly*) Mornin', Mrs. Medlock.

MRS. MEDLOCK: Good morning, Mrs. Sowerby.

MRS. SOWERBY: How's the little girl gettin' on, Mrs. Medlock? The one who come from India. (*To daughter*) Go and help your brother.

MRS. MEDLOCK: (*grim*) There are times when her rudeness and arrogance make me wish she had never left India, but I'm sure Martha's told you that.

MRS. SOWERBY: My Martha don't gossip about what's goin' on up at the manor, though she did ask my advice about how to deal with the little girl.

MRS. MEDLOCK: I could use your advice, Mrs. Sowerby. After all, you have had ten children.

MRS. SOWERBY: No two are alike.

MRS. MEDLOCK: Yes, but even so.

MRS. SOWERBY: Well, then, if I'm not bein' too forward, I'll tell you what I told Martha. A firm hand is needed, but there's also the need to see what's behind it when a child acts up. From what Martha said, there's a lot of hurt inside the little girl. Seems to me she's like one of those wild creatures my Dickon sometimes finds out on the moors caught in a snare or trap. It strikes out at Dickon whilst he's tryin' to help it, but in the end he wins their trust with his gentleness.

MRS. MEDLOCK: (*politely*) The carriage is waiting, so I'll be running along. Good morning, Mrs. Sowerby.

[*As* MRS. MEDLOCK *moves off,* MRS. SOWERBY *looks after her. She knows that although* MRS. MEDLOCK *"got the message," she's not quite ready as yet to take* MARY *to her bosom.*]

72. Ext. secret garden—day
The garden glistens from a recent rain. Some of the dead branches on the trees and bushes have been cut away and lie in neat piles on the ground. MARY *and* DICKON, *holding hands, move quickly into the garden.*

MARY: How did you get so much done?! It's been raining for two days!
DICKON: I like the rain. So does the garden. Come. I've somethin' to show you.

[*The daffodils, crocuses, and snowdrops have bloomed.*]

MARY: (*joyfully*) They bloomed!
DICKON: Aye. Crocuses an' snowdrops an' daffydowndillies is always the first to say spring's on the way.
MARY: (*eager*) When will the roses bloom?
DICKON: Not till June.
MARY: (*disappointed*) It's only the beginning of April. June's such a long way away.
DICKON: Aye, but when they bloom, there'll be curtains an' fountains of roses.
MARY: (*overwhelmed*) Curtains and fountains of roses?
DICKON: Aye, but not unless the dead wood's cut away an' the earth is softened so it can drink in the rain. (*Surveying the garden*) There's lots to be done . . .
MARY: Well, tell me what you want me to do and I'll do it.
DICKON: If you'll clean out the flower urns, I'll bring fresh earth to put in 'em.

[*As* MARY *and* DICKON *move off, the camera moves with them.*]

MARY: I'm going to tell you another secret, Dickon. There's a sick boy who lives in Misselthwaite Manor and no one is allowed to see him, but I saw him.
DICKON: It's Master Colin you're talkin' about.

[MARY *pauses, astonished.*]

MARY: You know about him?
DICKON: Aye.
MARY: Did Martha tell you?
DICKON: My mother. Mrs. Craven fell from a tree an' the fall brought on her baby too soon. My mother knows midwifin',[1] so she was called in to help the doctor with the birthin'. It was a miracle, my mother said, how Mrs. Craven held on to life long enough to bring her baby into the world.

73. Ext. path outside secret garden—day
DICKON *closes and locks the garden door, and the children move off.* MARY's *lost in thought.*

DICKON: You're still thinkin' about Master Colin . . .
MARY: He said he's going to have a lump on his back like his father and he'd rather be dead.
DICKON: I doubt he means that, though he probably wishes he'd never been born, an' that's just as bad.
MARY: Why?

---

1. **midwifin'** or **midwifing:** A midwife helps women in childbirth.

DICKON: Those that feel unwanted scarce ever thrive.

MARY: I thrived and I didn't feel wanted. My mother didn't like me.

DICKON: Did you like yourself? It's where likin' has to begin.

MARY: I didn't like myself. I wasn't pretty, and I wanted to be because my mother only liked pretty things. Colin thinks he's ugly, too, and that's why his father can't bear to look at him and never comes to see him.

DICKON: Poor lad. There's not been much joy in his life. Have you told him about your secret garden?

MARY: No. (*Suddenly decisive*) But I'm going to, Dickon. It will give him something to think about besides feeling sorry for himself. (*Concerned*) What time do you think it is?

[DICKON *looks up at the sun.*]

DICKON: Well past three.

MARY: I've been out all day without stopping for lunch! Someone may be looking for me! (*As she runs*) Bring your animals tomorrow!

DICKON: If they don't want to play on the moors again like today!

74. **Int. manor house—entry hall—angle to Martha—day**
MARTHA *is hurrying down the stairs as* MARY *runs up the stairs. In the background, we can hear* COLIN *shouting for* MARY.

MARTHA: Master Colin is causin' a terrible fuss 'cause you've not been to see him all day!

MARY: I don't have to see him if I don't want to!

MARTHA: (*pleading*) Nurse Boggs is just back from her holiday an' has things to see to. You'd be doin' her a kindness.

75. **Int. Colin's room—on Colin—day**
COLIN *is pounding his bed and shouting.* MARY *is furious as she enters.*

COLIN: I waited and waited! Where were you all day?!

MARY: With Dickon.

COLIN: If you go to him instead of coming to me, I'll have him banished![2]

MARY: Who do you think you are, the Rajah of Punjab?![3]

COLIN: If you don't come, I'll have you dragged here! You're mean and selfish!

MARY: You're the one who's selfish! All you think about is yourself and feeling sorry for yourself!

COLIN: You'd feel sorry for yourself too, if you had a lump on your back and you were going to die!

MARY: You say things like that because you want people to feel sorry for you!

[COLIN, *outraged, throws his pillow at* MARY.]

MARY: (*continuing*) I was going to tell you something special . . . and now I'm not!

COLIN: I hate you!

MARY: Good! Now I don't have any reason to come and see you again and I won't!

---

2. **banished:** sent away from one's home or country.
3. **Rajah of Punjab:** prince of Punjab, a large region in northwest India.

[MARY, *fuming, emerges from behind the tapestry. She runs right into Nurse Boggs, who has been listening to the embattled children.*]

NURSE BOGGS: I'm Master Colin's nurse.

MARY: (*sarcastic*) I feel sorry for you.

NURSE BOGGS: (*wryly*) If he had a vixen of a sister like you, he might get well.

MARY: I don't care if he doesn't get well! If we were in India, I'd put a snake in his bed!

Fade-out.

For Study and Discussion

IDENTIFYING FACTS

1. What is Colin's **conflict,** or problem? Why does he stay in bed all day?

2. How do the servants feel about Mary's discovery of Colin? Describe the reactions of Mrs. Medlock, Martha, Betty, and Nurse Boggs.

3. What advice does Mrs. Sowerby give Mrs. Medlock about Mary?

4. Do Colin's tantrums "work" on Mary? What does Mary do when he has a fit?

INTERPRETING MEANINGS

5. In what ways is Colin like Mary when we first met her?

6. When Dickon says, "Those that feel unwanted scarce ever thrive," what truth does Mary **discover** about herself? What does she discover about Colin?

7. What do you think Colin's real **problem** is? What does he really want?

APPLYING MEANINGS

8. "You can't order someone to be your friend," says Mary. "They have to want to be." How do you think friends are made? How do you make someone *want* to be your friend? Or can you?

Act Five

Fade-in:

76. Int. Mary's sitting room—night

MARY, *in her nightgown and robe, sits on the floor in front of the fire, reading. At the sound of screams, hurrying feet, and slamming doors, MARY hurries to the door, opens it, and looks out.*

77. Int. corridor outside Mary's sitting room—night

NURSE BOGGS *is hurrying toward MARY's room.*

NURSE BOGGS: (*agitated*) Master Colin's worked himself up into a terrible state and I can't calm him! I'm afraid he's going to do himself harm!

78. Int. Colin's room—Colin and Mrs. Medlock—night

COLIN *is screaming and struggling with MRS. MEDLOCK, who is trying to hold him down as he thrashes around the bed. MARY runs into the room and to the bed, NURSE BOGGS after her.*

MARY: (*screaming at the top of her lungs*) Stop it, you nasty, hateful boy! It would be a good thing if everyone went away and let you scream yourself to death!

[COLIN's *so astounded he stops screaming.*]

MARY: (*continuing; grim*) That's better. If you scream again, I'll scream, too, and I can scream much louder and longer than you can.

COLIN: (*weeping*) I only screamed because I felt the lump on my back growing bigger.

MARY: (to MRS. MEDLOCK) Can I feel the lump?

MRS. MEDLOCK: (*horrified*) Certainly not!

COLIN: I want her to!

NURSE BOGGS: (*grim*) Oh, let her, Mrs. Medlock, or there'll be no end to this.

MARY: (to COLIN) Turn over.

[COLIN *turns on his side.* MARY *draws her hand across and down* COLIN's *back.*]

MARY: (*continuing*) There's no lump.

COLIN: Yes, there is!

MARY: You've just got a knobby spine and knobby ribs like I have, so if you ever talk about lumps again, I'm going to laugh.

COLIN: I'm going to die!

MARY: (to NURSE BOGGS) Is he?

NURSE BOGGS: The specialist from London said Master Colin would improve if he ate well and got out into the air.

COLIN: (to MRS. MEDLOCK) You tell her!

MRS. MEDLOCK: You've been frail and sickly since you were born, Master Colin, and that's all I know. I've always hoped you'd outgrow your ailments, and I still hope. (*To* NURSE BOGGS) I'm worn out. Can you manage without me now?

COLIN: I want you to go! (*To* NURSE BOGGS) You, too! Only Mary can stay!

MRS. MEDLOCK: That's up to Miss Mary to decide.

COLIN: (*pleading*) Will you stay with me, Mary? Please?

MARY: Well, since you said please. But if

you scream again, I'll smother you with a pillow!

NURSE BOGGS: (*sotto*)[1] And she would, too.

MRS. MEDLOCK: Thank God Mr. Archibald's still away or we'd be answering to him for this brouhah.[2]

NURSE BOGGS: Thank God, indeed. I'd just as soon be spared this distressing business.

[MRS. MEDLOCK *and* NURSE BOGGS *exit.* COLIN, *exhausted from his tantrum, lies back on his pillow.*]

COLIN: You said you had something wonderful to tell me. Will you tell me now?

MARY: (*tart*) You don't deserve to be told, but I will if you swear not to tell anyone else.

[COLIN *nods.*]

MARY: (*continuing*) Nodding doesn't count.

COLIN: All right. I swear.

MARY: There's a secret garden and I've been in it.

COLIN: (*confused*) A secret garden?

MARY: Yes. The door was hidden and it took me forever to find it but I did. No one had taken care of it for so long that it became a wild tangle. Everything looked dead, but Dickon said some of the roses were still alive, and that when they bloomed, there'd be curtains and fountains of roses.

[COLIN's *overwhelmed.*]

MARY: (*continuing*) The first time I saw it, it was like an evil witch's garden, ugly and scary. But Dickon and I have worked and worked and now it's beginning to get beautiful.

[COLIN *tries to picture the garden in his mind's eye.*]

MARY: (*fading*) Everything was gray, but now it's like a green veil hanging over the garden. A robin's made his nest there . . . in one of the trees. I call him "Beggar" . . .

[*Reaction shot of* COLIN *smiling brightly.*]

79. *Ext. the secret garden—day*
MARY *and* DICKON *are busily knocking away dead brush and logs.*

MARY: There are holy men in India called dervishes who whirl and whirl until they go mad.[3] That's what Colin was like last night.

DICKON: It's bein' lonely that makes him act like he does.

MARY: I was lonely in India, but I didn't have fits like that . . . (*Continuing*) That's not true. If my ayah or governesses didn't do what I wanted, I'd have terrible fits. (*Sighs*) No wonder they didn't like me.

Cut to:

80. *Int. Colin's room—Colin—day*
COLIN, *propped up in bed, studies the*

---

1. *sotto* as in *sotto voce* (sot′ō vō′chā): Italian for "in a quiet voice"; "under one's breath."
2. **brouhah** (broo′hä): uproar.

3. **dervishes** (dûr′vish·əs): members of various Muslim orders, who whirl themselves into a religious frenzy.

pages of a large book filled with beautifully illustrated flowers. Under each flower is its Latin name. MARY *enters and moves to the bed.*

MARY: I thought reading makes your head ache.

COLIN: I'm just looking at the pictures. I told Nurse to get me a book with flowers, and she brought this one from the library. But I can't tell what the names are.

MARY: Flower books always use the Latin names.

COLIN: Do you know Latin?

MARY: No, but I know a poem that was first written in Latin. (*Beat*) "I do not love thee, Doctor Fell. The reason why I cannot tell. But this alone I know full well, I do not love thee, Doctor Fell."

COLIN: (*delighted*) I like that. Do you know any other poems?

MARY: Oh, there are lots of other poetry books in your father's library.

COLIN: Will you read some of the poems to me?

MARY: I'll think about it.

COLIN: You smell nice.

MARY: It's the wind from the moors you smell. It's the springtime an' out-o-doors as smells so graidely.

COLIN: (*confused*) I never heard you talk that way before.

MARY: I'm givin' thee a bit o' Yorkshire. (*Sternly*) Tha's a Yorkshire lad. Tha' should understand Yorkshire talk. It's a wonder tha's not ashamed o' thy face.

[COLIN *bursts into laughter.*]

MARY: Sometimes Dickon forgets and talks Yorkshire to me. I like it.

COLIN: (*eager*) I'd like to hear him talk Yorkshire.

MARY: How can you if you don't want anyone to look at you?

[COLIN *stares at* MARY. *This is a big decision and it doesn't come easy. Then slowly, after a long moment:*]

COLIN: I don't think I'd mind if Dickon looked at me . . .

MARY: You mean that?

COLIN: (*firmly now*) Yes. Yes.

MARY: (*awed*) Well, wonders never cease.

Cut to:

81. *Int. Colin's room—day*

COLIN *is propped up on the sofa.* MARY *enters, followed by* DICKON. *They both carry* DICKON's *animals.*

MARY: Colin . . . Dickon's here!

DICKON: I've brought along my creatures.

[DICKON *moves to sofa and puts the lamb in* COLIN's *lap.*]

DICKON: Speak gentle and he'll take to you.

[COLIN *looks down at the lamb with wonder. Then he looks up at* DICKON *and smiles radiantly.* MARY *smiles, happy for* COLIN. *The protective wall she built around her emotions is coming down. As they pet the animals, all three youngsters smile broadly.*]

COLIN: The squirrel looks sleepy. I didn't know animals are so friendly, Dickon.

Cut to:

82. Ext. manor house—day

A wicker carriage chair (wheelchair) sits in the driveway. MARY *and* DICKON *walk up to the wheelchair, followed by* JOHN, *the footman, who is carrying* COLIN *in his arms.* NURSE BOGGS *and* MRS. MEDLOCK *follow behind* JOHN. *As* JOHN *sets* COLIN *in the wheelchair:*

COLIN: (*glaring*) You hurt me!
MARY: Stop being such a crybaby!

[NURSE BOGGS *tucks the blanket around* COLIN.]

NURSE BOGGS: (*firm*) This is your first time out, so it's to be only for an hour.
COLIN: It'll be for as long as I want! (*To* DICKON) Don't stand there like a stick! Push me!

[DICKON *moves off, pushing the carriage chair,* MARY *walking alongside.* MRS. MEDLOCK, NURSE BOGGS, *and* JOHN *look after the retreating children.*]

NURSE BOGGS: I'm all for it. It's wrong for the boy to be locked away like he wasn't fit to be seen.
MRS. MEDLOCK: John is right, Nurse. Master Colin can't spend his whole life in a world of his own making.
JOHN: (*grim*) His making or his father's?
MRS. MEDLOCK: It comes to the same thing. (*Continuing*) One thing is sure. Mary Quite Contrary isn't about to take any guff from Master Colin.

83. Ext. driveway—day

The children come into shot, with DICKON *pushing the carriage chair.*

COLIN: All clear?
MARY: Safe as churches!
COLIN: I wasn't really yelling at you, Dickon . . .
MARY: (*giggling*) We talked it over and decided if we were nasty, no one would get suspicious.
DICKON: (*grinning*) Ah, I figured that out myself.

84. Ext. secret garden path—day

The children approach the secret garden. DICKON *is pushing the carriage chair slowly.*

COLIN: (*impatient now*) Go faster, Dickon!
MARY: No! In case someone happens to see us, we don't want them to know we're going somewhere special!

85. Ext. secret garden path and doorway—day

DICKON *opens the door and* MARY *pushes the carriage chair through.*

86. Ext. the secret garden—day

It's April and the spring flowers have all bloomed: pink and lavender, yellow and white. The tender green of new ivy covers the high walls. Bushes and trees wear a "green veil." Though the roses haven't bloomed, the "curtains and fountains" are greening. The fruit trees are budding. Much still remains to be done—there's still wild growth and tangle—but the garden is already lovely. MARY *watches* COLIN, *waiting for his reaction.* COLIN'S *eyes move over the garden and his face lights up.*

COLIN: This is a magic garden. It will make me well and I will live forever and ever.

Cut to:

87. Int. scullery—Betty—night

BETTY *stands at the table polishing brass pots.* MARTHA *enters.*

MARTHA: I'm done turnin' down the beds, so I'll give you a hand if you like.
BETTY: I'm not about to say no.

[MARTHA *gets a towel and joins in the polishing.*]

MARTHA: Ya know, I was lookin' at Miss Mary tonight. She was all plain an' scrawny an' she's gettin' pretty.
BETTY: It's our Yorkshire rain. Makes the flowers an' children bloom.
MARTHA: (*thoughtful*) She's changin' in other ways, too. She's still haughty sometimes, but not nearly as much.
BETTY: Her airs come from bein' spoiled when she lived in India.
MARTHA: I think it was the other way 'round. I think it was hurt and neglect made her act so badly.
BETTY: (*teasing*) You're deep as a river an' twice as murky . . .

[JOHN *enters the scullery.*]

JOHN: Mr. Archibald's back.
BETTY: (*tartly*) If you can't bring good news, don't bring any.
JOHN: (*grinning*) Well, this'll cheer you. Mr. Pitcher said they'll be off again soon.

Montage:

88. Ext. the secret garden—day

MARY *picks some flowers from the now-blossoming garden. She trots over to* COLIN, *who is sitting cheerfully in his carriage chair, and hands him the flowers. He smiles broadly.*

DICKON *discovers a bluejay feather and runs over to show it to* COLIN *and* MARY. *He points to a tree, where we see a robin's nest with several newly hatched fledglings.* DICKON *happily tries to balance the feather on his nose.*

DICKON *and* MARY *are dueling with branch stocks.* MARY *runs off, and* DICKON *runs, trying to catch her.* COLIN *sits in his chair, smiling. The smile suddenly turns to a look of sorrow as* COLIN *realizes he is unable to run with the others.*

End montage

89. Int. Colin's room—night

Moonlight streams into the room. COLIN *lies in bed, sleepless, unhappy because he can't be a part of* MARY'S *and* DICKON'S *world.* COLIN *suddenly senses that someone has entered the room.* ARCHIBALD *enters and quietly moves to a covered portrait hanging on the wall. He pulls the cord and the drape over the portrait parts. The portrait is one of Lilias Craven, an exquisite young woman.* ARCHIBALD *stares at the painting, agonizing over his loss. Slowly he closes the drapes again. As he exits,* ARCHIBALD *looks* down at COLIN *with a forlorn look on his face.* COLIN *buries his face in his pillow and begins to weep.*

90. *Ext. driveway—day*

ARCHIBALD *enters his carriage. The driver takes his seat up top.* MRS. MEDLOCK *walks to the carriage together with* PITCHER. PITCHER *is also dressed for traveling.*

MRS. MEDLOCK: Mr. Pitcher, did you find the sleeping powders?

PITCHER: Fortunately, or there'd be no rest for him tonight.

MRS. MEDLOCK: Any idea when you'll be returning?

PITCHER: It may be months. We're to travel on the Continent.[4] Italy. Spain. Wherever.

MRS. MEDLOCK: (*sighs*) He'd rather be anywhere than here.

PITCHER: (*bitter*) With good reason. (*Glancing toward carriage*) The trunks are strapped. Good-bye, Mrs. Medlock.

MRS. MEDLOCK: Safe journey, Mr. Pitcher.

[MRS. MEDLOCK *looks on sadly as the carriage pulls away.*]

Cut to:

91. *Ext. the secret garden—day*

COLIN *sits in his chair watching* MARY *and* DICKON *working in the garden. He appears unhappy that he can't work with them.*

MARY: Do you think we'll ever get finished, Dickon?

DICKON: What's been left undone for years can't be done in weeks.

COLIN: I wish I could help . . .

[COLIN *turns away. He's close to tears and doesn't want* MARY *to see. Suddenly, he spots* BEN WEATHERSTAFF *at the top of the garden wall.*]

COLIN: (*continuing; angry*) We're being spied on! (*To* BEN) Come in here!

MARY: He knows now. We'll be driven out like from the Garden of Eden . . .

DICKON: (*to* BEN) This way . . . look at all the work we've done.

BEN: The hours you must have put in. I was up on the ladder . . . (*Turning to* COLIN) Poor crippled boy . . .

COLIN: (*furious*) I'm not a poor crippled boy!

[*Holding the arms of the carriage chair,* COLIN *struggles to his feet, stands for a fraction of a moment, then falls back in the chair.*]

MARY: (*numbly*) You stood up . . .

BEN: You're frail, but you're no cripple, an' you're not dimwitted . . .

COLIN: (*outraged*) Who said I was dimwitted?

[BEN *pulls himself together.*]

BEN: Fools, that's who! But why've you locked yourself away . . .

COLIN: I thought I was going to have a lump on my back and my father hates me.

BEN: (*distressed*) Your father doesn't hate you, Master Colin.

COLIN: (*bitter*) Then why doesn't he come

---

4. **Continent:** Europe, apart from the British Isles.

Cut to:

95. Ext. the secret garden—day

MARY *and* DICKON *are supporting* COLIN *as he tries to walk.* COLIN's *feet drag uselessly on the ground.*

MARY: Pick up your feet, Colin! It won't work unless you pick up your feet!

COLIN: I'm trying!

MARY: Try harder.

COLIN: I'm tired. Take me back to my chair.

[MARY *and* DICKON *continue to half drag* COLIN *back to the carriage chair and ease him down.* BEN *watches the three youngsters in amazement.*]

DICKON: It comes hard 'cause your muscles are soft from not bein' used. We've a neighbor, Bob Haworth, whose legs was all spindly once, an' now he's a champion runner. Came from the exercises he done.

[COLIN *stares at* DICKON.]

COLIN: Could you show me how to do the exercises? Could you, Dickon!

DICKON: Aye! Give me your leg. Now push against me.

COLIN: Ow . . . that hurts, Dickon.

[MARY *looks at the birds' nest. The babies have grown bigger and* MARY *giggles in delight.*]

96. Ext. the secret garden—day

MARY *and* DICKON *are again supporting* COLIN *as he tries to walk.* COLIN *is obviously having a tough go of it.*

DICKON: Come on, Colin . . .

COLIN: Wait . . . wait . . . wait a minute.

[COLIN *slowly removes his arms from around* MARY *and* DICKON's *shoulders. He begins walking on his own— takes several steps and falls forward. In frustration,* COLIN *pounds the ground with his fists.* MARY *and* DICKON *rush over to him.*]

MARY: Stop . . . no, you can't get mad . . . you've got to try harder.

Fade-out.

For Study and Discussion

IDENTIFYING FACTS

1. What trick do the children play on the adults to hide their trip to the secret garden?

2. According to Ben Weatherstaff, why doesn't Colin's father come to see him very often?

3. What **discovery** does Mary make about Colin's lump?

4. Colin has finally found some friends and begins to go out. Why is he still unhappy?

INTERPRETING MEANINGS

5. How does Colin's **character** begin to change in Act Five? Does he become more likable?

6. How is Mary also changing?

APPLYING MEANINGS

7. Betty thinks Mary is difficult because she was spoiled. Martha thinks Mary is difficult because she was hurt and neglected. What do you think?

to see me except when he thinks I'm sleeping?

BEN: (*gently*) Maybe it's because he wants to spare you his pain an' grief.

[COLIN *stares at* BEN; *then:*]

COLIN: I want you to promise me that you won't tell anyone else about our secret garden.

BEN: It was me that worked beside your mother to make the garden, an' I'll work again to make it like it once was.

MARY: You mean you'll help us?!

BEN: Aye.

COLIN: (*defeated*) Now I'm the only one who can't help.

DICKON: (*to* MARY) Get the little spade an' the rose I potted this mornin'.

[MARY *understands what's in* DICKON's *mind and she smiles as she hurries away.* DICKON *lifts* COLIN *out of the carriage chair and puts him on the ground.*]

COLIN: (*confused*) What are you doing? . . .

[MARY *hurries into shot. She gives* DICKON *the potted rose, then hands the spade to* COLIN.]

MARY: Dig a little hole. The earth's soft.

[COLIN's *confused, but he digs the little hole.* DICKON *shakes the plant out of the pot and hands the plant to* COLIN.]

DICKON: Hold it firm with one hand, push the earth around it, an' tamp it down.

[COLIN *follows the instructions, then looks up.*]

MARY: You just planted your first rose.

Cut to:

92. *Int. Colin's room—day*
COLIN *is propped up on the sofa, the doctor and* NURSE BOGGS *standing next to him.*

DR. CRAVEN: (*concerned*) Nurse Boggs tells me you've been going out every day. You mustn't overdo, Master Colin.
COLIN: (*curt*) I'll do as I please.

93. *Int. tapestry corridor—day*
The door to COLIN's *room is ajar and* MARY *stands next to the tapestry waiting to go in.*

DR. CRAVEN'S VOICE: Your father has entrusted me with your care, Master Colin.
COLIN'S VOICE: Well, I don't trust you, so go away!
NURSE BOGGS'S VOICE: (*distressed*) I'll see you out, Doctor . . .

[MARY *quickly presses herself into the corner next to the tapestry, reluctant to let the doctor and* NURSE BOGGS *know she's been eavesdropping.* DR. CRAVEN *and* NURSE BOGGS *emerge from behind the tapestry. As they move off:*]

DR. CRAVEN: (*hopelessly*) Why does he dislike me so? I only want him to be well. It's all I've wanted since the day I brought him into the world and breathed life into him . . .

[MARY *looks at the doctor leaving, touched by his anguish. She runs back to* COLIN's *room.*]

94. *Int. Colin's room—day*

MARY: You're wrong about Dr. Craven. He wants you to get well. He wouldn't let you be so rude to him if you weren't such a poor, pitiful thing.
COLIN: I'm not a poor, pitiful thing! I stood up for a whole minute yesterday, didn't I?! (*Continues*) And from now on, I'm going to try to stand every day, and when I'm good at it, I'm going to try walking!
MARY: (*sanguine*[5]) It's about time.

---

5. **sanguine** (sang'gwin): cheerful, hopeful.

Act Six

Fade-in:

97. Int. Colin's room—day
> COLIN *has taken to his bed again. He is withdrawn, detached. Camera pulls back to include* MARY *standing next to the bed.*

MARY: (*brightly*) It's nice out. You're not going to stay in bed all day, are you, Colin?

> [COLIN *doesn't respond.*]

98. Ext. the moors—day
> MARY *and* DICKON *walk slowly across the moor.*

MARY: (*despondent*) Colin doesn't care anymore if I come to see him or not. I don't know what to do, Dickon.

> [DICKON *pauses. Looks off. He seems to be searching beyond this time and place. After a long moment:*]

DICKON: Colin'll find his way, an' you'll be the one that helps him find it. (*Smiles at* MARY) The way will come to you.

Cut to:

99. Int. Colin's room—day
> NURSE BOGGS *helps* COLIN *into the chair.*

COLIN: (*listless*) What're you doing . . . ?
MARY: We're just gonna go up and down the corridors because it's raining and I don't have anything else to do.

> [MARY *pushes* COLIN *out of the room.* NURSE BOGGS *looks after them.*]

NURSE BOGGS: (*distressed*) He'd been doing so well . . .

100. Int. portrait gallery—day
> COLIN *sits looking at the portrait of the boy in the velvet suit.*

MARY: The boy in the picture looks like you. That's why I thought you were a ghost the first time I saw you. He's dead, of course, but you're alive.

> [COLIN *glances at the portrait, then turns away indifferently.*]

Dissolve to:

101. Int. Lilias's bedroom—day

COLIN: (*whispers*) I smell roses . . .
MARY: This was your mother's room, Colin. She loved the secret garden, so she must have loved roses.

> [COLIN *looks up at* MARY. *His eyes fill.*]

MARY: (*continuing*) Sometimes it's all right to cry, Colin . . .

102. Int. Colin's room—day
> MARY *has just drawn the drape over the fireplace open and is looking up at Lilias's portrait.*

MARY: She's beautiful, Colin. As beautiful as a princess in a fairy tale. (*Turning to* COLIN) Why did you let your father cover your picture?
COLIN: I'm the one had it covered. I didn't want my mother to see the lump growing on my back.
MARY: Oh, Colin, she would've loved you even if you did have a lump. But I think

she wants you to try to keep on walking, too.

103. *Int. Colin's room—Colin—night*
Moonlight illuminates the room and portrait. COLIN *lies in bed looking at the portrait. The moments pass, then* COLIN *pushes his light covers aside and swings his legs over the side of the bed. Holding on to the nightstand, he stands. He releases his hold, takes a step, and he falls. He crawls to a chair and pulls himself up. Again and again, until he's soaked with perspiration, falling, pulling himself up, clinging to chairs and tables for support,* COLIN *struggles to walk until, finally, exhausted, he reaches the fireplace. Holding on to the mantle, he looks up at his mother's portrait.*

COLIN: Till I can walk, really walk, no one will know but you . . .

Cut to:
104. *Ext. the secret garden—day*
The roses have bloomed, a still-wild but glorious profusion of pink, coral, and deep velvet red. DICKON *pushes* COLIN's *chair as* BEN *works in the garden.*

MARY: Well . . . the roses bloomed even though it's been raining for days and days!
DICKON: They knew it was June.
BEN: Where you tend a rose, a thistle[1] canna' grow.

_____
1. **thistle** (this'əl): prickly plant.

[MARY *glances at* BEN *as though sensing something beyond his words.*]

105. *Ext. outside garden—day*
COLIN *sits in his chair with* MARY *at his side.*

MARY: I'm just thinking about what Ben Weatherstaff said about roses and thistles. He was talking about us.
COLIN: (*confused*) About us?
MARY: Yes. Ugly thoughts are like thistles, and beautiful thoughts are like roses. As long as my head was filled with ugly thoughts, I didn't have room for pretty ones and I was mean all the time. As long as you thought about a lump growing on your back, you were nasty and rude.

[COLIN *considers this, then he smiles.*]

COLIN: Thistles and roses.
MARY: Thistles and roses.

Cut to:
106. *Ext. the secret garden—day*
It's July and the roses and summer flowers are in full bloom. BEN *and* DICKON *look around, admiring the fruits of their hard work.* MARY *walks over to* COLIN, *who is seated in his chair. She carries the fox in her arms and sings.*

MARY: (*singing*)
"She is coming, my dove, my dear;
She is coming, my life, my fate . . .
The red rose cries, she is near.
She is near, and the white rose weeps,
    she is late."

Cut to:

107. Int. Colin's room—night
COLIN *lies on the bed.* MARY *sits next to him and continues to sing.*

MARY: (*singing*)
"The larkspur listens
I hear, I hear . . ."
COLIN: (*whispering*)
"And the lily whispers, I wait."

[COLIN *and* MARY *smile at one another.*]

Cut to:

108. Ext. the secret garden—day
COLIN *sits in his chair with* MARY, DICKON, *and* BEN *standing nearby.*

COLIN: Come here, everyone . . . hurry up . . . come on. I have an announcement to make. I have decided that when I grow up, I am going to do important experiments with magic. (*To* MARY) You know a little bit about magic because you grew up in India, where there are fakirs.[2] (*To* DICKON) You can charm animals, so you know some magic, too. (*Beat*) I am now going to show you my first magic experiment.

[COLIN *rises from the carriage chair. As* MARY, DICKON, *and* BEN *watch, astounded,* COLIN, *though somewhat unsteady, walks a few feet to a flower bush, picks a flower, brings it to* MARY, *then sinks down in his chair, tired but triumphant.*]

---

2. **fakirs** (fə·kirz'): Muslim or Hindu holy men who are beggars. Many claim they can perform miracles.

COLIN: (*continuing*) That is my first experiment!
MARY: (*numb*) You walked. You walked all by yourself . . .
COLIN: (*elated*) I've been practicing! Every night after Nurse Boggs went to bed, I practiced!

[DICKON *smiles.* BEN's *eyes fill.*]

BEN: Praise God . . .

[*Unnoticed,* MRS. SOWERBY *has entered the garden.*]

MRS. SOWERBY: (*overcome by emotion*) Amen.
DICKON: (*to his mother, wryly*) You're in, so you might as well come all the way . . .

[*As* MRS. SOWERBY *moves forward:*]

MRS. SOWERBY: I was passin' an' heard voices, but never did I envision what I just saw—Master Colin up an' walkin'!
DICKON: (*to* COLIN) No cause to worry. She's my mother, Susan Sowerby.
COLIN: Since you're Dickon's mother, I guess I don't mind your knowing I can walk now. I don't want anyone else to know.
BEN: (*dismayed*) Surely, you wants your father to know.
COLIN: Not yet. I want to surprise him. When he comes home, I shall walk to him and say, "I can walk now, Father, and I shall grow up and make you proud of me!" (*Firmly*) It has to be that way. That's part of the magic.
BEN: (*moved*) I never knew it by that name, but what does a name matter? Call

it magic or a miracle or the touch of God's hand . . .

MRS. SOWERBY: (*loving*) It's the Good Big Thing, Master Colin, an' I hope you'll never stop believin' in it.

MARY: Oh, he won't.

[DICKON *smiles.*]

Cut to:

109. *Int. Colin's room—night*

NURSE BOGGS *is turning down the bed.* COLIN *is propped on the sofa.* MARY *sits on the low stool beside him, books scattered on the floor around her.* NURSE BOGGS *finishes and moves toward the door.*

NURSE BOGGS: I'll be back in a little while to put you to bed, Master Colin.

[NURSE BOGGS *exits.*]

COLIN: (*worried*) I hope Dr. Craven isn't getting suspicious. When he was here before, he noticed my legs look stronger and that I'm getting fatter. (*Hoping*) Maybe he'll think I'm bloated.[3] Sick people get bloated, don't they?

MARY: Dead people get bloated when they're left out in the sun. I once saw a dead beggar in India who was so bloated he looked like a melon about to burst.

COLIN: I don't like to talk about dead people or dying.

MARY: I know, but you used to. You're not rude to Dr. Craven anymore, either.

COLIN: I know. I used to think he wanted me to die, and now I know he doesn't.

(*Hesitates*) Mary, do you like Dickon more than you like me? (*Quickly*) I don't mind if you like Dickon. I just want you to like me, too.

MARY: I like you the same but different.

Cut to:

110. *Ext. the secret garden—angle to Dickon—day*

DICKON *marches around the garden playing his panpipe. Soot is on his shoulder, the squirrel peeps out of his pocket.*

MARY *and* COLIN *sit under a tree watching* DICKON, *delighted with the "performance."* COLIN *suddenly reaches into his pocket.*

COLIN: (*suddenly shy*) I have a present for you.

[COLIN *takes a small velvet box out of his pocket, hands it to* MARY, *and she opens it. Inside the box is a small heart-shaped locket suspended from a thin gold chain.* MARY *is absolutely astonished.*]

MARY: Oh, Colin . . . it's beautiful.

COLIN: (*proudly*) I picked it out myself from a catalogue, and Mrs. Medlock ordered it for me all the way from London.

[MARY *puts the locket on.*]

MARY: I shall wear it always.

[COLIN *smiles and* MARY *responds. Though neither fully understands, both seem to sense they've made a commitment to each other.*]

---

3. **bloated:** puffed up, swollen.

Cut to:

111. Ext. sanitarium[4]—day

ARCHIBALD *is asleep on a lounge, covered with a blanket. Several medicine bottles, a water carafe,[5] and glass are on the low table beside the lounge.* ARCHIBALD *stirs in his sleep. He dreams. The picture distorts, and as though through a clouded mirror, we share his dream:*

112. Ext. secret garden—day

We see LILIAS *standing in the garden.* LILIAS *is lovely in her airy white dress.* ARCHIBALD *takes her in his arms and they're lost in a kiss. Then* LILIAS *frees herself, smiles, and moves off. She pauses abruptly and turns to* ARCHIBALD, *deeply troubled now. The picture distorts. When it comes into focus:*

113. Ext. sanitarium balcony—day

ARCHIBALD *is suddenly awakened by the sound of* PITCHER *calling to him. He holds a letter in his hand.*

PITCHER: It's time for your medicine, Mr. Archibald. Also, this letter just arrived from your solicitor.[6] Shall I see what it is?

[ARCHIBALD *nods, still caught up in his dream.* PITCHER *opens the envelope and takes out a smaller envelope.*]

---

4. **sanitarium** (san′ə·târ′ē·əm): a place where people live and receive treatment while recovering from illnesses. Archibald has gone to a sanitarium in Europe.
5. **carafe** (kə·raf′): glass bottle used to hold water, wine, or another drink.
6. **solicitor** (sə·lis′ə·tər): British term for lawyer.

PITCHER: (*continuing; confused*) Another letter is enclosed. Shall I read it?

[ARCHIBALD *nods indifferently.* PITCHER *takes the letter out of the envelope, puts on his spectacles, then reads:*]

PITCHER: (*continuing; reading*) "Dear Sir: I am Susan Sowerby who is Martha's mother who works for you in Misselthwaite Manor. I am making bold to speak to you. Please sir, I would come home if I were you. I think you would be glad you came, and if you will excuse me, sir, I think your lady would want you to come if she were here. Your obedient servant, Susan Sowerby."

[ARCHIBALD *stares at* PITCHER *in shocked disbelief.*]

PITCHER: (*continuing; frightened*) What is it?

ARCHIBALD: (*whispers*) I dreamed of Lilias . . .

Cut to:

114. Ext. the secret garden—day

Summer is drawing to a close. Petals from the overblown roses are scattered on the ground. COLIN *sits cheerfully in his carriage chair as* MARY *picks some flowers.*

DICKON: I've an errand to run, so I'm off to Thwaite Village now.

COLIN: (*concerned*) You'll come back, won't you? You have to push me back to the house.

DICKON: Aye, I'll be back. (*Teasing*) The game's not played out yet.

COLIN: (*laughing*) I like that. The game's not played out. I'm glad you're my friend, Dickon. You'll always be my friend, won't you?

[*For a fleeting moment, a shadow falls across* DICKON's *face, as though the sun's gone behind a cloud.*]

DICKON: (*quietly*) We'll be parted, you an' me, but remembrance will keep us friends.

COLIN: (*frowning*) Mary, why did Dickon say we'd be parted? How can he know that?

MARY: Dickon knows things no one else knows.

[COLIN *gets up from the carriage chair and walks with* MARY *through the garden. As they circle the garden,* MARY *looks at the overblown roses with regret.*]

MARY: Summer's almost over.

COLIN: I know. What will we do all winter, Mary?

MARY: We'll probably go to school. We're both too old for governesses, and you're well now.

COLIN: (*hoping*) Perhaps we can go to the same school.

MARY: No. Girls go to girls' schools and boys to boys'.

COLIN: I suppose there's no help for it.

MARY: You better sit down for a bit . . .

[COLIN *seats himself in the carriage chair.*]

COLIN: I wish we didn't have to go to different schools . . .

MARY: We'll write letters to each other.

COLIN: (*disconsolate*) But it won't be the same. And we won't be able to come to our secret garden.

MARY: Oh, our garden will be here when we come back. And while we're away, we can think about how beautiful it is. And how it's waiting for us.

[*Suddenly* ARCHIBALD *walks into the garden. His eyes are fixed on* COLIN *with stunned disbelief.* MARY, COLIN, *and* ARCHIBALD *are frozen in place. Immobilized. The shock is mutual.* ARCHIBALD's *eyes fill.*]

ARCHIBALD: (*whispers*) Colin . . . son . . .

[COLIN *stares at his father. This is the moment he's been waiting for, and he's rigid. Unable to move.* MARY *whispers to* COLIN.]

MARY: (*desperately*) Get up. Get up and walk! Come on, you know you can do it.

[COLIN *remains rigid, his eyes fixed on his father.*]

MARY: (*continuing*) You know you can. Please, Colin . . . go. Come on, go.

[COLIN *stirs. Then slowly, his eyes fixed on his father,* COLIN *rises out of the carriage chair. As* COLIN *moves slowly, tentatively, toward his father,* ARCHIBALD *is overcome with emotion. Weeping tears of joy, he opens his arms to receive* COLIN. *Enfolds him.*]

ARCHIBALD: (*weeping*) My boy . . . my son . . .

COLIN: Don't cry, Father. I'm well now! I can walk, and I'm going to live forever!

[MARY *smiles in delight.*]

COLIN: (*continuing*) It was the secret garden that made me well, Father. My mother's garden. And it was Mary who made me walk.

[MARY *walks over to* ARCHIBALD. *He clasps her hand in appreciation.*]

ARCHIBALD: (*to* MARY) Thank you.

COLIN: Come see our garden.

[*Hand in hand,* ARCHIBALD *and the two youngsters begin to stroll through the garden.*]

Cut to:

115. *Ext. vegetable garden—day* (1918)
MARY, *the lovely young woman in the Red Cross uniform, is seated on a bench under a tree. Suddenly, a gnarled hand reaches out and touches her shoulder. She turns, rises, and embraces* BEN WEATHERSTAFF.

MARY: Ben! Ben Weatherstaff!

[BEN *holds out the rusted key for the secret garden.*]

BEN: You'll be needin' this to unlock the garden.

MARY: (*overjoyed*) Ben, it's been so long!

BEN: I didn't know you, you've changed so . . .

MARY: (*laughing*) I grew up.

[*A shadow crosses* BEN's *face.*]

BEN: (*somber*) You know about Dickon?

MARY: Mrs. Medlock wrote to me. She wrote with such love. Such compassion.

BEN: You touched her heart an' warmed it . . . (*Heavily*) Killed in the war. Dickon. In a forest called the Argonne[7] . . .

MARY: If Dickon had to die, he would have chosen a place where there were green and growing things.

BEN: Aye. But to die so young. Who was to know . . .

MARY: (*gently*) Dickon knew.

BEN: (*managing a smile while fighting back tears*) Aye. Dickon knew. Come. I'll unlock the garden for you.

116. *Ext. the secret garden—day*
The garden is as we have never seen it before, a mystical and magical place. Roses cascade like waterfalls. Bushes have been transformed into the exquisite forms of woodland creatures. Low-growing flowers are a pink and lavender carpet. Lilies are massed against the walls and the walls are covered with tender green ivy. Pastel flowers tumble out of the stone urns. A little stream meanders through the garden; violets grow in the damp and shadowed crevices of the lichen-covered [8] *rocks that border it.* MARY *is filled with wonder, beyond words. Finally:*]

---

7. **Argonne** (är·gän′): the site in France of a famous and bloody battle during World War I.

8. **lichen** (lī′kən): mosslike plant that grows on rocks and trees.

MARY: I dreamed about the garden, but even in my dreams, it was never this beautiful . . .

[MARY *smiles tremulously at* BEN.]

MARY: (*continuing*) You did it, Ben. All these years . . .

BEN: There was a promise to be kept. As Mr. Archibald lay dyin', he said to me, "Tend the garden, Ben. Someday the children'll be comin' back an' when they do, their garden must be a magic place . . ."

MARY: (*loving*) And it is.

MAN'S VOICE (COLIN): Where you tend a rose, a thistle cannot grow . . .

[MARY *wheels toward the door.*]

MARY: (*joyful*) Colin!

[COLIN *stands in the garden door. Twenty-five now,* COLIN *is tall and handsome. He wears the uniform of a British officer and is leaning on a cane.* MARY *moves to* COLIN; *they embrace and kiss.*]

MARY: I wasn't sure the hospital would release you!

COLIN: (*teasing*) Did you think I'd let a little shrapnel⁹ stop me?

[COLIN *studies* MARY, *sober now.*]

COLIN: (*continuing*) When I was at Oxford,¹⁰ I asked you to marry me. When I was in France, I wrote and asked you to marry me. Why wouldn't you give me an answer, Mary?

MARY: I wanted you to ask me here, in our garden.

[COLIN *looks at* MARY *with love.*]

COLIN: I should have known. Will you marry me, Mary Lennox?

MARY: Of course.

[MARY *and* COLIN *join hands and stroll in the garden as* BEN *moves forward to congratulate them both. Camera pulls back as the three of them enjoy the sights and memories of the secret garden.*]

For Study and Discussion

IDENTIFYING FACTS

1. What meaning does Mary discover behind Ben's words: "Where you tend a rose, a thistle canna' grow"?

2. Describe Colin's first "magic experiment."

3. Explain why Archibald returns to Misselthwaite Manor.

4. Summarize what happens when we return to the present, 1918.

INTERPRETING MEANINGS

5. Why does Archibald weep when his son walks toward him? Do you think Archibald changed his attitudes toward Colin, Misselthwaite, and his own life?

6. **Foreshadowing** is the use of hints or clues to suggest what will happen later on in a

---

9. **shrapnel** (shrap′nəl): an artillery shell that explodes in the air and shatters a quantity of small metal balls.
10. **Oxford:** Oxford University, a well-known university in England.

story. *Foreshadowing* literally means "shadows of things to come." In Act Six, what details foreshadow Dickon's death? Were you surprised when you heard this news?

7. Early in Act One, we hear a little girl's voice saying, "I shall wear it always." By the end of the play, what do you discover this means?

8. Did you **predict** that Mary would marry Colin? Or did you think she really loved Dickon?

APPLYING MEANINGS

9. Do you like the way the story ends? If you were the director and screenwriter, would you change the last scene at all? Exchange your ideas in class.

The Play as a Whole

INTERPRETING MEANINGS

1. Why are Mary and Colin (who are rich) so unpleasant, while Martha and Dickon (who are poor) are so cheerful? What might the play be saying about what makes people happy? You might talk about this remark made by Dickon in Act Four (page 510): "Those that feel unwanted scarce ever thrive."

2. Think of what the secret garden stands for in this story. How is the **transformation** (or change) of the garden like the transformations that take place in Colin and Mary? The children break through the wall that protects and hides the garden. What "walls" have Colin and Mary built around themselves?

3. In the Bible, the Garden of Eden is an enclosed world where the first human beings are perfectly happy. There they live forever and are loved by God. Is the secret garden at all like the Garden of Eden, in your opinion? Where in Acts One and Five does Mary compare their garden to Eden?

4. The **theme** of a story is its meaning—the main idea it reveals about our lives. What does this play reveal to you about the power love has to change our lives and open us up to others—just as love transforms and opens up the secret garden?

5. The novel doesn't tell us what happens to Mary, Dickon, and Colin when they grow up. What do you think of the way the play changes the book?

APPLYING MEANINGS

6. Do you think children with Colin's problems exist today? Do you know of any people who are "thistles," like Mary? What makes people that way?

7. The garden is very important in helping Mary and Colin discover their true selves. Do you think people can live without nature? How important are flowers and green things to people today?

Writing About Literature

WRITING ABOUT CHARACTERS

The secret garden is an important influence on both Mary's and Colin's **characters.** Write a paragraph in which you explain how the garden helped change both Mary and Colin. Did the garden help them focus on something else besides their own problems? Did bringing new life to the garden encourage them to find new life in themselves?

Before you write, you might organize your ideas by filling out the charts below.

Mary:

Three adjectives describing Mary when she first arrives at Misselthwaite Manor.	1. 2. 3.
How Mary changes after finding the garden.	
Meaning of the garden to Mary.	

Colin:

Three adjectives describing Colin when we first meet him.	1. 2. 3.
Actions Colin takes to help with the garden that change his life.	
Meaning of the garden to Colin.	

Making a Diorama

A **diorama** is a box in which you place miniature characters and objects so that they re-create a scene. The box stands on its side, so that when you look inside, the diorama looks like a real stage set. Construct a diorama to illustrate a setting from *The Secret Garden*. It could be a setting in Misselthwaite Manor (remember the tapestries, the gloom, all the furniture), or in the garden, before or after its magical transformation. Before you begin, list all the details from the play that describe this setting. If your class acts out the play, you can use your diorama as a model for a stage set.

Acting It Out

(A Group Activity)
Many words in the stage directions tell how the characters are feeling as they say their lines. For example, in scene 23 (Act One) we read that Mary feels *annoyed* and *haughty*, Col. McGraw feels *distressed* and then *compassionate*, and Lieut. Barney feels *shaken*. How could the actors use their voices to suggest these feelings?

Form groups and let each group select a scene to present to the class. Look for words in the stage directions that tell how the characters are feeling. Practice saying the lines aloud until you think you have found the best way to express these feelings. Present the scenes in front of the class to see if your audience can interpret the characters' emotions. Here are some scenes you might try: 28, 37, 38, 60, and 69.

Language and Vocabulary

A SEMANTIC CHART
(A Group Project)
On page 472 you saw how to do a semantic

chart. A **semantic chart** helps you compare the meanings of several words. It helps you see how the words are both similar and different.

Here are some words from the first scenes of *The Secret Garden.* They are all words telling how the various characters feel. Working with a partner or group, make a semantic chart for each group of words.

Group 1:
angered
frustrated
annoyed

Group 2:
arrogant
superficial
indifferent

1. Your first step is to write out a brief definition of each word. (You'll find most of the words defined in the Glossary at the back of this book. Some words you will already be very familiar with. If necessary, use a dictionary.)

2. List some of the features or meanings shared by the words across the top of your chart. You might add situations in which you would have a particular feeling.

3. List your words at the left.

4. Check off the features or meanings that apply to each word.

Do these charts help you see how the words are both alike and different? Be sure to compare your charts with those done by your classmates.

About the Author

Frances Hodgson Burnett (1849–1924) was born in England to a well-to-do-family. When she was sixteen years old, an event occurred that changed her life: She and her family

moved to Knoxville, Tennessee, to join an uncle who owned a store there. The family now lived, not in a comfortable house off a city square, but in a log cabin, and without servants. Frances began earning money from her writing when she was only eighteen years old. Her first big success was a novel called *Little Lord Fauntleroy,* the story of a poor American boy who later inherits his noble father's title. Her novel *A Little Princess* is about an orphaned girl from India who lives in a cruel boarding school in London until it is discovered she is an heiress.

As for gardens, Frances Burnett always found them fascinating and mysterious, especially the overgrown gardens behind walls she longed to explore as a child in England. She also loved gardening: "I love to dig. I love to kneel down on the grass at the edge of a flower bed and pull out the weeds fiercely and throw them into a heap by my side. . . . And when at last . . . it seems as if I had beaten them . . . , I go away feeling like an army with banners."

Riddles in the Dark

Dramatized by PATRICIA GRAY
Based on the novel The Hobbit *by* J. R. R. TOLKIEN

Before You Read

This scene is from Act One of a play version of *The Hobbit*. *The Hobbit* takes place in Middle Earth, an imaginary world of long ago that is populated by wizards, dwarves, elves, trolls, goblins, dragons, and—hobbits. Hobbits are small furry-footed folk who live in a place called the Shire. They love peace, comfort, and food (not necessarily in that order). They avoid adventure and danger.

The hero of this tale, Bilbo Baggins, is a hobbit who finds himself in a very un-hobbit-like situation. The mysterious wizard Gandalf has persuaded Bilbo to join him and thirteen dwarves on a dangerous quest. Their aim is to retrieve the dwarves' ancient treasure from the evil dragon Smaug.

At this point in the play, Bilbo, Gandalf, the dwarf Thorin, and the other dwarves have narrowly escaped being eaten by hungry trolls. Now, resting in a cave in the Misty Mountains, they are about to be attacked by goblins. This portion of the play is adapted from Chapter 5 in the original novel. (Tolkien continues his tales of Middle Earth in his trilogy—a series of three related books—*The Lord of the Rings*.)

As you read, use the stage directions to help you visualize the strange setting. Try to picture the stage and what the characters are doing on it. When you produce the play for your classroom theater, you will want to assign someone to design sets and provide "props," those movable objects that the actors use on stage. One prop you'll need, for example, is a book that can serve as Bilbo's diary.

The character Gollum has a peculiar way of speaking. Once you "hear" his voice, with its strange hissing sounds and unusual grammar, you'll never forget it. As you read the play, first try to imagine what Gollum's voice should sound like. Then practice acting out some of his lines with a friend.

Gollum in the movie *The Lord of the Rings* (1978). All stills are from this Saul Zaentz production.

Stage Terms

Stage plays contain special directions that the director and actors must understand and follow. Stage directions usually appear in parentheses or brackets. They tell actors where to stand on stage, when to enter and exit, how to say their lines, and so on. Theater people use a large vocabulary of stage direction terms; some of the most common ones are listed below. A hint: "left" and "right" always refer to the actor's left and right as he or she is facing the audience.

R (stage right).

L (stage left).

C (center): the center of the stage.

D (downstage): toward the audience.

U (upstage): away from the audience.

UC (upstage center): the center of the stage, farthest from the audience.

DC (downstage center): the center of the stage, closest to the audience.

UR (upstage right): the upper right-hand corner of the stage, farthest from the audience.

Off (offstage): those parts of the stage that are outside the boundaries of the setting.

ad lib: a term that comes from a Latin phrase meaning literally "at pleasure." To *ad lib* means to "improvise, or make up." Usually, actors ad lib in scenes in which many characters are talking at once.

Cast of Characters

BILBO BAGGINS: a hobbit.

THORIN: a dwarf, grandson of the old dwarf king from whom Smaug stole the treasure long ago.

GLOIN, BALIN, BOFUR, OIN AND ORI: other dwarves.

GANDALF: a mysterious wizard who is leading the quest for the dragon's treasure.

GOBLINS: evil creatures who want to destroy the dwarves.

GOLLUM: a fishlike creature who lives in a cave.

SCENE:

A cave in the Misty Mountains. Lightning flashes. Sounds of thunder.

At rise of curtain:

Lights come up on platform at stage L. The DWARVES *and* GANDALF *are huddled together, talking in hushed tones.* BILBO *sits downstage on platform, writing in his diary. He scribbles industriously, then holds book off and reads impressively.*

BILBO: (*reading his entry*) "This is the first chance I've had to write in ages. We've been driven before the storm for twelve days and nights." (*There is a distant roll of thunder and more lightning.*) "The mountain path is steep and long. We are now resting in a smelly cave." (*He again scribbles rapidly.*)

THORIN: (*in a low voice*) This is awful!

GLOIN: (*holding his nose*) Phew!

BALIN: At least it's dry!

GANDALF: (*to* THORIN) If you know a better place, take us there!

BILBO: (*holding his script off and reading again*) "We don't dare to talk too loud—there are goblins in these mountains. All this misery for their gold—and my pride—hardly seems worthwhile. The next time anyone calls me a coward, I'll agree with him and stay home. I'd gladly trade my share of the treasure this minute for a steaming bowl of mutton soup!"

GANDALF: Keep your voices down! Thorin, look, your blade glows—that means goblins are nearby. Keep your eyes and ears open. Goblins are swift as weasels in the dark and make no more noise than bats.

(*They huddle together, peering in all directions; lightning flashes and sounds of thunder.*) Are your guards posted?

THORIN: (*nodding*) Four of them, Gloin north, Bofur south, Oin east, and Ori west.

[*Lights dim on platform L and come up on platform R. Drumbeats are heard off. The* GREAT GOBLIN *steps out on the platform, followed by an attendant.*]

GREAT GOBLIN: (*bellowing in a stony voice*) Who are those miserable persons?

ATTENDANT GOBLIN: (*bowing and scraping*) Dwarves, I believe, O Truly Tremendous One.

GREAT GOBLIN: What are they doing in my domain?

ATTENDANT GOBLIN: (*shaking*) I'll go and ask them, O Truly Tremendous One.

GREAT GOBLIN: (*with an awful howl of rage*) Ask them? (*Kicks the* ATTENDANT GOBLIN *and bats him over the head*) Beat them! Gnash them! Squash them! Smash them! (*Gesturing L*) After them!

[*The drumbeats increase as many* GOBLINS *rush on R with bloodcurdling cries. As they reach C, the lights come up on platform L.*]

OIN: (*reporting*) Goblins coming!

ORI: I think they're going to rush us!

GOBLINS: (*chanting and cracking whips*)
Swish, smack! Whip, crack!
Clash, crash! Crush, smash!

THORIN: (*drawing his sword*) Ready, my Goblin-cleaver! (*He stands on the edge of the platform.*) Ready, Dwarves—and Mr. Baggins. (GANDALF, *arms folded, stands aloof watching intently. The* GOBLINS *rush at the* DWARVES. THORIN *stabs one with his blade. The other* DWARVES *back up* THORIN, *and there are hand-to-hand conflicts.* BILBO *trips up a* GOBLIN *who is about to stab* THORIN *from behind.* THORIN *stabs another. All conflicts must be rehearsed with extra care so that the tempo is very fast. The* GOBLINS *fall, howling.*)

GOBLINS: (*ad lib*) Aie! He's got a Goblin-cleaver! Watch out! Stay back! (*The* GOBLINS *back off in terror.*)

GANDALF: (*to* DWARVES *and* BILBO) Quick. Now's our chance! Everyone follow me! (*Runs off L. Others follow,* BILBO *last. From off.*) Quicker, quicker! (GOBLINS *run after them, howling and hooting.*)

Blackout

[*Lights come up very dimly in cave.* BILBO *is discovered lying on the ground DC.*]

BILBO: (*sitting up, holding his head in pain*) Oooh! My head! Where am I! My head—I must have run into a tree! (*Groping*) It's so dark in here I can't see a thing. (*Calls loudly*) Anyone here?

ECHO: (*getting progressively fainter*) Here—here—here.

BILBO: (*getting frightened*) Who's that?

[*Now gleams appear in the darkness. They prove to be always in pairs, of yellow or green or red eyes. They seem to stare awhile and then slowly fade out and disappear and shine out again in another place. Sometimes they shine down from above. Some of them are bulbous.*]

BILBO: Now I remember. The goblins!

ECHO: 'Oblins, 'oblins—'oblins—'oblins.

BILBO: And what are those awful eyes watching me for? (*Lowers voice*) I was on Dori's back and someone tackled him and he dropped me!

ECHO: 'Opped me—'opped me—'opped me—'opped me.

BILBO: (*frightened, to the eyes*) Keep away from me, eyes! I wonder what happened to the dwarves? I hope the goblins didn't get them! (*Gasps*) My sword! (*Holding it up*) It hardly glows. That means the goblins aren't near and yet they're still around. Ugh! What a nasty smell! Go away, you horrible eyes! (*Realizing, stage whisper*) I know where I am. I'm still in the goblins' cave! They smell that way and these may be just the eyes of bats and mice and toads and slimy things like that. (*More naturally*) Cheer up, Bilbo. Fear always helps the thing you're afraid of. You're alive and you've been in holes before. You live in one. This is just an ordinary, black, foul, disgusting hole. So blah! (*The eyes begin to flicker out, pair by pair, until all are gone.* BILBO *brightens further.*) If this place were aired and decorated it would be nice and cozy. So now I'll just figure out how to get out of here. (BILBO *crawls around on his hands and knees toward stage R.*) Seems to be a lake over here—no use heading that way. Ouch! Something hurt my knee—— (*Picks up small object*) It's a ring! Someone's lost a ring. Well, finders keepers. I'll just stick it in my pocket so I don't lose it myself. (*Pockets ring. Lights come up a little*) I can see

better now. (*Stands and turns toward stage L*)

[*An unobtrusive black rubber float is pulled on stage R. On it sits a slimy creature, dressed in black tights or a shiny rubber diving suit, touched up with vaseline to make it glisten, complete with cap and goggles painted a pale watery green. He sits with a leg dangling over each side of the raft, or with knees bent, and holds a short paddle as if rowing.*]

GOLLUM: (*making a swallowing sound as he is pulled on*) Gollum! Gollum!

BILBO: (*whirling around*) What's that!

GOLLUM: It's me—Gollum!

BILBO: (*peering nervously in Gollum's direction*) Who's there?

GOLLUM: (*in full view now*) Bless us and splash us, my preciousss! Here's something to eat! (*Guttural*) Gollum!

BILBO: (*brandishing his blade, while shaking and backing off*) Stay back!

GOLLUM: (*swaying his head from side to*

Gollum: Cross it is. The Baggins is getting cross, preciouss, but it must wait, yes, it must. We can't go up the tunnels so hasty. We must go and get somethings first, yess, things to help us. My birthday present, that's what we wants now—then we'll be quite safe! (*He steps out of his raft and waddles UR.*) We slips it on and it won't see us, will it, my preciouss. No, it won't see us and its nassty little sword will be useless, yess—Sssss. (*Exits R*)

Bilbo: (*calling*) Hurry up!

Gollum: (*off, letting out a horrible shriek*) Aaaaaah! Where iss it! Lost! Lost!

Bilbo: What's the matter?

Gollum: (*offstage, wailing*) Gone—must find it! Lost! Lost!

Bilbo: Well, so am I!

[Gollum *waddles on from R, on his hands and knees, searching wildly.*]

Gollum: Cursesss! Must find it!

Bilbo: You can look for whatever it is later. You never guessed my riddle. You promised!

Gollum: Never guessed—never guessed— — (*Light dawns*) What has it got in its pocketses? Tell us! (*Advances toward* Bilbo)

Bilbo: What have you lost?

Gollum: We guesses, we *guesses*, precious, only guesses. He's got it and the goblinses will catch it and take the present from it. (*Makes a lunge at* Bilbo) They'll find out what it can do. The Baggins doesn't know what the present can do. It'll just keep it in its pocketses. It's lost itself, the nassty, nosey thing.

Bilbo: I better put that ring on or I'll lose it. (*Puts his hand into his pocket and slips the ring on his finger and holds it up.*) This?

Gollum: (*rushing right past* Bilbo, *wailing*) Cursess, the Baggins is *gone*—my precious. It has my ring! The ring of *power!*

Bilbo: (*alone on stage*) He ran right past— as if he didn't see me—as if I weren't there— Maybe I'm not! The ring! I wonder if it made me invisible! (*Inspects himself*) I can still see me.

[Gollum *rushes on again from L.*]

GOLLUM: Give it back like a good Baggins! Where isss it? (*Rushes off R*)

BILBO: A magic ring! I've heard of such things in Gandalf's stories—but to *find* one! What luck!

GOLLUM: (*offstage, shrieking*) Thief!

BILBO: I could stab him with my blade, but that would be wrong when he can't see me.

[GOLLUM *waddles on R, worn out and weeping.*]

GOLLUM: (*sitting downstage*) It's gone! (*Guttural sobs*) Gollum! Gollum! Thief! Thief Baggins! We hates it, we hates it, hates it forever! S-s-s-s-s. (*Recovering*) But he doesn't know the way out—he said so. (BILBO *nods silently and sits beside him.*) But he's tricksy. He doesn't say what he means—like what was in his pocketses— he knows! He knows a way *in*. He must know a way *out!* Yesss—he's off to the back door, that's it! (*Springs up*) After him! Make haste! (*Runs off L*) Gollum! Gollum!

BILBO: I'll follow him to the exit. Then with luck I can slip out the door! (*Runs off L after* GOLLUM)

Curtain

About the Author

John Ronald Reuel Tolkien (tōl'kĕn) (1892–1973) was born to English parents in South Africa. As a child he was fascinated by the sounds and meanings of words. Early in life he tried to learn all he could about such languages as Latin, Greek, German, Welsh, and Old English. Like many highly imaginative children, he also made up his own

imaginary languages. In adulthood, Tolkien became a noted professor of the languages and literature of the Middle Ages at Oxford University in England. One of his friends was C. S. Lewis, the author of the Narnia series (see page 10 of this book).

Tolkien was not only a brilliant scholar. He was also an imaginative storyteller who loved myths and fantastic tales. Throughout Tolkien's life, part of him remained a child who "desired dragons with a profound desire." Eventually, he combined his knowledge of myths and languages with his keen imagination to create perhaps the most famous fantasies of the twentieth century, *The Hobbit* and the trilogy called *Lord of the Rings*. These books tell of an epic battle between good and evil fought long ago in the quiet of Middle Earth. They have been read and loved by millions of readers, young and old.

DRAWING INFERENCES

Many writers rely on you to make **inferences,** or educated guesses, about the characters, situations, and setting in a story or play. For example, if you were watching the first scene of *The Secret Garden* on television, you would not be told directly when and where the story's opening scene is set. However, you could use clues from details like the touring car, the characters' costumes, and the house to draw an inference about the time and place of the action.

Reread the passages from Act Six of *The Secret Garden* below. Then use a separate sheet of paper to answer the question marked with this symbol ■ after each passage.

1. **COLIN:** *(worried)* I hope Dr. Craven isn't getting suspicious. When he was here before, he noticed my legs look stronger and that I'm getting fatter.

   ■ What inference is Colin afraid that Dr. Craven has drawn?

2. **PITCHER:** *(continuing; reading)* "Dear Sir: I am Susan Sowerby who is Martha's mother who works for you in Misselthwaite Manor. I am making bold to speak to you. Please sir, I would come home if I were you. I think you would be glad you came, and if you will excuse me, sir, I think your lady would want you to come if she were here. Your obedient servant, Susan Sowerby."

   ■ What do you infer Susan Sowerby really means in her letter?

3. **DICKON:** *(quietly)* We'll be parted, you an' me, but remembrance will keep us friends.

   ■ What inference do you draw about Dickon's real meaning here?

4. **BEN:** There was a promise to be kept. As Mr. Archibald lay dyin', he said to me, "Tend the garden, Ben. Someday the children'll be comin' back an' when they do, their garden must be a magic place . . ."

   ■ What inference do you think Mr. Archibald has drawn about the importance of the magic garden?

WRITING A SCENE

A **play** is a story acted out on a stage by actors and actresses who take the parts of characters. A play is different from a short story because in a play the writer has to use dialogue, rather than description or narration, to move the plot forward. In this unit you have studied some of the basic elements of drama. Now you will have the chance to write a dramatic scene of your own.

Prewriting

1. Just like a good short story, a dramatic scene explores a **conflict** or struggle. To find an idea for a scene, get together with a small group of classmates and brainstorm to fill in a chart like the one below. Some sample ideas have been filled in for you.

Idea Chart for a Dramatic Scene		
Character A	*Character B*	*Conflict*
Father	Daughter	Why can't you keep your room neat?
Space Alien	Earth Host	Why can't I stay with you forever?

2. Join with a group of partners and use **improvising** to explore one of the ideas on your chart. Assign each role in advance. Then relax and make up lines that you think are appropriate for your character and for the situation. If you wish, ask one group member to take notes on the dialogue. See if your improvisation leads to a turning point and a resolution for the conflict. [See **Focus** assignment on page 531.]

3. Write an **outline** for your scene. On your outline, cover the points listed on the diagram below:

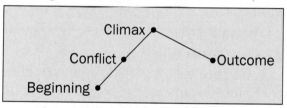

4. Make notes for the **setting** of your scene—the specific time and place of the action. Decide if the setting may be related to the atmosphere or mood of the scene.

Writing

1. Use **stage directions** to describe the scenery, lighting, and characters that the audience will see at the beginning of your scene. As a model, you can use the stage directions at the beginning of *Riddles in the Dark* (see page 537).

2. Follow your outline and write the **dialogue** for your scene. Remember to use the rules for identifying speakers and punctuating dialogue in drama. Here is an example from *The Monsters Are Due on Maple Street* (page 468):

   STEVE: I don't understand it. It was working fine before—

   DON: Out of gas?

   STEVE: *(shakes his head)* I just had it filled up.

3. Here are some guidelines to use when you write dialogue:

   - Be sure that the dialogue moves the plot forward.
   - Make the speeches sound natural—the way people speak in real life. Say your dialogue out loud to see that it meets this test.
   - Make the dialogue suit the speaker's character. For example, in *The Secret Garden* Dickon is gentle and patient. Notice that his speeches are never bossy or sarcastic.

4. Write **stage directions** to show information about the characters' feelings or emotions, tones of voice, movements, and gestures. Stage directions can also refer to props and important elements of scene design. When you write your stage directions, try to **visualize** how your scene would actually be played on stage in a theater.

5. Give your scene a title that hooks the reader's interest and sums up the action or problem.

Evaluating and Revising

1. When you have finished a first draft, put your scene aside for a while. Then try to evaluate it as objectively as you can. If you wish, join with a group of classmates. Organize a group reading of each member's scene. Give each other suggestions on how to improve dialogue and stage directions.

Here is how one writer revised part of a dramatic scene:

school

(On the ~~playground~~: late morning.)

glaring

PAUL: (~~looking~~ at Jeff) You were never

really my friend, were you? Why'd you tell

Mr. Samuels about the missing money?

JEFF: (feeling torn) Come off it, Paul. You

know we shouldn't have taken the money.

Samuels was always nice to us. He even

for the club headquarters.

let us use his garage.

PAUL: (losing his confidence and feeling

ashamed) I guess you're right. I don't feel

so good about having taken that money

, ya

now. What ~~do you~~ think we should do?

2. You may wish to use the following checklist as you revise your scene:

Checklist for Evaluation and Revision

✔ Have I clearly identified the setting and the characters?

✔ Does the scene explore a strong conflict?

✔ Does the scene have a high point and a resolution?

✔ Does the dialogue sound natural? Is this the way the characters would speak in real life?

✔ Do the stage directions give important information?

✔ Have I used the proper format?

Proofreading and Publishing

Proofread your scene and correct any errors you find in grammar, usage, and mechanics. (Here you may find it helpful to refer to the **Handbook for Revision** on pages 750–785.) Then prepare a final version of your scene by making a clean copy.

Consider some of the following ways to share your scene:

- illustrate your scene and post it on the class bulletin board
- join with a group to present a dramatic reading of your scene
- prepare a full staging of your scene, complete with scenery, costumes, and props

Portfolio If your teacher approves, you may wish to keep a copy of your work in your writing folder or portfolio.

Isfandiyar Slays the Dragon by Qasim (c. 1525–1530). From the Persian manuscript of the *Shahnamah*. Silver, gold, and ink on paper.

The Metropolitan Museum of Art, New York City. Gift of Arthur A. Houghton, Jr., 1970. (1970.301.51)

Myths and Folk Tales

The first stories that people ever told are called myths. **Myths** are stories about gods—stories that ancient people once believed were true. Myths were probably first told to explain natural mysteries, such as the changes in the seasons. Myths also explained why people had certain rituals. By suggesting that the gods paid attention to them, myths made human beings feel a bit more important in a world where survival was difficult.

Folk tales are entertaining stories that people have handed down, mostly by word of mouth, from generation to generation. Folk tales have much in common with myths. Just like myths, folk tales are often about magic transformations or about people with supernatural powers. Like myths, folk tales are exaggerated. But there is one big difference between myths and folklore. Myths are religious stories: folk tales are not. Myths explain the relationships between gods and humans. Folk tales are fantastic stories told mostly to teach lessons and to entertain.

Close Reading OF A FOLK TALE

*T*he oldest folk tales belong to oral tradition. No one knows who composed them. They were passed down from generation to generation by being recited. Many folk tales existed for centuries before they were collected and published. As you might expect, details of the stories changed as the tales were told and retold. This is why you will often find different versions of the same tale.

Guidelines for Close Reading

1. Read actively, asking yourself questions about characters and situations. Try to draw inferences as you read.

2. Make predictions about what will happen next.

3. Try to figure out unfamiliar words from context and other clues.

4. Look for qualities or traits that the characters represent. The characters in folk tales may be animals who speak and behave like people, yet retain their identity as animals.

5. Think about the message or point of the tale and how it applies to your own life.

The following tale about a pheasant (fĕz′ənt) is from Korea. The notes alongside the selection represent one reader's response.

The Pheasant's Bell
A Korean Folk Tale

Retold by KIM SO-UN

Deep in a lonely forest there once lived a woodcutter. One day the woodcutter was at work felling trees, when he heard the cry of a pheasant and the fluttering of wings nearby. He wondered what was happening and went to see what the commotion was about. Under the shade of a bush he saw a pheasant nest with many eggs inside it. A great snake was poised to strike at a mother pheasant, who was bravely trying to defend her nest. The woodcutter picked up a stick and tried to scare the snake away, crying: "Go away! Go away!" But the snake wouldn't move, so the woodcutter struck it with his stick and killed it.

Some years after this, the woodcutter one day set out on a distant journey. Twilight found him walking along a lonely mountain path. Soon it became completely dark. He was hungry and tired. Suddenly, far ahead of him in the woods he saw a dim light. He walked toward this light and came to a large and beautiful straw-thatched house. The woodcutter was surprised, for he had never expected to find such a fine house so deep in the forest. He knocked on the door, and a beautiful girl, about nineteen or twenty years of age, came out.

"I am hungry and tired," the woodcutter told her. "I have walked a long way today and have no place to stay. I wonder if you would put me up for the night?"

The girl answered in a kind tone: "I am alone in this house, but please do come in."

She welcomed the woodcutter inside and spread out a grand feast for him. But the woodcutter felt very ill at ease. He could not understand why such a beautiful young girl should be living all alone in the middle of a forest. He couldn't help wondering if he hadn't entered a haunted house. But he was so hungry that he ate the fine food put before him and asked no questions. Only when he was quite full did he finally speak.

"Why should such a young person as you live all alone here in such a large house?" he asked.

"I am waiting to take my revenge against my enemy," the girl answered.

"Your enemy?" he asked. "Where would he be?"

"He is right here," she said. "See, you are my enemy!" Then she opened a great red mouth and laughed loudly.

The woodcutter was astounded and asked her why he should be her enemy.

The girl reminded him of the time he had saved the mother pheasant and her nest, and added: "I am the snake you killed that time. I've waited a long long time to meet up with you. And now I'm going to take your life. Then finally I'll have the revenge I've dreamed of so long."

When the woodcutter heard this, his heart sank. "I had nothing against you at that time," he said in a quavering voice. "It was simply because I couldn't bear to see helpless beings hurt by someone strong like you were. That's why I saved the pheasant. But I really didn't mean to kill you. Don't say I'm your enemy. Please, please spare my life."

At first the girl kept laughing at him and would not listen to his pleas. But he kept on pleading, from bended knees, with tears flowing down his cheeks.

"All right then," the girl said, "I'll give you one chance. Deep in the forest and high in the mountains there is a temple ruin. Not a single soul lives there. However, a huge bell hangs in that temple. If, before dawn, you are able to ring that bell without moving from the place where you're sitting now, then I'll spare your life."

When the woodcutter heard this, he was even more frightened. "How can I ring that bell while I'm still sitting here in this room?" he sighed. "You're unfair. I'm no better off than

Why does she have a great red mouth? I get a weird picture of this girl.

This is magic. The snake turned into a girl.

She's set a test for him that is impossible to pass. This often happens in fairy tales.

A Korean Temple.

before. Please don't say such a cruel thing. It's the same as killing me right now. Please let me go home.''

The girl firmly refused: ''No! You are the enemy I've waited for so long. Yes, I've waited a long time for this chance to avenge myself. Now that I have you in my hands, why should I let you go? If you can't ring the bell, resign yourself to death. I shall eat you up."

The woodcutter gave up all hope. He realized that he was as good as dead.

Suddenly, the quiet night air vibrated with the sound of a distant bell. "Bong!" the bell rang. Yes, it was the bell in the crumbling old mountain temple!

When the girl heard the bell, she turned white and gnashed her teeth. "It's no use," she said. "You must be guarded by the gods."

No sooner had she said this than she disappeared from sight. The fine house in which the woodcutter was sitting also disappeared in a puff of smoke.

The woodcutter, whose life had been so miraculously saved, could hardly wait for daylight to break. With the first sign of dawn he set off toward the mountains in search of the ruined temple, filled with gnawing curiosity.

Sure enough, as he had been told, there he found a temple in which hung a great bell. But there was not a single soul in sight. The woodcutter looked at the bell in wonder. On it he noticed a stain of blood. He looked down to the floor. There, with head shattered and wings broken, lay the blood-stained body of a pheasant.

What happened? How did it ring?

What is "gnashed her teeth"?

More magic. The house and girl disappear.

Well, what happened? Why is the pheasant dead? Did the pheasant ring the bell? How? The story has a good moral: The man's kindness to the pheasant was rewarded.

Looking at Yourself as a Reader

Compare your own responses with those in the notes alongside the selection. Using the **Guidelines** on page 550, evaluate the reader's responses. Do you agree or disagree with any of the reader's ideas?

1. Which of these statements do you think most accurately states the moral or lesson of this folk tale? Discuss your choice with a partner.
   a. A person's act of kindness will be rewarded.
   b. If you have faith, even the most hopeless situation can come to a good end.
   c. A person who is harmed will always seek revenge.

2. Magical events often occur in folk tales. Name two magical events in "The Pheasant's Bell."

A Pair of Birds on a Cinnamon Tree by Ch-i Bai-Shih (1940). Ink and color on paper.

THINKING ABOUT WORDS

USING CONTEXT CLUES

In a myth in this unit, you will read that a king

. . . locked . . . his only daughter in a tower with brass doors, guarded by a *savage* dog. . . .

If you didn't know that *savage* means "wild and fierce," the context would give you clues to uncover its meaning. Let's think about how you could have figured out that meaning.

Thinking It Out. The words *locked* and *brass doors* provide strong clues that the king does not want his daughter to get out, or anyone to get in. In fact, the door is *guarded* by some kind of dog. Certainly, a sweet and friendly dog would not stop someone from going in or out. So *savage* has to describe the kind of dog that could prevent someone from entering or exiting. A wild and fierce dog could do that.

Below are two passages from "Quetzalcoatl," another myth you will read in this unit. The passages provide some good clues to help you get a general sense of what the underscored words mean. (They are related.) Use context clues to try to uncover their meanings. Check with the Glossary at the back of this book or a dictionary to see how close you got.

They were ruled by Quetzalcoatl, the great god of the sun and the wind, who had left his home in the land of the Sunrise so that he might teach the Toltecs and help them to become a happy and <u>prosperous</u> nation. . . .

. . . while he reigned over them, the Toltecs were very happy. Everything in the country <u>prospered</u>. The maize crops were more abundant than they had ever been before; the fruits were larger and more plentiful. . . .

In the world of myth, heroes do the things we wish we could do and the things we are glad we don't have to do. Heroes in myths represent the hopes and fears of the people who create them.

Heroes in myths are often helped by gods. Sometimes they are even gods themselves. The heroes usually have supernatural powers, and they are always opposed by monsters and other difficulties. Often the mythic hero saves a whole society from ruin. In many myths, the people wait for their hero to return someday, to help them again in their hour of need.

Hercules shown on a Greek plate (5th century B.C.).

Etruscan Museum in the Vatican, Rome.

Glooscap Fights the Water Monster

A Micmac Myth

Retold by RICHARD ERDOES and ALFONSO ORTIZ

Micmac medicine doll. Wood.

Courtesy of the National Museum of
the American Indian, Smithsonian Institution.

Before You Read

Many myth-makers tell stories about a god-teacher who teaches the people all the skills they need to survive on Earth. The great friend and teacher of the Micmac people of North America was a divine being called Glooscap. Glooscap taught his people all that was wise and good.

The Micmacs still live in eastern Canada, and they still tell Glooscap stories. The Micmacs say that when the famous Admiral Peary finally discovered the North Pole on April 6, 1909, he found Glooscap sitting on top of it.

After you read the first paragraph of this story about one of Glooscap's adventures, pause to discuss how the people felt about Glooscap. How would these beliefs comfort the Micmac people?

Connotations (kan′ə·tā′shəns) are all the feelings and associations that become attached to a word as it is used over a period of time. For example, suppose you wanted to describe a wet creature with a word that would make your readers' flesh creep. You might use the word *slimy*. But suppose, instead, that you liked this creature and you wanted your readers to like it too. Then you might describe it as *slippery*. As you read this myth, look for descriptions of the water monster that make you feel it is very disgusting.

Courtesy of the National Museum of the American Indian, Smithsonian Institution.

Glooscap yet lives, somewhere at the southern edge of the world. He never grows old, and he will last as long as this world lasts. Sometimes Glooscap gets tired of running the world, ruling the animals, regulating nature, instructing people how to live. Then he tells us, "I'm tired of it. Good-bye; I'm going to make myself die now." He paddles off in his magic white canoe and disappears in misty clouds. But he always comes back. He cannot abandon the people forever, and they cannot live without him.

Glooscap is a spirit, a medicine man,[1]

a sorcerer. He can make men and women smile. He can do anything.

Glooscap made all the animals, creating them to be peaceful and useful to humans. When he formed the first squirrel, it was as big as a whale. "What would you do if I let you loose on the world?" Glooscap asked, and the squirrel attacked a big tree, chewing it to pieces in no time. "You're too destructive for your size," said Glooscap, and remade him small. The first beaver also was as big as a whale, and it built a dam that flooded the country from horizon to horizon. Glooscap said, "You'll drown all the people if I let you loose like this." He tapped the beaver on the back, and it shrank to its present size. The first moose was so tall that it reached to the sky and looked altogether different from the way it looks now. It trampled everything in its path—forests, mountains, everything. "You'll ruin everything," Glooscap said. "You'll step on people and kill them." Glooscap tapped the moose on the back to make it small, but the moose refused to

---

1. **medicine man:** someone with supernatural powers over the natural world.

become smaller. So Glooscap killed it and re-created it in a different size and with a different look. In this way Glooscap made everything as it should be.

Glooscap had also created a village and taught the people there everything they needed to know. They were happy hunting and fishing. Men and women were happy in love. Children were happy playing. Parents cherished their children, and children respected their parents. All was well as Glooscap had made it.

The village had one spring, the only source of water far and wide, that always flowed with pure, clear, cold water. But one day the spring ran dry; only a little bit of slimy ooze issued from it. It stayed dry even in the fall when the rains came, and in the spring when the snows melted. The people wondered, "What shall we do? We can't live without water." The wise men and elders held a council and decided to send a man north to the source of the spring to see why it had run dry.

The man walked a long time until at last he came to a village. The people there were not like humans; they had webbed hands and feet. Here the brook widened out. There was some water in it, not much, but a little, though it was slimy, yellowish, and stinking. The man was thirsty from his walk and asked to be given a little water, even if it was bad.

"We can't give you any water," said the people with the webbed hands and feet, "unless our great chief permits it. He wants all the water for himself."

"Where is your chief?" asked the man.

Micmac Indians by an unknown Canadian artist (c. 1850).

Glooscap Fights the Water Monster **561**

"You must follow the brook farther up," they told him.

The man walked on and at last met the big chief. When he saw him, he trembled with fright, because the chief was a monster so huge that if one stood at his feet, one could not see his head. The monster filled the whole valley from end to end. He had dug himself a huge hole and dammed it up, so that all the water was in it and none could flow into the stream bed. And he had fouled the water and made it poisonous, so that stinking mists covered its slimy surface.

The monster had a mile-wide grinning mouth, going from ear to ear. His dull yellow eyes started out of his head like huge pine knots. His body was bloated and covered with warts as big as mountains. The monster stared dully at the man with his protruding eyes and finally said in a fearsome croak, "Little man, what do you want?"

The man was terrified, but he said, "I come from a village far downstream. Our only spring ran dry, because you're keeping all the water for yourself. We would like you to let us have some of this water. Also, please don't muddy it so much."

The monster blinked at him a few times. Finally he croaked:

> *Do as you please,*
> *Do as you please,*
>
> *I don't care,*
> *I don't care,*
>
> *If you want water,*
> *If you want water,*
>
> *Go elsewhere!*

The man said, "We need the water. The people are dying of thirst." The monster replied:

> *I don't care,*
> *I don't care,*
>
> *Don't bother me,*
> *Don't bother me,*
>
> *Go away,*
> *Go away,*
>
> *Or I'll swallow you up!*

The monster opened his mouth wide from ear to ear, and inside it the man could see the many things that the creature had killed. The monster gulped a few times and smacked his lips with a noise like thunder. At this the man's courage broke, and he turned and ran away as fast as he could.

Back at his village the man told the people, "Nothing can be done. If we complain, this monster will swallow us up. He'll kill us all."

The people were in despair. "What shall we do?" they cried. Now, Glooscap knows everything that goes on in the world, even before it happens. He sees everything with his inward eye. He said, "I must set things right. I'll have to get water for the people!"

Then Glooscap girded himself for war. He painted his body with paint as red as blood. He made himself twelve feet tall. He used two huge clamshells for his earrings. He put a hundred black eagle feathers and a hundred white eagle feathers in his scalp lock. He painted yellow rings around his eyes. He twisted his mouth into

"Crooked Mouth" mask of False Face Society,
Seneca, New York.

Courtesy of the National Museum of the American Indian,
Smithsonian Institution.

a snarl and made himself look ferocious. He stamped, and the earth trembled. He uttered his fearful war cry, and it echoed and re-echoed from all the mountains. He grasped a huge mountain in his hand, a mountain composed of flint, and from it made himself a single knife sharp as a weasel's teeth. "Now I am going," he said, striding forth among thunder and lightning, with mighty eagles circling above him. Thus Glooscap came to the village of the people with webbed hands and feet.

"I want water," he told them. Looking at him, they were afraid. They brought him a little muddy water. "I think I'll get more and cleaner water," he said. Glooscap went upstream and confronted the monster. "I want clean water," he said, "a lot of it, for the people downstream."

Ho! Ho!
Ho! Ho!

All the waters are mine!
All the waters are mine!

Go away!
Go away!

Or I'll kill you!

"Slimy lump of mud!" cried Glooscap. "We'll see who will be killed!" They fought. The mountains shook. The earth split open. The swamp smoked and burst into flames. Mighty trees were shivered into splinters.

The monster opened its huge mouth wide to swallow Glooscap. Glooscap made himself taller than the tallest tree, and even the monster's mile-wide mouth was too small for him. Glooscap seized his great flint knife and slit the monster's bloated belly. From the wound gushed a mighty stream, a roaring river, tumbling, rolling, foaming down, down, down, gouging out for itself a vast, deep bed, flowing by the village and on to the great sea of the east.

"That should be enough water for the people," said Glooscap. He grasped the monster and squeezed him in his mighty palm, squeezed and squeezed and threw him away, flinging him into the swamp. Glooscap had squeezed this great creature into a small bullfrog, and ever since, the bullfrog's skin has been wrinkled because Glooscap squeezed so hard.

Myths and Folk Tales

Perseus
A Greek Myth

Retold by ROBERT GRAVES

Before You Read

There are four great quest myths in Greek mythology. You might know some of them. One tells about the strong man Hercules, whose quests consisted of twelve horrible labors. One is about the hero of Athens called Theseus (thē′sē·əs), who killed the half-man, half-bull called the Minotaur. One is about a hero named Jason, who paid dearly for the Golden Fleece. And one is about Perseus (pur′sē·əs), who "faced" the gorgon Medusa (mə·dōo′sə), a famous female monster living in Libya. You can see her face on the opposite page.

The idea of fate is important in the Perseus story. You learn right away that a king has been told by an *oracle* (a priest or priestess who could foretell the future) that one day he will be killed by his own grandson. Think about this for a minute or two. In your journal, write down two or three sentences telling what *you* would do if you had learned this was to be your fate. Then read this myth to see what King Acrisius did.

A relief sculpture of Medusa's head at the temple at Didyma, Turkey (Greco-Turkish, 2nd century A.D.).

changed Medusa into a gorgon—a winged monster with glaring eyes, huge teeth, and snakes for hair. Whoever looked at her would turn to stone.

Athene helped Perseus by handing him a polished shield to use as a mirror when he cut off Medusa's head, so as not to be turned into stone; and Hermes[2] gave him a sharp sickle.[3] But Perseus still needed the god Hades's[4] helmet of invisibility, also a magic bag in which to put the head, and a pair of winged sandals. All these useful things were guarded by the Naiads of the River Styx.[5]

Perseus went to ask the Three Gray Sisters for the Naiads' secret address. It was difficult enough to find the Three Gray Sisters, who lived near the Garden of the Hesperides, and had only a single eye and a single tooth between them. When Perseus eventually reached their house, he crept up behind them as they passed the eye and the tooth from one to the other. Then he snatched both these treasures and refused to return them until the Gray Sisters gave him the Naiads' address.

He found the Naiads in a pool under a rock near the entrance of Tartarus, and threatened to tell all the world about them, unless they lent him the helmet, the sandals, and the bag. The Naiads hated anyone to know that, though otherwise good-looking, they had dogs' faces; so they did as Perseus asked.

Perseus, now wearing the helmet and the sandals, flew unseen to Libya. Coming upon Medusa asleep, he looked at her reflection in the polished shield and cut off her head with his sickle. The only unfortunate accident was that Medusa's blood, trickling from the bag in which the head lay, turned into poisonous snakes as it hit the earth. This made the land of Libya unsafe forever afterward. When Perseus stopped to thank the Three Gray Sisters, the Titan Atlas[6] called out, "Tell your father Zeus that unless he frees me pretty soon, I shall let the heavens fall—which will be the end of the world."

Perseus showed Medusa's head to Atlas, who at once turned to stone and became the great Mount Atlas.

As he flew on to Palestine, Perseus saw a beautiful princess named Andromeda chained to a rock at Joppa, and a sea serpent, sent by the god Poseidon, swimming toward her with wide-open jaws. Andromeda's parents, Cepheus and Cassiopeia, the king and queen of the Philistines, were ordered by an oracle to chain her there as food for the monster. It seems that Cassiopeia had told the Philistines, "I am more beautiful than all the Nereids[7] in the sea"— a boast which angered the Nereids' proud

---

2. **Hermes** (hûr′mēz): messenger of the gods.
3. **sickle**: a kind of sword with a curved blade.
4. **Hades** (hā′dēz): god of the underworld, or **Tartarus** (tär′tər·əs).
5. **Naiads** (nā′ads) **of the River Styx** (stiks): nymphs who live in the river that surrounds the underworld.

6. **Atlas**: a member of a race of giants called Titans. Atlas has been made to hold up the sky by Zeus.
7. **Nereids** (nir′ē·ids): the fifty sea nymphs who attend the sea god Poseidon.

Perseus carrying Medusa's head (5th century B.C.). Red figure vase painting.

father, the god Poseidon. Perseus dived at the sea serpent from above and cut off its head. Afterward he unchained Andromeda, took her home, and asked permission to marry her. King Cepheus answered, "Impudence! She is already promised to the king of Tyre."

"Then why did the king of Tyre not save her?"

"Because he was afraid to offend Poseidon."

"Well, I feared no one. I killed the monster. Andromeda is mine."

As Perseus spoke, the king of Tyre arrived at the head of his army, shouting, "Away, stranger, or we shall cut you into little pieces!"

Perseus told Andromeda, "Please shut your eyes tight, Princess!"

Andromeda obeyed. He pulled Medusa's head from his bag and turned everyone but Andromeda to stone.

Andromeda chained to her rock. A mosaic on the floor of the House of the Stags at Herculaneum, Italy.

When Perseus flew back to Seriphos, carrying Andromeda in his arms, he found that Polydectes had cheated him after all. Instead of marrying the princess on the mainland, he was still pestering Danaë. Perseus turned him and his whole family to stone, and made the friendly fisherman king of the island. Then he gave Medusa's head to Athene, and asked Hermes would he kindly return the borrowed helmet, bag, and sandals to the Naiads of the Styx? In this way Perseus showed far greater sense than Bellerophon,[8] who had gone on using the winged horse Pegasus after killing the Chimera. The gods decided that Perseus deserved a long, happy life. They let him marry Andromeda, become king of Tiryns, and build the famous city of Mycenae near by.

As for King Acrisius, Perseus met him one afternoon at an athletic competition. "Good day, Grandfather! My mother Danaë asks me to forgive you. If I disobey her, the Furies will whip me, so you are safe from my vengeance."

Acrisius thanked him, but when Perseus took part in the quoit-throwing competition, a sudden wind caught the quoit he had thrown and sent it crashing through Acrisius's skull. Later Perseus and Andromeda were turned into constellations, and so were Andromeda's parents, Cepheus and Cassiopeia.

---

8. **Bellerophon** (bə·ler′ə·fon): a hero who killed the dreaded monster called **Chimera** (kə·mir′ə), using the magical winged horse **Pegasus** (peg′ə·səs). Bellerophon got into trouble when he dared to ride Pegasus up to Olympus, home of the gods. The gods made him wander alone on Earth till he died.

IDENTIFYING FACTS

1. Like many heroes, Perseus's life is threatened as a child. Explain how Perseus and his mother came to be on the island of Seriphos.

2. The evil King Polydectes tricks Perseus into going on a **quest** for the head of the gorgon named Medusa. Why is Medusa so dangerous?

3. Heroes of myth and folklore often receive **supernatural** help on their quests. What gods assist Perseus? What **magic objects** do they donate to his project?

4. Describe what is very odd about the Three Gray Sisters. What information does Perseus need from them?

5. The Naiads give three **magic objects** to Perseus. Explain how these objects, plus the shield given to him by Athene, help Perseus accomplish his quest.

6. At the end of a fairy tale, the evildoers are usually punished and good is triumphant. What happens at the end of this myth?

INTERPRETING MEANINGS

7. Do you think that this myth proves that no one can escape fate? What do you think of the idea that everything in life is preordained (determined in advance) by fate?

APPLYING MEANINGS

8. Movie and TV quest stories are closely related to the ancient quest myths. Can you think of any movies or TV shows that are like this story of Perseus? Talk about these features:
   a. The hero threatened at birth
   b. The woman or girl who is in danger
   c. The awful monster
   d. The role played by magic
   e. The people who help the hero
   f. The perils of the journey
   g. The triumph of good at the end

9. The people who go on heroic quests in most of the ancient myths are men. Could a woman be cast in the role of Perseus? What heroes of quest movies and TV shows today are women?

Focus on Reading

IDENTIFYING MAJOR EVENTS

Can you remember the important events in this quest story? Test yourself by filling in the blanks that follow with the missing events.

1. Acrisius is told he will be killed by his grandson.

2.

3. Zeus visits Danaë as a shower of gold.

4. Perseus and his mother are cast out to sea.

5.

6. Perseus tells King Polydectes that he will bring back Medusa's head.

7.

8. Perseus finds the Three Gray Sisters.

9.

10. Perseus visits the Naiads.

11.

12. Perseus finds Medusa asleep.

13.

14. Perseus sees Andromeda chained to a rock.

15.

16. Perseus changes the king of Tyre's army to stone.

17.

18. Perseus marries Andromeda and builds the city of Mycenae.

19.

Literary Elements

MYTHS AND ORIGINS
Like many myths, this one explains the **origins** of several natural features of the world.

1. Why is Libya full of poisonous snakes? (Is it, really?)

2. What is the origin of Mount Atlas? (A real mountain in northwest Africa)

3. How did four of the constellations come to be in the heavens?

Language and Vocabulary

WORDS FROM THE MYTHS
The god Hermes has several names. The Romans called him Mercury, which is where we got the name for the chemical element.

1. Perhaps you've seen the figure of Hermes in his winged helmet and winged sandals, and carrying his staff entwined with serpents (snakes), used by various mes-

senger services. Why is Hermes a good emblem for such businesses?

2. The sight of Medusa's face changed the giant Atlas into a mountain. How is the word *atlas* used today? Can you find out why it came to be used this way?

3. The Greek and Roman names for the gods have been borrowed to name many things in modern life. Discuss how these gods' and goddesses' names have been used. Are some names used for more than one thing?

a. Mars	**e.** Mercury
b. Venus	**f.** Jupiter
c. Saturn	**g.** Athena
d. Apollo	**h.** Vulcan

4. In the natural world, what does the jellyfish called medusa look like? (Why is the name a good one?)

Focus on Writing a Book Report

TAKING NOTES ON A BOOK
In a **book report,** you summarize the contents of a book and discuss a main idea of your own about it.

When you prepare to write a book report, you will find it helpful to take close-reading **notes** on the book as you read it. At least some of these notes should be related to the major literary elements of the book. For example, if "Perseus" were part of a collection of myths you were reading, you might take notes on the major story events and on the character of the hero.

Choose a short book that you would like to read: for example, a collection of myths, a brief novel, or a book of essays. Use a

sheet of paper to make a chart with the following headings:

Major Elements	Reactions/Notes
———	———
———	———

As you read the first twenty pages or so of the book, fill out the chart. Save your notes.

Illustrating the Myth

Many famous artists have been inspired by the myth of Perseus. Some have drawn pictures of the agonized face of Medusa. Others have painted or sculpted figures of Perseus holding up the dripping snaky head. Draw or paint Medusa as you visualize her. Write a caption for your illustration.

About the Author

Robert Graves (1895–1985) was a British poet and novelist who was always very interested in mythology and in the history of Greece and Rome. Two of his popular novels, *I, Claudius* and *Claudius the God*, are about an emperor of ancient Rome. Graves's story of Claudius was later made into a popular TV miniseries. Claudius was a very efficient emperor whose life made exciting drama. Some historians believe he was murdered by his wife so that his corrupt nephew Nero could become ruler. Graves's retelling of the Perseus myth appears in *Greek Gods and Heroes*, a paperback book written especially for young adults. In that book, you'll also find retellings of the other great quest myths of Greece.

Quetzalcoatl
A Mexican Myth

Retold by AMY CRUSE

Aztec mask representing Quetzalcoatl. Turquoise mosaic (12th–16th century).

British Museum, London.

Before You Read

It is 1519. The great Spanish explorer Hernando Cortés (kor·tez') has landed on the coast of Mexico. He is marching with his soldiers inland, to the mountain cities of the Aztecs. Cortés is looking for one thing: gold. He is willing to slaughter the Aztecs to get their fabled treasures. But when Cortés and his soldiers reach the palace of the Aztec king Montezuma, they are amazed to find that they are received with respect, even awe. What can this mean?

It seems that Montezuma thought Cortés was the god Quetzalcoatl (ket·säl'kwäht''l), returning at last to save his people. Why did the great Aztec king make such a mistake? Montezuma's god was identified with the sun: Cortés was white and his armor glittered like the sun. The Aztecs had never seen such a man. Perhaps, to them, he looked like a sun god.

The myth that follows will tell you about this famous sun god who was worshipped by almost every civilization in Mexico. The Toltecs first told the myth of Quetzalcoatl. The Toltecs were an older group of people who first brought civilization to Mexico; the Aztecs took over the Toltec religion.

Talk for a few minutes about heroes. Do you know of any people or group of people today who wish that a hero would return to help them in time of trouble? Do any heroes in movies or even in cartoons return to help a people in need?

Xipe (zī'pē), the Toltec god of spring (left), and Quetzalcoatl as a serpent (right) (15th century). From an Aztec calendar.

The Bibliothèque Palais Bourbon, Paris.

Quetzalcoatl **577**

Language and Vocabulary

Today, Mexican words are entering the English language very rapidly, especially words relating to food. You all know what chili is, and tamale, tortilla, taco, and mesquite. Many Mexican words come from the Spanish language (tortilla, taco); others come from an older language spoken in Mexico called Nahuatl (nä'wät'l). The name of the hero of this myth is from the Nahuatl language. *Quetzalcoatl* means "plumed or feathered serpent." The word *quetzal* is still used to name a bird native to Central America. The bird is brilliantly colored with emerald green and crimson feathers, and the male has a three-foot train. One legend about this bird says that it loves freedom too much to survive captivity.

Long, long ago, hundreds of years before the people of Europe knew anything about the great land of America, a race of people called the Toltecs lived in the southern part of that country which we now call Mexico. They were ruled by Quetzalcoatl, the great god of the sun and the wind, who had left his home in the land of the Sunrise so that he might teach the Toltecs and help them to become a happy and prosperous nation. He was an old man with a flowing white beard, and he wore a long black robe fringed with white crosses. He was kind and wise, and while he reigned over them, the Toltecs were very happy. Everything

in the country prospered. The maize[1] crops were more abundant than they had ever been before; the fruits were larger and more plentiful. It is even said that the cotton grew in all sorts of colors, richer and rarer than could be produced by any dyes. The hills and valleys were gay with flowers, and bright-colored birds flitted through the air, filling the land with joyous song.

But the god Quetzalcoatl knew that if his people were to be really happy, they must not spend their days in the idle enjoyment of all this loveliness and plenty. They must work, and learn to take a pride in working as well as they possibly could. So he taught them many useful arts—painting and weaving and carving and working in metals. He taught them how to fashion the gold and silver and precious stones (which were found in great abundance

---

1. **maize** (māz): corn.

A fresco from the Temple of Cazacol, Teotihuacán, Mexico (Toltec).

Museum of Anthropology, Mexico City.

throughout the country) into beautiful vessels and ornaments, and how to make marvelous many-tinted garments and hangings from the feathers of birds. Everyone was eager to work, and because each man did his share, there was plenty of leisure for all. No one was in want, and no one was unhappy. It seemed as if, for these fortunate Toltecs, the Golden Age had really come.

The people of the neighboring states, who were living almost like savages, were very jealous when they saw the prosperity of the Toltecs. The gods of these people were fierce and warlike, and they hated Quetzalcoatl because he was so unlike themselves. They plotted together to destroy the peace and good government which he had established.

Tezcatlipoca,[2] the chief of these gods,

2. **Tezcatlipoca** (tez′kat·lē·pō′kə).

Quetzalcoatl   **579**

disguised himself as a very old man and went to the palace of Quetzalcoatl.

"I desire to speak with your master, the King," he said to the page who admitted him.

"That you cannot do," replied the page, "for the King is at present ill, and can see no one."

"Nevertheless, go and take my message," said Tezcatlipoca, "and come back and tell me what he says."

The page soon returned, saying that the King would see his visitor, and Tezcatlipoca went in. He bowed low and respectfully before the god, and said that he had come to bring him a drug that would at once cure him of his illness.

"I have been expecting you for some days," answered Quetzalcoatl, "and I will take your medicine, for my illness troubles me exceedingly."

Then Tezcatlipoca poured out a cupful of his medicine, which was really nothing but the strong wine of the country. Quetzalcoatl tasted it, and liked it very much; he did not know what it was, for he never drank wine. After drinking the cupful, he declared that he already felt better, so that it was easy to induce him to drink cupful after cupful of this new, pleasant-tasting medicine. Very soon the wine had its effect, and he could no longer think clearly or act wisely, or take his usual place as the ruler of the country. Tezcatlipoca took care to keep him supplied with plenty of the tempting drink, so that he remained for some time in this state of intoxication.

This was Tezcatlipoca's opportunity,

and he used it to the full. He set to work to bring upon the happy Toltecs every kind of misery that he could devise. He stirred up strife between them and their neighbors, and in many cunning ways he used his magic arts to lure large numbers of them to destruction. He brought plagues[3] upon them, and disasters in which many lost their lives; until at last, by his wicked devices, the once happy land was brought to a state even worse than that of its barbarous[4] neighbors.

When Quetzalcoatl shook off the evil influence of the wine given to him by his enemy and came to his true self once more, the grief which he felt at seeing all his work undone made him resolve to leave the Toltecs and go back whence he had come. But first he determined to destroy what he could of the gifts he had given to the people. He burned the houses he had built, and changed the cacao trees[5] from which the Toltecs had obtained so much valuable food into useless mesquites.[6] He buried his treasures of gold and silver in one of the deep valleys. All the bright-plumaged birds he commanded to follow him back to his own country; and, full of anger and grief, he set out on his long journey, taking with him a train of pages and musicians to lighten the way with their flute playing. On the road, as he passed through the neigh-

---

3. **plagues** (plāgz): horrible, deadly illnesses.
4. **barbarous** (bär′bər·əs): like barbarians, or uncivilized and rough savages.
5. **cacao** (kə·kā′ō) **trees:** Cocoa and chocolate are made from the seeds of these trees.
6. **mesquites** (mes·kēts′): thorny bushes or trees found in the southwestern United States and Mexico.

boring states, he was met by some of the gods of the land. These gods were his enemies, and were glad to see him depart; but before he went, they hoped to gain from him some of his secrets.

"Why are you going away," asked one, "and whither are you bound?"

"I am going back to my own country," Quetzalcoatl answered.

"But why?" the other asked again.

"Because my father, the Sun, has called for me."

"Go then," replied the gods. "But first tell us some of the secrets, which are known to you alone, concerning the arts you practice; for we know there is no one who can paint and weave and work in metals as you can."

"I will tell you nothing," replied Quetzalcoatl. He took all the treasures he had brought with him and cast them into a fountain nearby, which was called the Water of Precious Stones; and he went on his way, paying no heed to the entreaties of the disappointed gods.

As they journeyed on, the road grew ever harder and more dangerous, but Quetzalcoatl, his staff in his hand, pressed steadily forward; and his train, though they were weary and nearly exhausted, followed him. Only once did they stop to rest, and that was when an enchanter met Quetzalcoatl and gave him a cup of wine. The wine sent the god into a deep sleep, but in the morning he had recovered from its effects and was ready to set out once more.

That day was a terrible one for the wayfarers. At each step, it grew colder and

Xipe, the Toltec god of spring. Ceramic. Museum of Anthropology, Mexico City.

Plumed serpent heads decorate the staircase at the Pyramid of the Sun, Teotihuacán, Mexico (6th–8th century A.D.). Built by either the Olmecs or the Aztecs.

colder, and the poor pages, used to the sunny skies of their native land, felt their limbs gradually becoming numb and useless. At length, Quetzalcoatl led the way through a narrow valley between a volcano and the Sierra Nevada, or Mountain of Snow. Here the cold was so intense that the pages, one by one, sank down and died. Quetzalcoatl mourned over them with many tears and sang wild songs of lamentation; then sadly he went on his way, still weeping bitterly.

He had now to cross a great mountain. He climbed up one side, then, when he had reached the summit, he slid down the opposite slope to the bottom. After this, he soon reached the seashore, and there, awaiting him, was a raft. It was not made of timber, as most rafts are, but of serpents, twined together, with writhing bodies and lifted, hissing heads. Onto this strange raft Quetzalcoatl stepped, and was borne away back to his own land.

The Mexicans believe that one day he will come again, and once more rule over his people and bring back to them the Golden Age. When Cortés and his companions, in 1519, landed at Veracruz, which was the very place from which Quetzalcoatl was supposed to have departed centuries before, the people believed that here was their god returning to help them. Only slowly and reluctantly did they come to understand that he was a Spaniard, bent on conquest.

IDENTIFYING FACTS

1. The sun god Quetzalcoatl brings a Golden Age to the Toltecs. Describe some of the ways in which the Toltecs prosper under his rule.

2. How are the gods of the Toltecs' neighbors different from Quetzalcoatl?

3. Like many myths, this one explains the origin of evil on earth. What evils are explained by Tezcatlipoca's cunning and Quetzalcoatl's anger?

4. Why does Quetzalcoatl leave the Toltecs?

5. Describe the hardships of Quetzalcoatl's perilous journey back to his own land.

INTERPRETING MEANINGS

6. One of the tragic episodes in history is the way the Aztecs allowed Cortés into their mountain city and then were brutally conquered by him. Explain how their hope for their god's return led to their destruction.

7. Quetzalcoatl is often shown with serpents. According to this myth, why would this be?

APPLYING MEANINGS

8. Why did the people look forward to Quetzalcoatl's return? Have other people wished for heroes to return and save them?

9. According to their myths, the Toltecs are destroyed for two reasons: (a) their neighbors are jealous of their prosperity, and (b) the neighbors hate the Toltec god because he is so different from their own gods. Have other people in history been threatened for these same reasons? Talk about your answers in class.

Focus on Reading

FINDING THE MAIN IDEA

Most paragraphs are written around at least one main idea. This main idea is often directly stated in one sentence in the paragraph, usually at its beginning or its end. The rest of the paragraph contains details to support this main idea, or to explain it.

The second paragraph of this myth provides a good example of a paragraph organized around one main idea. Go back now and reread that paragraph.

When you come to a sentence like the last one in that paragraph, it is most important to stop and ask yourself a question: "Now, *how* was this a Golden Age? Did I catch all the details that lead up to this summarizing statement?"

Find at least four details in the paragraph that explain what made this age "golden."

Literary Elements

CONNECTIONS BETWEEN MYTHS

Many myths from different parts of the world show similar features. The myths of Quetzalcoatl and of Glooscap show some resemblances. Following are five statements about similarities between these two great hero stories. What details in the myths support these statements?

1. Both heroes teach the people skills.

2. Both save their people from danger.

3. Both have supernatural powers.

4. Both create a "Golden Age" or paradise for the people.

5. Both are expected to return some day.

Language and Vocabulary

WORDS FROM MEXICO

In the seventeenth century, as the settlers in America pushed westward, they picked up many new words. They needed these words to name all the strange new things they saw—things that they had not known back East or in Europe. Several of the new words they picked up came from the native languages, including Nahuatl, the principal Aztec tongue. All of these "English" words are from the Nahuatl language. What does each word mean?

chili	mesquite
chocolate	tamale
cocoa	tomato
coyote	

A good dictionary will tell you how each word was spelled in Nahuatl.

Focus on Writing a Book Report

DECIDING ON YOUR MAIN IDEA

To give your book report a focus, you need to identify a **main idea** for your writing. Here are some examples of main ideas:

> an overall evaluation or judgment of the book

> an opinion about an important element, such as plot, characters, or setting

> a statement that identifies or clarifies a unifying theme in the book

For example, a possible main idea for a book report discussing a collection of myths like "Quetzalcoatl" might be: "All these myths try to explain the origin of evil."

Take notes on some more of the book you started reading for the assignment on page 574, or choose another short book for a report. Experiment with two or three one-sentence statements of a main idea for your report. Save your writing.

"How and why" tales give us entertaining explanations of unexplainable things. Here you will learn how the possum lost the hair on its tail, how the whale got its peculiar throat, and why the tortoise has a cracked-looking shell. "How and why" stories often have animal characters. As you read these stories, think of how these animals are like the cartoon characters you see on television or in comics today.

Navajo sand painting by Joe Ben, Jr., showing the harmony between humans and nature.

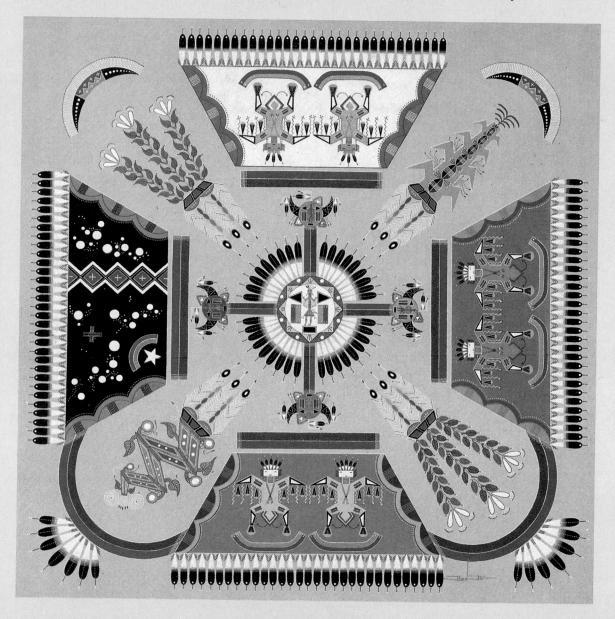

How the Possum Lost the Hair on Its Tail

An African American Folk Tale

Retold by ZORA NEALE HURSTON

Before You Read

Although most folk tales now appear in written form, you need to remember that they were created for speaking. As you read this tale, think of the storyteller face to face with an audience. How does the tale capture the actual speech of the storyteller?

© C. C. Lockwood/DRK Photo

Dialect is the language spoken in a certain place or by a certain group of people. The dialect in this folk tale was recorded by Zora Neale Hurston, who made field trips and collected oral narratives in her native state of Florida. As you will see, she is careful to preserve the speech patterns of her storyteller.

Yes, he did have hair on his tail one time. Yes, indeed. De possum had a bushy tail wid long silk hair on it. Why, it useter be one of de prettiest sights you ever seen. De possum struttin' 'round wid his great big ole plumey tail. Dat was 'way back in de olden times before de big flood.

But de possum was lazy—jus' like he is today. He sleep too much. You see Ole Nora[1] had a son name Ham and he loved to be playin' music all de time. He had a banjo and a fiddle and maybe a guitar too. But de rain come up so sudden he didn't have time to put 'em on de ark. So when rain kept comin' down he fretted a lot 'cause he didn't have nothin' to play. So he found a ole cigar box and made hisself a banjo, but he didn't have no strings for it. So he seen de possum stretched out sleeping wid his tail all spread 'round. So Ham slipped up and shaved de possum's tail and made de strings for his banjo out de hairs. When dat possum woke up from his nap, Ham was playin' his tail hairs down to de bricks and dat's why de possum ain't got no hair on his tail today. Losin' his pretty tail sorta broke de possum's spirit too. He ain't never been de same since. Dat's how come he always actin' shame-faced. He know his tail ain't whut it useter be; and de possum feel mighty bad about it.

---

1. **Ole Nora:** Noah was told to build an ark so that he, his family, and pairs of living creatures might survive the flood (Genesis 6-9).

For Study and Discussion

IDENTIFYING FACTS

1. Why is Ham without his musical instruments?

2. Why does Ham choose the possum's tail for his banjo strings?

INTERPRETING MEANINGS

3. Why was the possum's spirit broken?

4. The animals in folk tales often talk and act like people. What type of person does the possum remind you of?

APPLYING MEANINGS

5. "To play possum" is to pretend to be dead or asleep. How do you think this expression came about?

Writing About Literature

MAKING UP YOUR OWN TALE

Many of the stories Zora Neale Hurston collected in *Mules and Men* are called "lies"—wild exaggerations. After a speaker concludes a tale, someone else takes up the challenge of telling another tale that contains even greater exaggerations. Try your hand at "besting" the story about the possum's tail. Write your own folk tale explaining how the possum lost the hair on its tail. Then read your story out loud to the class.

About the Author

Zora Neale Hurston (1891–1960) was born in Eatonville, Florida, the first incorporated black township in the United States. She became interested in African American folk traditions while she was attending Barnard College in New York City. After graduation she returned to Florida to study oral traditions. Her research was published in *Mules and Men* (1935). Hurston, who wrote plays, novels, short stories, and articles, is best known for her second novel, *Their Eyes Were Watching God* (1937).

Paul Bunyan's Cornstalk
An American Tall Tale

Retold by HAROLD COURLANDER

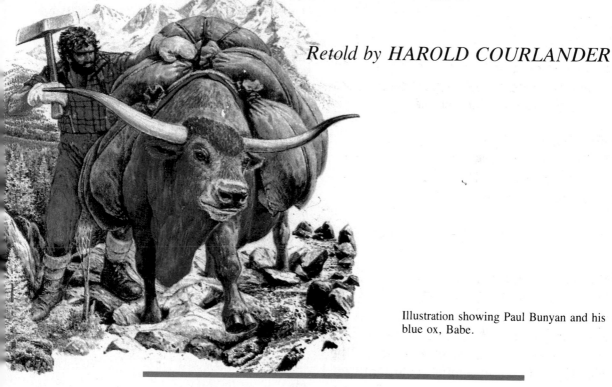

Illustration showing Paul Bunyan and his blue ox, Babe.

Before You Read

Paul Bunyan is an American folk hero known for his superhuman size and strength. Tales about Paul Bunyan were first told in the northern lumber camps. In these tales Paul accomplishes incredible feats with the help of his gigantic blue ox, Babe. Many legends tell how he changed the geography of North America.

The following story is an example of a *tall tale*, a wildly exaggerated and humorous story. As you read, ask yourself why tales about Paul Bunyan appeal so strongly to the imagination.

Paul Bunyan was the fellow who invented the ax with two edges so a man could stand between two trees and chop them both down at the same time. As it turned out, Paul was the only man who could do that trick, but the other lumberjacks used the double-bitted ax anyway, because they didn't have to sharpen the blades so often. Paul Bunyan also had other tricks. Most lumberjacks used to cut off the tops of the pines before they felled them. But when Paul was in a hurry, he'd wait till a tree started falling; then he'd get set with his ax and lop off the top of the tree as it came down.

Nothing Paul Bunyan ever did was small. He had an ox named Babe, who used to help him with his logging work. Babe was just about the most phenomenal ox in Michigan. His color was blue, and he stood ninety hands high. If you happened to hang on the tip of one horn, it's doubtful if you could have seen the tip of the other, even on a clear day. One day when Paul had Babe out plowing, the ox was stung by a Michigan deer fly about the size of a bushel basket. Babe took off across the country dragging the plow behind him, right across Indiana, Illinois, and Missouri, with the deer fly bringing up the rear. After a while Babe veered south and didn't stop till he got to the Rio Grande. The plow that Babe was hitched to dug a furrow four miles wide and two hundred miles long. You can check it in your own geography book. They call it Grand Canyon nowadays.

Even the storms that Paul was in were big. The biggest of all was the one they call the Big Blue Snow. It snowed for two months straight, and the way the drifts piled up only the tops of the tallest pines were showing. Lumberjacks went out that winter on their snowshoes and cut off all the pine tops. It saved them a lot of time when spring came around. Babe the blue ox didn't get a wink of sleep, though, from December till the first of March. It seems that standing out there in the weather the way he was, the snow that fell on his back melted and ran down his tail, and once it got there it froze into ice. Babe's tail kept getting heavier and heavier, and it drew on his hide so hard it just pulled his eyelids wide open and kept that way. Babe never did get his eyes closed until the spring thaw came and melted the ice off his tail.

But the Big Blue Snow wasn't anything compared to the big drouth that started in Saginaw County and spread out as far as the Alleghenies in the East and the Rockies in the West. It all started with Paul Bunyan's vegetable garden. Paul planted some corn and some pumpkins. One of those cornstalks was six feet high before the others had sprouted. In two weeks it was tall as a house and growing like crazy. About the time it was as big as a fifty-year-old pine, people began to come in from all over the county to see it. It was growing out of the ground so fast it was pulling up stones that even the frost couldn't heave out. Same kind of thing, more or less, happened to one of the pumpkin vines. It grew so fast it just darted around like a Massauga rattlesnake. It climbed into any place where there was an opening. People had to keep their windows closed. The ones that didn't had to cut their way out of their beds with a brush knife. Sometimes that vine would grow into one window and out another between sunset

Paul Bunyan by William Gropper (1939). Lithograph.

and sunrise. Things weren't too bad until the vine blossomed and the pumpkins came out. They were about the size of hogsheads—the *little* pumpkins, that is—and when the vine whipped back and forth looking for someplace to grow it just snapped the pumpkins around like crab apples on a string. People had to be mighty alert to keep from getting hit by those pumpkins. One man lost a team of horses that way, and half a dozen good barns and one silo were stoved in.

But the real problem started when the corn and pumpkin roots began to soak up all the water out of the ground. Farms for sixty miles around went dry—fields, springs, and wells. The pine woods turned yellow from lack of moisture. The Au Sable River just turned into a trickle, and pretty soon there wasn't anything there but dry mud. The next thing that happened was that the water in the Great Lakes began to go down. It went down so fast in Lake Huron it left the fish hanging in the air. When things began to look real bad, folks came and told Paul Bunyan he'd just have to get rid of his corn and pumpkins. Paul was reasonable about it. First he went after the pumpkin vine. He spent four hours racing around trying to catch hold of the end, and finally did it by trapping it in a barn. He hitched Babe up to the end of the vine, but as fast as Babe pulled the vine grew. Babe ran faster and faster, and he was near Lake Ontario before he had the vine tight enough to pull it out.

Then Paul sized up his cornstalk. He figured he'd have to chop it down. He sharpened up his ax and spit on his hands. He made a good deep cut in that stalk, but before he could chip out a wedge the stalk grew up six feet, cut and all. Every time he made a cut it would shoot up out of reach before he could swing his ax again. Pretty soon he saw there wasn't any use going on this way. "Only way to kill this stalk is to cut off the top," he said. He hung his ax in his belt and started climbing. In about two hours he was completely out of sight. People just stood around and waited. They stood around two and a half days without any sight of Paul. Lars Larson called, "Paul!" but there was no answer. Erik Erikson and Hans Hanson called, "Paul!" But there wasn't any word from Paul Bunyan. So they waited some more. Two more days went by. No word from Paul. They decided that if everyone yelled at once maybe the sound would carry. So all together the two thousand eight hundred men and boys hollered, "Paul!" And sure enough, they heard his faint voice from up above.

"When you going to top that cornstalk?" they yelled back at him.

"Hasn't that top come down yet?" Paul hollered back. "I cut it off three days ago!"

And it was the truth, too. The stalk stopped growing, the water in the Great Lakes stopped falling, the Au Sable River began to run, the springs began to flow again, and things came back to normal. But it was a narrow escape.

IDENTIFYING FACTS

1. Why did the other lumberjacks decide to use the double-bladed ax that Paul invented?

2. According to this story, how was the Grand Canyon created?

3. Why was it necessary for the giant cornstalk to be cut down?

INTERPRETING MEANINGS

4. What is the speaker's tone of voice (serious, sarcastic, humorous?)

APPLYING MEANINGS

5. What do you think is the reason for Paul Bunyan's popularity as a folk hero? Can you think of other characters like him?

Focus on Reading

ANECDOTES

An **anecdote** is a brief, entertaining narrative. The narrator tells a number of anecdotes that lead up to the incident with the cornstalk. Identify the different anecdotes in "Paul Bunyan's Cornstalk." How does each one relate to the final episode of the tale? How do these anecdotes contribute to your understanding of Paul Bunyan's character?

Literature and Geography

Changing Landscapes

In this tall tale Paul Bunyan gets credit for changing the American landscape. In other stories Paul digs a canal that turns out to be the Mississippi River and uses the dirt to create the Rocky Mountains and the Appalachians.

Making Connections: Activities

Read additional tales about Paul Bunyan and find out how he affected the geography of North America. Some sources to consult are *Ol' Paul* by Glen Rounds, *Paul Bunyan* by Esther Shepherd, and "Paul Bunyan: An American Hercules" by James Stevens.

Connecting Cultures

Tales About Giants

Some historians believe that the Paul Bunyan stories originated in Canada. They may have been adaptations of old French folk tales about giants. There are myths and legends about giants from many cultures around the world.

Making Connections: Activities

1. In your library locate tales about the following figures:

   Jack the Giant Killer
   Goliath
   Cyclops

   How do the stories about these giants compare with those about Paul Bunyan?

2. Read "A Voyage to Lilliput" in *Gulliver's Travels* by Jonathan Swift. How does Lemuel Gulliver seem to become a giant? What does he discover about people when he is bigger than they are?

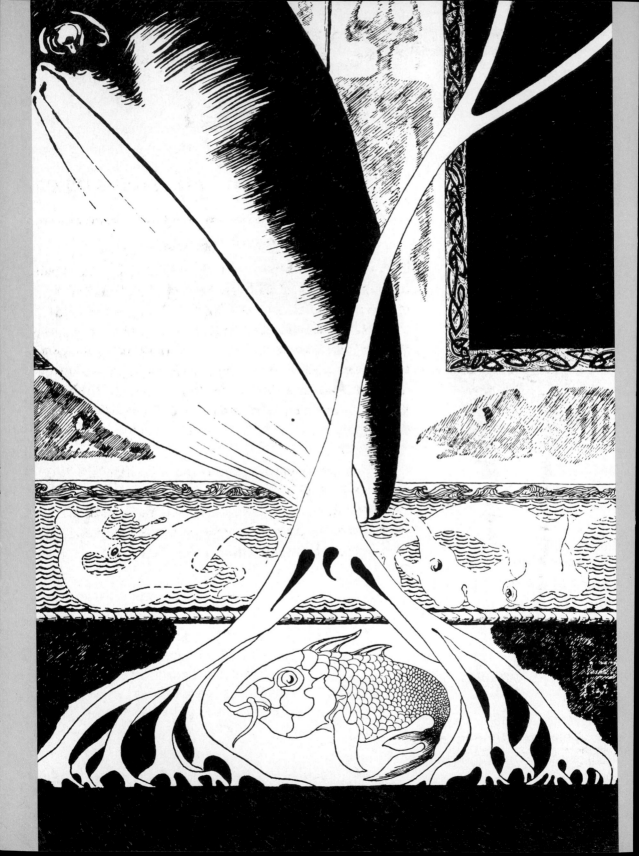

How the Whale Got His Throat

RUDYARD KIPLING

Before You Read

Before you read about this Mariner (sailor) and the Whale, look up the word *whale* in an encyclopedia. You should discover that there are two kinds of whales, baleen and toothed. Instead of teeth, the baleens have hundreds of tiny "plates" that hang down from their upper jaws. Big as it is, a baleen whale can eat only tiny fish and plants, which it must sift through these plates (they are made of material like our fingernails). This story explains how whales came to have this "screen" in their mouths (Kipling calls it a "grating").

"How the Whale Got His Throat" is one of the *Just So Stories* that Kipling wrote for his own three children. As you read this story (or listen to a good reader read it aloud), look for places where the person telling the tale seems to be speaking as a parent to a child.

The illustrations for this story are the original drawings done by Rudyard Kipling for his *Just So Stories*.

onomatopoeia, words whose sounds echo their meaning. He **repeats** words and phrases for a rhythmic effect. He even uses words that **rhyme**.

1. Find and read aloud four passages that use some of these techniques.

2. Write one sentence (it can be a silly sentence) in which you use at least three onomatopoetic words. Here are some words for ideas:

buzz	drip	lap	slurp
cluck	hiss	lick	snap
crack	holler	pop	squawk
crash	hoot	purr	whir
crunch	hum	rattle	whisper

3. Write one sentence in which you repeat one consonant sound at least four times. (It can be a silly sentence.)

Illustrating the Tale

Make a comic strip of "How the Whale Got His Throat." First decide which incidents you will illustrate; each incident will get one frame. Then write the dialogue that will be in those "conversation bubbles." You can't use all of Kipling's dialogue, so you will have to decide which parts of it are most important.

About the Author

Rudyard Kipling (1865–1936) was born in Bombay, India. His father, an illustrator, taught at the Lahore School of Industrial Art. One of Rudyard's earliest memories was of listening to his Indian baby sitters as they told him folk tales about jungle animals.

Rudyard Kipling by Sir Philip Burne-Jones (1899). Oil on canvas.

National Portrait Gallery, London.

When Rudyard was five years old, his parents sent him and his younger sister to England. They did this to protect them from the fevers that killed so many youngsters in India. For the next twelve years, Rudyard lived a very hard life, first in a foster home, where he was cruelly treated, and then at a boarding school, where he was bullied and beaten. When he was seventeen, he returned to India and began publishing humorous poems and short stories. By the time he returned to England, only a few years later, he was already famous. Kipling married an American and lived in Vermont for four years. There he wrote his best-known books for children: *The Jungle Books* and a novel called *Captains Courageous*. Kipling won the Nobel Prize for literature in 1907.

Why Tortoise's Shell Is Not Smooth

An African Folk Tale

CHINUA ACHEBE

hard shell, full of food and wine, but without any wings to fly home. He asked the birds to take a message for his wife, but they all refused. In the end, Parrot, who had felt more angry than the others, suddenly changed his mind and agreed to take the message.

" 'Tell my wife,' said Tortoise, 'to bring out all the soft things in my house and cover the compound[3] with them so that I can jump down from the sky without very great danger.'

"Parrot promised to deliver the message, and then flew away. But when he reached Tortoise's house, he told his wife to bring out all the hard things in the house.

---

3. **compound**: a fenced yard with buildings in it.

And so she brought out her husband's hoes, machetes, spears, guns, and even his cannon. Tortoise looked down from the sky and saw his wife bringing things out, but it was too far to see what they were. When all seemed ready, he let himself go. He fell and fell and fell until he began to fear that he would never stop falling. And then, like the sound of his cannon, he crashed on the compound."

"Did he die?" asked Ezinma.

"No," replied Ekwefi. "His shell broke into pieces. But there was a great medicine man in the neighborhood. Tortoise's wife sent for him, and he gathered all the bits of shell and stuck them together. That is why Tortoise's shell is not smooth."

For Study and Discussion

IDENTIFYING FACTS

1. Why is Tortoise especially eager to go to the feast in the sky?

2. What **problem** does he have in getting to the feast? How does he solve it?

3. Why does Tortoise say that everyone needs a new name? What name does he take?

4. Why does Tortoise have to jump down from the sky? How does Parrot trick him?

INTERPRETING MEANINGS

5. At the beginning of the folk tale, what is the birds' opinion of Tortoise? Does the story show that this opinion is right or wrong? Explain why you think so.

6. Which of the following statements expresses an important **idea** in this story?
   a. Everyone deserves a second chance.
   b. A person who makes trouble for others is also making it for himself or herself.
   c. A generous person will be rewarded.

APPLYING MEANINGS

7. What is it about a tortoise that might make people think it could be a good **trickster**? What is it about birds that might make people think they could be easily fooled? What other animals would be good tricksters?

Writing About Literature

MAKING UP A "HOW AND WHY" STORY

Think of three things in nature that might seem mysterious to a young child. Write a how or why question a child might ask about each of these things. Here are some examples: Why do dogs wag their tails? How did the giraffe get its long neck? Why do mosquitoes buzz?

After you've written three questions, ask a classmate to choose one of them to answer. Then you choose one of your classmate's three questions to answer. Let your imagination supply the answer, not science. Write your answer in one or two paragraphs. Try to think of a young child as your audience.

About the Author

Chinua Achebe (chin'yōō·ä a·chē'bē) (1930–) grew up during the time when Nigeria was ruled by the British. He was born in Ogidi, a large village in eastern Nigeria. He graduated from University College and worked in radio broadcasting for several

years in Lagos, the former capital of Nigeria. His first and most famous novel, which he wrote for adults, is called *Things Fall Apart.* This story is set in a village of the Ibo people in Nigeria in the early 1900s. In the novel, Achebe shows how folklore helps to keep things from falling apart, as the modern world forces changes on traditional ways of life. Achebe's other works include the novels *No Longer at Ease* and *Arrow of God,* and a collection of short stories, *Girls at War and Other Stories.*

Rapping About Story Forms

A popular African American writer talks about the origin of stories:

Behind the Scenes

One of the earliest forms of the story that we made up in Africa was the fable. A fable is a tale about animals . . . but really about people. It instructs us; it teaches us something about human behavior. But people do not like to be told straight out about themselves, so the storyteller acts as if he's just talking about buzzards or rabbits or something. When we came to these shores years ago, we brought these tales along. We even made up new ones, for there was much peculiar behavior on the part of people here to talk about and to teach about. So often, while drumming in the yard, we would tell stories about crafty foxes or sly monkeys or big dumb bears. We were often talking about our situation as slaves, trying to survive through our wits, trying to instruct each other through a ''code'' language.

This technique—this way of talking about one thing while really talking about another—is called ''signifyin'.'' For instance, a beautiful sister in her beautiful Afro walks past a group of brothers. Right away they start signifyin'.

''Mmmm, what a fine spring day, right, Joe?''

''Sure is. Can't remember when we've had such beautiful weather.''

''Yesirree. Such a lovely day, I feel I could fly.''

''Well fly, brother, fly.''

In other words—the girl is fine.

—Toni Cade Bambara

TALES THAT AMUSE AND AMAZE

Tales told to amuse and amaze come from all parts of the world. The most popular of these tales is the fairy tale. For generations, fairy tales have given form to our nightmares and our hopes. Most of all, of course, fairy tales have amused and amazed us with their extraordinary imagination. This is the imagination of the human family, the imagination of the "folk," who cannot resist the magic of the words "Once upon a time . . ."

Bluebeard gives his wife the keys to the castle. Colored engraving by Gustave Doré (1867).

The Granger Collection, New York.

Illustration for "The Story of the King of the Ebony Isles" from *The Arabian Nights*. Watercolor by Edmund Dulac (1882–1953).

© British Museum.

Ali Baba and the Forty Thieves

A Middle Eastern Folk Tale

Retold by ELISABETH GILLE

Before You Read

This folk tale is from a collection of Persian, Indian, and Arabian stories called *The Thousand and One Nights* (also known as *The Arabian Nights*). The first tale in the collection tells about Scheherazade (shə·her′ə·zäd′), the daughter of the king's adviser. This king hated all women because his beloved first wife had betrayed him. And so the king killed his first wife. Then, to get even with females in general, he married a different girl every day and had her killed the next morning. Scheherazade eventually was married to the king. But being clever as well as beautiful, she thought of a plan to stay alive. On the night of her marriage, Scheherazade began telling her husband a story. When she got to the most exciting part, she told him he must wait until the following night to find out what happened next. Because her stories hooked his interest, the king didn't want to kill his storyteller. And so the clever Scheherazade went on telling part of a story every night for a thousand and one nights. By that time, the king had fallen in love with her, and "they lived happily ever after."

"Ali Baba and the Forty Thieves" is set in ancient Persia (modern-day Iran). As you read this story of Scheherazade's, notice how it rises to one exciting point after another. There are at least four places in this story where Scheherazade might have stopped. Can you find them?

Language and Vocabulary

A prefix is a group of letters added to the beginning of a word or word root to change its meaning. (A **root** is the basic part of the word from which other words can be built.) You can figure out the meaning of some new words if you know what their prefixes mean. Many prefixes came into English from the Latin language. For example, the prefix *dis-* comes from a Latin word meaning "apart" or "away." It also signals "opposite meaning." When you put the prefix *dis-* in front of the root *like*, you get *dislike*, the opposite of *like*. Another useful Latin prefix is *re-*, meaning "back" or "again." You'll find the prefixes *dis-* and *re-* as you read this story.

Once upon a time in ancient Persia, there were two brothers. One, named Cassim, having married an heiress,[1] had become one of the richest merchants in the city. The other, Ali Baba, having married a young girl as poor as he was, had as his only means of livelihood whatever he could earn chopping wood in the nearby forest, loading it onto the three donkeys which were his only worldly goods, and bringing it to the city to sell. One day, while working in the forest, Ali Baba saw a large troop of horsemen galloping toward him. Fearing they might be thieves, he dispersed[2] his donkeys and climbed a tall tree from which he could watch, yet not be seen. The horsemen dismounted, each unloading a bag from behind his saddle. Their leader walked over to a great rock close to the

tree where Ali Baba had taken refuge, and pronounced these words: "Open Sesame!"[3] Instantly, a door swung open, and the whole troop disappeared through it.

Half an hour later, the door reopened. The thieves (there were forty of them) came out of the cave and the door closed behind them as the leader pronounced the words: "Close Sesame!"

As soon as they were out of sight, Ali Baba climbed down the tree and out of curiosity walked over and stood in front of the rock. Barely had he spoken the magic words "Open Sesame!" when the door opened wide. Ali Baba entered the cave. To his amazement, he discovered heaps of rich merchandise, bolts of fine silks and brocades,[4] carpets of great worth, leather purses full of gold and silver! Here was the

---

1. **heiress:** a woman who has inherited a lot of money.
2. **dispersed:** scattered.

3. **sesame** (ses'ə·mē): a plant. (You've probably tasted food coated with sesame seeds.)
4. **brocades** (brō·kāds'): rich woven fabrics.

treasure the thieves had collected during many years. Without hesitating, Ali Baba gathered up as much as his three donkeys could carry, strapped the bags on their backs, and placed some firewood on top in order to conceal the gold. He then returned to the city and told his wife of his adventure. As he emptied the sacks in front of her, great piles of gold pieces lay at her feet. She could hardly believe her eyes. As soon as she recovered from her surprise, she ran over to her sister-in-law's to borrow a scale to determine the exact value of this fortune.

But Cassim's wife, wondering what the poor Ali Baba could possibly own worth weighing, secretly coated the scale with tallow[5] before giving it to her. When her sister-in-law returned the scale, one goldpiece had indeed stuck to the tallow. His wife told Cassim of her trick and he ran to his brother, who had to tell him how he happened to discover the thieves' hideout, and where it was. Cassim immediately saddled ten mules, loaded them with huge chests, and went to the forest. Standing in front of the rock Ali Baba had described, he pronounced the magic words and the door opened. But alas! When he was ready to leave, the door which he had closed would not open. He could no longer remember the necessary words! In vain he shouted, "Open Barley!" "Open Millet!"[6] The door obstinately remained shut.

---

5. **tallow:** the fat of certain animals, used to make candles and soap (a sticky substance).
6. **barley . . . millet** (mil'it): other kinds of grasses whose seeds are used for food.

The thieves soon returned. They discovered Cassim, killed him, and cut his body into four pieces which they placed at the entrance to the cave in order to frighten off anyone else. Ali Baba, worried by his brother's long absence, went to find him. Horrorstruck when he saw what had happened, he carried the corpse back to his house. There he ordered his faithful slave, Morgiana, to have the body sewn together by a skillful cobbler so that the neighbors would believe Cassim had died a natural death, and the thieves would not recognize him. Actually, finding that the body had been removed, the thieves realized somebody now knew the location of their retreat. The leader came to the city to inquire about the missing body, and the cobbler, who could not keep a secret, blurted out the whole story.

Returning to his comrades, the leader said, "A certain person named Ali Baba knows of our secret hiding place. He must die! Here is my plan. I will go to him disguised as an honest merchant. I'll take with me twenty mules, each carrying two enormous oil jars. Of these forty jars, only one will be filled with oil; the others will each hide one of you, armed to the teeth. Ali Baba will certainly offer me shelter for the night, and I will have the jars placed in rows in the courtyard. Once darkness has fallen, and when all in the house are asleep, I'll toss some pebbles down from my window. At this signal, you are to split open your jars with the knives with which you will have been provided. Then, fully armed, we will throw ourselves upon Ali

Baba and his servants, who, taken thus by surprise, will not offer much resistence.''

Accordingly, twenty mules were loaded with two jars apiece. Thirty-nine jars held a thief, and the last jar was filled with oil. The leader then led them to the city. They arrived about an hour after sundown, as had been planned, and went at once to Ali Baba's house. They found him outside his doorway enjoying the evening air. The leader said, ''My lord, I'm taking these oil jars to sell in the market. But darkness has overtaken me, and I do no know where to seek lodging. I would be most grateful if you could put me up for the night.''

Ali Baba, suspecting nothing, courteously welcomed the false merchant, offered him supper, had a bed prepared, and ordered his slaves to set the jars in the courtyard. Before retiring, Morgiana wanted to make preparations for next morning's breakfast. But her lamp went out. As there was no more oil in the house, she decided to draw some from one of the jars in the courtyard. She had barely reached the first jar when she heard a whisper: ''Has the time come?'' Sensing danger, but without showing alarm, she calmly answered, ''No, not yet.'' She then guessed the truth, that probably only one of the jars contained oil. Cleverly locating it, she drew off enough to fill a large caldron[7] and put it on the stove to boil.

When it was ready, she carried it to the courtyard and silently poured enough boiling oil into each jar to suffocate and kill the thief inside. A little later, the leader, feeling the time was ripe, gave the agreed signal. When there was no response, he thought his comrades must have fallen asleep and he came down to wake them up himself. Overcome when he saw what had happened, he took to his heels and fled.

Next morning, Morgiana told her master everything. Ali Baba, deeply impressed and filled with gratitude, said, ''I pledge you my word that before I die I will recompense[8] you as you deserve. In the meantime, I grant you your freedom as of this moment. But let us hurry to bury the thieves secretly so that no one may suspect their fate. For if any hint of this were to leak out, it might easily be connected with my new riches.''

Meanwhile the leader of the thieves had gone back to the forest and was thinking up a plan of revenge. He found one before long. At dawn he put on clean clothes, procured a horse upon which he packed all sorts of fine silks and linens, and went back to the city. Here he rented a shop directly across the street from the one which Ali Baba had recently bought for his son and struck up a friendship with him. He showered him with gifts, ingratiating[9] himself so well that Ali Baba's son invited him to dine at his father's house.

---

7. **caldron** (kôl′drən): large kettle or pot.

8. **recompense** (rek′əm·pəns): reward.
9. **ingratiating** (in·grā′shē·āt′ing): pleasing someone to gain favor.

Illustration for "The Magic Horse" from *Tales from the
Arabian Nights*. Watercolor by Edmund Dulac (1882–1953).

Illustration for "Ali Baba and the Forty Thieves" from *Tales from the Arabian Nights*. Watercolor by Edmund Dulac (1882–1953).

Harry Ransom Humanities Research Center, The University of Texas at Austin.

The leader had disguised himself so successfully that Ali Baba didn't recognize him as the imposter who, only a few days before, had tried to murder him. He welcomed him warmly, thanked him for all his kindness to his son, and led him into a great hall where a feast had been prepared.

Morgiana, however, while serving the meal, noticed the gleam of a dagger hidden under the guest's robe. Taking a closer look, she saw through his disguise and became suspicious.

When dinner was over, she put on a dancing costume and a suitable headdress, and buckled on a silver-gilt belt in which she slipped a dagger of the same metal. She then requested the honor of dancing before her master. Delighted at this opportunity of providing such entertainment for his guest, he accepted heartily. Morgiana ranked second to none among dancers. She drew the dagger from her belt and performed so many different motions, so many airy gestures, and so many intricate steps that her audience was enchanted. At times she waved the dagger in front of her as if to strike, at times she waved it as if to stab herself. Suddenly, she sprang upon the false merchant and, without allowing him time to move, sank the dagger up to the hilt into his heart! Ali Baba and his son, utterly dismayed, cried out, "Oh, wretched creature! What have you done?"

Whereupon Morgiana drew back the merchant's robe, pointed to the dagger with which he was armed, and said, "I only did this to save you. Examine more closely the face of the man whom you welcomed at your table. You will recognize the false oil merchant, the leader of the forty thieves! I saw through his disguise while I was serving him, and I devised this means of preventing him from carrying out his sinister plans."

Ali Baba gratefully embraced Morgiana and said, "When I freed you, Morgiana, I promised my favors would not stop there. I am now so deeply indebted that I see only one way of repaying you; namely, to present you in marriage to my son. He, too, owes you his life. I feel sure he will gladly accede to my wishes."

Ali Baba's son, far from opposing this marriage, replied that he consented, not only in order to obey his father, but also because, having fallen in love with Morgiana, he could ask for nothing better.

A few days later, Ali Baba celebrated their wedding with pomp and splendor. There was a sumptuous banquet, followed by dancing and pageantry.[10]

At the end of a year, Ali Baba went back to the cave and pronounced the words "Open Sesame!" which he had not forgotten. He was able to verify that the treasure was intact, and that no one else had any hint of its existence.

He passed the secret words on to his son, who, in turn, passed them on to his own children. Ali Baba and his heirs used the fortune with wisdom and moderation, and thus were able to live out their lives in comfort and in luxury.

---

10. **pageantry** (paj′ən·trē): splendid display.

IDENTIFYING FACTS

1. How does Ali Baba get into the cave? What does he find inside?

2. How is Cassim's death important to the **plot?** That is, if he had not been killed, what might have happened in the story?

3. What plan does the leader of the thieves make to sneak his thirty-nine followers into Ali Baba's courtyard? How does the clever Morgiana find out the truth?

4. Ali Baba gives Morgiana two rewards. What are those rewards? What had Morgiana done to get each?

5. **Disguises** which hide a person's true nature are often found in folk tales. Find three places in this story where characters disguise themselves.

INTERPRETING MEANINGS

6. What details show that hospitality to strangers was an important value to the people who told this story?

7. Do you think this story was told mostly to entertain listeners? Or does it also teach a **moral lesson?** If you think it does, what is that moral?

APPLYING MEANINGS

8. In this story, as in almost all folk tales, the good are rewarded and the evil are punished. Judged by the standards of their own people, Ali Baba and Morgiana are admirable and heroic. Suppose that the setting of this story was not ancient Persia, but twentieth-century America. What criminal charges might Ali Baba and Morgiana have to face? If you were in their place, what would you have done to solve the problems without committing any "crimes"?

Focus on Reading

CAUSE AND EFFECT

The events that take place in a story are connected by **cause and effect.** This means that one event causes another event to happen. This event in turn causes another event to happen. See if you can answer these questions about cause and effect in Scheherazade's expertly plotted story.

1. Ali Baba sees the thieves open the cave door by saying the magic words.
   Effect:

2. Cassim's wife wonders why Ali Baba's wife wants to weigh something on her scale.
   Effect:

3. Cassim gets into the cave but can't remember the magic words to get out again.
   Effect:

4. The thieves return to find Cassim's body missing.
   Effect:

5. Morgiana's lamp runs out of oil.
   Effect:

6. The leader of the thieves strikes up a friendship with Ali Baba's son and is invited to dine at Ali Baba's house.
   Effect:

Literary Elements

THE SUPERNATURAL IN FOLK TALES

All folk tales contain elements of the supernatural. This means that things happen in folk tales that could not happen in the world as we know it. Our world is governed by certain laws of nature. Our laws of nature, for example, do not allow a cave door to open when it hears certain words.

1. List the events in this story that *definitely* could not happen in real life.

2. Which key events or situations in the story are perfectly realistic and could exist in real life?

Language and Vocabulary

A PREFIX GAME

A **prefix** is a group of letters added to the beginning of a word or word root. A prefix changes the meaning of a word. Many prefixes came into English from the Latin language. Here are two such prefixes:

dis- meaning "apart, away, opposite"
re- meaning "again, back"

Below, six mystery words or word parts are listed at the left, *without* their prefixes. At the right, in scrambled order, is a list of what the words mean *after* the correct prefix has been added (*dis-* or *re-*). All of the mystery words come from the story. See how many you can complete by using one of the prefixes. Then match the words to their correct meanings.

1. —opened   **a.** Scattered or spread apart

2. —compense   **b.** Opened again
3. —persed   **c.** The opposite of "climbed on"
4. —tiring   **d.** Going back to bed
5. —mounted   **e.** Pay back
6. —treat   **f.** Hiding place to go back to

Focus on Writing a Book Report

SUPPORTING THE MAIN IDEA

You need to support your main idea in a book report with **details.** You can use the following details in a book report.

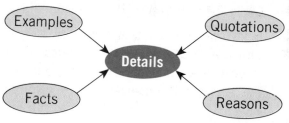

Suppose, for example, that you were presenting an opinion that Morgiana was the true hero of "Ali Baba." You might use a framework like the one below to support your opinion:

> In my opinion, the true hero of "Ali Baba" is Morgiana. My reasons for believing this are _____ and _____. One example of Morgiana's heroism is _____ _____.

Write a one-sentence statement of a main idea for a book report. Then list as many specific details as you can to support and develop this idea. Save your notes.

Momotaro: Boy-of-the-Peach

A Japanese Folk Tale

Retold by YOSHIKO UCHIDA

ももたろう

Before You Read

In Japan, people love to listen to the old tales told by professional storytellers. At one time, whole families would go to the *yose* to hear the storyteller, or *Hanashi-ka*, tell his tale—just as American families go to the movies today. A favorite story of Japanese children is this story of the boy who was born from a peach—Momotaro. As you read this tale, look for places where the storyteller would act out the story, or where he would change his voice to scare or amuse his listeners. Notice also what the folktale teaches about human values and family love. Before you read, talk about how we teach values to children today. Do parents still use stories to teach children what is important in life?

The illustrations for this story were done by Akasaka Sanko for a children's book written in Japanese.

© Miyoshi Akasaka

English has borrowed many words from other languages. Some of the words borrowed from Japanese are *judo*, *kimono*, and *tycoon*. Other words more recently borrowed from Japanese name many kinds of things, from foods (*sushi*) to furniture (*futon*). You probably know of at least three cars that have Japanese names. As you read this story, look for two Japanese words. You will find one of them easily. It is printed in italic type. Can you guess what this Japanese word means from the **context**, that is, from the rest of the sentence?

Once long, long ago, there lived a kind old man and a kind old woman in a small village in Japan.

One fine day they set out from their little cottage together. The old man went toward the mountains to cut some firewood for their kitchen, and the old woman went toward the river to do her washing.

When the old woman reached the shore of the river, she knelt down beside her wooden tub and began to scrub her clothes on a round, flat stone. Suddenly she looked up and saw something very strange floating down the shallow river. It was an enormous peach, bigger than the round wooden tub that stood beside the old woman.

Rumbley-bump and a-bumpety-bump . . . Rumbley-bump and a-bumpety-bump. The big peach rolled closer and closer over the stones in the stream.

"My gracious me!" the old woman said to herself. "In all my long life I have never seen a peach of such great size and beauty. What a fine present it would make for the old man. I do think I will take it home with me."

Then the old woman stretched out her hand just as far as she could, but no matter how hard she stretched, she couldn't reach the big peach.

"If I could just find a long stick, I would be able to reach it," thought the old woman, looking around, but all she could see were pebbles and sand.

"Oh, dear, what shall I do?" she said to herself. Then suddenly she thought of a way to bring the beautiful big peach to her side. She began to sing out in a sweet, clear voice:

The deep waters are salty!
The shallow waters are sweet!
Stay away from the salty water,
And come where the water is sweet.

She sang this over and over, clapping her hands in time to her song. Then, strangely enough, the big peach slowly began to bob along toward the shore where the water was shallow.

Rumbley-bump and a-bumpety-bump . . . Rumbley-bump and a-bumpety-bump. The big peach came closer and closer to the old woman and finally came to a stop at her feet.

The old woman was so happy she picked the big peach up very carefully and quickly carried it home in her arms. Then she waited for the old man to return so she could show him her lovely present. Toward evening the old man came home with a big pack of wood on his back.

"Come quickly, come quickly," the old woman called to him from the house.

"What is it? What is the matter?" the old man asked as he hurried to the side of the old woman.

"Just look at the fine present I have for you," said the old woman happily as she showed him the big round peach.

"My goodness! What a great peach! Where in the world did you buy such a peach as this?" the old man asked.

The old woman smiled happily and told him how she had found the peach floating down the river.

"Well, well, this is a fine present indeed," said the old man, "for I have worked hard today and I am very hungry."

Then he got the biggest knife they had so he could cut the big peach in half. Just as he was ready to thrust the sharp blade into the peach, he heard a tiny voice from inside.

"Wait, old man! Don't cut me!" it cried, and before the surprised old man and woman could say a word, the beautiful big peach broke in two, and a sweet little boy jumped out from inside. The old man and woman were so surprised they could only raise their hands and cry out, "Oh, oh! My goodness!"

Now the old man and woman had always wanted a child of their own, so they were very, very happy to find such a fine little boy, and decided to call him "Momotaro," which means boy-of-the-peach. They took very good care of the little boy and grew to love him dearly, for he was a fine young lad. They spent many happy years together, and before long Momotaro was fifteen years old.

One day Momotaro came before the old man and said, "You have both been good and kind to me. I am very grateful for all you have done, and now I think I am old enough to do some good for others too. I have come to ask if I may leave you."

"You wish to leave us, my son? But why?" asked the old man in surprise.

"Oh, I shall be back in a very short time," said Momotaro. "I wish only to go to the Island of the Ogres,[1] to rid the land of those harmful creatures. They have killed many good people, and have stolen and robbed throughout the country. I wish to kill the ogres so they can never harm our people again."

"That is a fine idea, my son, and I will not stop you from going," said the old man.

So that very day Momotaro got ready

---

1. **ogres** (ō′gərs): in fairy tales, giants or monsters that eat people.

to start out on his journey. The old woman prepared some millet[2] cakes for him to take along on his trip, and soon Momotaro was ready to leave. The old man and woman were sad to see him go and called, "Be careful, Momotaro! Come back safely to us."

"Yes, yes, I shall be back soon," he answered. "Take care of yourselves while I am away," he added, and waved as he started down the path toward the forest.

He hurried along, for he was anxious to get to the Island of the Ogres. While he was walking through the cool forest where

2. **millet** (mil′it): a kind of grass. Millet seeds are used to make certain foods in Asia.

the grass grew long and high, he began to feel hungry. He sat down at the foot of a tall pine tree and carefully unwrapped the *furoshiki* which held his little millet cakes. "My, they smell good," he thought. Suddenly he heard the tall grass rustle and saw something stalking through the grass toward him. Momotaro blinked hard when he saw what it was. It was a dog as big as a calf! But Momotaro was not frightened, for the dog just said, "Momotaro-san,[3] Momotaro-san, what is it you are eating that smells so good?"

"I'm eating a delicious millet cake which my good mother made for me this morning," he answered.

---

3. In Japanese, the suffix *san* is often added to names as a mark of respect.

The dog licked his chops and looked at the cake with hungry eyes. "Please, Momotaro-san," he said, "just give me one of your millet cakes, and I will come along with you to the Island of the Ogres. I know why you are going there, and I can be of help to you."

"Very well, my friend," said Momotaro, "I will take you along with me." And he gave the dog one of his millet cakes to eat.

As they walked on, something suddenly leaped from the branches above and jumped in front of Momotaro. He stopped in surprise and found that it was a monkey who had jumped down from the trees.

"Greetings, Momotaro-san!" called the monkey happily. "I have heard that you

are going to the Island of the Ogres to rid the land of these plundering creatures. Take me with you, for I wish to help you in your fight."

When the dog heard this, he growled angrily. "Grruff," he said to the monkey. "*I* am going to help Momotaro-san. We do not need the help of a monkey such as you! Out of our way! Grruff, grruff," he barked angrily.

"How dare you speak to me like that?" shrieked the monkey, and he leaped at the dog, scratching with his sharp claws. The dog and the monkey began to fight each other, biting, clawing, and growling. When Momotaro saw this, he pushed them apart and cried, "Here, here, stop it, you two! There is no reason why you both cannot go with me to the Island of the Ogres. I shall have two helpers instead of one!" Then he took another millet cake from his *furoshiki* and gave it to the monkey.

Now there were three of them going down the path to the edge of the woods—the dog in front, Momotaro in the middle, and the monkey walking in the rear. Soon they came to a big field, and just as they were about to cross it, a large pheasant[4] hopped out in front of them. The dog jumped at it with a growl, but the pheasant fought back with such spirit that Momotaro ran over to stop the dog. "We could use a brave bird such as you to help us fight the ogres. We are on our way to their island this very day. How would you like to come along with us?"

"Oh, I would like that indeed, for I would like to help you rid the land of these evil and dangerous ogres," said the pheasant happily.

"Then here is a millet cake for you, too," said Momotaro, giving the pheasant a cake, just as he had the monkey and the dog.

Now there were four of them going to the Island of the Ogres, and as they walked down the path together, they became very good friends.

Before long they came to the water's edge and Momotaro found a boat big enough for all of them. They climbed in and headed for the Island of the Ogres. Soon they saw the island in the distance, wrapped in gray, foggy clouds. Dark stone walls rose up above towering cliffs, and large iron gates stood ready to keep out any who tried to enter.

Momotaro thought for a moment, then turned to the pheasant and said, "You alone can wing your way over their high walls and gates. Fly into their stronghold[5] now, and do what you can to frighten them. We will follow as soon as we can."

So the pheasant flew far above the iron gates and stone walls and down onto the roof of the ogres' castle. Then he called to the ogres, "Momotaro-san has come to rid the land of you and your many evil deeds. Give up your stolen treasures now, and perhaps he will spare your lives!"

When the ogres heard this, they laughed and shouted, "HO, HO, HO! We

---

4. **pheasant** (fez'ənt): a long-tailed bird.

5. **stronghold**: fortress.

are not afraid of a little bird like you! We are not afraid of little Momotaro!"

The pheasant became very angry at this, and flew down, pecking at the heads of the ogres with his sharp, pointed beak. While the pheasant was fighting so bravely, the dog and monkey helped Momotaro to tear down the gates, and they soon came to the aid of the pheasant.

"Get away! Get away!" shouted the ogres, but the monkey clawed and scratched, the big dog growled and bit the ogres, and the pheasant flew about, pecking at their heads and faces. So fierce were they that soon the ogres began to run away. Half of them tumbled over the cliffs as they ran, and the others fell pell-mell into the sea. Soon only the Chief of the Ogres remained. He threw up his hands, and then

bowed low to Momotaro. "Please spare me my life, and all our stolen treasures are yours. I promise never to rob or kill anyone again," he said.

Momotaro tied up the evil ogre, while the monkey, the dog, and the pheasant carried many boxes filled with jewels and treasures down to their little boat. Soon it was laden with all the treasures it could hold, and they were ready to sail toward home.

When Momotaro returned, he went from one family to another, returning the many treasures which the ogres had stolen from the people of the land.

"You will never again be troubled by the ogres of Ogre Island!" he said to them happily.

And they all answered, "You are a kind and brave lad, and we thank you for making our land safe once again."

Then Momotaro went back to the home of the old man and woman with his arms full of jewels and treasures from Ogre Island. The old man and woman were so glad to see him once again, and the three of them lived happily together for many, many years.

For Study and Discussion

IDENTIFYING FACTS

1. Right away, this storyteller plunges us into the fabulous world of folklore. What miraculous thing does the old woman find in the stream?

2. Describe the **quest** that Momotaro goes on. Why does he undertake it?

3. As often happens in folk tales, the hero meets characters along the way who assist him on the quest. Who assists Momotaro? Tell exactly how each friend helps the Peach Boy get what he wants.

4. This is truly a tale that "amazes." Make a list of all the things in this tale that couldn't happen in real life.

INTERPRETING MEANINGS

5. What is the outcome of Momotaro's **quest**? Who benefits from his quest?

6. Many folk tales are stories of wish fulfillment. What wishes or fantasies come true for the people in this story?

APPLYING MEANINGS

7. Uchida's grandfather was a samurai in Japan before he became a teacher. The samurai were military leaders who had a strict code of conduct. In some ways, the samurai were like the knights of King Arthur's Round Table. The samurai code stressed bravery, loyalty, self-discipline, politeness, and respect for anyone in authority (such as parents, ancestors, and rulers). Which of these qualities does Momotaro have? Which of these qualities are important in our world today?

Focus on Reading

SUMMARIZING

When you **summarize** a story, you tell about its most important events. Here are some steps you can follow:

1. Divide the story into a beginning, a middle, and an end.

2. Look for a major event in each part of the story.

3. Tell about each major event in your own words. Use a complete sentence to describe each. If there are two major events in a part of the story, you may want to put both of them into one sentence.

4. Reread your summary. Have you used **transitions**—words and phrases like *then, after, as a result of* that help your reader know when and where events happened?

In the following summary, every other sentence has been left out. What sentences would you add to make a complete summary of the story?

a. An old woman finds a large peach and takes it home. _____

b. _____

c. When Momotaro is fifteen, he leaves the old people because he wants to rid the land of ogres. _____

d. _____

e. The animals go with him, and they all become good friends. _____

f. _____

g. Momotaro returns home. _____

h. _____

Literary Elements

COMMON FEATURES IN FOLK TALES

One of the supernatural elements in this story has to do with the unusual origin of the hero—he was found in a large peach.

1. Can you think of any other hero who has strange or mysterious origins? (Where did Superman come from? Where do the Ninja turtles come from?)

2. Do you recall other heroes or heroines who have unusual friends who help them accomplish a difficult task? (Think of Dorothy's helpers as she journeys to Oz. How about Luke Skywalker in *Star Wars*?)

Language and Vocabulary

JAPANESE WORDS

Japanese and English look and sound quite different. For example, Japanese is spoken with an even beat on each syllable. Instead of stressing certain syllables the way English speakers do, Japanese speakers vary the pitch of their voice. Here are some Japanese words and their English meanings:

1. *arigato* (ä·re·gä·to)—thank you

2. *ha-ha* (hä·hä)—mother

3. *otoh* (au·to)—father

4. *hai* (hi)—yes

5. *iye* (yeh)—no

6. *ohayo* (o·hi·o)—good morning

7. *dozo* (do·zo)—please

8. *san* (sähn)—a word that, added to a person's name, shows respect, like Mr., Mrs., or Ms. in English.

9. *sayonara* (si·o·nä·rä)—good-bye (means "if it must be so")

10. *yoi* (yoy)—good

Choose three of the English meanings from the list above. Then find out how to say these words in another language. If you know people who speak a foreign language, you may ask them. If you can speak a foreign language yourself, of course, you won't have to ask anyone! See how many different foreign words you and your classmates can find for these English meanings. Do any of the words resemble English or Japanese?

Writing About Literature

EXTENDING THE STORY

Where did the Peach Boy come from? How did he get into the huge juicy peach? How long had he been inside the peach, floating down the river? How did he know he had to go on his quest? Write three or four sentences in which you tell the beginning of the story.

About the Author

Yoshiko Uchida (1921–1992) was born in Alameda, California, and grew up in Berkeley. Her parents were Japanese immigrants and leaders in the Japanese American community. Uchida attended the University of California at Berkeley, but just before she graduated, World War II broke out. She and her family, along with most other Japanese living on the West Coast, were sent to internment camps like the one where she was in Topaz, Utah. Several of Uchida's books tell about the hardships that the Japanese

Americans endured in these camps. Uchida heard the story of Momotaro from her own mother. Uchida wrote many books for young people, among them *The Dancing Kettle, A Jar of Dreams, and Other Japanese Folk Tales* and *The Invisible Thread: A Memoir.*

A Writer's Journal

Behind the Scenes

It seems to me I've been interested in books and writing for as long as I can remember. I was writing stories when I was ten, and being the child of frugal[1] immigrant parents, I wrote them on brown wrapping paper which I cut up and bound into booklets, and because I am such a saver, I still have them. The first is titled, "Jimmy Chipmonk and His Friends: A Short Story for Small Children."

I not only wrote stories, I also kept a journal of important events which I began the day I graduated from elementary school. Of course my saver self kept that journal as well, and even today I can read of the special events of my young life, such as the times my parents took us to an opera or concert in San Francisco, or the day I got my first dog, or the sad day it died, when I drew a tombstone for him in my journal and decorated it with floral wreaths.

By putting these special happenings into words and writing them down, I was trying to hold on to and somehow preserve the magic as well as the joy and sadness of certain moments in my life, and I guess that's really what books and writing are all about.

—Yoshiko Uchida

---

1. **frugal** (frū′gəl): careful with money.

Nana Miriam

An African Folk Tale

Retold by HANS BAUMANN

Before You Read

Many folk tales tell about the deeds of a hero who saves the people from a great evil. Long ago, some of these stories may have had some basis in fact. For example, suppose that in years of drought, there was not enough water to grow crops. Suppose somebody figured out how to get water from a river to the fields. The people then praised their hero in songs and stories. As time passed, the tale changed—and became more interesting. The hero might have gained supernatural power. The drought might have become a monster.

As you read this folk tale from Nigeria, notice how it combines events that could happen with magic events that could never happen. Can you imagine what real disaster the story might be based on?

In most African groups, there are no family names, but people may get two or three more names as they become older. The additional names usually tell how someone looks, what one believes in, or what one stands for. Among the Yoruba, people may be given names that tell about something outstanding they have done. The Yoruba call these additional names "praise names." As you read this African folk tale, be thinking of a good praise name for Nana Miriam.

Fara Maka was a man of the Songai tribe, who lived by the River Niger.[1] He was taller than the other men and he was also stronger. Only he was very ugly. However, no one thought that important, because Fara Maka had a daughter who was very beautiful. Her name was Nana Miriam and she too was tall and strong. Her father instructed her in all kinds of things. He went with her to the sandbank and said, "Watch the fish!" And he told her the names of all the various kinds. Everything there is to know about fish he taught her. Then he asked her, "What kind is the one swimming here, and the other one over there?"

"This is a so-and-so," replied Nana Miriam. "And that is a such-and-such."

"Male or female?" asked Fara Maka.

"I don't know," said Nana Miriam.

"This one is a female, and so is the other one," explained Fara Maka. "But the third one over there is a male." And each time he pointed to a different fish.

That was how Nana Miriam came to learn so much. And in addition she had magic powers within her, which no one suspected. And because her father also taught her many magic spells, she grew stronger than anyone else in the Land of the Songai.

Beside the great river, the Niger, there lived a monster that took the form of a hippopotamus. This monster was insatiable.[2] It broke into the rich fields and devoured the crops, bringing famine to the Songai people. No one could tackle this hippopotamus, because it could change its shape. So the hunters had all their trouble for nothing and they returned to their villages in helpless despair. Times were so bad that many died of hunger.

One day, Fara Maka picked up all his lances and set out to kill the monster. When he saw it, he recoiled in fear, for huge pots of fire were hung around the animal's neck. Fara Maka hurled lance after lance, but

---

1. **Niger** (nī′jər): river in West Africa, flowing from Guinea through Mali, Niger, and Nigeria.

2. **insatiable** (in·sā′shə·bəl): never getting enough; greedy.

each one was swallowed by the flames. The hippopotamus monster looked at Fara Maka with scorn. Then it turned its back on him and trotted away.

Fara Maka returned home furious, wondering who he could summon to help him. Now there was a man of the Tomma tribe who was a great hunter. His name was Kara-Digi-Mao-Fosi-Fasi, and Fara Maka asked him if he would hunt the hippopotamus with his one hundred and twenty dogs. "That I will," said Kara-Digi-Mao-Fosi-Fasi.

So Fara Maka invited him and his one hundred and twenty dogs to a great banquet. Before every dog, which had an iron chain around its neck, was placed a small mound of rice and meat. For the hunter, however, there was a huge mound of rice. None of the dogs left a single grain of rice uneaten, and neither did Kara-Digi-Mao-Fosi-Fasi. Well fortified,[3] they set out for the place where the monster lived.

As soon as the dogs picked up the scent, Kara-Digi-Mao-Fosi-Fasi unchained the first one. The chain rattled as the dog leaped forward towards its quarry.[4] One chain rattled after the other, as dog after dog sprang forward to attack the hippopotamus. But the hippopotamus took them on one by one, and it gobbled them all up. The great hunter Kara-Digi-Mao-Fosi-Fasi took to his heels in terror. The hippopotamus charged into a rice field and ate that too.

When Fara Maka heard from the great hunter what had happened, he sat down in the shadow of a large tree and hung his head.

"Haven't you been able to kill the hippopotamus?" Nana Miriam asked him.

"No," said Fara Maka.

"And Kara-Digi-Mao-Fosi-Fasi could not drive it away either?"

"No."

"So there is no one who can get the better of it?"

"No," said Fara Maka.

"Then I'll not delay any longer," said Nana Miriam. "I'll go to its haunts and see what I can see."

"Yes, do," said her father.

Nana Miriam walked along the banks of the Niger, and she soon found the hippopotamus eating its way through a rice field. As soon as it saw the girl it stopped eating, raised its head and greeted her.

"Good morning," replied Nana Miriam.

"I know why you have come," said the hippopotamus. "You want to kill me. But no one can do that. Your father tried, and he lost all his lances. The great hunter Kara-Digi-Mao-Fosi-Fasi tried, and all his dogs paid with their lives for his presumption.[5] And you are only a girl."

"We'll soon see," answered Nana Miriam. "Prepare to fight with me. Only one of us will be left to tell the tale."

---

3. **fortified** (fôr′tə·fīd): strengthened (by the food).
4. **quarry**: an animal that is being hunted.

5. **presumption** (pri·zump′shən): here, the hunter's too great confidence that he could kill the monster.

"Right you are!" shouted the hippopotamus and with its breath it set the rice field afire. There it stood in a ring of flame through which no mortal could pass.

But Nana Miriam threw magic powder into the fire, and the flames turned to water.

"Right!" shouted the hippopotamus, and a wall of iron sprang up making a ring around the monster. But Nana Miriam plucked a magic hammer from the air, and shattered the iron wall into fragments.

Now for the first time the hippopotamus felt afraid, and it turned itself into a river that flowed into the Niger.

Again Nana Miriam sprinkled her magic powder. At once the river dried up and the water changed back into a hippopotamus. It grew more and more afraid and when Fara Maka came up to see what was happening, the monster charged him blindly. Nana Miriam ran after it, and when it was only ten bounds away from her father, she seized it by its left hind foot and flung it across the Niger. As it crashed against the opposite bank, its skull was split and it was dead. Then Fara Maka, who had seen the mighty throw, exclaimed, "What a daughter I have!"

Very soon, the whole tribe heard what had happened, and the Dialli, the minstrel[6] folk, sang the song of Nana Miriam's adventure with the hippopotamus, which used to devastate[7] the rice fields. And in the years that followed, no one in the Land of the Songai starved any more.

---

6. **minstrel:** musician.
7. **devastate** (dev′ə·stāt′): destroy.

For Study and Discussion

IDENTIFYING FACTS

1. Explain how Nana Miriam came to learn so much. In what two ways is she stronger than anyone else?

2. What **magic** power did the monster have? In what way was it like a human being?

3. Folk tales often tell about a people in danger, who need someone to save them. Why was the monster a terrible threat to the Songai? If Nana Miriam had not killed the monster, what might have happened to the Songai?

4. In folk tales the world over, things often happen in **threes.** (Three is thought of as a "mystical" number.) Name the three people who fight this monster. Who wins each **conflict**?

5. List three **facts** about the Songai that you learned from this tale. For example, what crop did they depend on?

INTERPRETING MEANINGS

6. What magic tools does Nana Miriam use? in what other folk tales does a character use a magic tool, such as a wand that grants wishes, or boots that can travel a great distance?

7. In many folk tales, we are surprised at the person who turns out to be the hero. Often the hero starts out as an unknown orphan, or as the youngest child. Is Nana Miriam an unlikely hero? Why?

APPLYING MEANINGS

8. What qualities did the Songai admire? Which of these qualities is most important to you? Which is least important?

Language and Vocabulary

PRAISE NAMES

Many young people in the United States have names from African languages. Here are some African names and their meanings. These names were often added to a person's original name as a praise name.

Girls' Names

Aisha (ä·ē′shä)
 (Swahili, E. Africa)   Life
Amadi (ä·mä′dē)
 (Ibo, Nigeria)   Rejoicing
Femi (fē′mē)
 (Yoruba, Nigeria)   Love me
Naila (nä·ē′lä)
 (Arabic, N. Africa) One who succeeds
Shani (shä′nē)
 (Swahili, E. Africa) Marvelous

Boys' Names

Akiiki (ä·kē·ē′kē)
 (Muneyankole, Uganda) Friend
Andwele (än·dwē′lē)
 (Nyakysa, Tanzania) God brought me
Bakari (bä·kä′rē)
 (Swahili, E. Africa) Of noble promise
Kamau (kä·mä′oo)
 (Kikiyu, Kenya) Quiet warrior
Mudada (moo·dä′dä)
 (Shona, Zimbabwe) The provider

1. Make up praise names for three of the heroes in this book.

2. Suppose you are in your thirties. You are living in a society that adds praise names to the name you were given at birth. What three praise names would you like?

3. Make up praise names for three friends.

Focus on Writing a Book Report

ORGANIZING A BOOK REPORT

When you write your book report, follow an outline like the one below.

 I. Identify book's author and title
 II. Summarize book's contents briefly
 III. State your main idea and support it with details
 IV. Conclude with brief restatement of main idea

 Write an outline for a book report. State your main idea for the report in a complete sentence and list your supporting details in a logical order. Save your notes.

About the Authors

The real authors of this story are the **Songai.** Songai (also spelled Songhay and Songhai) was a great empire that controlled the trade routes from North Africa through the Sahara Desert. Songai was at its height from the eleventh to the sixteenth century. The capital of the empire was Gao, on the River Niger. The empire included cities and vast grasslands, which were farmed by tribespeople. On the empire's eastern boundary, the principal city was Timbuktu (tim·buk·too′), a center of wealth and learning. Today the Songai people, who now number about 900,000, live mostly in the Republic of Mali.

The End of the World
A Sioux Myth

JENNY LEADING CLOUD

(Opposite page) Painted buffalo robe (1875). Made by the Dakota Cheyenne or the Sioux.

Courtesy Colter Bay Indian Arts Museum, Grand Teton National Park, Wyoming.

Before You Read

Myth makers have always told stories about the end of the world. But in most of these stories, a renewed world eventually is born from the old one. The Native Americans in particular have many of these end-of-the-world myths. In almost all of these stories, a dreaded event is prevented from happening, or the destruction is followed by renewal. Perhaps these myths remind us that optimism and courage and faith are the most human of all our characteristics—no matter where we live, or when.

Read the first paragraph of this myth. Then stop, and write in your journal your own prediction of what lies in this mysterious hidden cave. Write your own myth about the "end of the world."

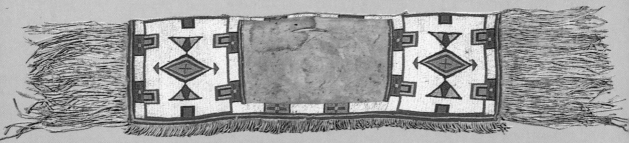

Saddle blanket made out of beaded and fringed leather (c. 1875–1900). Made by the Northern Cheyenne or the Sioux.

Courtesy Colter Bay Indian Arts Museum, Grand Teton National Park, Wyoming.

Somewhere at a place where the prairie and the Maka Sicha, the Badlands, meet, there is a hidden cave. Not for a long, long time has anyone been able to find it. Even now, with so many highways, cars, and tourists, no one has discovered this cave.

In it lives a woman so old that her face looks like a shriveled-up walnut. She is dressed in rawhide, the way people used to be before the white man came. She has been sitting there for a thousand years or more, working on a blanket strip for her buffalo robe. She is making the strip out of dyed porcupine quills, the way our ancestors did before white traders brought glass beads to this turtle continent. Resting beside her, licking his paws, watching her all the time is Shunka Sapa, a huge black dog. His eyes never wander from the old woman, whose teeth are worn flat, worn down to little stumps, she has used them to flatten so many porcupine quills.

A few steps from where the old woman sits working on her blanket strip, a huge fire is kept going. She lit this fire a thousand or more years ago and has kept it alive ever since. Over the fire hangs a big earthen pot, the kind some Indian peoples used to make before the white man came with his kettles of iron. Inside the big pot, *wojapi* is boiling and bubbling. *Wojapi* is berry soup, good and sweet and red. That soup has been boiling in the pot for a long time, ever since the fire was lit.

Every now and then the old woman gets up to stir the *wojapi* in the huge earthen pot. She is so old and feeble that it takes her a while to get up and hobble over to the fire. The moment her back is turned, the huge black dog starts pulling the porcupine quills out of her blanket strip. This way she never makes any progress, and her quillwork remains forever unfinished. The Sioux people used to say that if the old woman ever finishes her blanket strip, then at the very moment that she threads the last porcupine quill to complete the design, the world will come to an end.

About the Authors

This myth was told to Alfonso Ortiz and Richard Erdoes (see the note on page 565) in White River, South Dakota, by a Sioux woman named **Jenny Leading Cloud.**

The great **Sioux** people, lords of the Northern Plains, were fantastic horsemen and buffalo hunters and famed for their bravery. The Sioux produced the heroes Red Cloud, Sitting Bull, and Crazy Horse. In 1876, the Sioux defeated General George Custer at the bloody Battle of Little Bighorn in Montana. The Sioux fought their last battle against overwhelming odds, and in the face of cannon, at Wounded Knee, South Dakota, in 1891.

Reading and Critical Thinking

IDENTIFYING THE MAIN IDEA

A **generalization** is a universal statement. That means it's a statement that applies to many individuals or experiences.

A **fable** is a brief story, usually with animal characters, that teaches a practical lesson about how to behave in life. The fable's lesson is called a **moral.** This moral might be considered the **main idea** of the fable. Some fables, like those by Aesop, state the moral directly. Other fables present the moral indirectly. As you read the following fable, think about the lesson it teaches. What is its main idea?

Two Frogs and the Milk Vat

CLAUDE BROWN

There were two frogs sitting on a milk vat one time. The frogs fell into the milk vat. It was very deep. They kept swimming and swimming around, and they couldn't get out. They couldn't climb out because they were too far down. One frog said, "Oh, I can't make it, and I'm going to give up." And the other frog kept swimming and swimming. His arms became more and more tired, and it was harder and harder and harder for him to swim. Then he couldn't do another stroke. He couldn't throw one more arm into the milk. He kept trying and trying; it seemed as if the milk was getting hard and heavy. He kept trying; he knew that he was going to die, but as long as he had that little bit of life in him, he was going to keep on swimming. On his last stroke, it seemed as though he had to pull a whole ocean back, but he did it and found himself sitting on a vat of butter.

Identifying the Main Idea

1. What is the difference between the two frogs in the fable?

2. The frog who keeps on struggling to survive succeeds in getting out of the vat. How does he manage to solve his problem?

3. Make up a sentence that expresses the main idea of the fable. Here are some possibilities to consider:

   - If you keep on struggling and keep your optimism, you can triumph over life's problems.
   - Sometimes just when things seem darkest, the light shines through.

WRITING A BOOK REPORT

*I*n a **book report,** you present information about a book and present a main idea or evaluation of your own. In this unit you have had a chance to study some of the important elements of a book report. Now you will write your own report on a book of your choice.

Prewriting

1. For your report, select a book that you think you would enjoy reading. Before you choose a book, ask yourself:

   - What subjects do I really like? What issues are important?
   - What are my favorite types of reading? Myths? Poetry? Novels?
   - Can I get some ideas from movies or magazines?
   - Can my friends or classmates recommend a good book?

2. As you start to read, take close-reading **notes** on the book you have chosen. You may find it helpful to prepare a chart for your notes like the one below.

Major Elements of a Book	Reactions/ Notes
Plot _____	Opinions _____
Characters _____	Quotations _____
Setting _____	Questions _____
Theme _____	Evaluation _____

[See **Focus** assignment on page 574.]

3. Develop a **main idea** to focus your report. Use one or two sentences to state this idea as clearly as you can. Your main idea could be one of the following:

   - an overall evaluation of the book

   Example: Ashley Bryan's *Lion and the Ostrich Chicks and Other African Tales* is a wide-ranging collection of legends that never fails to entertain the reader.

   - an opinion about one of the book's major elements

   Example: In *The Rainbow People*, a collection of tales originally told by Chinese immigrants in California, Laurence Yep shows a flair for creating a magical, mysterious atmosphere.

   - a statement that identifies an important or unifying theme in the book

   Example: The myths of the Greek heroes in this collection often feature a seemingly impossible task or quest.

   [See **Focus** assignment on page 584.]

4. Gather **details** to support your main idea. Fill out a chart like the one below:

   Main Idea: _____
   Supporting Details
   Facts: _____
   Examples: _____
   Reasons: _____
   Quotations: _____

[See **Focus** assignment on page 617.]

Writing

1. Follow an outline like the one below when you write your report.

   I. Identify book's author and title
   II. Briefly summarize book's contents
   III. State main idea and give supporting details
   IV. Restate main idea in conclusion

   [See **Focus** assignment on page 637. If you need help with summarizing, see **Focus on Reading** on page 629.]

2. Remember to use **transitions** to make the relationship of events and ideas clear. Here are some helpful transition words:

after	next
as a result	then
finally	therefore
first	when
most important	

Evaluating and Revising

1. After you finish your first draft, exchange papers with a partner and read each other's book report. Share ideas with your partner about how to improve your reports. For example, ask your partner to tell you if you have given a clear summary of your book's contents. Also ask if you have stated your main idea clearly and supported it convincingly.

   Finally, ask what kind of impression your description and evaluation made on the reader. Did reading your book report stimulate your classmate's interest enough so that he or she would want to read the book?

   Here is an example of how one student writer revised a paragraph in a book report on the novel *Sounder* by William Armstrong.

The novel's main character is the boy.

The boy has to grow up ~~when~~ his father *during the years* *from place to place* *in the chain gang* is taken ~~to prison~~. ~~He~~ *The boy* helps his mother

with crops so the family will not ~~lose~~ the *be put off* farm. He learns about kindness and hope *the value of education. He also learns*

when a teacher helps him and gives him

a chance to go to school. The boy's

character development is related to one

of the novel's main themes. Armstrong's

story reveals how some people have the

faith never to give up, *or become bitter* no matter how

hard life may be.

2. You may find the following checklist helpful as you revise your report:

Checklist for Evaluation and Revision

✔ Do I identify the book's author and title at the beginning?

✔ Do I give a brief summary of the contents?

✔ Do I clearly state my main idea in the report?

✔ Have I supported the main idea with examples, facts, reasons, and quotations from the book?

✔ Have I arranged my supporting details clearly?

✔ Do I end with a strong conclusion?

Proofreading and Publishing

1. Proofread your report and correct any errors you find in grammar, usage, and mechanics. (Here you may find it helpful to refer to the **Handbook for Revision** on pages 750–785.) Then prepare a final version of your report by making a clean copy.

2. Consider some of the following publication methods for your report:

- deliver your report orally to the class
- make your report the centerpiece of an illustrated poster for the book
- organize a round table with a few classmates and take turns discussing each other's books and reports

Portfolio If your teacher approves, you may wish to keep a copy of your work in your writing folder or portfolio.

The Libraries Are Appreciated by Jacob Lawrence
(1943). Gouache on watercolor on paper.

The Novel

Novels are long stories about characters who face **conflicts** of some kind. These conflicts might be **external:** that is, they might involve the characters in physical struggles with forces like fire-breathing dragons or sub-zero temperatures. Or, the conflicts might be **internal:** the characters might have to struggle with feelings like fear, doubt, or loneliness. Most novels include both kinds of conflicts.

Like a short story, a novel reveals a theme. **Theme** is a truth about life that we discover by watching the characters and the way they respond to the things that happen to them.

As you probably have already discovered, the most satisfying elements in most novels are the **characters** themselves. In a successful novel, we care deeply about the fates of the main characters. We worry about them. We cheer when they succeed, and we weep when they fail. Some characters in fiction, in fact, are so vivid that we add them to that endless parade of real, live people we will never forget.

Philadelphia Museum of Art.
The Louis E. Stern Collection.

You read a novel in almost the same way you read a short story or play or biography. You take pleasure in experiencing a good story, told by a talented storyteller. You enjoy the feeling of suspense building up. You enjoy watching the characters perform for you. When you're busy washing the dishes, you think, "I can't wait to get back to that novel."

Guidelines for Reading a Novel

1. Ask questions as you read. Ask about unfamiliar words or terms. Ask about situations or references that puzzle you. Ask questions when the writer drops clues.

2. Make predictions. Think about what might happen next.

3. Relate what you read to your own life. Compare the characters and events with people and situations in your own experience. Are the characters believable?

4. Think about the underlying meaning or theme. Relate the theme to life as you know it. Decide if it's a good theme or if it's overworked.

You might have a pad of paper and pencil handy as you read the following novel. Write down your questions and your responses to the problems faced by Sara, Wanda, and Charlie on this extraordinary day that starts out in such an ordinary way.

THINKING ABOUT WORDS

HOW TO OWN A WORD

In an earlier unit (page 76), you were introduced to the notion of "owning" a word. The idea is that when you know a lot about a word, you "own it" because you can use it comfortably in many ways. *Astute* is a marvelous word that is well worth "owning."

In the last unit, in "How the Whale Got His Throat" (page 595) you read about a 'stute fish. At the bottom of the page on which the 'stute fish is introduced, there is a little note explaining that *'stute* is short for *astute,* meaning "clever." *Clever* is a good synonym for *astute,* but someone who is astute is often more than clever. People who are astute are clever at understanding behavior and situations and at using this knowledge to their own advantage. That is certainly what the 'stute fish was like.

Below is a chart that organizes some ideas about *astute.* Think of ideas you might add.

Describe some situations in which characters from stories act astutely.

- When the third pig in the fairy tale builds his house of bricks.
-
-

ASTUTE

What are some words that might describe the way people who are astute act?

- cagey
-

Describe some situations in which you might try especially hard to be astute.

- If I made a bet with a friend that I would be the first to solve a tricky math problem.
-

What might you say if you were watching two people play a game of checkers and one of them made an astute play?

- That was a smooth move!
-
-

The Summer of the Swans

BETSY BYARS

Before You Read

This novel, which won the Newbery Award in 1971, is an example of realistic fiction. It's fiction because it came out of Betsy Byars's imagination. It's realistic because it shows life as it really is. All of the events that occur in *The Summer of the Swans* could really have happened. The story is set in a realistic small town in West Virginia, where abandoned coal mines dot the outlying hills. The characters in the story experience the needs, wishes, and fears of real people.

The main character in *The Summer of the Swans* is fourteen-year-old Sara Godfrey. The whole story covers a crisis in the Godfrey family that is over in just a little more than twenty-four hours. Yet in that time, Sara's feelings about herself and her whole outlook on life change.

This is also a story about a ten-year-old boy who has very special needs. Charlie is mentally handicapped, and his problems are often a trial to his sisters and aunt. But Charlie is the one who helps the family understand the tragedy of loss and the value of love.

Before you read, write a few sentences in your journal telling how you think families can be affected by special children in their midst. How might they have to adjust their lives to accommodate a child with special needs?

Dialogue refers to the characters' quoted conversation. If a story is to be believable, its dialogue has to sound just the way people talk in real life. If you're like many readers, you'll immediately realize that Betsy Byars has a great talent for writing dialogue that is natural, realistic, even witty. Her young characters, and her older ones, all are able to say things in ways that make us laugh, or cry.

Sara Godfrey was lying on the bed tying a kerchief on the dog, Boysie. "Hold your chin up, Boysie, will you?" she said as she braced herself on one elbow. The dog was old, slept all the time, and he was lying on his side with his eyes closed while she lifted his head and tied the scarf.

Her sister Wanda was sitting at the dressing table combing her hair. Wanda said, "Why don't you leave Boysie alone?"

"There's nothing else to do," Sara answered without looking up. "You want to see a show?"

"Not particularly."

"It's called 'The Many Faces of Boysie.' "

"Now I know I don't want to see it."

Sara held up the dog with the kerchief neatly tied beneath his chin and said, "The first face of Boysie, proudly presented for your entertainment and amusement, is the Russian Peasant Woman. Taaaaaa-daaaaaa!"

"Leave the dog alone."

"He likes to be in shows, don't you, Boysie?" She untied the scarf, refolded it and set it carefully on top of the dog's head. "And now for the second face of Boysie, we travel halfway around the world to the mysterious East, where we see Boysie the Inscrutable Hindu, Taaaaaaa-daaaaaa!"

With a sigh Wanda turned and looked at the dog. "That's pathetic. In people's age that dog is eighty-four years old." She shook a can of hair spray and sprayed her hair. "And besides, that's my good scarf."

"Oh, all right." Sara fell back heavily against the pillow. "I can't do anything around here."

"Well, if it's going to make you that miserable, I'll watch the show."

"I don't want to do it any more. It's no fun now. This place smells like a perfume factory." She put the scarf over her face and stared up through the thin blue material. Beside her, Boysie lay back down and curled himself into a ball. They lay without moving for a moment and then Sara sat up on the bed and looked down at her long, lanky legs. She said, "I have the biggest feet in my school."

"Honestly, Sara, I hope you are not going to start listing all the millions of things wrong with you because I just don't want to hear it again."

"Well, it's the truth about my feet. One time in Phys Ed the boys started throwing the girls' sneakers around and Bull Durham got my sneakers and put them on and they fit perfectly! How do you think it feels to wear the same size shoe as Bull Durham?"

"People don't notice things like that."

"Huh!"

"No, they don't. I have perfectly terrible hands—look at my fingers—only I don't go around all the time saying, 'Everybody, look at my stubby fingers, I have stubby fingers, everybody,' to *make* people notice. You should just ignore things that are wrong with you. The truth is everyone else is so worried about what's wrong with *them* that—"

"It is very difficult to ignore the fact that you have huge feet when Bull Durham is dancing all over the gym in your shoes. They were not stretched the tiniest little bit when he took them off either."

"You wear the same size shoe as Jackie Kennedy Onassis if that makes you feel any better."

"How do you know?"

"Because one time when she was going into an Indian temple she had to leave her shoes outside and some reporter looked in them to see what size they were." She leaned close to the mirror and looked at her teeth.

"Her feet *look* littler."

"That's because she doesn't wear orange sneakers."

"I like my orange sneakers." Sara sat on the edge of the bed, slipped her feet into the shoes, and held them up. "What's wrong with them?"

"Nothing, except that when you want to hide something, you don't go painting it orange. I've got to go. Frank's coming."

She went out the door and Sara could hear her crossing into the kitchen. Sara lay back on the bed, her head next to Boysie. She looked at the sleeping dog, then covered her face with her hands and began to cry noisily.

"Oh, Boysie, Boysie, I'm crying," she wailed. Years ago, when Boysie was a young dog, he could not bear to hear anyone cry. Sara had only to pretend she was crying and Boysie would come running. He would whine and dig at her with his paws and lick her hands until she stopped. Now he lay with his eyes closed.

"Boysie, I'm crying," she said again. "I'm really crying this time. Boysie doesn't love me."

The dog shifted uneasily without opening his eyes.

"Boysie, Boysie, I'm crying, I'm so sad, Boysie," she wailed, then stopped and sat up abruptly. "You don't care about anybody, do you, Boysie? A person could cry herself to death these days and you wouldn't care."

The Summer of the Swans   651

She got up and left the room. In the hall she heard the tapping noise of Boysie's feet behind her and she said without looking at him, "I don't want you now, Boysie. Go on back in the bedroom. Go on." She went a few steps farther and, when he continued to follow her, turned and looked at him. "In case you are confused, Boysie, a dog is supposed to comfort people and run up and nuzzle them and make them feel better. All you want to do is lie on soft things and hide bones in the house because you are too lazy to go outside. Just go on back in the bedroom."

She started into the kitchen, still followed by Boysie, who could not bear to be left alone, then heard her aunt and Wanda arguing, changed her mind, and went out onto the porch.

Behind her, Boysie scratched at the door and she let him out. "Now quit following me."

Her brother Charlie was sitting on the top step and Sara sat down beside him. She held out her feet, looked at them, and said, "I like my orange sneakers, don't you, Charlie?"

He did not answer. He had been eating a lollipop and the stick had come off and now he was trying to put it back into the red candy. He had been trying for so long that the stick was bent.

"Here," she said, "I'll do it for you." She put the stick in and handed it to him. "Now be careful with it."

She sat without speaking for a moment, then she looked down at her feet and said, "I hate these orange sneakers. I just *hate* them." She leaned back against the porch railing so she wouldn't have to see them and said, "Charlie, I'll tell you something. This has been the worst summer of my life."

She did not know exactly why this was true. She was doing the same things she had done last summer—walk to the Dairy Queen with her friend Mary, baby-sit for Mrs. Hodges, watch television—and yet everything was different. It was as if her life was a huge kaleidoscope, and the kaleidoscope had been turned and now everything was changed. The same stones, shaken, no longer made the same design.

But it was not only one different design, one change; it was a hundred. She could never be really sure of anything this summer. One moment she was happy, and the next, for no reason, she was miserable. An hour ago she had loved her sneakers; now she detested them.

"Charlie, I'll tell you what this awful summer's been like. You remember when that finky Jim Wilson got you on the seesaw, remember that? And he kept bouncing you up and down and then he'd keep you up in the air for a real long time and then he'd drop you down real sudden, and you couldn't get off and you thought you never would? Up and down, up and down, for the rest of your life? Well, that's what this summer's been like for me."

He held out the candy and the stick to her.

"Not again!" She took it from him. "This piece of candy is so gross that I don't even want to touch it, if you want to know the truth." She put the stick back in and handed it to him. "Now if it comes off again—and I mean this, Charlie Godfrey— I'm throwing the candy away."

Charlie looked at the empty sucker stick, reached into his mouth, took out the candy, and held them together in his hand. Sara had said she would throw the candy away if this happened again and so he closed his fist tightly and looked away from her.

Slowly he began to shuffle his feet back and forth on the step. He had done this so many times over the years that two grooves had been worn into the boards. It was a nervous habit that showed he was concerned about something, and Sara recognized it at once.

"All right, Charlie," she said wearily. "Where's your sucker?"

He began to shake his head slowly from side to side. His eyes were squeezed shut.

"I'm not going to take it away from you. I'm going to fix it one more time."

He was unwilling to trust her and continued to shake his head. The movement was steady and mechanical, as if it would continue forever, and she watched him for a moment.

Then, with a sigh, she lifted his hand and attempted to pry his fingers loose. "Honestly, Charlie, you're holding onto this grubby piece of candy like it was a crown jewel or something. Now, let go." He opened his eyes and watched while she took the candy from him and put the stick

in. The stick was now bent almost double, and she held it out to him carefully.

"There."

He took the sucker and held it without putting it into his mouth, still troubled by the unsteadiness of the bent stick. Sara looked down at her hands and began to pull at a broken fingernail. There was something similar about them in that moment, the same oval face, round brown eyes, brown hair hanging over the forehead, freckles on the nose. Then Charlie glanced up and the illusion was broken.

Still holding his sucker, he looked across the yard and saw the tent he had made over the clothesline that morning. He had taken an old white blanket out into the yard, hung it over the low clothesline, and then got under it. He had sat there with the blanket blowing against him until Sara came out and said, "Charlie, you have to fasten the ends down, like this. It isn't a tent if it's just hanging in the wind."

He had thought there was something wrong. He waited beneath the blanket until she came back with some clothespins and hammered them into the hard earth, fastening the edges of the blanket to the ground. "Now, *that's* a tent."

The tent had pleased him. The warmth of the sun coming through the thin cotton blanket, the shadows of the trees moving overhead had made him drowsy and comfortable and now he wanted to be back in the tent.

Sara had started talking about the summer again, but he did not listen. He could tell from the tone of her voice that she was

not really talking to him at all. He got up slowly and began to walk across the yard toward the tent.

Sara watched him as he walked, a small figure for his ten years, wearing faded blue jeans and a striped knit shirt that was stretched out of shape. He was holding the sucker in front of him as if it were a candle that might go out at any moment.

Sara said, "Don't drop that candy in the grass now or it's really going to be lost."

She watched while he bent, crawled into the tent, and sat down. The sun was behind the tent now and she could see his silhouette. Carefully he put the sucker back into his mouth.

Then Sara lay back on the hard boards of the porch and looked up at the ceiling.

disliked. It was everything—the way she bossed them, the way she never really listened, the way she never cared what she said. She had once announced loud enough for everyone in Carter's Drugstore to hear that Sara needed a good dose of magnesia.

"It isn't a motorcycle, it's a motor *scooter*." Wanda was speaking patiently, as if to a small child. "They're practically like bicycles."

"No."

"All I want to do is to ride one half mile on this perfectly safe motor scooter—"

"No. It's absolutely and positively no. No!"

"Frank is very careful. He has never had even the tiniest accident."

No answer.

"Aunt Willie, it is perfectly safe. He takes his mother to the grocery store on it. Anyway, I am old enough to go without permission and I wish you'd realize it. I am nineteen years old."

No answer. Sara knew that Aunt Willie would be standing by the sink shaking her head emphatically from side to side.

"Aunt Willie, he's going to be here any minute. He's coming all the way over here just to drive me to the lake to see the swans."

"You don't care *that* for seeing those swans."

"I do too. I love birds."

"All right then, those swans have been on the lake three days, and not once have you gone over to see them. Now all of a sudden you *have* to go, can't wait one min-

In the house Wanda and Aunt Willie were still arguing. Sara could hear every word even out on the porch. Aunt Willie, who had been taking care of them since the death of their mother six years ago, was saying loudly, "No, not on a motorcycle. No motorcycle!"

Sara grimaced. It was not only the loudness of Aunt Willie's voice that she

"If he does, no one's ever heard him, not since his illness. He can understand what you say to him, and he goes to school, and they say he can write the alphabet, but he can't talk."

Charlie did not hear them. He put his ear against his watch and listened to the sound. There was something about the rhythmic ticking that never failed to soothe him. The watch was a magic charm whose tiny noise and movements could block out the whole clamoring world.

Mrs. Weicek said, "Ask him what time it is, Ernestine. He is so proud of that watch. Everyone always asks him what time it is." Then without waiting, she herself said, "What time is it, Charlie? What time is it?"

He turned and obediently held out the arm with the watch on it.

"My goodness, it's after eight o'clock," Mrs. Weicek said. "Thank you, Charlie. Charlie keeps everyone informed of the time. We just couldn't get along without him."

The two women sat in the rocking chairs on the porch, moving slowly back and forth. The noise of the chairs and the creaking floor boards made Charlie forget the watch for a moment. He got slowly to his feet and stood looking up the street.

"Sit down, Charlie, and wait for Sara," Mrs. Weicek said.

Without looking at her, he began to walk toward the street.

"Charlie, Sara wants you to wait for her."

"Maybe he doesn't hear you, Allie."

"He hears me all right. Charlie, wait for Sara. Wait now." Then she called, "Sara, your brother's leaving."

Sara looked out the upstairs window and said, "All right, Charlie, I'm coming. Will you wait for a minute? Mary, I've got to go."

She ran out of the house and caught Charlie by the arm. "What are you going home for? Don't you want to see the swans?"

He stood without looking at her.

"Honestly, I leave you alone for one second and off you go. Now come on." She tugged his arm impatiently.

As they started down the hill together she waved to Mary, who was at the window, and said to Charlie, "I hope the swans are worth all this trouble I'm going to.

"We'll probably get there and they'll be gone," she added. They walked in silence. Then Sara said, "Here's where we cut across the field." She waited while he stepped carefully over the narrow ditch, and then the two of them walked across the field side by side, Sara kicking her feet restlessly in the deep grass.

There was something painfully beautiful about the swans. The whiteness, the elegance of them on this dark lake, the incredible ease of their movements made Sara catch her breath as she and Charlie rounded the clump of pines.

"There they are, Charlie."

She could tell the exact moment he saw them because his hand tightened; he

In his room Charlie lay in bed still kicking his foot against the wall. He was not asleep but was staring up at the ceiling where the shadows were moving. He never went to sleep easily, but tonight he had been concerned because a button was missing from his pajamas, and sleep was impossible. He had shown the place where the button was missing to Aunt Willie when he was ready for bed, but she had patted his shoulder and said, "I'll fix it tomorrow," and gone back to watching a game show on television.

"Look at that," Aunt Willie was saying to herself. "They're never going to guess the name. How can famous celebrities be so stupid?" She had leaned forward and shouted at the panelists, "It's Clark Gable!" Then, "Have they never heard of a person who works in a store? A person who works in a store is a *clerk*—Clerk Gable—the name is *Clerk Gable*!"

Charlie had touched her on the shoulder and tried again to show her the pajamas.

"I'll fix it tomorrow, Charlie." She had waved him away with one hand.

He had gone back into the kitchen, where Sara was dyeing her tennis shoes in the sink.

"Don't show it to me," she said. "I can't look at anything right now. And Mary, quit laughing at my tennis shoes."

"I can't help it. They're so gross."

Sara lifted them out of the sink with two spoons. "I know they're gross, only you should have told me that orange tennis shoes could not be dyed baby blue. Look

at that. That is the worst color you have ever seen in your life. Admit it."

"I admit it."

"Well, you don't have to admit it so quickly. They ought to put on the dye wrapper that orange cannot be dyed baby blue. A warning."

"They do."

"Well, they ought to put it in big letters. Look at those shoes. There must be a terrible name for that color."

"There is," Mary said. "Puce."

"What?"

"Puce."

"Mary Weicek, you made that up."

"I did not. It really is a color."

"I have never heard a word that describes anything better. Puce. These just look like puce shoes, don't they?" She set them on newspapers. "They're—Charlie, get out of the way, please, or I'm going to get dye all over you."

He stepped back, still holding his pajama jacket out in front of him. There were times when he could not get anyone's attention no matter what he did. He took Sara's arm and she shrugged free.

"Charlie, there's not a button on anything I own, either, so go on to bed."

Slowly, filled with dissatisfaction, he had gone to his room and got into bed. There he had begun to pull worriedly at the empty buttonhole until the cloth had started to tear, and then he had continued to pull until the whole front of his pajama top was torn and hung open. He was now holding the jacket partly closed with his hands and looking up at the ceiling.

It was one o'clock and Charlie had been lying there for three hours.

He heard a noise outside, and for the first time he forgot about his pajamas. He stopped kicking his foot against the wall, sat up, and looked out the window. There was something white in the bushes; he could see it moving.

He released his pajamas and held onto the window sill tightly, because he thought that he had just seen one of the swans outside his window, gliding slowly through the leaves. The memory of their soft smooth-ness in the water came to him and warmed him.

He got out of bed and stood by the other window. He heard a cat miaowing and saw the Hutchinsons' white cat from next door, but he paid no attention to it. The swans were fixed with such certainty in his mind that he could not even imagine that what he had seen was only the cat.

Still looking for the swans, he pressed his face against the screen. The beauty of them, the whiteness, the softness, the silent splendor had impressed him greatly, and he felt a longing to be once again by the lake, sitting in the deep grass, throwing bread to the waiting swans.

It occurred to him suddenly that the swan outside the window had come to find him, and with a small pleased smile he went around the bed, sat, and slowly began to put on his bedroom slippers. Then he walked out into the hall. His feet made a quiet shuffling sound as he passed through the linoleumed hall and into the living room, but no one heard him.

The front door had been left open for coolness and only the screen door was latched. Charlie lifted the hook, pushed open the door, and stepped out onto the porch. Boysie, who slept in the kitchen, heard the door shut and came to the living room. He whined softly when he saw Charlie outside on the porch and scratched at the door. He waited, then after a moment went back to the kitchen and curled up on his rug in front of the sink.

Charlie walked across the front porch and sat on the steps. He waited. He was patient at first, for he thought that the swans would come to the steps, but as time passed and they did not come, he began to shuffle his feet impatiently back and forth on the third step.

Suddenly he saw something white in the bushes. He got up and, holding the banister, went down the steps and crossed the yard. He looked into the bushes, but the swans were not there. It was only the cat, crouched down behind the leaves and looking up at him with slitted eyes.

He stood there, looking at the cat, unable to understand what had happened to the swans. He rubbed his hands up and down his pajama tops, pulling at the torn material. The cat darted farther back into the bushes and disappeared.

After a moment Charlie turned and began to walk slowly across the yard. He went to the gate and paused. He had been told again and again that he must never go out of the yard, but those instructions, given in daylight with noisy traffic on the street, seemed to have nothing to do with the present situation.

In the soft darkness all the things that usually confused him—speeding bicycles, loud noises, lawn mowers, barking dogs, shouting children—were gone, replaced by silence and a silvery moonlit darkness. He seemed to belong to this silent world far more than he belonged to the daytime world of feverish activity.

Slowly he opened the gate and went out. He moved past the Hutchinsons' house, past the Tennents', past the Weiceks'. There was a breeze now, and the smell of the Weiceks' flowers filled the air. He walked past the next house and hesitated, suddenly confused. Then he started through the vacant lot by the Akers' house. In the darkness it looked to him like the field he and Sara had crossed earlier in the evening on their way to see the swans.

He crossed the vacant lot, entered the wooded area, and walked slowly through the trees. He was certain that in just a moment he would come into the clearing and see the lake and the white swans gliding on the dark water. He continued walking, looking ahead so that he would see the lake as soon as possible.

The ground was getting rougher. There were stones to stumble over now and rain gullies and unexpected piles of trash. Still the thought of the swans persisted in his mind and he kept walking.

Charlie was getting tired and he knew something was wrong. The lake was gone. He paused and scanned the field, but he could not see anything familiar.

He turned to the right and began to walk up the hill. Suddenly a dog barked behind him. The sound, unexpected and loud, startled him, and he fell back a step and then started to run. Then another dog was barking, and another, and he had no idea where the dogs were. He was terribly frightened and he ran with increasing awkwardness, thrashing at the weeds with his hands, pulling at the air, so that everything about him seemed to be running except his slow feet.

The sound of the dogs seemed to him to be everywhere, all around him, so that he ran first in one direction, then in another, like a wild animal caught in a maze. He ran into a bush and the briers stung his face and arms, and he thought this was somehow connected with the dogs and thrashed his arms out wildly, not even feeling the cuts in his skin.

He turned around and around, trying to free himself, and then staggered on, running and pulling at the air. The dogs'

barking had grown fainter now, but in his terror he did not notice. He ran blindly, stumbling over bushes and against trees, catching his clothing on twigs, kicking at unseen rocks. Then he came into a clearing and was able to gain speed for the first time.

He ran for a long way, and then suddenly he came up against a wire fence that cut him sharply across the chest. The surprise of it threw him back on the ground, and he sat holding his hands across his bare chest, gasping for breath.

Far down the hill someone had spoken to the dogs; they had grown quiet, and now there was only the rasping sound of Charlie's own breathing. He sat hunched over until his breathing grew quieter, and then he straightened and noticed his torn pajamas for the first time since he had left the house. He wrapped the frayed edges of the jacket carefully over his chest as if that would soothe the stinging cut.

After a while he got slowly to his feet, paused, and then began walking up the hill beside the fence. He was limping now because when he had fallen he had lost one of his bedroom slippers.

The fence ended abruptly. It was an old one, built long ago, and now only parts remained. Seeing it gone, Charlie felt relieved. It was as if the fence had kept him from his goal, and he stepped over a trailing piece of wire and walked toward the forest beyond.

Being in the trees gave him a good feeling for a while. The moonlight coming through the leaves and the soft sound of the wind in the branches were soothing,

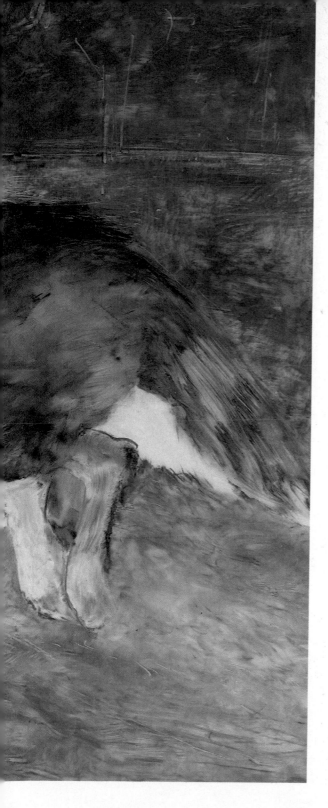

but as he went deeper into the forest he became worried. There was something here he didn't know, an unfamiliar smell, noises he had never heard before. He stopped.

He stood beneath the trees without moving and looked around him. He did not know where he was. He did not even know how he had come to be there. The whole night seemed one long struggle, but he could not remember why he had been struggling. He had wanted something, he could not remember what.

His face and arms stung from the brier scratches; his bare foot, tender and unused to walking on the rough ground, was already cut and sore, but most of all he was gripped by hopelessness. He wanted to be back in his room, in his bed, but home seemed lost forever, a place so disconnected from the forest that there was no way to get from one to the other.

He put his wrist to his ear and listened to his watch. Even its steady ticking could not help him tonight and he wrapped the torn pajamas tighter over his chest and began to walk slowly up the hill through the trees. As he walked, he began to cry without noise.

In the morning Sara arose slowly, letting her feet hang over the edge of the bed for a moment before she stepped onto the floor. Then she walked across the room, and as she passed the dressing table she paused to look at herself in the mirror. She smoothed her hair behind her ears.

One of her greatest mistakes, she thought, looking at herself critically, was cutting her hair. She had gone to the beauty school in Bentley, taking with her a picture from a magazine, and had asked the girl to cut her hair exactly like that.

"And look what she did to me!" she had screamed when she got home. "Look! Ruined!"

"It's not that bad," Wanda had said.

"Tell the truth. Now look at that picture. Look! Tell the truth—do I look anything, anything at *all,* even the tiniest little bit, like that model?"

Wanda and Aunt Willie had had to admit that Sara looked nothing like the blond model.

"I'm ruined, just ruined. Why someone cannot take a perfectly good magazine picture and cut someone's hair the same way without ruining them is something I cannot understand. I hope that girl fails beauty school."

"Actually, your *hair* does sort of look like the picture. It's your face and body that don't."

"Shut up, Wanda. Quit trying to be funny."

"I'm not being funny. It's a fact."

"I didn't make smart remarks the time they gave you that awful permanent."

"You did too. You called me Gentle Ben."

"Well, I meant that as a compliment."

"All right, girls, stop this now. No more arguing. Believe me, I mean it."

Sara now looked at herself, weighing the mistake of the hair, and she thought suddenly: I look exactly like that cartoon cat who is always chasing Tweetie Bird and who has just been run over by a steam roller and made absolutely flat. This hair and my flat face have combined to make me look exactly like—

"Sara!" Aunt Willie called from the kitchen.

"What?"

"Come on and get your breakfast, you and Charlie. I'm not going to be in here fixing one breakfast after another until lunch time."

"All right."

She went into the hall and looked into Charlie's room.

"Charlie!"

He was not in his bed. She walked into the living room. Lately, since he had learned to turn on the television, he would get up early, come in, and watch it by himself, but he was not there either.

"Charlie's already up, Aunt Willie."

In the kitchen Aunt Willie was spooning oatmeal into two bowls.

"Oatmeal again," Sara groaned. "I believe I'll just have some Kool-Aid and toast."

"Don't talk nonsense. Now, where's Charlie?"

"He wasn't in his room."

She sighed. "Well, find him."

"First I've got to see my shoes." She went over to the sink and looked at the sneakers. "Oh, they look awful. Look at them, Aunt Willie. They're gross."

"Well, you should have left them alone. I've learned my lesson about dyeing clothes, let me tell you. You saw me, I hope, when I had to wear that purple dress to your Uncle Bert's funeral."

"What color would you say these were?"

"I haven't got time for that now. Go get your brother."

"No, there's a name for this color. I just want to see if you know it."

"I don't know it, so go get your brother."

"I'll give you three choices. It's either, let me see—it's either pomegranate, Pomeranian, or puce."

"Puce. Now go get your brother."

"How did you know?"

"Because my aunt had twin Pomeranian dogs that rode in a baby carriage and because I once ate a piece of pomegranate. Go get your brother!"

Sara put down the shoes and went back into the hall. "Charlie!" She looked into his room again. "Oh, Charlie!" She went out onto the front porch and looked at Charlie's tent. It had blown down during the night and she could see that he wasn't there.

Slowly she walked back through the hall, looking into every room, and then into the kitchen.

"I can't find him, Aunt Willie."

"What do you mean, you can't find him?" Aunt Willie, prepared to chide the two children for being late to breakfast, now set the pan of oatmeal down heavily on the table.

"He's not in his room, he's not in the yard, he's not anywhere."

"If this is some kind of a joke—" Aunt Willie began. She brushed past Sara and went into the living room. "Charlie! Where are you, Charlie?" Her voice had begun to rise with the sudden alarm she often felt in connection with Charlie. "Where could he have gone?" She turned and looked at Sara. "If this is a joke . . ."

"It's not a joke."

"Well, I'm remembering last April Fool's Day, that's all."

"He's probably around the neighborhood somewhere, like the time Wanda took him to the store without saying anything."

"Well, Wanda didn't take him this morning." Aunt Willie walked into the hall and stood looking in Charlie's room. She stared at the empty bed. She did not move for a moment as she tried to think of some logical explanation for his absence. "If anything's happened to that boy—"

"Nothing's happened to him."

"All right, where is he?"

Sara did not answer. Charlie had never left the house alone, and Sara could not think of any place he could be either.

"Go outside, Sara. Look! If he's not in the neighborhood, I'm calling the police."

"Don't call until we're sure, Aunt Willie, please."

"I'm calling. Something's wrong here."

Sara was out of her pajamas and into her pants and shirt in a minute. Leaving her pajamas on the floor, she ran barefoot into the yard.

"Charlie! Charlie!" She ran around the house and then stopped. Suddenly she remembered the swans and ran back into the house.

"Aunt Willie, I bet you anything Charlie went down to the lake to see the swans."

Aunt Willie was talking on the telephone and she put one hand over the receiver and said, "Run and see."

"You aren't talking to the police already?" Sara asked in the doorway.

"I'm not talking to the police, but that's what I'm going to do when you get back. Now quit wasting time."

"Just let me get my shoes."

She ran back into the kitchen and put on the sneakers, which were still wet. Then she ran out of the house and down the street. As she passed the Weiceks', Mary came out on the porch.

"What's the hurry?" she called.

"Charlie's missing. I'm going to see if he's down at the lake."

"I'll go with you." She came down the steps, calling over her shoulder, "Mom, I'm going to help Sara look for Charlie."

"Not in those curlers you're not."

"Mom, I've got on a scarf. Nobody can even tell it's rolled."

"Yeah, everyone will just think you have real bumpy hair," Sara said.

"Oh, hush. Now what's all this about Charlie?"

"We couldn't find him this morning and I think he might have got up during the night and gone to see the swans. He acted awful when we had to leave."

"I know. I saw you dragging him up the street last night."

"I had to. It was the only way I could get him home. It was black dark. You couldn't even see the swans and he still wouldn't come home."

"I hope he's all right."

"He's probably sitting down there looking at the swans, holding onto the grass, and I'm going to have to drag him up the hill screaming all over again. He's strong when he wants to be, you know that?"

"Hey, you've got your shoes on."

"Yeah, but they're still wet."

"You'll probably have puce feet before the day's over."

"That's all I need."

They turned and crossed the field at the bottom of the hill.

"Let's hurry because Aunt Willie is at this moment getting ready to call the police."

"Really?"

"She's sitting by the phone now. She's got her little card out with all her emergency numbers on it and her finger is pointing right to *POLICE*."

"Remember that time the old man got lost in the woods? What was his name?"

"Uncle somebody."

"And they organized a posse of college boys and the Red Cross brought coffee and everything, and then they found the old man asleep in his house the next morning. He was on a picnic and had got bored and just went home."

"Don't remind me. Probably as soon

as Aunt Willie calls the police we'll find Charlie in the bathroom or somewhere."

They came through the trees and into the clearing around the lake. Neither spoke.

"Yesterday he was sitting right here," Sara said finally. "Charlie! Charlie!"

There was no answer, but the swans turned abruptly and began to glide to the other side of the lake. Sara felt her shoulders sag and she rammed her hands into her back pockets.

"Something really has happened to him," she said. "I know it now."

"Probably not, Sara."

"I *know* it now. Sometimes you just know terrible things. I get a feeling in my neck, like my shoulders have come unhinged or something, when an awful thing happens."

Mary put one hand on her arm. "Maybe he's hiding somewhere."

"He can't even do that right. If he's playing hide-and-seek, as soon as he's hidden he starts looking out to see how the game's going. He just can't—"

"Maybe he's at the store or up at the Dairy Queen. I could run up to the drugstore."

"No, something's happened to him."

They stood at the edge of the water. Sara looked at the swans without seeing them.

Mary called, "Charlie! Charlie!" Her kerchief slipped off and she retied it over her rollers. "Charlie!"

"I was so sure he'd be here," Sara said. "I wasn't even worried because I knew he would be sitting right here. Now I don't know what to do."

"Let's go back to the house. Maybe he's there now."

"I know he won't be."

"Well, don't get discouraged until we see." She took Sara by the arm and started walking through the trees. "You know who you sound like? Remember when Mary Louise was up for class president and she kept saying, 'I know I won't get it. I know I won't get it.' For three days that was all she said."

"And she didn't get it."

"Well, I just meant you sounded like her, your voice or something," Mary explained quickly. "Now, come on."

When Sara entered the house with Mary, Aunt Willie was still sitting at the telephone. She was saying, "And there's not a trace of him." She paused in her conversation to ask, "Did you find him?" and when Sara shook her head, she said into the telephone, "I'm hanging up now, Midge, so I can call the police. Sara just came in and he wasn't at the lake."

She hung up, took her card of emergency phone numbers and began to dial.

There was something final about calling the police and Sara said, "Aunt Willie, don't call yet. Maybe—"

"I'm calling. A hundred elephants couldn't stop me."

"Maybe he's at somebody's house," Mary said. "One time my brother went in the Hutchinsons' to watch TV and we—"

"Hello, is this the police department? I want to report a missing child."

She looked up at Sara, started to say something, then turned back to her telephone conversation. "Yes, a missing child, a boy, ten, Charlie Godfrey. G-o-d-f-r-e-y." Pause. "Eighteen-oh-eight Cass Street. This is Willamina Godfrey, his aunt. I'm in charge." She paused, then said, "Yes, since last night." She listened again. "No, I don't know what time. We woke up this morning, he was gone. That's all." She listened and as she answered again her voice began to rise with concern and anger. "No, I could not ask his friends about him because he doesn't have any friends. His brain was injured when he was three years old and that is why I am so concerned. This is not a ten-year-old boy who can go out and come home when he feels like it. This is not a boy who's going to run out and break street lights and spend the night in some garage, if that's what you're thinking. This is a boy, I'm telling you, who can be lost and afraid three blocks from home and cannot speak one word to ask for help. Now are you going to come out here or aren't you?"

She paused, said, "Yes, yes," then grudgingly, "And thank you." She hung up the receiver and looked at Sara. They're coming."

"What did they say?"

"They said they're coming. That's all." She rose in agitation and began to walk into the living room. "Oh, why don't they hurry!"

"Aunt Willie, they just hung up the telephone."

"I know." She went to the front door and then came back, nervously slapping her hands together. "Where can he *be*?"

"My brother was always getting lost when he was little," Mary said.

"I stood right in this house, in that room," Aunt Willie interrupted. She pointed toward the front bedroom. "And I promised your mother, Sara, that I would look after Charlie all my life. I promised your mother nothing would ever happen to Charlie as long as there was breath in my body, and now look. Look! Where is this boy I'm taking such good care of?" She threw her hands into the air. "Vanished without a trace, that's where."

"Aunt Willie, you can't watch him every minute."

"Why not? Why can't I? What have I got more important in my life than looking after that boy? Only one thing more important than Charlie. Only one thing—that devil television there."

"Aunt Willie—"

"Oh, yes, that devil television. I was sitting right in that chair last night and he wanted me to sew on one button for him but I was too busy with the television. I'll tell you what I should have told your mother six years ago. I should have told her, 'Sure, I'll be glad to look after Charlie except when there's something good on television. I'll be glad to watch him in my spare time.' My tongue should fall out on the floor for promising to look after your brother and not doing it."

She went back to the doorway. "There are a hundred things that could have happened to him. He could have fallen into one of those ravines in the woods. He could be lost up at the old mine. He could be at the bottom of the lake. He could be kidnapped." Sara and Mary stood in silence as she named the tragedies that could have befallen Charlie.

Sara said, "Well, he could not have been kidnapped, because anybody would know we don't have any money for ransom."

"That wouldn't stop some people. Where are those policemen?"

Sara looked down at the table beside the television and saw a picture Charlie had drawn of himself on tablet paper. The head and body were circles of the same size, the ears and eyes overlapping smaller circles,

the arms and legs were elongated balloons. He had started printing his name below the picture, but had completed only two letters before he had gone out to make the tent. The *C* was backward.

Wanda had bought him the tablet and crayons two days ago and he had done this one picture with the brown crayon. It gave Sara a sick feeling to see it because something about the picture, the smallness, the unfinished quality, made it look somehow very much like Charlie.

Aunt Willie said, "When you want the police they are always a hundred miles away bothering criminals."

"They're on their way. They said so," Mary said.

"All right then, where are they?"

Mary blinked her eyes at this question to which she had no answer, and settled the rollers beneath her scarf.

"I still can't get it out of my head that Charlie went back to see the swans," Sara said.

"He really was upset about having to go home. I can testify to that," Mary said.

Aunt Willie left the room abruptly. When she came back she was holding a picture of Charlie in one hand. It was a snapshot of him taken in March, sitting on the steps with Boysie in front of the house.

"The police always want a photograph," she said. She held it out so Mary and Sara could see it. "Mrs. Hutchinson took that with her Polaroid."

"It's a real good picture of him," Mary said.

Sara looked at the picture without speaking. Somehow the awkward, unfinished crayon drawing on the table looked more like Charlie than the snapshot.

"It was his birthday," Aunt Willie said mournfully, "and look how proud he was of that watch Wanda bought him, holding his little arm straight out in the picture so everyone would notice it. I fussed so much about Wanda getting him a watch because he couldn't tell time, and then he was so proud just to be wearing it. Everyone would ask him on the street, 'What time is it, Charlie? Have you got the time, Charlie?' just to see how proud he was to show them."

"And then those boys stole it. I think that was the meanest thing," Mary said.

"The watch was lost," Aunt Willie said. "The watch just got lost."

"Stolen," Sara snapped, "by that crook Joe Melby."

"I am the quickest person to accuse somebody, you know that. You saw me, I hope, when I noticed those boys making off with the Hutchinsons' porch chairs last Halloween; but that watch just got lost. Then Joe Melby found it and, to his credit, brought it back."

"Huh!"

"There was no stealing involved."

Mary said, giggling, "Aunt Willie, did Sara ever tell you what she did to Joe?"

"Hush, Mary," Sara said.

"What did she do?"

"She made a little sign that said *FINK* and stuck it on Joe's back in the hall at school and he went around for two periods without knowing it was there."

"It doesn't matter what I did. Nobody's going to pick on my brother and I mean it. That fink stole Charlie's watch and then got scared and told that big lie about finding it on the floor of the school bus."

"You want revenge too much."

"When somebody *deserves* revenge, then—"

"I take my revenge same as anybody," Aunt Willie said, "Only I never was one to keep after somebody and keep after somebody the way you do. You take after your Uncle Bert in that."

"I hope I always do."

"No, your Uncle Bert was no good in that way. He would never let a grudge leave him. When he lay dying in the hospital, he was telling us who we weren't to speak to and who we weren't to do business with. His dying words were against Jeep Johnson at the used-car lot."

"Good for Uncle Bert."

"And that nice little Gretchen Wyant who you turned the hose on, and her wearing a silk dress her brother had sent her from Taiwan!"

"That nice little Gretchen Wyant was lucky all she got was water on her silk dress."

"Sara!"

"Well, do you know what that nice little Gretchen Wyant did? I was standing in the bushes by the spigot, turning off the hose, and this nice little Gretchen Wyant didn't see me—all she saw was Charlie at the fence—and she said, 'How's the *retard* today?' only she made it sound even uglier, 'How's the *reeeeetard*,' like that. Nothing

ever made me so mad. The best sight of my whole life was nice little Gretchen Wyant standing there in her wet Taiwan silk dress with her mouth hanging open."

"Here come the police," Mary said quickly. "But they're stopping next door."

"Signal to them," Aunt Willie said.

Before Mary could move to the door, Aunt Willie was past her and out on the porch. "Here we are. This is the house." She turned and said over her shoulder to Sara, "Now, God willing, we'll get some action."

Sara sat in the living room wearing her cut-off blue jeans, an old shirt with *Property of State Prison* stamped on the back which Wanda had brought her from the beach, and her puce tennis shoes. She was sitting in the doorway, leaning back against the door with her arms wrapped around her knees, listening to Aunt Willie, who was making a telephone call in the hall.

"It's no use calling," Sara said against her knees. This was the first summer her knees had not been skinned a dozen times, but she could still see the white scars from other summers. Since Aunt Willie did not answer, she said again, "It's no use calling. He won't come."

"You don't know your father," Aunt Willie said.

"That is the truth."

"Not like I do. When he hears that Charlie is missing, he will . . ." Her voice trailed off as she prepared to dial the telephone.

Sara had a strange feeling when she thought of her father. It was the way she felt about people she didn't know well, like the time Miss Marshall, her English teacher, had given her a ride home from school, and Sara had felt uneasy the whole way home, even though she saw Miss Marshall every day.

Her father's remoteness had begun, she thought, with Charlie's illness. There was a picture in the family photograph album of her father laughing and throwing Sara into the air and a picture of her father holding her on his shoulders and a picture of her father sitting on the front steps with Wanda on one knee and Sara on the other. All these pictures of a happy father and his adoring daughters had been taken before Charlie's illness and Sara's mother's death. Afterward there weren't any family pictures at all, happy or sad.

When Sara looked at those early pictures, she remembered a laughing man with black curly hair and a broken tooth who had lived with them for a few short golden years and then had gone away. There was no connection at all between this laughing man in the photograph album and the gray sober man who worked in Ohio and came home to West Virginia on occasional weekends, who sat in the living room and watched baseball or football on television and never started a conversation on his own.

Sara listened while Aunt Willie explained to the operator that the call she was making was an emergency. "That's why I'm not direct dialing," she said, "because I'm so upset I'll get the wrong numbers."

"He won't come," Sara whispered against her knee.

As the operator put through the call and Aunt Willie waited, she turned to Sara, nodded emphatically, and said, "He'll come, you'll see."

Sara got up, walked across the living room and into the kitchen, where the breakfast dishes were still on the table. She looked down at the two bowls of hard, cold oatmeal, and then made herself three pieces of toast and poured herself a cup of cherry Kool-Aid. When she came back eating the toast Aunt Willie was still waiting.

"Didn't the operator tell them it was an emergency, I wonder," Aunt Willie said impatiently.

"Probably."

"Well, if somebody told me I had an emergency call, I would run, let me tell you, to find out what that emergency was. That's no breakfast, Sara."

"It's my lunch."

"Kool-Aid and toast will not sustain you five minutes." She broke off quickly and said in a louder voice, "Sam, is that you?" She nodded to Sara, then turned back to the telephone, bent forward in her concern. "First of all, Sammy, promise me you won't get upset—no, promise me first."

"He won't get upset. Even *I* can promise you that," Sara said with her mouth full of toast.

"Sam, Charlie's missing," Aunt Willie said abruptly.

Unable to listen to any more of the

conversation, Sara took her toast and went out onto the front porch. She sat on the front steps and put her feet into the worn grooves that Charlie's feet had made on the third step. Then she ate the last piece of toast and licked the butter off her fingers.

In the corner of the yard, beneath the elm tree, she could see the hole Charlie had dug with a spoon; all one morning he had dug that hole and now Boysie was lying in it for coolness. She walked to the tree and sat in the old rope swing and swung over Boysie. She stretched out her feet and touched Boysie, and he lifted his head and looked around to see who had poked him, then lay back in his hole.

"Boysie, here I am, look, Boysie, look."

He was already asleep again.

"Boysie—" She looked up as Aunt Willie came out on the porch and stood for a minute drying her hands on her apron. For the occasion of Charlie's disappearance she was wearing her best dress, a bright green bonded jersey, which was so hot her face above it was red and shiny. Around her forehead she had tied a handkerchief to absorb the sweat.

Sara swung higher. "Well," she asked, "is he coming?" She paused to pump herself higher. "Or not?"

"He's going to call back tonight."

"Oh," Sara said.

"Don't say 'Oh' to me like that."

"It's what I figured."

"Listen to me, Miss Know-it-all. There is no need in the world for your father to come this exact minute. If he started driving right this second he still wouldn't get here till after dark and he couldn't do anything then, so he just might as well wait till after work and then drive."

"Might as well do the sensible thing." Sara stood up and really began to swing. She had grown so much taller since she had last stood in this swing that her head came almost to the limb from which the swing hung. She caught hold of the limb with her hands, kicked her feet free, and let the swing jerk wildly on its own.

"Anyway," Aunt Willie said, "this is no time to be playing on a swing. What will the neighbors think, with Charlie missing and you having a wonderful time on a swing?"

"I knew he wouldn't come."

"He is going to come," Aunt Willie said in a louder voice. "He is just going to wait till dark, which is reasonable, since by dark Charlie will probably be home anyway."

"It is so reasonable that it makes me sick."

"I won't listen to you being disrespectful to your father, I mean that," she said. "I know what it is to lose a father, let me tell you, and so will you when all you have left of him is an envelope."

Aunt Willie, Sara knew, was speaking of the envelope in her dresser drawer containing all the things her father had had in his pockets when he died. Sara knew them all—the watch, the twenty-seven cents in change, the folded dollar bill, the brown plaid handkerchief, the three-cent stamp, the two bent pipe cleaners, the half pack of stomach mints.

"Yes, wait till you lose your father. Then you'll appreciate him."

"I've already lost him."

"Don't you talk like that. Your father's had to raise two families and all by himself. When Poppa died, Sammy had to go to work and support all of us before he was even out of high school, and now he's got this family to support too. It's not easy, I'm telling you that. *You* raise two families and then I'll listen to what you've got to say against your father."

Sara let herself drop to the ground and said, "I better go. Mary and I are going to look for Charlie."

"Where?"

"Up the hill."

"Well, don't *you* get lost," Aunt Willie called after her.

From the Hutchinsons' yard some children called, "Have you found Charlie yet, Sara?" They were making a garden in the dust, carefully planting flowers without roots in neat rows. Already the first flowers were beginning to wilt in the hot sun.

"I'm going to look for him now."

"Sawa?" It was the youngest Hutchinson boy, who was three and sometimes came over to play with Charlie.

"What?"

"Sawa?"

"What?"

"Sawa?"

"*What?*"

"Sawa, I got gwass." He held up two fists of grass he had just pulled from one of the few remaining clumps in the yard.

"Yes, that's fine. I'll tell Charlie when I see him."

S ara and Mary had decided that they would go to the lake and walk up behind the houses toward the woods. Sara was now on her way to Mary's, passing the vacant lot where a baseball game was in progress. She glanced up and watched as she walked down the sidewalk.

The baseball game had been going on for an hour with the score still zero to zero and the players, dusty and tired, were playing silently, without hope.

She was almost past the field when she heard someone call, "Hey, have you found your brother yet, Sara?"

She recognized the voice of Joe Melby and said, "No," without looking at him.

"What?"

She turned, looked directly at him, and said, "You will be pleased and delighted to learn that we have not." She continued walking down the street. The blood began to pound in her head. Joe Melby was the one person she did not want to see on this particular day. There was something disturbing about him. She did not know him, really, had hardly even spoken to him, and yet she hated him so much the sight of him made her sick.

"Is there anything I can do?"

"No."

"If he's up in the woods, I could help

look. I know about as much about those hills as anybody." He left the game and started walking behind her with his hands in his pockets.

"No, thank you."

"I *want* to help."

She swirled around and faced him, her eyes blazing. "I do not want your help." They looked at each other. Something twisted inside her and she felt suddenly ill. She thought she would never drink cherry Kool-Aid again as long as she lived.

Joe Melby did not say anything but moved one foot back and forth on the sidewalk, shuffling at some sand. "Do you—"

"Anybody who would steal a little boy's watch," she said, cutting off his words, and it was a relief to make this accusation to his face at last, "is somebody whose help I can very well do without." Her head was pounding so loudly she could hardly hear her own words. For months, ever since the incident of the stolen watch, she had waited for this moment, had planned exactly what she would say. Now that it was said, she did not feel the triumph she had imagined at all.

"Is that what's wrong with you?" He looked at her. "You think I stole your brother's watch?"

"I know you did."

"How?"

"Because I asked Charlie who stole his watch and I kept asking him and one day on the school bus when I asked him he pointed right straight at you."

"He was confused—"

"He wasn't that confused. You probably thought he wouldn't be able to tell on you because he couldn't talk, but he pointed right—"

"He *was* confused. I gave the watch *back* to him. I didn't take it."

"I don't believe you."

"You believe what you want then, but I didn't take that watch. I thought that matter had been settled."

"Huh!"

She turned and started walking with great speed down the hill. For some reason she was not as sure about Joe Melby as she had been before, and this was even more disturbing. He did take the watch, she said to herself. She could not bear to think that she had been mistaken in this, that she had taken revenge on the wrong person.

Behind her there were sudden cheers as someone hit a home run. The ball went into the street. Joe ran, picked it up, and tossed it to a boy in the field. Sara did not look around.

"Hey, wait a minute," she heard Joe call. "I'm coming."

She did not turn around. She had fallen into that trap before. Once when she had been walking down the street, she had heard a car behind her and the horn sounding and a boy's voice shouting, "Hey, beautiful!" And she had turned around. She! Then, too late, she had seen that the girl they were honking and shouting at was Rosey Camdon on the opposite side of the street, Rosey Camdon who was Miss Batelle District Fair and Miss Buckwheat

Queen and a hundred other things. Sara had looked down quickly, not knowing whether anyone had seen her or not, and her face had burned so fiercely she had thought it would be red forever. Now she kept walking quickly with her head down.

"Wait, Sara."

Still she did not turn around or show that she had heard him.

"Wait." He ran, caught up with her, and started walking beside her. "All the boys say they want to help."

She hesitated but kept walking. She could not think of anything to say. She knew how circus men on stilts felt when they walked, because her legs seemed to be moving in the same awkward way, great exaggerated steps that got her nowhere.

She thought she might start crying so she said quickly, "Oh, all right." Then tears did come to her eyes, sudden and hot, and she looked down at her feet.

He said, "Where should we start? Have you got any ideas?"

"I think he's up in the woods. I took him to see the swans yesterday and I think he was looking for them when he got lost."

"Probably up that way."

She nodded.

He paused, then added, "We'll find him."

She did not answer, could not, because tears were spilling down her cheeks, so she turned quickly and walked alone to Mary's house and waited on the sidewalk until Mary came out to join her.

IDENTIFYING FACTS

1. Explain why Charlie is unable to sleep. Why does he leave the house?

2. What further details do you learn in this section about the children's father?

3. How does Sara's father react to Charlie's disappearance?

4. Who is Joe Melby? Why does Sara dislike him?

INTERPRETING MEANINGS

5. Why does Sara say she's already "lost" her father? How does Aunt Willie respond to Sara's complaint?

6. Charlie's disappearance immediately creates **suspense**. It makes us anxious to find out what will happen next. List three questions you hope the rest of the novel will answer.

7. How do you feel about Charlie so far?

APPLYING MEANINGS

8. What's your opinion of the way Sara punished Gretchen Wyant for her cruelty to Charlie? If Charlie were your brother, how would you have handled this incident?

9. This novel does not have chapter titles. Choose any one of the chapters you've read so far. Make up an interesting title for that chapter.

Literary Elements

POINT OF VIEW
Point of view is the vantage point from which a story is told. There are two main points of

view: first person and omniscient (om·nish'ənt).

1. **First-person point of view:** The story is told by a character inside the story. Suppose that Sara were telling this story. She would refer to herself as "I," which is called the first-person pronoun. ("You" is the second-person pronoun. "He, she, it" are third-person pronouns.) If Sara were telling the story, we would not be able to share Charlie's private thoughts and feelings. We would only know what Sara could tell us.

2. **Omniscient point of view:** The narrator is someone outside the events of the story. This all-knowing narrator knows everything about the story and can take us back and forth in time. An omniscient narrator can tell us the unspoken thoughts of all the characters.

The point of view in *The Summer of the Swans* is omniscient. Whose private thoughts and feelings does the narrator tell about in each of the following passages?

1. "The beauty of them, the whiteness, the softness . . . had impressed him greatly, and he felt a longing to be once again by the lake, sitting in the deep grass, throwing bread to the waiting swans." (Pages 671–672)

2. "The whole night seemed one long struggle, but he could not remember why he had been struggling." (Page 675)

3. "One of her greatest mistakes, she thought, looking at herself critically, was cutting her hair." (Page 676)

Whose thoughts and feelings does the narrator of this novel tell you most about?

Focus on Persuasive Writing

SUPPORTING YOUR OPINION

How would you convince Sara that Joe Melby didn't take Charlie's watch? You would probably need to use supporting arguments. At the beginning of the next section, you will see how Mary persuades Sara (see pages 690–691).

To persuade your readers or listeners to agree with your opinion on a topic, your argument needs **support.** Here are some types of support you can use:

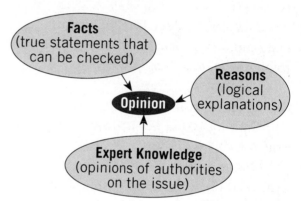

Choose a topic for a persuasive speech to your classmates. For example, you might want to persuade your listeners to support recycling or to start a pen pal program. Write a one-sentence opinion statement. Then list as many facts, reasons, and expert opinions as you can to support your view. Save your notes.

She and Mary were almost across the open field before Sara spoke. Then she said, "Guess who just stopped me and gave me the big sympathy talk about Charlie."

"I don't know. Who?"

"Joe Melby."

"Really? What did he say?"

"He wants to help look for Charlie. He makes me sick."

"I think it's nice that he wants to help."

"Well, maybe if he'd stolen your brother's watch you wouldn't think it was so nice."

Mary was silent for a moment. Then she said, "I probably shouldn't tell you this, but he didn't steal that watch, Sara."

"Huh!"

"No, he really didn't."

Sara looked at her and said, "How do you know?"

"I can't tell you how I know because I promised I wouldn't, but I *know* he didn't."

"How?"

"I can't tell. I promised."

"That never stopped you before. Now, Mary Weicek, you tell me what you know this minute."

"I promised."

"Mary, tell me."

"Mom would kill me if she knew I told you."

"She won't know."

"Well, your aunt went to see Joe Melby's mother."

"What?"

"Aunt Willie went over to see Joe Melby's mother."

"She didn't!"

"Yes, she did too, because my mother was right there when it happened. It was about two weeks after Charlie had gotten the watch back."

"I don't believe you."

"Well, it's the truth. You told Aunt Willie that Joe had stolen the watch—remember, you told everybody—and so Aunt Willie went over to see Joe's mother."

"She wouldn't do such a terrible thing."

"Well, she did."

"And what did Mrs. Melby say?"

"She called Joe into the room and she said, 'Joe, did you steal the little Godfrey boy's watch?' And he said, 'No.'"

"What did you expect him to say in front of his mother? 'Yes, I stole the watch'? Huh! That doesn't prove anything."

"So then she said, 'I want the truth now. Do you know who did take the watch?' and he said that nobody had *stolen* the watch."

"So where did it disappear to for a week, I'd like to know."

"I'm coming to that. He said some of the fellows were out in front of the drugstore and Charlie was standing there waiting for the school bus—you were in the drugstore. Remember it was the day we were getting the stamps for letters to those pen pals who never answered? Remember the stamps wouldn't come out of the machine? Well, anyway, these boys outside the store started teasing Charlie with some candy, and while Charlie was trying to get the candy, one of the boys took off Charlie's watch without Charlie noticing it. Then they were going to ask Charlie what time it was and when he looked down at his watch, he would get upset because the watch would be gone. They were just going to tease him."

"Finks! *Finks!*"

"Only you came out of the drugstore right then and saw what they were doing with the candy and told them off and the bus came and you hustled Charlie on the bus before anybody had a chance to give back the watch. Then they got scared to give it back and that's the whole story. Joe didn't steal the watch at all. He wasn't even in on it. He came up right when you did and didn't even know what had happened. Later, when he found out, he got the watch back and gave it to Charlie, that's all."

"Why didn't you tell me before this?"

"Because I just found out about it at lunch. For four months my mother has known all about this thing and never mentioned it because she said it was one of those things best forgotten."

"Why did she tell you now?"

"That's the way my mom is. We were talking about Charlie at the dinner table, and suddenly she comes up with this. Like one time she casually mentioned that she had had a long talk with Mr. Homer about me. Mr. Homer, the principal! She went over there and they had a long discussion and she never mentioned it for a year."

"That is the worst thing Aunt Willie has ever done."

"Well, don't let on that you know or I'll be in real trouble."

"I won't, but honestly, I could just—"

"You promised."

"I know. You don't have to keep reminding me. It makes me feel terrible though, I can tell you that." She walked with her head bent forward. "Terrible! You know what I just did when I saw him?"

"What?"

"Accused him of stealing the watch."

"Sara, you didn't."

"I did too. I can't help myself. When I think somebody has done something mean to Charlie I can't forgive them. I want to keep after them and keep after them just like Aunt Willie said. I even sort of suspected Joe Melby hadn't really taken that watch and I still kept on—"

"Shh! Be quiet a minute." Mary was carrying her transistor radio and she held it up between them. "Listen."

The announcer was saying: "We have a report of a missing child in the Cass section—ten-year-old Charlie Godfrey, who has been missing from his home since sometime last night. He is wearing blue pajamas and brown felt slippers, has a watch on one wrist and an identification bracelet with his name and address on the other. He is a mentally handicapped child who cannot speak and may become alarmed when approached by a stranger. Please notify the police immediately if you have seen this youngster."

The two girls looked at each other, then continued walking across the field in silence.

Mary and Sara were up in the field by the woods. They had been searching for Charlie for an hour without finding a trace of him.

Mary said, "I don't care how I look. I am taking off this scarf. It must be a hundred degrees out here."

"Charlie!" Sara called as she had been doing from time to time. Her voice had begun to sound strained, she had called so often. "Charlie!"

"Sara, do you know where we are?" Mary asked after a moment.

"Of course. The lake's down there and the old shack's over there and you can see them as soon as we get up a little higher."

"*If* we get up a little higher," Mary said in a tired voice.

"You didn't have to come, you know."

"I wanted to come, only I just want to make sure we don't get lost. I have to go to Bennie Hoffman's party tonight."

"I know. You told me ten times."

"So I don't want to get lost." Mary walked a few steps without speaking. "I still can't figure out why I was invited, because Bennie Hoffman hardly knows me. I've just seen him two times this whole summer at the pool. Why do you think he—"

"Come on, will you?"

"It seems useless, if you ask me, to just keep walking when we don't really know which way he went. Aunt Willie thinks he went in the old coal mine."

"I know, but she only thinks that because she associates the mine with tragedy because her uncle and brother were killed in that coal mine. But Charlie wouldn't go in there. Remember that time we went into the Bryants' cellar after they moved out, and he wouldn't even come in there because it was cold and dark and sort of scary."

"Yes, I do remember because I sprained my ankle jumping down from the window and had to wait two hours while you looked through old *Life* magazines."

"I was not looking through old magazines."

"I could hear you. I was down there in that dark cellar with the rats and you were upstairs and I was yelling for help and you kept saying, 'I'm going for help right now,' and I could hear the pages turning and turning and turning."

"Well, I got you out, didn't I?"

"Finally."

Sara paused again. "Charlie! Charlie!" The girls waited in the high grass for an answer, then began to walk again. Mary said, "Maybe we should have waited for the others before we started looking. They're going to have a regular organized posse with everybody walking along together. There may be a helicopter."

"The longer we wait, the harder it will be to find him."

"Well, I've got to get home in time to bathe and take my hair down."

"I know. I *know*. You're going to Bennie Hoffman's party."

"You don't have to sound so mad about it. I didn't *ask* to be invited."

"I am not mad because you were invited to Bennie Hoffman's party. I couldn't care less about Bennie Hoffman's party. I'm just mad because you're slowing me up on this search."

"Well, if I'm slowing you up so much, then maybe I'll just go on home."

"That suits me fine."

They looked at each other without speaking. Between them the radio began announcing: "Volunteers are needed in the Cass area in the search for young Charlie Godfrey, who disappeared from his home sometime during the night. A search of the Cheat woods will begin at three o'clock this afternoon."

Mary said, "Oh, I'll keep looking. I'll try to walk faster."

Sara shrugged, turned, and started walking up the hill, followed by Mary. They came to the old fence that once separated the pasture from the woods. Sara walked slowly beside the fence. "Charlie!" she called.

"Would he come if he heard you, do you think?"

Sara nodded. "But if they get a hundred people out here clomping through the woods and hollering, he's not going to come. He'll be too scared. I know him."

"I don't see how you can be so sure he came up this way."

"I just know. There's something about me that makes me understand Charlie. It's like I know how he feels about things. Like sometimes I'll be walking down the street and I'll pass the jeweler's and I'll think that if Charlie were here he would want to stand right there and look at those watches all afternoon and I know right where he'd

stand and how he'd put his hands up on the glass and how his face would look. And yesterday I knew he was going to love the swans so much that he wasn't ever going to want to leave. I know how he feels."

"You just think you do."

"No, I *know*. I was thinking about the sky one night and I was looking up at the stars and I was thinking about how the sky goes on and on forever, and I couldn't understand it no matter how long I thought, and finally I got kind of nauseated and right then I started thinking, Well, this is how Charlie feels about some things. You know how it makes him sick sometimes to try to print letters for a long time and—"

"Look who's coming," Mary interrupted.

"Where?"

"In the trees, walking toward us. Joe Melby."

"You're lying. You're just trying to make me—"

"It is him. Look." She quickly began to tie her scarf over her rollers again. "And you talk about *me* needing eyeglasses."

"Cut across the field, quick!" Sara said. "No, wait, go under the fence. Move, will you, Mary, and leave that scarf alone. Get under the fence. I am not going to face him. I mean it."

"I am not going under any fence. Anyway, it would look worse for us to run away than to just walk by casually."

"I cannot walk by casually after what I said."

"Well, you're going to have to face

him sometime, and it might as well be now when everyone feels sorry for you about your brother.'' She called out, ''Hi, Joe, having any luck?''

He came up to them and held out a brown felt slipper and looked at Sara. ''Is this Charlie's?''

Sara looked at the familiar object and forgot the incident of the watch for a moment. ''Where did you find it?''

''Right up there by the fence. I had just picked it up when I saw you.''

She took the slipper and, holding it against her, said, ''Oh, I *knew* he came up

this way, but it's a relief to have some proof of it.''

"I was just talking to Mr. Aker," Joe continued, ''and he said he heard his dogs barking up here last night. He had them tied out by the shack and he thought maybe someone was prowling around.''

"Probably Charlie," Mary said.

"That's what I figured. Somebody ought to go down to the gas station and tell the people. They're organizing a big search now and half of the men are planning to go up to the mine.''

There was a pause and Mary said,

"Well, I guess I could go, only I don't know whether I'll have time to get back up here." She looked at Joe. "I promised Bennie Hoffman I'd come to his party tonight. That's why my hair's in rollers."

"Tell them I found the slipper about a half mile up behind the Akers' at the old fence," Joe said.

"Sure. Are you coming to Bennie's tonight?"

"Maybe."

"Come. It's going to be fun."

Sara cleared her throat and said, "Well, I think I'll get on with my search if you two will excuse me." She turned and started walking up the hill again. There seemed to be a long silence in which even the sound of the cicadas in the grass was absent. She thrashed at the high weeds with her tennis shoes and hugged Charlie's slipper to her.

"Wait a minute, Sara, I'll come with you," Joe Melby said.

He joined her and she nodded, still looking down at the slipper. There was a picture of an Indian chief stamped on the top of the shoe and there was a loneliness to the Indian's profile, even stamped crudely on the felt, that she had never noticed before.

She cleared her throat again. "There is just one thing I want to say." Her voice did not even sound familiar, a tape-recorded voice.

He waited, then said, "Go ahead."

She did not speak for a moment but continued walking noisily through the weeds.

"Go ahead."

"If you'll just wait a minute, I'm trying to think how to say this." The words she wanted to say—I'm sorry—would not come out at all.

They continued walking in silence and then Joe said, "You know, I was just reading an article about a guru over in India and he hasn't spoken a word in twenty-eight years. *Twenty-eight years* and he hasn't said one word in all that time. And everyone has been waiting all those years to hear what he's going to say when he finally does speak because it's supposed to be some great wise word, and I thought about this poor guy sitting there and for twenty-eight years he's been trying to think of something to say that would be the least bit great and he can't think of anything and he must be getting really desperate now. And every day it gets worse and worse."

"Is there supposed to be some sort of message in that story?"

"Maybe."

She smiled. "Well, I just wanted to say that I'm sorry." She thought again that she was going to start crying and she said to herself, You are nothing but a big soft snail. Snail!

"That's all right."

"I just found out about Aunt Willie going to see your mother."

He shrugged. "She didn't mean anything by it."

"But it was a terrible thing."

"It wasn't all that bad. At least it was different to be accused of something I *didn't* do for a change."

"But to be called in like that in front

of Aunt Willie and Mary's mother. No, it was terrible." She turned and walked into the woods.

"Don't worry about it. I'm tough. I'm indestructible. I'm like that coyote in 'Road Runner' who is always getting flattened and dynamited and crushed and in the next scene is strolling along, completely normal again."

"I just acted too hastily. That's one of my main faults."

"I do that too."

"Not like me."

"Worse probably. Do you remember when we used to get grammar-school report cards, and the grades would be on one part of the card, and on the other side would be personality things the teacher would check, like 'Does not accept criticism constructively'?"

Sara smiled. "I always used to get a check on that one," she said.

"Who didn't? And then they had one, 'Acts impetuously and without consideration for others,' or something like that, and one year I got a double check on that one."

"You didn't."

"Yes, I did. Second grade. Miss McLeod. I remember she told the whole class that this was the first year she had ever had to give double checks to any student, and everyone in the room was scared to open his report card to see if he had got the double checks. And when I opened mine, there they were, two sets of double checks, on acting impetuously and on not accepting criticism, and single checks on everything else."

"Were you crushed?"

"Naturally."

"I thought you were so tough and indestructible."

"Well, I am"—he paused—"I think." He pointed to the left. "Let's go up this way."

She agreed with a nod and went ahead of him between the trees.

There was a ravine in the forest, a deep cut in the earth, and Charlie had made his way into it through an early morning fog. By chance, blindly stepping through the fog with his arms outstretched, he had managed to pick the one path that led into the ravine, and when the sun came out and the fog burned away, he could not find the way out.

All the ravine looked the same in the daylight, the high walls, the masses of weeds and wild berry bushes, the trees. He had wandered around for a while, following the little paths made by dirt washed down from the hillside, but finally he sat down on a log and stared straight ahead without seeing.

After a while he roused enough to wipe his hands over his cheeks where the tears and dirt had dried together and to rub his puffed eyelids. Then he looked down, saw his bare foot, put it on top of his slipper, and sat with his feet overlapped.

There was a dullness about him now. He had had so many scares, heard so many frightening noises, started at so many shadows, been hurt so often that all his senses were worn to a flat hopelessness. He would just sit here forever.

It was not the first time Charlie had been lost, but never before had there been this finality. He had become separated from Aunt Willie once at the county fair and had not even known he was lost until she had come bursting out of the crowd screaming, "Charlie, Charlie," and enveloped him. He had been lost in school once in the hall and could not find his way back to his room, and he had walked up and down the halls, frightened by all the strange children looking out of every door, until one of the boys was sent out to lead him to his room. But in all his life there had never been an experience like this one.

He bent over and looked down at his watch, his eyes on the tiny red hand. For the first time he noticed it was no longer moving. Holding his breath in his concern, he brought the watch closer to his face. The hand was still. For a moment he could not believe it. He watched it closely, waiting. Still the hand did not move. He shook his hand back and forth, as if he were trying to shake the watch off his wrist. He had seen Sara do this to her watch.

Then he held the watch to his ear. It was silent. He had had the watch for five months and never before had it failed him. He had not even known it could fail. And now it was silent and still.

He put his hand over the watch, covering it completely. He waited. His breathing had begun to quicken again. His hand on the watch was almost clammy. He waited, then slowly, cautiously, he re-moved his hand and looked at the tiny red hand on the dial. It was motionless. The trick had not worked.

Bending over the watch, he looked closely at the stem. Aunt Willie always wound the watch for him every morning after breakfast, but he did not know how she did this. He took the stem in his fingers, pulled at it clumsily, then harder, and it came off. He looked at it. Then, as he attempted to put it back on the watch, it fell to the ground and was lost in the leaves.

A chipmunk ran in front of him and scurried up the bank. Distracted for a moment, Charlie got up and walked toward it. The chipmunk paused and then darted into a hole, leaving Charlie standing in the shadows trying to see where it had gone. He went closer to the bank and pulled at the leaves, but he could not even find the place among the roots where the chipmunk had disappeared.

Suddenly something seemed to explode within Charlie, and he began to cry noisily. He threw himself on the bank and began kicking, flailing at the ground, at the invisible chipmunk, at the silent watch. He wailed, yielding in helplessness to his anguish, and his piercing screams, uttered again and again, seemed to hang in the air so that they overlapped. His fingers tore at the tree roots and dug beneath the leaves and scratched, animal-like, at the dark earth.

His body sagged and he rolled down the bank and was silent. He looked up at the trees, his chest still heaving with sobs, his face strangely still. After a moment, his eyelids drooped and he fell asleep.

"Charlie! Charlie!"

The only answer was the call of a bird in the branches overhead, one long tremulous whistle.

"He's not even within hearing distance," Sara said.

For the past hour she and Joe Melby had been walking deeper and deeper into the forest without pause, and now the trees were so thick that only small spots of sunlight found their way through the heavy foliage.

"Charlie, oh, Charlie!"

She waited, looking down at the ground.

Joe said, "You want to rest for a while?"

Sara shook her head. She suddenly wanted to see her brother so badly that her throat began to close. It was a tight feeling she got sometimes when she wanted something, like the time she had had the measles and had wanted to see her father so much she couldn't even swallow. Now she thought that if she had a whole glass of ice water—and she was thirsty—she probably would not be able to drink a single drop.

"If you can make it a little farther, there's a place at the top of the hill where the strip mining is, and you can see the whole valley from there."

"I can make it."

"Well, we can rest first if—"

"I can make it."

She suddenly felt a little better. She thought that if she could stand up there on top of the hill and look down and see, somewhere in that huge green valley, a small plump figure in blue pajamas, she would ask for nothing more in life. She thought of the valley as a relief map where everything would be shiny and smooth, and her brother would be right where she could spot him at once. Her cry, "There he is!" would ring like a bell over the valley and everyone would hear her and know that Charlie had been found.

She paused, leaned against a tree for a moment, and then continued. Her legs had begun to tremble.

It was the time of afternoon when she usually sat down in front of the television and watched game shows, the shows where the married couples tried to guess things about each other and where girls had to pick out dates they couldn't see. She would sit in the doorway to the hall where she always sat and Charlie would come in and watch with her, and the living room would be dark and smell of the pine-scented cleaner Aunt Willie used.

Then "The Early Show" would come on, and she would sit through the old movie, leaning forward in the doorway, making fun, saying things like, "Now, Charlie, we'll have the old Convict Turning Honest scene," and Charlie, sitting on the stool closer to the television, would nod without understanding.

She was good, too, at joining in the dialogue with the actors. When the cowboy would say something like, "Things are quiet around here tonight," she would join in with, "Yeah, *too* quiet," right on cue. It seemed strange to be out here in the woods with Joe Melby instead of in the living room with Charlie, watching *Flame of Ar-*

aby, which was the early movie for that afternoon.

Her progress up the hill seemed slower and slower. It was like the time she had won the slow bicycle race, a race in which she had to go as slow as possible without letting a foot touch the ground, and she had gone slower and slower, all the while feeling a strong compulsion to speed ahead and cross the finish line first. At the end of the race it had been she and T. R. Peters, and they had paused just before the finish line, balancing motionless on their bicycles. The time had seemed endless, and then T. R. lost his balance and his foot touched the ground and Sara was the winner.

She slipped on some dry leaves, went down on her knees, straightened, and paused to catch her breath.

"Are you all right?"

"Yes, I just slipped."

She waited for a moment, bent over her knees, then she called, "Charlie! Charlie," without lifting her head.

"Oh, Charleeeeee," Joe shouted above her.

Sara knew Charlie would shout back if he heard her, the long wailing cry he gave sometimes when he was frightened during the night. It was such a familiar cry that for a moment she thought she heard it.

She waited, still touching the ground with one hand, until she was sure there was no answer.

"Come on," Joe said, holding out his hand.

He pulled her to her feet and she stood looking up at the top of the hill. Machines had cut away the earth there to get at the veins of coal, and the earth had been pushed down the hill to form a huge bank.

"I'll never get up that," she said. She leaned against a tree whose leaves were covered with the pale fine dirt which had filtered down when the machines had cut away the hill.

"Sure you will. I've been up it a dozen times."

He took her hand and she started after him, moving sideways up the steep bank. The dirt crumbled beneath her feet and she slid, skinned one knee, and then slipped again. When she had regained her balance she laughed wryly and said, "What's going to happen is that I'll end up pulling you all the way down the hill."

"No, I've got you. Keep coming."

She started again, putting one foot carefully above the other, picking her way over the stones. When she paused, he said, "Keep coming. We're almost there."

"I think it's a trick, like at the dentist's when he says, 'I'm almost through drilling.' Then he drills for another hour and says, 'Now, I'm really almost through drilling,' and he keeps on and then says, 'There's just one more spot and then I'll be practically really through.' "

"We must go to the same dentist."

"I don't think I can make it. There's no skin at all left on the sides of my legs."

"Well, we're really almost practically there now, in the words of your dentist."

She fell across the top of the dirt bank on her stomach, rested for a moment, and then turned and looked down the valley.

She could not speak for a moment. There lay the whole valley in a way she had never imagined it, a tiny finger of civilization set in a sweeping expanse of dark forest. The black treetops seemed to crowd against the yards, the houses, the roads, giving the impression that at any moment the trees would close over the houses like waves and leave nothing but an unbroken line of black-green leaves waving in the sunlight.

Up the valley she could see the intersection where they shopped, the drugstore, the gas station where her mother had once won a set of twenty-four stemmed glasses which Aunt Willie would not allow them to use, the grocery store, the lot where the yellow school buses were parked for the summer. She could look over the valley and see another hill where white cows were all grouped together by a fence and beyond that another hill and then another.

She looked back at the valley and she saw the lake and for the first time since she had stood up on the hill she remembered Charlie.

Raising her hand to her mouth, she called, "Charlie! Charlie! Charlie!" There was a faint echo that seemed to waver in her ears.

"Charlie, oh, Charlie!" Her voice was so loud it seemed to ram into the valley.

Sara waited. She looked down at the forest, and everything was so quiet it seemed to her that the whole valley, the whole world was waiting with her.

"Charlie, hey, Charlie!" Joe shouted.

"Charleeeeee!" She made the sound of it last a long time. "Can you hear meeeeee?"

With her eyes she followed the trail she knew he must have taken—the house, the Akers' vacant lot, the old pasture, the forest. The forest that seemed powerful enough to engulf a whole valley, she thought with a sinking feeling, could certainly swallow up a young boy.

"Charlie! Charlie! Charlie!" There was a waver in the last syllable that betrayed how near she was to tears. She looked down at the Indian slipper she was still holding.

"Charlie, oh, Charlie." She waited. There was not a sound anywhere. "Charlie, where are you?"

"Hey, Charlie!" Joe shouted.

They waited in the same dense silence. A cloud passed in front of the sun and a breeze began to blow through the trees. Then there was silence again.

"Charlie, Charlie, Charlie, Charlie, Charlie."

She paused, listened, then bent abruptly and put Charlie's slipper to her eyes. She waited for the hot tears that had come so often this summer, the tears that had seemed so close only a moment before. Now her eyes remained dry.

I have cried over myself a hundred times this summer, she thought, I have wept over my big feet and my skinny legs and my nose, I have even cried over my stupid shoes, and now when I have a true sadness there are no tears left.

She held the felt side of the slipper against her eyes like a blindfold and stood there, feeling the hot sun on her head and the wind wrapping around her legs, conscious of the height and the valley sweeping down from her feet.

"Listen, just because you can't hear him doesn't mean anything. He could be—"

"Wait a minute." She lowered the slipper and looked down the valley. A sudden wind blew dust into her face and she lifted her hand to shield her eyes.

"I thought I heard something. Charlie! Answer me right this minute."

She waited with the slipper held against her breasts, one hand to her eyes, her whole body motionless, concentrating on her brother. Then she stiffened. She thought again she had heard something—Charlie's long high wail. Charlie could sound sadder than anyone when he cried.

In her anxiety she took the slipper and twisted it again and again as if she were wringing water out. She called, then stopped abruptly and listened. She looked at Joe and he shook his head slowly.

She looked away. A bird rose from the trees below and flew toward the hills in the distance. She waited until she could see it no longer and then slowly, still listening for the call that didn't come, she sank to the ground and sat with her head bent over her knees.

Beside her, Joe scuffed his foot in the dust and sent a cascade of rocks and dirt down the bank. When the sound of it faded, he began to call, "Charlie, hey, Charlie," again and again.

For Study and Discussion

IDENTIFYING FACTS

1. Why did Aunt Willie visit Joe Melby's mother?

2. Explain what really happened to Charlie's watch.

3. Why does Sara want to find Charlie before the search party starts out?

INTERPRETING MEANINGS

4. What is Sara's friend Mary most concerned about? How is Sara different from Mary at this point in the novel?

5. On page 693, Sara says to Mary that she knows how Charlie *feels*. Reread the passage beginning "No, I *know*." In your own words, explain how Charlie feels about some things.

6. Why do you think Sara feels that the picture of the Indian chief on Charlie's slipper is so lonely? (See page 696.)

7. Why do you think Joe tells Sara the story about the guru who hadn't spoken for twenty-eight years? (See page 696.)

8. Charlie undergoes a crisis when his watch stops. Why does this minor event affect him so strongly? How did this description of Charlie's anguish make you feel about him? (See page 698.)

9. When Sara and Joe stand on the hill overlooking the valley, Sara wants to cry but can't. What does she realize about herself? (See page 701.)

APPLYING MEANINGS

10. Why do you think some people are cruel to people like Charlie?

Charlie awoke, but he lay for a moment without opening his eyes. He did not remember where he was, but he had a certain dread of seeing it.

There were great parts of his life that were lost to Charlie, blank spaces that he could never fill in. He would find himself in a strange place and not know how he had got there. Like the time Sara had been hit in the nose with a baseball at the Dairy Queen, and the blood and the sight of Sara kneeling on the ground in helpless pain had frightened him so much that he had turned and run without direction, in a frenzy, dashing headlong up the street, blind to cars and people.

By chance Mr. Weicek had seen him, put him in the car, and driven him home, and Aunt Willie had put him to bed, but later he remembered none of this. He had only awakened in bed and looked at the crumpled bit of ice-cream cone still clenched in his hand and wondered about it.

His whole life had been built on a strict routine, and as long as this routine was kept up, he felt safe and well. The same foods, the same bed, the same furniture in the same place, the same seat on the school bus, the same class procedure were all important to him. But always there could be the unexpected, the dreadful surprise that would topple his carefully constructed life in an instant.

The first thing he became aware of was the twigs pressing into his face, and he put his hand under his cheek. Still he did not open his eyes. Pictures began to drift into his mind; he saw Aunt Willie's cigar box which was filled with old jewelry and buttons and knickknacks, and he found that he could remember every item in that box—the string of white beads without a clasp, the old earrings, the tiny book with souvenir fold-out pictures of New York, the plastic decorations from cakes, the turtle made of sea shells. Every item was so real that he opened his eyes and was surprised to see, instead of the glittering contents of the box, the dull and unfamiliar forest.

He raised his head and immediately felt the aching of his body. Slowly he sat up and looked down at his hands. His fingernails were black with earth, two of them broken below the quick, and he got up slowly and sat on the log behind him and inspected his fingers more closely.

Then he sat up straight. His hands dropped to his lap. His head cocked to the side like a bird listening. Slowly he straightened until he was standing. At his side his fingers twitched at the empty air as if to grasp something. He took a step forward, still with his head to the side. He remained absolutely still.

Then he began to cry out in a hoarse excited voice, again and again, screaming now, because he had just heard someone far away calling his name.

At the top of the hill Sara got slowly to her feet and stood looking down at the forest. She pushed the hair back from her forehead and moistened her lips. The wind dried them as she waited.

Joe started to say something but she reached out one hand and took his arm to stop him. Scarcely daring to believe her ears, she stepped closer to the edge of the bank. Now she heard it unmistakably—the sharp repeated cry—and she knew it was Charlie.

"Charlie!" she shouted with all her might.

She paused and listened, and his cries were louder and she knew he was not far away after all, just down the slope, in the direction of the ravine.

"It's Charlie, it's Charlie!"

A wild joy overtook her and she jumped up and down on the bare earth and she felt that she could crush the whole hill just by jumping if she wanted.

She sat and scooted down the bank, sending earth and pebbles in a cascade before her. She landed on the soft ground, ran a few steps, lost her balance, caught hold of the first tree trunk she could find, and swung around till she stopped.

She let out another whoop of pure joy, turned and ran down the hill in great strides, the puce tennis shoes slapping the ground like rubber paddles, the wind in her face, her hands grabbing one tree trunk after another for support. She felt like a wild creature who had traveled through the forest this way for a lifetime. Nothing could stop her now.

At the edge of the ravine she paused and stood gasping for breath. Her heart was beating so fast it pounded in her ears, and her throat was dry. She leaned against a tree, resting her cheek against the rough bark.

She thought for a minute she was going to faint, a thing she had never done before, not even when she broke her nose. She hadn't even believed people really did faint until this minute when she clung to the tree because her legs were as useless as rubber bands.

There was a ringing in her ears and another sound, a wailing sirenlike cry that was painfully familiar.

"Charlie?"

Charlie's crying, like the sound of a cricket, seemed everywhere and nowhere.

She walked along the edge of the ravine, circling the large boulders and trees. Then she looked down into the ravine where the shadows lay, and she felt as if something had turned over inside her because she saw Charlie.

He was standing in his torn pajamas, face turned upward, hands raised, shouting with all his might. His eyes were shut tight. His face was streaked with dirt and tears. His pajama jacket hung in shreds about his scratched chest.

He opened his eyes and as he saw Sara a strange expression came over his face, an expression of wonder and joy and disbelief, and Sara knew that if she lived to be a hundred no one would ever look at her quite that way again.

She paused, looked down at him, and

then, sliding on the seat of her pants, went down the bank and took him in her arms.

"Oh, Charlie."

His arms gripped her like steel.

"Oh, Charlie."

She could feel his fingers digging into her back as he clutched her shirt. "It's all right now, Charlie, I'm here and we're going home." His face was buried in her shirt and she patted his head, said again, "It's all right now. Everything's fine."

She held him against her for a moment and now the hot tears were in her eyes and on her cheeks and she didn't even notice.

"I know how you feel," she said. "I know. One time when I had the measles and my fever was real high, I got lost on my way back from the bathroom, right in our house, and it was a terrible feeling, terrible, because I wanted to get back to my bed and I couldn't find it, and finally Aunt Willie heard me and came and you know where I was? In the kitchen. In our kitchen and I couldn't have been more lost if I'd been out in the middle of the wilderness."

She patted the back of his head again and said "Look, I even brought your bedroom slipper. Isn't that service, huh?"

She tried to show it to him, but he was still clutching her, and she held him against her, patting him. After a moment she said again, "Look, here's your slipper. Let's put it on." She knelt, put his foot into the shoe, and said, "Now, isn't that better?"

He nodded slowly, his chest still heaving with unspent sobs.

"Can you walk home?"

He nodded. She took her shirttail and wiped his tears and smiled at him. "Come on, we'll find a way out of here and go home."

"Hey, over this way," Joe called from the bank of the ravine. Sara had forgotten about him in the excitement of finding Charlie, and she looked up at him for a moment.

"Over this way, around the big tree," Joe called. "That's probably how he got in. The rest of the ravine is a mass of brier bushes."

She put one arm around Charlie and led him around the tree. "Everybody in town's looking for you, you know that?" she said. "Everybody. The police came and all the neighbors are out—there must be a hundred people looking for you. You were on the radio. It's like you were the President of the United States or something. Everybody was saying, 'Where's Charlie?' and 'We got to find Charlie.'"

Suddenly Charlie stopped and held up his hand and Sara looked down. "What is it?"

He pointed to the silent watch.

She smiled. "Charlie, you are something, you know that? Here we are racing down the hill to tell everyone in great triumph that you are found, *found,* and we have to stop and wind your watch first."

She looked at the watch, saw that the stem was missing, and shook her head. "It's broken, Charlie, see, the stem's gone. It's broken."

He held it out again.

"It's *broken,* Charlie. We'll have to take it to the jeweler and have it fixed."

He continued to hold out his arm.

"Hey, Charlie, you want to wear my watch till you get yours fixed?" Joe asked. He slid down the bank and put his watch on Charlie's arm. "There."

Charlie bent his face close and listened.

"Now can we go home?" Sara asked, jamming her hands into her back pockets.

Charlie nodded.

They walked through the woods for a long time, Joe in the lead, picking the best path, with Charlie and Sara following. From time to time Sara turned and hugged Charlie and he smelled of trees and dark earth and tears and she said, "Everybody's going to be so glad to see you it's going to be just like New Year's Eve."

Sara could not understand why she suddenly felt so good. It was a puzzle. The day before she had been miserable. She had wanted to fly away from everything, like the swans to a new lake, and now she didn't want that any more.

Down the hill Mr. Rhodes, one of the searchers, was coming toward them and Joe called out, "Mr. Rhodes, Sara found him!"

"Is he all right?" Mr. Rhodes called back.

"Fine, he's fine."

"Sara found him and he's all right. He's all right." The phrase passed down the hill from Dusty Rhodes, who painted cars at the garage, to Mr. Aker to someone Sara couldn't recognize.

Then all the searchers were joining them, reaching out to pat Charlie and to say to Sara, "Oh, your aunt is going to be so happy," or "Where *was* he?" or "Well, now we can all sleep in peace tonight."

They came through the woods in a big noisy group and out into the late sunlight in the old pasture, Sara and Charlie in the middle, surrounded by all the searchers.

Suddenly Sara sensed a movement above her. She looked up and then grabbed Charlie's arm.

The swans were directly overhead, flying with outstretched necks, their long wings beating the air, an awkward blind sort of flight. They were so low that she thought they might hit the trees, but at the last moment they pulled up and skimmed the air just above the treetops.

"Look, Charlie, look. Those are the swans. Remember? They're going home."

He looked blankly at the sky, unable to associate the heavy awkward birds with the graceful swans he had seen on the water. He squinted at the sky, then looked at Sara, puzzled.

"Charlie, those are the swans. Remember? At the lake?" she said, looking right at him. "They're going home now. Don't you remember? They were—"

"Hey, there's your aunt, Charlie. There's Aunt Willie coming."

Sara was still pulling at Charlie's arm, directing his attention to the sky. It seemed urgent somehow that Charlie see the swans once again. She said, "Charlie, those are—"

He looked instead across the field and

he broke away from Sara and started running. She took two steps after him and then stopped. Aunt Willie in her bright green dress seemed to shine like a beacon, and he hurried toward her, an awkward figure in torn blue pajamas, shuffling through the high grass.

There was a joyous yell that was so shrill Sara thought it had come from the swans, but then she knew that it had come from Charlie, for the swans were mute.

"Here he is, Willie," Mrs. Aker called, running behind Charlie to have some part in the reunion.

Aunt Willie was coming as fast as she could on her bad legs. "I never thought to see him again," she was telling everyone and no one. "I thought he was up in that mine. I tell you, I never thought to see him again. Charlie, come here to your Aunt Willie."

Charlie ran like a ball rolling downhill, bouncing with the slope of the land.

"I tell you this has been the blackest day of my life"—Aunt Willie was gasping—"and I include every day I have been on earth. Charlie, my Charlie, let me look at you. Oh, you are a sight."

He fell into Aunt Willie's arms. Over his head Aunt Willie said through her tears to Mrs. Aker, "May you never lose your Bobby, that's all I got to say. May you never lose your Bobby, may none of you ever lose anybody in the woods or in the mine or anywhere."

Sara stood in the pasture by the old gray shack and watched the swans disappear over the hill, and then she watched Charlie and Aunt Willie disappear in the crowd of people, and she felt good and loose and she thought that if she started walking down the hill at that moment, she would walk with the light movements of a puppet and never touch the ground at all.

She thought she would sit down for a moment now that everyone was gone, but when she looked around she saw Joe Melby still standing behind her. "I thought you went with the others."

"Nope."

"It's been a very strange day for me." She looked at the horizon where the swans had disappeared.

"It's been one of my stranger days too."

"Well, I'd better go home."

Joe walked a few steps with her, cleared his throat, and then said, "Do you want to go to Bennie Hoffman's party with me?"

She thought she hadn't heard him right for a moment, or if she had, that it was a mistake, like the boy who shouted, "Hey, beautiful," at Rosey Camdon.

"What?"

"I asked if you wanted to go with me to the party."

"I wasn't invited." She made herself think of the swans. By this time they could probably see the lake at the university and were about to settle down on the water with a great beating of wings and ruffling of feathers. She could almost see the long perfect glide that would bring them to the water.

"I'm inviting you. Bennie said I could

bring somebody if I wanted to. He begged me to bring someone, as a matter of fact. He and Sammy and John and Pete have formed this musical group and they're going to make everybody listen to them."

"Well, I don't know."

"Why not? Other than the fact that you're going to have to listen to some terrible guitar playing. Bennie Hoffman has had about one and a half lessons."

"Well . . ."

"It's not any big deal, just sitting in Bennie Hoffman's back yard and watching him louse up with a two-hundred-dollar guitar and amplifier."

"I guess I could go."

"I'll walk over and pick you up in half an hour. It won't matter if we're late. The last fifty songs will sound about the same as the first fifty."

"I'll be ready."

When Sara came up the walk Wanda was standing on the porch. "What is going on around here, will you tell me that? Where is Charlie?"

"We found him. He's with Aunt Willie, wherever that is."

"Do you know how I heard he was lost? I heard it on the car radio when I was coming home. How do you think that made me feel—to hear from some disc jockey that my own brother was missing? I could hardly get here because there are a hundred cars full of people jamming the street down there."

"Well, he's fine."

"So Mr. Aker told me, only I would like to see him and find out what happened."

"He got up during the night sometime—this is what I think happened—to go see the swans and ended up in a ravine crying his heart out."

Wanda stepped off the porch and looked across the street, leaning to see around the foliage by the fence. She said, "Is that them over there on the Carsons' porch?"

Sara looked and nodded.

"Honestly, Charlie still in his pajamas, and Aunt Willie in her good green dress with a handkerchief tied around her forehead to keep her from sweating, and both of them eating watermelon. That beats all."

"At least he's all right."

Wanda started down the walk, then paused. "You want to come?"

"No, I'm going to a party."

"Whose?"

"Bennie Hoffman's."

"I didn't think you were invited."

"Joe Melby's taking me."

"Joe Melby? Your great and terrible enemy?"

"He is not my enemy, Wanda. He is one of the nicest people I know."

"For three months I've been hearing about the evils of Joe Melby. Joe Melby, the thief; Joe Melby, the fink; Joe Melby, the—"

"A person," Sara said coldly, "can occasionally be mistaken." She turned and went into the living room, saw Boysie sleeping by the door and said, "Boysie, we found Charlie." She bent and rubbed him behind the ears. Then she went into the kitchen, made a sandwich, and was starting into the bedroom when the phone rang.

"Hello," she said, her mouth full of food.

"Hello, I have a long-distance call for Miss Willamina Godfrey," the operator said.

"Oh, she's across the street. If you'll wait a minute I'll go get her."

"Operator, I'll just talk to whoever's there," Sara heard her father say.

She said quickly, "No, I'll go get her. Just wait one minute. It won't take any time. She's right across the street."

"Sara? Is this Sara?"

"Yes, this is me." The strange feeling came over her again. "If you wait a minute I'll go get Aunt Willie."

"Sara, did you find Charlie?"

"Yes, we found him, but I don't mind going to get Aunt Willie. They're over on the Carsons' porch."

"Is Charlie all right?"

"He's fine. He's eating watermelon right now."

"Where was he?"

"Well, he went up into the woods and got lost. We found him in a ravine and he was dirty and tired and hungry but he's all right."

"That's good. I was going to come home tonight if he hadn't been found."

"Oh."

"But since everything's all right, I guess I'll just wait until the weekend."

"Sure."

"So I'll probably see you Saturday, then, if nothing turns up."

"Fine."

"Be sure to tell Willie I called."

"I will."

A picture came into her mind of the laughing, curly-headed man with the broken tooth in the photograph album, and she suddenly saw life as a series of huge, uneven steps, and she saw herself on the steps, standing motionless in her prison shirt, and she had just taken an enormous step up out of the shadows, and she was standing, waiting, and there were other steps in front of her, so that she could go as high as the sky, and she saw Charlie on a flight of small difficult steps, and her father down at the bottom of some steps, just sitting and not trying to go further. She saw everyone she knew on those blinding white steps and for a moment everything was clearer than it had ever been.

"Sara?"

"I'm still here."

"Well, that was all I wanted, just to hear that Charlie was all right."

"He's fine."

"And I'll see you on Saturday if nothing happens."

"Sure."

"Good-bye."

She sat for a minute still holding the receiver and then she set it back on the telephone and finished her sandwich. Slowly she slipped off her tennis shoes and looked down at her feet, which were dyed blue. Then she got up quickly and went to get ready for the party.

IDENTIFYING FACTS

1. Why is routine so important to Charlie?

2. Explain how Charlie is found.

3. After the crowd of people leaves them alone, what does Joe ask Sara?

4. At the end of the novel, Sara seems quite different from the person she was at the beginning. Find the passages that describe how Sara feels she has **changed.**

INTERPRETING MEANINGS

5. The **climax** of a novel is that exciting or emotional moment when you find out how the main problem will turn out. What is the climax of this novel? How did you feel at this moment?

6. On page 710 Sara compares life to a series of steps. How is her flight of steps different from Charlie's? What is her father's flight of steps like?

7. At the end of this passage, Sara sees that "everything was clearer than it had ever been." What do you think is now clear to Sara?

8. Is Charlie different from the person he was at the beginning of the novel? Give a reason for your answer.

9. Are all the problems or **conflicts** in the story resolved by the end of the novel? For example, is Sara's problem concerning her father resolved?

APPLYING MEANINGS

10. Suppose Sara had not experienced the loss of her brother. Do you think she would have come to realize what was of true worth in life anyway? What other experiences could make a person "see life clearly"?

Literary Elements

THEME

Theme is the idea or truth about human life revealed in a story or novel. Here are some questions that will help you identify the theme in *The Summer of the Swans.*

1. The **title** of a novel often has something to do with its theme. What are some characteristics of the swans? In what ways is Charlie like the swans?

2. How does Sara, the main character, **change** in the story? What causes the change?

3. Think of how Sara's search for Charlie is like a **quest.** Even before Charlie leaves the house on his own quest for the swans, what is Sara searching for? Sara finds Charlie, but what else has she **discovered** at the end of the novel?

Discuss in class what the novel has revealed to you. As part of your discussion, compose two possible statements of the novel's theme. (Remember that there is no one true way to state a theme.)

Language and Vocabulary

DIALOGUE

Byars's witty dialogue sounds, to most readers, exactly the way real people talk. Among the characteristics of her dialogue are the use of slang and exaggeration.

Slang is a kind of informal language that is usually spoken by a particular group of people. Teenagers are particularly good at making up new slang words.

Two of Sara's favorite slang words are *fink* and *gross*. Sometimes she makes an adjective out of *fink* and says *finky*. Can you write a dictionary definition for each of these slang words? After each definition, write a sentence using the word. Identify each word's part of speech.

One characteristic of slang is that it is not welcome in formal situations. Someone delivering a formal speech to the School Board would not use slang. What words could you use in these sentences to replace the slang words *finky, gross,* and *tuff?*

1. "You remember when that *finky* Jim Wilson got you on the seesaw?"

2. "This piece of candy is so *gross* that I don't even want to touch it . . ."

3. "Their clothes are so *tuff* and they're invited to every party . . .

Exaggeration stretches the truth by describing things as much greater than they really are. Sometimes the characters in this novel use exaggeration for comic effect. Sometimes they use exaggeration to emphasize how they feel. Explain why the characters use exaggeration in each of these speeches. (What point is each one making?)

1. After Aunt Willie gets off the motor scooter, Frank says "there's not a drop of blood circulating" in his arms. (Page 658)

2. Sara complains to Mary that her awful orange sneakers make her look "like Donald Duck." (Page 661)

3. Sara tells Wanda, "The peak of my whole life so far was in third grade when I got to be milk monitor." (Page 667)

Writing About Literature

USING ANOTHER POINT OF VIEW
Suppose Charlie is telling his own story. Charlie can't speak, but he certainly can think and he certainly has feelings. Narrate the events that take place in one part of this novel, but let Charlie tell the story, using the first-person pronoun *I.* You might have Charlie tell about the time he sees the swans; the time he loses his way; the time his watch breaks; the day after he is found.

ANALYZING A CHANGE IN CHARACTER
Betsy Byars says that early in her career, a teacher told her that in a good children's novel, the main character had to be different by the end of the book. "That made instant sense to me," said Byars. "If what happened to your character was important enough, then the person would be changed . . . I take characters, ordinary people, and throw them into a crisis, and I think that is one reason I haven't done a sequel—I feel one crisis is enough for anybody."

Write at least one paragraph in which you explain how Sara has changed in this novel, and why she changed. Before you write, you might fill out a chart like the one on page 714 to gather your details.

Sara	Story at start	Story at end
1. Feelings about Charlie.		
2. Feelings about Joe.		
3. Feelings about herself.		
4. Feelings about her father.		
Crisis in Sara's life:		

Open your paragraph with a sentence that states your general topic. Note that the example below includes the title and author.

In *The Summer of the Swans* by Betsy Byars, Sara is a character who changes as a result of a crisis in her life.

Focus on Persuasive Writing

ORGANIZING A PERSUASIVE PAPER
Use an outline like the one below to organize your ideas for a persuasive essay:

I. Introduction
   A. Attention grabber
   B. Opinion statement
II. Body
   Supporting reasons, facts, expert opinions
III. Conclusion
   A. Restatement of opinion
   B. Call to action (if appropriate)

Organize your supporting details in a logical way. You may want to use **order of importance.** In this method, you present details from least to most important, or the reverse.

Remember to use **transitions** to help your readers or listeners understand the connections between ideas. Here are some helpful transitions for order of importance:

first	mainly	second
last	most important	third

Choose a topic for a persuasive paper. Write a one-sentence opinion statement that expresses your view. Then prepare an outline for your essay, using the one above as a guideline. Next, exchange outlines with a partner. Give each other suggestions for making your papers clearer and more persuasive. Save your notes.

About the Author

Betsy Byars (1928–   ), one of the most popular of all young adult novelists, was born in Charlotte, North Carolina, and graduated from Queens College there. She began writing mystery stories and magazine articles when her husband was in graduate school in Illinois and her children were very young. Her first successful children's novel was *The Midnight Fox* (1968), a realistic story about a city boy who overcomes his fear of animals.

Byars says that she always asked her four children to read her manuscripts, and she admits that they were not tactful about what they didn't like.

Many of her books began with a newspaper story or an event from her own children's lives. The character of Charlie in her most famous novel, *The Summer of the Swans,* grew out of some volunteer work she was doing with children with mental retardation. The plot for the novel came from an article that Byars read in a local newspaper. The article told about the search for an elderly man who wandered away from a picnic and got lost. The swans, she says, came from an article about swans at the university in Greenville, South Carolina, who "persist in leaving their beautiful lake and flying to less desirable ponds." *The Summer of the Swans* not only won the Newbery Award, but also was named a Junior Literary Club book, a *Horn Book* honor book, and an American Library Association Notable Book. Her other works include *Seven Treasure Hunts, Wanted . . . Mud Blosson,* and *McMummy.*

Byars now lives in Clemson, South Carolina. "There is no activity in my life," she has said, "which has brought me more pleasure than my writing." How does it feel to have a mother who is a famous young adult novelist? When one of Byars' daughters was fourteen years old and was asked this question, she replied, "Well, it's no big deal."

Behind the Scenes

Winning the Newbery

In 1968, I participated in a volunteer program sponsored by West Virginia University. Anybody who was interested—truck drivers, housewives, miners—signed up to help kids who were having learning difficulties in school. I got a third-grade girl and a first-grade boy.

This was a stunning experience for me. Up until this time I had never been around kids who were having real problems in learning. I had not been aware of how much they suffered, not only because they had learning difficulties, but—more importantly—because of the way other kids treated them.

Charlie, the character in *The Summer of the Swans,* was neither of the kids I tutored, but I would never have written the book if I had not known them.

I did a lot of research on the character of Charlie in the Medical Library of W.V.U. I found three case histories of kids who had had brain damage because of high-fevered illnesses when they were babies, and that's where Charlie came from. All the details of his life were from those three case histories. I made nothing up.

I worked hard on the book and I was proud of it. It was published in April of 1970 to a sort of resounding thud. It didn't sell well, it didn't get great reviews; in some papers it didn't get reviewed at all.

I went through a very discouraging period. Maybe, I thought, I am just not going to make it as a first-rate writer. Maybe I never will be good enough. Maybe I should consider doing something else. That fall I enrolled at West Virginia University to get my master's degree in special education.

I had now published seven books, but I had never had one of those long editorial lunches at a swanky New York restaurant that you read about. I had never been in a publisher's office. I had never even met an editor. My contacts with my editors had consisted of long letters and brief phone calls. I did not know a single other writer. Despite having published seven books, I was as green as grass.

I was leaving for class one morning in January when the phone rang. I answered it, and a woman's voice said, "This is Sara Fenwick and I'm Chairman of the Newbery-Caldecott Committee." My heart rose. "We've been in Los Angeles for the past week going over possible Newbery-Caldecott winners." My heart sank. I realized what she wanted now. She wanted to ask me some questions about writing *The Summer of the Swans,* and I would not be able to answer the questions intelligently and she would go back to the committee and say, "The woman is an idiot."

"And," she continued, "I am so pleased to tell you that your book *The Summer of the Swans* has won the Newbery Award."

I was stunned. I went blank. I couldn't say a word. She said, "Mrs. Byars, are you there?"

I managed to say, "Yes."

She said, "Mrs. Byars, have you ever heard of the Newbery Award?"

I said, "Yes."

Obviously, it was not one of my shining hours. At the end of the conversation, she said, "We're having a champagne reception on Thursday and we wish you could be with us."

I uttered my first complete sentence of the conversation. "I wish I could too."

It was midafternoon before my editor called. She said, "What time are you leaving for Los Angeles?"

I said I wasn't planning to go.

She said, "Of course you're going. Get your reservations and call me back."

I got the reservations, rushed downtown and bought two Newbery Award-type outfits. The next morning at seven o'clock I was on my way to Los Angeles. I was a nervous wreck.

When I got out there, it turned out that I had to be hidden for a day and a half to keep people from suspecting I was the new winner. Actually I could have passed freely among all the librarians, not once falling under suspicion. In fact, one of the things someone said after the announcement was, "It's so refreshing to have someone win that nobody ever heard of."

The announcement of the Newbery Award literally changed my life overnight. Up until this time I had had a few letters from kids. Now we had to get a bigger mailbox. I got tapes, questionnaires, invitations to speak, invitations to visit schools, requests for interviews. For the first time in my life, I started feeling like an author.

—Betsy Byars

DISTINGUISHING BETWEEN FACTS AND OPINIONS

A fact is something that has happened or is true. An **opinion** is a statement of belief or judgment. Facts can be checked or verified. People can (and do) disagree about opinions. For example, the statement that Washington, D.C., is our nation's capital is a fact. The statement that Washington is a beautiful city, on the other hand, is an opinion.

Good readers are able to distinguish between facts and opinions. Read the passage below from the essay "Wetlands" by Seymour Simon. Then use a separate sheet of paper to answer the questions that follow.

> Wetlands range in size from those that cover only a fraction of an acre to the huge swamps and marshes of Florida, the Carolinas, Georgia, and Louisiana. The large prairie potholes of the midwestern United States and Canada provide nesting places for two-thirds of the more than ten million North American ducks and other waterfowl, while millions more nest in the swamps and marshes of the southeastern United States.
>
> Wetlands are important to people. They act like natural sponges, helping protect against floods. They recycle decaying plant and animal materials and allow the chemicals in them to be used again by living things. Wetlands filter pollutants and cleanse fresh waters better than any sewage-treatment plant ever built. Wetlands are places for fishing and small boats and are also spots of peace and quiet beauty. . . .
>
> Many people and nature organizations are working to save our remaining wetlands. All of us can help, too, by learning about our local wetlands and telling our friends and families how wonderful wetlands really are and how they need to be protected. You may not want to live in a swamp or a bog, but wetlands are some of the world's most interesting places to explore and treasure.

Distinguishing Between Facts and Opinions—from *Wetlands*

1. Which paragraph consists entirely of facts?

2. List four facts from the passage about wetlands.

3. In which paragraph does the author try to persuade you to do something? What does he want you to do?

4. Use a sentence of your own to state the author's opinion about wetlands.

FOCUS ON *Writing*

WRITING A PERSUASIVE ESSAY

*W*hat do a campaign speech, a movie advertisement, and a sermon have in common? They are all examples of persuasion. In **persuasive writing** you state an opinion on an issue and then try to convince your audience. In the writing assignments in this unit, you have learned some of the key elements of persuasion. Now you will have a chance to write a persuasive essay of your own.

Prewriting ～～

1. List some topics that you care about. Then jot down your opinion on each one. The topic you choose for your paper should be a subject about which people can disagree, rather than a matter of fact. Remember how to distinguish between facts and opinions:

   - A **fact** is something that has happened or is true.
   - An **opinion** is a statement of belief or judgment.

   For your persuasive essay, choose an issue that you think is important and that also matters to your audience.

2. Use one sentence to state your opinion on the issue. This **opinion statement** will be the **main idea** of your essay. [See **Focus** assignment on page 669.]

3. Think about how to make the best appeal to your **audience.** Ask yourself questions like these:

   - What are my readers likely to know already about the topic?
   - What opinions are they likely to have?
   - What reasons will appeal to them most?
   - Will I ask them to take an action?

4. Find support for your opinion. Here are some kinds of support you can use in a persuasive essay or speech:

   - facts ▪ reasons ▪ expert opinions

   [See **Focus** assignment on page 689.]

5. Evaluate your support. The following are two misleading types of support that you should avoid in your paper:

   - **Bandwagon:** urging people to think or do something simply because "everybody" believes or does it. Example: "Don't be the only holdout. Join the In-Line Skating Club today!"
   - **Testimonial:** using the statement of a celebrity or another person who doesn't know very much about the topic. Example: "Singer Paul Lorenzo thinks in-line skates are cool!" [Notice that testimonial is an emotional appeal quite different from the logical appeal of *expert* opinion.]

Writing

1. When you write your first draft, use an **outline** like the one below.

   I. Introduction
      A. Attention-grabber
      B. Opinion statement
   II. Body
      A. Most important fact, reason, or expert opinion
      B. Next supporting detail
      C. Additional support, if necessary
   III. Conclusion
      A. Restatement of opinion
      B. Call to action (if appropriate)

(If you wish, you can reverse the order in the body of your paper, starting with the least important supporting argument and ending with the most important detail.)

2. **Word choices** are especially important for a persuasive writer. As you work on your draft, pay special attention to the impact your choice of words might have on your audience. For example, if you were trying to persuade a parents' association to buy new uniforms for a sports team, would you refer to the uniforms as *hot, comfortable, fashionable,* or *neat?* If you were giving a speech about recycling to a community group, would you use the pronouns *you* and *your* or the pronouns *we, us,* and *our?* When you choose your words, remember that the purpose of persuasive writing and speaking is to convince your audience to identify with you and to adopt your point of view.

3. Use **transitions** to make the relation-ship of your ideas clear. Some helpful **transitional words and phrases** include the following:

also	first	second
another	last	then
but	mainly	therefore
finally	most important	third

[See **Focus** assignment on page 714.]

Evaluating and Revising

1. When you revise your essay, pay special attention to evaluating your reasons. Have you presented strong, specific evidence to support your opinion? Have you arranged your ideas clearly?

Here is how one writer revised a paragraph in a persuasive paper about recycling.

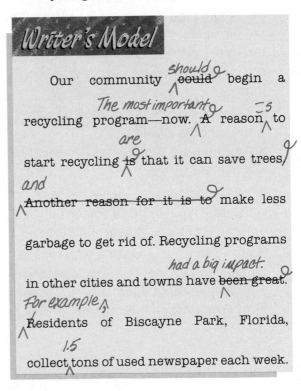

Writer's Model

Our community ~~could~~ *should* begin a recycling program—now. ~~A~~ *The most important* reason *—s* to start recycling ~~is~~ *are* that it can save trees *and* ~~Another reason for it is to~~ make less garbage to get rid of. Recycling programs in other cities and towns ~~have been great~~ *had a big impact.* *For example,* Residents of Biscayne Park, Florida, collect *1.5* tons of used newspaper each week.

2. You may find the following checklist helpful as you revise your essay.

Checklist for Evaluation and Revision

✔ Does the beginning grab the reader's attention?

✔ Do I state my opinion clearly?

✔ Do I use supporting details such as facts, reasons, and expert opinions?

✔ Is my reasoning sound?

✔ Have I organized my support in a logical way?

✔ Do I end with a strong conclusion?

Proofreading and Publishing ∿

1. Proofread your persuasive essay and correct any errors you find in grammar, usage, and mechanics. (Here you may find it helpful to refer to the **Handbook for Revision** on pages 750–785.) Then prepare a final version of your essay by making a clean copy.

2. Consider some of the following ways to publish and share your essay:

- post your essay on the class bulletin board
- organize a debate with one or more classmates
- deliver your essay as a speech in class
- send your essay as an editorial to the school or local paper

Portfolio If your teacher approves, you may wish to keep a copy of your work in your writing folder or portfolio.

Books FOR *Further Reading*

Some selections in this anthology (such as *Julie of the Wolves* by Jean Craighead George on page 3) are taken from novels or other book-length works. If you enjoy these excerpts, you will enjoy reading the books they come from. Here are some other books that will almost certainly give you a lot to think about.

CHARACTERS

Byars, Betsy, *Cracker Jackson* (Viking, 1985; paperback, Puffin)

When a twelve-year-old boy gets an anonymous note, he realizes that his former babysitter is in big trouble. You can't make a bad choice reading any of Byars's novels. She takes young people seriously and makes you feel that you too can make a difference.

Lord, Bette Bao, *In the Year of the Boar and Jackie Robinson* (Harper & Row, 1984)

This novel tells about a spunky Chinese girl who emigrates with her family to the United States in 1947. Shirley Temple Wong finds acceptance when she excels at baseball.

Mohr, Nicholasa, *Going Home* (Dial, 1986)

In this sequel to *Felita,* a twelve-year-old girl learns a lot about herself when she visits her parents' birthplace in Puerto Rico. You will especially enjoy Felita's warm and caring family.

Soto, Gary, *Baseball in April* (Harcourt Brace Jovanovich, 1990)

These stories are based on Soto's experiences growing up Latino in central California.

QUESTS

Alexander, Lloyd, *The High King* (Henry Holt, 1968; paperback, Dell)

This is the final book in the Prydain series. The others are *The Book of Three, The Black Cauldron, The Castle of Llyr,* and *Taran Wanderer.* In *The High King,* Taran, an orphan and former pig-keeper, completes his marvelous quest to save Prydain from its evil enemies. After you read this series, if you're hungry for more high fantasy, try *The Dark Is Rising* (Harcourt Brace Jovanovich, 1966), the first in a wonderful six-book series by Susan Cooper.

L'Engle, Madeline, *A Wrinkle in Time* (Farrar, Straus & Giroux, 1962; paperback, many editions)

This is the first of four fascinating fantasies about three young people whose quest for a kidnapped scientist (the father of two of them) takes them into a time warp. The other books in this series are *A Wind in the Door, A Swiftly Tilting Planet,* and *Many Waters.*

O'Dell, Scott, *Island of the Blue Dolphins* (Houghton Mifflin, 1960; paperback, Dell)

> You won't be able to forget Karana, a nineteenth-century Native American girl who survives all alone on an island for eighteen years. This novel is based on real historical events.

Rawls, Wilson, *Where the Red Fern Grows* (Doubleday, 1961; paperback, Bantam)

> A ten-year-old boy saves for two years to buy hunting dogs. This is an exciting and sad story of a boy's coming-of-age.

Speare, Elizabeth, *The Sign of the Beaver* (Houghton Mifflin, 1983; paperback, Dell)

> This gripping quest for survival is set in Maine before the Revolutionary War. Matt's father has to leave him alone to guard the family's cabin. Winter sets in and Matt has very little food left. Will the Penobscot boy he meets save his life—or take it?

SHORT STORIES

Aiken, Joan, *The Last Slice of Rainbow, and Other Stories* (Harper, 1988)

> Joan Aiken's imaginative stories are always different from anything you have read before.

Singer, Isaac Bashevis, *Stories for Children* (Farrar, Straus & Giroux, 1984)

> This fine collection includes more than 30 stories set long ago in the Jewish district of Warsaw, in Poland.

Yolen, Jane, Martin B. Greenberg, and Charles G. Waugh, *Dragons & Dreams: A Collection of New Fantasy and Science Fiction Stories* (Harper & Row, 1986)

> Some of the best-known writers of science fiction and fantasy contributed stories to this collection.

POETRY

Atwood, Ann, *Haiku: The Mood of the Earth* (Scribner, 1971)

> Each of the twenty-five haiku in this collection is illustrated with two full-color photographs. Atwood teaches you about haiku, as well as providing beautiful examples of it.

Giovanni, Nikki, *Spin a Soft Black Song* (Hill & Wang, 1985)

> This popular collection includes poems about family relationships and events that are important to all children.

Silverstein, Shel, *Where the Sidewalk Ends* (Harper, 1974) and *A Light in the Attic* (Harper, 1981)

> Silverstein needs no introduction. Both of these collections are more popular than the fiction books at many libraries. This poet seems to know exactly how to appeal to young people.

Sneve, Virginia Driving Hawk, *Dancing Teepees* (Holiday House, 1989)

> This beautifully illustrated collection combines traditional Native American

poetry and poems written by tribal poets today.

BIOGRAPHY AND AUTOBIOGRAPHY

Kerr, M. E., *Me Me Me Me Me: Not a Novel* (Harper & Row, 1983)

A well-known author of young adult novels tells about her teenage years. If you think you want to become a writer some day, you should read this often humorous autobiography.

Lawson, Robert, *Ben and Me* (Little, Brown, 1939; paperback, Dell)

This book is told from the unique point of view of a mouse, Amos, who enjoyed the friendship of the great Ben Franklin.

HISTORY

Fisher, Leonard Everett, *Pyramid of the Sun, Pyramid of the Moon* (Macmillan, 1988)

If you want to know more about the Indian civilizations of Mexico, this is the book for you. It takes you through the invasion of Cortés in 1520.

SCIENCE

Macaulay, David, *The Way Things Work* (Houghton Mifflin, 1988)

This clearly written text explains complicated machinery in a fascinating way. Look also for his book *Pyramid* (Houghton Mifflin, 1975).

PERSONAL ESSAYS

Bombeck, Erma, *Family: The Ties That Bind . . . and Gag* (McGraw-Hill, 1987)

These wise and witty essays about family life are fun for all ages to read.

PLAYS

George, Richard, *Roald Dahl's Charlie and the Chocolate Factory: A Play* (Penguin, 1983)

A sixth-grade teacher did this adaptation of the well-known story by Roald Dahl, and his class enacted it. Dahl liked the adaptation so much that he wrote an introduction for it.

Winther, Barbara, *Plays from Folktales of Africa and Asia* (Plays, Inc., 1975)

This collection includes six plays based on folktales from Africa, six based on folktales from India and the Near East, and seven from the Far East.

MYTHS AND FOLK TALES

Bryan, Ashley, *Lion and the Ostrich Chicks and Other African Tales* (Macmillan, 1986)

This book contains retellings of legends from the Bushman, Masai, Hausa, and Angolan peoples of Africa.

Caduto, Michael J., and Joseph Bruhac, *Keepers of the Earth* (Fulcrum, Inc., 1988)

This collection unites each Native American folktale with related environmental activities. If you are interested in ecology, and if you want to understand more about how Native

Americans respected and celebrated nature, you must read this book.

D'Aulaire, Ingri, and Edgar Parin, *D'Aulaire's Book of Greek Myths* (Doubleday, 1962)

This beautifully illustrated book contains the best-known Greek myths. If you are interested in Norse, or Scandinavian, mythology, see *D'Aulaire's Norse Gods and Giants* (Doubleday, 1986).

Riordan, James, *The Woman in the Moon and Other Tales of Forgotten Heroines* (Dial, 1985)

These traditional stories feature strong, capable women.

Yep, Laurence, *The Rainbow People* (Harper & Row, 1989)

Yep retells twenty magical and mysterious tales originally told by Chinese immigrants in Oakland, California.

NOVELS

Babbitt, Natalie, *Tuck Everlasting* (Farrar, Straus & Giroux, 1975)

Ten-year-old Winnie meets the mysterious Tuck family and learns their amazing secret—but what will she do with it? This novel raises some profound questions.

Banks, Lynn Reid, *The Indian in the Cupboard* (Doubleday, 1981; paperback, Avon)

Omri isn't too excited about his birthday present—a little plastic Indian figure. Then, he finds out how to make the toy come to life. The sequel is *The Return of the Indian* (Doubleday, 1986).

Boyd, Candy Dawson, *Forever Friends,* originally titled *Breadsticks and Blessing Places* (Penguin, 1986)

A sixth grader has trouble accepting her best friend's death in an accident, but her family helps her when she needs it most. This is the second book by an African American writer who grew up in Chicago.

Cleaver, Bill, and Vera Cleaver, *Where the Lilies Bloom* (Lippincott, 1969; paperback, New American Library)

A fourteen-year-old girl in Appalachia struggles to keep her brother and three sisters together. After their father dies, the children pretend to the neighbors that he is still alive and taking care of them.

Howe, James, *Bunnicula: A Rabbit Tale of Mystery* (Atheneum, 1974; paper, Avon)

This is the first in a comical series featuring a family cat and dog who talk like humans. The cat suspects that the new pet, a rabbit, is a vampire. Other books in this series are *The Celery Stalks at Midnight, Howliday Inn,* and *Nighty Nightmare.*

Taylor, Mildred, *Roll of Thunder, Hear My Cry* (Dial, 1976; paperback, Bantam)

This unforgettable novel tells about a close-knit African American family that endures prejudice during the 1930s. It is also about bravery and love. The sequel is *Let the Circle Be Unbroken* (Dial, 1981).

WRITING ABOUT LITERATURE

Reasons for Writing About Literature

You will often be asked in English class to write about the literature you read. Sometimes you will be given a topic to work on: for example, as a homework assignment or in response to an examination question. At other times you may have to choose your own subject.

Writing about a literary work is a good way of getting to know it better. Before you write a composition about a story, a poem, or a play, you must study the selection carefully. Usually, you will want to examine its literary elements, such as characters, setting, point of view, conflict, and suspense. Your appreciation and enjoyment of a work will grow as your understanding of it deepens.

Another reason for writing about literature is that it develops your skills in critical thinking. In writing an analysis or an evaluation of a work, you sharpen your ability to think in certain ways, such as identifying cause and effect or comparing and contrasting. Before you write, you must sort out your thoughts and reach conclusions. You will find all these skills valuable in many areas throughout your life.

Finally, writing about literature can be a way to explore your own ideas and feelings and to express your personal reactions. How do you respond to a certain character, and why? What are the reasons for your own evaluation, or judgment, of a work? How would you persuade your family or friends to read a certain piece of literature (or *not* to read it)? When you write about literature, these are some of the questions you can ask and answer.

Using the Writing Process

Writing is called a *process* because it involves several steps, or stages. Here is a summary of the stages of the writing process.

1. *Prewriting.* Gather your information and organize your ideas.

2. *Writing.* Put your ideas down on paper or on a word processor.

3. *Evaluating and Revising.* Look critically at your writing and decide how it can be made clearer and more forceful. Then make changes to improve your writing.

4. *Proofreading and Publishing.* Correct errors in grammar, usage, punctuation, capitalization, and spelling. Then share your work with others, either in written form or orally.

As you write, you will move freely back and forth among these stages. When you are proofreading, for example, you may find that you need to add some new ideas in a part of your essay. Then you will have to move back to the prewriting stage.

The following pages contain more information about each step in the writing process.

PREWRITING

The first stage, prewriting, can be divided into three important steps.

1. *Be sure you understand the assignment.* Words such as *analyze, describe, discuss, explain, compare,* and *contrast* often appear in writing assignments. These words describe your *purpose* in writing. Before you begin to write, make certain that you understand what these words mean.

Often, your teacher will ask you to write about the elements of a story, poem, or play. You might be asked to write about *plot, setting, character,* or *theme.* You will find these elements defined in *Literary Terms and Techniques,* pages 738–749.

2. *Gather your ideas.* You might gather ideas by brainstorming or clustering. *Brainstorming* means jotting down ideas as quickly as they come to you. Do not stop to decide if the ideas are helpful. (You can evaluate your ideas later.) If your teacher approves, brainstorm with a classmate. If you brainstorm in a small group, one person should write down all the ideas that the group members suggest.

In *clustering,* you use a visual kind of brainstorming. Write your subject in the center of a piece of paper and draw a circle around it. Then, around the subject, write related ideas and circle these. Draw lines to connect them with the subject or with each other. Keep going by writing additional ideas, circling them, and drawing lines to show connections.

Here is an example of a cluster diagram about Sara in Betsy Byars' novel *The Summer of the Swans* (page 648).

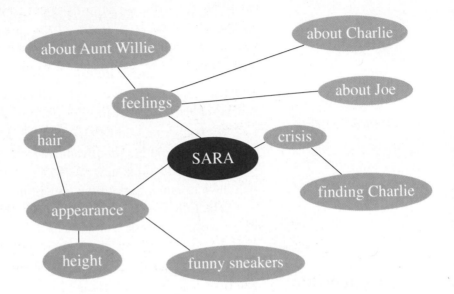

You can also gather ideas by using *character wheels* (see page 733) or *reporter's questions* (Who? What? When? Where? Why? How?).

3. *Organize your ideas.* Next, think about how you are going to organize all your information. One way to do this is to look over your material and write a sentence that states the main idea you want to focus on. A *topic sentence* states the main idea of a paragraph; a *thesis statement* states the main idea of an essay or report. A topic sentence or thesis statement should be followed up with details that support the main idea. For example, here is a rough outline for a paragraph on Ray Bradbury's story, "All Summer in a Day" (page 194).

Topic Sentence: In "All Summer in a Day" by Ray Bradbury, the children have strong reasons for disliking Margot.

Reason 1: She stays separate and alone.

Reason 2: She's the only one who remembers the sun.

Reason 3: She has acted strangely, and her parents plan to take her back to Earth.

The topic sentence usually comes at the beginning of a paragraph, but it can also come at the end.

WRITING

Use your prewriting plan and notes to write a first draft of your essay. As you write, don't worry about correcting mistakes. You can do that at several later stages of the process—for example, when you revise and proofread. The important thing now is just to get your ideas down on paper or on a word processor.

EVALUATING AND REVISING

When you *evaluate* your writing, you decide what changes you need to make in your first draft. You may evaluate your writing alone, or you may exchange papers with a classmate and evaluate each other's work. It's a good idea to reread your first draft at least twice. The first time, evaluate your *content:*

1. Have you answered the question or done what the assignment asks?

2. Have you stated your main idea clearly?

3. Have you supported or explained the main idea with specific details?

On your second reading, evaluate your *writing style:*

4. Is the order of your ideas clear and logical?

5. Have you included a conclusion that states the main idea again or that summarizes the main points?

6. Are your ideas clearly stated and easy to understand?

7. Have you used transitional words and phrases to show relationships of ideas?

8. Have you been too wordy or unnecessarily repetitious?

9. Does your paragraph (or essay) read smoothly?

When you *revise,* you write your changes on your first draft. Evaluating and revising often occur at the same time. You actually make the changes as you decide what needs to be done. Here are four helpful methods you can use to revise an essay.

1. You can add details or restate them.

2. You can delete (take out) details.

3. You can move details around.

4. You can replace some details with others.

PROOFREADING AND PUBLISHING

When you *proofread* your paper, you correct errors in grammar, usage, punctuation, capitalization, and spelling. Keep these rules in mind as you proofread.

1. Titles of short stories, poems, and essays should have quotation marks around them. Titles of long works like plays and novels should be underlined.

2. Each sentence should begin with a capital letter.

3. Each sentence should end with a period, a question mark, or an exclamation point.

4. Proper nouns and proper adjectives should be capitalized.

5. All words should be spelled correctly.

6. Verb forms should be correct.

7. Verbs should agree with their subjects.

8. Pronouns should be used correctly. The referents or pronouns should be clear (see page 564).

9. Quotation marks should be placed around direct quotations from a story, poem, play, essay, or novel.

10. Commas or periods should go *inside* the closing quotation marks.

Below is a chart showing some useful proofreading symbols.

Symbol	Example	Meaning of Symbol
≡	Pine street	Capitalize a lowercase letter.
∧	fabulus	Insert a word, letter, or punctuation mark.
ℛ	I am am here.	Cut a word, letter, or punctuation mark.
⌒	Here's my key.	Leave out and close up.
⟲	Please give us the books and them.	Transfer the circled material.
¶	It was early.	Begin a new paragraph.
⊙	Take this pen	Add a period.
⋀	Oh I'm not so sure.	Add a comma.

The paragraph below shows the changes that one writer made while revising and proofreading an essay about "All Summer in a Day." Notice that the writer has added some details, changed some wording, and moved a sentence around. The writer has also corrected some spellings and punctuation marks.

In "All Summer in a Day" the children have strong reasons for dislikeing Margot. She keeps to herself, *separated and alone.* she refuses to play games with them "in the echoing tunnels of the underground city." ~~She is different from them in many ways.~~ Margot looks strange, too she is pale, *and thin and washed-out looking.* But the children hate Margot most of all for two reasons. First, she is different because she remembers Earth, *and what the sun is like.* Second, her parents plan to take her back to Earth. Bradbury sums up *the children's* there reasons for hatred by saying: They hated her pale snow face, her waiting silence, her thinness, and her possible future."

[For additional examples of revising and proofreading, see the model essays on pages 734–737, and in the *Handbook for Revision,* pages 750–785.]

When you *publish* your writing, you share it with an audience. Here are some publication methods you can consider:

1. Submitting your paper in an essay contest or to the school or community newspaper

2. Reading your essay aloud, either in class or to another appropriate audience

3. Joining with classmates to create an illustrated booklet or anthology of essays

4. Posting your essay on the class or hall bulletin board

5. Making your essay the basis for a performance, a slide show, or a video

Writing on a Topic of Your Own: A Character Sketch

A *character* in literature is usually a person, but characters may also be animals (like Hank the Cowdog) or fantasy creatures (like Heath the dragon). A *character sketch* describes someone's personality traits. A **trait** is a quality, such as intelligence, humor, stubbornness, or shyness. A character sketch answers the question, "What is this character like?"

Writers reveal a person's character in several ways:

1. By letting us hear what a character says

2. By letting us know a character's thoughts

3. By describing the appearance of a character

4. By describing the actions of a character

5. By letting us know what others say about the character

6. By telling us directly what a character is like (nasty, sweet, naive, stupid, wacky, and so on)

ASSIGNMENT: Write a short character sketch of Becky in "Becky and the Wheels-and-Brake Boys" by James Berry (page 220). Mention at least two of Becky's character traits.

PREWRITING Reread James Berry's story. Find passages where the author reveals something about Becky. Look at her words and thoughts and actions. Examine what other people say about her.

Then you could make a *character wheel* like the one on the opposite page. In your wheel, write a few of the character's important traits in wider sections. Underneath each section, list details and events from the story that illustrate each trait. (You could also gather ideas by using a cluster diagram.)

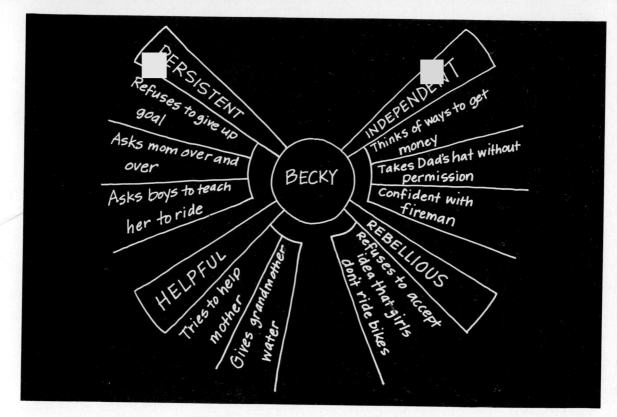

The diagram shows "BECKY" in the center with traits radiating out:

PERSISTENT
- Refuses to give up goal
- Asks mom over and over
- Asks boys to teach her to ride

INDEPENDENT
- Thinks of ways to get money
- Takes Dad's hat without permission
- Confident with fireman

HELPFUL
- Tries to help mother
- Gives grandmother water

REBELLIOUS
- Refuses to accept idea that girls don't ride bikes

WRITING   In a short character sketch, you should discuss only two or three character traits. Begin by writing a topic sentence that names the story or play you are writing about. In your first paragraph, identify the character you are describing, as well as the traits which you will discuss. Then explain or illustrate each trait with specific details, events, examples, or quotations.

On the next two pages is a model essay that presents a character sketch of Becky. The notes in the margin show important parts or features of the essay.

Final Copy

Title

GETTING HER OWN WAY

Introduction

Thesis

In "Becky and the Wheels-and-Brake Boys" by James Berry, Becky's words and actions show that she is a strong character who is determined to get her own way. When Becky sets out to get the bicycle she wants so badly, three of her character traits are especially important. She is persistent, independent, and rebellious.

Body

Topic sentence

Supporting details

Quotations

First, Becky shows her persistence by refusing to give up her goal—a bike of her own. Becky asks her mother over and over for a bike, and she refuses to take "no" for an answer. When her mother asks Becky if she still thinks about "that foolishness," Becky honestly answers, "I can't get rid of it, mam."

Topic sentence

Supporting details

Quotation

When Becky thinks of a way to earn money, she shows her independence. Without asking anyone's permission, she takes her father's sun helmet to sell, and she approaches the fireman all on her own. Becky knows exactly what she wants, and her instincts tell her to go straight to the top. Typically, when she arrives at the fire station she says, "I'd like to talk to the head man." Both her mother and the fireman seem amazed at Becky's behavior, but neither one scolds or punishes her.

Topic sentence

Becky is also rebellious. She refuses to accept the idea that there is "proper behavior" for a girl, although her mother, grandmother, and the

Supporting details

boys all believe that girls should restrict themselves to traditional roles like sewing and washing clothes. Although she risks the disapproval of her family and the boys, Becky still clings to making her dream of a bike come true.

Conclusion

Becky's persistence, independence, and rebelliousness pay off, because she gets what she wants in the end. She may have had a one-track mind about her bike, but it is hard not to admire her spirit.

EVALUATING AND REVISING

Use these questions to help you evaluate and revise your character sketch.

1. Do you begin with a strong topic sentence? In your introduction, do you name the work, the character, and two or three character traits?

2. Do you use specific details from the story to show how each trait is developed?

3. Have you arranged all your details in logical order?

4. Have you used transitional words and phrases to help your readers understand the connections between events and ideas?

5. Do you end with a strong conclusion?

PROOFREADING AND PUBLISHING

Use the guidelines on page 730 to proofread your work. Then write or type a clean copy and proofread *that* version as well. Finally, think of an appropriate way to share your writing.

Below you will find a rough draft of the essay that appears on pages 734–735. The notes in the margin show revision techniques, as well as the reasons for proofreading corrections. Study the two versions of the essay. Notice how the writer has revised the draft for greater clarity and accuracy.

MODEL ESSAY

Rough Draft

GETTING HER OWN WAY

Title

Comma after introductory phrases

In "Becky and the Wheels-and-Brake Boys" by James Berry Becky's words and actions show that she is a strong character who is determined

Additional detail

to get her own way. When Becky sets out to get the bicycle she wants so badly three of her character traits are especially important. She is persistent, independent, and rebellious.

Transition

First Becky shows her persistence by refusing to give up her goal—a bike of her own. Becky asks her mother over and over for a bike, and she refuses to take "no" for an answer. When her mother asks Becky if she

Direct quote

still thinks about "that foolishness," Becky answers honestly "I can't get rid of it, mam."

Transition; Sentences combined

When Becky thinks of a way to earn money, She shows her independence.

Added for clarity

Without asking anyone's permission, she takes her father's sun helmet to sell, and she approaches the fireman, all on her own. Becky knows exactly what she

Spelling

wants, and her instincts tell her to go straight to the top. Typicaly, when she arrives at the fire station she says, "I'd like to talk to the head man."

Subject-verb agreement

Both her mother and the fireman seems amazed at Becky's behavior, but neither one scolds or punishes her.

Transition

Becky is *also* rebellious. She refuses to accept the idea that there is

Commas with series

"proper behavior" for a girl, although her mother, grandmother, and the

Spelling

boys all believe that girls should restrict themselves to traditional roles like sewing and washing clothes. Although she risks the disapproval of

Comma after introductory adverb clause

her family and the boys, Becky still clings to making her dream of a bike come true.

Added for clarity

Becky's persistence, independence, and rebelliousness pay off, *because she gets what she wants in the end.* She may have had a one-track mind about her bike, but it is hard not to admire her spirit.

Literary Terms and Techniques

ALLITERATION *The repetition of the same, or very similar, sounds in words that are close together.* Alliteration usually occurs at the beginning of words, as in the phrase "*busy* as a *bee*." It can also occur within or at the ends of words. The following poem repeats the sounds of "s" and "p."

January

In January
it's so nice
while slipping
on the sliding ice
to sip hot chicken soup
with rice.
Sipping once
sipping twice
sipping chicken soup
with rice.
—Maurice Sendak

Alliteration can establish a mood, emphasize words, and serve as a memory aid. If you ever twisted your tongue around a line like "Suzy sells shells by the sea shore" or "How much wood could a woodchuck chuck if a woodchuck could chuck wood," you have already had some fun experiences with alliteration.

See page 300.

ALLUSION *A reference to something, such as a statement, a person, a place, or an event, that is known from literature, history,* religion, mythology, politics, sports, or science. Writers expect readers to recognize an allusion and to think almost at the same time about the literary work it comes from. In the excerpt from *The Lion, the Witch and the Wardrobe* (page 10), Mr. Tumnus calls Lucy "daughter of Eve." The Narnian faun is making an allusion to the Biblical story of Adam and Eve. The cartoon below makes an allusion you will recognize right away.

"Someone's been sleeping in my bed, too, and there she is on Screen Nine!"

Drawing by Shanahan; © 1989
The New Yorker Magazine, Inc.

AUTOBIOGRAPHY *An account of the writer's own life, or part of it.* The Diary of a Young Girl, a journal kept by Anne Frank as she and her family hid from the Nazis during World War II, is a well-known autobiographical work (see page 393). Bill Cosby's hilarious account of his own experiences parenting is called *Fatherhood* (see page 453). Roald Dahl (you might know him as the author of *Charlie and the Chocolate Factory*) writes about his experiences growing up in England in *Boy*. Benjamin Franklin tells the story of his own life in his famous *Autobiography*.

See pages 385, 393.
See also *Biography*.

BIOGRAPHY *An account of a real person's life, or part of it, written or told by another person.* A classic American biography is Carl Sandburg's life of Abraham Lincoln. In a library or bookstore you can find biographies of movie stars, television personalities, politicians, sports figures, self-made millionaires, and artists. Today, biographies are among the most popular forms of literature.

See pages 385, 393.
See also *Autobiography*.

CHARACTER *A person or an animal in a story, play, or other literary work.* In some works, such as the tales told by African Americans when they labored as slaves, animals are characters. In other works, such as fairy tales, a fantastic creature like a dragon is a character (see "Dragon, Dragon" on page 166). In still other works, a character is a god or a hero (see "Quetzalcoatl" on page 576). Most often, a character is an ordinary human being, as in *The Summer of the Swans* (page 648).

The way a writer reveals the personality of a character is called **characterization.** A writer can reveal character in six ways:

1. By describing how the character looks and dresses.
2. By letting us hear the character speak.
3. By showing us how the character acts.
4. By letting us know the character's inner thoughts and feelings.
5. By revealing what other people in the story think or say about the character.
6. By telling us directly what the character's personality is like (cruel, kind, sneaky, brave, and so on).

See pages 1, 157, 645.

CONFLICT *A struggle or clash between opposing characters or between opposing forces.* In an **external conflict,** a character struggles against some outside force. This outside force might be another character, a society as a whole, or a natural force like bitter cold weather or a ferocious shark. An **internal conflict,** on the other hand, takes place within the character's own mind. A character with an internal conflict might be struggling against fear or loneliness or even being a sore loser.

See pages 95, 157, 645.

CONNOTATION *Emotions or associations that have come to be attached to certain words.* For example, the words *inexpensive, cheap,* and *a bargain* all are used to describe something that is not costly. Their dictionary definitions, or **denotations,** are roughly the same. However, a manufacturer of VCR's would not use *cheap* when advertising its latest model, since the word *cheap* is associated with something that is not well made. *Bargain* would be a better choice. Connotations can be especially important in poetry.

See page 565.

DESCRIPTION *Writing intended to create a mood or emotion, or to recreate a person, a place, a thing, an event, or an experience.* Description works through **images,** words that appeal to the senses of sight, smell, taste, hearing, or touch. Writers use description in all forms of writing—in fiction, nonfiction, and poetry. Here is a description of a famous character who has wormed her way into the hearts of readers everywhere. The writer's description appeals to our sense of sight, but it also gives us a hint of the girl's character. Viewing this lone figure in a deserted train station, an "ordinary observer" would see:

> A child of about eleven, garbed in a very short, very tight, very ugly dress of yellowish gray wincey. She wore a faded brown sailor hat and beneath the hat, extending down her back, were two braids of very thick, decidedly red hair. Her face was small, white, and thin, also much freckled; her mouth was large and so were her eyes, that looked green in some lights and moods and gray in others.
>
> —from *Anne of Green Gables,*
> L. M. Montgomery

See page 100.

DIALECT *A way of speaking characteristic of a particular region or of a particular group of people.* A dialect may have a distinct vocabulary, pronunciation system, and grammar. In a sense, we all speak dialects. The dialect that is dominant in a country or culture becomes accepted as the standard way of speaking. Writers often reproduce regional dialects, or dialects that reveal a person's economic or social class. The characters in *Sounder* (page 114) use an African American dialect spoken in the rural South. In "Jody's Discovery" (page 129), the characters speak a dialect common in the backwoods of Florida. Below, a spunky young girl gets up the courage to ask her uncle a hard question (she is speaking an African American urban dialect):

> So there I am in the navigator seat. And I turn to him and just plain ole ax him. I mean I come right on out with it . . . And like my mama say, Hazel—which is my real name and what she remembers to call me when she bein serious—when you got somethin on your mind, speak up and let the chips fall where they may. And if anybody don't like it, tell em to come see your mama. And Daddy look up from the paper and say, You hear your mama good, Hazel. And tell em to come see me first. Like that. That's how I was raised.
>
> So I turn clear round in the navigator seat and say, "Look here, . . . you gonna marry this girl?"
>
> —from "Gorilla, My Love,"
> Toni Cade Bambara

See pages 126, 230, 587.

DIALOGUE *Conversation between two or more characters.* Most plays consist entirely of dialogue. Dialogue is also an important element in most stories and novels. Dialogue is very effective in revealing character. It can also add realism and humor to a story.

In the written form of a play, dialogue appears without quotation marks. In prose or poetry, however, dialogue is normally enclosed in quotation marks.

See pages 464, 712.

DRAMA *A story written to be acted in front of an audience.* (A drama can also be appreciated and enjoyed in written form, however.) The action of a drama is usually caused by a character who wants something very much, who takes steps to get it, and who then meets with complications.

See page 463.
See also *Dialogue.*

ESSAY *A short piece of nonfiction prose.* An essay usually examines a subject from a personal point of view. Most essays are short. The French writer Michel de Montaigne (1533–1592) is supposed to have invented the essay. James Thurber, also in this book (page 446), is one of America's greatest humorous essayists.

See page 446.

FABLE *A very brief story in prose or verse that teaches a moral or a practical lesson about how to succeed in life.* The characters of most fables are animals that behave and speak like human beings. Some of the most popular fables are those supposedly told by Aesop, who was a slave in ancient Greece. You may have heard his fable about the sly fox who praises the crow for her beautiful voice. The fox begs the crow to sing for him, which she does. But when the crow opens her mouth, she lets fall the piece of cheese in her beak that the fox had been after the whole time.

See page 640.

FANTASY *Imaginative writing that carries the reader into an invented world where the laws of nature as we know them do not operate.* In fantasy worlds, supernatural forces are often at play. Characters may wave magic wands, cast spells, or appear and disappear at will. These characters may seem almost like ordinary human beings—or they may be witches, Martians, elves, giants, or fairies. Some of the oldest fantasy stories are called **fairy tales.** "Cinderella" and "The Emperor's New Clothes" are fairy tales. A newer type of fantasy, which deals with the changes that science may bring in the future, is called **science fiction.** "All Summer in a Day" (page 194) is Ray Bradbury's science fiction story about life as he imagines it on the planet Venus.

See page 18.
See also *Science Fiction.*

FICTION *A prose account that is basically made-up rather than factually true.* The term usually refers to novels and short stories.

See also *Fantasy, Nonfiction, Science Fiction.*

FIGURE OF SPEECH *A word or phrase that describes one thing in terms of something* else and is not literally true. Figures of speech always involve some sort of imaginative comparison between seemingly unlike things. Some 250 different types of figures of speech have been identified. The most common by far are the **simile** ("My heart is like a singing bird"), the **metaphor** ("The road was a ribbon of moonlight"), and **personification** ("The leaves were whispering to the night").

See page 443.

See also *Metaphor, Personification, Simile.*

FLASHBACK *Interruption in the present action of a plot to flash backward and tell what happened at an earlier time.* A flashback breaks the normal chronological movement of a narrative. A flashback can be placed anywhere in a story, even at the very beginning. There it usually gives background information. *The Secret Garden* (page 474) is almost one entire flashback. Although it starts out in the present when the main character is an adult, it soon flashes back to her childhood.

See pages 474, 495.

FOLK TALE *A story with no known author that originally was passed on from one generation to another by word of mouth.* Folk tales generally differ from myths in that they are not about gods and they were never connected with religion or belief. "The Pheasant's Bell" (page 551), and "Momotaro: Boy-of-the-Peach" (page 618) are both folk tales. Some folk tales tend to travel.

The old European folk tale of Cinderella has turned up in hundreds of other cultures (see "The Algonquin Cinderella" on page 147.)

See pages 549, 617, 630.

FORESHADOWING *The use of clues or hints suggesting events that will occur later in the plot.* Foreshadowing builds suspense or anxiety in the reader or viewer. In a movie, for example, strange alien creatures glimpsed among the trees may foreshadow later danger for the exploring spacemen.

See pages 165, 470.

FREE VERSE *Poetry that is "free" of a regular meter and rhyme scheme.* Poets writing in free verse try to capture the natural rhythms of ordinary speech. The following poem is written in free verse.

The City

If flowers want to grow
right out of the concrete sidewalk cracks
I'm going to bend down to smell them.

—David Ignatow

See pages 358, 362, 366.

IMAGERY *Language that appeals to the senses.* Most images are visual—that is, they create pictures in our minds by appealing to our sense of sight. Images can also appeal to our senses of hearing, touch, taste, or smell. Images can appeal to several senses at once. While imagery is an element in all types of writing, it is especially important in poetry. The following poem is full of rainy images:

FROM The Rainy Day

The day is cold, and dark, and dreary;
It rains, and the wind is never weary;
The vine still clings to the moldering
   wall,
But at every gust the dead leaves fall,
   And the day is dark and dreary.
       —Henry Wadsworth Longfellow

See page 250.

IRONY *A contrast between what appears to be true and what is really true, or a contrast between expectation and reality.* Irony can create powerful effects, from humor to horror. Here are some examples of situations that would make us feel irony:

1. We would feel irony if the shoemaker goes around with holes in his shoes.
2. We would feel irony if the children of a famous dancer trip over their own feet.
3. We would feel irony if it rains on the day the weather forecasters schedule their picnic.
4. We would feel irony if someone asks "How's my driving?" after going through a stop sign.
5. We would feel irony if a huge Great Dane runs away from a tiny mouse.
6. We would feel irony if a person who lives in the desert keeps a boat in the yard.
7. We would feel irony if the relative of a law enforcer is a bank robber.
8. We would feel irony if someone walked out in the midst of a hurricane and said "Nice day."

See page 408.

LEGEND *A story, usually based on some historical fact, that has been handed down from one generation to the next.* Legends often grow up around famous figures or events. The stories about King Arthur and his knights are legends based on the exploits of a real Celtic warrior-king who probably lived in Wales in the 500s. The story "Where the Buffaloes Begin" (page 252) is about a legend told around the campfires of the Native Americans of the Great Plains. As you can tell from that story, legends often make use of fantastic details.

METAPHOR *A comparison between two unlike things in which one thing becomes another thing.* A metaphor is an important type of figure of speech. Metaphors are used in all forms of writing and are common in ordinary speech. When you say about your grumpy friend, "He's such a bear today," you do not mean that he is growing bushy black fur. You mean that he is in a bad mood and taking his feelings out on everybody else.

Metaphors differ from **similes,** which use specific words to make their comparisons (words such as *like, as, than,* and *resembles*). "He is behaving like a bear" would be a simile.

The following famous poem compares fame to an insect:

> Fame is a bee.
> It has a song—
> It has a sting—
> Ah, too, it has a wing.
>   —Emily Dickinson

See pages 44, 53.
See also *Figure of Speech, Simile.*

Literary Terms and Techniques

MOOD *The overall emotion created by a work of literature.* Mood can often be described in one or two adjectives, such as eerie, dreamy, mysterious, depressing. The mood created by the poem below is sad and lonely:

Since Hanna Moved Away

The tires on my bike are flat.
The sky is grouchy gray.
At least it sure feels like that
Since Hanna moved away.

Chocolate ice cream tastes like prunes.
December's come to stay.
They've taken back the Mays and Junes
Since Hanna moved away.

Flowers smell like halibut.
Velvet feels like hay.
Every handsome dog's a mutt
Since Hanna moved away.

Nothing's fun to laugh about.
Nothing's fun to play.
They call me, but I won't come out
Since Hanna moved away.

—Judith Viorst

See page 112.

MYTH *A story that usually explains something about the world and involves gods and other supernatural beings.* Myths are deeply connected to the traditions and religious beliefs of the culture that produced them. Myths often explain certain aspects of life, such as what thunder is or where sunlight comes from or why people die. **Creation myths** explain how the world came to exist. Most myths are very old and were handed down orally for many centuries before being put in writing. The story of the hero Perseus on page 567 is a famous Greek myth. "Quetzalcoatl" (page 576) is a Mexican myth, and "Glooscap Fights the Water Monster" (page 558) is a popular Native American myth.

See page 549.
See also *Folk Tale.*

NARRATION *The kind of writing that tells "what happened."* Narration (also called *narrative*) is the form of writing most used by storytellers. Narration is also used in nonfiction, whenever a series of events are related.

See pages 63–65.

NONFICTION *Prose writing that deals with real people, events, and places without changing any facts.* Popular forms of nonfiction are the autobiography, the biography, and the essay. Other examples of nonfiction include newspaper stories, magazine articles, historical writing, travel writing, scientific reports, and personal diaries and letters.

See page 385.
See also *Fiction.*

NOVEL *A long fictional story, whose length is normally somewhere between one hundred and five hundred book pages.* A novel uses all the elements of storytelling—**plot, character, setting, theme,** and **point of view.** Because of its length, a novel usually has a more complex plot and more characters, settings, and themes than a short story has.

See page 645.

ONOMATOPOEIA (on′ə·mat′ə·pē′ə) *The use of a word whose sound imitates or suggests its meaning.* Onomatopoeia is so natural to us that we begin using it at a very early age. *Boom, bang, sniffle, rumble, hush, ding,* and *snort* are all examples of onomatopoeia. Onomatopoeia helps create the music of poetry. In the following poem, the poet had a lot of fun using onomatopoeia:

Our Washing Machine

Our washing machine went whisity whirr
Whisity whisity whisity whirr
One day at noon it went whisity click
Whisity whisity whisity click
Click grr click grr click grr click
　　Call the repairman
　　Fix it . . . quick.

　　　　　　　—Patricia Hubbell

See pages 337, 596, 600.
See also *Alliteration.*

PARAPHRASE *A restatement of a poem or a story, in which the meaning is expressed in other words.* You might be asked to paraphrase a work of literature to be sure you have understood exactly what it says. When you paraphrase a poem, you should tell what it says, line by line, in your own words. When you paraphrase a work of prose, you should give a brief summary of the major events or ideas. Here is the first stanza of a very famous poem, followed by a paraphrase:

Once upon a midnight dreary, while I
　　pondered, weak and weary,
Over many a quaint and curious volume
　　of forgotten lore—
While I nodded, nearly napping, sud-
　　denly there came a tapping,

As of someone gently rapping, rapping
　　at my chamber door.
"'Tis some visitor," I muttered, "tap-
　　ping at my chamber door—
　　　　Only this, and nothing more."
　　　　　　　—from "The Raven,"
　　　　　　　　Edgar Allan Poe

One midnight, I was tired but I stayed up late to read some interesting old books that I hadn't looked at in a while. As I was dozing off, I suddenly heard a sound as if someone were tapping at the door. "Just someone stopping by," I said, annoyed, "knocking at the door—that's all."

Notice that the paraphrase is neither as eerie nor as elegant as the poem.

PERSONIFICATION *A special kind of metaphor in which a nonhuman thing or quality is talked about as if it were human.* You are using personification if you say, "The leaves danced along the sidewalk." Of course leaves don't dance—only people do. The poem below personifies the night wind.

Rags

The night wind
rips a cloud sheet
into rags,
then rubs, rubs
the October moon
until it shines
like a brass doorknob.
　　　　　—Judith Thurman

See also *Figure of Speech, Metaphor, Simile.*

PLOT *The series of related events that make up a story.* Plot tells "what happens" in a short story, novel, play, or narrative poem. Most plots are built on these bare bones: An **introduction** tells us who the characters are and what their **conflicts,** or problems, are. **Complications** arise as the characters take steps to resolve their conflicts. Eventually, the plot reaches a **climax,** the most exciting moment in the story, when the outcome of the conflict is decided one way or another. The final part of the story is the **resolution.** This is when the characters' problems are solved and the story is closed.

See page 157.

POETRY *A kind of rhythmic, compressed language that uses figures of speech and imagery to appeal to our emotions and imaginations.* Poetry often has a regular pattern of rhythm, and it may have a regular rhyme pattern. **Free verse** is poetry that has no regular pattern of rhythm or rhyme.

See page 281.
See also *Alliteration, Figure of Speech, Free Verse, Imagery, Refrain, Rhyme, Speaker, Stanza.*

POINT OF VIEW *The vantage point from which a story is told.* Two common points of view are the omniscient (om·nish'ənt) and the first person.

1. In the **omniscient,** or "all-knowing," point of view, the narrator knows everything about the characters and their problems. This all-knowing narrator can tell us about the past, the present, and the future. Below is an example of the omniscient point of view:

> Once upon a time, in a small village, there were three houses built by three brother pigs. One was made of straw, one was made of twigs, and one was made of brick. Each pig thought his house was the best and the strongest. A wolf—a very hungry wolf—lived just outside of town. He was practicing his blowing techniques and trying to decide which pig's house was the weakest.

2. In the **first-person point of view,** one of the characters is telling the story, using the personal pronoun *I.* We become very familiar with this narrator, but we can only know what this character knows. We can observe only what this character observes. All our information about the story must come from this one narrator. In some cases the information this narrator gives us is not correct.

> As soon as I found out some new pigs had moved into the neighborhood, I started to practice my blowing. I like to blow down houses and eat whoever is inside. The little pigs have built their houses out of different materials—but I know I can blow 'em down in no time. That brick house looks especially weak.

See page 229.

PROSE *Any writing that is not poetry.* Essays, short stories, novels, news articles, and letters are all usually written in prose.

PUN *A play on words.* Puns are based on either (1) the multiple meanings of a word, or (2) two words that sound alike but have different meanings. There's a pun in the famous "Knock Knock" joke: Who's there? *Orange.* Orange who? *Orange you glad I came?* Puns are often used by poets. Here is a "prehistoric riddle" that uses a pun.

Question: Why did dinosaurs turn into fossils?

Answer: When the band started to play, the music made the dinosaurs rock.

This riddle puns on two meanings of the word *rock:* (1) a hard substance, and (2) a slang term for dancing to music.

REFRAIN *A repeated sound, word, phrase, line, or group of lines.* Refrains are usually associated with songs and poems, but they are also used in speeches and other forms of literature. Refrains are often used to cre-ate rhythm. Refrains are also used for emphasis and emotional effects.

See pages 300, 304.

RHYME *The repetition of accented vowel sounds and all sounds following them, in words that are close together in a poem.* *Trouble* and *bubble* are rhymes, as are *clown* and *noun.* Rhymes in poetry help create rhythm, they lend a songlike quality to the poem, they emphasize ideas, they provide humor or delight, and they aid memory.

End rhymes are rhymes at the ends of lines. **Internal rhymes** are rhymes within lines. Here is an example of a poem with both kinds of rhymes.

> In days of *old* when knights caught *cold,*
> They were not quickly *cured;*
> No aspirin *pill* would check the *ill,*
> Which had to be *endured.*
> —from "Thoughts on Progress,"
> David Daiches

See pages 300, 319, 596, 600.

RHYTHM *A musical quality produced by the repetition of stressed and unstressed syllables or by the repetition of other sound patterns.* Rhythm occurs in all language—written and spoken—but it is particularly important in poetry. The most obvious kind of rhythm is the regular repetition of stressed and unstressed syllables called **meter.** If you say the following lines aloud you'll hear a strong, regular rhythm. (Crowns, pounds, and guineas are British currency.)

> When I was one-and-twenty
> I heard a wise man say,

"Give crowns and pounds and guineas
But not your heart away . . ."
——from "When I Was One-and-
Twenty," A. E. Housman

See pages 292, 300, 316.

SCIENCE FICTION *A kind of fantasy usually based on changes that science or technology may bring in the future.* While science fiction creates imaginary worlds—often on other planets or in Earth's future—these worlds are usually governed by physical laws as we know them. "All Summer in a Day" (page 194) is Ray Bradbury's science fiction story about life on the planet Venus. It is based on the idea that someday our space technology will be advanced enough for people to set up civilizations on distant planets. Popular young adult science fiction books include *The Martian Chronicles* by Ray Bradbury, *A Wrinkle in Time* by Madeleine L'Engle, and *Sweetwater* by Laurence Yep.

See also *Fantasy.*

SETTING *The time and place of a story or play.* The setting can help create mood or atmosphere in a story. Some examples of vivid settings are the bleak and spooky mansion in *The Secret Garden* (page 474), the empty, vast tundra in *Julie of the Wolves* (page 3), the deserted wilderness in *Hatchet* (page 99), and the crumbling Fadgin house in "Nancy" (page 233).

See pages 157, 233, 262.

SHORT STORY *A short fictional prose narrative that usually takes up less than twenty book pages.* Short stories are usually built on a plot that consists of these elements: **introduction, conflict, complications, climax,** and **resolution.** Short stories are more limited than novels. They usually have only one or two major characters and one setting.

See page 157.
See also *Fiction, Plot.*

SIMILE (sim′ə·lē) *A comparison between two unlike things, using a word such as* like, as, resembles, *or* than. The simile is an important type of figure of speech. "His voice is as loud as a trumpet" and "Her eyes are like the blue sky" are both similes. In the following poem, the poet uses a simile to help us see a winter scene in a new way:

Scene
Little trees like pencil strokes
black and still
etched forever in my mind
on that snowy hill.
——Charlotte Zolotow

See pages 36, 40, 196, 204, 333.
See also *Figure of Speech, Metaphor.*

SPEAKER *The voice talking to us in a poem.* Sometimes the speaker is identical to the poet, but often the speaker and the poet are not the same. A poet may speak as a child, a woman, a man, a whole people, an animal, or even an object. In "Life Doesn't Frighten Me" (page 303), the speaker is a little girl. The unexpected speaker of "Interview" (page 370) is Cinderella's stepmother.

See pages 304, 362.

STANZA *A group of lines in a poem that form a unit.* A stanza in a poem is something like a paragraph in prose; it often expresses a unit of thought. The word *stanza* is an Italian word meaning "stopping place" or "place to rest."

SUSPENSE *The uncertainty or anxiety we feel about what will happen next in a story.* Any kind of writing that has a plot evokes some degree of suspense. Our sense of suspense is awakened in "Jody's Discovery" (page 129), for example, when Penny gets bitten by the rattlesnake. Jody's horror and disbelief make us anxious to read on to see whether his father will live or die.

See pages 443, 470, 688.
See also *Plot.*

THEME *An idea about life revealed in a work of literature.* A theme is not the same as a subject. A subject can usually be expressed in a word or two—love, childhood, death. A theme is the idea the writer wishes to reveal about that subject. Theme has to be expressed in a full sentence. A work can have more than one theme. A theme is usually not stated directly in the work. Instead, the reader has to think about all the elements of the work and then make an inference, or educated guess, about what they all mean. One theme of *The Secret Garden* (page 474) might be stated this way: "We cannot like ourselves until we learn to respect and care about others."

See pages 157, 204, 274, 645, 712.

TONE *The attitude a writer takes toward an audience, a subject, or a character.* Tone is conveyed through the writer's choice of words and details. A tone can be light and humorous, serious and sad, friendly or hostile toward a character, and so forth. The poem "The Sneetches" (page 285) is light and humorous in tone. The excerpt from *Sounder* (page 114) has a serious tone.

See pages 371, 400.

HANDBOOK FOR *Revision*

Contents

Each of the essays on pages 752–759 is shown in two versions: a rough draft and a final copy. In the draft, the writer has evaluated and revised the essay for logic, clarity, style, and specific support. The writer has also proofread the essay for errors in grammar, usage, punctuation, spelling, and capitalization. The writer's corrections are shown on the draft. The reasons for many of the changes are shown in the margin. Marginal annotations in the final copy identify important parts of each essay.

Symbols for Revising and Proofreading

Symbol	Example	Meaning of Symbol
≡	Pine street	Capitalize a lowercase letter.
/	Mae's Mother	Lowercase a capital letter.
/	revizing	Change a letter.
∧	fabulus	Insert a word, letter, or punctuation mark.
℘	I am am here.	Cut a word, letter, or punctuation mark.
⌇	Here is my key.	Leave out and close up.
⟨tr⟩	Please give us the books and them.	Transfer the circled material.
⟨¶⟩	¶ It was early.	Begin a new paragraph.
⊙	Take this pen	Add a period.
⋀	Oh I'm not so sure.	Add a comma.
⋁	Tanyas voice	Add an apostrophe.
⊙	as follows	Add a colon.
⋀	Rob Pinzio, Jr. Paula Fong, M.D.	Add a semicolon.

MODEL 1: A PERSUASIVE ESSAY
Rough Draft

EARTHLINGS, UNITE!

What happened on April 22, 1970, to bring people all over

Question mark

the world together? That date marked the first celebration of Earth

Day. Every April 22 since then, people in record-breaking numbers

have used this day to show their common concern for our

environment. Our school should organize a full schedule of Earth

Commas with series

Day activities for students, parents, and other members of the

community.

Transition; Spelling

most important

The reason for observance of Earth Day is that the holiday

draws attention to environmental problems on our planet. Toxic

chemicals, hazardous wastes, and other pollutants are choking our

Run-on sentence

air and water. Many of our fellow creatures on earth, including

some of the rarest animals and plants, may die out completely

because they are losing their natural surroundings. Celebration of

Capital letter needed

Earth day would help to make us all more aware of environmental

problems and how we might solve them.

Transition

A second reason for   to

Our school should observe this holiday because Earth Day

is that

activities would allow students, parents, teachers, and community

MODEL 1: A PERSUASIVE ESSAY
Final Copy

EARTHLINGS, UNITE!

Title

Introduction

What happened on April 22, 1970, to bring people all over the world together? That date marked the first celebration of Earth Day. Every April 22 since then, people in record-breaking numbers have used this day to show their common concern for our environment. Our school should organize a full schedule of Earth Day activities for students, parents, and other members of the community.

Opinion statement

The most important reason for observance of Earth Day is that the holiday draws attention to environmental problems on our planet. Toxic chemicals, hazardous wastes, and other pollutants are choking our air and water. Many of our fellow creatures on earth, including some of the rarest animals and plants, may die out completely because they are losing their natural surroundings. Celebration of Earth Day would help to make us all more aware of environmental problems and how we might solve them.

Body

Supporting reasons

A second reason for our school to observe this holiday is that Earth Day activities would allow students, parents, teachers,

Additional support

Sentence fragment	members, To be involved together on an issue that concerns
Apostrophe	everyone. Students could benefit from the adults knowledge and
	practical experience on environmental topics. Adults would be
	exposed to the ideas of teachers and students. Fresh solutions
	would be the result.

and activities

Style; Question mark	What are some possible projects for an Earth Day program,
Comma with interrupter	you ask. Students and adults could work together in teams for
Sentence fragment	example to clean up trash, plant young trees, Or learn more about
	recycling. Community members could share slides and
Spelling	videocasettes about remote but important areas of the earth's
	environment, such as tropical rain forests. Teachers could
	organize special classes on topics such as the destruction of the
	rain forest and the recycling of garbage.
	So, Earthlings, unite! If you agree that we can help to make
Pronoun reference	a difference by celebrating Earth Day at your school, write a letter
	to the school board or the administration today. All of us take life
Contraction	from the earth. Now lets start to give something back in return.

and community members to be involved together on an issue that concerns everyone. Students could benefit from the adults' knowledge and practical experience on environmental topics. Adults would be exposed to the ideas of teachers and students. Fresh solutions would be the result.

What are some possible projects and activities for an Earth Day program? Students and adults could work together in teams, for example, to clean up trash, plant young trees, or learn more about recycling. Community members could share slides and videocassettes about remote but important areas of the earth's environment, such as tropical rain forests. Teachers could organize special classes on topics such as the destruction of the rain forest and the recycling of garbage.

So, Earthlings, unite! If you agree that we can help to make a difference by celebrating Earth Day at our school, write a letter to the school board or the administration today. All of us take life from the earth. Now let's start to give something back in return.

Practical suggestions

Conclusion

Call to action

MODEL 2: AN INFORMATIVE ESSAY

Rough Draft

IN THE LAND OF THE GWICH'IN

In northeast Alaska, amid the tall peaks and the winding

river valleys of the Brooks Range, stands the small town of Arctic

Village. This collection of log houses, together with a school, a

Subject-verb agreement — church, and a community center, ~~are~~ *is* home to one of the most

endangered peoples on earth. They are the Gwich'in.

Spelling — The norther*n*most Indians of North America, the Gwich'in

Combine sentences — live in fifteen settlements, *that* ~~These settlements~~ stretch from Alaska

Capital letter needed — into Canada, roughly a hundred miles south of the Arctic *o*cean.

Although experts believe humans have lived here for more than

Comma after introductory clause — 25,000 years today the Gwich'in number only about 5,000.

Possessive pronoun — Their*'*s is a harsh land, frozen and dark for much of the year.

Double comparison — There is an even ~~more~~ harsher prospect for the Gwich'in, however:

Spelling — they may lo*s*e their traditional way of life.

Transition — *For thousands of years, these* ~~The~~ people have depended on the caribou, or reindeer.

Commas with interrupter — Caribou meat for example provides 75 percent of the protein in the

Gwich'in diet. Skins are sewn into boots and clothing, and bones

Capitalization — are made into tools. ~~according~~ to traditional stories the Gwich'in

756 Handbook for Revision

MODEL 2: AN INFORMATIVE ESSAY
Final Copy

IN THE LAND OF THE GWICH'IN

In northeast Alaska, amid the tall peaks and the winding river valleys of the Brooks Range, stands the small town of Arctic Village. This collection of log houses, together with a school, a church, and a community center, is home to one of the most endangered peoples on earth. They are the Gwich'in.

The northernmost Indians of North America, the Gwich'in live in fifteen settlements. These settlements stretch from Alaska into Canada, roughly a hundred miles south of the Arctic Ocean. Although experts believe that humans have lived here for more than 25,000 years, today the Gwich'in number only about 5,000. Theirs is a harsh land, frozen and dark for much of the year. There is an even harsher prospect for the Gwich'in, however: they may lose their traditional way of life.

For thousands of years, these people have depended on the caribou, or reindeer. Caribou meat, for example, provides 75 percent of the protein in the Gwich'in diet. Skins are sewn into boots and clothing, and bones are made into tools. According to

Title

Introduction

Body

Specific details

Additional details

Handbook for Revision

Subject-verb agreement

still tell, long ago they and the caribou ~~was~~ *were* one. After humans and animals became separate beings, they say, every caribou kept some of the human heart, and every human kept some of the caribou heart.

It is oil exploration that threatens to end the close ties of the Gwich'in and the caribou. After oil was discovered in Prudhoe Bay

Spelling; Apostrophe

in 1968, the Gwich'in suceeded for a while in protecting the caribou's grazing lands. Some of the world's leading oil companies, however, want to drill in the lands where the herds raise their young. This

Capitalization

land lies within the arctic national wildlife refuge. Aside from the direct threat to the caribou calves, the Gwich'in worry about the

Sentence fragment

dangers of oil spills, And toxic chemicals if the companies' plan is approved.

The Gwich'in have organized themselves to protect their way of life. They have the strongest motivation of all, their own survival.

Commas with appositive

As Sarah James a Gwich'in leader put it: "Caribou are not just what

Close quotation marks

we eat; they are who we are. Without caribou we wouldn't exist.

traditional stories the Gwich'in still tell, long ago they and the caribou were one. After humans and animals became separate beings, they say, every caribou kept some of the human heart, and every human kept some of the caribou heart.

It is oil exploration that threatens to end the close ties of the Gwich'in and the caribou. After oil was discovered in Prudhoe Bay in 1968, the Gwich'in succeeded for a while in protecting the caribou's grazing lands. Some of the world's leading oil companies, however, want to drill in the lands where the herds raise their young. This land lies within the Arctic National Wildlife Refuge. Aside from the direct threat to the caribou calves, the Gwich'in worry about the dangers of oil spills and toxic chemicals if the companies' plan is approved.

Cause-and-effect explanation

The Gwich'in have organized themselves to protect their way of life. They have the strongest motivation of all, their own survival. As Sarah James, a Gwich'in leader, put it: "Caribou are not just what we eat; they are who we are. Without caribou we wouldn't exist."

Conclusion

Part 2: Sentence Structure

- Sentence Fragments
- Run-on Sentences
- Comparisons

SENTENCE FRAGMENTS

A **sentence** is a group of words that expresses a complete thought. A sentence has a subject and a predicate. A group of words that looks like a sentence but that doesn't make sense by itself is a **sentence fragment.**

1. **Correct a fragment by adding the necessary sentence parts. Usually you will need to add a verb, a subject, or both.**

   Fragment
   By running to get help from the Forresters, Jody. [verb missing: What about Jody, or what did he do?]

   Sentence
   By running to get help from the Forresters, Jody **shows** responsibility.

   Fragment
   In the dream, is making a fire at a barbecue pit. [subject missing: Who is making a fire?]

   Sentence
   In the dream, Brian's friend **Terry** is making a fire at a barbecue pit.

   Fragment
   Acting like a young dog again. [subject and verb missing]

   Sentence
   Acting like a young dog again, **Sounder rushes** to greet his master.

2. **Correct a fragment by connecting it to an independent clause.**

   Fragment
   Because Tom hates to go to school, especially on Monday mornings. He pretends to be sick.

   Sentence
   Because Tom hates to go to school, especially on Monday mornings**, he** pretends to be sick.

RUN-ON SENTENCES

A **run-on sentence** consists of two complete sentences run together as if they were one sentence. Most run-ons are *comma splices*—or two complete thoughts separated only by a comma. Other run-ons are *fused sentences*—two complete thoughts separated by no punctuation.

1. **Correct a run-on sentence by using a period to form two complete sentences.**

   Run-on
   During his childhood, Abraham Lincoln lived in Kentucky and Indiana he had less than a year of formal schooling.

   Corrected
   During his childhood, Abraham Lincoln lived in Kentucky and Indiana**. He** had less than a year of formal schooling.

2. **Correct a run-on by using a comma and a coordinating conjunction (such as *and, but,* or *yet*) to create a compound sentence.**

   Run-on
   Cinderella's stepmother treated her badly life turned out well for her because she married a handsome prince and lived with him happily ever after.

   Corrected
   Cinderella's stepmother treated her badly**, but** life turned out well for her because she married a handsome prince and lived with him happily ever after.

COMPARISONS

1. Avoid incomplete comparisons.

Incomplete
The team played better today. [better than what?]

Complete
The team played better today **than it did yesterday.**

2. Avoid double comparisons.

Nonstandard
Nana Miriam is **more stronger** than anyone else because she has magic powers.

Standard
Nana Miriam is **stronger** than anyone else because she has magic powers.

Part 3: Pronouns

- Pronoun-Antecedent Agreement
- Case Forms of Personal Pronouns

PRONOUN-ANTECEDENT AGREEMENT

The noun or pronoun to which a pronoun refers is called its **antecedent.**

1. A pronoun must agree with its antecedent in number and in gender.

Example
Ali Baba frees Morgiana and also rewards **her.**

2. Use a singular pronoun to refer to an antecedent that is a singular indefinite pronoun. Use a plural pronoun to refer to an antecedent that is a plural indefinite pronoun.

Examples
Each of the daughters has **her** own hobbies.

Some of these poets use metaphors in **their** works.

3. When the antecedent may be either masculine or feminine, rephrase the sentence to avoid an awkward construction, or use both the masculine and the feminine forms.

Standard
All the heroes were known for **their** great deeds.

Standard
Each of the heroes was known for **his or her** great deeds.

4. Use a plural pronoun to refer to two or more antecedents joined by *and*.

Nonstandard
In the end, **Ben** and the other **boys** allowed Becky to join **his** group.

Standard
In the end, **Ben** and the other **boys** allowed Becky to join **their** group.

5. Use a singular pronoun to refer to two or more singular antecedents joined by *or* or *nor*.

Nonstandard
Neither **Gwendolyn Brooks** nor **Maya Angelou** wrote **their** poems in the nineteenth century.

Standard
Neither **Gwendolyn Brooks** nor **Maya Angelou** wrote **her** poems in the nineteenth century.

Sentences of this type can sound awkward if the antecedents are of different genders. If a sentence sounds awkward, revise it to avoid the problem.

Awkward

Each of the rich children in *The Secret Garden* has **his or her** internal conflicts.

Revised

Both the rich children in *The Secret Garden* have **their** internal conflicts.

CASE FORMS OF PERSONAL PRONOUNS

Use the correct case for personal pronouns that are part of compound constructions.

Nonstandard

Wanda says that **her** and Frank are going for a ride on the scooter. [object form used as subject]

Standard

Wanda says that **she** and Frank are going for a ride on the scooter.

Nonstandard

Did Mr. Ramos ask you and **she** to give a report on Vietnamese refugees? [subject form used for direct object]

Standard

Did Mr. Ramos ask you and **her** to give a report on Vietnamese refugees?

Nonstandard

Between you and **I,** did you think "The Jumblies" was funny? [subject form used for object of preposition]

Standard

Between you and **me,** did you think "The Jumblies" was funny?

Part 4: Verbs

- Missing or Incorrect Verb Endings
- Subject-Verb Agreement
- Sequence of Tenses

MISSING OR INCORRECT VERB ENDINGS

1. A *regular verb* forms the past and past participle by adding *-d* or *-ed* to the infinitive form. Don't make the mistake of leaving off or doubling the *-d* or *-ed* ending.

   Nonstandard

   Sara was **suppose** to take Charlie to see the swans.

   Standard

   Sara was **supposed** to take Charlie to see the swans.

   Nonstandard

   During their attempt to escape, some refugees **drownded.**

   Standard

   During their attempt to escape, some refugees **drowned.**

2. An *irregular verb* forms the past and past participle in some other way than by adding *-d* or *-ed* to the infinitive form. Irregular verbs form their past and past participle by

   - changing a vowel
   - changing consonants
   - adding *-en*
   - making no change at all

   Examples

Infinitive	Past	Past Participle
catch	caught	(have) caught

know	knew	(have) known
speak	spoke	(have) spoken
cut	cut	(have) cut

When you proofread your writing, check your sentences to determine which form—past or past participle—is called for. Remember that many nonstandard verb forms sound quite natural. Keep a dictionary handy to check any verb forms you're not sure about.

Nonstandard
The Mexicans did not believe that Quetzalcoatl **had went** away for good.

Standard
The Mexicans did not believe that Quetzalcoatl **had gone** away for good.

Nonstandard
When he was driving down the road, Maibon **seen** an old man hobbling along.

Standard
When he was driving down the road, Maibon **saw** an old man hobbling along.

Nonstandard
Brian **throwed** his hatchet at the porcupine.

Standard
Brian **threw** his hatchet at the porcupine.

SUBJECT-VERB AGREEMENT

1. A verb must agree with its subject in number—either singular or plural.

Nonstandard
Beterli **try** to bully Keevan, and the two **boys quarrels.**

Standard
Beterli **tries** to bully Keevan, and the two **boys quarrel.**

2. When a sentence contains a verb phrase, the first helping verb in the verb phrase agrees with the subject.

Nonstandard
The **actors has** memorized their parts.

Standard
The **actors have** memorized their parts.

3. The number of a subject is not changed by a phrase or clause coming between the subject and the verb.

Nonstandard
The **effects** of the volcano's eruption **was** serious.

Standard
The **effects** of the volcano's eruption **were** serious.

4. Use a singular verb to agree with the following singular indefinite pronouns: *anybody, anyone, each, either, everybody, everyone, neither, nobody, no one, one, somebody,* **and** *someone.*

Nonstandard
Everyone in the play **grow** to love the secret garden.

Standard
Everyone in the play **grows** to love the secret garden.

Nonstandard
Rena likes those poems because **each** of them **use** clever rhymes.

Standard
Rena likes those poems because **each** of them **uses** clever rhymes.

5. Use a plural verb to agree with the following plural indefinite pronouns: *both, few, many,* **and** *several.*

Nonstandard
Many of E. E. Cummings' poems **has** unusual punctuation.

Standard
Many of E. E. Cummings' poems **have** unusual punctuation.

Nonstandard
Several of my classmates **has** seen the movie version of *The Yearling.*

Standard
Several of my classmates **have** seen the movie version of *The Yearling.*

6. The following indefinite pronouns are singular when they refer to singular words and plural when they refer to plural words: *all, any, most, none,* **and** *some.*

Nonstandard
Most of the story **are** easy to read.

Standard
Most of the story **is** easy to read.

Nonstandard
Most of these poems **has** lively rhythms.

Standard
Most of these poems **have** lively rhythms.

Nonstandard
All of these novels **is** available at the public library.

Standard
All of these novels **are** available at the public library.

7. Subjects joined by *and* **usually take a plural verb.**

Nonstandard
Frank and **Wanda goes** to his sister's house.

Standard
Frank and **Wanda go** to his sister's house.

8. Singular subjects joined by *or* **or** *nor* **take a singular verb.**

Nonstandard
At the beginning of the play, neither **Mary** nor **Colin are** happy.

Standard
At the beginning of the play, neither **Mary** nor **Colin is** happy.

9. When a singular subject and a plural subject are joined by *or* **or** *nor,* **the verb agrees with the subject nearer the verb.**

Nonstandard
Neither **Roger** nor the other **boys knows** that Jerry sold Rollie Tremaine the card.

Standard
Neither **Roger** nor the other **boys know** that Jerry sold Rollie Tremaine the card.

10. When the subject follows the verb, as in questions and in sentences beginning with *here* **and** *there,* **identify the subject and make sure that the verb agrees with it.**

Nonstandard
Here **are** a **list** of the world's tallest volcanoes.

Standard
Here **is** a **list** of the world's tallest volcanoes.

Nonstandard
When **does** summer **classes** start?

Standard
When **do** summer **classes** start?

11. A verb should always agree with its subject, not with its predicate nominative.

Nonstandard
Grandfather's **words was** a precious legacy.

Standard
Grandfather's **words were** a precious legacy.

12. The contractions *don't* **and** *doesn't* **must agree with their subjects.**

Examples
At the beginning of James Berry's story, the **Wheels-and-Brake Boys don't** allow Becky to join them.

According to James Thurber, **Rex doesn't** hesitate to jump fences.

SEQUENCE OF TENSES

Changing verb tense in mid-sentence or from sentence to sentence without good reason creates awkwardness and confusion. Be sure that the verb tenses in a single sentence or in a group of related sentences are consistent.

Awkward
When Jody **searches** for the abandoned fawn, he **risked** the danger of an attack by a rattlesnake or a panther.

Better
When Jody **searches** for the abandoned fawn, he **risks** the danger of an attack by a rattlesnake or a panther.

Part 5: Comma Usage

- Compound Structure
- Items in a Series
- Two or More Adjectives
- Nonessential Elements
- Introductory Elements
- Interrupters

COMPOUND STRUCTURE

Use a comma before a coordinating conjunction (*and, but, or, nor, for, so,* and *yet*) that joins two independent clauses. If the clauses are very short, you may omit the comma.

Examples

The voice was as loud as an earthquake, **and** the eldest son's knees knocked together in terror.

—Gardner, "Dragon, Dragon" (p. 169)

Little Wolf was only ten years old, **but** he could run faster than any of his friends.

—Baker, "Where the Buffaloes Begin" (p. 254)

He felt perfectly sure he could slay the dragon by simply laying into him, **but** he thought it would be only polite to ask his father's advice.

—Gardner, "Dragon, Dragon" (p. 171)

The President cards were a roaring success **and** the cowboy cards were quickly forgotten.

—Cormier, "President Cleveland, Where Are You?" (p. 184)

ITEMS IN A SERIES

Use commas to separate words, phrases, and clauses in a series.

Examples

Thousands of people came to **hike, picnic, camp, fish, paint, bird watch,** or just enjoy the scenery.

—Lauber, "Volcano" (p. 435)

Maibon **flung down the stone, spun around, and set off as fast as he could.**

—Alexander, "The Stone" (p. 215)

My seven sisters helped by **working in the garden, gathering eggs, or taking water to the cattle.**

—Nhuong, "The Land I Lost" (p. 413)

In front, behind, and on both sides of him, a heaving mass of buffaloes billowed like the sea.

—Baker, "Where the Buffaloes Begin" (p. 260)

All the floors were full of greenish light reflected from the maple trees outdoors; **the floors were dark and gleaming, the carpets had been taken up for the summer, and the furniture had linen dresses on.**

—Enright, "Nancy" (p. 235)

TWO OR MORE ADJECTIVES

Use a comma to separate two or more adjectives preceding a noun. However, do *not* use a comma before the final adjective in a series if the adjective is thought of as being part of a noun. Determine if the adjective and noun form a unit by inserting the word *and* between the adjectives. If *and* fits sensibly, use a comma.

Examples

"We need **warm, soapy** water," the teacher said. [warm *and* soapy; comma needed]

—Armstrong, from *Sounder* (p. 119)

Meg got her **large chocolate** milkshake and I had a small one. [*And* sounds awkward.]

—Namioka, "The All-American Slurp" (p. 272)

NONESSENTIAL ELEMENTS

A *nonessential* (or *nonrestrictive*) clause or participial phrase contains information that is not necessary to the meaning of the sentence. Use commas to set off nonessential clauses and nonessential participial phrases. An *essential* (or *restrictive*) clause or participial phrase is not set off by commas, because it contains information that is necessary to the meaning of the sentence.

Nonessential Clause

I have relations, aunts and uncles, **who are darlings too,** a good home, no—I don't seem to lack anything. [The clause can be omitted without changing the main idea.]

—Frank, from *The Diary of a Young Girl* (p. 394)

Essential Clause

That particular egg was the one **Beterli had marked as his own.** [The clause is necessary to identify which egg is meant.]

—McCaffrey, "The Smallest Dragonboy" (p. 82)

Nonessential Phrase

That selection, **written by Marjorie Kinnan Rawlings,** comes from her novel *The Yearling.*

Essential Phrase

The selection **written by Marjorie Kinnan Rawlings** comes from her novel *The Yearling.*

INTRODUCTORY ELEMENTS

Use a comma after *yes, no,* or any mild exclamation such as *well* or *why* at the beginning of a sentence. Also use a comma after an introductory participial phrase, after two or more introductory prepositional phrases, and after an introductory adverb clause.

Examples

Yes, being the smallest candidate was not an enviable position.

—McCaffrey, "The Smallest Dragonboy" (p. 81)

"**Well,** *has* there ever been a case where a dragon didn't choose?"

—McCaffrey, "The Smallest Dragonboy" (p. 85)

In the still darkness of the shelter in the middle of the night, his eyes came open and he was awake and he thought there was a growl.

—Paulsen, from *Hatchet* (p. 103)

Whenever she thought of the handbills, she walked faster. [introductory adverb clause]

—Petry, "Harriet Tubman" (p. 29)

INTERRUPTERS

1. Nonessential appositives and appositive phrases are usually set off by commas.

We had been invited to dinner by our neighbors, **the Gleasons.**

—Namioka, "The All-American Slurp" (p. 265)

Yet Little Wolf knew well that his enemies, **the Assiniboins,** could come creeping along the hollows of the prairie like wolves.

—Baker, "Where the Buffaloes Begin" (pp. 255–256)

I told her that this was America and yelled that Debbie, **my sister,** didn't have a jacket like mine.

—Soto, "The Jacket" (p. 39)

She told her of the panic-stricken talk in the quarter, told her that the slaves were afraid that the master, **Dr. Thompson,** would start selling them.

—Petry, "Harriet Tubman" (p. 24)

2. Words used in direct address are set off by commas.

Examples

"**Father,** have you any advice to give me?" he asked.

—Gardner, "Dragon, Dragon" (p. 172)

"And may I ask, **O Lucy, daughter of Eve,**" said Mr. Tumnus, "how you have come into Narnia?"

—Lewis, "Mr. Tumnus" (p. 12)

"Thanks, **Jerry,**" he said. "I hate to take your last cent."

—Cormier, "President Cleveland, Where Are You?" (p. 182)

3. Use commas to set off parenthetical expressions.

Examples

And then, **of course,** the biggest crime of all was that she had come here only five years ago from Earth.

—Bradbury, "All Summer in a Day" (p. 197)

Yes, I'm still alive, **indeed,** but don't ask where or how.

—Frank, from *The Diary of a Young Girl* (p. 395)

But even if she fell asleep, **she thought,** the Lord would take care of her.

—Petry, "Harriet Tubman" (p. 26)

Part 6: Style

- Sentence Variety
- Stringy Sentences
- Overwriting
- Creative Use of Synonyms
- Vivid Words
- Clichés
- Levels of Language

SENTENCE VARIETY

1. Create sentence variety in length and rhythm by using different kinds of clauses, as well as simple sentences.

Little Variation

In "Becky and the Wheels-and-Brake Boys," Becky wants a bike badly. Her mother says no. The family is too poor. Becky does not give up. She tries to raise some money. She takes her father's sun helmet to the fire station. She wants to sell the helmet to the fireman, Mr. Dean. Mr. Dean laughs. He drives Becky home.

More Variation

In "Becky and the Wheels-and-Brake Boys," Becky wants a bike badly. Her mother says no, telling Becky that the family is too poor. Becky does not give up, however, and she tries to raise some money by taking her father's sun helmet to the fire station. When she tells the fireman, Mr. Dean, that she wants to sell the helmet to him, he laughs and drives Becky home.

2. Expand short, choppy sentences by adding details.

Choppy

Lensey Namioka was born in China. She came to America. She now lives in Seattle, Washington. She has written several novels. Her autobiography is called *Life with Chaos.*

More Detailed

Lensey Namioka was born in 1929 in Beijing, China. She came to America with her parents and now lives in Seattle, Washington. She has written several novels about the adventures of Japanese samurai warriors. The title of her autobiography, *Life with Chaos,* is a pun on Namioka's Chinese family name, *Chao.*

3. Vary sentence openers by using appositives, single-word modifiers, phrase modifiers, clause modifiers, and transitional words.

Little Variation

Harriet's brothers force her to return on the first attempt to escape. Harriet decides to go North alone. She tells her sister Mary of her decision. She slips away from the plantation in the middle of the night. She comes to the farmhouse where the white woman lives. Harriet approaches carefully. The woman opens the door. She does not seem surprised to see Harriet.

More Variation

Because Harriet's brothers force her to return on the first attempt to escape, Harriet decides to go North alone. **After telling her sister Mary of her decision,** she slips away from the plantation. **In the middle of the night,** she comes to the farmhouse where the white woman lives and approaches carefully. **When the woman opens the door,** she does not seem surprised to see Harriet.

STRINGY SENTENCES

Simplify stringy sentences by writing as concisely as you can. Cut down your use of prepositional phrases. Reduce clauses to phrases, if possible. If you can, reduce clauses and phrases to single words.

Stringy

Tom Sawyer experienced misery on Monday morning because he didn't want to go to school, so he thought for a while and then he decided to create a pretense that he was sick, and he started to groan so that Sid would wake up.

Better

Tom Sawyer was miserable on Monday morning. He didn't want to go to school, so after thinking for a while, he decided to pretend to be sick. He started to groan so that Sid would wake up.

OVERWRITING

1. Get rid of unnecessary words.

Wordy

That poem has a lively **rhythm and beat.**

Better

That poem has a lively **rhythm.**

Wordy

At the end of the story, the boy's father **unexpectedly and surprisingly** returns.

Better

At the end of the story, the boy's father **unexpectedly** returns.

2. Avoid complicated words where plain, simple ones will do.

Pretentious

Langston Hughes was the author of many distinguished literary **creations.**

Simpler

Langston Hughes was the author of many distinguished literary **works.**

CREATIVE USE OF SYNONYMS

Avoid awkward repetition by using synonyms creatively.

Awkward

While Brian looks at the **bear,** he wonders if the **bear** will attack him.

Better

While Brian looks at the **bear,** he wonders if the **beast** will attack him.

VIVID WORDS

1. Whenever possible, replace vague words with specific ones.

Vague

The light in the forest and the sound of the trees were nice, but as he went along he became worried.

Specific

The moonlight coming through the leaves and the soft sound of the wind in the branches were soothing, but as he went deeper into the forest he became worried.

—Byars, *The Summer of the Swans* (p. 673)

2. Replace abstract words with vivid, concrete words that appeal to the senses.

Abstract

Her pallor was striking, and if she spoke her voice would be tiny.

Concrete/Sensory

She was an old photograph dusted from an album, whitened away, and if she spoke at all, her voice would be a ghost.

—Bradbury, "All Summer in a Day" (p. 197)

CLICHÉS

A **cliché** is a tired expression. Replace clichés in your writing with fresh, vivid expressions.

Cliché

They were as fast as lightning.

Vivid

They were as fast as sprinting cheetahs.

LEVELS OF LANGUAGE

Depending on your purpose, audience, and form of writing, you should use an appropriate level of language. For example, *formal English* is appropriate for serious essays, reports, and speeches on solemn occasions. *Informal English* is suitable for personal letters, journal entries, and many articles. The following chart gives an outline of formal and informal levels of language.

	Formal	Informal
Words	longer, rare, specialized	shorter, colloquial

Spelling	in full	contractions
Grammar	complex, complete	compound, fragmentary

Formal English usually creates a serious tone. Informal English tends to have a friendlier, more personal tone.

Formal

Once on Sunday after the usual slow, massive dinner, as Fiona lay in the extremity of boredom counting mosquito bites and listening to herself yawn, she heard another sound: a new one that might promise much.

—Enright, "Nancy" (p. 236)

Informal

"Oh! Given themselves a name as well, have they? Well, Becky, answer this. How d'you always manage to look like you just escaped from a hair-pulling battle? Eh? And don't I tell you not to break the backs down and wear your canvas shoes like slippers? Don't you ever hear what I say?"

—Berry, "Becky and the Wheels-and-Brake Boys" (p. 223)

Part 7: Glossary of Usage

a, an Use the indefinite article *a* before words beginning with a consonant sound. Use the indefinite article *an* before words beginning with a vowel sound.

Examples

Lucy finds herself in *a* dark wood.

Jamaica is *an* island in the Caribbean Sea.

accept, except *Accept* is a verb meaning "to receive." *Except* may be either a verb or a preposition. As a verb, *except* means "to leave out." As a preposition, *except* means "excluding."

Examples

Do you *accept* the idea that everything is determined by fate in advance?

No one *except* Margot remembers the sun clearly. [preposition]

The swift, destructive mudflows from the volcano *excepted* no obstacle in their path. [verb]

affect, effect *Affect* is a verb meaning "to influence." As a verb, *effect* means "to bring about" or "to accomplish." As a noun, *effect* means "the result of an action."

Examples

How did Gwendolyn Brooks's description *affect* your opinion of Narcissa?

Maibon's magic stone *effected* some mysterious changes on his farm. [verb]

In "Nancy," the house in which Fiona lived with her grandparents had a confining *effect* on her. [noun]

all, all of The word *of* can usually be omitted, except before some pronouns.

Examples

All my friends liked reading "Ali Baba and the Forty Thieves." [preferable to *all of*]

All of us wanted to see the movie. [*Of* is necessary.]

among, between Use *between* when you are referring to two things at a time. Use *among* when you are referring to more than two items.

Examples

Bruce wanted to memorize a short poem, but he couldn't decide *between* "The Sea" and "Dream Variations."

Among the folktales we read, which did Reggie like best?

amount, number Use *amount* to refer to a singular word. Use *number* to refer to a plural word.

Examples

Tom Sawyer had a great *amount* of ingenuity.

Robert Cormier has written a *number* of novels for young adults.

anxious, eager *Anxious* means "worried" or "uneasy." *Eager* means "feeling keen desire or strong interest."

Examples

Aunt Willie becomes *anxious* about Charlie when no one can find him.

Bharati liked "Perseus" so much that she is *eager* to read more ancient Greek myths about heroes.

as, like *Like* is a preposition. In formal situations, do not use *like* for the conjunction *as* to introduce a subordinate clause.

Examples

Poets *like* Shel Silverstein create funny verses about unusual subjects.

Did C. S. Lewis' story "Mr. Tumnus" end *as* you expected?

awhile, a while *Awhile* is an adverb meaning "for a short time." *A while* is made up of an article and a noun and means "a period or space of time."

Examples

Shirl and Nikki read *awhile* in the library.

Mark Twain worked for *a while* as a cub pilot.

bad, badly *Bad* is an adjective. *Badly* is an adverb. In standard English, only the adjective form should follow a sense verb, such as *feel, see, hear, taste, look,* or another linking verb.

Examples

Sara thinks that Joe Melby has played a *bad* trick on Charlie by taking his watch.

In "The Smallest Dragonboy," the bully Beterli behaved *badly* to Keevan.

When he sits by his father's bed and thinks of the motherless fawn, Jody feels *bad.*

because In formal situations, do not use the construction *reason . . . because*. Instead, use *reason . . . that.*

Informal
The reason nothing frightens the speaker is *because* she has a magic charm.

Formal
The reason nothing frightens the speaker is *that* she has a magic charm.

beside, besides *Beside* is a preposition meaning "by the side of" or "next to." *Besides* may be used as either a preposition or an adverb. As a preposition, *besides* means "in addition to" or "also." As an adverb, *besides* means "moreover."

Examples

Did you sit *beside* Dihundra at the play rehearsal?

Besides "Habits of the Hippopotamus," which other poems did you enjoy? [preposition]

Langston Hughes was a poet and playwright; he was an outstanding writer of fiction, *besides.* [adverb]

between See **among, between.**

bring, take *Bring* means "to come carrying something." *Take* means "to go carrying something."

Examples

"Please *bring* your textbooks to class tomorrow," said Ms. Owens.

Mr. Ortega said, "Please *take* these books to Room A302."

compare to, compare with Use *compare to* when you want to stress either the similarities or the differences between two things. Use *compare with* when you wish to stress both similarities and differences.

Examples

The metaphor in the first line of James Reeves's poem compares the sea *to* a hungry dog.

Stu's report compared Rudyard Kipling's "How the Whale Got His Throat" *with* Chinua Achebe's "Why Tortoise's Shell Is Not Smooth."

convince, persuade *Convince* means "to win someone over through argument." *Convince* is usually followed by *that* and a subordinate clause. *Persuade* means to move someone to act in a certain way. *Persuade* is often followed by *to*.

Examples

Frank wants to convince Aunt Willie *that* his motor scooter is safe.

Frank *persuades* Aunt Willie *to* take a ride on the scooter.

could of Do not write *of* with the helping verb *could*. Write *could have*. Also avoid *had of, ought to of, should of, would of, might of,* and *must of*.

Example

Jerry *could have* [not *could of*] spent the money himself, but he gave it to his brother Armand.

different from, different than Use *different from*, not *different than*.

Example

An autobiography is *different from* a biography because in an autobiography the writer tells about his or her own life.

doesn't, don't *Doesn't* is the contraction of *does not. Don't* is the contraction of *do not*. Use *doesn't*, not *don't*, with *he, she, it, this, that,* and singular nouns.

Examples

Sarah Cynthia Sylvia Stout *doesn't* like dealing with the garbage.

Harriet Tubman's three brothers *don't* want to escape with her.

eager See **anxious, eager.**

effect See **affect, effect.**

everyday, every day *Everyday* is an adjective meaning "daily" or "common." *Every day* is an adverbial phrase meaning "each day."

Examples

Moderate exercise should be part of *everyday* life.

Sara thinks that *every day* of the summer has been awful.

everyone, every one *Everyone* is an indefinite pronoun. *Every one* consists of an adjective and a pronoun and means "every person or thing of those named."

Examples

Everyone in my class loved "The Sneetches."

Every one of my friends enjoys science fiction.

except See **accept, except.**

farther, further *Farther* refers to geographical distance. *Further* means "in addition to" or "to a greater degree."

Examples

The boat was taking Tran to Thailand, but Tran's mother wanted him to travel even *farther*, all the way to America.

Because the sudden eruption puzzled scientists, they researched its causes *further*.

fewer, less Use *fewer*, which tells "how many," to modify a plural noun. Use *less*, which tells "how much," to modify a singular noun.

Examples

With each passing year, the buffaloes on the plain grew *fewer* and *fewer*.

If Mary had possessed *less* curiosity, she might not have discovered the secret garden.

good, well *Good* is an adjective. *Well* may be used either as an adjective or an adverb. The expressions *feel good* and *feel well* mean different things. *Feel good* means "to feel happy or pleased." *Feel well* means "to feel healthy."

Examples

At the end of the novel, Sara feels *good* about Joe.

Tom Sawyer pretends to Sid and Aunt Polly that he doesn't feel *well*.

Avoid using *good* to modify an action verb. Instead, use *well* as an adverb meaning "capably" or "satisfactorily."

Nonstandard

John Gardner uses humor *good* in "Dragon, Dragon."

Standard

John Gardner uses humor *well* in "Dragon, Dragon."

had of See **could of.**

hardly, scarcely The words *hardly* and *scarcely* convey negative meanings. Never use with another negative word.

Example

The people *can* [not *can't*] *hardly* believe that Momotaro has saved them from the ogres.

Abe Lincoln's family *had* [not *hadn't*] *scarcely* any money.

he, she, they Do not use an unnecessary pronoun after the subject of a clause or a sentence. This error is called the *double subject.*

Nonstandard

At the end of the story, Mr. Dean *he* will probably marry Becky's mother.

Standard

At the end of the story, Mr. Dean will probably marry Becky's mother.

how come In informal situations, *how come* is often used instead of *why.* In formal situations, *why* should always be used.

Informal

How come the narrator says that her family disgraced themselves at the dinner party with the Gleasons?

Formal

Why does the narrator say that her family disgraced themselves at the dinner party with the Gleasons?

imply, infer *Imply* means "to suggest something indirectly." *Infer* means "to get a certain meaning from a remark or an action."

Examples

Writers often do not directly state the theme of a story or poem; instead, they *imply* it.

Did you *infer* from the end of Robert Cormier's story that Jerry would eventually feel better about his actions?

in, into, in to *In* means "within." *Into* means "from the outside to the inside." *In to* refers to motion with a purpose.

Examples

"Jody's Discovery" takes place *in* the Florida backwoods.

The porcupine stuck some of its quills *into* Brian's leg.

Did Ms. Lopez come *in to* your classroom to make the announcement?

its, it's *Its* is a possessive pronoun. *It's* is the contraction for *it is* or *it has.*

Examples

Anne McCaffrey's story is enjoyable because of *its* use of fantasy.

It's clear in the play that both Mary and Colin are very unhappy children.

kind(s), sort(s), type(s) With the singular form of each of these nouns, use *this* or *that.* With the plural form, use *these* or *those.*

Examples

Do you like *this type* of essay?

Those kinds of tales are about a leader who instructs the people in survival skills.

lay, lie The verb *lay* means "to put (something) in a place." *Lay* usually takes an object. The past tense of *lay* is *laid.* The verb *lie* means "to rest" or "to stay in one position." *Lie* never takes an object. The past tense of *lie* is *lay.*

Examples

Please *lay* [place] those books on the table.

After Wanda leaves the room, Sara *lies* [rests] on her bed and complains to the dog Boysie.

leave, let *Leave* means "to go away." *Let* means "to permit" or "to allow."

Nonstandard
Please *leave* us watch TV till 9:00!

Standard
Please *let* us watch TV till 9:00!

Standard
The bus was supposed to *leave* at 6:30.

less See **fewer, less.**

might of, must of See **could of.**

number See **amount, number.**

on, onto, on to *On* refers to position and means "upon," "in contact with," or "supported by." *Onto* implies motion and means "to a position on." Do not confuse *onto* with *on to.*

Examples

The waves broke *on* the seashore.

The crocodile dragged Lan's body *onto* an island.

The author goes *on to* discuss the eruption itself.

or, nor Use *or* with *either.* Use *nor* with *neither.*

Examples

Consuelo's report will be *either* on Leroy V. Quintana *or* on Pat Mora.

Neither Sara *nor* Aunt Willie can find Charlie.

ought to of See **could of.**

principal, principle *Principal* is an adjective meaning "first" or "main." It can also be a noun meaning the head of a school. *Principle* is a noun meaning "rule of conduct" or "a fact or general truth."

Examples

The *principal* characters in "President Cleveland, Where Are You?" are Jerry, Rollie, Roger, and Jerry's brother Armand.

Tricksters like Tortoise have very few *principles.*

real In informal situations, *real* is often used as an adverb meaning "very" or "extremely." In formal situations, *very* or *extremely* is preferred.

Informal
The speaker in "Abuelito Who" feels *real* close to her grandfather.

Formal
The speaker in "Abuelito Who" feels *very* close to her grandfather.

rise, raise *Rise* means "to go up" or "to get up." *Rise* never takes an object. The past tense of *rise* is *rose.* *Raise* means "to cause (something) to rise" or "to lift up." *Raise* usually takes an object. The past tense of *raise* is *raised.*

Examples
When the volcano erupted, the magma *rose* to the surface.

Fiona *raised* herself to her elbows and saw that Nana was asleep.

scarcely, hardly See **hardly, scarcely.**

should of See **could of.**

sit, set *Sit* means "to rest in an upright, seated

position." *Sit* seldom takes an object. The past tense of *sit* is *sat*. *Set* means "to put (something) in a place." *Set* usually takes an object. The past tense of *set* is *set*.

Examples
In fine weather, Ben likes to *sit* outside and read.

Ali Baba orders his slaves to *set* the jars in the courtyard.

some, somewhat In writing, do not use *some* for *somewhat* as an adverb.

Nonstandard
The end of that story surprised me *some*.

Standard
The end of that story surprised me *somewhat*.

than, then *Than* is a conjunction used in comparisons. *Then* is an adverb telling *when*.

Examples
Nana Miriam was stronger *than* anyone else in two ways.

Quetzalcoatl mourns for the dead pages and *then* goes on his way.

that See **who, which, that**.

this here, that there The words *here* and *there* are unnecessary after *this* and *that*.

Example
This [not *this here*] figure of speech is a simile, but *that* [not *that there*] one is a metaphor.

try and In informal situations, *try and* is often used instead of *try to*. In formal situations, *try to* should be used.

Informal
Try and draw inferences from clues in the story.

Formal
Try to draw inferences from clues in the story.

use to, used to Be sure to add the *d* to *use*.

Example
Many different peoples around the world *used to* [not *use to*] tell myths and folk tales orally.

well See **good, well**.

when, where Do not use *when* or *where* to begin a definition.

Nonstandard
Onomatopoeia is *when* you use a word whose sound imitates or suggests its meaning.

Standard
Onomatopoeia is the use of a word whose sound imitates or suggests its meaning.

Nonstandard
A pun is *where* there is a play on words.

Standard
A pun is a play on words.

where Do not use *where* for *that*.

Nonstandard
Roxy read *where* James Thurber grew up in Columbus, Ohio.

Standard
Roxy read *that* James Thurber grew up in Columbus, Ohio.

who, which, that *Who* refers to persons only. *Which* refers to things only. *That* may refer to either persons or things.

Examples
The poet *who* wrote "Cynthia in the Snow" was Gwendolyn Brooks.

The strange land, *which* was called Narnia, was ruled by the White Witch.

A writer *that* Jay enjoyed was Lensey Namioka.

One poem *that* uses an ingenious shape is "Concrete Cat."

who, whom *Who* is used as the subject of a verb or as a predicate nominative. *Whom* is used as an object of a verb or as an object of a preposition. The use of *who* or *whom* in a subordinate clause depends on how the pronoun functions within the clause.

Examples

Who wrote ''The Sneetches''?

Armand, *who* is Jerry's older brother, wants to take Sally to a dance.

The writer *whom* Carlos liked best was Bill Cosby.

Of *whom* were the children jealous in Bradbury's story?

whose, who's   *Whose* is the possessive form of *who. Who's* is a contraction for *who is* or *who has.*

Examples

Whose son is Jody?

Who's the true hero of the tale, Ali Baba or Morgiana?

would of   See **could of.**

your, you're   *Your* is the possessive form of *you. You're* is the contraction of *you are.*

Examples

Is *your* class putting on a play this spring?

You're a Ray Bradbury fan, aren't you?

Part 8: Grammar Reference Guide

SUBJECT-VERB AGREEMENT

A verb should agree with its subject in number—singular or plural.

The **waves were** not big now.
—Ashabranner, ''The Most Vulnerable People'' (p. 424)

The **slaves were** right about Dr. Thompson's intention.
—Petry, ''Harriet Tubman'' (p. 24)

Among these people **were** many natural **scientists.**
—Lauber, ''Volcano'' (p. 442)

If a **family wants** to get through the day with a minimum of noise and open wounds, the **parents have** to impose order on the domestic scene.
—Cosby, ''Fatherhood'' (p. 454)

NOUNS

A **noun** is a word used to name a person, place, thing, or idea. Nouns can function in sentences as subjects, direct objects, indirect objects, objects of prepositions, predicate nominatives, and appositives.

The **king's knights** were all **cowards** who hid under their **beds** whenever the **dragon** came in

sight, so they were of no **use** to the **king** at all.
—Gardner, ''Dragon, Dragon'' (p. 167)

Dian Fossey studied the **behavior** of **Coco** and **Pucker,** orphan **gorillas.**

To fling my **arms** wide
In some **place** of the **sun,**
To whirl and to dance
Till the white **day** is done.
—Hughes, ''Dream Variations'' (p. 350)

PRONOUNS

A **pronoun** is a word used in place of a noun or of more than one noun. **Personal pronouns** refer to the person speaking (first person), the person spoken to (second person), or the person, place, or thing spoken about (third person).

	Singular		
	Subject Form	**Object Form**	**Possessive Form**
First Person	I	me	my, mine
Second Person	you	you	your yours
Third Person	he	him	his
	she	her	her, hers
	it	it	its

	Plural		
	Subject Form	**Object Form**	**Possessive Form**
First Person	we	us	our, ours
Second Person	you	you	your yours
Third Person	they	them	their theirs

They stopped running and stood in the great jungle that covered Venus, that grew and never stopped growing, tumultuously, even as **you** watched **it.**

> —Bradbury, "All Summer in a Day" (p. 201)

"Pray that **we** reach the refugee camp," the woman told **him.**

> —Ashabranner, "The Most Vulnerable People" (p. 426)

He licked at our hands and, staggering, fell, but got up again.

> —Thurber, "Snapshot of a Dog" (p. 450)

A **reflexive pronoun** ends in -*self* or -*selves* and refers back to the subject of a verb.

> On the other side of the wardrobe, Lucy finds **herself** in Narnia.

A **relative pronoun** is used to introduce adjective and noun clauses.

> It was difficult enough to find the Three Gray Sisters, **who** lived near the Garden of the Hesperides.
>
> > —Graves, "Perseus" (p. 570)

> At this signal, you are to split open your jars with the knives with **which** you will have been provided.
>
> > —Gille, "Ali Baba and the Forty Thieves" (p. 611)

> The catastrophe **that** might take his father had made it motherless.
>
> > —Rawlings, "Jody's Discovery" (p. 139)

An **interrogative pronoun** is used to begin questions.

> **who** knows if the moon's
> a balloon, coming out of a keen city
> in the sky—filled with pretty people?
>
> > —Cummings, "who knows if the moon's" (p. 314)

"**What**'s the matter?" I asked.

> —Cormier, "President Cleveland, Where Are You?" (p. 182)

A **demonstrative pronoun** is used to point out a specific person or thing.

> "Well, well, **this** is a fine present indeed," said the old man.
>
> > —Uchida, "Momotaro: Boy-of-the-Peach" (p. 621)

> **These** he knew because there were some raspberry bushes in the park and he and Terry were always picking and eating them when they biked past.
>
> > —Paulsen, from *Hatchet* (p. 100)

An **indefinite pronoun** is used to refer to people or things in general.

> Dickon's not like **anyone** in the world.
>
> > —Hanalis, *The Secret Garden* (p. 507)

VERBS

A **verb** is a word that expresses action or a state of being. An **action verb** tells what action someone or something is performing.

> Wandering wolves **caught** it, **threw** their long noses to the moon, and **howled** an answering cry.
>
> > —Baker, "Where the Buffaloes Begin" (p. 259)

A **linking verb** helps to make a statement by serving as a link between two words (for example, subject with predicate nominative or predicate adjective). The most commonly used linking verbs are forms of the verb *be*.

> This monster **was** insatiable.
>
> > —Baumann, "Nana Miriam" (p. 634)

> He never **grows** old.
>
> > —Erdoes and Ortiz, "Glooscap Fights the Water Monster" (p. 559)

A **helping verb** is a verb that can be added to another verb to make a verb phrase.

> The people of the neighboring states, who **were living** almost like savages, were very jealous when they saw the prosperity of the Toltecs.
>
> > —Cruse, "Quetzalcoatl" (p. 579)

ADJECTIVES

An **adjective** is a word used to modify a noun or pronoun. Adjectives tell *what kind, which one,* or *how many.*

> But McBean was quite **wrong.** I'm quite **happy** to say
> That the Sneetches got really quite **smart** on **that** day.
>
> —Dr. Seuss, "The Sneetches" (p. 291)

The articles *the, a,* and *an* are adjectives. *An* is used before a word beginning with a vowel sound or with an unsounded *h.*

ADVERBS

An **adverb** is a word used to modify a verb, an adjective, or another adverb. Adverbs tell *how, when, where,* and *to what extent.*

> Let me put it **more clearly,** since no one will believe that a girl of thirteen feels herself **quite** alone in the world, nor is it so.
>
> —Frank, from *The Diary of a Young Girl* (p. 394)

PREPOSITIONS

A **preposition** is a word that shows the relationship of a noun or a pronoun to some other word in the sentence. Prepositions are almost always followed by nouns or pronouns. A group of words that begins with a preposition and ends with a noun or pronoun is called a **prepositional phrase.**

> The look **in Pierre's eyes** stopped him.
>
> —Reynolds, "A Secret for Two" (p. 161)

> They went **to sea in a Sieve,** they did.
> **In a Sieve** they went **to sea:**
> **In spite of all their friends could say,**
> **On a winter's morn, on a stormy day,**
> **In a Sieve** they went **to sea!**
>
> —Lear, "The Jumblies" (p. 295)

> The two dogs eventually worked their way **to the middle of the car tracks,** and **after a while** two or three streetcars were held up **by the fight.**
>
> —Thurber, "Snapshot of a Dog" (p. 448)

CONJUNCTIONS

A **conjunction** is a word used to join words or groups of words. **Coordinating conjunctions** join equal parts of a sentence or similar groups of words.

> That winter the elbows began to crack **and** whole chunks of green began to fall off.
>
> —Soto, "The Jacket" (p. 39)

Correlative conjunctions are used in pairs to join similar words or groups of words.

> **Both** Tezcatlipoca **and** Quetzalcoatl were Toltec gods.

A **subordinating conjunction** is used to introduce a clause that has less importance than the main clause in a sentence.

> I was twelve years old **when** I made my first trip to the jungle with my father.
>
> —Nhuong, "The Land I Lost" (p. 413)

A **conjunctive adverb** is an adverb used as a conjunction to connect ideas.

> **Besides,** no one knew exactly what impressed the baby dragons as they struggled from their shells in search of their lifetime partners.
>
> —McCaffrey, "The Smallest Dragonboy" (p. 81)

INTERJECTIONS

An **interjection** is a word that expresses emotion and has no grammatical relation to other words in the sentence.

> "**Oh**, Mr. Tumnus—I'm so sorry to stop you, and I do love that tune—but really, I must go home."
>
> —Lewis, "Mr. Tumnus" (p. 15)

> Mary was silent for a moment. Then she said, "I probably shouldn't tell you this, but he didn't steal that watch, Sara."
> "**Huh!**"
>
> —Byars, *The Summer of the Swans* (p. 690)

PHRASES

A **phrase** is a group of words that does not contain a subject and a verb.

A **prepositional phrase** is a group of words that begins with a preposition and ends with a noun or pronoun.

in the story   **to** the lake
outside the house   **with** them

An **appositive** is a noun or pronoun placed beside another noun or pronoun to identify or explain it. An **appositive phrase** is made up of an appositive and its modifiers.

> "We have a report of a missing child in the Cass section—**ten-year-old Charlie Godfrey**."
> —Byars, *The Summer of the Swans* (p. 691)

A **participial phrase** consists of a participle and its complements or modifiers. The entire participial phrase acts as an adjective.

> Bad dogs **barking loud**
> Big ghosts in a cloud
> Life doesn't frighten me at all.
> —Angelou, "Life Doesn't Frighten Me" (p. 303)

> Now Maibon began to be truly distressed, not only for the toothless baby, the calfless cow, the fruitless tree, and the hen **sitting desperately on her eggs**, but for himself as well.
> —Alexander, "The Stone" (p. 213)

> The mighty voice rolled out upon the valley, each flutelike bark **echoing from slope to slope**.
> —Armstrong, from *Sounder* (p. 125)

> His tongue, **stained with berry juice**, stuck to the roof of his mouth and he stared at the bear.
> —Paulsen, from *Hatchet* (p. 100)

An **infinitive phrase** consists of an infinitive together with its modifiers and complements. The entire phrase can be used as a noun, an adjective, or an adverb.

> Monday was the best day **to buy the cards.** [infinitive phrase used as an adjective modifying *day*]
> —Cormier, "President Cleveland, Where Are You?" (p. 181)

CLAUSES

A **clause** is a group of words that has a subject and a verb. An **independent clause** expresses a complete thought and can stand by itself as a sentence.

> **The rattler struck him** from under the grapevine without warning.
> —Rawlings, "Jody's Discovery" (p. 131)

A **subordinate clause** does not express a complete thought and cannot stand by itself as a sentence.

> **When the woman opened the door**, she did not seem at all surprised to see her.
> —Petry, "Harriet Tubman" (p. 28)

Part 9: Mechanics

- Capitalization
- Punctuation
- Letters

CAPITALIZATION

1. FIRST WORDS

▋ **Capitalize the first word of every sentence.**

Examples
My clothes have failed me.
—Soto, "The Jacket" (p. 36)

When Tom reached the little isolated frame schoolhouse, he strode in briskly, with the manner of one who had come with all honest speed.
—Twain, from *The Adventures of Tom Sawyer* (p. 48)

▋ **Capitalize the first word of a direct quotation when the word begins with a capital letter in the original. If the writer has not** used a capital letter, do not capitalize the first word of the quotation.

Examples

Penny shouted, "Git back! Hold the dogs!"

—Rawlings, "Jody's Discovery" (p. 131)

"It's only just round the corner," said the faun, "and there'll be a roaring fire—and toast—and sardines—and cake."

—Lewis, "Mr. Tumnus" (p. 13)

■ **Traditionally, the first word in a line of poetry is capitalized, although some writers do not follow this rule for reasons of style.**

Examples

The sea is a hungry dog,
Giant and gray.
He rolls on the beach all day.

—Reeves, "The Sea" (p. 335)

Abuelito who throws coins like rain
and asks who loves him
who is dough and feathers . . .

—Cisneros, "Abuelito Who" (p. 345)

2. THE PRONOUN *I*

■ **Capitalize the pronoun *I*.**

Example

This here phizzog—somebody handed it to you —am **I** right?

—Sandburg, "Phizzog" (p. 368)

3. PROPER NOUNS AND PROPER ADJECTIVES

■ **A *proper noun* names a particular person, place, or thing. A *proper adjective* is formed from a proper noun. Capitalize proper nouns and proper adjectives.**

Examples

| Jamaica | Spain | Japan | Poland |
| Jamaican | Spanish | Japanese | Polish |

■ **In proper nouns consisting of two or more words, do not capitalize articles (*a, an, the*), short prepositions (those with fewer**

than five letters, such as *at, of, for, with*), and coordinating conjunctions (*and, but, for, nor, or, so, yet*).

Examples

San Antonio	Isle of Man
Caribbean Sea	President Clinton
Mayor Ruiz	Truth or Consequences

If you are not sure whether to capitalize a word, check in an up-to-date dictionary.

4. NAMES OF PEOPLE

■ **Capitalize the names of people. Note that some names may contain more than one capital letter.**

Examples

Blanche Hanalis	Scott O'Dell
L. M. Montgomery	Nikki Giovanni
Leroy V. Quintana	Harriet Tubman

5. GEOGRAPHICAL NAMES

■ **Capitalize geographical names, such as towns, cities, counties, townships, states, regions, countries, continents, islands, mountains, bodies of water, parks, roads, highways, and streets.**

Examples

San Francisco	Albemarle Sound	Interstate 90
North America	Catalina Island	Dade County
Panama Canal	Lake Huron	Third Avenue
Michigan	Route 110	Costa Rica

■ **Note that words such as *south, east,* and *northwest* are *not* capitalized when they indicate direction.**

Examples

| east of the Rockies | northwest of the airport |
| west of Tulsa | southeast of the mall |

6. ORGANIZATIONS

■ **Capitalize the names of organizations, teams, businesses, institutions, buildings, and government bodies.**

Examples

Chicago Bulls	Girl Scouts
Willis Intermediate School	General Electric
	Holiday Inn
Regent Hotel	Treasury Department
University of Texas	Empire State Building

7. HISTORICAL EVENTS

▌ Capitalize the names of historical events and periods, special events, and calendar items.

Examples

New Deal	Middle Ages	Flag Day
Stone Age	Wednesday	Tulip Festival
Earth Day	World Series	Korean War

8. NATIONALITIES, RACES, AND RELIGIONS

▌ Capitalize the names of nationalities, races, and peoples.

Examples

Chippewa	Bantu	Turkish
Aztec	African American	Navajo
Dominican	Micronesian	Vietnamese

▌ Capitalize the names of religions and their followers, holy days, sacred writings, and specific deities.

Examples

Islam	the Talmud	the Koran
Lutheran	Taoism	Pentecost
Good Friday	Presbyterian	Purim
the Bible	Lent	Hindu
Judaism	Allah	
Lakshmi	Potlatch	

9. BRAND NAMES

▌ Capitalize the brand names of business products. Do not capitalize the noun that often follows a brand name.

Examples

Chevrolet cars	Canon cameras
Ritz crackers	Tide detergent

10. PARTICULAR PLACES, THINGS, AND EVENTS

▌ Capitalize the names of ships, trains, airplanes, spacecraft, monuments, buildings, awards, planets, and any other particular places, things, or events.

Examples

Voyager 2	Tower of London	*Monitor*
Nobel Prize	Silver Crescent	*Concorde*
Uranus	*Pinta*	Niagara Falls

11. SPECIFIC COURSES, LANGUAGES

▌ Do *not* capitalize the names of school subjects, except for languages and for course names followed by a number.

Examples

chemistry	history	mathematics
biology	Spanish	Science 2

12. TITLES OF PEOPLE

▌ Capitalize a title belonging to a particular person when it comes before a person's name.

Examples

President Suharto	Professor Stern
General Powell	Principal Larson
Ms. Oates	Dr. Rao

▌ Do not capitalize a title used alone or following a person's name, especially if the title is preceded by *a* or *the*.

Examples

Rosa Santos, mayor of Galveston
the governor's mansion
a duke's title

▌ Capitalize a word showing a family relationship when the word is used with a person's name but *not* when it is preceded by a possessive.

Examples

Aunt Pia	Uncle Roger	their aunt Dot

13. TITLES OF LITERARY AND OTHER CREATIVE WORKS

▮ **Capitalize the first and last words and all important words in titles of books, magazines, newspapers, short poems, stories, historical documents, movies, television programs, works of art, and musical compositions.**

Unimportant words within titles are articles (*a, an, the*), short prepositions (fewer than five letters, such as *at, of, for, to, from, with*) and coordinating conjunctions (*and, but, for, nor, or, so, yet*).

Examples

The Summer of the Swans
The Secret Garden
"Life Doesn't Frighten Me"
"Nancy"
"Nana Miriam"
"Volcano"
Newsweek
Beauty and the Beast

▮ **The word *the* written before a title is capitalized only when it is the first word of a title.**

Examples

"The Jacket"   *Julie of the Wolves*

PUNCTUATION

1. END MARKS

▮ **End marks—*periods, question marks,* and *exclamation points*—are used to indicate the purpose of a sentence. (A period is also used at the end of many abbreviations.) Use a period to end a statement (or declarative sentence).**

Example

He was fourteen, three years older than I, and a freshman at Monument High School.

—Cormier, "President Cleveland, Where Are You?"
(p. 181)

▮ **A question (or interrogative sentence) is followed by a question mark.**

Examples

Did your father ever tell you about Misselthwaite Manor?

—Hanalis, *The Secret Garden* (p. 484)

"Then why did the king of Tyre not save her?"

—Graves, "Perseus" (p. 571)

You'll not repeat what I tell you?

—Hanalis, *The Secret Garden* (p. 491)

▮ **Use an exclamation point after an exclamation.**

Examples

"My goodness! What a great peach!"

—Uchida, "Momotaro: Boy-of-the-Peach" (p. 621)

"Bless you!" cried the king.

—Gardner, "Dragon, Dragon" (p. 169)

"Pa! You'll bleed to death!"

—Rawlings, "Jody's Discovery" (p. 134)

▮ **An imperative sentence may be followed by either a period or an exclamation point.**

Examples

Hold it firm with one hand, push the earth around it, an' tamp it down.

—Hanalis, *The Secret Garden* (p. 520)

"Well, don't wait around here!" cried the boy savagely.

—Bradbury, "All Summer in a Day" (p. 198)

▮ **Use a period after an abbreviation.**

Examples

Personal Names: M. R. Cox
Titles Used with Names: Rev., Dr., Mr., Mrs., Ms.
States: N.M., S.D., N.C., Ala.
Time of Day: A.M., P.M.
Years: B.C., A.D.
Addresses: St., Ave.
Organizations and Companies: Co., Inc.
Units of Measure: lb., oz., in., ft., yd., mi.

▮ **No periods are used in abbreviations with states when the zip code is included.**

Example

NC 28211

■ Abbreviations in the metric system are often written without periods: for example, km for kilometer, kg for kilogram, ml for milliliter. Abbreviations for government agencies and international organizations and some other frequently used abbreviations are written without periods: for example, NBA, NAACP, FBI, PTA.

2. COMMAS: CONVENTIONAL USES

■ Use a comma to separate items in dates and addresses.

Examples

I wrote to Darlene on June 26, 1995.
I sent the letter to 450 Springs Blvd., Scottsdale, AZ 85258.

■ Notice that a comma also separates the final item in a date and in an address from the words that follow it. A comma does *not* separate the month from the day, the house number from the street name, or the state name from the ZIP code.

■ Use a comma after the salutation of a friendly letter and after the closing of any letter.

Examples

Dear Rev. Sanchez,   My dear Gloria,
Sincerely yours,   Love,

For other uses of commas, see **Part 5** (pp. 765–766).

3. SEMICOLONS

■ Use a semicolon between independent clauses that are closely related in thought and that are not joined by *and, but, or, nor, for, so,* or *yet.*

Example

The maize crops were more abundant than they had ever been before; the fruits were larger and more plentiful.

—Cruse, "Quetzalcoatl" (p. 578)

4. COLONS

■ Use a colon before a list of items, especially after expressions like *as follows* and *the following.*

Example

Marcia's favorite writers were the following: Maya Angelou, Pat Mora, Robert Cormier, and Elizabeth Enright.

■ Use a colon in certain conventional situations: between the hour and the minute, between chapter and verse in a Biblical citation, and after the salutation of a business letter.

Examples

10:30 A.M.   Exodus 4:10   Dear Dr. Long:

5. ITALICS

■ When writing or typing, indicate italics by underlining. Use italics for titles of books, plays, periodicals, films, television programs, long musical compositions, ships, aircraft, and spacecraft.

Examples

BOOK: *Island of the Blue Dolphins*
PLAY: *Carousel*
PERIODICAL: *People*
FILM: *The Last Emperor*
TELEVISION PROGRAM: *Safari*
LONG MUSICAL COMPOSITION: *A Little Night Music*
SHIP: *Queen Mary*
AIRCRAFT: *Spirit of St. Louis*
SPACECRAFT: *Discovery*

■ Use italics for words, letters, and figures referred to as such.

Examples

All right should always be written as two words.

Double the *p* and add *-ed* to form the past participle of the verb *hop.*

Many people think that *7* is a lucky number.

Vaca is Spanish for cow.

6. QUOTATION MARKS

■ **Use quotation marks to enclose a direct quotation—a person's exact words.**

Example

"Maibon, it's the fault of that stone!" wailed his wife.

—Alexander, "The Stone" (p. 212)

■ **Do not use quotation marks to enclose an indirect quotation—a rewording of a direct quotation.**

Example

I wondered what was happening to me, because I did not know whether to laugh or cry.

—Cormier, "President Cleveland, Where Are You?" (p. 183)

■ **Begin a direct quotation with a capital letter.**

Example

Sara looked down into his eyes and said, "**Oh**, come on," and drew him to his feet.

—Byars, *The Summer of the Swans* (p. 659)

■ **When an expression identifying the speaker interrupts a quoted sentence, the second part of the quotation begins with a small letter.**

Example

"Okay," I said, "what do *you* want for breakfast?"

—Cosby, "Fatherhood" (p. 454)

■ **A direct quotation is set off from the rest of the sentence by a comma or by a question mark or an exclamation point.**

Examples

"Janice Gordon has a bike," I reminded her.
—Berry, "Becky and the Wheels-and-Brake Boys" (p. 226)

"Did he die?" asked Ezinma.
—Achebe, "Why Tortoise's Shell Is Not Smooth" (p. 604)

"Charlie!" she shouted with all her might.
—Byars, *The Summer of the Swans* (p. 704)

■ **Commas and periods are always placed inside closing quotation marks.**

Examples

"I am going back to my country," Quetzalcoatl answered.

—Cruse, "Quetzalcoatl" (p. 581)

At last he said, "I want to go home."

—Ashabranner, "The Most Vulnerable People"

■ **Question marks and exclamation points are placed inside closing quotation marks if the quotation is a question or an exclamation. Otherwise, they are placed outside.**

Examples

"A girl from the North Side?" I asked, incredulous.

—Cormier, "President Cleveland, Where Are You?" (p. 186)

"Babes don't give orders to candidates around here, babe!"

—McCaffrey, "The Smallest Dragonboy" (p. 88)

Did you like Edward Lear's "The Jumblies"?

Let's all read "Habits of the Hippopotamus"!

■ **When you write dialogue (conversation), begin a new paragraph every time the speaker changes, and enclose each speaker's words in quotation marks.**

Example

The cobbler scratched his chin and considered it. "It's not enough," he said at last. "It's a good enough kingdom, you understand, but it's too much responsibility."

"Take it or leave it," the king said.

"I'll leave it," said the cobbler. And he shrugged and went home.

—Gardner, "Dragon, Dragon" (pp. 168–169)

■ **When a quotation consists of several sentences, place quotation marks at the beginning and at the end of the whole quotation.**

Example

"Why, it is she that has got all Narnia under her thumb. It's she that makes it always winter. Always winter and never Christmas—think of that!"

—Lewis, "Mr. Tumnus" (p. 16)

■ Use single quotation marks to enclose a quotation within a quotation.

Example

Donna reminded us, "At the end of the play, Colin's exact words are, 'When I was at Oxford, I asked you to marry me.' "

■ Use quotation marks to enclose titles of short works, such as short stories, short poems, articles, songs, episodes of television programs, and chapters and other parts of books.

Examples

SHORT STORY: "Dragon, Dragon"
SHORT POEM: "Beach Stones"
ARTICLE: "Splendors of Coral"
SONG: "Yankee Doodle"
TV EPISODE: "Nest of Vipers"

7. APOSTROPHES

POSSESSIVE CASE

■ To form the possessive of a singular noun, add an apostrophe and an *s*. Add only the apostrophe to a proper noun ending in an *s* sound if the addition of *'s* would make the name awkward to pronounce.

Examples

the **sun's** rays   **Roberta's** bike
a **bird's** wings   Mr. **Rodriguez'** class

■ To form the possessive of a plural noun that does not end in *s*, add an apostrophe and an *s*.

Examples

the **children's** toys   **women's** hats

■ To form the possessive of a plural noun ending in *s*, add only the apostrophe.

Examples

the **trees'** leaves   the **jars'** lids

■ Do not use an apostrophe with possessive personal pronouns.

Incorrect

Are these hats **our's**?

Correct

Are these hats **ours**?

■ To form the possessive of some indefinite pronouns, add an apostrophe and an *s*.

Examples

Everyone's vote counts.
Someone's books are on that table.

CONTRACTIONS

■ Use an apostrophe to show where letters or numerals have been left out in a contraction.

Examples

We're here. [We are]   **I'm** not sure. [I am]
Let's go. [Let us]   **He'd** arrived. [He had]
in the **'90s** [1990s]   **You'll** see. [You will]

PLURALS

■ Use an apostrope and an *s* to form the plurals of letters, numerals, signs, and of words referred to as words.

Examples

That word has four *s***'s**.
Write your *4***'s** more clearly, please.
Use *@***'s** on the invoice.
Take out some of the *and***'s** in that sentence.

8. HYPHENS

■ Use a hyphen to divide a word at the end of a line.

Example

Many of Anne McCaffrey's books are **available** in foreign languages.

■ Divide a word only between syllables.

Incorrect

Rawlings' *The Yearling* became a very succe-ssful movie.

Correct

Rawlings' *The Yearling* became a very **successful** movie.

■ Do not divide a one-syllable word.

Incorrect

Nonfiction deals with real people and events: fa-cts are not changed.

Correct

Nonfiction deals with real people and events: **facts** are not changed.

■ **Do not divide a word so that one letter stands alone.**

Incorrect

Language that appeals to the sense is called i-magery.

Correct

Language that appeals to the senses is called **im-agery.**

■ **Use a hyphen with compound numbers from *twenty-one* to *ninety-nine* and with fractions used as modifiers.**

Examples

fifty-two cards   a **two-thirds** vote

LETTERS

1. PERSONAL AND SOCIAL LETTERS

■ **Follow the format below for a personal or social letter.**

Your Address
Today's Date

Dear ———,

——————————————————
——————————————————
——————————————————

———————,
(Your Signature)

2. BUSINESS LETTERS

■ **Use either of the two formats below for a business letter.**

Block Style

Heading (Your Address and Today's Date)

Inside Address (Name and Address of the Person or Company You Are Writing)

(Salutation):

——————————————————
——————————————————
——————————————————.
——————————————————
——————————————————.

(Closing),
(Your Signature and Typed Name)

Modified Block Style

Heading (Your Address
and Today's Date)

Inside Address (Name and Address of the Person or Company You Are Writing)

(Salutation):

——————————————————
——————————————————.
——————————————————
——————————————————
——————————————————.

(Closing),
(Your Signature and Typed Name)

Glossary

The words listed in this Glossary are found in the selections in this book. Use this Glossary as you would a dictionary—to look up unfamiliar words. Strictly speaking, the word *glossary* means a collection of technical, obscure, or foreign words found in a certain field of work. The words in this Glossary are not "technical, obscure, or foreign," but are those that might present difficulty as you read the selections in this book.

Many words in the English language have several meanings. This Glossary gives the meanings that apply to the words as they are used in the selections in the book. Words closely related in form and meaning are generally listed together in one entry (**arrogance** and **arrogant**), and the definition is given for the first form. Regular adverbs (ending in -*ly*) are defined in their adjective form; the adverb form is shown at the end of the definition.

The following abbreviations are used:

    adj., adjective   *n.*, noun
    adv., adverb   *v.*, verb

For more information about the words in this Glossary, consult a dictionary.

A

abrupt (ə·brupt′) *adj.* **1.** Sudden; hasty. **2.** Rude or curt, as in speech.

abundant (ə·bun′dənt) *adj.* Existing in plentiful supply.

accede (ak·sēd′) *v.* To give consent or agreement; say yes.

accommodation (ə·kom′ə·dā′shən) *n.* A willingness to help or oblige.

accompany (ə·kum′pə·nē) *v.* To come or go along with. —**accompaniment** *n.*

accord (ə·kôrd′) *v.* To give as due or earned. —**of one's own accord** By one's own choice.

accumulation (ə·kyoom′yə·lā′shən) *n.* A collecting or gathering together.

accurate (ak′yər·it) *adj.* Making no error; exact; true. —**accurately** *adv.*

acquaintance (ə·kwān′təns) *n.* A person with whom one is slightly familiar.

acquire (ə·kwīr) *v.* To come into possession of; to get.

adjacent (ə·jā′sənt) *adj.* Lying near or close by.

adjoin (ə·join) *v.* To be next to. —**adjoining** *adj.*

affected (ə·fek′tid) *adj.* Not natural; artificial.

aggravate (ag′rə·vāt′) *v.* **1.** To make

worse, more serious, more un-pleasant. **2.** To make angry; annoy.

aghast (ə·gast') *adj.* Shocked; horrified.

agony (ag'ə·nē) *n.* A terrible suffering of body or mind.

ailment (āl'mənt) *n.* An illness.

albeit (ôl·bē'it) *conj.* Even though.

alert (ə·lurt') **1.** *v.* To warn or prepare, as if for danger or attack. **2.** *adj.* Very watchful and ready.

alleviate (a·lē'vē·āt') *v.* To make lighter or easier to bear; relieve.

aloof (ə·loof') *adj.* Cool or distant in manner or action; unsympathetic.

altitude (al'tə·tood) *n.* Height.

amateur (am'ə·choor) *n.* A person who does something without sound training or skill.

ambush (am'boosh) **1.** *n.* A concealed place where troops, or others, lie hidden to attack. **2.** *v.* To hide in order to attack.

anchorage (ang'kər·ij) *n.* Something that gives support or steadiness.

anguish (ang'gwish) *n.* Great suffering of mind or body; agony.

animated (an'ə·mā'tid) *adj.* Having spirit or zest; lively. —**animatedly** *adv.*

animosity (an'ə·mos'ə·tē) *n.* Strong dislike or hatred.

antic (an'tik) *n.* (*usually plural*) A prank or funny act.

anvil (an'vil) *n.* A heavy block of iron or steel on which heated metal is hammered into shape.

apparatus (ap'ə·ra'təs) *n.* All the devices or equipment for a particular use.

apparent (ə·par'ənt) *adj.* Obvious.

application (ap'li·kā'shən) *n.* **1.** Something put on, especially a medicine or treatment. **2.** A formal request.

arrogance (ar'ə·gəns) *n.* Too much pride and too little regard for others. — **arrogant** *adj.*

aspire (ə·spīr') *v.* To have great hope or ambition for something; seek.

assent (ə·sent') *v.* To agree or consent.

assortment (ə·sôrt'mənt) *n.* A collection or group of various things; variety.

astound (ə·stound') *v.* To stun with amazement.

attire (ə·tir') *n.* Clothing.

avenge (ə·venj') *v.* To get revenge for.

avid (av'id) *adj.* **1.** Enthusiastic; eager. **2.** Greedy. —**avidly** *adv.*

awe (ô) *n.* A feeling of fear and wonder, as at the size or power of something.

awry (ə·rī') *adj.* **1.** Leaning or turned to one side. **2.** Not right; amiss.

B

baleful (bāl'fəl) *adj.* Evil or threatening.

banish (ban'ish) *v.* To drive away; get rid of; dismiss.

bawl (bôl) *v.* **1.** To call out loudly; shout. **2.** To cry or sob noisily.

a	add	i	it	o͝o	took	oi	oil
ā	ace	ī	ice	o͞o	pool	ou	pout
â	care	o	odd	u	up	ng	ring
ä	palm	ō	open	û	burn	th	thin
e	end	ô	order	yo͞o	fuse	th	this
ē	equal					zh	vision

ə = { a in *above* e in *sicken* i in *possible*
{ o in *melon* u in *circus*

beacon (bē′kən) *n.* Any light for warning or guiding.

beckon (bek′ən) *v.* To summon or signal by a movement of the hand or head.

bellow (bel′ō) *v.* To utter a loud, hollow cry.

betray (bi·trā′) *v.* **1.** To fail, desert, or be unfaithful to. **2.** To give away; disclose.

bewilder (bi·wil′dər) *v.* To puzzle or confuse.

billow (bil′ō) *v.* To rise or roll in waves; swell.

bison (bi′sən) *n.* A large wild animal related to the ox. The North American bison is called a buffalo.

blistering (blis′tər·ing) *adj.* Extremely strong or intense.

bloat (blōt) *v.* To puff up; swell.

blurt *v.* To say abruptly or without thinking.

bog 1. *n.* Wet and spongy ground, such as a swamp. **2.** *v.* To sink or cause to sink in, as if in a bog.

boisterous (bois′tər·əs) *adj.* Noisy and wild. —**boisterously** *adv.*

brandish (bran′dish) *v.* To wave triumphantly or threateningly.

brier (brī′ər) *n.* A prickly bush or shrub.

brisk *adj.* Acting or moving quickly; lively. —**briskly** *adv.*

brood *n.* All of the young of the same mother.

buffet (buf′it) *v.* To strike over and over.

bulbous (bul′bəs) *adj.* Shaped like a bulb.

C

cajole (kə·jōl′) *v.* To coax or persuade by flattery or deceit.

callous (kal′əs) *adj.* **1.** Thickened and hardened. **2.** Unfeeling; hardhearted.

candidate (kan′də·dāt′) *n.* A person who seeks, or is proposed for, an office or honor.

canvass (kan′vəs) *v.* To examine, discuss, or debate.

carcass (kar′kəs) *n.* The dead body of an animal.

cascade (kas·kād′) *n.* **1.** A small waterfall. **2.** Something that looks like a waterfall.

casual (kazh′ōō·əl) *adj.* **1.** Happening by chance; not planned. **2.** Informal and relaxed.

catastrophe (kə·tas′trə·fē) *n.* A sudden and widespread misfortune or disaster.

caustic (kôs′tik) *adj.* **1.** Capable of eating or burning away living tissue. **2.** Sarcastic; biting.

cautious (kô′shəs) *adj.* Careful not to take chances or make mistakes. —**cautiously** *adv.*

cavern (kav′ərn) *n.* A large cave.

ceaseless (sēs′lis) *adj.* Going on without pause; continual. —**ceaselessly** *adv.*

chastise (chas′tīz) *v.* To punish, scold, or condemn.

chide (chīd) *v.* To scold mildly.

clamber (klam′bər) *v.* To climb up or down with effort, using both hands and feet.

clamor (klam′ər) *n.* A loud and continuous noise, especially a loud protest or outcry.

commend (kə·mend′) *v.* To speak highly of; praise.

commitment (kə·mit′mənt) *n.* A pledge; promise.

commotion (kə·mō′shən) *n.* Great confusion; excitement; disturbance.

compassion (kəm·pash′ən) *n.* Pity for the suffering or distress of another and the desire to help. —**compassionate** *adj.*

compensation (kom′pən·sā′shən) *n.* Something paid, given, or done to balance something else.

complement (kom′plə·mənt) **1.** *n.* Something that completes or perfects. **2.** *v.* To make complete.

complexion (kəm·plek′shən) *n.* The color and appearance of the skin, especially of the face.

compose (kəm·pōz′) *v.* **1.** To make up; form. **2.** To create. **3.** To make calm.

compound (kom·pound′) *v.* To mix; put together.

compulsion (kəm·pul′shən) *n.* An irresistible, sometimes irrational, urge.

comrade (kom′rad) *n.* A close companion or friend.

concealment (kən·sēl′mənt) *n.* A place or means of hiding.

conceivable (kən·sē′və·bəl) *adj.* Imaginable; capable of being thought of.

conduct 1. *n.* (kon′dukt) A person's behavior. **2.** *v.* (kən·dukt′) To act or behave.

confront (kən·frunt′) *v.* To stand face to face with; face boldly. —**confrontation** *n.*

conquest (kon′kwest′) *n.* The act of winning over or defeating by force.

consciousness (kon′shəs·nis) *n.* The condition of being awake and aware.

consensus (kən·sen′səs) *n.* Agreement of a majority or of everyone; general opinion.

console (kən·sōl′) *v.* To comfort in sorrow or disappointment; cheer.

constellation (kon′stə·lā′shən) *n.* A group of stars to which a name has been assigned.

constrict (kən·strikt′) *v.* To draw together; make narrower; squeeze. —**constriction** *n.*

constructive (kən·struk′tiv) *adj.* Helping to build up or improve. —**constructively** *adv.*

consumption (kən·sump′shən) *n.* The act of using up or destroying.

contempt (kən·tempt′) *n.* The feeling that a person, act, or thing is low, dishonorable, or disgusting.

contemptuous (kən·temp′chōō·əs) *adj.* Full of scorn; disdainful.

contortion (kən·tôr′shən) *n.* The act of twisting.

a	add	i	it	o͝o	took	oi	oil
ā	ace	ī	ice	o͞o	pool	ou	pout
â	care	o	odd	u	up	ng	ring
ä	palm	ō	open	û	burn	th	thin
e	end	ô	order	yo͞o	fuse	th	this
ē	equal					zh	vision

ə = { a in *above*   e in *sicken*   i in *possible*
{ o in *melon*   u in *circus*

contraption (kən·trap′shən) *n.* An odd or puzzling device or gadget.

conventional (kən·ven′shən·əl) *adj.* **1.** Established by custom; usual. **2.** Behaving in an expected way.

converse (kən·vûrs′) *v.* To take part in a conversation.

convict 1. *n.* (kon′vikt) A person found guilty of a crime and serving a prison sentence. **2.** *v.* (kən·vikt′) To prove guilty.

cordial (kôr′jəl) *adj.* Warm and hearty; sincere.

corridor (kôr′ə·dər) *n.* A long hallway.

courteous (kûr′tē·əs) *adj.* Polite and considerate. —**courteously** *adv.*

cradle (krād′əl) *v.* To hold and rock as if in a baby's cradle.

crane *v.* To stretch out (one's neck), especially to try to look at something.

crater (krā′tər) *n.* **1.** A bowl-shaped hollow around an opening of a volcano. **2.** A hole made by an explosion.

crave (krāv) *v.* To want very much.

crestfallen (krest′fô′lən) *adj.* Low in spirits; downcast.

crevice (krev′is) *n.* A narrow opening due to a crack or split, as in a rock or wall.

crouch *v.* To bend down in a shrinking or cowering position.

crude (krōōd) *adj.* **1.** Lacking good taste; uncouth. **2.** Roughly made; not well finished. —**crudely** *adv.*

curt (kûrt) *adj.* Short and somewhat rude in tone or manner.

D

dam *n.* A wall or other barrier that is built to hold back flowing water.

debris (də·brē′) *n.* **1.** Scattered fragments or remains; rubble. **2.** Something discarded; rubbish.

decisive (di·sī′siv) *adj.* Showing decision; firm.

dedicate (ded′ə·kāt′) *v.* **1.** To set aside or devote to a special purpose. **2.** To write or say publicly that a thing has been done as a sign of affection or respect for a person named.

defiant (də·fī′ənt) *adj.* Boldly resisting to obey or submit.

dejection (di·jek′shən) *n.* Lowness of spirits; sadness.

delectable (di·lek′tə·bəl) *adj.* Delicious.

deliberation (di·lib′ə·rā′shən) *n.* Long and careful thought.

delve *v.* **1.** To dig with a spade. **2.** To make a careful search for information.

demote (di·mōt′) *v.* To reduce to a lower grade, rank, or position. —**demotion** *n.*

deposit (di·poz′it) *v.* **1.** To set down; place. **2.** To give over for safekeeping. **3.** To make a partial payment.

descend (di·send′) *v.* To go or move from a higher to a lower point; to go down.

descent (di·sent′) *n.* The action of going down or coming down to a lower point.

desolate 1. *adj.* (des′ə·lit) Dreary; empty. **2.** *v.* (des′ə·lāt′) To make sorrowful or miserable. —**desolation** *n.*

desperation (des′pə·rā′shən) *n.* A state of despair that causes reckless behavior.

despondent (di·spon′dənt) *adj.* Discouraged or depressed.

destination (des′tə·nā′shən) *n.* The place toward which someone is going; goal.

destruction (di·struk′shən) *n.* Ruin or great damage.

detached (di·tacht′) *adj.* **1.** Standing alone; separate. **2.** Not favoring a certain side.

detest (di·test′) *v.* To hate.

devastate (dev′ə·stāt′) *v.* To leave in ruins; destroy.

device (di·vīs′) *n.* **1.** An instrument or tool. **2.** A scheme or plan. —**leave to his or her own devices** To let someone do as he or she pleases.

dignity (dig′nə·tē) *n.* **1.** The quality of character or worth that commands respect. **2.** Stately manner.

dimension (di·men′shən) *n.* Any measurable extent, as length, width, depth.

diminish (di·min′ish) *n.* To make smaller or less; decrease.

disastrous (di·zas′trəs) *adj.* Causing great distress or damage.

discard (dis·kard′) *v.* To throw away or get rid of.

discourse (dis′kôrs) *n.* **1.** A formal speech. **2.** Conversation.

disdain (dis·dān′) *n.* Scorn or haughty contempt, especially toward someone considered inferior.

disembodied (dis′em·bod′ēd) *adj.* Existing apart from a body.

disgrace (dis·grās′) **1.** *n.* A condition of shame or dishonor. **2.** *v.* To bring shame or dishonor to.

dismal (diz′məl) *adj.* **1.** Very bad. **2.** Dark, gloomy, and depressing. **3.** Sad and miserable.

dismantle (dis·man′təl) *v.* **1.** To remove all equipment or furnishings from. **2.** To take apart.

dismay (dis·mā′) **1.** *n.* Alarm, uneasiness, and confusion. **2.** *v.* To fill with uneasiness and alarm.

disoblige (dis′ə·blīj′) *v.* To act against the wishes of.

disposition (dis′pə·zish′ən) *n.* Someone's usual mood or spirit; temperament.

dispute (dis·pyo͞ot′) **1.** *v.* To quarrel. **2.** *n.* An argument or debate.

disrepair (dis′rə·pâr′) *n.* A run-down condition due to neglect.

dissipate (dis′ə·pāt′) *v.* To break up and scatter or dissolve.

distort (dis·tôrt′) *v.* **1.** To twist out of normal shape. **2.** To alter in a way that creates a false impression.

a	add	i	it	o͝o	took	oi	oil
ā	ace	ī	ice	o͞o	pool	ou	pout
â	care	o	odd	u	up	ng	ring
ä	palm	ō	open	û	burn	th	thin
e	end	ô	order	yo͞o	fuse	th	this
ē	equal					zh	vision

ə = { a in *above*   e in *sicken*   i in *possible*
{ o in *melon*   u in *circus*

distraught (dis·trôt′) *adj.* Extremely upset; crazed.

distress (dis·tres′) **1.** *n.* Extreme suffering or its cause. **2.** *v.* To cause to suffer or worry.

divulge (dī·vulj′) *v.* To tell; reveal.

domain (dō·mān′) *n.* **1.** Land belonging to one ruler or government. **2.** Any field of action, interest, or knowledge.

dome (dōm) *n.* A round roof shaped somewhat like an upside-down cup.

domestic (də·mes′tik) *adj.* Of or having to do with the home or family.

dominate (dom′ə·nāt′) *n.* To control or rule over.

dour (dŏor) *adj.* Gloomy and sullen.

dreary (drir′ē) *adj.* Full of or causing sadness or gloom.

drone *v.* **1.** To make a deep humming or buzzing sound. **2.** To speak in a dull manner.

drought (drout) *n.* A lack of rain for a long period; a severe dry spell.

drouth (drout) *n.* Another word for **drought.**

drowsy (drou′zē) *adj.* Sleepy.

dwarf (dwôrf) *n.* **1.** In fairy tales, a tiny person having some special skill or magical power. **2.** A person, animal, or plant that is much smaller than normal size.

E

eavesdrop (ēvz′drop′) *v.* To listen secretly to things being said in private.

ebullient (i·bŏol′yənt) *adj.* Bubbling over with high spirits.

edible (ed′ə·bəl) *adj.* Fit to eat.

eerie (ir′ē) *adj.* Causing or arousing fear; weird; strange. —**eerily** *adv.*

elate (i·lāt′) *v.* To cause to feel full of joy or pride.

elegant (el′ə·gənt) *adj.* Tasteful, luxurious, and beautiful.

elicit (i·lis′it) *v.* To call forth or draw out.

eligible (el′ə·jə·bəl) *adj.* Capable of or legally qualified for something.

eliminate (i·lim′ə·nāt′) *v.* **1.** To get rid of. **2.** To remove from competition.

elixir (i·lik′sər) *n.* A sweetened liquid.

elongate (i·long′gāt′) *v.* To increase in length; stretch out.

eloquent (el′ə·kwənt) *adj.* Effective or skillful in expressing feelings or ideas.

elude (i·lōōd′) *v.* To escape from by quickness or cleverness.

emaciated (i·mā′shē·āt′id) *adj.* Abnormally thin. —**emaciation** *n.*

embed (im·bed′) *v.* To set firmly in a surrounding substance.

emerge (i·mûrj′) *v.* To come forth or come out, so as to be visible.

emigrate (em′ə·grāt′) *v.* To move from one country or section of a country to settle in another.

emit (i·mit′) *v.* To send forth or give off.

emphatic (em·fat′ik) *adj.* Spoken or done with emphasis. —**emphatically** *adv.*

endure (in·dŏor′) *v.* To put up with; bear; tolerate.

engulf (in·gulf′) *v.* To swallow up; overwhelm completely.

enhance (in·hans′) *v.* To add to; increase.

ensue (in·sσō′) *v.* To follow in time; to come next.

entice (in·tīs′) *v.* To attract by tempting with something attractive or desirable.

entreaty (in·trē′tē) *n.* An earnest request or plea.

enviable (en′vē·ə·bəl) *adj.* So excellent as to be envied or much desired.

envious (en′vē·əs) *adj.* Feeling discontent or jealousy because of someone else's good fortune. —**enviously** *adv.*

epidemic (ep′ə·dem′ik) *n.* The sudden spread of a disease among many people.

epitome (i·pit′ə·mē) *n.* A person or thing that possesses all of the qualities or characteristics of something.

erect (i·rekt′) *adj.* Upright; not stooping or leaning.

erupt (i·rupt′) *v.* To cast forth (as lava or steam).

etiquette (et′ə·kət) *n.* The rules established for behavior in polite society or in official or professional life.

evasion (i·vā′zhən) *n.* The act of getting away from, especially the avoiding of something unpleasant by tricks or cleverness.

evoke (i·vōk′) *v.* To call forth.

exasperation (ig·zas′pə·rā′shən) *n.* The feeling of being annoyed or irritated almost to the point of anger.

exceedingly (ik·sē′ding·lē) *adv.* Extremely; very.

exertion (ig·zûr′shən) *n.* Great effort.

exhalation (eks′hə·lā′shən) *n.* The process of breathing out.

exhaust (ig·zôst′) *v.* **1.** To make extremely tired. **2.** To use up entirely. **3.** To study or discuss thoroughly.

exhilarate (ig·zil′ə·rāt′) *v.* To fill with happiness or high spirits.

exquisite (eks′kwi·zit) *adj.* **1.** Finely and delicately made. **2.** Extremely beautiful.

extravagant (ik·strav′ə·gənt) *adj.* **1.** Going beyond reason or proper limits. **2.** Spending too much.

extremity (ik·strem′ə·tē) *n.* **1.** The most distant point or part. **2.** Something extreme, such as distress, need, or danger.

F

facet (fas′it) *n.* One of the small, smooth surfaces cut upon a gem. —**faceted** *adj.*

falter (fôl′tər) *v.* To hesitate, be uncertain.

famine (fam′in) *n.* A widespread lack of food which causes starvation.

a	add	i	it	o͝o	took	oi	oil
ā	ace	ī	ice	o͞o	pool	ou	pout
â	care	o	odd	u	up	ng	ring
ä	palm	ō	open	û	burn	th	thin
e	end	ô	order	yo͞o	fuse	th	this
ē	equal					zh	vision

ə = { a in *above* e in *sicken* i in *possible*
       { o in *melon* u in *circus*

fate *n.* What happens to a person; fortune.

favoritism (fā′vər·ə·tiz′əm) *n.* An unfair favoring of one or a few out of a group.

feeble (fē′bəl) *adj.* **1.** Lacking strength; weak. **2.** Not adequate or effective.

fell (fel) *v.* To cut down.

ferocious (fə·rō′shəs) *adj.* Extremely fierce or savage.

filter (fil′tər) *v.* **1.** To act as a device that strains out impurities from a liquid or gas. **2.** To leak out slowly.

fleeting (flēt′ing) *adj.* Passing quickly.

flexible (flek′sə·bəl) *adj.* **1.** Capable of being bent or twisted without breaking. **2.** Easily changed; adaptable.

flippant (flip′ənt) *adj.* Not respectful or serious; too smart or pert.

flirt (flûrt) *v.* To act in an affectionate or loving way without being serious. —**flirtation** *n.*

flourish (flûr′ish) *v.* To wave about.

fluster (flus′tər) *v.* To make confused or upset.

foal (fōl) *n.* A young horse, donkey, zebra, or similar animal.

foliage (fō′lē·ij *or* fō′lij) *n.* The leaves of trees or plants.

forlorn (fôr·lôrn′) *adj.* Sad or pitiful because alone or neglected.

fracture (frak′chər) *v.* To break or crack.

frail (frāl) *adj.* Easily damaged in body or structure; weak.

frantic (fran′tik) *adj.* Wild with fear, worry, pain, or rage.

frazzle (fraz′əl) *v.* To tire out, exhaust.

frenzied (fren′zēd) *adj.* Wildly excited. —**frenziedly** *adv.*

frenzy (fren′zē) *n.* A wild, excited fit or condition.

frustrate (frus′trāt′) *v.* To baffle the efforts of or bring to nothing.

furtive (fûr′tiv) *adj.* Done in secret; stealthy.

futile (fyōō′təl) *adj.* Useless.

G

gape (gāp) *v.* To stare with the mouth open, as in surprise.

garb *n.* Clothing.

garish (gâr′ish) *adj.* Too showy or bright; gaudy.

gaunt (gônt) *adj.* Very thin and bony, as from illness.

genuine (jen′yōō·in) *adj.* **1.** Being as it appears; not false. **2.** Sincere.

gesture (jes′chər) *n.* A motion of the hands or other part of the body that expresses some feeling or idea.

gingerly (jin′jər·lē) *adv.* In a cautious, careful, or reluctant manner.

gird (gûrd) *v.* To get ready for action.

glisten (glis′ən) *v.* To shine or sparkle.

gnarled (närld) *adj.* Knotty or twisted.

gnash (nash) *v.* To grind or strike the teeth together, as in a rage.

gnaw (nô) *v.* **1.** To bite or eat away little by little. **2.** To trouble persistently.

goad (gōd) *v.* To drive into action; to urge on.

gouge (gouj) *v.* To scoop out.

gratify (grat′ə·fī′) *v.* To satisfy; indulge.

gratitude (grat′ə·tood′) *n.* Thankfulness for a gift or favor; appreciation.

grimace (gri·mās′) *n.* A twisting of the face expressing pain, annoyance, disgust, or other feelings.

grudging (gruj′ing) *adj.* Reluctant; unwilling. **—grudgingly** *adv.*

guarantee (gar′an·tē′) *n.* **1.** A pledge to repair, replace, or refund payment for something. **2.** A promise.

gusto (gus′tō) *n.* Keen enjoyment.

guttural (gut′ər·əl) *adj.* Having a throaty, grating sound; harsh.

H

habituate (hə·bich′oo āt′) *v.* To accustom or make used to.

hallucination (hə·loo′sə·nā′shən) *n.* The impression of seeing or hearing something that is not really present.

hamper *v.* To interfere with the movements of.

harass (hə·ras′) *v.* To trouble, as with cares or worries.

hasty (hās′tē) *adj.* **1.** Quick. **2.** Acting or done on impulse; rash.

haughty (hô′tē) *adj.* Satisfied with one's self and scornful of others; arrogant.

haze *n.* **1.** Fine droplets, as of water or dust particles, suspended in air. **2.** Mental confusion; muddle.

heartily (här′tə·lē) *adv.* Sincerely and enthusiastically.

heir (âr) *n.* A person who inherits or is likely to inherit property upon the death of the person possessing it.

hogan (hō′gən) *n.* A Navaho hut made of sticks and branches and covered with earth.

hogshead (hogz′hed′ *or* hôgz′hed′) *n.* A barrel or cask large enough to hold from 63 to 140 gallons.

hoist *v.* To raise or lift, especially by mechanical means.

homage (hom′ij) *n.* Respect or honor given or shown.

hostile (hos′təl) *adj.* **1.** Having to do with the enemy. **2.** Showing dislike; unfriendly.

humiliate (hyoo·mil′ē·āt′) *v.* To strip of pride or self-respect; embarrass.

hysterical (his·ter′ə·kəl) *adj.* Showing uncontrolled excitement or emotion.

I

idle (īd′əl) *adj.* **1.** Not busy. **2.** Lazy; unwilling to work.

ignite (ig·nīt′) *v.* To set on fire.

illuminate (i·loo′mə·nāt′) *v.* **1.** To light up. **2.** To make clear.

illusion (i·loo′zhən) *n.* A deceiving appearance or the false impression it gives.

imperative (im·per′ə·tiv) *adj.* Urgently necessary; unavoidable.

a	add	i	it	oo	took	oi	oil
ā	ace	ī	ice	oo	pool	ou	pout
â	care	o	odd	u	up	ng	ring
ä	palm	ō	open	û	burn	th	thin
e	end	ô	order	yoo	fuse	th	this
ē	equal					zh	vision

ə = { a in *above*   e in *sicken*   i in *possible*
     { o in *melon*   u in *circus*

imperious (im·pir′ē·əs) *adj.* Proud and haughty.

impetuous (im·pech′oo·əs) *adj.* Acting on impulse and without thought; rash. —**impetuously** *adv.*

imposing (im·pō′zing) *adj.* Impressive, as in manner, appearance, or size.

impostor (im·pos′tər) *n.* A person who deceives, especially one who pretends to be someone else.

impudence (im′pyə·dəns) *n.* Offensive boldness; rudeness.

impulse (im′puls) *n.* **1.** A driving force. **2.** A sudden desire or feeling which makes one want to act.

incision (in·sizh′ən) *n.* A cut or gash, especially one made in surgery.

incoherent (in′kō·hir′ənt) *adj.* Not clear; confused. —**incoherently** *adv.*

incompetent (in·kom′pə·tənt) *adj.* Lacking in ability or skill.

inconsolable (in′kən·sō′lə·bəl) *adj.* Not to be comforted or cheered; broken-hearted.

incredulous (in·krej′ə·ləs) *adj.* Feeling, having, or showing doubt or disbelief. —**incredulously** *adv.*

indebted (in·det′id) *adj.* Owing gratitude or thanks, as for a favor.

indifference (in·dif′rəns) *n.* Lack of interest; unconcern. —**indifferent** *adj.*

indignant (in·dig′nənt) *adj.* Angry because of something that is not right, just, or fair. —**indignation** *n.*

indistinct (in′dis·tingkt′) *adj.* Not clear; vague; dim.

indomitable (in·dom′ə·tə·bəl) *adj.* Not easily defeated or overcome; persevering.

induce (in·doos′) *v.* To persuade.

industrious (in·dus′trē·əs) *adj.* Working hard.

inevitable (in·ev′ə·tə·bəl) *adj.* Certain; unavoidable.

inexplicable (in·eks′pli·kə·bəl) *adj.* Impossible to explain.

infest (in·fest′) *v.* To overrun or occupy in large numbers so as to be annoying or dangerous.

infinite (in′fə·nit) *adj.* Having no limits; endless. —**infinity** *n.*

ingest (in·jest′) *v.* To swallow.

inhabit (in·hab′it) *v.* To live in; occupy.

initial (in·ish′əl) *adj.* Coming at the beginning; earliest; first.

inquisitive (in·kwiz′ə·tiv) *adj.* Full of questions; curious.

inscrutable (in·skroo′tə·bəl) *adj.* Incapable of being understood; mysterious; puzzling.

inseparable (in·sep′ər·ə·bəl) *adj.* Incapable of being separated.

integrity (in·teg′rə·tē) *n.* Great sincerity, honesty, and virtue; strength of character.

intense (in·tens′) *adj.* Very strong, great, or deep. —**intensity** *n.*

intent (in·tent′) *adj.* Firmly directed or fixed; earnest. —**intently** *adv.*

intention (in·ten′shən) *n.* Plan, purpose.

intermix (in′tər·miks′) *v.* To mix together.

interspecific (in′tər·spi·sif′ik) *adj.* Relating to similar behavior patterns among different species.

intervene (in′tər·vēn′) *v.* **1.** To come in to change a situation. **2.** To come or be between two places or times.

intricate (in′tri·kit) *adj.* Complicated or involved.

intrigue 1. *v.* (in·trēg′) To arouse the interest of. **2.** *n.* (in′trēg) A secret, crafty plot or scheme.

intrude (in·trood′) *v.* To come in without being invited or wanted. —**intrusion** *n.*

J

jaunty (jôn′tē) *adj.* Having a lively or self-confident air or manner.

jeer (jir) *v.* To make fun of with insulting words; mock.

jostle (jos′əl) *v.* To push or crowd against; shove; bump.

jubilant (joo′bə·lənt) *adj.* Expressing great joy. —**jubilation** *n.*

K

kaleidoscope (kə·lī′də·skōp′) *n.* **1.** A tubelike device containing loose bits of colored glass. **2.** Any changing pattern, view, or scene.

kerchief (kûr′chif) *n.* A piece of fabric, usually square, worn over the head or around the neck.

L

labor (lā′bər) *v.* To work hard.

laden (lād′ən) *adj.* Weighed down; loaded; burdened.

lair (lâr) *n.* The den of a wild animal.

lamentation (lam′ən·tā′shən) *n.* The act of expressing great sorrow; wail; moan.

larva (lar′və) *n., pl.* (lar′vē) The early stage of an insect's life after hatching; for example, a caterpillar before it turns into a moth.

lavish (lav′ish) *adj.* **1.** Generous or too generous. **2.** Provided or used up in great supply. —**lavishly** *adv.*

legitimate (lə·jit′ə·mit) *adj.* **1.** Lawful. **2.** Logical; reasonable; justified.

leisurely (lē′zhər·lē) *adj.* Relaxed and unhurried. —**leisureliness** *n.*

linger (ling′gər) *v.* To stay on as if unwilling to go.

listless (list′lis) *adj.* Lacking energy or interest in anything.

lofty (lôf′tē) *adj.* **1.** Very high. **2.** Proud.

lull 1. *n.* A time of quiet or calm during a period of noise or activity. **2.** *v.* To quiet or put to sleep by soothing sounds or motions.

luminous (loo′mə·nəs) *adj.* Full of light; glowing.

lunge (lunj) *v.* To make a quick movement or plunge forward.

lure (loor) *v.* To attract, especially into danger.

luscious (lush′əs) *adj.* **1.** Very good to

a	add	i	it	oo	took	oi	oil
ā	ace	ī	ice	o͞o	pool	ou	pout
â	care	o	odd	u	up	ng	ring
ä	palm	ō	open	û	burn	th	thin
e	end	ô	order	yoo	fuse	th	this
ē	equal					zh	vision

ə = { a in *above*　e in *sicken*　i in *possible*
{ o in *melon*　u in *circus*

taste and smell; delicious. **2.** Pleasing to any sense or to the mind.

M

malice (mal′is) *n.* A desire to injure someone; ill will.

maneuver (mə·nōō′vər) **1.** *n.* Any skillful move or action. **2.** *v.* To use planned moves skillfully.

manifest (man′ə·fest′) *v.* To reveal; show.

meander (mē·an′dər) *v.* To wander aimlessly.

meek *adj.* Lacking courage or spirit.

melancholy (mel′ən·kol′ē) **1.** *adj.* Very gloomy; sad. **2.** *n.* Low spirits; sadness; depression.

mellow (mel′ō) *adj.* **1.** Rich and soft in quality, as colors or sounds. **2.** Made gentle by age or experience.

menace (men′is) **1.** *n.* A threat. **2.** *v.* To threaten with evil or harm.

merchandise (mûr′chən·dīs′) *n.* Goods bought and sold for profit.

merely (mir′lē) *adv.* Nothing more than; only.

mimic (mim′ik) *v.* To imitate the speech or actions of someone, usually to make fun.

minimal (min′ə·məl) *adj.* Smallest or least possible in size, amount, or degree.

mire (mīr) **1.** *n.* Swampy ground or deep mud. **2.** *v.* To sink or stick in mire.

moderation (mod′ə·rā′shən) *n.* The condition of not being extreme or excessive.

modify (mod′ə·fī) *v.* To change moderately.

molest (mə·lest′) *v.* To harm or bother.

monarch (mon′ərk) *n.* A ruler, as a king or queen.

mooring *n.* The line, cable, or anchor that holds something in place.

mope *v.* To be gloomy and depressed; sulk.

mortify (môr′tə·fī′) *v.* **1.** To deprive of self-respect or pride; humiliate. **2.** To become dead or decayed.

mottle (mot′′l) *v.* To mark with spots of different colors; blotch.

mournful (môrn′fəl) *adj.* Showing or causing grief; sorrowful.

muddle (mud′′l) *n.* A condition of confusion; mix-up.

murky (mûr′kē) *adj.* **1.** Dark, gloomy. **2.** Foggy, misty.

mutual (myōō′chōō·əl) *adj.* Having the same attitude toward or relationship with each other or others.

N

nectar (nek′tər) *n.* **1.** A sweet liquid found in flowers, collected by bees to make honey. **2.** A sweet drink.

niche (nich) *n.* A hollow in a wall.

nobility (nō·bil′ə·tē) *n.* The condition of showing outstanding or impressive qualities.

noncommittal (non′kə·mit′əl) *adj.* Not binding one to an opinion or plan of action.

nymph (nimf) *n.* In Greek and Roman myths, any of a group of lesser goddesses who lived in woods, fountains, or trees.

O

oblige (ə·blīj′) *v.* **1.** To compel; force. **2.** To do a favor or service for.

oblivious (ə·bliv′ē·əs) *adj.* Not conscious or aware.

obscure (əb·skyŏŏr′) *v.* To make dim or indistinct.

obsess (əb·ses′) *v.* To fill or trouble the mind of excessively; haunt.

obstinate (ob′stə·nit) *adj.* **1.** Stubbornly holding to one's opinions. **2.** Hard to overcome or control. —**obstinately** *adv.*

offensive (ə·fen′siv) *adj.* Unpleasant or disagreeable.

officious (ə·fish′əs) *adj.* Too forward in offering service or advice; meddlesome. —**officiously** *adv.*

ooze *v.* To flow or leak out slowly or gradually.

optimistic (op′tə·mis′tik) *adj.* Full of hope and cheerfulness.

orator (ôr′ə·tər) *n.* A person who delivers a public speech.

ostentation (os′tən·tā′shən) *n.* Too great a display of something in order to attract attention or admiration.

outrageous (out·rā′jəs) *adj.* Fantastic; unbelievable. —**outrageousness** *n.*

overwhelm (ō′vər·welm′) *v.* To overcome completely.

P

pallid (pal′id) *adj.* Pale in appearance; lacking in color or strength; weak.

pant *v.* To breathe quickly and jerkily.

paralysis (pə·ral′ə·sis) *n.* **1.** The loss of the power of movement or feeling in a part of the body. **2.** Any stopping of normal activities.

parasite (par′ə·sīt′) *n.* A plant that lives on and gets its food from another. —**parasitic** *adj.*

parch *v.* **1.** To make or become dry with heat. **2.** To make or become thirsty.

pathetic (pə·thet′ik) *adj.* Arousing, expressing, or deserving pity or sympathy.

perennial (pə·ren′ē·əl) *adj.* Everlasting.

perky (pûr′kē) *adj.* Lively.

persistent (pər·sis′tənt) *adj.* Enduring or continuing.

perturb (pər·tûrb′) *v.* To disturb greatly; alarm; agitate.

petulant (pech′ŏŏ·lənt) *adj.* Showing annoyance over little things; fretful.

phenomenal (fi·nom′ə·nəl) *adj.* Marvelous; extraordinary.

philosophy (fi·los′ə·fē) *n.* **1.** Wisdom and strength in dealing with difficult experiences.

pinion (pin′yən) *v.* To bind or hold the

a	add	i	it	ŏŏ	took	oi	oil
ā	ace	ī	ice	ōō	pool	ou	pout
â	care	o	odd	u	up	ng	ring
ä	palm	ō	open	û	burn	th	thin
e	end	ô	order	yōō	fuse	th	this
ē	equal					zh	vision

ə = { a in *above* e in *sicken* i in *possible*
       o in *melon* u in *circus*

arms of (someone) to make the person helpless.

piteous (pit′ē·əs) *adj.* Arousing or deserving pity.

pivot (piv′ət) **1.** *n.* A point, shaft, or pin on which something turns. **2.** *v.* To turn as if on a pivot.

placate (plā′kāt′) *v.* To calm the anger of; soothe.

plague (plāg) **1.** *v.* To trouble, torment. **2.** *n.* A contagious, often fatal, disease that spreads rapidly.

plaintive (plān′tiv) *adj.* Expressing sadness; mournful.

plight (plīt) *n.* An awkward, bad, or dangerous situation.

plumage (ploo′mij) *n.* The feathers of a bird.

plunder (plun′dər) *v.* To rob of goods or property by force.

ply (plī) *v.* To work at; be engaged in.

pollen (pol′ən) *n.* A yellow powder containing the male reproductive cells of plants.

pomegranate (pom′gran′it) *n.* A tropical fruit about the size of an orange, having many seeds.

pomp *n.* Magnificent display; splendor.

posse (pos′ē) *n.* A force of people summoned by a sheriff to help in some official duty.

precede (pri·sēd′) *v.* To be, go, or come before.

prestige (pres·tēzh′) *n.* Fame, importance, or respect based on a person's reputation or power.

prey (prā) *n.* Any animal killed by another for food.

primate (prī′māt′) *n.* An order of mammals including apes, monkeys, lemurs, and humans.

procure (prō·kyoor′) *v.* To get by some effort or means; acquire.

profile (prō′fīl′) *n.* **1.** The outline of a human face as seen from the side. **2.** A short biographical sketch.

profusion (prə·fyoo′zhən) *n.* A large supply.

propellers (prə·pel′ərs) *n.* Rotating blades that move an aircraft or vessel through the air or water.

prospect (pros′pekt′) *n.* The act of looking ahead; expectation.

prosperous (pros′pər·əs) *adj.* Successful; thriving.

protrude (prō·trood′) *v.* To jut out; project.

provoke (prə·vōk′) *v.* To cause or bring about.

prowess (prou′is) *n.* **1.** Great skill or ability. **2.** Strength and courage.

psyche (sī′kē) *n.* The human soul or mind.

psychiatry (sī·kī′ə·trē) *n.* The branch of medicine that deals with the treatment of mental illness.

puce (pyoos) *adj.* A dark brownish purple or purplish brown.

punctual (pungk′choo·əl) *adj.* Acting, finished, or arriving on time.

pursuit (pər·soot′) *n.* A chase.

Q

quaver (kwā′vər) *v.* To tremble or shake in an uncertain way, as a voice.

queasy (kwē′zē) *adj.* Sick or causing sickness at the stomach.

quiver (kwiv′ər) *v.* To make a slight trembling motion; vibrate.

R

radiant (rā′dē·ənt) *adj.* **1.** Beaming, as with joy, love, or energy. **2.** Very bright and shining; brilliant.

rancid (ran′sid) *adj.* Having the bad taste or smell of spoiled fat or oil.

random (ran′dəm) *adj.* Not planned or organized; chance.

ransom (ran′səm) *n.* The price demanded or paid for the release of a person held captive.

ravage (rav′ij) *v.* To hurt or damage severely; destroy.

recess (rē′ses) *n.* **1.** A short period of time when work is stopped. **2.** A hollow place.

recoil (ri·koil′) *v.* To react suddenly, as to pain or fear, by leaping or shrinking back.

reconcile (rek′ən·sīl′) *v.* **1.** To bring back to friendship after a quarrel. **2.** To make adjusted to; resign.

recover (ri·kuv′ər) *v.* **1.** To get back after losing. **2.** To make up for, as a loss. **3.** To get well.

recreation (rek′rē·ā′shən) *n.* Amusement, relaxation, or play.

reference (ref′ər·əns) *n.* **1.** The act of calling attention. **2.** Something that provides information or help.

reflective (ri·flek′tiv) *adj.* Thoughtful.

refuge (ref′yo͞oj) *n.* Shelter or protection from danger or distress.

register (rej′is·tər) *v.* **1.** To show; express. **2.** To enter one's name in an official record; enroll.

regulate (reg′yə·lāt′) *v.* To control according to certain rules.

relent (ri·lent′) *v.* To become gentler or more compassionate.

relentless (ri·lent′lis) *adj.* **1.** Without pity; unforgiving; harsh. **2.** Continuing; persistent.

reluctant (ri·luk′tənt) *adj.* Unwilling; not eager.

remote (ri·mōt′) *adj.* Distant in time or relationship.

render (ren′dər) *v.* **1.** To perform; do. **2.** To cause to be or become.

replenish (ri·plen′ish) *v.* To provide with a new supply; fill up again.

reproach (ri·prōch′) *v.* To blame for some wrong.

repulsive (ri·pul′siv) *adj.* Disgusting or horrifying.

resent (ri·zent′) *v.* To feel or show anger or ill will based on real or imagined wrong or injury.

resign (ri·zīn′) *v.* To give up; submit.

resilient (ri·zil′yənt) *adj.* Springing back to former shape or position.

resound (ri·zound′) *v.* To be filled with sound or echo back.

a	add	i	it	o͞o	took	oi	oil
ā	ace	ī	ice	o͞o	pool	ou	pout
â	care	o	odd	u	up	ng	ring
ä	palm	ō	open	û	burn	th	thin
e	end	ô	order	yo͞o	fuse	th	this
ē	equal					zh	vision

ə = { a in *above*   e in *sicken*   i in *possible*
{ o in *melon*   u in *circus*

resource (ri·sôrs′) *n.* **1.** The ability to act usefully and well in a difficulty. **2.** A supply of something.

restless (rest′lis) *adj.* Unable to rest or be still; nervous; uneasy.

restore (ri·stôr′) *v.* To bring back to a former or original condition.

resume (ri·zōōm′) *v.* To begin again after stopping.

reticent (ret′ə·sənt) *adj.* Reserved; quiet.

retort (ri·tôrt′) *v.* To reply sharply.

retrieve (ri·trēv′) *v.* To get back; regain.

revelation (rev′ə·lā′shən) *n.* Something made known, especially something surprising.

reverberation (ri·vûr′bə·rā′shən) *n.* A reflecting, as of sound waves, light, or heat.

rigor (rig′ər) *n.* Harshness or discomfort.

riotous (rī·ət·əs) *adj.* Loud; uproarious. **—riotously** *adv.*

rival (rī′vəl) *n.* A person who tries to outdo another; competitor.

rivulet (riv′yə·lit) *n.* A brook.

S

sanctuary (sangk′chōō·er′ē) *n.* A place of safety and peace.

scald (skôld) *v.* To burn with hot liquid or steam.

scour (skour) *v.* **1.** To clean by washing and rubbing hard. **2.** To clean or clear, as by flowing water.

seizure (sē′zhər) *n.* A sudden, violent attack, as of a disease.

shear (shir) *v.* **1.** To cut the hair or fleece from. **2.** To take something away from; deprive.

sheepish (shē′pish) *adj.* Awkwardly shy or embarrassed.

shingle (shin′gəl) *n.* A pebbly beach.

shorn An alternative past participle of *shear.*

sidle (sīd′′l) *v.* To move sideways, especially in a cautious or sly manner.

silhouette (sil′ōō·et′) *n.* The outline of a person or object seen against a light or a light background.

sinister (sin′is·tər) *adj.* **1.** Wrong, wicked, or evil. **2.** Threatening evil, trouble, or bad luck.

skirmish (skûr′mish) *n.* A brief fight or encounter between small groups.

skirt *v.* To go around, not through; pass along the edge of.

slacken (slak′ən) *v.* To make or become slower, less active, or less forceful.

sluggish (slug′ish) *adj.* Not active or energetic; lazy or dull. **—sluggishly** *adv.*

sly (slī) *adj.* Clever in a secret, stealthy, or sneaky way; crafty; cunning. **— slyly** *adv.*

smolder (smōl′dər) *v.* To burn slowly with smoke but no flame.

snarl *v.* To growl, showing the teeth.

sober (sō′bər) *adj.* **1.** Serious, calm, thoughtful, and well-balanced. **2.** Solemn.

sociable (sō′shə·bəl) *adj.* Liking to be with people; pleasant in company; social.

solitary (sol'ə·ter'ē) *adj.* **1.** Living, being, or going alone. **2.** Single; sole.

sorrowful (sor'ə·fəl) *adj.* Sad, distressed. —**sorrowfully** *adv.*

souvenir (soō'və·nir') *n.* Something that is kept as a reminder of the past.

spasm (spaz'əm) *n.* A sudden, involuntary contraction of a muscle.

spate *n.* **1.** A sudden flood or rush. **2.** A large number occurring or appearing together.

speculation (spek'yə·lā'shən) *n.* The act of thinking or wondering seriously.

sprite *n.* A fairy, elf, goblin, or similar creature.

stagger (stag'ər) *v.* To walk or run unsteadily; sway; reel.

stalk (stôk) *v.* **1.** To approach secretly or stealthily. **2.** To walk in a stiff or angry manner.

stampede (stam·pēd') *n.* A sudden rushing off or flight through panic, as of a herd of cattle or horses.

stealthy (stel'thē) *adj.* Done in a secret or underhand way. —**stealthily** *adv.*

strenuous (stren'yoō·əs) *adj.* Taking much effort or energy.

strife (strīf) *n.* Angry fight, quarrel, or conflict.

sturdy (stûr'dē) *adj.* Vigorous; strong.

substantial (səb·stan'shəl) *adj.* **1.** Actual; real; having substance. **2.** Solid; strong; firm.

succession (sək·sesh'ən) *n.* A group of things or persons that follow one after another.

sullen (sul'ən) *adj.* Glumly silent because ill-humored or resentful. —**sullenly** *adv.*

sultry (sul'trē) *adj.* Uncomfortably hot, humid, and still.

summit (sum'it) *n.* The highest point; top.

summon (sum'ən) *v.* To send for or order to come.

sumptuous (sump'choō·əs) *adj.* Very expensive and luxurious.

superficial (soō'pər·fish'əl) *adj.* **1.** Of, on, or affecting only the surface; not deep. **2.** Not genuine.

suspicious (sə·spish'əs) *adj.* Having a feeling or idea, not based on real proof, that something is wrong.

T

tactic (tak'tik) *n.* A device or maneuver used to achieve a specific goal.

tantalize (tan'tə·līz') *v.* To torment by making something desirable almost but never quite available.

tapestry (tap'is·trē) *n.* A heavy ornamental cloth with designs or pictures woven into it, usually hung on a wall.

tart *adj.* **1.** Having a sharp, sour taste. **2.** Sharp and biting in meaning or tone.

a	add	i	it	ŏŏ	took	oi	oil
ā	ace	ī	ice	ōō	pool	ou	pout
â	care	o	odd	u	up	ng	ring
ä	palm	ō	open	û	burn	th	thin
e	end	ô	order	yōō	fuse	th	this
ē	equal					zh	vision

ə = { a in *above*   e in *sicken*   i in *possible*
{ o in *melon*   u in *circus*

taunt (tônt) *v.* To insult or make fun of with scornful, mocking, or sarcastic remarks.

tempo (tem′pō) *n.* **1.** The pace or rate of activity. **2.** The speed at which a piece of music is played.

tenacious (ti·nā′shəs) *adj.* **1.** Holding or grasping firmly. **2.** Not forgetting.

tentative (ten′tə·tiv) *adj.* Hesitant; half-hearted. —**tentatively** *adv.*

terrorist (ter′ə·rist) *n.* A person who uses threats and violence to frighten others.

terse (tûrs) *adj.* Short and to the point.

testify (tes′tə·fī) *v.* To give evidence; bear witness.

testy (tes′tē) *adj.* Easily made angry.

thicket (thik′it) *n.* A thick, dense growth, as of trees or bushes.

threadbare (thred′bâr′) *adj.* So badly worn that the threads show, as a rug or garment.

thrive *v.* **1.** To prosper or be successful. **2.** To grow vigorously; flourish.

timid (tim′id) *adj.* Fearful or shy.

toil *v.* To work hard.

token (tō′kən) *n.* A sign or symbol.

tolerate (tol′ər·āt′) *v.* **1.** To allow to be or permit without opposition. **2.** To bear or endure.

torrent (tôr′ənt) *n.* Water flowing with great speed and violence.

totter (tot′ər) *v.* To walk feebly and unsteadily.

tranquil (trang′kwil) *adj.* Calm; serene. —**tranquillity** *n.*

transcend (tran·send′) *v.* To go beyond; overstep the limits of.

transfix (trans·fiks′) *v.* To make motionless, as with horror or fear.

traverse (trə·vûrs′) *v.* To pass or travel over, across, or through.

tremor (trem′ər) *n.* **1.** A quick, vibrating movement. **2.** A quivering feeling.

tremulous (trem′yə·ləs) *adj.* Showing fear; timid. —**tremulously** *adv.*

trench *n.* A long, narrow opening dug into the earth; ditch.

trundle (trun′dəl) *v.* To roll or propel as if by rolling.

turmoil (tûr′moil) *n.* A condition of great agitation; disturbance.

tyrant (tī′rənt) *n.* **1.** A ruler having absolute power. **2.** Any person who exerts power in such a way.

U

unconscious (un·kon′shəs) *adj.* Not able to feel or think; not awake.

unison (yōō′nə·sən) *n.* Agreement.

unobtrusive (un′əb·trōō′siv) *adj.* Not demanding notice; inconspicuous.

unwieldy (un·wēl′dē) *adj.* Hard to handle or manage; awkward.

urgency (ûr′jən·sē) *n.* Need or demand for prompt action or attention.

urn *n.* A large vase used for flowers and plants.

V

vacancy (vā′kən·sē) *n.* An empty place.

vacant (vā′kənt) *adj.* Empty or unfilled.

vague (vāg) *adj.* Not definite, clear, precise, or distinct.

vain (vān) *adj.* Unsuccessful; useless. —**in vain** Without success.

veer (vir) *v.* To change direction.

vengeance (ven′jəns) *n.* Punishment inflicted in return for a wrong done; revenge.

venomous (ven′əm·əs) *adj.* Poisonous.

vent *v.* To relieve or express freely.

veranda (və·ran′də) *n.* A long, open, outdoor porch, usually roofed.

verge (vûrj) *n.* **1.** The edge of something. **2.** The point at which some action is likely to occur.

verify (ver′ə·fī) *v.* To prove to be true or accurate.

vessel (ves′əl) *n.* **1.** A hollow container, as a bowl. **2.** A ship or boat larger than a rowboat.

vicious (vish′əs) *adj.* **1.** Dangerous or likely to attack. **2.** Spiteful or mean.

vigil (vij′əl) *n.* The act of staying awake to observe or protect; watch.

vinyl (vī′nəl) *n.* A plastic used in making records, combs, floor coverings, and other items.

vital (vīt′′l) *adj.* **1.** Lively and energetic. **2.** Necessary or essential to life.

vitality (vī·tal′ə·tē) *n.* Physical or mental energy.

vixen (vik′sən) *n.* An ill-tempered, quarrelsome person.

vocalize (vō′kəl·īz′) *v.* To make sounds with the voice. —**vocalization** *n.*

vulnerable (vul′nər·ə·bəl) *adj.* Capable of being hurt, injured, or wounded.

W

waive (wāv) *v.* To give up voluntarily, as a claim or right.

waver (wā′vər) *v.* **1.** To sway; flutter. **2.** To be uncertain or undecided.

wayfarer (wā′fâr′ər) *n.* A traveler.

weary (wir′ē) *adj.* Tired; fatigued. —**wearily** *adv.*

whimper (wim′pər) *v.* To cry with low, mournful, broken sounds.

whittle (wit′əl) *v.* To cut or shave bits from wood.

wilt *v.* To lose or cause to lose freshness or energy; to become limp.

wily (wī′lē) *adj.* Sly; cunning.

wince (wins) *v.* To shrink or draw back, as from a blow or a pain.

wistful (wist′fəl) *adj.* Wishful; longing. —**wistfully** *adv.*

witness (wit′nis) *n.* A person who has seen or knows something and can give evidence concerning it.

writhe (rīth) *v.* To twist or distort the body or part of the body, as in pain.

wry (rī) *adj.* **1.** Bent or twisted. **2.** Grim, bitter, or ironic. —**wryly** *adv.*

Y

yield (yēld) *v.* **1.** To give up; surrender. **2.** To give forth; produce.

a	add	i	it	o͝o	took	oi	oil
ā	ace	ī	ice	o͞o	pool	ou	pout
â	care	o	odd	u	up	ng	ring
ä	palm	ō	open	û	burn	th	thin
e	end	ô	order	yo͞o	fuse	th	this
ē	equal					zh	vision

ə = { a in *above*   e in *sicken*   i in *possible*
       o in *melon*   u in *circus*

Outline of Concepts and Skills

LITERATURE AND HISTORY
The Underground Railroad 34

LITERATURE AND SCIENCE
Fact Versus Fiction 205
Myths and Scientific Words 445

CONNECTING CULTURES
Myths About Dragons 96
Tales About Giants 593

Index OF *Contents* BY *Types*

Poetry

Short Stories

Index of Fine Art and Illustrations